# PROGRESSIVE CENTURY

# PROGRESSIVE CENTURY

## The American Nation in Its Second Hundred Years

**Paul W. Glad** *University of Wisconsin*

D. C. HEATH AND COMPANY

LEXINGTON. MASSACHUSETTS / TORONTO / LONDON

Cover painting: John Kane, *Turtle Creek Valley, No. 1.*
Photo courtesy ACA Galleries, New York.

Maps prepared by Richard D. Pusey.

Published simultaneously in Canada.

Printed in the United States of America.

International Standard Book Number: 0–669–90407–X

Library of Congress Catalog Card Number: 74–12873

To the memory of two friends:

OSCAR OSBURN WINTHER

and

CHASE C. MOONEY

# PREFACE

An interest in history, wrote Professor Herbert J. Muller in *The Uses of the Past,* "begins as a childlike interest in the obvious pageantry and exciting event; it grows as a mature interest in the variety and complexity of the drama, the splendid achievements and the terrible failures; it ends as a deep sense of the mystery of man's life—of all the dead, great and obscure, who once walked the earth, and of the wonderful and awful possibilities of being a human being." This is a poetic way of suggesting that our perceptions of the past change as we mature and acquire the information to reflect upon our own and society's relationship to historical influences. The stages of growth and perception are not necessarily the same for everyone, yet in a broad sense everyone is a historian. Even those who believe that they act outside historical processes have some awareness of their behavior in relationship to time and to past experience. A major purpose of systematic historical study is to sharpen our comprehension of the way we respond to various stimuli and, in the end, to gain understanding of "the wonderful and awful possibilities of being a human being."

It happens that when I was growing up during the 1930s, I discovered on our family bookshelf *The Beginner's American History,* by D. H. Montgomery. Published in 1902, the small volume was one that my mother had used when she was a girl in elementary school and had saved. I was captivated by its engravings and, after developing adequate reading skills, charmed by its hero tales. In twenty-eight chapters the book moved with great Americans from the discovery of the New World to the Civil War. The final chapter on the years after 1865 concluded by describing the great seal of the United States, emphasizing the symbolism of the reverse side. The unfinished pyramid had been well begun by builders of the American nation, suggested Montgomery, and he exhorted his youthful readers to do their part by making sure "that the pyramid, as it rises, shall continue to stand square, and strong, and true."

Having cut my eye teeth on the didacticism of that beginner's history, I suppose I have always to some extent shared assumptions of the pre-World War I years in which elementary schoolchildren studied it. Americans then believed that they would proceed from one achievement to another in advancing toward fulfillment of the national destiny, and historians have labeled the era *progressive.* But whatever the assumptions associated with my youthful introduction to American history, they do not fully explain my giving this book the title I have. Few people who have survived the traumas of our recent past could retain such naive confidence in either the nation's righteousness or its triumphant future.

Progressivism nevertheless contained many ideas about how the society should be organized, who should do the organizing, and what the ends of organization should be. It seems to me that some of those ideas have remained vital and have influenced the course of recent history. Not all of them, as I have tried to indicate in the pages that follow, have worked themselves out in the way a 1902 beginner's American history anticipated. There have indeed been splendid achievements. There have also been terrible failures. I have written this book neither to glory in the achievements nor to castigate the failures, but rather to provide explanations of both. Perhaps the subject is so various and complex as to foredoom any such effort. Yet this study of the American nation in its second century may at least suggest some of the wonderful as well as some of the awful possibilities in our existence as human beings.

Although I have aimed at the truth in what I have written, I may have missed the mark through inadvertence or ignorance. If so, I ruefully accept blame. At the same time I cheerfully acknowledge the aid of those whose criticism reduced error to a minimum. To colleagues in my own department who did not take flight when they saw me approaching, typescript in hand, I extend my thanks. Professors Paul K. Conkin, Stanley I. Kutler, Edward M. Coffman, Diane Lindstrom Jacobsen, Stanley K. Schultz, and Morton Rothstein all had the courage to stand their ground and offer suggestions for the improvement of what they read. Similarly, during a stimulating year as a visitor at the University of Oklahoma, I exploited the considerable critical abilities of Professors David Levy, Robert Shalhope, and Russell Buhite.

Both graduate and undergraduate seminars at the University of Wisconsin read portions of the manuscript with a critical intelligence that commands respect. Clay McShane of the Department of History and Zachary Cooper of the Department of Afro-American Studies commented on portions of the work, providing me with invaluable suggestions for bringing certain points into sharper focus.

Criticism by correspondence has been as helpful as criticism tête à tête. I am under heavy obligation to Professor Charles K. Cannon of Coe College for pointing out ambiguities in style and interpretation. And I am profoundly grateful to Professor Thomas K. McCraw of the University of Texas for his perceptive and painstaking commentary; no critic could have been more helpful in sharpening my own understanding.

To Professor Herbert Wiese of Coe College and to George Talbot, Curator of Iconographic Collections at the State Historical Society of Wisconsin, I owe a special thanks for their inestimable assistance in the selection of photographs and other illustrative material. For the skillful editing of this book, as well as for important suggestions on its content, Barbara Hamelburg, Donna Bouvier, and Jeanne Rainoldi deserve more than perfunctory acknowledgment. Without their proficiency, the volume would not have gone to press.

In yet a different way I have been aided by members of my own family.

My wife, Carolyn, has comforted me in despair, deflated me in arrogance, scorned me in self-pity, and sustained me in hope. My children, now young adults, have learned by their mother's example.

Finally, I acknowledge the importance of many friends and associates by naming two in particular: Professor Merle Curti and Professor Merrill Jensen. My two revered colleagues at the University of Wisconsin have taught, as did my two revered professors at Indiana University, to whose memory this book is dedicated, by example as well as by precept. Characterizing all these men is their respect for individual personality, their sensitive and solicitous concern, and their capacity to rejoice with those who rejoice. To have such friends (different though they may be in manner, style, and professional interest) is to understand the wonderful possibilities of being a human being, and to have such friends is to have a standard for historical inquiry.

PAUL W. GLAD
Madison, Wisconsin

# CONTENTS

## Part Four    A Time of War, Affluence, Disruption, and Judgment

# Maps

# Tables

# PART ONE

Modernizing America

# 1

# Times and Tensions of a Developing Industrial Society

Time, like mass, length, and temperature, is a fundamental dimension of the physical world, important for the measurement of forces and stresses. The acceleration of gravity, for example, is approximately thirty-two feet per second per second. The rhythmic events of the physical universe—the rising and falling of tides, the turning of the earth on its axis, or the rotation of planets around the sun—must be expressed as the number of them that occur in a given length of time. The standard, internationally recognized time unit is the second, and elaborate astronomical calculations have been required to establish its duration. Although neither days nor years are absolutely constant in duration, various adjustments now permit comparison of events timed in a given year with similar events timed in other years.

While historians do not require the precision in measurement demanded by astronomers and physicists, they do use physical time to date happenings that concern them. From the historian's point of view, what is important about physical time is that it flows metrically and is (despite theories of relativity and the fourth dimension) irreversible. Treated as a homogeneous medium, physical time is independent of all that happens within it; it therefore provides an ordered dimension that forms the basis for historical chronology. Events may occur simultaneously, but no two instants can occur simultaneously. When events are not simultaneous, historians can establish their sequence. And sequence is obviously important in dealing with problems of causation: if A came before B, then B could not have caused A.

**History, Culture, Cosmology, and Time**

Although historical thought places heavy reliance on the concept of physical or absolute time, those who would understand the past must also appreciate time in its subjective and relative character. One's sense of time—one's feeling about it—depends to some extent upon what occurs during a given period. Time spent in waiting seems to pass more slowly than time spent in strenuous activity. Subjective feelings surge and eddy in irregular rhythms that do not synchronize with the steady ticking of a clock, and in moments of reverie the past, present, and future may intertwine. Societies, like individuals, have ideas about time that derive in large part from their experience. Where traditional patterns of behavior dominate, the society tends to think of time as unchanging. In the classical languages of India there are no words for the concept *to become*. (The verb formed from the Sanskrit root *bhū* translates as both "to become" and "to exist.") There is no distinction between being born and being alive, for becoming is a part of existing.

Such a static conception of time never characterized the Western thought that took shape over centuries out of a synthesis of Greek and Hebrew ideas. Judeo-Christian religious beliefs rested on the assumption of a meaningful dynamic in human affairs. After describing the creation of the universe, the Book of Genesis presents man's original condition in the Garden of Eden as unrelated to time. When Adam and Eve eat the forbidden fruit, the Old Testament goes on to show God's designs working themselves out within time and against a background of human weakness and instability. Christianity, with its emphasis on ultimate union with God, looked toward the future as well as toward the past. The Western religious heritage therefore stressed both the beginning of a time dimension (man's expulsion from the garden) and its end (the day of judgment). It also stressed the progression of mankind on that dimension from one point to the next.

The ancient Greek philosophers, on the other hand, thought that cosmic and historic time are infinite in both directions. Like the early Christians and their Hebrew forebears, Plato believed that God transcends time and in that sense is eternal. Yet unlike them, he and his Greek contemporaries believed that the human race has no beginning and will have no end. History, in their view, follows a long-term cyclical pattern that coincides with planetary movements. That pattern is a reflection of God's eternity, but it has no other meaning.

During the Middle Ages, scholars and theologians assumed the task of reconciling Greek and Hebrew points of view in a Christian synthesis. The feudal world, with its blend of certainty and mystery, could understand the concept of an infinite and all-powerful God but not the notion that God's purposes were directly discernible to mortal man. While medieval thinkers affirmed Judeo-Christian ideas of creation and judgment—which, of course, imply that for mankind time has limits—they rejected the Greek idea that history moves in cyclical patterns. Believing in a divine plan of history without knowing precisely what it entailed, they were sure that it did not involve repeated recurrence. The crucifixion of Christ, in particular, was conceivable only as a unique event. Yet the Greek conception of time did have enormous influence within the limits imposed by Christian theology. More consistent with the relatively rigid medieval social structure than was the idea of human progress through history, it certainly seemed valid for at least the earthly careers of individual men. The Greek conception of time survived in the Renaissance to find expression in the line from Shakespeare's *Cymbeline:*

> Golden lads and girls all must
> As chimney-sweepers, come to dust.

The cosmology of Shakespeare's world was, however, undergoing significant change in ways that would eventually modify perceptions of time. Copernicus had already revived an ancient theory that the earth was only one of a number of planets revolving about the sun. Although Shakespeare and his contemporary poets rejected the heliocentric idea, Galileo did not —and neither did other astronomers, physicists, and mathematicians who were busy establishing scientific foundations of the modern era. In 1643, a year after Galileo died, Isaac Newton was born. Forty-five years later he published his *Mathematical Principles of Natural Philosophy,* a work that provided a verifiable explanation of the movements of celestial bodies. To contemporaries, Newton seemed to have discovered the underlying principles of the natural order (the design of the Creator), his system justifying the patterned rationality characteristic of the eighteenth-century Enlightenment.

Founding Fathers of the American republic, like almost everyone else in the Western world, accepted Newton's system and elaborated on its social implications. Their reflections suggest a conception of time divided into periods corresponding to human generations. The design of the Creator had established the species and the process of nature. That design—not the troubles, laws, fluctuations, and institutions of man—was what had shaped conditions of life. Each generation, thought Thomas Jefferson, must come to terms with those conditions in its own way. John Adams believed that the life of a man could have moral meaning only insofar as he lived it in harmony with nature's scheme of things. The generation that carried on the American Revolution was ready to break tradition and to abandon mistakes of the past in order to create new institutions that would be consistent with the universal design.

During the nation's formative years Americans were conscious of physical time just as they were aware of order in the universe. But their sense of uniqueness in the American experience led them to stress the present rather than either the past or the future. "No society can make a perpetual constitution, or even a perpetual law," observed Thomas Jefferson. "The earth belongs always to the living generation: they may manage it, then, and what proceeds from it, as they please, during their usufruct." Because the first American generations after the Revolution believe that their continent had never been managed before the arrival of Europeans, they saw themselves as standing outside historical development as well as on virgin land. They were conducting an enterprise that was both distinctive and in harmony with the design of creation.

Indeed, they never really conceived of a historical process. In studying past cultures, they looked for evidence of American uniqueness rather than for evidence of American development out of Western traditions. Little concerned with problems of historical causation, they sometimes found historical parallels. These they tended to fashion into symbols. Thus the columned portico became a familiar embellishment of public buildings, not because it was well suited to the American climate or because it emerged out of Western architectural development; it enjoyed its popularity in part because the American republic identified itself with a rational order, an identification that paralleled the love of order in ancient Greece. What could be more fitting than the appropriation of Greek architectural styles?

The Newtonian physics of the Enlightenment and the unique experience of creating a new nation on American soil help to explain the segmented time sense of the early republic. Yet that sense of time came in the nineteenth century to be transformed by new scientific insights and by the way in which Americans used technology to conquer a wilderness empire. Biological speculations about the origins of man and the concurrent development of new means of transportation were especially important in bringing about a new concept of time.

**Darwin and the Sense of Time**

Charles Darwin, born at Shrewsbury, England, in 1809, went to the University of Edinburgh to study medicine and then to Cambridge to study for the Anglican ministry. Repelled by the thought of practicing surgery without anaesthetics, and indifferent to theology, he distinguished himself in neither endeavor. Yet the young man did show some promise. In 1831 he had the good fortune to be assigned as a naturalist to the *Beagle,* a naval vessel responsible for mapping the coasts of South America, in a sojourn of five years duration. When he returned to England with his carefully collected notes and specimens, he was already persuaded that the generally accepted ideas about creation and universal design required modification.

The work of Thomas Malthus and Sir Charles Lyell provided Darwin with a conceptual model for his own study. Lyell's *Principles of Geology* had shown how geological processes—volcanic activity, erosion, earthquakes, land almost everywhere sinking and rising—accounted for the structure of the earth's surface. Fossil remains and other evidence were soon to indicate that such processes had taken place over millions of years. The renowned geologist, Louis Agassiz (who, ironically, became an outspoken critic of the Darwinian formulation) liked to tell his Harvard classes that the earth was much older than men had once thought: "Its age is as if one were gently to rub a silk handkerchief across Plymouth Rock once a year until it were reduced to a pebble."

Darwin's findings were consistent with Lyell's emphasis on natural processes and with the idea that biblical chronology grossly underestimated the age of the earth. Yet there remained the problem of accounting for biological change, the disappearance and emergence of countless species of organisms. In reading the *Essay on Population* by Thomas Malthus, Darwin found the explanation he sought. The essential argument of the essay was that population increases faster than all the possible means of subsistence. His argument, Malthus admitted, had "a melancholy hue." Indeed it did, for only premature death could counterbalance human fecundity and assure the adequacy of food supplies. The inevitable consequences of population growth were pestilence, war, famine, even infanticide.

Darwin seized upon the Malthusian idea of struggle for survival to explain the development of species. Extinction was the fate of those that could not compete, but those that successfully adapted to their environment survived to reproduce their kind. Species changed through the inheritance of variant characteristics that enabled some organisms to wage successfully the battles of an overpopulated nature. This process of natural selection, operating over long periods of time and throughout environmental changes, accounted for the infinite varieties of life and also for the striking similarities among those varieties. The central idea of Darwin's theory of evolution, then, was that animal and vegetable species, in all their diversity of form, developed out of a common source. The process required eons; Darwin found no evidence to suggest separate acts of creation.

MAN·IS·BVT·A·WORM·

As this cartoon emphasized, Darwin's *On the Origin of Species* (1859) had a profound cosmological impact. To explain the evolution of man, time's meter had to be extended and coiled over eons. The caricature of Darwin himself (bearing a resemblance to the Creator in Michelangelo's Sistine frescoes) suggested the challenge to traditional religious belief that evolutionary theory implied.

Publication of Darwin's *On the Origin of Species* in 1859 provoked excitement and agitated controversies in America and Europe. No one, not even Darwin himself, was able to concentrate exclusively on the biological implications of evolutionary theory. Americans, although more immediately concerned with sectional strife and the Civil War, eventually found themselves forced to cope with the cosmological issues Darwin raised. Debates about evolution undermined the notion of purposeful design in nature. Men still talked about God, but even churchmen began to experience difficulty in conceiving of a God who at one stroke created the species in immutable perpetuity. As the idea of cosmic design slowly gave way to the idea of gradual evolution over time, the American culture's concept of time itself began to change. The generation of Thomas Jefferson had thought in the present tense about its relationship to a natural order. The post-Civil War generations thought in all tenses about where they stood in an evolutionary process that demanded the instinct and the capacity to survive struggle.

This change in the way that Americans conceived of time found expression in the way they viewed their own past. For some 250 years American historians had been amateurs, many of them men of God or of leisure who found personal satisfaction in collecting documents and recording their impressions. Their skills and purposes varied widely. Yet their work, from William Bradford's celebration of Plymouth plantation in the seventeenth century to the romantic nationalism of George Bancroft or Francis Parkman in the nineteenth, tended to emphasize the uniqueness rather than the continuity of American experience. Viewing history as "a thing of shreds and patches"—the phrase employed by Justin Winsor (1831–1897)—they could use episodes of the past to recount tales of adventure and courage, to teach moral lessons, to glorify the Founding Fathers, to stimulate local pride, or to inculcate patriotism. The ever-present inclination to idealize history was never stronger than in the period when men believed in the rational and purposeful design of nature.

After the dissemination of Darwinian ideas, the concept of history as a thing of shreds and patches gave way to the concept of history as a study of continuous and cumulative *change*. The events of the past and the activities of men did, to be sure, give character to discrete segments of time. Yet they also had to be seen in connected sequence, in a cause-and-effect relationship over continuously flowing time. To seize upon an event, tear it out of its place in time, and use it for some moral or practical purpose might be a justifiable activity for preachers, politicians, and even some academicians. For those who called themselves historians, however, it would never do. As Professor John Higham has aptly put it, "History became Darwinian while biology became historical." Yet at the point when scholars began discussing the evolution of history, they also began to think more and more about history as a discipline with its own standards and canons. The American Historical Association, formed in 1884, was in part the product of a new sense of time.

Posed at the kitchen door, these women display—perhaps unconsciously—obvious symbols of daily responsibilities such as washing, scrubbing, sweeping, and child care. Timepieces were important to Gro Svendsen and to other housewives whose chores were endless. The household clock provided a means of regulating daily tasks and measuring domestic accomplishments (State Historical Society of Wisconsin).

**Geography,
Technology, and
Time**

Gro Nilsdatter grew up in Hallingdal, Norway, married Ole Svendsen, and emigrated to America in 1862. She and her husband settled near Estherville, Iowa, where Gro bore ten children, kept house, and helped with farm chores. A woman of great curiosity and sensitivity, she wrote lively, informative letters to her family in Norway. They reveal, among other things, a deep concern for the phenomena of nature: "The night of the nineteenth of July we had a terrible storm, the worst storm we have ever had, and for the first time I feared that our house would be blown down and dashed to pieces"; "We have had exceptionally fine weather this winter with very little snow, so the work in the fields this spring was finished before Easter"; "This spring the locusts ravaged our fields. . . . In many places there will be no harvest"; "On the twenty-fourth of this month, all the prairie grass in this county was burned." As even a cursory reading of such letters would indicate, weather patterns, locusts, and prairie fires were something to write home about; they were also a life-and-death matter.

If Gro Svendsen ever heard of Darwin's theory of evolution, she never mentioned it. Neither did she make reference to Sir Isaac Newton or, except in traditional religious terms, to any concept of cosmic order. But Gro was, like all rural people, sensitive to changing seasons; she seldom failed to note the date of an important event such as a storm or a drought-ending rain. In a way that was typical of sparsely settled areas, where there was always more work to be done than time to do it, the Svendsens struggled against the fleeting hours. "The clock is striking the hour before midnight," wrote Gro, fatigued after a long, hard day on March 4, 1869. Then, characteristically, her spirit brightened. "This reminds me that I should tell you that this fall we bought a clock that cost nine dollars. It is a beautiful clock and keeps excellent time."

The Svendsens were not the only pioneer family to exchange hard-won savings for a clock. Back in 1844, George W. Featherstonhaugh, a British geologist who traveled widely in the United States, had been struck by rural America's interest in timepieces: "Wherever we have been, in Kentucky, in Indiana, in Illinois, in Missouri, and . . . in every dell of Arkansas, and in cabins where there was not a chair to sit on, there was sure to be a Connecticut clock." The earliest clocks on the frontier usually ran poorly, if at all, for their parts, carved of wood, required constant temperature and unchanging relative humidity. Yet people bought them, even though that form of wooden nutmeg did little to improve the Yankee peddler's reputation for sharp trading. Not until the 1830s, when Connecticut clockmaker Chauncey Jerome began mass-producing brass works, did clocks that were both inexpensive and reliable become readily available. From that point on, Americans became increasingly precise in their measurement of time and therefore increasingly conscious of time's passage.

That Yankee peddlers found the unreliable wooden clock a salable item on the frontier is only in part an indication of the concern for time shared by most rural folk. It is also an indication of their interest in gadgetry, an interest that relieved the tedium of an isolated existence. A remarkable number of rural pleasures were, in fact, related to time. Foot racing provided a simple, yet exciting form of athletic activity. And horse racing was, if anything, even more popular.

Contests of speed against one another were even more important in the nation's transportation services. When technology created the steam locomotive and the steamboat, racing added interest to labor that otherwise might have been dull and monotonous. The greater its speed, the more sporting the vehicle. Indeed, the speed with which transportation was accomplished sometimes took on greater importance than the transportation itself. Americans did not become significantly more mobile as a result of more rapid transportation, but their lives became more exciting. "They go and come," wrote Henry David Thoreau of the trains that passed Walden Pond, "with such regularity and precision, and their whistle can be heard so far, that the farmers set their clocks by them, and thus one well-regulated institution regulates a whole country. Have not men improved somewhat in punctuality since the railroad was invented? Do they not talk and think faster in the depot than they did in the stage-office?" The developing railway network and the speed of movement it made possible had the effect of reinforcing a new feeling about time, a new sense of momentum, throughout American society.

The geographic expanse over which that railway network extended also influenced the way Americans thought about time. A small country such as England—or indeed all of Europe west of Russia—can operate with a single standard time. Some 2,500 miles separate the Atlantic and Pacific coastlines of the United States, however; and when east-west distances are that great, no single standard time is practicable. But as speed of travel increased, the custom of allowing every community to establish its own time, a custom

## Go and See
## THE GREAT AMERICAN
## PANORAMA.

OVER THE

PACIFIC

RAILWAY

3,500 MILES

FROM

NEW YORK

TO

CALIFORNIA

3,500 MILES

PULLMAN'S PALACE RAILWAY DINING CAR.

After completion of the first transcontinental railroad in 1869, advertising posters of the Central Pacific
acknowledged distances and even
exaggerated them. Railroad accommodations (dining and sleeping
cars) relieved the fatigue of travel,
and long distance railway journeys
served to make coordinates of time
and space (State Historical Society
of Wisconsin).

The details of Edward Lamson Henry's 1867 painting, "The 9:45 Accommodation,
Stratford, Connecticut," reinforced Thoreau's suggestion that railroads brought a new
sense of urgency to people having to meet train schedules (Metropolitan Museum of
Art).

that prevailed until after the Civil War, proved equally unworkable. If a trip from Boston to San Francisco takes two or three months, changes in time require no great effort of adjustment and several changes are possible. If traveling time is reduced to a week or less, however, the adjustments come in more rapid succession; they are more unsettling and therefore more consciously made.

Thus, by reducing the time required for travel, the expansion of the railway network made inevitable the post-Civil War movement to standardize time. Prior to 1870 railroad companies generally followed the time standard of their most important terminus, although some of them operated—whimsically, it seemed—on times of their own. The chaos of making connections was both unnerving and costly, but not until 1872 did a conference of railroad managers focus on the problem of correlating time and train schedules. That initial effort led to the founding of the General Time Convention, which held regular meetings after 1874. Finally, in 1883, when the convention proposed a standard time for Canada and the United States, the railroads accepted it almost unanimously.

The time system adopted by railroads and supported by an international congress held in Washington in 1884 is the time system of today: a global system based on standard time meridians spaced at intervals of 15 degrees eastward and westward from the meridian of Greenwich, England. For the United States, this means an hour's difference between the meridians of 75, 90, 105, and 120 degrees. Time changes halfway between those meridians, and each of the four zones thus created has its own standard time. All sections of the country accepted the new system after the 1884 conference. By the end of the century Americans had grown accustomed to relating time and place according to a well-devised scheme, although it received no official government sanction until 1918. First, Darwinism raised doubts about man's being created but a little lower than the angels; next, the acceptance of the standard time system made man see the hours of his days relative to his location. If he wished to think of his hours as golden by comparison with those of other people, he had to view his location as being peculiarly blessed.

**The Land: Coordinate of Time**

Americans had never doubted the richness of the land in which they lived. Prominent among those who chanted its praises was Arnold Guyot, Swiss friend of Louis Agassiz and distinguished member of the Princeton faculty. Shortly after his arrival in the United States in 1848, Guyot delivered a series of lectures in French at the Lowell Institute in Boston. Subsequently translated and published under the title *The Earth and Man,* the lectures struck a favorable response, going through several printings. The vogue that Guyot enjoyed was at least in part attributable to his telling Americans what they already believed was true of their environment. Few would quarrel with his detailed list of geopolitical advantages enjoyed by the United States: "The fertility of the soil; its position, in the midst of the oceans, between the two extremes of Europe and Asia, facilitating commerce with these two worlds; the proximity of the rich tropical countries of Central and South America, towards which, as by a natural descent, it is borne by the waters of the majestic Mississippi, and of its thousand tributary streams; all these advantages seem to promise its labor and activity a prosperity without example."

Prosperity arrived. And statistics of nineteenth-century economic development yield an impression of its magnitude. In the period 1869–1873, the gross national product averaged $9.11 billion, as measured in constant 1929 dollars. By 1897–1901, GNP had risen to an annual average of $37.1 billion, and by 1907–1914 it was up to $55.0 billion a year. The per capita increase went from an annual $223 in 1869–1873 to $496 in 1897–1901. In the years 1907–1914, the average annual per capita share of GNP stood at $608. The extraordinary growth of the American economy from the Civil War to World War I certainly seemed to justify Guyot's optimistic predictions.

Remarkable though that growth was, however, it did not proceed without reverses in every decade to the end of the century. The depressions of the seventies and the nineties were especially severe. If bank clearings are taken as a measure of economic prosperity, the nation's progress was fitful indeed. In 1873 New York clearings stood at $35.5 billion but fell to $21.6 million in 1876. In the nation as a whole they were $61 billion in 1882, but they declined to $37.8 billion by 1885. Mounting again to a high of $60.9 billion in 1892, they fell off to $45 billion by 1894. Prices followed the same cyclical pattern. The general price index, standing at 100 in 1873, declined to 77 in the depression that followed the panic of that year. The index went from 87 to 76 in the mid-eighties, and from 78 to 71 in the nineties. The downward trend of prices from the Civil War to the end of the century is worth noting. Together with the cyclical fluctuations that brought periodic unemployment, business losses, social unrest, and anxiety, it raised questions about the soundness of the American economy despite significant increases in gross national product.

One of the first to pose such questions was a jack-of-all-trades named Henry George. Born in Philadelphia in 1839, he left school at thirteen to work for an importing house and then as a foremast boy on a ship bound for Australia and Calcutta. Back in Philadelphia by 1856, he learned how to set type. But once more his wanderlust got the better of him, and he signed on as a steward of a lighthouse tender ordered to service on the Pacific coast. Soon wearying of that, too, he jumped ship in San Francisco and joined the gold rush to the Frasier River in Canada. Though he found no gold, upon his return to San Francisco he did find a wife, and for years he struggled to feed his growing family. He worked as a reporter and editor for several newspapers and was active in Democratic politics. His was a probing, restless intelligence, and he set for himself the task of explaining why a nation of such enormous wealth contained, at the same time, so much wretched poverty. A political sinecure as inspector of gas meters gave him the time he needed to write out his conclusions. *Progress and Poverty,* the book that George published in 1879, became a best seller. For some readers it became much more: the basis for a creed.

A voracious reader, George was familiar with Darwinian ideas. He did not question their validity in the field of biology, but he did not believe that evolution of the species greatly affected the progress of civilization, for man had not changed significantly as a biological organism since the beginning of recorded history. Should Homer or Virgil, Demosthenes or Cicero, Alexander, Hannibal or Caesar, Plato or Lucretius, Euclid or Aristotle miraculously reenter life, George argued, no one could assume that they would be inferior to men of the nineteenth century. Society changed over time; civilizations rose and fell. The differences between the people of one era as against those of another, however, were differences that inhered in the society and not in the individual. What accounted for differences between civilizations was not genetics or heredity, but rather the "body of traditions, beliefs, customs, laws, habits, and associations, which arise in every community and which surround every individual."

George also affirmed the idea that "human nature is human nature all the world over." He was singularly unimpressed by claims to racial superiority. A white child reared by Indians would be perfectly attuned to Indian culture. That such was not the case with black or Indian children in white societies was, he thought, attributable "to the fact that they are never

Henry George commented on the way white men's guns deprived red men of game. This 1874 photograph of a buffalo hunters' camp in the Texas Panhandle shows fresh hides staked and stretched on the ground. Tongues were dried on a rack, but most of the meat was left for buzzards to consume (Western History Collections, University of Oklahoma Library).

treated precisely as white children." George rejected the view that significant innate differences distinguished the races; character was shaped by society. To undermine the foundations of a society was to weaken the character of its people. Anglo-Saxon conquest of the American continent had destroyed the conditions to which Indian habits and customs were well adapted, but whites had done little to help Indians adjust to a new environment. Thus the American Indian had become "a hunter in a land stripped of game; a warrior deprived of his arms and called on to plead in legal technicalities." He learned the vices of civilization, but not its virtues. "He loses his accustomed means of subsistence, he loses self-respect, he loses morality; he deteriorates and dies away." Why had the Anglo-Saxon exterminated the Indian? "Simply because he has not brought the Indian into his environment."

George never denied that civilizations progressed, but he could not ignore the poverty that existed in civilized societies. What, then, was the law of progress? And why did poverty develop? Men progressed, he thought, as they drew together in cooperative association and by that association increased the "mental power" directed toward improvement. Difficulties arose when a dominant class concentrated wealth and political power in its own hands. When that occurred, "the masses of the community are compelled to expend their mental powers in merely maintaining existence." At the same time, within the privileged class, "mental power is expended in keeping up and intensifying the system of inequality, in ostentation, luxury, and warfare." Thus the power that association set free for progress was wasted. Barriers to further progress were raised, and retrogression began.

George's explanation of the rise and fall of civilizations was not entirely his own, for others had also noted the decadence of economic inequality. The program that George derived from his understanding of why inequality had developed was, however, peculiarly his own. He believed that throughout all history privileged classes had obtained their power from possession of land. The progress of a civilization brings an increase in land values, and those fortunate enough to hold property in land need do nothing to benefit from that increase. People who work for wages must constantly struggle to subsist because "with increases in productive power, rent tends to even greater increase, thus producing a constant tendency to the forcing down of wages." All the benefits resulting from the march of progress in the United States, then, went to the owners of land. Because of this, land speculation had been rife, and such speculation had, in turn, been a major cause of the periodic depressions Americans had suffered.

What did George propose as a solution? What was necessary for the use of land, he thought, was not its private ownership, but security of improvements. One did not have to turn over title to the land to induce a man to improve it; one had only to say "whatever your labor or capital produces on this land shall be yours." Furthermore, since the value of land increased in proportion to population growth, the community had a legitimate claim to the increase in value. George urged that the community make good its

Concerned with extremes of wealth and want (the subject of an 1889 cartoon in *Frank Leslie's Illustrated Newspaper*), George wrote *Progress and Poverty* to show how the extremes might be reduced and a just society established. In his analysis he observed that "as the value of land increases, so does the contrast between wealth and want appear." Where land values were highest (that is, in large cities), "civilization exhibits the greatest luxury side by side with the most piteous destitution."

Poverty and want were all too apparent on Manhattan's lower east side at the close of the nineteenth century (George Eastman House).

claim by a single tax, that is, by appropriating for public use the unearned increment from an increase in land value. To do that, he argued, would eliminate the need for any other form of taxation. And, what is more important, the basic cause of inequality—of the suffering that came with poverty and the debility that came with privilege—would also be eliminated. Every citizen in the country would have ample opportunity to realize his full potential: "To remove want and the fear of want, to give to all classes leisure, and comfort, and independence, the decencies and refinements of life, the opportunities of mental and moral development, would be like turning water into a desert. The sterile waste would clothe itself with verdure, and the barren places where life seemed banned would ere long be dappled with the shade of trees and musical with the song of birds."

Small wonder that *Progress and Poverty* enjoyed such popularity! Argued with logic and conviction, if not with complete understanding of economic forces, it gave rise to single-tax clubs and discussion groups made up of true believers. George's remedy for the ills of society would do nothing less than break the cycle of history, a cycle that marked the decline of every civilization to which human cooperation had given rise. The single tax made coordinates of land and time. Without it, the time of American civilization would end just as the time of other civilizations had ended. With it, the progress of American civilization would continue into an unlimited future.

## The Myth of the Self-Made Man

*Progress and Poverty* was a seminal book; other criticisms of American society appeared in rapid succession. Few of them incorporated George's single-tax proposal as a remedy for social and economic ills, but they did ring the changes on comparisons of rich and poor, the life of ease enjoyed by the privileged and the life of toil endured by the downtrodden. Unequal distribution of wealth was real—and only too apparent. According to one estimate published in the December 1893 number of the *Political Science Quarterly,* "sixty-seven per cent of the wealth is owned by nine per cent of the families." As if to give meaning to such figures, George W. Vanderbilt was at the time completing the chateau on his 200 square-mile estate at Asheville, North Carolina. It had forty bedrooms, a Norman banquet hall with a seventy-five foot ceiling, a print room, a tapestry gallery, and a library built to hold twenty-five thousand books. The other side of the statistical divide was equally impressive, though, of course, in a very different way. At the turn of the century, an investigating committee of the City Homes Association of Chicago found that in the Polish district, where dwellings contained an average 3.16 apartments, the population density was 339.8 people per acre. The committee pointed out by way of comparison that the density of Chicago's Polish quarter was three times that of the most crowded portions of Tokyo and Calcutta.

The late nineteenth century was a period when evidence of unequal distribution of wealth could be found on every hand. It was also a period that echoed with paeans to the self-made man, the rugged individualist who held an honored place in the hagiocracy of industrial America. In 1897, when Vanderbilt University honored the memory of its benefactor by placing his statue on the campus, Chauncey Depew spoke at the unveiling. "The American Commonwealth is built upon the individual," he intoned. "It recognizes neither classes nor masses. . . . We have thus become a nation of self-made men." Nothing could have been more fitting than for the university to erect the statue of Cornelius Vanderbilt. He had been "a conspicuous example of the products and possibilities of our free and elastic conditions." And so it went. Depew's remarks exemplified an essential part of the litany endlessly repeated in such ceremonial observances across the land.

In point of fact, as the findings of several investigators have shown, only a fraction of the men of wealth could claim to have made themselves. Basing their study on a sample of 303 industrial leaders of the 1870s, historians Frances Gregory and Irene Neu drafted a composite portrait. The industrial leader, they concluded, was American by birth, English in national origin, and Protestant (Congregational, Presbyterian, or Episcopalian) in religious affiliation. He was city born and "bred in an atmosphere in which business and a relatively high social standing were intimately associated with his family life." He did not begin to work at a regular job until after his eighteenth birthday because he was preoccupied with school and college. His formal education was well above average for the period. Clearly, the man who fit such a description was hardly the hero of rags-to-riches fables.

Why, then, did business and industrial leaders seek to identify themselves as self-made men? John William Ward has pointed out that status in society may be described in several ways, but all of them emphasize objective (birth, wealth, authority, power) and subjective (character, intellect, diligence) characteristics. Men who obviously had the objective attributes of wealth or power could not simply enjoy their perquisites. They had to think that they had personal characteristics justifying them. Good fortune, not enough in itself, had to be merited. Or, as Max Weber put it, "Good fortune thus wants to be 'legitimate' fortune."

The process of legitimizing fortune was not carried out through a centrally directed campaign of propaganda. Nor were those who sought to justify themselves always clear in their own minds about what it was they were doing. That so much of the driving force behind it was subconscious helps to explain why the self-justification of the rich drew heavily upon—to use Henry George's terminology—"the body of traditions, beliefs, customs, laws, habits, and associations" of an earlier America. Back in the 1830s Alexis de Tocqueville had seen equality of social conditions in the United States producing men who, though they lacked the power to influence others, nevertheless secured the education and fortune necessary to satisfy their own wants. The "individualism" that Tocqueville identified (he was among the first to use the word) "disposes each member of the community to sever himself from the mass of his fellows and to draw apart with his family and his friends, so that after he has thus formed a little circle of his own, he willingly leaves society at large to itself." Emerson spoke for such men when he observed that "whoso would be a man must be a nonconformist."

But Emerson had not stopped there. He had gone on to discover unity in the great Over-Soul, which was the ultimate reality transcending all nature. To stand apart from one's neighbors is a chilling experience unless one can find a more meaningful relationship with nature than he can find in society. Emerson found such a relationship in the order of the universe, an order that lay beyond particular societies. "Within man," he wrote, "is the soul of the whole; the wise silence; the universal beauty, to which every part and particle is equally related; the eternal One." The individual, he concluded, was but an instrument for carrying out purposes far larger than those of any artificial society.

Men of wealth at the turn of the century did not often justify themselves by quoting Emersonian aphorisms, but they did appeal to the tradition that had made those aphorisms seem plausible. What Chauncey Depew meant when he said that the American Commonwealth was built upon the individual was that the American government interfered as little as possible with the relationship between man and the natural order. What the captain of industry meant when he talked about being a self-made man was that his success resulted from skillful operations that were consistent with the laws of nature but at the same time uninhibited by artificial contrivances of government or society. His understanding of the natural order enabled him to adopt the language of Darwinism without really comprehending the essential idea of evolution. He could talk about "the survival of the fittest" as a sociological phenomenon because economic competition was natural and socially beneficial; he thought more about how society rewarded able competitors than he did about how the less able were wiped out. He thought little, if at all, about the biological implications of Darwin's theories.

Looking back at the thinking of captains of industry in the late nineteenth century, at their ceremonial pronouncements and their rhetorical self-justification, one cannot escape the conclusion that they were inconsistent. On the one hand, they did much to break down static conceptions of time and society. As men who furthered the advancement of technology, they helped to revolutionize American thinking about time and history. On the other hand, in the realm of social theory—which they developed out of a need for self-justification rather than out of any particular expertise—they reverted to a static conception of natural order. Thus, until they could revise their understanding of what individualism implied, they were singularly unprepared to cope with forces of change, with the fluctuations of business, or with the consequences of their own achievement. John Maynard Keynes, who encountered opposition to his own new ideas during the Great Depression of the 1930s, commented on the phenomenon. "Practical men, who believe themselves to be quite exempt from any intellectual

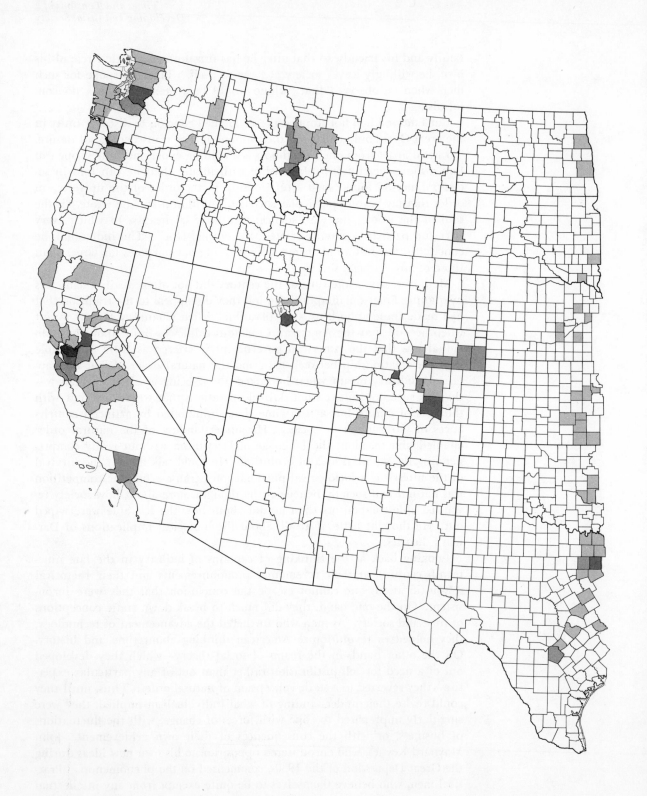

# Concentration of Manufacturing, 1900

## by Counties

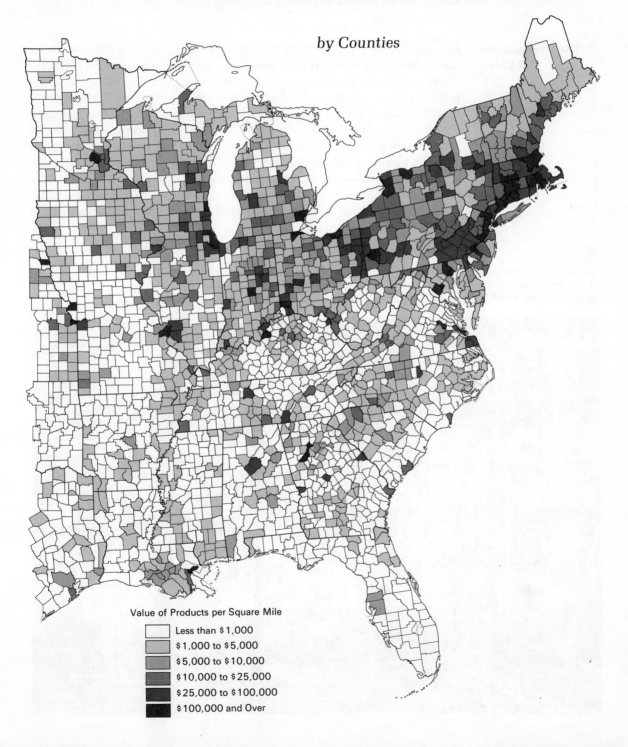

Value of Products per Square Mile

- Less than $1,000
- $1,000 to $5,000
- $5,000 to $10,000
- $10,000 to $25,000
- $25,000 to $100,000
- $100,000 and Over

influences," he observed, "are usually the slaves of some defunct economist." He might well have been describing the late nineteenth century captain of industry.

**The Organization of Labor**

Changes taking place in American life during the nineteenth century resulted from several interrelated processes and developments. Inventions—the steam engine, the Bessemer process, the reaper, or the telephone—supplied the tools of economic change. Not many inventions were entirely self-generating; nearly all of them grew out of borrowing from, and experimenting with, different combinations of ideas. Working closely with inventors were innovators in techniques of production, men more concerned with the uses of technology than with technology itself. Andrew Carnegie was one such innovator. He invented nothing, but under his guidance the steel industry provided essential materials for industrial expansion in all directions. The variety of economic possibilities created by inventors and

The belts and shafting of industrial plants made for dangerous working conditions, as an artist's impression of the lathe and press room at the McCormick reaper factory in 1885 would suggest (State Historical Society of Wisconsin).

Women and children had always shared in the work on farms. With the migration from rural to urban areas, they found employment in factories, usually in low-paying, unskilled jobs. This Gulf Coast cannery relied heavily on such cheap labor (George Eastman House).

innovators required a third order of activity: the coordination of capital resources and finance with production and distribution of goods. Functional diversity within the business and industrial elite should have been a warning against the simplistic suggestion that individualism explained nineteenth-century economic change.

It should have been a warning, too, against simplistic conceptions of class structure and class interest. Yet industrial development did have a profound effect on those who worked in the new industrial plants, men who in preindustrial society had been artisans, mechanics, and craftsmen. Competition with larger, more powerful, or more efficient producers and distributors forced many artisans to abandon entrepreneurial activities. Seeking employment in factories, they entered a wage system that often seemed unfair and exploitative.

Competition among the sellers of labor could be just as ruthless as competition among entrepreneurs. Selling their labor rather than the products of their labor, they sold their time as much as their skill; while sacrificing a part of their lives, they also sacrificed activities that could give meaning to life. Thus they gave up the psychic satisfactions that artisans and craftsmen were presumed to derive from exercising their talents. Having little power to make decisions for themselves during that part of the day set off by the shrill sound of the opening and closing whistle, workers often misunderstood and perhaps mistrusted those who made decisions that affected their well-being both on the job and off. If they believed ceremonial pronouncements on the virtues of individualism, they had either to think that they were destined for better things or that they lacked the character and ability to succeed. One line of thought led to temporary acceptance of their lot; the other led to self-hatred and its psychological hazards. If, on the other hand, they could not accept the myth of the self-made man, their one logical course was to organize themselves, thus developing the power to escape the worst effects of the wage system or possibly to escape the wage system itself.

The first attempt to organize workers nationally came with the formation of the National Labor Union in 1866. Although it failed to achieve its major objectives, the union's six years of activity served to indicate the magnitude of labor's problems. Under the leadership of William H. Sylvis, who became its president in 1868, the NLU sought to provide an alternative to the wage system by entering into cooperative enterprises. Workers pooled their resources, supplied their labor, and managed factories and stores themselves. But such schemes, however high-minded and enthusiastic their proponents, had little chance of success. Capitalization was insufficient, managers were inexperienced, and plants had limited productive capacity. Sylvis and other supporters of the cooperative idea believed that the basic difficulty lay in the reluctance of bankers to grant loans to cooperatives. They therefore began to agitate for a government-operated banking system, one that would loan funds for the general welfare rather than for private gain. In search of support for such a program, the NLU drifted into independent politics—and then disintegrated. By broadening its appeal in order to attract votes, and by soliciting the support of reformers who rode a variety of hobbies, the NLU lost cohesion. Trade unions that stressed more specific working-class objectives, such as the eight-hour day, were only lukewarm about generalized reform. They deserted the ranks, leaving NLU leaders to ponder the reasons for their union's failure.

A second and more important attempt to unite workers in opposition to the wage system developed under the auspices of the Knights of Labor. Founded in 1869 through the efforts of Uriah S. Stephens, a Philadelphia garment worker and religious humanitarian, the Knights sought to unite "all who gained their bread by the sweat of their brow." A secret organization with an elaborate ritual that affirmed the nobility and holiness of labor, the order grew slowly during the depression years of the seventies. But then, with the labor unrest of 1877, the Knights were able to take advantage of nationwide dissatisfaction of workingmen. The following year they held their first national convention.

The organization never fully approved of strikes or the use of force. Terence V. Powderly, who replaced Stephens as Grand Master Workman in 1879, constantly emphasized the solidarity of society. Although the order became more militant in the eighties than it had been in the seventies, Powderly always used his influence to avoid strikes unless he could find no other alternative. What he sought instead was a refurbished cooperative movement. He and the Knights were no more successful in that effort than the NLU had been, however, and labor organizations never again made cooperation a major objective.

In other respects, too, the experience of the Knights of Labor paralleled that of the National Labor Union. Both movements lacked the unity essential to coherent policy. The Knights did not discriminate among those who labored for their daily bread, but welcomed both skilled and unskilled workers. In the early days even farmers and small businessmen could belong. But the Knights discovered what the NLU had also learned to its sorrow: that a broad reform movement which appeared attractive at its inception could become divisive in implementation. Many of the workers who joined the union during its aggressive phase in the eighties had little sympathy for Powderly's dream of cooperation among all economic classes. Skilled craftsmen, especially, were jealous of prerogatives that they believed should be theirs; they were suspicious of talk about labor's solidarity. Defections occurred, then, as an increasing number of workers came to believe that they had more to gain by fighting their battles within the wage system than by reshaping the whole society into a cooperative commonwealth.

**The Farmers'
Search for Solidarity**
The technology that made industrialization possible was by no means confined to manufacturing. New farm machinery brought changes in agriculture, too. The mechanization of agriculture was not, of course, something that occurred overnight. An abundance of land, along with a scarcity of labor to till it, had always served as a powerful stimulus to mechanization. Farmers necessarily placed great emphasis on inventions that might increase their efficiency and on machines that might allow them to till more land with less labor. The use of machinery had little effect on productivity per acre; increased yields per acre could be had from the use of fertilizer, irrigation systems, contour plowing, and the like. No farmer would ever scorn better yields, but throughout the nineteenth century the standard of progress was productivity per man-hour rather than productivity per acre. American agriculture was extensive, not intensive; time was its measure of success.

To buy the machines they needed, farmers often had to go into debt, but the possible rewards of extensive farming seemed to make the risk one worth taking. Borrowing against time, they acquired means to increase the productivity of their hours of toil. For the most part the risk paid off, although mechanization did bring some unsuspected hazards. It led to premature cultivation of subhumid areas in the West, where farmers could grow only a limited number of crops. Cash crop cultivation, which had long prevailed in the South, came to characterize the West as well. The trouble with such an agriculture—whether in corn and wheat growing regions or in tobacco and cotton areas—was that it took the farmer into a cash market economy and, by reducing his options, increased the hazards he faced. He was more likely to be hurt by falling prices, more inclined to fail during years of drought, and more dependent on railroads and distributive facilities than were those who carried on a diversified agriculture.

Farmers, an agrarian cartoon implied, were quick to perceive hazards in developments that accompanied the modernization of American life. The alert Granger tried to warn a preoccupied populace of approaching danger as the "consolidation train" (pulling boxcars of extortion, bribery, usurpation and depression) came round the bend.

Farmers with financial resources adequate to meet periods of economic crisis were able to succeed. So were those who, like the farmers of Illinois, Wisconsin, and Iowa, learned to diversify their operations. But too many farmers of the West and South continued to suffer from too much specialization and too little capital. They could not bargain effectively either with industrialists and merchants who sold to them or with grain dealers and processors who bought from them. That they should come to think of themselves as pawns in a national economic chess game was hardly surprising. If anything seemed clear to them, it was that they were being manipulated by influences that they could not control. In a fundamental sense, then, the problems of farmers appeared to parallel the problems of industrial workers. Both groups, despite their size, were economically weak. Many farmers reasoned that, like workers in factories, they would have to organize if they were to acquire the power necessary for securing at least some of their objectives.

A year after the founding of the National Labor Union in 1866, the Patrons of Husbandry, also known as the Grange, came into existence. Centering in the east north-central states, the new organization sought to improve the position of farmers through programs of education, cooperation, and social activity. Although it consciously avoided political action as an organization, individual members exerted a powerful influence in several states during the depression years of the seventies. They were especially successful in securing legislation designed to control railroads and monopolies. But in their cooperative enterprises they ran into the same difficulties that brought the downfall of labor cooperatives. The failure of such enterprises, along with improvement of agricultural methods and the return of good times, helped to bring about a precipitous decline in Granger influence. Membership dropped from about 800,000 in 1874 to 150,000 in 1880.

In the meantime, the center of agricultural unrest had shifted west and south into the high-risk areas where a balanced agriculture had not been developed. New organizations began to form there, beginning with the Texas Alliance, chartered in 1880. After the Texas Alliance merged with a Louisiana farmers' organization in 1887 and with an Arkansas group in 1889, the National Farmers' Alliance and Industrial Union came into being. Popularly known as the Southern Alliance, it was to become the largest farm organization in the United States, with a membership of some three million in the nineties. But in the North another farmers' alliance was rapidly taking shape. The logic of organization led inevitably to discussion of merging the two groups. They shared a common agrarian belief in the virtues of farming as a way of life, a common hatred for the way in which railroads and monopolies dealt with farmers, and a common conviction that only by standing together could farmers secure redress of their grievances.

The mechanization of agriculture, which encouraged extensive farming, was readily associated with economic progress. This rural family took obvious pride in its sod-busting plow and steam tractor, perhaps unaware that both contributed to the problems as well as the progress of farmers (State Historical Society of Wisconsin).

Yet the two alliance groups were not identical in their interests and convictions. The Southern Alliance was a secret organization limited to whites, while the Northern Alliance was open and even enrolled people who were not farmers. The extent to which blacks should participate in the movement became an issue that worked against consolidation and that also helps to explain differences in tactics between the two groups. Southerners were willing to recognize a separate Colored Farmers' Alliance, but they were reluctant to become involved in biracial political activity in defiance of southern tradition. To do that would, so it seemed to the Southern Alliance, raise new issues that had little to do with the farmers' issues they were bent on discussing. Thus the Southern Alliance concentrated on developing economic reforms, while leaders of the Northern Alliance urged political action in cooperation with other dissatisfied elements in American society.

The economic enterprises of the Alliance movement expanded on the cooperative idea. Farmers first organized agencies for cooperative buying. They then turned to stock-company schemes for marketing manufactured goods. Finally they attempted even to set up plants for manufacturing agricultural machinery. Few of these ventures proved successful. Alliancemen succumbed to the difficulties so familiar to others who had tried cooperatives: insufficient capital, high interest rates, the distrust of bankers, and the sometimes ruthless competition of established firms. Yet the Alliances moved beyond experimentation with old ideas. The Southern Alliance, for example, proposed what it called the "subtreasury plan," which would establish warehouses in all rural counties. These warehouses could accept nonperishable farm products for storage and grant loans up to 80 per cent of the value of the stored product. The subtreasury plan, argued its supporters, would provide a hedge against seasonal gluts while helping to prevent gyrations of the economy as a whole. Although the idea was never implemented, it did survive to influence agricultural programs during the New Deal era.

Failure of the Alliance cooperatives and other ventures cleared the way for advocates of political action. In December 1889 the two Alliance groups held simultaneous annual meetings in St. Louis. The Colored Alliance and the Knights of Labor also had representatives on the scene. Though these groups did not merge as a result of the joint sessions, they did reach agreement on some common objectives, and their platforms constituted a summary of agrarian demands. They called for the reclamation of lands held by foreign syndicates and railroads and for legislation against alien land ownership. Both Alliances urged government ownership and operation of railroads and telegraph lines. They agreed in urging financial reforms to abolish national banks, to expand the amount of currency in circulation, and to institute an income tax. The momentum for a new political party was beginning to build, and political activists within the Alliance movement were beginning to sniff victory in the air.

**Classes and the
Future: Utopia or
Cataclysm?**

Americans could not help but be impressed by the technological and industrial achievements of the United States during the nineteenth century. Changes that accompanied those achievements were everywhere apparent. By the decade of the nineties trolleys clattered along bustling Boston streets that had once been cowpaths, while part of the Common that had been used as pasture was dug up for construction of the nation's first subway. The stars that had shone over the site of General Braddock's defeat on the banks of the Monongahela River in western Pennsylvania were dimmed by the orange glow from the furnaces of Andrew Carnegie's steel plant at Homestead. Smoke-belching locomotives moved across the plains where Indians had followed herds of bison at midcentury, and steam-powered monsters threshed ripened grain in fields where the shaggy animals had grazed. Portland, Oregon, not yet fifty years old in 1890, had streets well lighted by hydroelectric current generated at Willamette Falls fourteen miles away.

Accelerating technological change prodded the mind and stirred the imagination. Did men not "talk and think faster in the depot than they did in the stage-office"? Accelerating technological change also seemed to exacerbate social cleavages that began with industrialization. Did the conflict between labor and the captains of industry have any chance of working itself out? Or would social stability give way to revolutionary social change? Would farmers unite with others who thought themselves oppressed? What did the future hold? Such questions intruded on American sensibilities toward the close of the nineteenth century, giving rise to a spate of books that attempted to provide answers. Some prophets optimistically predicted a resolution of social antagonisms and the formation of a utopian society. Others of more melancholy turn of mind foresaw a violent denouement, a cataclysmic struggle.

The most widely read prophecy in the utopian genre—indeed, the most popular of all futuristic books published in the late nineteenth century—was Edward Bellamy's *Looking Backward: 2000–1887*. Taking a position sympathetic to the poor, the exploited, and the powerless, Bellamy nevertheless wrote without the stridency of indignation. Whatever anger he felt in contemplating economic injustice was tempered by a charity that encompassed all classes and by a belief in the salutary effects of a technology properly pursued. Reared in the faith of his father, a Baptist clergyman in Chicopee Falls, Massachusetts, Bellamy had moved away from traditional theology to a profound interest in social ethics. In an essay written at the age of twenty-four, he had emphasized the idea of human solidarity made possible through brotherly love. *Looking Backward,* which he brought out fifteen years later, provided a description of how in the year 2000 American society might operate without class or economic rivalries and their attendant evils.

In Bellamy's utopia the State would assume responsibility for the production and distribution of goods; and, by eliminating the waste of competition, it would multiply national wealth. The State would therefore guarantee economic security for all. Machines would relieve Americans of the arduous tasks that, sapping energy, prevented full development of the human potential. With no need to worry about securing basic necessities of existence—and surrounded by books, music, and art—every citizen could satisfy his individual desires, achieving the good life in his own way.

The society that Bellamy envisioned did not lack discipline. Like all boys his age (he had just celebrated his eleventh birthday when Confederate guns opened fire on Fort Sumter), he had been fascinated by the armies of North and South locked in combat. Later in life, he turned his attention from warfare to military organization, and his happy society of the future bore the marks of his mature interest. There, in that society, the first twenty-five years of a person's life were devoted to education. Then, moving into one of the labor battalions set up to produce goods on which the society depended, he served for a period of twenty years. Finally, upon reaching the age of forty-five, he was permitted to spend his leisure as he chose. At this stage of life he also assumed political responsibilities denied him at earlier stages. Bellamy's state was run by the elders who chose from among their own number the president and the council that together governed the nation. Thus did the Chicopee romancer look forward to a highly structured society. But it was in such a society—one that eliminated competition—that the individual man could best achieve a sense of his humanity. Although in its organization the United States would resemble an army, it would no longer need to fight wars. World brotherhood would make such barbarous practice obsolete.

Bellamy, far more interested in the structure of utopia than in the process of change, avoided a detailed description of how Americans might move toward a new order. Yet in one of the book's dialogues he had Dr. Leete, universal man of the year 2000, outline the steps by which the great transition could take place. After about 1875, according to the doctor, there was no chance "for individual enterprise in any important field of industry, unless backed by great capital." As a consequence, Americans had witnessed the movement of capital toward larger and larger aggregations. They had seen the rich grow richer and the poor become poorer. They had observed small businessmen wiped out by trusts, syndicates, and monopolies. "Was there, then, no way of commanding the services of the mighty wealth-producing principle of consolidated capital without bowing down to a plutocracy like that of Carthage?" To ask the question, suggested Dr. Leete, was to answer it. The final step in the process of consolidation came when the nation itself became "the one great business corporation in which all other corporations were absorbed." The transition from the "epoch of trusts" to the formation of "the Great Trust" had been gradual and bloodless. The great corporations themselves had taught people to recognize the economies and advantages of scale. And when the final consolidation came, it "implied nothing which seemed impracticable even to the timid."

Seers who, like Bellamy, looked forward to a benign transformation of American society sometimes found themselves linked in uneasy tandem with those who anticipated violent, revolutionary change. The utopians shared with the cataclysmists a jaundiced view of nineteenth-century industrial society in the United States. Both groups tended to view it as materialistic, exploitative, hypocritical, and corrupt. Both were impressed with its instability and expected it to change. While the utopians anticipated a happy resolution of social and economic problems, however, the cataclysmists believed that the antagonisms of American civilization impelled it toward chaos. They concentrated their attention, therefore, on the holocaust to which, as they read them, all signs of the times were pointing.

In the troubled last decade of the nineteenth century, Ignatius Donnelly took his place with the cataclysmists. He had not always played the role of a Cassandra, and a lifetime of disappointments never completely quenched the hope that spasmodically burst into flame and fired his enthusiasm. Born in Philadelphia in 1831, Donnelly went west as a young man confident of securing a fortune in Minnesota land development. He invested in Nininger City, seventeen miles south of St. Paul, in the expectation that boom times were on their way. That dream evaporating during the panic of 1857, Donnelly turned to politics. After a term as lieutenant-governor of Minnesota, he served six years in Congress. Always a champion of the underprivileged—farmers, immigrants, Indians, blacks, women—Donnelly found six years ample time to antagonize the Republican party to which he belonged. After losing his bid for a fourth term in 1868, he spent the rest of his life writing books, farming, and conducting frequent forays onto political battlefields.

The three books produced by the Sage of Nininger in the 1880s gave evidence of research as prodigious as it was undisciplined. The first of them, *Atlantis: The Antediluvian World,* was an effort to prove that the Atlantic island of ancient legend had actually existed and that it had nurtured a sophisticated civilization. *Ragnarok: The Age of Fire and Gravel* presented an argument for the notion that deposits of sand and gravel were not produced by glacial drift but were, rather, the debris of an enormous comet that struck prehistoric earth with incredible force. In *The Great Cryptogram,* Donnelly developed his version of the thesis that Francis Bacon actually wrote the plays attributed to Shakespeare.

At his best Donnelly could write with rhetorical flourish, but at his worst he would scarcely have done credit to pulp magazines featuring advertisements for liver pills and trusses. His choices of subject in themselves suggest a mind enchanted by the bizarre. And in the way that he handled his materials he betrayed a penchant for opposing learned opinion. For Donnelly, reality was never quite what it seemed. His method was to assume the truth of one of his eccentric propositions and then to scratch around beneath a crust of academic scholarship for proof of his initial assumption. Perhaps because of his own frustrations, combined with a tendency to find

The cover design for an early edition of Edward Bellamy's *Looking Backward* captured his belief that American society would pass from dark, depressing economic exploitation to the sunshine of utopian community.

The clatter, bustle, and overcrowding of cities increased the psychological pressures on people who lived and worked in urban areas. Ignatius Donnelly saw the metropolis as a locus of disruptive ferment in a future he described with bleak pessimism. The scene at Dearborn and Randolph on a busy day in Chicago might well have reinforced his conviction that the metropolis was heading toward revolution (State Historical Society of Wisconsin).

the causes of his disappointment in the fates and not in himself, his books also suggest a fascination with catastrophic upheaval: worlds in collision, volcanic eruptions, convulsions of nature.

In *Caesar's Column, A Story of the Twentieth Century,* his futuristic novel depicting the likely consequences of worsening social and economic conditions in America, Donnelly gave free rein to his proclivities. He began by describing the terrible stresses of 1988 through letters written by Gabriel Weltstein, his protagonist. The sinister arrogance and brutality of the oligarchy that had come to dominate the country are matched by the sufferings of the exploited workers: "Toil, toil, toil, from early morn until late at night; then home they swarm; tumble into their wretched beds; snatch a few hours of disturbed sleep, battling with vermin, in a polluted atmosphere; and then up again and to work; and so on, and on, in endless, mirthless, hopeless round. . . ." Brutality begets brutality.

A conspiracy, known as the Brotherhood of Destruction, forms to counter the crimes of the oligarchy. Acts of bloodcurdling viciousness multiply and lead eventually to desperate, holocaustic struggle. At its conclusion the oligarchy and its minions are annihilated. Caesar Lomellini, leader of the Brotherhood, has their bodies piled up and covered with cement so as to form a great column "in commemoration of the death and burial of modern civilization." The anticlimactic last chapter of the book, containing some of Donnelly's suggestions for salvation, takes a few humane and decent people off to an agrarian paradise in Africa.

Published in 1890, two years after *Looking Backward,* Donnelly's novel appealed to those who found Bellamy's vision too bland and tepid to bear much relationship to social trends as they understood them. "Bellamy looks backward on what is impossible as well as improbable," commented Milton George, agrarian radical and founder of the Northern Alliance. *"Caesar's Column* looks forward to what is not only possible, but probable." With such approval the book did well as a publishing venture. Selling some 700,000 copies, it ranked second only to *Looking Backward* in the markets of prophecy.

Neither Bellamy nor Donnelly would get high marks for accuracy in predicting the future. Each author incorporated a romantic theme that would seem absurd if written today. The theme centered on stock figures drawn from Victorian melodrama, such as chaste beauties whose maidenly blushes stir the hearts of virtuous young men. Although they did better in forecasting technological achievements—Bellamy has music piped into the home of Dr. Leete, and Donnelly's hero and his friends escape to Africa on board a giant airship—even their wildest imaginings seem quaint in the space age. But far more important than the prescience of the authors is what *Looking Backward* and *Caesar's Column* reveal about the times in which they were written. Both books emphasized disparities of wealth and power that had grown in proportion to the expansion of industry. And both insisted that social and economic change was unavoidable. For Bellamy the winds of change blew softly; his hero slept his way into the year 2000. For Donnelly change would come with hurricane force; he would not go gently into any bright utopia, nor would he rage against the dying of a dark and sinister system.

# 2

# Issues and Interests:
# American Society
# at the End of an Era

A sense of crisis pervaded the country as it entered the last decade of the nineteenth century. Politicians discussed public issues such as the tariff or the monetary system, but their observations seemed to bear little relationship to the realities that impinged on the lives of ordinary citizens. Although the first years of the nineties were prosperous ones, the forces of change were gathering momentum. Discontented groups had already begun to organize themselves for the reconstruction of American society when a panic on the New York Stock Exchange in 1893 initiated a prolonged and severe depression. A new urgency infused political debates of the depression years. The times appeared to favor radical change; and, while leaders of the two major parties pontificated on public platforms, leaders of a new radical party waited impatiently in the wings.

None of the changes that Edward Bellamy anticipated came to pass in the nineties; neither did the cataclysm that Ignatius Donnelly had foreseen. Several developments account for failure of a radical thrust. For one thing, radical leaders made disastrous miscalculations in their timing. Waiting too long to strike their telling blow in the political campaign of 1896, they never received another opportunity. For another, they attempted to exploit popular discussions by taking a position on the major public issue of the nineties, the free coinage of silver. Using that issue to capture support, they hoped to gain the power necessary for implementing a much broader reform program. The strategy backfired. Instead of winning support, they found themselves in the position of having to give support to the party that had preempted the silver cause. Their efforts were instrumental in changing the character of the Democratic party, but that was very far from what they had in mind. Finally, neither the radicals nor the candidate whose nomination they ratified ever fully understood or appreciated the growing complexity of the society in which they lived. A formal yet unsophisticated view of that society led to a limited set of

34

objectives. Looking toward amalgamation of exploited economic classes, they failed to reckon with the compelling power of divergent and rapidly multiplying interest groups.

**Populists Organize**     The Populist (or People's) party, growing out of agrarian unrest and organizing itself in the nineties, appeared to some troubled Americans as a bellwether of cataclysmic change. To others, less worried about change because they were more profoundly impressed by the need for it, the People's party seemed to offer a means of righting the wrongs and eliminating the injustices of a new industrial society. The 1889 alliance conventions at St. Louis had served to emphasize the unity of dissident agrarians. Sustained by the thought of a common purpose, leaders of embattled farmers began to muster their forces for congressional and state elections in 1890. With support from the Knights of Labor, the Patrons of Husbandry, and other interested groups, they formed independent parties in Kansas, Nebraska, the Dakotas, Minnesota, Colorado, Michigan, and Indiana. In the South, dissidents concentrated on winning control of the Democratic party rather than on establishing new parties.

Expansion of agriculture over the subhumid Great Plains involved high risk and hardship for proud farm families such as this one. When depression added to their burdens in the 1890s, many of them gave enthusiastic support to the Populist movement (Solomon D. Butcher Collection, Nebraska State Historical Society).

Results of agrarian efforts encouraged those who had become disenchanted with economic experimentation and had urged political action. The People's party in Kansas elected five congressmen and one senator; it also controlled the lower house of the state legislature. Nebraska Independents gained control of the lower house of the legislature and sent an Independent to Congress. In the South, candidates backed by the Alliance dominated the legislatures of eight states, and the Alliance helped to elect governors in South Carolina, Georgia, Tennessee, and Texas.

With such an impressive showing, the December convention of the Alliance at Ocala, Florida, buzzed with talk of a new political party. But southern representatives, arguing that the times were ripe for gaining control of the democracy, proved reluctant to plunge into third-party politics. They managed to pass a resolution postponing any major political move. Third-party men were not so easily deterred. Their drive for organization culminated in February 1892, when a St. Louis gathering voted to form the People's party and to hold a nominating convention in Omaha the following summer. Ignatius Donnelly jubilantly announced the objectives of the new party: "We propose to wipe the Mason and Dixon line out of our geography; to wipe the color line out of politics; to give Americans prosperity, that the man who creates shall own what he creates; to take the robber class from the throat of industry; to take possession of the government of the United States, and put our nominee in the White House."

At Omaha the Populists nominated Iowa's James B. Weaver and with clamorous enthusiasm adopted a platform calling for remedial action in the three areas of land, transportation, and finance. Specific planks included demands for free coinage of silver, an increase in the circulating medium, a graduated income tax, postal savings banks, government ownership and operation of all railroad and telegraph lines, reclamation of alien land holdings, and abolition of corporate land holding in excess of actual need. Shortly after his nomination Weaver told a Des Moines audience that the Populist position could be summed up in a single phrase: "Equal rights for all and special privileges for none."

Populist success in the 1892 election was not so great as some agrarians had anticipated. Senator Kyle of South Dakota, for example, had believed that, running a presidential candidate of its own, the party might force the election into the House of Representatives. As it turned out, however, the Grover Cleveland–Adlai Stevenson ticket of the Democrats won an easy victory over Republicans Benjamin Harrison and Whitelaw Reid. Cleveland swept into office with 277 electoral votes as compared with 145 for Harrison and 22 for Weaver. Democrats also won majorities in both houses of Congress. While Populists did not accomplish all that they had hoped for, their candidate did carry four states—Kansas, Colorado, Nevada, and Idaho—enough to persuade them that they were riding the wave of the future. It was, after all, the first time since the Civil War that a third party had captured any electoral votes.

**The Depression of
the Nineties**

Events soon provided substance for the belief that change was in order. Shortly after Cleveland entered the White House in 1893, the nation confronted a major depression. Business failures—notably of railroads, iron and steel companies, and banks—followed one after the other with distressing frequency. Before the end of the year nearly sixteen thousand businesses had closed their doors. The depression of the nineties was at least as severe as any before the Great Depression of the 1930s, and far more traumatic than most. A graph of economic activity for the decade would show two troughs occurring in 1893–1894 and 1896–1897. The substantial recovery that came in 1895 was both partial and short-lived. During the worst months the economy functioned at 25–30 per cent below capacity, while complete recovery did not come until after the turn of the century.

Business cycles, including periods of prosperity as well as depression, are easier to describe than to explain. The depression of the nineties posed peculiar challenges to those who sought an explanation, in part because it came in a period of long-range income and production increases. One modern economist, Edwin Frickey, estimated that between the Civil War and World War I the average annual rate of growth in all industrial and commercial production was 5.38 per cent. Another, Simon Kuznets, focusing his attention on income, found that total national income, measured in 1929 dollars, was 9.4 billion in the decade 1869–1878; by 1909–1918, it had increased to 50.3 billion. National income per capita went from $216 in the decade 1869–1878 to $515 in 1909–1918. Americans were clearly far better off at the beginning of World War I than they had been at the close of the Civil War.

Yet the depression of the nineties was a harsh and palpable reality. With unemployment hovering around three million in 1893–1894, some 17 to 19 per cent of the work force found itself directly affected. Many of those who held their jobs had to work for lower wages. Taken together, pay cuts and unemployment meant drastic reduction in per capita real earnings of non-farm employees in the period 1892–1894. Industrial workers, along with farmers who had long suffered from declining agricultural prices, increased the ranks of the discontented. Few persons escaped the depression's influence. Henry Adams, returning home from Switzerland, found "everyone . . . in a blue fit of terror." New York City counted nearly seventy thousand unemployed and twenty thousand homeless and vagrant. Thousands of job-seekers flocked to Chicago, where the Columbian Exposition (the "White City" built as a glistening monument to American achievement) had just opened its gates. But the exposition provided only limited unemployment relief; policemen patroled railroad stations to discourage transients. And still they came. Reports had it that a hundred thousand persons were out of work in Chicago during the winter of 1893–1894.

Puzzled by the depression, Americans groped for explanation of the crisis. As in most periods of economic disturbance, public statements abounded in metaphor and analogy: alternating prosperity and depression was like the swing of a pendulum; the cloudy skies of depression would give way to the sunshine of prosperity; depression was a disease of the nervous system or the circulatory system. But analogy is no substitute for analysis, and the search for explanation gave rise to one of the great debates in American history. Discussions of the crisis pitted the rural West and South against the urban East as agrarian leaders pointed accusing fingers at Wall Street and the money power. Labor representatives charged that capital in its short-sighted quest for profits had helped to bring on the crisis by ignoring workers' demands for shorter hours and better pay. Businessmen countered with attacks on radical proposals advanced by Populists, labor unions, and an assortment of malcontents such as Henry George and Edward Bellamy. Shrewd businessmen, they contended, had no interest in undermining prosperity; to argue that they had deliberately plotted to bring on the crisis was an absurdity.

A few sympathetic observers of the business community attempted to cut through the vilification that accompanied social unrest in the nineties. Focusing their attention on economic forces, they concluded that the fundamental cause of depression lay in agricultural and industrial over-production. American manufacturers and farmers were producing more than the domestic market was capable of absorbing. The obvious solution to the crisis, in this view, was to expand markets overseas. But in 1893 those who advocated such a program did not have the influence over policy that they would exert later in the decade.

Ultimately, the great public debate of the depression years centered on merits and shortcomings of the American monetary system. One reason for the deep concern over currency was that, for more than thirty years after the Civil War, prices had declined steadily. The long period of deflation was hard on farmers who complained of shrinking incomes and on debtors who complained that their obligations, when measured in constant dollars, had actually increased. Indeed, argued proponents of a reformed currency system, deflation was hard on everyone affected by the depression crisis, for the downward movement of prices was a major cause of the depression's severity.

Those who urged monetary reform saw a direct correlation between prices and the amount of money in circulation. Scarce or dear money, ran the argument, meant low prices and economic contractions. Gold was dear and it was deflationary; gold monometallism was inadequate to sustain prices at a level that would assure agricultural profits and keep within reasonable bounds the obligations of debtors. During the depression of the nineties, therefore, monetary reform implied bimetallism, or supplementing gold with silver coinage. All participants in currency debates of the period agreed that bimetallism would have an inflationary effect. Soft-money men argued that some inflation was necessary to restore monetary stability and hasten the return of prosperity. Defenders of the gold stand-

Bimetallists adopted a sepulchral
view of monetary policies that eliminated the silver dollar and—as silver cartoonists understood them—
brought on the depression of the
nineties.

ard, on the other hand, thought that inflation would cheat creditors, persons living on fixed incomes, and workers whose wages would lag behind
prices.

**The Silver Crusade**     Arguments over money were nothing new in American history. Those who
recalled currency discussions of the Civil War and Reconstruction period
found much that was familiar in the controversy of the nineties. At the
beginning of the Civil War the currency consisted of gold coins, subsidiary
silver coins, and the notes of some 1,500 state banks. By the time Lee had
surrendered to Grant at Appomattox, gold and silver had largely disappeared from circulation, and state bank notes were being withdrawn because of heavy taxes placed on them. To meet its wartime obligations the
United States Treasury had issued a fiat currency popularly called greenbacks. Since the government did not take the further step of nationalizing
gold and silver, greenbacks fell to a discount that fluctuated with the fortunes of war. At one time a $10 gold piece would buy nearly $30 in greenbacks; at the close of hostilities the greenback had recovered considerably
but it was still worth only about 80 cents on the dollar.

Given the peculiarities of American currency at the close of the war, advocates of hard money began to urge abandonment of greenbacks and a
return to gold. Proponents of soft money argued with equal vehemence for
continuation or expansion of greenback issues. But what led some men to
favor gold while others urged greenbacks? Alignments of the Reconstruction period were complicated by a variety of influences. Not all businessmen, for example, wanted a deflationary gold standard. Many of those who

looked forward to industrial growth and economic fulfillment believed that greenbacks could help bring on a new age of industrial prosperity. Jay Cooke, a leading financier of the war years and a venturesome speculator in land, life insurance, and railroads after the war, insisted that currency expansion was essential to economic development. "Why," asked Cooke, "should this Grand and Glorious Country be stunted and dwarfed—its activities chilled and its very life blood curdled by these miserable 'hard coin' theories—the musty theories of a bygone age . . . ?" Men such as Cooke made uneasy alliance with agrarians, labor reformers, and congenital dissenters who held to the view that greenbacks might be used as an instrument of economic justice. It was a motley crowd that gathered under the soft-money umbrella.

Although hard-money men were also a mixed group—and certainly not all of one mind—most of them thought of money questions as moral questions. Using greenbacks to manipulate the currency, it seemed to them, would open the way for corruption and dishonesty. The New York *Christian Advocate* went so far as to suggest that "atheism is not worse in religion than an unstable or irredeemable currency in political economy." The churchmen who supported gold had natural allies among academic economists who held professorships in colleges supported by churches. Monetary theories taught by professional economists were usually linked with the ethical convictions of a well-educated class that had few doubts about its proper place in American society. On the whole it was the Best People—an older elite of eastern merchants, commercial bankers, textile manufacturers, professional men, and gentlemen reformers—who identified gold as the only honest money.

To characterize hard- and soft-money interests in this way, however, comes close to making both groups appear more homogeneous than they actually were. Both hard and soft money enjoyed widespread support, and that fact helps to explain the seemingly inconsistent nature of monetary policy worked out by Congress in the years from the depression of the 1870s to the depression of the 1890s. Four pieces of legislation—the Resumption Act, the Coinage Act of 1873, the Bland-Allison Act, and the Sherman Silver Purchase Act—assumed special importance as political leaders and parties turned their attention to monetary questions.

Congress passed the Resumption Act in 1875. Although in later years it came to be regarded as a victory for hard money, the act included provisions calculated to please both hard- and soft-money interests. For soft-money men there was a section that permitted free banking, or modification of the national banking system so as to end all bank note limitation and to make note expansion as free as deposit expansion. For those who favored hard money, there was a commitment to resume specie payments for greenbacks after January 1, 1879. After that date, under the terms of the act, holders of greenbacks would be able to exchange greenbacks for gold at par.

While the act itself constituted a compromise between the two interest groups in 1875, events of the following years made its hard-money provisions more effective than its soft-money sections. Free banking during the depression seventies did not produce the results that soft-money men had predicted. But the Treasury Department did make good the commitment to redeem greenbacks in gold. On the January day in 1879 when resumption went into effect, the New York Subtreasury held over $100 million in coin reserves to meet possible demands. The precaution proved unnecessary, for confidence in convertibility was so great that by closing time the Subtreasury had actually exchanged more paper for gold than gold for paper. Proponents of soft money then charged that convertibility placed the United States on a de facto gold standard. They were correct. But they either forgot or chose to ignore the fact that when Congress passed the Resumption Act in 1875, it had seemed to offer more to the soft-money interest through free banking than it did to the hard-money interest through the promise of specie payments.

Advocates of soft money were even more disquieted by the Coinage Act of 1873, which eliminated silver dollars from coinage lists used by the United States Mint. Passage of the act resulted in part from an awareness of the great difficulties involved in maintaining a bimetallic monetary standard. Under the old coinage law of 1837, the ratio between gold and silver coins had been pegged at 15.9884 units of silver to one unit of gold. This coinage ratio reflected the market prices then prevailing; in 1837, in other words, the market price of gold was roughly sixteen times that of silver. But formal adoption of bimetallism is one thing; maintaining bimetallism as a standard is quite another. What happened, of course, is that the market prices of silver and gold fluctuated at different rates. Increased production of gold, especially after the California Gold Rush of 1849, caused its market value to decline in relation to silver. Money overvalued at the mint tends to drive out of circulation money undervalued at the mint. At a 16 to 1 coinage ratio, silver was worth more on the market than it was at the mint, and in the thirty years prior to 1873 very little silver came into the mint for coinage.

By 1872, however, several signs indicated to those who chose to read them that silver was about to make a monetary comeback. American silver production that year was more than twice what it had been in 1869, while continued increases in production would, of course, affect the market price. Only a few government officials—notably George S. Boutwell, the Secretary of the Treasury; Henry R. Linderman, a coinage expert in the Treasury Department; and John Sherman, chairman of the Senate Finance Committee—were aware of the impending decline in the market price of silver. And because they feared the effects of coining depreciated silver bullion into legal-tender silver dollars, they cooperated in drafting a coinage bill that would do away with silver dollars. Introduced without fanfare, the bill received final congressional approval in February 1873.

Had soft-money men been privy to the information that shaped the Coinage Act, they would not have accepted demonetization of silver without a struggle. As it turned out, three years elapsed before a significant decline in the market price of silver made them conscious of the act's implications. At last aware of having been deprived of an opportunity to secure inflation through coinage of depreciated silver, they then raised a great hue and cry about the sinister motives of those who had perpetrated "the Crime of '73." Disappointed in the results of free banking, disturbed by the demonetization of silver, and distressed by the depression that followed the financial panic of 1873, they began to agitate for a return to "the dollar of our daddies."

Greenback sentiment remained strong throughout the decade of the seventies; but, as the market price of silver declined, advocates of bimetallism began to preempt the soft-money position. Their influence in Congress was strong enough in 1878 to secure passage of the Bland-Allison Act, which authorized the Secretary of the Treasury to purchase not less than $2 million and not more than $4 million of silver every month. The secretary could either coin the silver or issue silver certificates based upon the purchases. Although discussion of the silver purchase bill had been heated, economic effects of the act were negligible. It caused no shock

Polemics on the money question were legion, but none was more influential than William H. Harvey's 1894 tract, *Coin's Financial School.* The text featured a precocious adolescent named Coin, who confounded gold bugs with his persuasive arguments for silver, and the accompanying cartoons reflected a simple logic that won adherents among Harvey's readers.

waves on Wall Street; nor did it have much influence in bringing about the business recovery that began in the late seventies. The addition of such a limited amount of silver to the nation's currency could not have produced such a result so quickly. Yet with the return of prosperity and with partial remonetization of silver secured, agitation for soft money declined significantly.

The movement for more extensive coinage of silver did not, however, remain dormant for long. An economic slump in the middle eighties reawakened the demand for measures that would raise prices. Debates of the previous decade had provided silver men with arguments for increasing the amount of money in circulation. They now set about organizing themselves to exert political pressure for their objectives. A convention of silver activists, held at St. Louis in November 1889, formed the American Bimetallic League, electing Ohio's Adoniram J. Warner as its president. It passed a resolution, introduced by Missouri Congressman Richard "Silver Dick" Bland, calling for the free coinage of silver at a ratio of 16 to 1. It also sanctioned the appointment of an executive committee, which proceeded to set up a silver lobby in Washington early the next year.

The silver lobby pressed for free and unlimited coinage of silver, but it was practical enough to settle for half a loaf—at least temporarily. The lobby therefore supported the Sherman Silver Purchase Act, passed by Congress in 1890. The Sherman Act differed from the Bland-Allison Act in that it did not stipulate a dollar amount for silver purchases but instead directed the Secretary of the Treasury to buy 4.5 million ounces of silver monthly. The silver thus acquired was to be stored, while the Treasury was directed to issue treasury notes to cover the cost of the purchases. At 1890 prices the Sherman Act permitted the purchase of almost twice as much silver as did the Bland-Allison Act. Yet the market price of silver continued to decline so rapidly that by 1893 the dollar amount of monthly purchases was not much greater than it had been under the old act. By 1893, too, the severity of hard times greatly increased the demands for monetary reform.

As the silver movement grew stronger, its influence on politics increased proportionately. Until the depression of the nineties money issues had never been party issues; each of the two major parties had included both hard- and soft-money interests. The spreading agitation for silver, however, precluded the possibility of carrying on politics as usual. The American Bimetallic League, although functioning as a pressure group, provided evidence that it could become something more than that early in 1893 when its members gathered in Washington for what Warner termed its "first annual meeting." Casting its nets out on a sea of discontent, the convention voted to invite every labor and industrial organization in the United States—and the "civilized world" as well—to send delegates to future meetings of the league. The People's party, too, hoped to fish successfully in troubled waters. Populists never believed that free and unlimited coinage of silver was a panacea that would bring about social

Sound money advocates did their best to prevent free coinage of silver, in part because it would bring about an inflation that might prove disastrous. This broadside, directed primarily at working men, suggested that free silver would reduce real wages by 47 cents to the dollar (courtesy Chicago Historical Society).

justice as well as prosperity. But the party had always favored an increase in the stock of money and an increase in agricultural prices. If it could win support for its broader program by appealing to silverites, it had no reservations about making that appeal. One of the songs that Populists sang at their gatherings put the case succinctly:

> Silver free, sixteen to one,
> Is not all we stand upon,
> > Though we mean to split old parties with that wedge.
> But our platform shall abide
> When the wedge is thrown aside,
> > Then the gold and silver kings will have to "hedge."

With both the American Bimetallic League and the Populist party threatening the disruption of traditional politics, the Democratic and Republican parties would eventually find themselves forced to eliminate ambiguities from the monetary planks in their platforms.

**The Trials of a
President**

When Grover Cleveland entered the White House in 1893, he was convinced that all silver purchases would have to be stopped. As he read the signs of the times, silver was responsible for speculation, hoarding of gold, and an unfavorable balance of trade. Therefore, calling Congress into special session in August 1893, he urged repeal of the Sherman Silver Purchase Act. Despite determined and sometimes eloquent opposition of silver congressmen such as William Jennings Bryan of Nebraska, the president had his way. But he accomplished repeal at the cost of party unity. Indeed, discussion of the act divided the country as had nothing else since the Civil War. Beyond that, repeal produced negligible results. It certainly did not bring the return of prosperity. Prices and wages showed no evidence of improvement; unemployment remained high. Most alarming of all, abandonment of silver purchases had little effect on a crisis that was rapidly developing in the Treasury Department.

For years Treasury Department officials had considered a gold reserve of at least $100 million essential to sound fiscal policy. Having begun to decline before Cleveland took office, the reserve was down to $84 million when the Senate voted to repeal the Sherman Act. And, contrary to the president's expectations, the gold reserve continued to fall. During the gloomy January of 1894 it dropped to a new low of $62 million. "This don't [sic] help us," Cleveland told his cabinet. "I believe in taking the bull by the horns and coming out with an issue of bonds." Secretary of the Treasury John G. Carlisle therefore announced the sale of $50 million of 4 per cent bonds to shore up the reserve. When the move proved no more successful than had the repeal of the Sherman Act, Cleveland sought advice from financiers J. P. Morgan and August Belmont. They agreed to purchase $62 million in 4 per cent bonds at 104½, which would provide the Treasury with $65 million in gold. They further agreed to secure half the gold from abroad and to use their influence in helping to prevent further withdrawals. Once the agreement had been concluded, Morgan and Belmont lost no time in disposing of the bonds. Silver men then reacted with corresponding alacrity. "What is this contract?" asked an outraged Bryan in the House of Representatives. "It is a contract made by the Executive of a great nation with the representatives of foreign money loaners. It is a contract made with men who are desirous of changing the financial policy of this country."

Meanwhile, throughout controversies over money and the Treasury reserves, the Cleveland administration struggled with tariff reforms promised during the campaign of 1892. In February 1894 the House of Representatives passed a bill introduced by Congressman William L. Wilson with the president's approval. The measure would have reduced average rates from almost 50 per cent to about 30 per cent on dutiable goods; many raw materials—including wool, coal, iron ore, hemp, and flax—would have gone on the free list. In theory, free raw materials would have brought lower production costs for manufacturers and increased world markets for industrial goods. The Senate, however, accepted neither the theory nor the specifics of the Wilson bill. By rejecting any suggestion of compromise, Cleveland alienated Democrats who were not already offended by his hard-money position. The predictable result of the president's intransigence was a tariff bill that contained few changes in existing rates. Its only major innovation, provision for a tax on incomes, came to nothing when the Supreme Court declared it unconstitutional in 1895. Describing himself as "a man depressed and disappointed," Cleveland refused to sign the bill; it became law without his signature.

As if the president's troubles with the Treasury and with Congress were not enough, multiplying indications of widespread social and economic unrest added to his woes. The high unemployment rate provided recruits for industrial armies that wandered about the country in search of jobs or relief. The most notorious of the armies was organized by Jacob S. Coxey in Masillon, Ohio. It formed a "petition in boots" by marching on the nation's capital in support of Coxey's scheme to provide unemployment relief through construction of a new road system. Along with other armies it drifted into Washington during the summer of 1894, where it lost its momentum in what for the marchers must have been a disappointing anticlimax. Police arrested Coxey and his lieutenants for trespassing on the Capitol grounds. Nevertheless, when vagabonds could organize themselves in such efforts, the specter of revolution began to haunt men of property.

Far more violent than the meanderings of industrial armies was a strike at the Pullman Palace Car Company in Chicago during that dismal sum-

Extensive labor unrest characterized the depression nineties. When workers struck the Pullman Palace Car Company in 1894, Chicago became the center of conflict between Pullman employees and U.S. soldiers. These troops served, in effect, as strikebreakers (Library of Congress).

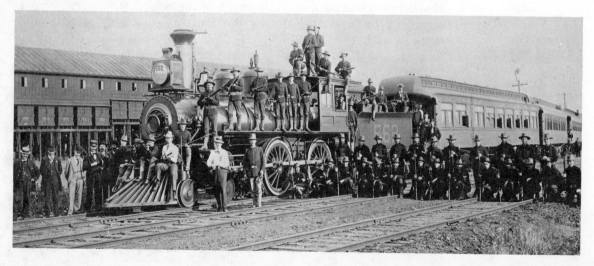

mer of 1894. Workers, who lived in the company town that George M.
Pullman had built on the shores of Lake Michigan, objected to paying
rents that remained high despite a series of wage cuts. At the point of
desperation some four thousand employees joined the American Railway
Union, electing a grievance committee to discuss their plight with Pullman.
He not only refused to listen but also discharged three members of the
committee. In the strike that resulted, the American Railway Union found
itself opposing the powerful Railway Managers' Association, which had
been organized by the heads of twenty-four railroads. The conflict threatened to spread far beyond the Chicago area, for, when workers refused to
move Pullman cars, the railroads refused to run trains. Such action, of
course, interfered with the movement of postal cars; thus Attorney General
Richard Olney felt justified in issuing an injunction barring the union
from obstructing the mails. Delivery of the injunction precipitated a riot
in the railroad yards at Blue Island, outside Chicago; the Federal government countered by calling out U.S. troops from nearby Fort Sheridan.
When the melee ended after nearly a week, the city of Chicago counted the
costs in broken windows, burned buildings, overturned railroad cars,
twelve dead, and hundreds injured. The strike had been broken, but the
price of restoring peace by such methods was exorbitant.

## The Elections of 1894

Identified with the arrival of hard times, apparently unable to restore
prosperity, divided over monetary and tariff issues, and now displaying
greater interest in breaking a strike than in the needs of workingmen, the
Democratic party suffered a severe setback in the congressional elections of
1894. Democrats lost 113 seats in the House of Representatives, with
Democratic membership in that body declining from 61.2 per cent to 29.4
per cent. Voting in every area of the country gave evidence of dissatisfaction over Democratic performance. The Northeast—including the New
England states, New York, New Jersey, and Pennsylvania—elected ninety-
two Republicans and only seven Democrats. In the five states of the Middle
West—Ohio, Indiana, Illinois, Michigan, and Wisconsin—where Democrats had elected forty-four congressmen in 1892, they were able to elect
but three in 1894. The number of Republican congressmen, on the other
hand, increased from thirty-four to seventy-five. In the plains region of the
West, the seven states north of Arkansas and the Indian Territory sent
forty-four Republicans, four Democrats and two Populists to the House of
Representatives. Party labels had less meaning in the Far West, but successful candidates were for the most part those who campaigned as Republicans; nearly all were advocates of free and unlimited coinage of silver at
a 16 to 1 ratio. In the South, too, the party label lost some of its meaning,
for there the tendency toward fusion of parties was prevalent. But Senator
John T. Morgan of Alabama voiced a common attitude toward President
Cleveland: "I hate the ground the man walks on."

Detailed examination of voting behavior in specific localities supports
the idea that a great number of citizens cast negative ballots; that is, they

tended to vote against Democrats rather than for opponents of Democrats. Traditional ethnic, religious, and political ties as well as class identification constituted important elements in negative voting patterns. In Milwaukee, for example, Democrats had done unusually well in German Lutheran wards in 1892, registering a substantial minority (a mean of 43.3 per cent) of the total vote. In November 1894, however, the Democratic mean in those same wards declined to 24.8 per cent. Catholic wards in the city had traditionally voted Democratic, but the party lost there, too. The mean Democratic vote declined from 69.6 per cent in 1892 to 51.8 per cent in 1894. Some of the German Lutherans and middle-class Catholics went over to the Republican party between 1892 and 1894, but shifts to the People's party were even more striking. In the city as a whole, the Populists' share of the total vote went from 2.7 to 21.3 per cent. Working-class Catholics, associating the Democratic party with the depression, could not bring themselves to cast their votes for Democrats as they usually did in normal times. But neither could they move over into the Republican column, for they had always thought of the GOP as the party of native American Protestants and therefore the enemy of the Catholic Church. The People's party benefited from the voting shift in Catholic wards, but that shift was more a rebuke to the Democrats than it was a commitment to Populism. Many German Lutheran workers, identifying Republicans with prohibition, also voted Populist. What the Milwaukee voting patterns in 1892 and 1894 suggest, then, is that working-class interests produced a heavy anti-Democratic vote; at the same time, cultural influences turned much of that vote toward the Populists rather than toward Republicans.

The elections of 1894 were important, not only because they established a context for the dramatic presidential election of 1896 but also because they marked the beginning of an eighteen-year Republican ascendancy in national politics. Capturing every major city in the northeastern quadrant of the United States in 1894, Republicans laid the groundwork for future dominance. Democrats, on the other hand, lost heavily in industrial cities in part because the depression cut ethnic ties that bound working-class wards to the Democratic party. Such losses would be difficult to recover. Populists, encouraged by a 42 per cent increase in the total vote they had polled in 1892, believed they had moved one step closer to major party status. That their hopes were well grounded, given Democratic disintegration in 1894, made their ultimate disappointment all the greater.

**The Election of 1896**    Meeting at St. Louis in June 1896, the Republican National Convention was the first to draft a platform and to nominate candidates for the fall election. A minority of the delegates, for the most part those representing silver-producing states in the West, attempted to secure Republican endorsement of a bimetallic monetary standard. The convention would not hear of it. The majority report of the platform committee supported "the existing gold standard" until such time as an international bimetallic agreement could be worked out. When the silver men sought to introduce a substitute monetary plank, they were greeted with hisses and catcalls. And after the convention voted overwhelmingly to adopt the majority report, silver supporters followed Colorado's Senator Henry Moore Teller out of the convention hall. The silver Republican bolt left the party united behind the gold standard and free to proceed with the nomination of candidates.

Front runner for the convention's endorsement was Governor William McKinley of Ohio. In his thoroughly planned campaign for the nomination, his supporters had worked effectively to win delegates to the McKinley cause. McKinley's nomination was nearly a foregone conclusion; but, aside from that, the party could hardly have chosen a candidate more likely to win election. Ohio born, McKinley had enlisted in the Union Army at the outbreak of the Civil War. During the four years of his service, he fulfilled every responsibility with exemplary devotion to duty and in 1865 was mustered out with a brevet commission of major. Having studied law, he hung out his shingle in Canton, Ohio, entering politics shortly thereafter. McKinley then carved out a career for himself in the United States House of Representatives; as chairman of the Ways and Means Committee, he was chiefly responsible for the tariff bill of 1890, which made his name almost synonymous with protection of American industry. After defeat in 1890, when the Ohio legislature gerrymandered his district, he entered the gubernatorial race in 1891. He won handily and was reelected in 1893.

McKinley's vote-getting ability was impressive, and only two features of his record might have aroused concern among Republicans. In the first place, he had voted for the Bland-Allison Act and the Sherman Silver Purchase Act. Until 1896, however, the party had never identified itself unequivocally with the hard-money position. McKinley's attitude was easy enough to explain to men who had exhibited similar ambivalence on monetary issues. In any case, his work on the tariff demonstrated an understanding of economic problems that put monetary manipulation in its proper place. The second consideration was personal rather than public: he had unwisely endorsed the notes of a friend whose tin-plate business failed during the depression of the nineties. Fortunately, with the help of other and better friends, McKinley was able to weather the financial crisis. As no one ever raised serious questions about his conduct in the matter, McKinley did not find embarrassing explanations necessary. If anything, the affair worked to his advantage, for it brought him into a closer relationship with Mark Hanna, a wealthy Cleveland industrialist who would soon manage with incomparable skill his campaign for the presidency.

Shortly after Republicans had adopted a gold platform and nominated McKinley, the Democrats met in national convention at Chicago. Like the GOP, the Democratic party had always been divided on the money question; and, like the GOP, it had never adopted a position favoring either gold or silver. Grover Cleveland had, of course, worked to repeal the Sherman Silver Purchase Act, and beyond that he had struggled doggedly to

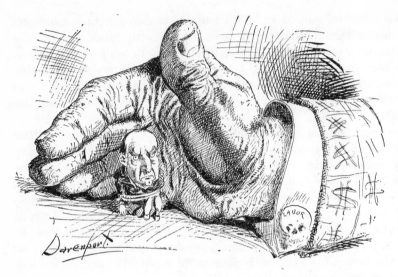

During the election of 1896, Democrats and Populists tried to suggest that Republican nominee William McKinley was under the thumb of Mark Hanna and the gold interests. The disparagement, misleading as it was, produced few changes in the shift of votes to the Republican party.

maintain the value of the American dollar. But, inasmuch as such tactics did not restore prosperity, the president faced an increasingly active opposition within party ranks. During the spring of 1896 the Bimetallic Democratic National Committee carried on a vigorous campaign in each of the states west of the Alleghenies and south of Maryland. Its efforts, along with those of other silver organizations, assured a silver majority at the Chicago convention.

Concentrating on monetary issues in the months before meeting in Chicago, Democrats had given relatively little thought to candidates. When the delegates finally convened, those who favored gold were depressed by the continuation of hard times and by their failure to seat a majority. They seemed too dispirited to care much about who won the nomination or what sort of money plank found its way into the platform. Yet they were willing at least to go through the motions of making a fight for gold. Ready to accept their own defeat within the party and defeat of the party in November, they could only hope that the election would bring a total repudiation of the silver heresy. Then, perhaps, their fidelity to sound money would have its reward. Silver men, on the other hand, exuded confidence. Knowing that their crusade had enlisted several worthy champions, they were willing to concentrate on the immediate task: winning the convention's approval of a silver plank. The platform debate, then, promised to become the most exciting event of the Chicago convention. It lived up to its promise. William Jennings Bryan delivered a powerful address in support of silver. "You shall not press down upon the brow of labor this crown of thorns," he thundered in warning to his opponents. "You shall not crucify mankind upon a cross of gold." The convention proceeded to adopt a silver plank; the following day it completed the repudiation of Cleveland when Bryan captured the presidential nomination.

The Democratic candidate was a young man barely old enough to meet the minimum age requirement of the presidency. He had been born and reared in central Illinois, the region where Lincoln had once practiced law and politics. Unlike the martyr president, however, the Bryans were always staunch Democrats. His family's religious convictions, like its political affiliations, made a deep and lasting impression on young William. From his parents he received training in the evangelical Protestantism (and the moralism through which it found expression) that was to shape much of his political thinking. Like other schoolchildren who took to heart the lessons of the McGuffey Readers, William understood the virtues of thoughtfulness and honesty, and the awful results of greed and intemperance. Never did he question the universal application of God's moral law, and never did he hesitate to confront political problems with the ethical principles he learned as a child.

Bryan was educated at Whipple Academy and Illinois College in Jacksonville, and from there he went to law school in Chicago. After two years' study at the Union College of Law and in the office of Lyman Trumbull, Bryan passed his bar examinations, married, and settled down in Jacksonville. Enjoying only modest success in his practice, he soon moved on to pursue more promising opportunities in Lincoln, Nebraska. Plunging into politics almost immediately, he won election to the United States House of Representatives in 1890. During his two terms in the House, the young Nebraskan earned a reputation for oratorical skill and for his advocacy of free silver. His enthusiasm for silver alienated President Cleveland, and for a time Bryan's political career seemed over. But, having committed himself to a cause, the young orator threw his prodigious energies into bringing about its success. No one in the silver movement attended more rallies or spoke more often and more effectively for bimetallism than did Bryan. The Boy Orator of the Platte was no stranger to the silver Democrats who nominated him.

Nor was he a stranger to the Populists who gathered in St. Louis for their convention, scheduled to begin on July 22. But Bryan's nomination brought consternation rather than joy to the People's party. After discussions with representatives of other dissident groups, party leaders had deliberately chosen to meet following adjournment of the Republican and Democratic conventions. Back in January, when they had made that decision, no one believed that the Democratic party would repudiate its president and nominate a silver candidate. Populists hoped, rather, that once they had announced a candidate and a program, the new party would be in a position to attract support from all those who were dissatisfied with standpat attitudes of the two major parties. Now the Democrats had done the unexpected and, in coming out for silver, had frustrated Populist strategy. "Mr. Bryan is a very gifted man," grumbled a newspaper with Populist sympathies, "but he is in very bad company." In the end there was little that the Populists could do but grumble. The People's Party Convention endorsed Bryan, sacrificing the broader planks of its platform in the process. That it nominated a different vice-presidential candidate, Thomas E.

William Jennings Bryan ran as the nominee of both the Democratic party and the Populist party in 1896. To at least one cartoonist he seemed like a circus performer astride two balky mounts. McKinley emphasized the point. "We have but one political party which is united," he told a group of Pennsylvania farmers. "Discord reigns in all others."

Watson of Georgia, helped to preserve party identity—but the cause had been lost.

The McKinley-Bryan campaign, once it got under way, provided abundant material for a study in contrasts. Bryan packed his bags and carried his cause to the people. He made, in all, three campaign trips that took him from Nebraska and the Dakotas to the Atlantic coast, and from Tennessee and North Carolina to Maine and Minnesota. He traveled eighteen thousand miles, delivering six hundred speeches to an estimated five million people. Without sizable financial backing, he carried most of the burdens of the campaign on his own broad shoulders. McKinley, on the other hand, remained at home in Canton to greet and talk informally with a series of delegations brought in by the trainload under Republican auspices. Campaign manager Mark Hanna was, in his own way, as indefatigable as the peripatetic Bryan. With the help of a well-staffed and enthusiastic speakers' bureau, he made certain that voters heard all the arguments for gold. Exercising great care to identify McKinley as "the advance agent of prosperity," GOP campaigners worked effectively among people who were tired of business stagnation and unemployment. Democrats, for all of Bryan's persuasive oratory, were kept constantly off balance. "I have kept them moving, kept them moving all the while," Hanna crowed exuberantly on election day. He had good reason to be exuberant. When the returns were in, McKinley polled 7,104,779 popular votes to 6,502,925 for Bryan.

**Election Returns and Their Meaning**

Geographic distribution of the 1896 vote indicated that McKinley's strength lay in the northeastern portion of the country, the area of greatest urban and industrial development. More than half the goods manufactured in the United States came from New England and the Middle Atlantic states.

Three-fourths of American industry centered in the manufacturing belt east of the Mississippi River and north of the Ohio River and the Mason-Dixon line. In that region, constituting only one-seventh of the nation's total area, lived three-fourths of the manufacturing wage earners. It was there that both Republicans and Democrats campaigned most vigorously in 1896. It was there that McKinley won the election, capturing all the states of the region. To that bloc of electoral votes he added those of the upper South (Delaware, Maryland, West Virginia, and all but one in Kentucky), those of the upper Middle West (Wisconsin, Iowa, Minnesota, and South Dakota), and those of Oregon and California on the Pacific coast. Back in 1892, Cleveland had fared much better in the Northeast than did Bryan four years later. He had carried New York, New Jersey, Indiana, Illinois, and Wisconsin; he had added five electoral votes from Michigan and one from Ohio.

The returns of 1896 suggest that Bryan's nomination meant a change in the character of the Democratic party. The Great Commoner, as he came to be known, tried to use the silver issue as an instrument for mobilizing

With his agrarian emphasis, Bryan was in his element when he addressed small town rallies such as this one. His voice had remarkable carrying power, an important asset in the days before public address systems. When he spoke, as the photograph suggests, even horses seemed to prick up their ears (Minnesota Historical Society).

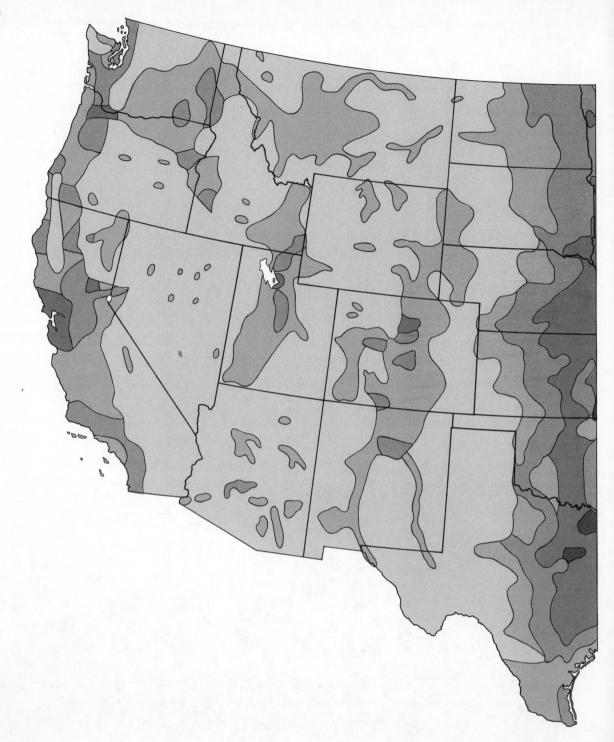

# U.S. Population Density, 1900

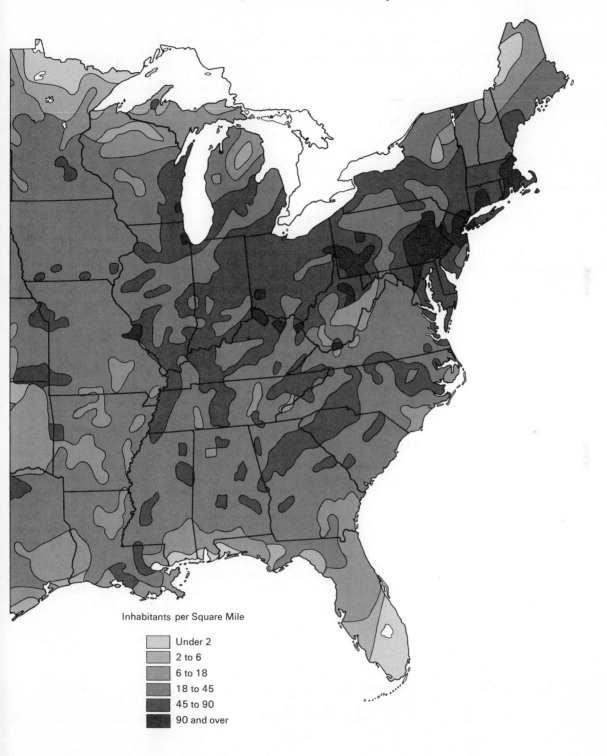

Inhabitants per Square Mile

Under 2
2 to 6
6 to 18
18 to 45
45 to 90
90 and over

the toiling masses of the country. And he failed. Free silver rhetoric, how-ever eloquent, bore little relationship to the problems of industrial workers as those workers saw them. Secular (or long-term) price declines were not nearly so important to them as the fact that depression brought unemploy-ment and reduction of wages. Furthermore, when Bryan associated his cause with a broader class of businessman—"the attorney in a country town," "the merchant at the cross-roads store," "the farmer who goes forth in the morning and toils all day," and "the miners who go down a thou-sand feet into the earth, or climb two thousand feet upon the cliffs"—he spoke a language that industrial laborers scarcely understood. Bryan's con-ception of the worker as producer did little to persuade those laborers that he understood their most fundamental difficulties. And when he suggested that meeting the needs of farmers would automatically produce a resolu-tion of urban problems, he seemed to be talking nonsense. "Burn down your cities and leave our farms, and your cities will spring up again as if by magic," he announced in the Cross of Gold speech at the Chicago con-vention; "but destroy our farms and the grass will grow in the streets of every city in the country." Never before had the Democratic party seemed so closely identified with the agrarian interests as opposed to urban inter-ests. The silver issue, with which Bryan sought to build a reform coalition of the toiling masses, became instead an issue that alienated many voters who had long supported the Democratic party.

For reasons in addition to his monetary reforms, Bryan's nomination aroused concern among people who had persistently cast their ballots for Democratic candidates. The most reliably Democratic wards had always been those where Irish and German Catholics had constituted a majority of the electorate. In some cities, German Lutherans were equally loyal. To voters within those ethnic and religious traditions the Democratic party had appeared as the party of personal liberty. Unlike the GOP, it had never associated itself with the moral reform of American society through temperance legislation and Sabbath laws, or with attacks on parochial schools and the use of foreign languages. In the eyes of many who felt threatened by such reforms, the Democratic party was a bulwark against cultural annihilation. Small wonder that they greeted Bryan's nomination with a notable lack of enthusiasm: his moralistic fervor, his religious back-ground, his attitude on temperance, and his appeals for reform all seemed consistent with the nativism they had always feared. The votes Bryan gained—and he won in some areas that had never before supported a Democratic candidate—fell far short of compensating for the votes he lost.

Nothing in William McKinley's campaign stirred the fears of ethnic groups; nothing he said to workers seemed so divorced from realities of the depression as did Bryan's appeal for silver. Long an advocate of a protec-tive tariff—in part because he believed it economically sound and in part because of its attractions for men of all classes—McKinley effectively har-monized protectionist and sound money themes. "Depression in agriculture always follows low tariff legislation," he told a delegation of farmers. "The

While Bryan went out on the hustings in 1896, McKinley remained at home in Canton, Ohio. There he cordially greeted pilgrims who, having taken advantage of special campaign excursion rates offered by railroads, called to pay their respects. The Republican candidate's personal warmth could not have been better displayed. "I think Major McKinley is just lovely," was the well-publicized remark of a woman from Wyoming, a state that had recognized female suffrage rights in 1889 (Ohio Historical Society).

farmer is suffering today because the number of his competitors has increased and his best customers are out of work." Increasing tariff rates would reduce competition and set factories to operating again. "You don't get customers through the mint," concluded McKinley; "you get them through the factory." And, in speaking to a group of Pennsylvania coal miners, he developed similar arguments, adding a counterthrust at silver that had special appeal for workingmen: "We do not want any cheap money, any more than we want cheap labor in the United States."

Bryan's attempt to unify the toiling masses behind free silver resulted in his failure to unify the party that had begun to fracture during Cleveland's second term (1893–1897). Indeed, his campaign seemed to point toward class conflict rather than toward restoration of party cohesion. That he attracted the support of some Populist leaders such as Ignatius Donnelly helped to maintain the party split for years to come. While the author of *Caesar's Column* won some votes for Bryan among the discontented, he aroused fears of revolution among people who had little to gain from such turmoil. At the same time, Bryan offered nothing to industrial workers who might have been persuaded that they would benefit from a radical change in the American economic system. And to ethnic and religious minorities the Boy Orator's preaching of reform sounded more like a threat of extinction than a promise of redemption.

McKinley's victory over Bryan occurred at a time when rural concepts of social justice still exercised a powerful influence; but it was also a time when industrial development and urban growth had shattered social patterns consistent with rural homogeneity. Many observers of the American scene were impressed by signs of a growing class consciousness. Some—Edward Bellamy among them—looked forward to a happy resolution of class differences in a cooperative commonwealth. Others—Ignatius Donnelly was typical—anticipated a cataclysmic struggle between oligarchs and revolutionaries. Bryan represented yet a third group that would use existing institutions to bring about a reform program cut to the pattern of an agrarian utopia envisioned by Thomas Jefferson a hundred years earlier. Neither Bellamy nor Donnelly nor Bryan fully understood that, with diversification of its economic activity, American society was moving toward a large number of narrow-interest groups rather than toward class consciousness. They were impressed by manifestations of broad social unrest and by attempts to organize that unrest. None of them saw that Samuel Gompers's American Federation of Labor—with its limited bread-and-butter, wages-and-hours objectives—would become the dominant labor organization of the twentieth century. None of them anticipated the emergence of an American Farm Bureau Federation, with its equally limited goals, two decades after the decline of Populism.

## The New Immigration

The American population was changing in composition as well as in its economic interests. The principal reason for the change in population makeup was, of course, the great influx of immigrants during the years between the close of the Civil War and the coming of World War I. A majority of new arrivals came from Europe; their move to the United States was part of a global phenomenon. In all, some 60 million people left European shores between 1821 and 1932. In that period nations of the Western Hemisphere recorded a total of 53.8 million immigrants, while Australia, New Zealand, South Africa, and other non-American areas listed 5.4 million. Within this general movement of peoples other significant patterns were becoming apparent at the time of the McKinley-Bryan campaign. Until 1890, more than half of all intercontinental migration originated in northern and western Europe. After 1890, an increased proportion of emigrants came out of the nations of southern and eastern Europe. The magnitude of the shift can be illustrated by a comparison of the decade 1901–1910 with the decade 1881–1890. In the eighties approximately 7 million Europeans left their homeland; of this number more than 5 million (more than 70 per cent) came from the British Isles, Germany and the Scandinavian countries. In the first decade of the twentieth century approximately 11.3 million people departed Europe; nearly 8 million (more than 70 per cent) left Austria-Hungary, Spain, Italy, and Russia.

Migration statistics are at best approximations, since not all emigrants were counted even in countries that maintained careful records. Nevertheless the changing general pattern of migration seems clearly established; it is certainly supported by immigration figures in reports of the United States Bureau of the Census. The peak of immigration from northern and western Europe arrived during the decade of the eighties, but even then there were

At the time of McKinley's election a new wave of immigrants had begun to reach American shores. The promise of free treats on Uncle Sam's ark of refuge was a powerful attraction; yet, as the cartoonist implied, push stresses were as powerful as pull forces. In America the newcomers encountered a rapidly changing society, and their arrival influenced the direction of social change.

signs of change as nearly one-fifth of the 4.7 million European immigrants came to America from areas outside the regions of traditional immigrant recruitment. And the flow from eastern and southern Europe increased sharply. In the 1901–1910 decade the Austro-Hungarian Empire, Russia, and Italy accounted for 5.8 million of the alien arrivals, while the British Isles, Germany, and the Scandinavian countries taken together supplied but 1.7 million. The change in patterns of immigration aroused concern, and eventually, in 1907, Congress authorized an Immigration Commission to make "full inquiry, examination, and investigation."

Predictably, the commission allowed its predispositions to color the findings in its forty-one-volume report issued in 1911. Headed by Vermont's William P. Dillingham, the commission suggested that the "old" immigrants arriving before 1890 had come as settlers to engage in agricultural pursuits. The report alleged that "they had mingled freely with the native Americans and were quickly assimilated." It went on to argue that such had not been the case with "new" immigrants arriving after 1890. The movement from southern and eastern Europe had been, rather, "largely a

# The "New" Immigrants in Urban America

The changing pattern of immigration at the turn of the century produced a nativist reaction calling for restrictions on the entry of newcomers from southern end eastern Europe. Gutzon Borglum (the sculptor whose notion of patriotism eventually led him to take on the peculiar task of defacing Mount Rushmore by enfacing it) vigorously supported restriction or even exclusion. "I am indeed against Mediterranean people coming into this country," he confessed to a friend. "They wear slippers, and they make an 8-inch blade on their knife . . . . I don't want the slippered assassin, the idol [sic] revolutionist, the loafer, and the dictator from any part of the world, in America . . . ."

A man of strong agrarian sympathies, Borglum objected to the new immigrants chiefly for their tendency to congregate in metropolitan areas where they formed cohesive ethnic associations. Along with many other Americans, the sculptor believed that such urban clusters inhibited the process of assimilation and constituted a threat to national unity.

Failing to recognize that settlement and technology had greatly reduced opportunities in agriculture, forcing farm workers to compete with immigrants for new opportunities in the metropolis, nativists tended to blame the new immigration for the ills they found in urban society. The reasoning was distorted and simplistic. Few of the newcomers were slippered assassins or loafers, and while some of them came to grief, their failure must be measured against the enormity of difficulties they encountered. Far more impressive than immigrant deficiencies is the evidence of an enduring toughness that assured survival.

Dedicated in 1886, the Statue of Liberty greeted new immigrants arriving in New York harbor. Inscribed on its base were the lines of a sonnet by Emma Lazarus, lines welcoming "your tired, your poor, your huddled masses yearning to breathe free." As immigrants soon discovered, however, pity mixed with condescension did little to ease their problems of adjustment (The Port of New York Authority).

Under the immigration laws, any alien who did not appear to be "clearly and beyond a doubt entitled to land shall be detained"; many of those placed in detention were eventually deported. In New York, steerage passengers of the new immigration were sent to Ellis Island, where they were questioned and given medical examinations. There they waited patiently, if often anxiously, for official approval. An estimated 3,000 suicides on the island over a forty-year period attests to the intensity of immigrant anxieties.

After authorities had completed the processing of immigrants, the newcomers approved for entry took the ferry to New York City or Hoboken. At the Barge Office in Battery Park these immigrants loaded their baggage on carts and prepared to begin life in a strange, new land. "I squared my shoulders against what was coming," Jacob Riis recalled of his own experience on reaching the United States. "I was ready and eager. But for a passing moment . . . I would have given it all for one familiar face, one voice I knew."

Fears of the immigrants were justified. The "golden door" of Lazarus's poem opened for many into living quarters that were unspeakably vile and filthy.

Sanitation and plumbing facilities in urban slums were grievously inadequate, and the passage of time brought few improvements. "We got water from a common hydrant in the yard and carried it upstairs," remembered AF of L president Samuel Gompers, who became a citizen in 1872. "The toilet was in the yard also." Forty years later, a barefoot boy (with cheeks that may have been dirty, but were certainly not tan) filled his wash basin at the community faucet that served the entire tenement in which he lived (George Eastman House).

When the backyard playground was a junk pile—and children went without shoes—injury and infection took their toll.

Inadequate wages challenged the spirit of immigrants and converted tenement apartments into places where entire families labored to produce items such as cigars, caps, shirts, and artificial flowers. Unskilled though most of the new immigrants may have been, many families such as this one managed to meet the challenge and maintain their dignity under trying circumstances (George Eastman House).

In 1910 an Italian woman hurried home to her tenement with a bundle of material ready for processing. Such labor, performed by the piece within households, provided a means of augmenting family income without violating traditional prejudices against the employment of women outside the home. Piece rates were low, however, and where such practices prevailed the organization of women into unions proved all but impossible (George Eastman House).

Tenement dwellers sometimes became scavengers in their struggle to meet domestic needs. Railroad yards were a source of wood and coal that might be used for fuel in cooking and heating.

Although most men sought jobs in the industrial plants of large cities, some of them followed other pursuits. Peddlers' carts and vendors' booths crowded the streets where immigrants lived; there one might buy almost anything from fresh fruit to used clothing. Itinerant scissors grinders were ubiquitous. This one was photographed as he made his rounds on Halstead Street in Chicago (George Eastman House).

Overcrowded living conditions usually produced squalor, but in some neighborhoods a sense of community helped to bring about a degree of neatness in tenement courtyards. In ethnic enclaves privacy was, to be sure, difficult to maintain. Yet the immigrant, in his loneliness, regarded privacy as a condition to be overcome rather than achieved.

Generational differences in the rate and manner of adjustment sometimes brought tensions to immigrant families. The popularity of stickball, a variety of baseball suitable for confined areas, provided evidence that children of immigrants could adapt to their surroundings and (in spite of them) enjoy the "national pastime" (George Eastman House).

Many of life's pleasures are relative. Occasionally immigrant children acquired pennies that did not have to be used for some family need. Those who accumulated such fortunes might taste delight in the soft drinks dispensed by a peddler from the container strapped to his back (George Eastman House).

The Statue of Liberty was a symbol of national unity. Yet the achievement of social homogeneity in a polyglot population required more than inspired words on the statue's base. Such, at least, was the conviction of those who led the settlement house movement. One of the most famous of the settlements was Hull House, pictured in this view from Halstead Street. Here in Chicago, Jane Addams worked to provide immigrants with a sense of individual worth—and an identification with their adopted country—by emphasizing the value of their distinctive contributions to American society (State Historical Society of Wisconsin).

movement of unskilled laboring men" who had shown little desire to establish permanent homes in the United States. Coming as transient industrial workers, they had "congregated together in sections apart from native Americans." And, in the urban ghettoes where they lived, assimilation had been well-nigh imperceptible.

The generalizations of the Dillingham Commission were flawed in many respects. For one thing, the commission failed to recognize the differences among specific nationality groups within both the old and the new immigrations. By purporting to show that Italian and Slavic immigrants tended to be predominantly male, unskilled, illiterate, and transient, the report provided at best incomplete information. Arrivals from the British Isles, Germany, and the Scandinavian countries included a larger percentage of males than did Jewish, Bohemian, and Portuguese arrivals. Percentages of illiterates were lower among Bohemians and Finns than among the Irish and Germans. Scandinavians exhibited a greater tendency to return home than did Jews or Portuguese. The percentage of skilled laborers was higher among Italian immigrants than it was among the Irish, and only the Scots included a larger percentage of skilled workers among their number than did the Jews.

Had the Commission been less inclined to draw value-laden generalizations from overaggregated data and more concerned with the demographic and technological influences on migration patterns, it might have been impressed by similarities rather than differences between the old and new migrations. The first-comers in every immigrant group included a high proportion of unaccompanied males; as each group's time of residence in the United States lengthened, the percentage of males tended to decline. The percentage of immigrants who returned to Europe increased in the period after the Civil War, but that trend had less to do with country of origin than with improvements in transportation.

The steamship greatly reduced hazards of the Atlantic crossing, but not until after the Civil War did the steamship have an important influence on migration of Europeans. As late as 1856 more than 96 per cent of the immigrants arriving in New York came in sailing vessels. By the middle seventies, however, sailing vessels had largely withdrawn from the immigrant carrying trade. What does much to explain the new immigration is that, with the emergence of highly competitive steamship lines, passage from Palermo, Italy, became as easy to obtain as passage from Bergen, Norway. The steamship companies, in other words, bridged the Atlantic from areas that had never before contributed significantly to the westward flow. Beyond increasing the safety of ocean travel and beyond making transportation more readily available for all Europeans, the steamship greatly reduced the time required for a voyage to America. Sailing ships took from one to three months, but steamships churned their way across the Atlantic in less than two weeks. Seasonal migrations—shuttling back and forth between Europe and the United States—increased in direct proportion to the use of steamships.

Increased use of steamships, however, does not in itself explain an increase in transiency among immigrants in the late nineteenth and early twentieth centuries. While some of the new immigrants were less likely to remain permanently in the United States than were the old, their greater instability suggests that the conditions they encountered in America were different from the conditions that old immigrants had faced. As the Dillingham Commission itself recognized, the old immigrants had come "during a period of agricultural development" and had "formed an important part of the great movement toward the West." After 1890 agricultural lands were no longer so readily available as they had once been. Although many of the new immigrants had been peasants at home, they discovered that opportunities for employment were much greater in American industry than in American agriculture. They therefore tended to cluster in urban centers. In adjusting to a new way of life as well as to a new country, their ethnic affiliations helped to assuage what Professor Oscar Handlin has called "the shock of alienation."

For some of the new immigrants ethnic ties were infinitely more binding than their strange occupational associations in a strange environment; those ties, exerting a constant pull, drew many an alien back to the land of his birth. Yet most of the immigrants remained in their new environment however much they might have wanted to return to the old. Ethnicity was as dominant an influence for those who remained as it was for those who returned to native lands; in providing the assurance of the familiar where everything else was strange, the retention of native customs and languages, along with traditional religious practices and associations, helped to meet the deep psychological needs of the outlander.

Groups that contributed to the old immigration were conscious of their ethnic associations, too, but their ethnic identification was less noticeable—in part because the old immigration extended over a longer period of time and in part because it was more diffused geographically. The ethnicity of the new immigrants, more obvious because of their tendency to concentrate in urban industrial centers, greatly increased the diversity of cultures in American society. When William Jennings Bryan sought to lead a general reform movement based on appeals to a broad economic class made up of the toiling masses, he overlooked or misunderstood that diversity. Thus, the Great Commoner's conception of the good society, shaped in the days of his Illinois youth, was already out of date by 1896. The possibility of achieving social homogeneity—at least by the methods Bryan employed—had disappeared.

**Drawing the
Color Line**

Unlike immigrants who came to the United States from Europe, black Americans had few, if any, written records (such as baptismal certificates) by which to establish strong association with a specific place. They did know that their ancestors had been transported from Africa, and the evidence of oral tradition suggests that many of them maintained a sense of tribal identification despite the efforts of slave owners to break up tribal groupings. One should not assume, then, that slavery totally obliterated all vestige of African culture, or that the experience in bondage wiped out all linkages among black people in American society. African colonization proposals had aroused the enthusiasm of free blacks even before the Civil War, and the idea of tribal reunification would continue to have a powerful appeal after emancipation.

For various reasons, perhaps mainly economic ones, a mass return migration never received serious consideration in the immediate post-Civil War period, and most freedmen prepared to exercise their newly won rights as American citizens. Yet the Reconstruction program, through which congressional and other reformers hoped to establish those rights, brought few lasting results. After withdrawal of the last Federal troops from the South in 1877, most Reconstruction gains rapidly slipped away. With them went the hopes of reformers and blacks alike. Under the leadership of "Redeemers," southern states forged a social system that favored whites and relegated black people to inferior status.

From time to time black aspirations would revive, only to be put down again. In 1886, for example, formation of the Colored Farmers' Alliance and Cooperative Union offered the possibility of overcoming sectional differences and racial prejudices through the coordinated pursuit of economic objectives. But the incipient coalition of black and white agrarians ran amuck in the intricacies of southern politics, and black farmers emerged from the agrarian movement with little to show for their involvement in it. Indeed, the hint of rural radical unity speeded a proliferation of Jim Crow regulations already under way, for election victories rewarded candidates who viewed with alarm a palpable black threat in depressed agricultural regions.

State after state moved to deprive southern blacks of political and civil rights during the last two decades of the nineteenth century. In 1881 the Tennessee legislature passed the first Jim Crow railroad transportation law forcing Negro travelers into second-class coaches, and other states enacted their own measures using the Tennessee law as a model. Extension of the segregation principle soon followed, gaining judicial sanction in the *Plessy v. Ferguson* case (1896), which enunciated the separate-but-equal doctrine. Before the turn of the century the practice of maintaining separate and nominally equal facilities for blacks had expanded to include waiting rooms, ticket windows, drinking fountains, theaters, boarding houses, hospitals, schools, jails, penitentiaries, and the like. In the nineties, too, southern states passed various laws ingeniously designed to deprive Negroes of the right to vote; they instituted poll taxes, literacy tests, grandfather clause provisions, and white primaries.

In segregation and the subversion of political rights Redeemers found means of maintaining white domination over southern blacks, means that were little better than slavery. Furthermore, resort to subterfuge in order to circumvent the Fourteenth and Fifteenth Amendments encouraged even harsher treatment of black citizens. The number of lynchings in the eight-

ies averaged about 150 annually; most of the victims were southern Negroes. During the next decade the frequency of such episodes declined to
about sixty or seventy a year, although the viciousness of specific lynchings,
of course, abated not at all. The perpetrators of such violence were quick
to justify their actions. According to the most common rationalization,
lynching protected white women from black rapists, but there was a
broader purpose behind extralegal punishment. Intimidation of "uppity
Nigras," the reasoning ran, would help preserve white supremacy. The
thinking that justified lynching was consistent with the thinking of people
who never took part in a lynching themselves and would have been horrified if invited to do so. Yet because they sanctioned its fundamental purpose, the practice attained a degree of approval in society that it could not
attain in law.

The Redeemers and their allies (including Congress, the Supreme Court,
and white northerners who had heard enough of racial equality and were
turning their attention to other matters) opened the way to segregation
and the abrogation of civil rights for black people. Blacks therefore found
themselves in the difficult position of having to choose between resistance
and martyrdom on the one hand or accommodation and its attendant psychological penalties on the other. Most of them opted for some form of
accommodation; those who did found a spokesman in Booker T. Washington. Born into slavery, but the son of a white father, Washington attended
Hampton Institute after the Civil War. In 1881 he became principal of the
Tuskegee Institute in Alabama, and in that position he won recognition—
at least among whites—as the nation's most influential black leader.

The key to Washington's success was his masterly articulation of arguments for accommodation. Never openly advocating political or social
equality, he continually preached the virtues of hard work, racial cooperation, and economic advancement. "The wisest among my race understand,"
he said in his celebrated address at the Atlanta Exposition in 1895, "that
the agitation of questions of social equality is the extremest folly, and that
progress in the enjoyment of all the privileges that will come to us must be
the result of severe and constant struggle rather than of artificial forcing."
On its denotative level Washington's message repeated a formula propa-
gated by white opinion makers in conjunction with arguments for white
supremacy: black people would advance as they proved themselves worthy.
Because Washington's public utterances echoed their own thoughts on the
matter, white philanthropists contributed to Tuskegee, white politicians
deferred to his recommendations, and white citizens elevated him to the
pantheon of national heroes.

Washington's enormous influence assured his preeminence among Negroes, and his strategy won widespread acceptance by black Americans
searching for a way to cope with discriminatory practices of the larger society. Yet black acceptance of white supremacy was minimal (if not nonexistent), and acceptance of accommodation even as a strategy was far from
universal. After 1900 William Edward Burghardt DuBois, holder of a

Booker T. Washington's address at the Cotton States and International Exposition in Atlanta was a brilliant expression of the accommodationist strategy for Negroes. Black poet Langston Hughes later used a telling aphorism to explain the meaning of accommodation: "When your head is in the lion's mouth, use your hand to pet him." How readily the lion responded to Washington's petting became immediately apparent, as when President Cleveland visited the Exposition's Negro Building in October 1895. Most black people, however, found their uncomfortable position little improved (*Harper's Weekly*).

Ph.D. degree in history from Harvard, emerged as Washington's most perceptive critic. In *The Souls of Black Folk* (1903), DuBois argued that because it accepted the fiction of Negro inferiority, the accommodationist program was doomed to ultimate failure. If Negroes did become businessmen and property owners, as Washington urged, their success would always be in jeopardy so long as they had neither the political nor social influence to protect it. And the effort to gain self-respect while accepting inferior status was so filled with contradictions as to be absurd. No, contended DuBois, it was time for blacks to speak out! They would stand a far better chance of gaining their rights by demanding them than by exchanging them for promises; they could never gain self-respect by constantly belittling themselves. Out of DuBois's thought came the Niagara Movement, initiated by a conference at Niagara Falls, Canada, in 1905. Also instrumental in founding the National Association for the Advancement of Colored People in 1910, DuBois used the organization to disseminate his ideas. Until World War I, however, Washington's accommodationist strategy continued to exercise a greater influence over the minds of black people.

One reason for Washington's continuing prominence was his ability to employ a rhetoric that conveyed ideas on more than one level. Never so tactless as to demand equality for blacks, he also avoided suggesting that

Negroes would forever occupy an inferior position. Using the language of success stories that were popular during the heyday of Horatio Alger, he appealed to racial solidarity and pride. Washington's white audiences were impressed by his conciliatory tone and his apparent refusal to rail against the Negro's place in American society; they could not quarrel with his appropriation of the success theme, for it echoed sentiments to which they had grown accustomed. His black followers, on the other hand, were most impressed by his emphasis on black achievement and the unlimited possibilities of self-help; they tended to dismiss his conciliatory phrasing as a sop to white opinion, a device for avoiding white hostility but otherwise meaningless.

To look at Washington's leadership in this way (an interpretation suggested by August Meier's *Negro Thought in America*) is to see him functioning more often as a shrewd manipulator than as an obsequious sycophant. Some blacks would later identify Washington with Uncle Tom, but more striking was his resemblance to Uncle Remus. The Negro folk tales recorded by Joel Chandler Harris were, like Washington's speeches and writings, open to more than one interpretation. Widely accepted as charming children's stories, the Uncle Remus tales were rich in symbolism. Br'er Rabbit, folklorists have shown, was a prototype of the trickster, a prominent figure in Negro jokes and stories from slavery down to the present.

Like another black favorite, the Signifying (that is, manipulative) Monkey, Br'er Rabbit was a creature who lived by his wits. It was the only way he could live, for the sassy little fellow operated in a terror-filled universe. Through his cleverness he managed to work his impish will, even to the point of killing his adversary and marrying the widow, "Ole Miss Fox." In the context of slavery, the black raconteur and his listeners relished the sometimes malicious triumphs of one of nature's weakest and most timid creatures. During the post-Reconstruction period of accommodation, tricksters continued to dominate such folk tales in the guise of animals usually characterized as weak or skittish. In time new heroes—especially the badmen whose meanness, strength, sexual prowess, and defiance of authority fascinated the residents of urban ghettoes—would emerge to rival Br'er Rabbit and the Signifying Monkey as folk heroes of American blacks. During the years of Booker T. Washington's ascendancy, however, it was the tricksters who had the greater appeal. Trickster jokes and stories dealt in the deepest and most profound longings of an oppressed people; they touched a level of reality that the vigorous discussion of political issues in the nineties would never plumb.

Political discussion are necessarily formal, that is to say, consistent with the norms of the society involved in making political decisions. Because it is public office for which candidates are contending, their debates are limited by socially sanctioned standards within their constituencies. The issues they discuss may be important ones; the issues they do not discuss may be equally important as determinants of individual behavior. But the issues that are not sanctioned by a major portion of the electorate are seldom debated openly. Thus it is easy to charge politicians with hypocrisy in failing to consider matters of great concern to particular groups, but the disparity between political discussions and behavioral determinants perhaps derives less from hypocrisy than from social heterogeneity. The more pluralistic the society, in other words, the less meaningful its political debates are likely to be for the separate groups within it. And if a segment of the population occupies a caste position—as black people did after Reconstruction—then its interests are scarcely mentioned except in negative ways during political campaigns. In the years after 1896 the fragmentation of the society would become a major concern of native white Americans, but they would continue largely to ignore the needs of their black compatriots. In fact, the subjugation of black people sometimes served as a means of overcoming differences among whites, and reforms of the years between 1897 and World War I did little to meliorate racial discrimination.

# PART TWO

A Time of Reform
Consensus at Home
and Conflict Abroad

# 3

# Prosperity and Progressivism: Emergence of a Reform Strategy

The depression of the 1890s was severe but transitional, and the recovery that followed McKinley's election marked the beginning of a new era in economic development. In 1897 the United States entered one of the longest cycles of business prosperity in American history; lasting until 1921, it was interrupted only by a minor recession in 1903, a sharp but limited panic in 1907, and a brief downturn in 1914. Standing at less than $33.3 billion in 1897, the gross national product more than doubled in the two decades before American entry into World War I (see Table 3.1). Population increased more than 40 per cent in that interval, and GNP per capita went from $462 to $675.

Several changes, many of them characteristic of a maturing economy, made the years of prosperity markedly different from the years that had preceded the depression. The trend toward consolidation of business, which had begun in the 1870s, accelerated rapidly after 1897 and shaped the organizational structure of American industry in the new century. Technological innovations, especially those that led to development of the automobile and to the widespread use of electric power, stimulated impressive growth in a variety of economic sectors. Banks and other financial institutions reached new levels of sophistication in their operations. American industry sought and found overseas markets for manufactured goods; exports and foreign investments made the United States a creditor nation by the end of World War I. The new prosperity even brought a reversal of the thirty-year decline in agricultural prices, and a majority of farmers experienced an unprecedented sense of well-being.

The extraordinary innovative energy of the prosperous years found release in enthusiastic experimentation with social and political institutions. Industrial development, technology, and urbanization all contributed to the demand for such experimentation. Institutions that had functioned reasonably well at a time when most Americans lived on farms and in villages required furbishing and renovation; institutions and regulatory agencies for which an agricultural society had little use became a necessity in

TABLE 3.1    Gross National Product, Population, and Per Capita GNP

| Year | Total GNP (millions of 1929 dollars) | Population (thousands) | Per Capita GNP (1929 dollars) |
|------|------|------|------|
| 1890 | 26,196 | 63,056 | 415 |
| 1891 | 27,365 | 64,361 | 425 |
| 1892 | 30,010 | 65,666 | 457 |
| 1893 | 28,569 | 66,970 | 427 |
| 1894 | 27,756 | 68,275 | 407 |
| 1895 | 31,082 | 69,580 | 447 |
| 1896 | 30,444 | 70,885 | 429 |
| 1897 | 33,327 | 72,189 | 462 |
| 1898 | 34,068 | 73,484 | 464 |
| 1899 | 37,172 | 74,799 | 497 |
| 1900 | 38,197 | 76,094 | 502 |
| 1901 | 42,587 | 77,585 | 549 |
| 1902 | 43,004 | 79,160 | 543 |
| 1903 | 45,123 | 80,632 | 560 |
| 1904 | 44,559 | 82,165 | 542 |
| 1905 | 47,870 | 83,820 | 571 |
| 1906 | 53,420 | 85,437 | 625 |
| 1907 | 54,277 | 87,000 | 624 |
| 1908 | 49,790 | 88,709 | 561 |
| 1909 | 55,893 | 90,492 | 618 |
| 1910 | 56,499 | 92,407 | 611 |
| 1911 | 58,312 | 93,868 | 621 |
| 1912 | 61,058 | 95,331 | 640 |
| 1913 | 63,475 | 97,227 | 653 |
| 1914 | 58,636 | 99,118 | 592 |
| 1915 | 60,424 | 100,549 | 601 |
| 1916 | 68,870 | 101,966 | 675 |
| 1917 | 67,264 | 103,266[a] | 651 |
| 1918 | 73,361 | 103,203[a] | 711 |
| 1919 | 74,158 | 104,512[a] | 710 |

SOURCE:  John W. Kendrick, *Productivity Trends in the United States* (Princeton, N.J.: Princeton University Press, 1961), pp. 298–99; U.S. Bureau of the Census, *Historical Statistics of the United States, Colonial Times to 1957* (Washington, D.C.: U.S. Government Printing Office, 1960), p. 7.

[a] Total population including armed forces overseas (in thousands), 1917: 103,414; 1918: 104,550; 1919: 105,063.

the twentieth century. A political system that was itself undergoing change became an instrument for change. It was a remarkable period. And Americans gave it a label that is remarkable for its imprecision. They called the era *progressive* and rested there, seemingly content that its meaning was woven into the fabric of a new society.

**The Consolidation and Division of American Business**

Of all the changes that took place in the postdepression period, none attracted more attention than the rapid consolidation of business. There were novelties in the form as well as in the rate of combination. During the decade of the 1870s businessmen and manufacturers had attempted to eliminate the hazards of sharp competition and overproduction by forming pools (informal and often secret understandings) that would assure each participant his share of a common market. Because of difficulties in enforcing those arrangements, however, the pool soon gave way to the trust as a favored form of combination. The trust was a merger that assigned to a group of trustees a majority of the voting stock in each constituent company. In exchange for their stock, the original owners of securities received trust certificates; those certificates returned a pro-rata share of the combined earnings of all companies subject to the agreement. Best known of the early trusts was Standard Oil, first formed under the leadership of John D. Rockefeller in 1879. At its inception the Standard controlled 90 per cent of the nation's refining; within three years it controlled nearly 90 per cent of the pipelines as well.

Trusts such as Standard Oil, while they promised greater stability and profits through elimination of competition, were nevertheless vulnerable to legal restrictions. Opponents of big business charged that trusts violated fair trade practices, and antitrust sentiment leading to legislative action made necessary the development of other forms of combination. Mergers achieved through outright purchase accounted for some of the late nineteenth century business consolidation, but here, too, there were disadvantages. Purchase usually required the consent of security holders in the acquired firm, and that consent was not always easy to obtain. Then, in 1889, the state of New Jersey came to the rescue of struggling consolidators by amending its law to allow a corporation to hold the stock of other corporations. "Business wise men," notes the economic historian Edward C. Kirkland, "read the meaning of this star in the East." The holding company—a corporation organized for the purpose of owning the securities of other corporations—had been born.

Opponents of large business combinations in any form won an important early victory when Congress passed the Sherman Anti-Trust Act in 1890. The act declared that a person would be guilty of a misdemeanor should he "monopolize, or attempt to monopolize, or combine or conspire . . . to monopolize any part of the trade or commerce among the several states, or with foreign nations." Then came the depression of the nineties, ruining weak competitors and chastening the strong. In the midst of those hard times the United States Supreme Court agreed to hear a case with significant implications for the organization of business. In 1895 the government brought suit against the American Sugar Refining Company on the ground that its control of more than 90 per cent of all refined sugar manufactured in the United States constituted a monopoly in violation of the Sherman law. Those who favored dissolution of the company were disappointed, however, for the Court held that manufacturing should be distinguished

Vienna born Joseph Keppler was perhaps the most influential color cartoonist of the late nineteenth century. In 1876 he started *Puck,* the first successful humorous weekly in the United States, and on its pages he lambasted comstockery, political machines, and big business. His 1889 masterpiece, "Bosses of the Senate," helped to increase popular demand for the regulation of business combinations.

from commerce. Chief Justice Fuller, speaking for the majority, argued that "commerce succeeds to manufacture, and is not a part of it." The American Sugar Refining Company was admittedly a monopoly; but, because it engaged in manufacture rather than in trade, it had not violated the law.

The election of McKinley and the return of prosperity sent business consolidators plunging down the path that the Court had cleared. Not all combinations formed during the post-1897 rush toward consolidation followed the holding-company pattern; pools and trusts continued to operate, while some corporations continued to merge or buy up others. But the form of consolidation mattered little to those not directly involved. What certainly did matter to a great many people was the rapid acceleration of the consolidation movement during the years from 1897 to 1904. The general public began to worry about dangers inherent in any concentration of power. Ignoring technical implications of the word *trust,* people applied the term generically to all types of big business combination and prepared to support a new antitrust crusade. That mammoth corporations such as the Standard Oil Company, the American Sugar Refining Company, and the American Tobacco Company had continued to pay dividends during the depression was both an inducement to consolidate other firms and a stimulus to the regulation of trusts. If merged corporations could sustain profits despite reduced demand, thought some businessmen, then large-scale operations must be more sound than small ones. Other citizens, however, taking a dim view of big business profits in a time of economic privation for the general population, readily associated trusts with unfair advantage.

In 1904, when concern about postdepression mergers was at its height, John Moody brought out a book he called *The Truth About the Trusts.* The title suggested a sensational exposé, and readers were not disappointed. Moody's statistics were indeed suggestive. They pointed to the existence of 318 important and active industrial trusts representing 5,288 distinct plants and "practically every line of productive industry in the United States." Of the 318 trusts, 236 came into existence after January 1, 1898; and, of those formed after that date, 170 were incorporated under New Jersey laws. If capitalization is an indication of size and scope of operation, then, according to Moody, the trusts formed after 1897 were much larger enterprises than were those appearing earlier. Aggregate capitalization of the eighty-two older trusts totaled $1,196,724,310, while those formed after 1897 represented a total capitalization of $6,049,618,223. The trend that Moody described seemed likely to continue indefinitely. Yet it turned out to be more sporadic than he anticipated, slowing down markedly in the same year he published *The Truth About the Trusts* and not picking up momentum again until World War I.

A possible reason for the temporary slowdown in business mergers was Theodore Roosevelt's response to demands for their curtailment. Assuming office as president after McKinley's assassination in 1901, TR knew a popular cause when he saw one. Within a year he launched a drive to break up combinations contrary to the public interest; his administration brought into the courts more antitrust suits than had any previous administration. For their part, jurists began to demonstrate a willingness to expand the Federal commerce power far beyond the limits imposed upon it in the Sugar Trust Case. In the Northern Securities decision of 1904, for example, Justice John Marshall Harlan's majority opinion held that any combination, "even among *private* manufacturers or dealers," was unlawful if it had a restraining effect upon commerce. "Liberty of contract," he wrote, "does not imply liberty in a corporation or individuals to defy the national will, when legally expressed." Although Harlan exaggerated the Supreme Court's readiness to apply the Sherman Act in antitrust cases, subsequent decisions by no means beat a retreat back to its 1895 position. In *Swift and Company v. United States* (1905), Justice Oliver Wendell Holmes distinguished between production and commerce, but he held that sales of cattle in local stockyards were not just local transactions. They were, rather, part of a "constantly recurring course" of commerce among the states. Holmes's "stream of commerce" doctrine justified application of the Sherman Anti-Trust Act to production as well as trade, and it could therefore be used to break down distinctions between the two kinds of activities.

Yet to suggest that Roosevelt's fervent trust-busting campaign was solely

responsible for a decrease in the number of mergers after 1904 is tantamount to converting the historical record into a morality play. Other less
high-minded influences were also at work. For one thing, not all industries
were equally susceptible to combination, and, for another, not all businessmen agreed that mergers should be formed. Some industrial leaders believed that consolidation promised more than it could deliver. A purveyor
of such opinion was *The Iron Age,* one of the most influential of trade and
industrial publications. In 1910, after taking a hard look at the merger
movement, the journal concluded "that very few of the promises of the promoters of consolidations have materialized." Events of the next decade
would not compel a total reversal of that judgment; several studies suggested that the profits of constituent firms before merger had at least
equaled the earnings of consolidations. After the turn-of-the-century movement toward concentration, therefore, very few industrial mergers attracted
attention until the end of World War I. Those that did were in new industries such as automobiles, motion pictures, aluminum, chemicals, or
electric light and power.

The emergence of great financial empires would have a more subtle and
more profound influence than the formation of industrial trusts. Methods
of financing railroads in the late nineteenth century had served to concen-

By the turn of the century many journalists and students of American business
believed that bankers and financiers—the "money trust"—had gained control
over the economy. Of the Wall Street nabobs, none appeared more powerful than J.
Pierpont Morgan. In 1902, after he had assembled the gigantic United States
Steel holding company, he announced plans for a British-American shipping combine. The announcement provoked a negative reaction from more than one
cartoonist (Culver Pictures).

trate the investment market in New York City, and the needs of consolidated corporations after 1897 further increased the power of investment bankers. It was such men who floated the securities that brought new mergers and companies into existence; banks, insurance companies, and investment trusts were their principal customers. Thus a common interest developed among the firms selling securities, the investment bankers marketing them, and the individuals and institutions buying them for their investment portfolios. The interest extended beyond services provided and profits shared. Investment bankers used their control of capital to gain seats on boards of directors; with that leverage they were able to exercise an influence in the management of corporations. The concentration of capital and power resulting from the complex operations of finance capitalism aroused hostility toward the "money trust" and in 1913 brought on an investigation by a committee of the House of Representatives under the chairmanship of Arsene Pujo. But the investigation did not counteract a significant shift of economic control from farmers, merchants, and manufacturers to financiers and bankers. As Columbia University scholars Adolph A. Berle and Gardiner C. Means argued in their astute 1932 analysis, *The Modern Corporation and Private Property,* the United States was moving toward a system in which there would be owners who exercised little influence over decisions concerning their property and managers who made decisions without appreciable ownership.

The concentration of economic power in the hands of finance capitalists did not mean that American business had become a gigantic monolith containing no cracks or stresses. Businessmen, Professor Robert Wiebe has convincingly demonstrated, did not all have identical objectives, problems, or methods of operation; certainly all of them did not worship at the House of Morgan. Many of them vigorously opposed the accumulation of economic power. George M. Reynolds, of the Continental and Commercial Bank of Chicago, was "inclined to think that the concentration having gone to the extent it has, does constitute a menace." Other critics contended that if the inner circle around Morgan was not actually a threat, it nevertheless exerted a negative influence in restricting technological innovation and productive efficiency. The obverse side of the investment bankers' concern for profits and dividends, according to this view, was a reluctance to take the risks that innovation implied.

Divisions that existed between bankers determined to secure a return on their investments and industrial leaders concerned about increasing productivity were not the only splits among American businessmen. Wiebe has shown how a rift developed between small-town banks serving rural areas on the one hand and the larger banks of metropolitan centers on the other. Urban-rural differences among businessmen to some extent overlapped sectional differences, but sectional differences also brought cleavages among businessmen. Struggles over control of the railroads, for example, pitted urban businessmen of the West (where shippers were numerous and sentiment for lower rates was strong) against urban businessmen of the East (where control of rail lines was centered and where opposition to rate regulation ran high). Small business interests were not the same as the interests of big business, nor were the interests of firms that performed varying functions always identical. Just as important as the concentration of industry in the trusts and the concentration of capital that accompanied the merger movement, therefore, were the stresses and cleavages that turned businessman against businessman and belied the existence of a coherent business community.

**Labor and the
AF of L**

While the American economic topography after 1897 followed contours of the combination movement and finance capitalism, business disunity provided a measure of its shifting faults. Economic profiles may also be taken from labor organizations, for conflicts within the work force yield significant readings of fluctuations in American society. As the estimates of occupation groups in Table 3.2 indicate, farmers and farm laborers made up a larger percentage of the work force in 1890 than in 1920. For industrial wage earners, professionals, and white-collar workers, the trend was in the opposite direction. In 1890 the number of farmers and farm laborers exceeded the number of industrial workers by more than a million; thirty years later, workers outnumbered farm proprietors and laborers by more than seven million. Just as significant as occupational change was a doubling of the total work force in the years from 1890 to 1920. In part through large-scale immigration the employable part of the population increased more rapidly than did the total population. Another important influence was the movement of women from the home into gainful employment. Between 1890 and 1920 the number of women who held jobs increased more than 200 per cent.

Rapid growth in the number of potential workers, as already noted, came at a time when most of the nation's arable land had been occupied. It was also a period when technological innovation had greatly reduced the demand for labor in agriculture while greatly increasing the demand for labor in factories and the secondary and tertiary industries. American manufacturing, the service trades, and the like were capable of absorbing a far larger number of immigrants, women, and other potential employees than was American agriculture. Job opportunities, then, account for both occupational change and the urban growth that accompanied it. Causal relationships moved in the other direction as well: urban growth increased markets for manufactured goods, leading, in turn, to an increased demand for labor in manufacturing and related nonagricultural industries.

The prosperous years after 1897 were, on the whole, propitious years for organized labor. According to one estimate, total union membership stood at 447,000 in 1897, but increased to more than three million in 1917 and then to more than five million by 1920. Growth came in spurts, largely in the years from 1897 to 1904 and from 1916 to 1919. It was, furthermore, unevenly distributed. At the time of American entry into World War I, unions were strongest in transportation, coal mining, the building trades,

TABLE 3.2   Occupations of American Workers

| Groups | 1890 | Per Cent | 1900 | Per Cent | 1910 | Per Cent | 1920 | Per Cent |
|---|---|---|---|---|---|---|---|---|
| Farm laborers[1] | 3,004,061 | 13.2 | 4,410,877 | 15.2 | 6,143,998 | 16.1 | 4,178,673 | 10.0 |
| Farmers[2] | 5,370,181 | 23.6 | 5,770,738 | 19.8 | 6,229,161 | 16.3 | 6,463,708 | 15.5 |
| Proprietors and officials[3] | 1,347,329 | 5.9 | 1,811,715 | 6.2 | 2,879,023 | 7.5 | 3,168,418 | 7.6 |
| Professional[4] | 1,114,507 | 4.9 | 1,565,686 | 5.4 | 2,074,992 | 5.4 | 2,760,190 | 6.6 |
| Lower salaried[5] | 965,852 | 4.3 | 1,329,928 | 4.6 | 2,393,620 | 6.3 | 3,985,306 | 9.6 |
| Servants | 1,454,791 | 6.4 | 1,453,677 | 5.0 | 1,572,225 | 4.1 | 1,270,946 | 3.1 |
| Industrial wage earners | 7,360,442 | 32.4 | 10,263,569 | 35.3 | 14,556,979 | 38.2 | 17,648,072 | 42.4 |
| Unclassified[6] | 2,118,498 | 9.3 | 2,467,043 | 8.5 | 2,317,538 | 6.0 | 2,138,971 | 5.1 |
| Total | 22,735,661 | . . . | 29,073,233 | . . . | 38,167,336 | . . . | 41,614,971 | . . . |

SOURCE:   Harold U. Faulkner, *The Decline of Laissez-Faire, 1897–1917* (New York: Rinehart & Company, 1951), p. 415.

[1] Members of the family working on the home farm and laborers working out.
[2] Farm owners and tenants.
[3] Managers, proprietors, officials, bankers and brokers, real-estate and insurance agents, commercial travelers, hucksters and peddlers, restaurant, hotel, and saloon keepers, etc.
[4] Not only the groups regularly referred to as professional but public-service workers of local, state, and federal governments.
[5] Foremen, overseers, bookkeepers, stenographers, agents and collectors, sales agents, ticket and express agents, mail carriers, chauffeurs and other groups.
[6] Largely occupations for which the census designation does not distinguish between proprietor and workman.

and printing; membership in the metal industries and needle trades was increasing. But unions were weak in manufacturing and virtually nonexistent in agriculture. Even in areas of their greatest strength, labor organizations enlisted only a small proportion of workers. Leaving farm laborers out of consideration, less than 4 per cent of the work force was organized in 1900, about 11 per cent in 1910, and slightly more than 20 per cent in 1920.

By far the most influential organization for workers was the American Federation of Labor. The AF of L had come into being in 1886, when representatives from thirteen national trade unions and twelve other labor groups met at Columbus, Ohio, to combine "for mutual protection and benefit." During the depression of the nineties the new workingmen's federation had experienced difficulty in adding to its membership. But it had not faltered despite hard times and dissension between labor organizers.

One reason for the federation's capacity to survive its many trials was the leadership of Samuel Gompers, who served as president from 1886 to 1894 and from 1895 until his death in 1924. Coming to the United States with his Dutch-Jewish parents in 1863, Gompers received very little formal education. A year after his arrival and shortly after his fourteenth birthday, he joined the Cigarmakers' union in New York. With some twenty years' experience as a labor organizer by the time he assumed the AF of L presidency, he developed clear ideas about what labor's course should be if workingmen were to achieve a good life in American society.

Gompers had little sympathy with the Knights of Labor, the Socialists, or anyone else who attempted to organize working classes into a single big

Samuel Gompers, save for one year the American Federation of Labor's president from its founding until his death in 1924, provided union leadership that was crafty, opportunistic, and concerned with bread and butter issues. Adopting a radical theoretical perspective, he believed, would have "concentrated all the forces of society against a labor movement and nullified in advance normal, necessary activity" (National Archives).

union or party. His stubborn opposition to the Socialists was one reason for his loss of the AF of L presidency in 1894. Returning to power the following year, however, he managed to lead AF of L members away from participation in the Socialist movement and toward what he and other federation leaders called "pure and simple unionism." The phrase was vague, but to the AF of L it meant a mixture of craft unionism, humanitarianism, social meliorism, and—most importantly—practical opportunism.

The organization was nothing if not realistic in developing a strategy. Gompers took a dim view of revolutionary movements; he could not believe that workers would ever succeed in taking over the American government. On the other hand, he had seen the power of government turned against labor too often to think that the AF of L could rely on politicians. He urged, therefore, that labor fight its own battles without interference. The AF of L would concentrate on the immediate struggle for higher wages, better working conditions, more education, more of anything that might increase the workers' status and standard of living. Its first tactical move was usually to secure recognition of affiliated unions. Once recognized, a union could enter into collective bargaining to secure a trade agreement. With such an agreement in hand, it was ready to move on to other goals.

AF of L objectives, as Gompers repeatedly pointed out, were always limited ones. The federation accepted the machine, the factory, and private capitalism, seeking only to secure better conditions for labor within the industrial system. This approach threw the AF of L back on its own resources. Determined to fight for its own narrow objectives, it had to be ready to negotiate continuously. It had to be prepared to compromise its demands and also to face the consequences of a breakdown in negotiations. This meant careful preparation for labor conflict, high dues, and large strike funds. It meant iron discipline at all times—and sometimes conciliation and arbitration. Above all, it meant a concern with wages and working conditions in the immediate future rather than with millenial hopes and class-conscious efforts to bring about a workers' utopia.

The aggressive opportunism that Gompers advocated helps to account for the AF of L's survival in the nineties and its growth after 1898. Membership increased from 265,000 in 1897 to 1,676,200 in 1904 and 2,021,000 by 1914. On the eve of World War I, nearly 80 per cent of organized labor was affiliated with the AF of L, although, to be sure, only a fraction of the work force was organized. Important as leadership and strategy were, other influences also help to explain such growth. Various associations contributed to an improved climate for labor activity. The National Civic Federation, founded in 1900 with Mark Hanna as president and Gompers as vice-president, worked to gain acceptance of unions and to promote harmony within American industry. Believing that "organized labor cannot be destroyed without debasement of the masses," the National Civic Federation attempted to unite employers, workers, and representatives of the general public in support of mediation, conciliation, and trade agreements. Other associations that aided in improving the status of labor were the National Consumers' League, formed in 1898 to combat sweatshops; the National Child Labor Committee, created in 1904 to prevent exploitation of children; and the American Association of Labor Legislation, organized in 1906 to encourage improvement of laws related to workingmen's problems.

Effective though such associations often were, they did not bring about harmony across the entire industrial front. The success of AF of L unions —which, of course, implied an increase in the number of negotiations and strikes—led employers' associations and citizens' alliances to launch a counteroffensive. The National Association of Manufacturers, originally set up to promote expansion of overseas markets, began to issue strong statements against union recognition and for the open shop. In 1903 NAM president David M. Parry became chairman of the Citizens' Industrial Association, and four years later the NAM organized another subsidiary, the National Council for Industrial Defense. Such groups offered aid and comfort to employers who were reluctant to follow so flexible a businessman as Mark Hanna into the National Civic Federation. The NAM and its institutional offspring provided assurances that closed shops were un-American and that breaking strikes was a heroic activity.

In the years from 1904 to World War I, when the rate of growth in union membership slacked off, the problems of labor resulted as much from dissension within the ranks as from employers' efforts to maintain the open shop. Gompers's pure and simple nonpolitical unionism had always been anathema to the Socialists. The Socialist Labor party, under the leadership of Daniel De Leon in the 1890s, thought that labor should become more class-conscious, endorse Socialist candidates for public office, and work to overthrow capitalism. Its failure to make much headway within the AF of L induced De Leon to form another organization, the Socialist Trade and Labor Alliance. The new group was no more successful, but it did break up the SLP. In 1901, De Leon's opponents formed the Socialist Party of America. Rejecting "dual unionism," or affiliation with both organized labor and socialism, which had antagonized AF of L leaders, they sought instead to win labor over to their cause. A measure of success crowned their efforts in 1912 when Eugene V. Debs, the Socialist party's candidate for president, polled 897,011 votes, setting his followers to dreaming of greater things to come.

The dream never became a reality, for groups that were more radical than the Socialist party had entered the competition for leadership among workingmen. The Industrial Workers of the World, formed at a Chicago meeting of labor and Socialist militants in 1905, presented what appeared to be a more direct challenge to AF of L conservatism. Declaring that "the working class and the employing class have nothing in common," the IWW urged direct action—the bomb and the torch if necessary—to overthrow an evil capitalist system. The new organization was to have a stormy history. Split by dissension, it soon broke into factions. One of them, led by the Western Federation of Miners, was less influenced by Karl Marx than by its frontier antecedents. While it supported radical programs, it was far more interested in organizing workers of the Far West. In 1907 it seceded from the IWW and in 1911 rejoined the AF of L. The remaining "Wobblies," as they were called, continued to bicker. In 1908 they split again. De Leon and his revolutionary-political followers were ousted, leaving a nonpolitical actionist residue headed by William D. Haywood. Aspiring to leadership in the class struggle, that residue—now the real IWW—set about organizing unskilled and migratory workers. The organization was small (at its peak it had fewer than sixty thousand members), but in several strikes it fought very effectively indeed. Its most notable triumph came with the textile workers' strike at Lawrence, Massachusetts, in 1912, but after that achievement the Wobblies encountered increasingly vigorous opposition. During World War I they were suspected of disloyalty; Big Bill Haywood, convicted of violating the Espionage Act, was deported to Russia, where he died in 1928.

"I declare it to you," Gompers had told the Socialists during the twenty-third annual convention of the AF of L in 1903, "I am not only at variance with your doctrines, but with your philosophy. Economically, you are unsound; socially, you are wrong; industrially, you are an impossibility." Nothing in the turbulent careers of radical leaders and their followers

WORKINGMEN !

INSIST UPON
THE
UNION LABEL

IT INSURES
SANITARY SHOPS,
FAIR PAY,
SHORTER HOURS,
RELIABLE CLOTHING

USED BY ALL LEADING MAKERS
OF MECHANICS CLOTHING
(SEE LIST OTHER SIDE.)

The United Garment Workers, for years the dominant union in men's clothing, was not as cohesive as its label implied. In 1914, after a series of quarrels, a majority of its members broke away from the AF of L (and its pure and simple unionism) to form the independent Amalgamated Clothing Workers. Later, during the depression thirties, the politically conscious Clothing Workers followed Sidney Hillman into the Congress of Industrial Organizations.

after 1905 caused him to change that assessment in any fundamental way. While the AF of L continued to oppose dual unionism, however, it did begin to modify its attitude toward political activity. Gompers could no longer ignore the challenge presented by Wobblies and Socialists on the one hand or by the NAM and the National Council for Industrial Defense on the other.

Beginning with the congressional elections of 1906, the AF of L became more deeply involved in political campaigns. Gompers urged his followers to "stand by our friends and administer a stinging rebuke to men or parties who are either indifferent, negligent, or hostile." In 1908, when parties were preparing for the presidential election of that year, the AF of L submitted its program to both the Republican and Democratic national conventions. The Democrats proving more receptive, Gompers enthusiastically endorsed William Jennings Bryan, who was making his third bid for the presidency. The federation remained sympathetic to the Democratic party four years later, when its support was a factor in the election of Woodrow Wilson.

While the AF of L may have become more active in politics because of pressure from Socialists and Wobblies, it did not feel compelled to go one step further. It never launched a vigorous campaign to bring the unorganized workingmen of the country into its ranks. Its preference for craft unions remained strong and prevented widespread recruitment of semiskilled and unskilled laborers. Whatever the reasons for AF of L dominance within the American labor movement, then, the meaning of that dominance was clear enough. It marked the failure of a broad, class-conscious effort to reshape the American economy and American society. Perhaps the radicals attempted too much. Torn by dissension and disagreement, they proved themselves incapable of mounting a full-scale revolutionary movement. The AF of L concentrated on narrower objectives that could be more easily realized; never questioning the basic social and economic structure within which it operated, it succeeded in holding the line for pure and simple unionism.

## Farm Organizations and Their Objectives

While the year 1897 marked the beginning of a wave of mergers and a new era in labor relations, it also brought a reversal of agricultural fortunes. The next two decades were years of unusual prosperity for American farmers. Farm production increased steadily as agriculture became more scientific and more mechanized. Yet demands for foodstuffs and other farm products remained high. Drought in France and storms and floods in Austria, Russia, and the Balkans reduced by nearly one-third the European wheat crop of 1897. Blessed with a bumper harvest that year, American farmers exported twice as much wheat (150,000,000 bushels) as they had exported in 1896. That development brought a significant shift in the balance of trade, as $120,000,000 in gold entered the country. Along with the revival of trade came a vast increase in the world's production of gold, following discovery of deposits in Africa and Yukon. The increased production, together with inflation of national bank notes and growth of population, helped to maintain agricultural prices. The nation's rural population increased from 45,614,142 to 51,406,017 in the years from 1900 to 1920; but in the same period urban population rose from 30,380,433 to 54,304,603. People living in burgeoning American cities had to be fed, and agricultural producers enjoyed the benefits of a steadily improving market. The defeat of silver in 1896, then, did not have the disastrous consequences that William Jennings Bryan had predicted. Indeed, as indicated in Table 3.3, gross farm income reached unprecedented levels.

Although Bryan and other advocates of free silver appeared to have been in error, farmers thought that they had learned some important lessons from the political battles of the nineties. Above all, they became disillusioned with broad-scale efforts to organize all farmers as a political force. Like the AF of L, they came to believe that, as Professor Grant McConnell has put it, "any circle of unity . . . must be of the smallest possible radius and must be drawn tight with the strongest bonds of immediate and obvious economic self-interest." Agrarian mass movements, in other words, died with the old century; farm organizations of the period from 1897 to 1920 concentrated on specific goals. If farmers differed from workingmen in their tactics, it was because they were becoming aware of their minority position in American society. But whatever their percep-

TABLE 3.3    Gross Farm Income

Gross Income from Various Groups of Farm Products and from Total Farm Production,
Including Estimates for Omitted Products (Millions of Current Dollars)

| Year | 12 Important Crops[1] | Staple Foodstuffs[2] | Dairy Products, Chickens, and Eggs | Meat Animals and Export of Live Cattle[3] | Total Farm Production[4] |
|------|------|------|------|------|------|
| 1890 | 1,273 | 438 | 551 | 765 | 3,072 |
| 1891 | 1,472 | 652 | 592 | 813 | 3,324 |
| 1892 | 1,258 | 513 | 611 | 776 | 3,041 |
| 1893 | 1,098 | 400 | 654 | 950 | 3,126 |
| 1894 | 1,033 | 361 | 584 | 787 | 2,773 |
| 1895 | 1,057 | 383 | 587 | 766 | 2,887 |
| 1896 | 978 | 353 | 593 | 699 | 2,728 |
| 1897 | 1,143 | 497 | 616 | 765 | 3,114 |
| 1898 | 1,315 | 628 | 649 | 823 | 3,438 |
| 1899 | 1,279 | 509 | 715 | 883 | 3,557 |
| 1900 | 1,458 | 486 | 771 | 1,023 | 3,974 |
| 1901 | 1,545 | 570 | 815 | 1,124 | 4,220 |
| 1902 | 1,645 | 603 | 897 | 1,185 | 4,506 |
| 1903 | 1,711 | 611 | 933 | 1,128 | 4,499 |
| 1904 | 1,972 | 715 | 947 | 1,030 | 4,695 |
| 1905 | 1,852 | 697 | 1,020 | 1,120 | 4,735 |
| 1906 | 1,992 | 675 | 1,024 | 1,264 | 5,146 |
| 1907 | 2,050 | 696 | 1,130 | 1,300 | 5,307 |
| 1908 | 2,159 | 793 | 1,189 | 1,285 | 5,447 |
| 1909 | 2,369 | 902 | 1,318 | 1,450 | 6,037 |
| 1910 | 2,368 | 762 | 1,429 | 1,646 | 6,539 |
| 1911 | 2,312 | 768 | 1,263 | 1,485 | 6,041 |
| 1912 | 2,480 | 860 | 1,446 | 1,572 | 6,629 |
| 1913 | 2,462 | 789 | 1,480 | 1,779 | 6,980 |
| 1914 | 2,241 | 988 | 1,503 | 1,775 | 6,890 |
| 1915 | 2,582 | 1,056 | 1,488 | 1,724 | 7,200 |
| 1916 | 3,223 | 1,265 | 1,668 | 2,130 | 8,587 |
| 1917 | 4,681 | 1,899 | 2,259 | 2,986 | 12,165 |
| 1918 | 5,688 | 2,244 | 2,730 | 4,008 | 14,842 |
| 1919 | 6,124 | 2,311 | 3,178 | 3,946 | 15,765 |

SOURCE:  Frederick Strauss and Louis H. Bean, *Gross Farm Income and Indices of Farm Production and Prices
in the United States, 1869–1937* (U.S. Department of Agriculture, *Technical Bulletin*, No. 703, Washington,
D.C.: Government Printing Office, 1940), pp. 24, 28.

[1] Wheat, corn, oats, barley, rye, buckwheat, flaxseed, hay, potatoes, sweet potatoes, cotton, tobacco.
[2] Wheat, rye, potatoes, sweetpotatoes, dry beans, rice.
[3] Slaughter of cattle, calves, hogs, sheep and lambs, and export of live cattle.
[4] Adjusted for changes in inventory values of meat animals.

tions of the farmer's position and role, farm organizations of the period
before World War I tended to avoid broad programs and the sort of political activity that brought frustration to the Populists in 1896.

Disillusionment with political action did not prevent farmers from organizing; what it did was to impose limits on the objectives of agricultural
societies. If anything, the number of farmers' associations increased after
the return of prosperity. The Gleaners, the National Dairy Union, the
National Conference on Marketing and Farm Credits, the National Milk
Producers' Federation, the Farmers' Mutual Benefit Association, the Farmers' Social and Economic Union, the Farmers' Relief Association, and many
other such societies attest to the continuing vitality of the organizing impulse. Agricultural associations of the prewar period did not repudiate
nineteenth-century antecedents. From time to time their rhetoric fanned
the flames of a lingering populism, turning the thoughts of farmers to renewed political activity. But never did they look upon themselves as the
universal champions of a downtrodden humanity, and never did they
dream of replacing one of the two major parties in national politics. The
character of agricultural associations in the first two decades of the twentieth century becomes apparent with detailed examination of specific
groups, and four of the most important—the Grange, the American Society

After the depression nineties, prosperity returned to the countryside. This bucolic
scene in Wisconsin (where farmers had never experienced the difficulties of farmers
on the Great Plains and in the South) bespeaks a quiet contentment with the increase in agricultural income after the turn of the century (State Historical Society
of Wisconsin).

Rural America experienced many changes during the years of prosperity before World War I. With the development of the internal combustion engine and gasoline tractors, farming became more mechanized than ever. Increased sophistication of agricultural operations encouraged regional specialization and therefore contributed to regional farm associations (State Historical Society of Wisconsin).

of Equity, the Non-Partisan League, and the Farmers' Union—merit special attention.

Of the four groups, only the Grange could trace its origins back to nineteenth-century agrarian unrest. But it had become docile with age, emphasizing educational and cultural activities. Granger ritual and symbolism gave it the appeal of a kind of rural Masonry, and its conservative agricultural program was most attractive to farmers of the New England and Middle Atlantic states. The Grange, to be sure, had a platform which it recommended to legislatures. Among other things, it urged Federal appropriations for highways, a parcel post system, postal savings banks, direct election of United States senators, and tariff revision. It listened sympathetically to the appeals of prohibitionists and, after the coming of war, to the pleas of pacifists. But national issues always seemed remote; the Grangers were more attentive to farm problems that lay closer to home. They resisted joining the National Board of Farm Organizations in 1919, preferring to work independently for desired legislation. The Washington representative of the National Grange lobbied effectively on matters that made few headlines—and few enemies. The quiet ways of Grangers won greater support nationally than did the more strident voices of other groups. With a membership of more than 540,000 by 1915, it became the nation's largest agricultural association.

The American Society of Equity was one of the first farm organizations founded after the turn of the century. It sought, initially, to boost agricultural prices by holding farm products off the market, but it soon began to concentrate on increasing the market efficiency of farmers. In line with that objective, Equity maintained a crop-reporting service for members. Also encouraging the construction of grain elevators, it helped to finance them. By 1907, however, Equity members had fallen out over the society's program. A dissident faction, favoring abandonment of crop-holding schemes and development of cooperative marketing, managed to gain control of the organization. With the shift in policy, Equity became an unwieldy collection of state and commodity associations with very little central direction. In some states, however, it was able to exercise a degree of influence. In 1911, for example, it claimed credit for legislative enactment of a long list of reforms in Wisconsin: an industrial commission, workmen's compensation, state life insurance, an income tax, a state binder-twine plant, and provisions for cooperative marketing. Even though its claim was exaggerated, Equity was a force that had to be taken into account. But not for long. Internally divided and hampered by poor business leadership of its cooperative programs, Equity gave way to the Non-Partisan League in north-central states, where it had its largest concentration of members.

In some respects, the Non-Partisan League was to farmers what the IWW was to workers. Founded in 1915, the league was perhaps the most rancorous of agricultural organizations. No Populist had ever denounced bankers and railroads more bitterly than did Non-Partisan Leaguers; and no Wobbly attacked "the interests" with more venom. But the parallel should not be pushed too far. While the IWW concentrated on direct action, the league sought to take over political machinery of the state by way of the ballot. Having gained political power, league leaders reasoned, they could enact a program including state ownership and operation of banks and elevators and so enable farmers to reap their just rewards.

Chief among the founding fathers of the Non-Partisan League was Arthur C. Townley, one of the most colorful organizers in the history of American agrarian movements. The Minnesota-born Townley had tasted success during two years as a flax grower in North Dakota. Heady with thoughts of even greater prosperity, he had expanded his operations and invested heavily in farm machinery, only to be ruined by drought and a poor harvest in 1912. He then worked for a time as an organizer for the Socialist party. He did not attempt to recruit members for the party itself, for North Dakota farmers were reluctant to sign the red card. The men he solicited joined, instead, the "organization department," which had been set up within the party to allow affiliation without membership. Townley's success was remarkable, but the North Dakota Socialist convention of 1915 discontinued the program because it did not seem consistent with the future welfare of the party. The disgruntled Townley then seized upon an idea suggested by one of his associates; he would work to organize a nonpartisan group having nothing to do with the Socialists.

Beginning in February 1915 Townley trained a band of skilled recruiters, sending them out in Model T Fords to cover the state of North Dakota.

The basic problem, as he saw it, was that the state legislature was controlled by "a bunch of wind-jamming, poker-playing, booze-fighting politicians" whose knowledge of agriculture was minimal. But it was not "sleek, smooth-tongued, bay-windowed fellows that looked well, talked well, lived well, lied well" who could best look after the interests of farmers. If farmers constituted 83 per cent of the state's population, then they should control 83 per cent of the government. League organizers had little difficulty in gaining a hearing. One of them left an account of the approach Townley urged him to use in recruiting a farmer: "Find out the damn fool's hobby, and then talk it. If he likes religion, talk Jesus Christ; if he is against the government, damn the democrats; if he is afraid of whiskey, preach prohibition; if he wants to talk hogs, talk hogs—talk anything he'll listen to, but talk, talk, until you get his god-damn John Hancock to a check for six dollars."

Within two years the Non-Partisan League had shifted into high gear, and by February 1917 it claimed thirty thousand members. By that time, too, it had succeeded in winning an 85 per cent majority in the lower house of the state legislature while capturing every elective state office save one. Despite opposition in the state senate, the league secured passage of some 254 laws during the legislative session of 1917. It was only a beginning. Townley, Governor Lynn Frazier, and other league leaders looked toward the creation of a system of state socialism, and by 1919 they had secured much of their program. In that year the legislature provided for creation of an industrial commission to supervise state industries and a Bank of North Dakota to finance them. It authorized an experimental creamery and construction of a mill, an elevator, and inexpensive homes for farmers and laborers. All improvements were exempted from the general property tax. At the same time, the state began to issue bonds for financing the state bank, mill, and elevator. A separate $10 million issue of bonds provided funds for rural-credit loans.

Success in North Dakota led to talk of expanding into other states, and before its demise the Non-Partisan League had penetrated thirteen of them. But, as adaptable as its program was to the conditions of North Dakota, it failed to make much headway elsewhere. Its leader charged with disloyalty and sedition during World War I (Townley spent six months in jail), the league had difficulty in recovering the momentum to broadcast its ideas. Rival organizations soon arose to challenge Non-Partisan leadership, even in North Dakota. The Farm Bureau movement would eventually gain the dominant position in American agriculture during the decade of the twenties, but in the meantime the Farmers' Union also extended its influence.

The Farmers' Educational and Cooperative Union was no Johnny-come-lately to the competition for agrarian support. First formed in Texas in 1902, it had concentrated its early activities in southern states. Echoes of the old Populism resonated in its demand for "equity" and its determination "to eliminate gambling in farm products by Boards of Trade, Cotton

Exchanges and other speculators." But the Farmers' Union made a tactical
break with Populism by refusing to be drawn into politics. It turned instead to a program of raising prices by withholding output. For several
years it managed to hold on at the ragged edge of survival; but, when it
began to expand into Great Plains states, its prospects improved. Organizing cooperative grain elevators, livestock shipping associations, and consumer stores, it appealed to small- and middle-size farmers who were dissatisfied with the more conservative policies of the Grange. During the
twenties it would become a competitor of the American Farm Bureau
Federation.

Agricultural organizations of the twentieth century's first two decades
were both numerous and diversified; but, whatever the differences that
divided them, they do justify several generalizations. In all the programs
advanced, there was a clear recognition of the fact that farmers were becoming a minority group in the United States as a whole. Since they could
no longer pretend to speak for a majority of Americans, agrarian leaders
began to identify themselves unequivocally with farmers as a class. Where
they advocated political action, they directed their attention to the agricultural states rather than to the national government. The agrarian mind
moved from the universal to the particular; concern for social and industrial justice gave way to a new interest in cooperatives and to new

Agrarian mythology emphasized the sturdy individualism of the farmer. Yet rural
people had always cooperated in barn raisings and similar endeavors. During the
twentieth century new forms of rural cooperation replaced the old, first with the
emergence of regional associations, and then with the rise of corporate agriculture
and agribusiness (State Historical Society of Wisconsin).

schemes for raising agricultural prices. "Farmers as a whole are a dumb lot," H. L. Mencken would remark in the twenties, "but they know which side of the bread has the butter." The insult was gratuitous; the suggestion that farmers were alert to economic self-interest was thoroughly justified by the activities of their organizations after 1896.

**Ethnic Religion and the Social Gospel**

While farmers formulated programs to achieve particular objectives, Americans became increasingly aware of challenges to the religious beliefs that had predominated during the years of agricultural expansion. At the time of the American Revolution about three-fourths of the population identified itself as Protestant, and throughout the frontier period Protestant denominations continued to flourish. They often engaged in sectarian rivalry but seldom in theological hairsplitting. Because there was no established church, religious institutions in the United States depended upon voluntary support. To secure that support, churches emphasized evangelical crusades, usually in the form of revivals or missionary enterprises. The appeal in such efforts was necessarily simple and direct; abstruse theological dissertations would have won few converts and few victories over frontier temptations. Throughout the nineteenth century, therefore, Protestant churchmen centered their attention on the number of souls saved rather than on what constituted salvation. Minimizing dogmatic distinctions, nineteenth-century American Protestantism came close to being a culture religion, exhibiting a tendency to associate itself with the American nation rather than with a theological position. Thus no one thought Senator Albert J. Beveridge either impious or profane (though his rhetoric might have seemed excessive) when he announced in 1900 that God had made the United States a paladin of civilization: "He has marked the American people as His chosen Nation to finally lead in the regeneration of the world . . . trustees of the World's progress, guardians of its righteous peace."

Yet at the very time that Beveridge spoke so confidently of the American mission, challenges to the Protestant culture religion were increasing significantly with the arrival of new immigrants at American ports. They did not, of course, come with a conscious determination to subvert religious convictions of the new land. In Europe the church or synagogue had been a meaningful center of community existence, and in a strange environment immigrants sought to re-create village religious observance complete with village dialect and customs. As they arrived, however, the intermingling of immigrants from many villages and provinces thwarted their effort to perpetuate local practices. Finding that other newcomers spoke Polish, Swedish, or Greek, they did the next best thing: they organized their churches by major language rather than by dialect. Thus they developed ethnic religious institutions in which they found identity as Poles, Swedes, or Greeks; the broader association might not have been as satisfying as identification with Poznan, Småland, or Thrace would have been, but it was

Not all ethnic communities were urban. On the plains of western Kansas, a group of Swedish immigrants established their homesteads and built a sod schoolhouse for their children. Inside the primitive structure, they stretched a piece of tent canvas across the ceiling to catch dirt, field mice, and snakes, as well as water from a roof that leaked badly during rainstorms. Conditions were not ideal for learning, but the children, knowing nothing better, made the most of what they had. Two of the six boys pictured here went on to Augustana Seminary in Rock Island, Illinois, became Lutheran pastors, and preached in both Swedish and English.

better than intolerable anonymity. The pattern varied from one ethnic group to another and from one religious tradition to another. Protestant, Catholic, and Jewish immigrants all formed distinctive religious associations that changed with the passage of time and with the arrival of shiploads of newcomers from different parts of Europe. Yet so long as the immigrant churches and synagogues provided an ethnic identification, they would have a character and serve a purpose that set them apart from the dominant culture religion of nineteenth-century American Protestantism.

The principal churches of non-English-speaking Protestants were the Lutheran and the Reformed. Most Scandinavians and Germans in the various Lutheran synods, like the Dutch and Germans of the Reformed churches, reached the United States long before the new immigration. They should have been, on the face of it, more readily assimilated into the receiving culture than were Catholic or Jewish immigrants. Yet they were remarkably slow to loosen ethnic bonds, several influences serving to keep their ethnic lines taut. Most important, perhaps, were the strong doctrinal convictions of Lutheran and Reformed churches, for those convictions led to a heavy emphasis on religious instruction, often in parochial schools using the mother tongue. Eventually, well into the twentieth century, both denominations would lose much of their ethnic character, but holding services in languages other than English remained a common practice until after World War II.

Indeed, in part because they were more willing to involve themselves in the political process, immigrant Catholics sometimes seemed more in tune with American society than were Lutheran or Reformed groups. The Catholic Church had been present in parts of the United States from the very beginning of settlement, but in the early nineteenth century it had begun to stagnate and lose members. Then, in the 1840s, came the great wave of Irish immigrants who revitalized the church; in that one decade membership increased from 650,000 to 1,600,000. By the end of the century the hierarchy of American Catholicism was almost entirely of Irish descent. Irish immigrants came from an English-speaking land. Largely because of that, they not only moved rapidly into the mainstream of American life (especially in cities) but also provided an important linkage between the Catholic Church as an alien body and the developing American culture.

Yet the later arrival of German, Italian, and Slavic Catholics presented enormous problems, for, in urging the church to reorganize its structure, they threatened Catholic unity. The issue came to a head in 1890. Peter Paul Cahensly, a German resident concerned with aiding Catholic emigrants to America, addressed a petition to the Holy See. He asked that parishes in the United States be organized by national origins, with each group represented in the episcopate. Pope Leo XIII rejected the idea of ethnic federation. In so doing, he prevented a fragmentation of the church; at the same time he also assured its more rapid acculturation of American influences. Yet, in having to forego the assistance of their own ethnic church, many German, Italian, and Slavic Catholics had to endure pressures that few other immigrant groups experienced.

A dissimilar yet not entirely discrepant development occurred within American Judaism. Jews, too, had lived in America since the seventeenth century, albeit in fewer number than Catholics. The first settlers were for the most part Sephardic, that is, from the Jewish populations driven out of Spain and Portugal after expulsion decrees in 1492 and 1497. American Jewry did not increase significantly, however, until the mid-nineteenth century when large numbers began to arrive from Central Europe. The new wave of German Jews (Ashkenazim) did not fuse with the handful of Sephardim, but at first associated with the German societies that had no religious qualifications for membership. They nevertheless gradually moved away from a German identification as German immigrants became acculturated, and before the Civil War they were building temples, hospitals, and other institutions for Jewish communities.

Much of that effort developed out of a fear that Jews would also succumb to the pressures of assimilation, and indeed, American Jewry split over the issue of Americanization. In the 1880s a group of modernist rabbis meeting in Pittsburgh adopted a liberal platform that became the program of Reform Judaism. The Reform departure from Judaic tradition—relegating the Hebrew language and the Talmud to the fringes of Jewish life, abandoning dietary and other rules of conduct—provoked a counterreaction. Some Jews who did not believe that life in the United States required giving up ancestral tradition organized themselves as a Conservative body "for the purpose of keeping alive the true Judaic spirit." For still others—the Orthodox—Reform was unthinkable, and to them even the Conservatives seemed only too willing to compromise their faith.

Jews of Conservative and Orthodox persuasion believed that assimilation posed a threat to Judaic traditions. Jacob Epstein's illustrations for Hutchins Hapgood's sensitive 1902 collection, *The Spirit of the Ghetto,* revealed the depth of their concern. In this sketch a Jewish boy prepares for morning prayer. The phylacteries he attaches to his left arm and forehead contain parchments inscribed, in part, with the injunction from Deuteronomy: "Hear, O Israel: The Lord our God is one Lord; and you shall love the Lord your God with all your heart, and with all your soul, and with all your might. And these words which I command you this day shall be upon your heart; and you shall teach them diligently to your children . . . . And you shall bind them as a sign upon your hand, and they shall be as frontlets between your eyes."

While American Jews were dividing over reform, a series of pogroms and anti-Semitic decrees in Russia stirred a mass migration that would bring a half-million Jews to the United States before the turn of the century, and an additional million and a quarter by 1914. The new arrivals came from a milieu that was entirely different from that of Central Europe. In eastern Europe there had been all-Jewish communities where traditions could be nurtured with little regard for the surrounding culture. The Judaism of the newcomers who adhered to religious practices was therefore more intense by many degrees than that of the Sephardim and Ashkenazim. But not all the immigrants from Eastern Europe adhered to the ancient faith. The ethnic diversity of that part of the world had led many of them to think of the Jews as a nation, for in their separate villages that is what they were. More than that, with anti-Semitism rampant, they were a nation oppressed. Their condition was made to order for radical leaders, and Jews who gave up traditional religious observances gravitated toward secular radical extremes. The east European immigrants, observes Nathan Glazer in his brief but excellent *American Judaism,* were frightening to the Ashkenazim in more ways than one: "their poverty was more desperate than German Jewish poverty, their piety more intense than German Jewish piety, their irreligion more violent than German Jewish irreligion, their radicalism more extreme than German Jewish radicalism."

Yet the extremism of the new Jewish immigrants was a measure of their intense suffering. Despite a distaste for east European radicalism and Orthodoxy, Jews who had established themselves in American society sought to provide help for the oppressed. An important agency for assistance to east European immigrants was the Henry Street Settlement, established on New York's Lower East Side by Lillian Wald in 1893. A trained nurse, she had taken up residence in the ghetto with the hope of giving aid to the sick and the infirm. The house on Henry Street provided that and much more. It became a meeting place, a recreation center, and an educational institution. Jacob Schiff, who headed Kuhn, Loeb and Company, was one of Lillian Wald's strongest supporters, and he assisted other causes as well. A Reform Jew himself, he recognized that, because Conservatives had not moved so far from Orthodoxy, they were in a better position to communicate with east Europeans than were Jews of Reform congregations. He therefore gave money to the Conservative Jewish Theological Seminary to assist in the training of rabbis who might effectively serve needs of the new immigrants.

Motivations behind the assistance that German Jews extended to east Europeans were obviously mixed. American Jewry was anxious to preserve its good name, and many feared that east European immigrants would tend to foster a negative stereotype from which they, too, would suffer. Beyond that, however, was a profound concern for suffering humanity that found expression in all three religious traditions at the turn of the century.

Among Protestants, that concern became the driving force of the Social Gospel Movement. Protestantism in the United States had long preached an individualistic piety that emphasized a decent life on earth and ultimate salvation as flowing from a personal decision to "get right with God." Highly successful in agricultural America, Protestantism's stress on individual responsibility comported well with the myth of the self-made man, that favorite theme of a developing industrial society. Yet there were limits to the appeal of American Protestantism's religious individualism, just as there were limits to the appeal of a secular Gospel of Wealth. With a stream of new immigrants flowing into the country, taking up residence in urban ethnic enclaves, working as unskilled laborers, and forming an ethnically divided proletariat, the shibboleths and formulas of individualistic piety began to seem remote if not trifling.

Within the Protestant churches—especially the Episcopal and Congregational denominations—were men and women of troubled conscience who sensed a need to shift the direction of Protestant thrust. "The first half of the [nineteenth] century was individualistic; the second half has tended to become collectivistic," noted a British observer in 1901. "Freedom was the earlier ideal, brotherhood is the latter." The way to bring about a day of brotherhood, believed advocates of the Social Gospel, was to translate the Sermon on the Mount into action. Belief without deeds was sterile, but those who took their Christian convictions to heart would work for social reconstruction.

Various Protestant denominations provided institutional structure for Social Gospel activities. The first and most effective organization was the Church Association for the Advancement of the Interests of Labor (CAIL), founded in 1887 by a group of Episcopal clergymen and laymen in New York. But there were others. The Congregational churches organized a Committee on Capital and Labor in 1892; in the same year the Baptists, led by Walter Rauschenbusch, founded the Brotherhood of the Kingdom. Later, in 1904, the Presbyterians created a Department of Church and Labor, while other churches established similar agencies in their national offices. The Social Gospel was not just a sectarian movement. In 1908 twenty-five Protestant denominations, with about two-thirds of the Protestants in the United States on their combined membership rolls, established the Federal Council of the Churches of Christ in America. Almost immediately the Council began to function as a social action organization.

With nearly every Protestant denomination becoming involved in causes promoted by the Social Gospel Movement, churchmen frequently paused to reflect upon the changes they thought it had brought about. One perceptive participant saw it as advocating a preventive Christianity in contrast to the remedial Christianity of an earlier day. In the past the social work of the Church had been "to remedy the effects of evils which have been left to work themselves out and multiply themselves in fresh evil effects." But the Social Gospel had aroused the Church to an awareness that "it is our business to strike deeper, to get at the roots of these evils and remove them." Walter Rauschenbusch, the preeminent figure of the Social Gospel Movement, summed up his sense of its purpose and his hope in a paraphrase of Paul's first letter to the Corinthians, thirteenth chapter: "The values created by love never fail; but whether there are class privileges, they shall fall; and whether there are millions [of dollars] gathered, they shall be scattered; and whether there are vested rights, they shall be abolished. For in the past strong men lorded it in ruthlessness and strove for their own power and pride, but when the perfect social order comes, the strong shall serve the common good." In the meantime, while followers of the Social Gospel set out to serve the common welfare, a new kind of popular magazine began publishing articles indicating where American society might be served to good effect.

**The Muckrakers**     Magazine publishing in the United States dates back to 1741, when Andrew Bradford brought out his *American Magazine.* For the next century and a half a great many periodicals were called into existence, but few were chosen by readers as worthy of their support. Those that continued to publish did so in spite of limited circulation. Not until after the Civil War did technological advances in the printing trades, favorable mailing rates under the Postal Act of 1879, and capital for investment combine to encourage new ventures in publishing. The average citizen did not become a magazine reader overnight, for until the nineties there remained a hiatus between the expensive monthlies such as *Harper's* and *Scribner's* and the cheap weeklies such as *Frank Leslie's Illustrated Newspaper* and *Detective Fiction.* But just before the turn of the century, awareness of a large potential market led enterprising publishers to begin turning out low-cost magazines that would appeal to popular tastes. By 1900 the availability of some fifty national magazines bore witness to the emergence of a new instrument for shaping public opinion.

Men who pioneered the development of that instrument—Frank Munsey, S. S. McClure, John Brisben Walker, George Horace Lorimer, and others—could not have been more favored by the times in which they lived. A new technology in printing had made possible the mass production methods that were a sine qua non for magazines of national circulation. By 1890 rotary presses were replacing the older, more cumbersome flatbed presses. In that year, too, R. Hoe and Company developed a rotary art press that printed halftone illustrations from curved plates; a multicolor rotary press followed soon after. Paper manufacturers made their contribution by producing from wood pulp a cheap glazed paper that had many of the characteristics of a more expensive rag-content product. Such improvements, inasmuch as they made possible the production of attractive magazines at a low unit cost, permitted competition with established publishers.

Innovative marketing practices, which aroused the enthusiasm of American industry in the late nineteenth century, served to enhance the new magazines' chances of success. The cracker barrel, that symbol of homespun profundity and bulk merchandising, could still be found in general stores across the land. But both manufacturers and retailers preferred packaged goods that promised greater profits than merchandise sold in bulk. After producers began packaging their products under brand names and trademarks, after they began spending large sums to advertise those brand names, and after chain stores began linking retail outlets for packaged products, the day of bulk merchandising was over. The new magazines played an important part in bringing about the revolution in retailing, for it was in their pages that advertisers sought to establish the identity of brand merchandise. And, of course, the magazines themselves profited from fees they received for the advertising services they performed.

Making a go of it in magazine publishing required much more than technical proficiency and advertisers, however, for circulation depended on content as well as format. If publishers were to retain advertising revenues and keep their rotary presses in operation, they had to edit their magazines to make them attractive to a wide readership. Not all of them followed the same formula. Edward W. Bok, editor of the *Ladies Home Journal,* offered suggestions on how to raise children, how to read the Bible as literature, how to decorate home interiors, and how to play the piano; he carried on crusades against public drinking cups, venereal disease, and French fashions. George Horace Lorimer, who edited another Curtis publication, the *Saturday Evening Post,* believed that the American businessman had become a whipping boy for reformers and that he deserved better treatment. Filled with stories of successful men and the romance of American enterprise, the *Post* vindicated Lorimer's judgment when its circulation passed the two million mark at the end of World War I.

One of the most widely used circulation-building formulas was that to which Theodore Roosevelt gave the name *muckraking.* In a 1906 speech he said that some journalists reminded him of the Man with a Muck-rake in Bunyan's *Pilgrim's Progress:* he would not look up even to receive a celestial crown but "continued to rake the filth on the floor." Although the president never revealed what journalists he had in mind, several writers proudly proclaimed themselves muckrakers. A term of opprobrium became a badge of honor, as reform-minded contributors to mass circulation magazines tried to outdo one another in exposing the abuses and shortcomings of American society.

Roosevelt was actually giving only belated recognition to a phenomenon that accompanied the rise of popular periodicals. The literature of exposure is, of course, as old as the bawdy planet, but it took on a new intensity when editors of national magazines recognized the universality of its appeal. *Collier's, Munsey's, Hampton's, Everybody's, Cosmopolitan, American Magazine, McClure's*—all these and others served up dishes that were far from dainty. They set them before a public that had a voracious appetite for information about the manipulations of big businessmen, the graft of urban political machines, the venality of national political leaders, and the willingness of labor unions to circumvent the law. The vigorous articles in which Thomas Lawson analyzed stock-market practices and Charles Edward Russell damned the beef trust appeared in *Everybody's*. Samuel Hopkins Adams shocked the readers of *Collier's* with his revelation of frauds perpetrated by the makers of patent medicines. *Cosmopolitan* published David Graham Phillips's widely read series, "The Treason of the

One reason for the preeminence of *McClure's Magazine* among muckraking journals was S. S. McClure's willingness to subsidize the research as well as the writing of his authors. Ida Tarbell, Lincoln Steffens, and others thus produced articles that were crammed with disturbing factual detail. Mr. Dooley (the fictional saloon keeper of journalist Finley Peter Dunne's feature articles) commented that the day had passed when magazines "was very ca'ming to the mind" and he could enjoy them as he did "a bottle iv white pop now an' thin."

Senate." Nothing slipped past the teeth of the rake; even women's clubs and churches did not escape.

Just as remarkable as the articles of exposure—and even more important—was the editorial position of muckraking journals. When *McClure's* published its January number in 1903, it happened to contain an article by Lincoln Steffens on "The Shame of Minneapolis," an installment of Ida Tarbell's history of Standard Oil, and a piece by Ray Stannard Baker revealing the extent to which laws had been evaded during a recent strike. After reading over copy before going to press, a bemused S. S. McClure wrote a reflective editorial. Observing that capitalists, workingmen, politicians, and citizens had all either broken the law or let it be broken, he posed an important question: "Who is left to uphold it?" Lawyers could not be trusted to uphold it because the best of them were hired by corporations to give advice on how to get around it. Judges could not be trusted to uphold it because they were so preoccupied with legal technicalities that they had lost sight of fundamentals. Churches could not be trusted to uphold it because the richest of them were no better than the corporations. The colleges? Institutions of learning, unfortunately, simply did not understand. "There is no one left; none but all of us," concluded McClure. "We all are doing our worst and making the public pay." But the public included everyone; with the striking of a balance, everyone would have to pay. "And in the end the sum total of our debt will be our liberty."

The muckrakers wrote with an eye toward reform, but for all their disgust with corruption and dishonesty, their vision was remarkably detached. They took no sides in the controversies of their time; they did not attack business malpractice to further the cause of labor, and they did not condemn labor malfeasance to justify business practices. What they sought were facts, and McClure and other publishers were willing to pay for accuracy. McClure estimated that each of Ida Tarbell's articles on Standard Oil cost him $4,000; the bill for each installment in Steffens's series on the shame of American cities was $2,000. Muckrakers ardently believed that, if reform was to be wise and equitable, it would have to be based on solid information. No one more clearly described the point of view than did Ray Stannard Baker, in a conversation with Jack London. When London chided him for not casting his lot with the Socialists, Baker replied:

You see, I'm not a reformer. I'm a reporter. I have only begun to look at the world. I want to see it all more clearly and understand it better, before I pledge myself to any final solution for the evils we both see. I'm not sure yet that if either you or I made over the world, it would be any better than the one we now have. We don't know enough.

Muckraking, as it appeared in *McClure's* and other mass circulation magazines, was thorough and unbiased. It suggested few specific solutions to the problems it probed and no sweeping alterations of the American social and economic system.

**Progressive Goals
for American Society**

Muckraking journalists did not originate what came to be known as the Progressive Movement, but their attitude toward the problems of American society was typical of citizens who identified themselves as progressives. Whether or not progressivism could accurately be described as a movement, it was a phenomenon that marked a change in the nature of American politics at the close of the nineteenth century. The old system had been characterized by close identification of voters with parties, effective mobilization of voters by parties, and an unusual level of voter participation in elections. Figures on turnout for presidential elections and drop-off in congressional and state elections, given in Table 3.4, indicate that

TABLE 3.4    Voter Participation

Mean Levels of National Turnout and Drop-Off by Periods

| Period (Presidential Years) | Mean Estimated Turnout | Period (Off Years) | Mean Estimated Turnout | Mean Drop-off |
|---|---|---|---|---|
| | (%) | | (%) | (%) |
| 1848–1872 | 75.1 | 1850–1874 | 65.2 | 7.0 |
| 1876–1896 | 78.5 | 1878–1898 | 62.8 | 15.2 |
| 1900–1916 | 64.8 | 1902–1918 | 47.9 | 22.4 |
| 1920–1928 | 51.7 | 1922–1930 | 35.2 | 28.7 |
| 1932–1944 | 59.1 | 1934–1946 | 41.0 | 27.8 |
| 1948–1960 | 60.3 | 1950–1962 | 44.1 | 24.9 |

SOURCE: Walter Dean Burnham, "The Changing Shape of the American Political Universe," *The American Political Science Review*, Vol. 59 (March 1965), pp. 7–28.

Americans were deeply involved in the political process during the nineteenth century. Citizen participation was more intense and more uniform than at any time after 1896. The system operated so as to permit resolution of divisive issues, in part because it made possible a majoritarian settlement of those issues. Its one great failure, marked by outbreak of the Civil War, should not detract from the system's general success in determining which of the competing sectional modes of organization should prevail.

One reason for the extent to which Americans became involved in nineteenth-century politics is that the political system rested upon a rural and small-town base; consequently, party affiliation had a social as well as political dimension. A preindustrial system, it related broad political questions to the everyday life of a predominantly rural society. It thus enclosed all citizens within a framework that encouraged comprehensible discussion of issues; contending parties did not agree, but they talked about the same things. Political discussions carried on in such manner served to increase party loyalties. Voters tended to commit themselves to a party first, and after that to the party position on issues of the day.

Then came a new era of industrial enterprise. The growth of manufacturing and of cities broke down the old system by destroying its base. Industrialization undermined the social homogeneity that predominated in an agricultural society; in so doing, it weakened the framework within which political discussions had taken place. In effect, industrial diversification complicated the task of mobilizing masses of citizens for participation in the political process. The election of 1896 demonstrated how difficult it had become, the demonstration discouraging further attempts to organize a mass movement of either the downtrodden or anyone else.

National politics tended to become sectional in orientation, with Democrats controlling the agricultural South and portions of the West, while Republicans dominated the industrial Northeast. Associated with the prosperity that followed McKinley's election, Republicans enjoyed greater success in national politics as Democrats tried to avoid being labeled the party of depression. More important to the progressives than party success, however, was the way in which industrialization and urbanization gave rise to narrow interest groups. Comparing the twentieth century's new political and social system with that of an earlier day led progressives to fear the fragmentation of American society. In business, labor, agriculture —indeed, in almost every area of activity—they saw emergent interests shaping their self-serving programs and contending with one another. To the progressives it seemed evident that harmony would never result from the spontaneous workings of a society made up of such competing groups. Nor could they place much confidence in a return to the old nineteenth-century party system, for the process of industrialization and urbanization could not be reversed.

The progressives did not, however, lose hope. Harmony could be created —from above. Left to itself, an industrializing American society could not produce the consensus that had been possible in a period of agricultural dominance. But the harmony of an earlier day could be made contemporary through a new kind of consensus management. For the progressives, a moral concern with the disintegration of society produced a practical desire for hard facts that might yield a sense of direction. "What is the need of a philosophy or an 'ism' when there is obvious wrong to be righted?" asked Charles McCarthy, who headed the legislative reference library in Wisconsin during the years when that state was making a name for itself as a leader in progressive activities. But how were progressives to right the obvious wrong? McCarthy and other progressives believed that making government more efficient would increase the efficiency of individual citizens, and that making individuals more efficient would increase their opportunities for achieving happiness and the good life.

Improving the efficiency of the state or national government required that men who wielded political power be advised by experts in taxation, land use, city planning, forestry, labor, transportation, and a thousand other areas of specialization. But officeholders and experts alike had to be disinterested; that is, they could not be controlled by any of the narrow-interest groups that were seeking special favors for themselves. The progressives worked hard for reforms that would give the people a greater voice in the selection and control of officeholders. Their enthusiasm for such reforms—the initiative, referendum, recall, direct primary, and the like—represented more than a desire to continue plebescitarian features of the nineteenth-century system on the one hand, and less than a resolute confidence in the efficacy of democratic government on the other. Giving the people a greater voice in government was, rather, a means of assuring the political influence of those who remained unorganized or unaffiliated with particular interest groups. In a population where direct democracy reforms had broken the political power of such groups, the progressives believed that the cooperating members of all classes might govern effectively with the help of expert advice. The reforms were introduced, therefore, not as an effort to invigorate a new mass movement, but as an effort to bring about rule by the disinterested and the detached. A powerful but neutral government would be the result of measures that expanded the influence of the general electorate. Such a government would function in the common interest of all citizens rather than in the special interests of particular groups.

One way to understand the influence of an emerging progressive point of view is to examine changes that took place in the movement for women's rights. In 1848 feminists, gathered at Seneca Falls, New York, adopted a Declaration of Sentiments and Resolutions. The Declaration asserted that "all men and women are created equal," and it attacked the tendency of a male-dominated society to "destroy woman's confidence in her own powers, to lessen her self-respect, and to make her willing to lead a dependent and abject life." To correct the effects of discrimination, the feminists proposed to make women the equal partners of men in every activity. During the summer of 1920, with ratification of the Nineteenth Amendment, women secured the right to vote. In the difference between what the feminists of 1848 hoped to achieve and what the suffragists of 1920 accomplished lies an explanation of what progressivism implied.

Nineteenth-century feminists favored woman suffrage, but they did not see it as a panacea. Elizabeth Cady Stanton, a founder of the women's rights movement, thought the vote a "superficial and fragmentary" reform because it left basic social and economic disabilities untouched. But what were the disabilities that troubled nineteenth-century feminists? Charlotte Perkins Gilman provided a cogent analysis in *Women and Economics,* a book published in 1898. Sex, she charged, had become for women the sole means of fulfillment. A man could engage in a variety of activities outside the home. A woman could only marry and have children; and, because rewards came to her only "through a small gold ring," she could not contribute effectively to the society. The result was a profound discontent from which everyone, including husbands and children, suffered.

Before the turn of the century a majority of American women avoided the feminist movement, in part because the changes it urged seemed such a radical departure from norms to which they had grown accustomed. But that did not mean they were content with their place. In 1890 the National American Woman's Suffrage Association (NAWSA) sought to unite the advocates of broad social reform with the advocates of limited political change by emphasizing the vote, that is, the least common denominator between the two groups. Coherence in the suffrage movement was not easy to achieve, however, because arguments that were effective in gaining support for the vote weakened the cause of broader social and economic reform. The nineteenth-century feminists had urged the equality of women and men. The suffragists emphasized instead that prominent female characteristics—purity, sensitivity, and social concern—would help to create a better society if women took part in the political process.

Frances Willard, president of the Women's Christian Temperance Union,

This poster from the Women's Trade Union League provides more than a hint of the depth and subtlety of problems that female workers faced. Formed in 1903 by a coalition of reformers and advocates of trade union membership, the WTUL directed its initial efforts toward the organization of women as workers. Perhaps because the League included "allies" as well as working women, however, it proved unable to adhere strictly to its initial purpose. Keenly aware as well of the problems of women qua women, the WTUL gradually moved in the direction of reform legislation and the suffrage (State Historical Society of Wisconsin).

In 1913 suffragists marched through the streets of Washington in demonstration of their cause. Feminism encompassed a variety of objectives during the nineteenth century. As the progressive point of view gained ascendancy, however, woman suffrage blossomed like Aaron's rod.

had once said that politics was "enlarged housekeeping." Suffragists expanded on the idea at the same time that progressives were urging that disinterested or neutral government assume a more active role in maintaining social coherence. The housekeeping metaphor had great appeal to progressives, for it suggested ties that bind the individual members of a family. And if activities of government were to be enlarged, there was indeed no reason why women should not participate in politics. For their part, women could expect to gain more from the suffrage alone, if progressives had their way, than they could ever before have gained from only the suffrage. The positive, neutral state envisioned by progressive reformers would see to it that justice was done. Women had never asked for more than that. The Nineteenth Amendment gave them the one reform they needed, or so the suffragists thought.

## Theodore Roosevelt and the Progressives

Progressivism, then, implied the unbiased exercise of political power to prevent social disruption by contending interest groups. It also aimed at promoting the general welfare of a society that was, if not harmonious, at least content with limiting its quarrels to issues that were less than cosmic. Theodore Roosevelt, who became president in 1901, was by disposition and temperament in tune with the main themes of progressivism. Born in 1858, the son of a New York banker and importer, little "Teedie" was a frail child whose struggle to overcome physical handicaps developed into a lifelong quest for adventure and strenuous endeavor. Educated for the most part by private tutors before he matriculated at Harvard, his intellectual interests extended over a variety of fields from the natural sciences to history. As a student of biology he accepted the idea of evolution through struggle, but he was clever enough to realize that Darwinian postulates needed refinement when applied to society. The welfare of society, he came to believe, should take precedence over individual interest. And a given society's capacity to insure fair competition among individuals was a measure of its ability to make progress along the pathways of civilization.

After graduating from Harvard in 1880, TR spent three years as a Republican assemblyman in the New York state legislature. Then, abandoning politics temporarily after the death of his first wife, he escaped to North Dakota, where he spent two years working feverishly at ranching and writing. In 1886 he returned to New York, remarried, and reentered the political arena. An unsuccessful campaign as Republican candidate for mayor of New York City did not keep him from helping out in the Harrison campaign of 1888; his reward was an appointment to the Civil Service Commission. From there he went first to a position as president of the New York City police board and then to a post as Assistant Secretary of the Navy in the McKinley administration. His exploits with the Rough Riders in Cuba during the Spanish-American War captured the public imagination, helping to assure his victory in New York's 1898 gubernatorial campaign. Two years later the Republican National Convention

Theodore Roosevelt gloried in the competition of politics, and audiences relished his vigorous platform manner. William Allen White, who knew him well, described the reaction that many Americans shared: "I felt the joy and delight of his presence and, knowing his weakness, still gave him my loyalty—the great rumbling, roaring, jocund tornado of a man, all masculine save sometimes a catlike glint, hardly a twinkle, in his merry eyes."

tapped the popular young governor as a vice-presidential candidate to improve McKinley's already excellent chances for reelection. Roosevelt was reluctant to run—he found the anonymity of the office depressing—but he finally agreed. And so, when McKinley died from an assassin's shot in Buffalo, TR enthusiastically grasped the reins of power.

The youngest president ever to hold office, Roosevelt had a reputation for brashness that furrowed the brows of Republican leaders on Capitol Hill. They need not have been worried, for TR was both a realist who recognized the need for congressional cooperation and an ambitious seeker after the GOP nomination in 1904. Had he not already been inclined to take a position above contending factions in Congress and contending interests throughout the country, the political realities of his first years in office would have tempered presidential policy. The program that Roosevelt formulated was therefore notable for its moderation. The Expedition Act added two assistants to the Attorney General's staff and cleared the way for trying suits under the Sherman Act. The Elkins Act of 1903 forbade railroad rebates to major industrial shippers. Both measures encountered little opposition; no one wanted to fight the first, and railroads themselves supported the second. The president had to exert more influence to secure passage of the Department of Commerce bill, creating a new administrative department, and a Bureau of Corporations to collect information on interstate industrial activities. When he announced in

February 1903 that Standard Oil was lobbying against the new bureau, however, popular outrage swamped congressional opponents of the measure.

After Roosevelt won election to the presidency in his own right in 1904, his legislative objectives encompassed further railroad regulation, the protection of consumers, and the conservation of natural resources. In 1906, after some adept parliamentary manipulation by the president, Congress passed the Hepburn Act. Under its provisions the Interstate Commerce Commission received power to set maximum rates for railroads and to order compliance after thirty days. District courts were granted authority to issue injunctions suspending ICC decisions, but only the circuit courts and the Supreme Court could reverse the commission's rulings, and the act authorized quick appeal to those agencies. The ICC findings were to be accepted until controverted by other evidence; in litigation, therefore, railroads had to assume the burden of proof. The Hepburn Act provided means for effective regulation of railroads; its provisions were later extended to include storage, express, pipe line, telephone, and telegraph companies.

Concern for the protection of consumers resulted in the Meat Inspection Act and the Pure Food and Drug Act, both passed in 1906. The prime mover behind passage of the pure food legislation was Dr. Harvey W. Wiley, chief chemist in the Department of Agriculture. Disturbed by the use of adulterants and undesirable preservatives in canned foods, Wiley prevailed upon the president to ask for corrective legislation in his annual message of 1905. Wiley was not, however, a lone crusader. In the pages of *Collier's,* Samuel Hopkins Adams had already opened his attack on patent medicine frauds when, in 1906, Upton Sinclair published *The Jungle,* a

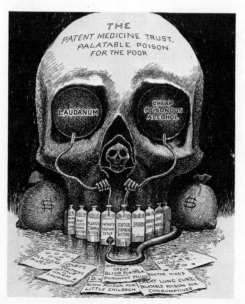

This cartoon accompanied "The Great American Fraud," a series of articles that Samuel Hopkins Adams began publishing in *Collier's* in 1905. The series, along with Upton Sinclair's *The Jungle,* contributed to passage of the Pure Food and Drug Act in 1906. "Gullible America," Adams wrote, "will spend this year some seventy-five million dollars in the purchase of patent medicines. In consideration of this sum it will swallow huge quantities of alcohol, an appalling amount of opiates and narcotics, a wide assortment of varied drugs ranging from powerful and dangerous heart depressants to insidious liver stimulants; and, far in excess of other ingredients, undiluted fraud."

Near the end of his presidency, Theodore Roosevelt and Gifford Pinchot were photographed on a Mississippi River excursion undertaken to promote plans for improving the nation's rivers. Although conservation and control of waterways were progressive measures—serving national rather than particular interests—the Inland Waterways Commission that TR appointed received little congressional support. Not until creation of the Tennessee Valley Authority in 1933 did his proposals reach fruition (U.S. Forestry Service).

didactic novel that described vile conditions in the Chicago packing houses. With the nation aroused, Roosevelt took advantage of the public outcry to press for control of food processors and drug peddlers.

The legislation that TR obtained was not precisely what Sinclair, at least, had in mind. The author had hoped to improve the working conditions of packing-house employees; pure food was at best a secondary consideration. "I aimed at the public's heart," he later observed, "and by accident I hit it in the stomach." But Sinclair was not a progressive; at the time he wrote *The Jungle* his sympathies lay more with the Socialists. Neither he nor others who looked toward the reorganization of industry ever really understood what was involved in Roosevelt's effort to prevent abuses without changing the system. The packers themselves supported inspection, and the president was delighted. The public interest, after all, had been well served.

Roosevelt's activities in behalf of conservation, a subject that lay close to his heart, are also indicative of what progressivism entailed. Making full use of the authorization provided by the Forest Reserve Act of 1891, TR created forest reserves out of nearly 150 million acres of unsold government timber lands and withdrew from public entry an additional 85 million acres in Alaska and the Northwest, areas rich in water and mineral resources. In 1907 he organized a national conference to discuss problems of conservation; out of its deliberations came the National Conservation Association. Some reformers interpreted those moves as an attack on large lumber companies and other despoilers of the American environment. That is certainly not what the president intended. As Professor Samuel P. Hays has shown, what motivated the conservation movement was a desire to prevent indiscriminate cutting that would eventually ruin the companies as well as the forests. Gifford Pinchot, who served Roosevelt as chief forester in the Department of Agriculture, developed a program of sustained yield planting that would assure an adequate supply of lumber through an indefinite future. Neither Pinchot nor Roosevelt believed that forests should stand untouched; conservation through judicious cultivation was their aim. The lumber companies—Weyerhaeuser, King Lumber, and the Northern Pacific—all supported the program even though Congress proved reluctant to provide necessary appropriations. But having to forego help from Capitol Hill, Roosevelt and Pinchot had still found a practical way to eliminate abuses by private companies without destroying the companies. Indeed, lumbermen stood to gain from the manner in which TR pursued the national interest.

Although Roosevelt appeared to be moving against big business in much of the legislation he requested, he never endorsed a sweeping program to cut business interests down in size. That he was not the enemy of big business became clear in discussions of the tariff, sometimes identified as "the mother of trusts." In Iowa, Governor Albert B. Cummins in 1901 proposed the removal of tariff protection from all trust-made products, and the idea gained currency throughout the Middle West. But Roosevelt could not be persuaded that tariffs were anything but a matter of expediency. In general, he favored the idea of reciprocity that McKinley had helped to popularize among Republican leadership; beyond that he wanted more than anything else to avoid taking a position that might split his party. Furthermore, whether or not the tariff was the mother of trusts, TR never believed that all trusts were bad.

The president's reputation as a trust-buster, stemming largely from his prosecution of the Northern Securities Company, was largely undeserved if not unsought. The company represented a merger of three large railroads (the Northern Pacific, the Great Northern, and the Chicago, Burlington and Quincy) that threatened to become a transportation monopoly extending over the entire Northwest. Behind it stood an association of staggering power and famous names: the House of Morgan, the Rockefeller interests, James J. Hill, and E. H. Harriman. Early in 1902 Roosevelt instructed Attorney General Philander C. Knox to start a suit under the Sherman Act to dissolve Northern Securities. Nearly two years passed before the Supreme Court upheld a Federal court decision ordering dissolution of the company; but, when it did, the president was ecstatic. The prosecution, he announced, was "one of the great achievements of my administration." And he went on to battles against Standard Oil, the American Tobacco Company, a combination of packing companies known as the "Beef Trust," and several other mergers. In all, he instituted proceedings against forty-four corporations.

Yet not once did the president ever contend that trust-busting was a definitive solution to the problems of industry. What best pleased him in the Northern Securities decision was that "the most powerful men in this country were held to accountability before the law." Like other progressives, he believed that special interests must be regulated and controlled in the national interest; whenever he saw power exercised in a way that threatened regulation and control, TR was ready to intervene. But he did not propose to break up every combination. In 1902 he explained his position by use of an analogy. The growth of big business, he argued, was natural, inevitable, beneficial, and irreversible. Congress could no more turn it back by legislation than it could reverse the spring floods of the Mississippi River. The floods could be regulated and controlled by levees, however, and so could the trusts. TR did not add, as he might have, that flood control demanded expertise; he certainly believed in the progressive idea that American social and economic controls should be developed by disinterested experts. While he did not always claim expert knowledge himself, he had no doubts about his impartiality.

The same year in which Roosevelt was talking about floods and levees provided him with yet another opportunity to demonstrate his unbiased concern for the general welfare. In northeastern Pennsylvania more than fifty thousand anthracite coal miners walked off their jobs after rejection of United Mine Workers' demands for a 20 per cent pay increase, recog-

The anthracite strike of 1902, provoked largely by the arrogance and obtuseness of mine owners, created a severe energy crisis as winter approached. Here New Yorkers lined up at a public distribution point to fill their sacks from a dwindling supply. Roosevelt's use of presidential power to end the strike received enthusiastic public support (Culver Pictures).

nition of the union, an eight-hour day, and other benefits. The six rail-roads that controlled most of the anthracite fields, led by George F. Baer of the Reading and W. H. Truesdale of the Lackawanna, refused to negotiate because they thought the union would crack under the pressure of mounting demands for coal. Though the strike dragged on from May to October, the UMW did not crack; indeed, its resolution seemed to grow firmer when Baer announced that the miners would be protected "not by the labor agitators but by the Christian men to whom God in His infinite wisdom, has given control of the property interests of the country." With winter coming on, Roosevelt decided to act. He began with a White House conference between mine owners and union leaders. After several days' haggling, he finally secured agreement to accept the findings of an arbitral commission that he himself would appoint. In the end the union won a 10 per cent pay increase, a nine-hour day, a permanent board of conciliation, and other demands. Few people other than the mine owners were prepared to argue that the settlement was not a fair one. And the owners had shown themselves to be so arrogant that even fewer people cared what they thought. In a letter to William Howard Taft, TR summed up his own reaction to Baer and his ilk: "May heaven preserve me from ever again dealing with so wooden headed a set, when I wish to preserve their interest."

Roosevelt believed that he could understand the real interests of mine owners better than the mine owners themselves did; he was no less confident of his ability to act in the real interests of labor. Repeatedly affirming labor's right to organize, he even carried a card of honorary membership in the railroad brotherhoods. But organizing and negotiating were one thing; violence and lawlessness were quite another. In a typical utterance TR said that he wanted "the labor people absolutely to understand that I set my face like flint against violence and lawlessness of any kind on their part, just as much as against arrogant greed by the rich." When the miners of Cripple Creek, Colorado, asked him to send troops to restrain mining corporations determined to destroy their union, Roosevelt demurred. Yet he more than once sent troops to other trouble spots when they were requested by management. Some critics argued that Roosevelt was, at heart, antilabor. He was not. He simply believed that the national interest always took precedence over special interest and that, in serving the national interest, he had to stand above special interest groups of any kind.

The paternalism characterizing much progressive activity frequently found its way into TR's pronouncements, but never more clearly than in a letter he wrote to Philander C. Knox in 1904:

The friends of property must realize that the surest way to provoke an explosion of wrong and injustice is to be shortsighted, narrow-minded, greedy and arrogant, and to fail to show in actual work that here in this republic it is peculiarly incumbent upon the man with whom things have prospered to be in a certain sense the keeper of his brother with whom life has gone hard.

Roosevelt did not invent progressivism. No more than the muckrakers did he originate the progressive view of society. Yet in his actions he practiced what progressivism preached.

**Wilson and the Progressives**

Roosevelt moved out of the White House in 1909 to make way for William Howard Taft, whose ability and affability had both so impressed TR that he had actively urged elevating the Secretary of War to the presidency. Unfortunately for Taft, his handling of presidential responsibilities alienated progressives within the party and throughout the country. He stepped up antitrust prosecutions, to be sure, and he threw his considerable weight behind more effective railroad regulation. Yet such activities were not enough to establish his progressive bona fides, for he also alienated TR's followers by helping to secure passage of the high Payne-Aldrich Tariff and by removing Gifford Pinchot as chief forester. At its 1912 convention, the Republican party split over the seating of delegates. Taft won renomination, but only after Roosevelt had led his followers out of the convention hall to begin making plans for a new party. A few weeks later, the "Bull Moose" progressives—so named because TR had said that he felt "fit as a bull moose"—met in Chicago to organize the Progressive party. They listened to their candidate proclaim, "We stand at Armageddon, and we battle for the Lord"; then they went out to campaign for TR with the convention's enthusiastic rendition of "Onward, Christian Soldiers" ringing in their ears.

In the meantime, Democrats at Baltimore, after sweltering through forty-five ballots, finally nominated Woodrow Wilson on the forty-sixth. The Democratic candidate was a newcomer to politics. Born in 1856, the son of a Presbyterian clergyman, he was reared in Virginia, Georgia, and South Carolina. After completing his undergraduate education at Princeton in 1879, he studied law at the University of Virginia. As much as he delighted in study, and as much as he dreamed of developing his persuasive powers, Wilson found the practice of law boring. Abandoning it after only a year, he went to Johns Hopkins for graduate work in history and government. From 1885, when he published his doctoral dissertation under the title *Congressional Government,* until 1910, when he became governor of New Jersey, Wilson pursued an academic career. Books and articles flowed steadily from his pen as he taught at Bryn Mawr, Wesleyan, and Princeton. Chosen president of Princeton in 1902, he remained in that position until he resigned to enter the New Jersey gubernatorial race in 1910. As governor, he soon captured progressive support with a program that included regulation of railroads and utilities, a workmen's compensation law, and amendment of the state's corporation laws. He won the endorsement of Bryan, and at the same time he appealed to Democrats who for years had searched in vain for an alternative to Bryan.

Confronting a divided opposition in 1912, Wilson became the first Democrat since Grover Cleveland to win election to the presidency. He campaigned as a progressive; and, while he attempted to demonstrate that his

In 1896, William Jennings Bryan had been hampered by divided support, but in
1912 the party tables were turned. When Roosevelt and the Bull Moosers bolted
the Republican party, this cartoon asserted, they assured the election of Woodrow Wilson.

vision of progressivism was superior to that of Roosevelt, the difference was
more one of style and manner than of content. Roosevelt argued that the
trusts should not be destroyed but regulated. Wilson contended that competition should be improved by breaking up the corporations that stifled it.
More important than the specific content of campaign arguments was Wilson's willingness to use the power of the presidency to bring about reform.
He did not have TR's dash and color, but he could scarcely be outdone in
moral fervor. "This is not a day of triumph," he said in his inaugural address; "it is a day of dedication." As he saw it, the duty of his administration was "to cleanse, to reconsider, to restore, to correct the evil without
impairing the good, to purify and humanize every process of our common
life without weakening or sentimentalizing it."

The "New Freedom"—the phrase was one that Wilson used to distinguish his program from Roosevelt's "New Nationalism"—found expression
in tariff revision, banking and currency reform, antitrust legislation, and an
agency to prevent unlawful suppression of competition. The tariff, which
had done much to bring about Taft's fall from progressive grace, was the
first item on the president's agenda. Working closely with Oscar Underwood, chairman of the House Ways and Means Committee, the Administration developed a bill that would bring about the first major reduction in
duties since the Civil War. An income tax, placed beyond constitutional
challenge by ratification of the Sixteenth Amendment, would compensate
for the loss of revenue. Growing in importance over the years, income
taxation emerged as one of the progressive period's major achievements.
But protectionists, for the time being, were less concerned with government
revenues than with the possibility of having to face stiffer competition from
abroad. When lobbyists began buttonholing senators after House passage
of the bill, Wilson responded much as Roosevelt had during the battle for
a Bureau of Corporations. He announced that "Washington has seldom
seen so numerous, so industrious, or so insidious a lobby." Again the tactic

worked. Forced by subsequent investigations to reveal their own financial interests, senators approved both an income tax and lowered tariff rates. It was Wilson's first and in many ways his most important victory for progressive reform.

At the same time that Wilson signed the Underwood Tariff into law, he faced a controversy over reorganization of the banking and currency system. Everyone agreed that the system needed reform. Based upon the bonded indebtedness of the United States, currency was inelastic. The banking structure had neither central control nor workable machinery for mobilizing banking reserves. To agree that a problem existed, however, was not the same thing as coming to an agreement on a solution. New York financial magnates, along with most other big businessmen, favored a banker-controlled central bank. Bankers of interior cities, particularly in the Middle West, were not opposed to a central bank, but they were concerned with the new system's controls. Country bankers feared domination either by big-city bankers or by government. The Bryan faction of the Democratic party urged a reserve system with currency controlled by the government as a means of preventing concentration of credit reserves in Wall Street. Those who considered Bryan a monetary heretic preferred a decentralized reserve system controlled by private bankers.

Woodrow Wilson was neither cold nor dispassionate, as those who did not know him frequently alleged, but he was circumspect and reserved in manner. Certainly no glad-hander, he could nevertheless communicate effectively with crowds. "I have a sense of power in dealing with men collectively which I do not feel always in dealing with them singly," he wrote in 1885, long before he became president. "In the former case the pride of reserve does not stand so much in my way as it does in the latter. One feels no sacrifice of pride necessary in courting the favour of an assembly of men such as he would have in seeking to please one man" (Underwood & Underwood).

Facing divided counsel, Wilson was determined to stand above class and sectional interest. Carter Glass, chairman of the House Banking Committee, prepared a preliminary bill to establish a system of reserve banks under private control and without central direction. Publication of the Glass bill led to considerable discussion within the Wilson Administration. Bryan and Secretary of the Treasury William Gibbs McAdoo, along with Robert L. Owen, chairman of the Senate Banking Committee, fought for a system owned and controlled entirely by the government. For his part, Wilson listened to the advice of Louis D. Brandeis, who suggested that bankers be denied representation on the proposed Federal Reserve Board and that Federal Reserve currency be made the obligation of the United States. At the same time, the idea that private banking interests should own and in some measure control the Federal Reserve banks remained intact. With the help of George Reynolds, former president of the American Bankers' Association, and Paul Warburg of Kuhn, Loeb and Company, the nation's bankers gradually came over to the compromise measure. The amended Glass bill passed both houses of Congress; Wilson signed it into law just before Christmas 1913.

The Federal Reserve Act created twelve Federal Reserve banks, each of them owned by the member banks in the region where it was located. All national banks were required to belong to the system; state banks were permitted to join if they wished. The member banks were required to keep a percentage of their assets on deposit in the Federal Reserve, and the Reserve banks were authorized to issue legal tender notes secured by commercial and agricultural loans of member banks and by a 40 per cent gold reserve. Reserve banks were, in other words, bankers' banks. Federal Reserve notes would provide a flexible currency that could expand with the needs of the business community; at the same time, control over the rediscount rate—the charge made by the system in exchanging currency for the secured paper of member banks—would permit some control over business cycles as well. Capping the whole system was a Federal Reserve Board, composed of the Secretary of the Treasury, the Comptroller of the Currency, and five members appointed by the President of the United States with the advice and consent of the Senate.

The Federal Reserve Act was entirely in harmony with New Freedom progressivism. Bankers retained private ownership of banks; opponents of concentration secured a degree of decentralization through creation of the Federal Reserve districts; farmers were pleased with the provision that agricultural paper could be discounted along with commercial paper; progressives secured an instrument of control over banking. The act, in sum, brought conflicting narrow-interest groups into harmony. Some historians have argued that the government controls built into the Federal Reserve System actually represented a triumph of conservatism because members of the Reserve Board (or the Board of Governors) were in large part drawn from, or sympathetic to, the community of big-city bankers. But adoption of the Federal Reserve Act did mark a break with the period of cumbersome banking practice. Later development of the system moved it toward a philosophy of managed currency that would more adequately meet the demands of an economy rapidly growing in size and complexity.

After passage of the Federal Reserve Act, Wilson turned his attention to the regulation of business. The President's antitrust program, embodied in the Clayton bill and the Federal Trade Commission bill, proved disappointing to men of progressive persuasion. The Clayton bill enumerated unfair trade practices, but it envisioned no modification of the nation's financial and industrial structure. Labor opposed it because its provisions could be applied to unions as well as to business. As originally drafted, the bill to create an interstate trade commission would create little more than another bureau of corporations, a fact-finding adjunct of the Justice Department. With the Bryan wing of the Democratic party urging annihilation of the business oligarchy and the United States Chamber of Commerce arguing for the self-regulation of business, Wilson turned again to Brandeis for guidance. Together they worked out what seemed a promising course of action. Unfair trade practices would be described in general terms, and a trade commission would be granted authority to cope with specific restraints of trade.

The president announced that a Federal Trade Commission would be the principal agency of his regulatory program, and with that announcement he seemed to lose interest in the Clayton bill. The Senate passed a watered-down version of the bill, exempting labor from its provisions. Wilson signed it into law, but as an antitrust measure it accomplished little. The Federal Trade Commission Act, also passed in 1914, prohibited interlocking directorates, forbade price discrimination, and outlawed stock purchases that reduced competition. From the progressive point of view the FTC was a failure in its early years. Brandeis, for one, attributed its shortcomings to the "stupid administration" appointed by the president. Instead of taking vigorous action against business abuses, the commissioners actually encouraged business rationalization through trade associations and price stabilization.

The progressive impulse seemed to have spent itself. As Wilson viewed it, however, progressivism had reached its culmination on a note of triumph. In a public letter to McAdoo, written in November 1914, he proclaimed that the era of turmoil and dissension had passed and that Americans were moving into a period of cooperation that would yield a common purpose. It would be "a time of healing because a time of just dealing." That vision of the future never fully materialized; but neither did progressives shuffle off toward oblivion. Their idea of a powerful but neutral state, one that would control special interests in its pursuit of the national interest, retained enough vitality to endure through the difficult early years of World War I. And when the United States finally entered that war to make the world safe for democracy, progressives flocked into the nation's capital to meet their destiny.

# 4

## Power, Commerce, Morality: The United States in World Politics

Historians looking back on nineteenth-century international relations through the smoke and fire of twentieth-century struggle have often reflected on the pacific character of the period from 1815 to 1914. For four decades after Waterloo the great powers of Europe avoided conflict with one another; and, when war did occur after 1854, it was always limited in scope and duration. The 1854–1856 struggle that pitted Russia against Turkey, Britain, and France was largely confined to the Crimean peninsula. The three wars of German unification against Austria, Denmark, and France were carefully contained; all ended within a matter of months, and neither Britain nor Russia intervened. Russian invasion of European Turkey in 1878 brought a more serious risk of general war, but the danger was quickly averted by a congress of the great powers meeting in Berlin. With that formal, if not fundamental, restoration of the international equilibrium, no disagreements seriously disrupted the peace of Europe until the summer of 1914.

Meanwhile, the United States enjoyed the benefits conferred by a century of comparative tranquility in the relations of great powers on the other side of the Atlantic. At a time when Americans were busy settling a continent, resolving sectional differences, and improving their industrial capabilities, they had little cause to worry about interference from abroad. Just as the United States seemed to be completing its internal development at the close of the nineteenth century, however, signs of instability in the balance of power began to appear. That instability, and the forces bringing it about, were to have a profound effect on relationships among America, Europe, and the world. Understanding of what led the United States to seek expanded influence in world politics necessarily begins with examination of the balanced power arrangements that served to insure peace throughout most of the nineteenth century.

**The Precarious Balance**    The system that operated in Europe from 1815 to 1914 had many characteristics helping to explain its success in maintaining peace, but three were of particular importance. In the first place, each of the five nations that dominated international relations—Austria, Britain, France, Prussia (or

Germany) , and Russia—exercised a power roughly the equivalent of power exercised by any of the other four. This is not to argue that Austria was as strong as Britain, or that France after 1871 was as strong as Germany. But none of the five could realistically hope to achieve what Napoleon had attempted: hegemony over the European continent. The balance was never static, but only toward the end of the peaceful century did its adjustment become difficult and then impossible.

The second feature of the system—its flexibility—was just as important as the first. Recognizing no power or authority superior to its own, each of the five states avoided irrevocable or perpetual commitments. The statesmen of Europe worked to keep themselves free of such entaglements because they found security in shifting alignments; when any one nation appeared to be headed toward expansion of its power, the others were free to unite against it. Thus the grandiose plans of Napoleon III aroused suspicions in other countries, and France found herself without allies when the armies of Prussia humiliated French forces in 1870–1871.

The third characteristic of the nineteenth-century system was less obvious, but the force of its influence was always important and sometimes decisive. Alliances and alignments, shifting and flexible though they might be, operated within a common European self-consciousness. Statesmen of the great powers seldom made explicit mention of European unity. And yet it was real—reinforced by economic development, political interest, historic tradition, and relationships with other parts of the world. The spread of machine industry across national boundaries and the creation of railroad linkages between industrial cities suggest achievement of a new economic solidarity. For a time that solidarity gave rise to optimistic talk of free trade and shared prosperity, the nineteenth-century equivalent of twentieth-century common market ideas. Industrialization also brought a sense of common purpose to the social classes that emerged within nations where population was shifting to industrial cities. To the growing numbers of workers in manufacturing, trade unionism and socialism promised redress of obvious wrongs in all countries; at the same time, politics fell increasingly under the influence of men who controlled economic development. Class interest, at least in the short run, imposed limitations on the exercise of national power and united in common cause the statesmen working to prevent class struggle.

European self-consciousness arose not only from continental development, but also from relationships with the world outside Europe. As industrialization tended to increase world trade, Europeans became ever more aware of their civilization, their Christianity, and their white skins. Confident of their moral and intellectual superiority—and the power to impose their will—they frequently employed standards of conduct with respect to "backward" peoples that they would not have dared to use at home. Turkey, a Moslem country, was never really treated as an equal until after World War I. When the Boxers sought to drive foreign devils out of China, the European states having interests there joined with the United

The work of French caricaturist and painter, Honoré Daumier (1808–1879), provides a memorable record of nineteenth-century society. His sense of irony, combined with his mastery of lithography, gave his political cartoons a rare quality of permanent merit. Global equilibrium, as he viewed it in this cartoon, depended upon an equal thrust of forces among the European powers.

States and Japan. Their purposes? Among other things, the powers were determined to keep the machinery of their European system well lubricated with resources from other parts of the world. Whatever antagonisms the expansion of Europe entailed, it certainly had the effect of reinforcing a sense of superiority, a generalized European self-consciousness.

Although the balance-of-power system functioning within that framework of self-consciousness did much to preserve peace in Europe, several fundamental changes made the balance increasingly difficult to maintain in the years after 1850. The most important changes found expression in statistics of population and economic growth. For centuries France had been the most populous country in Europe; in 1850 it still outranked all others except Russia. In the next sixty years, however, French population increased only 8.9 per cent; with less than 40 million people at the time of World War I, France had a smaller population than any other great power. The slow French growth rate seemed even slower when compared with Germany's 44.4 per cent increase between 1870 and 1910. With a population of more than 65 million in 1914, a united Germany stood second only to Russia among European nations. Such figures can be misleading (with its more balanced age grouping, France could muster nearly as many troops during World War I as Germany was able to put into the field), but population growth nonetheless took on great meaning in association with statistics of industrial production.

By reason of its uneven development the industrial revolution, which at first stimulated a sense of European unity, came to have an unbalancing effect. The great powers differed in their industrial growth potential; a glance at figures for coal, pig-iron, and steel production is enough to reveal significant disparities. Great Britain, the early leader in industrialization, maintained impressive growth rates in the three sectors: coal production increased from 57 million tons in 1850 to 292 million tons in 1914; pig-iron went from 2.2 million tons to 11 million; and steel production increased from 0.7 million tons in 1870 to 6.5 million tons in 1914. Even more impressive, however, was Germany's economic development. By 1914 she was producing 277 million tons of coal, 14.7 million tons of pig-iron, and 14 million tons of steel. In basic industries she had far outdistanced France and Russia combined. On the eve of World War I, then, perceiving the extent to which industrialization had shifted the balance-of-power fulcrum required no special wizardry.

The statesmen of Europe were not blockheads. Indeed, they had begun to display their concern back in the 1870s when they developed arguments and justifications for imperialistic expansion. The "new imperialism" of the late nineteenth century was not merely an economic phenomenon. National pride, missionary zeal, love of adventure, the lure of the unknown, and Darwinian ideas emphasizing competition for survival all contributed to imperialistic enthusiasm. But the desire for markets and for sources of raw materials reached a new intensity as great powers began to compete with one another for colonies overseas. Jules Ferry, founder of the second French Empire, laid great stress on both markets and investments: "I say that France, which is glutted with capital and which has exported considerable quantities, has an interest in looking at this side of the colonial question. . . . It is the same question as that of outlets for our manufactures." French, German, Italian, and other colonizers looked toward the establishment of self-contained empires surrounded by tariff walls. Supporters of free trade began to encounter unexpected opposition as nations of Europe joined in the scramble for colonies.

Englishmen, some of whom had earlier regarded the Empire as a burden, waxed enthusiastic about the need to maintain British colonial superiority. Lord Rosebery spoke to the point in 1888 when he observed: "We formerly did not have in our foreign affairs to trouble ourselves much with colonial questions, because we had a monopoly of colonies. That monopoly has ceased." The thought was almost too much for Joseph Chamberlain, most prominent of British imperialists, who believed that colonies were essential to trade and that trade was essential to civilization. "History teaches us that no nation has ever achieved real greatness without the aid of commerce," he remarked shortly before the author of the McKinley Tariff won election to the United States presidency, "and the greatness of no nation has survived the decay of its trade."

To what extent European powers benefited from the colonies they acquired has never been clearly established. Gains were certainly low compared with expectations, as trade with developed countries consistently brought greater profits than trade with colonies. But imperialistic rivalry did have the effect of increasing other rivalries among the great powers. The logic of international competition led to heightened concern for military capabilities. Ivan Bloch, a Polish financier who feared the possibility of unlimited war, estimated that total defense expenditures of the principal European powers increased by more than 50 per cent in the years between 1874 and 1896. Those of Germany rose by 79 per cent, and after 1890 her supremacy on the Continent was unquestioned. Only Russia tried to keep up, yet the government of Nicholas II enjoyed little success in the attempt. Britain, abandoning the effort to sustain her power on the Continent, concentrated on maintaining her control of the sea. That task alone was demanding enough, for new developments in naval technology—the transition from sail to steam, the construction of low-profile ironclads, and no-profile submarines—led other nations to expand their navies and diminish British supremacy.

Growth in military and naval expenditures, like colonial and industrial rivalries, made for a certain inflexibility in the relations of great powers. Having adopted programs of industrial, territorial, or military expansion, nations found no satisfactory alternative to escalation. Otto von Bismarck, whose leadership had been a major influence in the shaping of his times, wanted it both ways. He sought to establish German superiority on the continent without sacrificing advantages of the balance-of-power system. German superiority, achieved in the Franco-Prussian War of 1870–1871, depended for its maintenance on a foreign policy that would keep France from forming combinations with other powers. In 1882, therefore, Germany joined with Austria and Italy in the Triple Alliance. Terms of the agreement provided, among other things, that Germany and Austria would aid Italy in case of a French attack upon Italy, and that Italy would aid Germany should the French attack Germany. Fearful that Russia might be drawn into alliance with France, Bismarck negotiated a Reinsurance Treaty with Russia in 1887; it pledged the partners to neutrality if either were attacked by a third power.

Bismarck's alliance system worked well for a time, well enough to minimize the rigidity it imposed on international relations. German defensive arrangements isolated France without posing the offensive danger that might have provoked a counteralliance. But in 1890 Kaiser Wilhelm II, dismissing the Iron Chancellor, proceeded to follow a foreign policy that calcified the most critical working parts of the European system. Thus cast aside and isolated, Russians naturally looked westward toward France. An exchange of notes, in which the two powers agreed on mutual consultation in the event of an international crisis, established a basis for the Franco-Russian Alliance of 1894. Britain, in the meantime, was growing uneasy over German diplomacy and German naval expansion. Traditionally the British had never seen eye to eye with the French, but discretion now demanded a settlement of their long-standing differences. Anglo-French collaboration began with a rapprochement in 1904, culminating in the Triple

Entente. That agreement—signed in 1907 by representatives of Britain, France, and Russia—assured cooperation of the three powers in meeting the threat of the Triple Alliance. By 1907, then, Europe had become polarized into two armed camps—and the risk of war had been immeasurably increased.

**Global Politics and American Expansionism**

As the European balance of power became increasingly rigid, it became increasingly unstable, for weaker nations could not combine effectively to redress the imbalance that came with industrialization, German unification, and other developments. The United States, having few formal commitments to other countries, then began to assume a larger place in the thinking of world leaders. They could not have ignored her in any case, for rapid growth of American industry and population made the nation's power an essential factor in all major international equations. However much many Americans may have wanted to isolate themselves from world affairs, their involvement became difficult—indeed impossible—to avoid. Not everyone, of course, wanted to remain aloof; during the decade of the nineties a majority of citizens accepted the idea that American well-being and freedom of action depended on more than mere geographic position. Several considerations, many of them shaped by the rivalries of great powers and given direction by ideas that Americans shared with European contemporaries, seemed to justify a more aggressive foreign policy.

The new imperialism, in part because of the deterrent effect of American power and the United States's adherence to the Monroe Doctrine, did not penetrate the Western Hemisphere to the degree that it permeated Africa and Asia. Yet European nations did undertake various activities there. Great Britain carried on extensive trade with Latin America throughout most of the nineteenth century. After 1870 the newly formed German empire also developed commercial and investment outlets in the Americas. In 1879 a French company announced plans to build a canal across the Isthmus of Panama. Although the government of France claimed no direct interest in the project, leadership and capital were French, and the company would certainly rely on protection from France in time of need.

Such moves, along with others that would provide European navies with coaling stations in the Pacific, lent substance to the arguments of those concerned with meeting threats to American power. Especially prominent among the advocates of greater security was Alfred Thayer Mahan, a career officer in the Navy, who served for a time as lecturer and president of the Naval War College at Newport, Rhode Island. In preparing his lectures on naval history, Mahan developed the theme that sea power was essential to national greatness. The thesis was neither original nor, in view of the lecturer's profession, surprising. But it was cogently stated; and, beginning with publication of *The Influence of Sea Power on History,* Mahan's ideas received wide dissemination through books and articles that appeared regularly over the next twenty years.

For Mahan, sea power required more than gunboats and battle fleets.

Using England as a model for maritime greatness, he pointed out that the British system had been built upon a flourishing foreign commerce, a powerful navy to protect merchant shipping, overseas bases suitably located for refueling and repair, and a global empire to supply raw materials and markets. Although Mahan did not envision an empire of comparable size for the United States, he did believe that the national interest demanded American control of certain strategic positions. Of those positions, none seemed to him more important than that of the interoceanic canal. "Militarily speaking," he wrote in 1890, ". . . the piercing of the Isthmus [by French engineers] is nothing but a disaster to the United States, in the present state of her military and naval preparations." What the situation called for, thought Mahan, was American control of the canal and of Caribbean and Pacific bases that would safeguard approaches to that important waterway. In his mind, Cuba, the Isthmus, and the Hawaiian Islands were all linked together in a single system that was vital to American security. Beyond the establishment of American control over such a system, Mahan looked toward limited acquisition of colonies and bases that would make possible unlimited expansion of American commerce into all parts of the world.

Mahan was not alone in his concern for national security. In addition to the president, two members of Benjamin Harrison's administration (Secretary of State James G. Blaine and Secretary of the Navy Benjamin Tracy) pressed for expansion of the shipbuilding program begun in 1883 when Congress authorized construction of the Navy's first steel warships. Secretary Tracy, contemplating the dangers of an unguarded coast, conjured the possibility of an attack on New York. In an 1890 report, the Navy's Policy Board requested funds for new warships, arguing that "in the adjustment of our trade with a neighbor we are certain to reach out and obstruct the interests of foreign nations." Congressmen were not so easily persuaded that conflict was imminent, but they did approve construction of three first-class battleships.

The naval expansion program evidenced at least partial acceptance of the contention that American security was being threatened by European powers. In the spring of 1895, E. L. Godkin published an article in the *North American Review* attacking the idea, but he despaired of winning many debates with people who knew little about foreign affairs. Ignorance linked with patriotism, he thought, provided overwhelming support for jingo politicians and naval expansionists. Godkin's analysis, perceptive though it was, failed to take into account the full sweep of popular thought about the proper role of the United States in world affairs. The fact is that national security was only one consideration called into play to justify a more aggressive foreign policy. Americans soon moved beyond security arguments that were defensive in tone to more positive expansionist ideas. The notion that the United States needed more naval strength to avoid becoming a pawn in European power struggles involved policy decisions that ran counter to the nation's historic avoidance of such conflicts; ex-

The popular appeal of naval expansion is apparent in this photograph of a woman in her kitchen at the turn of the century. Hanging over the sink is a composite print of U.S. naval vessels in 1898, daily reminder of the power that justified increased American influence in world affairs. "There is no such thing as isolation in the world today," wrote Albert Beveridge. "They say that Cuba is not contiguous . . . that the Philippines are not contiguous. They are contiguous. Our navy will make them contiguous" (State Historical Society of Wisconsin).

pansionism, on the other hand, seemed consistent with the American past.

Ever since the planting of colonies on a raw Atlantic coastline in the seventeenth century, Americans had been moving westward to occupy virgin land and to establish their control over a continental domain. Now it was clear that the frontier period of American history was drawing to a close. In 1893 the Wisconsin historian, Frederick Jackson Turner, read his seminal paper on "The Significance of the Frontier in American History" at a meeting of the American Historical Association in Chicago. The burden of his essay was that "the existence of an area of free land, its continuous recession, and the advance of American settlement westward, explain American development." But in his conclusion Turner prophesied that even though free land had disappeared, "the American energy will continually demand a wider field for its exercise."

Five years after Turner read his paper, a young Indiana lawyer, campaigning for a seat in the United States Senate, delivered an oration giving eloquent expression to expansionist sentiments that survived the passing of the frontier. Recounting the great moments of manifest destiny—the purchase of Louisiana Territory, the conquest of Florida, the Texas Revolution, and the Mexican War—Albert J. Beveridge stirred his audience with a patriotic refrain: "And the march of the flag went on!" The settlement of a continent did not, in Beveridge's view, justify resting on laurels already won.

There are so many real things to be done—canals to be dug, railways to be laid, forests to be felled, cities to be builded, unviolated fields to be tilled, priceless markets to be won, ships to be launched, peoples to be saved, civilization to be proclaimed and the flag of liberty flung to the eager air of every sea.

The American people must press on. "We cannot fly from our world duties; it is ours to execute the purposes of a fate that has driven us to be greater than our small intentions." To men such as Beveridge, the new involvement of the United States in world affairs represented fulfillment of a historic mission.

Americans had always been impressed with the idea that they had a unique purpose to serve, but never had the concept been more enthusiastically received. On every hand people talked of the global mission of America. A distillation of such discussion appeared in Josiah Strong's little book, *Our Country: Its Possible Future and Its Present Crisis,* published in 1885. A Congregational minister and Secretary of the American Home Mission Society, Strong rode the currents of popular thought; his volume became one of the late nineteenth century's best sellers. The evangelical thrust of Christianity, he argued, had been entrusted to Anglo-Saxon peoples because their sensitive understanding of human liberty made them, of all races and nationalities, best qualified to carry on the work. "There can be no reasonable doubt," Strong confidently asserted, "that North America is to be the great home of the Anglo-Saxon, the principal seat of his power, the center of his life and influence." From the United States the Anglo-Saxon would "exercise the commanding influence in the world's future." The fittest of races (unlike some of his clerical brethren, Strong incorporated Darwinism into his vision of coming events) would stretch forth its hand "into the future with power to mold the destinies of unborn millions."

The ideas of *Our Country* found reinforcement in an outpouring of popular books and articles. John Fiske, John W. Burgess, and other writers emphasized relationships between Darwinism, Anglo-Saxonism, and expansionism. Ethan Allen, grandson and namesake of the Revolutionary War hero, spoke for millions of Americans when he argued that the United States had outgrown the Monroe Doctrine: "Our broad shoulders need a more ample garment; and this is to take in and incorporate territory that we need." But important as paeans to national greatness and missionary injunctions were in stimulating enthusiasm for global activities, the expansionists who delivered them almost invariably appealed to economic interests as well. "Among the most striking features of the Anglo-Saxon," Josiah Strong observed, "is his money-making power—a power of increasing importance in the widening commerce of the world's future." And in the depression years of the nineties no expansionist argument seemed more attractive than the promise of economic redemption through world trade.

Since the founding of the republic, large numbers of Americans had regarded overseas commercial expansion as a source of capital accumulation and a stimulus to economic development. In its beginnings, as Professor William Appleman Williams and others have shown, this commercialism emphasized markets for agricultural surpluses. But with the economic instability that accompanied the growth of industry—and with the nationalistic fervor that swelled to a crescendo in the nineties—foreign trade and economic expansion took on the character of a broad national enterprise. Economic trends, ideas, and programs interacted during the late nineteenth century. Post-Civil War business fluctuations prompted economic theorists, both professional and amateur, to develop explanations of recurrent crises. For most of the period between 1873 and 1896, as already noted in some

The circus meant many things to Americans of the late nineteenth century; it was, as an advertising poster put it with characteristic flamboyance, "a Brilliant, Gorgeous, Imposing and Magnificent Living Panorama, Resplendent with Glitter and Gold. . . ." The mystic appeal of the circus—with its lions, camels, elephants, and costumed performers—fed the imagination of a society reaching out to markets beyond the seas. Hamlin Garland wrote that as "a compendium of biologic research," the circus brought to mind the "mystery of the East" and "vague visions of vast deserts" and jungles (State Historical Society of Wisconsin).

detail, monetary theories held a dominant position in the arguments of economic analysts. In those same years, however, an alternate explanatory model attracted increasing attention. That model posited unlimited industrial and agricultural productivity on the one hand and a limited home market on the other. Given such conditions, demand would stagnate while stocks and inventories built up—unless farmers and businessmen found new outlets outside the home market.

Here, then, was a theory that provided not only an explanation of the business cycle but a program for action as well. It was a theory that bypassed the controversy over free coinage of silver; bimetallists and monometallists could support trade expansion with equal enthusiasm. Accepting commercial expansion as a recovery program, businessmen soon rid themselves of the notion that competition in world markets was feasible only during periods of depression. By the middle nineties they were contending that American technological and cost-production advantages over European rivals would permit retention of such markets in time of prosperity. Trade would then serve to reduce extreme fluctuations in the business cycle and perhaps even eliminate depressions altogether.

No one found overproduction and market expansion ideas more convincing than did William McKinley. In 1895 he delivered the keynote address to the fledgling National Association of Manufacturers at its organizational meeting. "We want our own markets for our manufactures and agricultural products," he told his enthusiastic audience; "we want a foreign market for our surplus products. . . . We want a reciprocity which will give us foreign markets for our surplus products, and in turn that will open our markets to foreigners for those products which they produce and which we do not." Two years later, after his victory over William Jennings Bryan, McKinley played variations on the same theme when he addressed the Philadelphia Commercial Museum: "No worthier cause [than] the expansion of trade . . . can engage our energies at this hour." By the time disturbances in Cuba led the United States to declare war against Spain, men with the influence to shape policy had reached agreement on the need for world markets to relieve industrial and agricultural glut at home. The search for markets coincided with the nation's quest for security and with activities of citizens determined to carry out the civilizing mission of America. Such were the influences that led the United States to play a more aggressive role in world politics during the 1890s.

## A Splendid Little War and Its Consequences

Not all Americans wished to see their nation become more deeply involved in world affairs. In the Pacific and in Latin America, the two areas that particularly attracted the attention of citizens and officials eager to play a more important role in world politics, expansionists had to contend with the resistence of antiexpansionists. But alignments were puzzling; international questions bore no obvious relationship to positions on domestic questions. Grover Cleveland, though capable of forceful diplomatic moves, was less sympathetic to the idea of an American empire than was William

McKinley. Andrew Carnegie stoutly opposed the acquisition of colonies, even attempting to form an antiimperialist coalition with the help of William Jennings Bryan. The ideological cement of political alignments, in other words, cracked under the stress of international pressures. Farmers, to whom the Populists had looked for support, were as interested in overseas markets as were manufacturers. Industrial workers, eager for a return to prosperity, could also muster enthusiasm for commercial expansion, although they were less attracted to the prospects of colonial acquisitions. Union leaders feared annexations that might lead to infiltration of a contract labor system and have a debilitating effect on their organizations.

Events of the nineties repeatedly demonstrated the ambivalence in American thinking about expansion. At the opening of the decade the nation found itself participating in an agreement that established a German-British-American protectorate over the Samoan Islands. It did not work well, and in 1899 it was replaced by a new accord that divided the archipelago between Germany and the United States. Although Germany gained control of the two largest islands, the island of Tutuila and its harbor (Pago Pago) went to the United States. Disciples of Mahan rejoiced, but men such as South Dakota senator Richard F. Pettigrew were not impressed. Speaking for the antiimperialists, the senator expressed his resentment of the move: "We blot out, then, a sovereign nation, a people with whom we have treaty obligations, and divide the spoils."

After working out the awkward three-power protectorate over Samoa in 1889, the Harrison administration had turned its attention to an even greater prize in the Pacific: the Hawaiian Islands. A treaty ratified in 1887 had already given the American navy an exclusive right to use Pearl Harbor, but in 1893 a revolution in the islands—a revolution encouraged by the American minister in Honolulu—brought to power a group that favored annexation of Hawaii by the United States. The McKinley Tariff had authorized a bounty of 2 cents a pound for American-grown sugar, and Hawaiian planters hoped to cash in on that largess. They were temporarily thwarted by the election results of 1892. Shortly after assuming office in March the following year, President Cleveland withdrew the annexation treaty from consideration by the Senate. Hawaii remained independent until Republicans regained control of the White House; then, in 1898, McKinley secured annexation by a joint resolution of Congress.

Although expansionists found Cleveland's Pacific policy disappointing, his stand in Latin America was much more to their liking. When a boundary dispute between Venezuela and British Guiana threatened peace in the Western Hemisphere, Cleveland urged arbitration. Britain rejected the proposal. Secretary of State Richard Olney expressed his vexation in a belligerent note: "Today the United States is practically sovereign on this continent, and its fiat is law upon the subjects to which it confines its interposition." In the end, British and Venezuelan negotiators reached a satisfactory settlement, but Englishmen had been startled by American truculence. As for American jingoes and expansionists, they could not have

This 1900 cartoon reflected the satisfaction that many citizens felt in contemplating American expansion. "By gum," remarked Uncle Sam as he pinned flags to the globe, "I rather like your looks." Not everyone agreed. "A self-governing state cannot accept sovereignty over an unwilling people," cautioned the Anti-Imperialist League platform in 1899. "The United States cannot act upon the ancient heresy that might makes right" (*Rocky Mountain News*, 1900).

been more pleased; Cleveland seemed to have forced the greatest of world powers to accede to American demands.

Americans flaunted their growing power, and events taking place in Cuba would soon provide an opportunity to use it. United States tariff policy was, if anything, even more important to the Spanish colony than it was to Hawaii. When the McKinley Tariff placed raw sugar on the free list and when a reciprocity treaty with Spain lowered other duties, trade with the island increased to some $100 million annually. But after the Wilson-Gorman Tariff of 1894 placed a 40 per cent duty on Cuban sugar, the island entered a severe depression. Dissatisfied and restless Cubans, convinced that they would fare much better under home rule, revolted against Spain early in 1895. The rebellion stirred the sympathetic interest of Americans who shared Cuban disdain for the inefficient and sometimes harsh Spanish government. Despite atrocity stories published in American newspapers, however, President Cleveland refused to become involved.

Then, after McKinley assumed office, two occurrences greatly increased the likelihood of intervention. In February 1898 the New York *Journal* published a letter from Enrique Dupuy de Lome, Spanish minister to the United States, to a friend in Cuba. The letter had been stolen, but what most impressed those who read it was its content. De Lome had described McKinley as "a bidder for the admiration of the crowd" and "a common politician who tries to leave a door open behind himself." The minister's gratuitous remarks were bad enough, but six days after their publication one of the new American battleships, the *Maine,* blew up and sank in Havana harbor. The destruction of the ship, which had been sent to Cuba to protect American property there, immediately became a cause célèbre. Although there was no evidence to suggest that Spain had anything to do with the disaster, many Americans agreed with Assistant Secretary of the Navy Theodore Roosevelt when he announced that "the *Maine* was sunk by an act of dirty treachery on the part of the Spaniards."

McKinley, reluctant to use force, carried on abortive negotiations with the feckless Spanish government, which was struggling to retain some semblance of control over the remnants of its once impressive New World empire. Finally, the president turned to Congress for advice. Spain had made important concessions, but McKinley's message was greeted as a call to arms. On April 19 Congress passed a joint resolution declaring Cuba independent and authorizing use of the Army and Navy to free the island from Spanish rule. The United States having thrown down the gauntlet, Spain reluctantly accepted the challenge.

After hostilities were over, Secretary of State John Hay rendered a judgment of the Spanish-American conflict. It had been, he said, "a splendid little war." In one respect the assessment was accurate: the war was little in the sense that it lasted only three months and American casualties were minimal. Yet to anyone familiar with the sophisticated military maneuvers of the twentieth century, the conflict seems more ludicrous than splendid. Bad management and poor logistics hampered operations; troops did not reach Cuba in force until June 22, less than a month before an armistice was signed. Disease wiped out more men than did Spanish guns. While Americans waged war inefficiently, however, the Spanish waged it ineptly. Without resources and industrially outclassed, Spain was incapable of effective military action. Therein lay an explanation for the United States's success. Admiral Dewey's crushing triumph over the Spanish fleet at Manila Bay in the Philippines, and—in the Cuban theater—the victory at San Juan Hill, the destruction of Spanish ships off Santiago, and the surrender of Santiago itself inspired celebrations throughout the land. It was not, however, such a splendid achievement to defeat so weak an enemy.

On February 15, 1898, an explosion of undetermined cause sank the *Maine* in Havana harbor with a loss of over 250 lives. By April 1, after an American Court of Inquiry reported that a submarine mine had blown up the vessel, the demand for war with Spain had become shrill. The New York *World* offered its advice to President McKinley: "DESTRUCTION OF THE MAINE BY FOUL PLAY should be the occasion of ordering our fleet to Havana and *demanding proper amends within forty-eight hours under threat of bombardment*" (The National Archives).

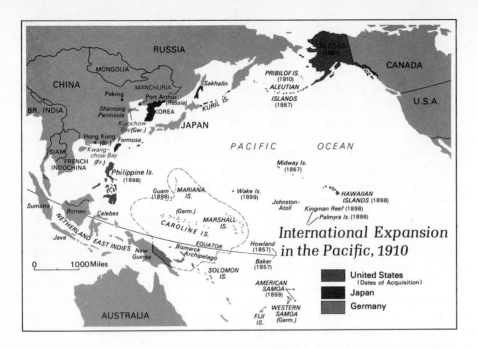

International Expansion in the Pacific, 1910

Small wars nevertheless may have important consequences. The results of the Spanish-American War made it a major event in the development of American foreign policy. The peace treaty, drawn up at Paris in the fall of 1898, provided for the independence of Cuba, of course, but it went beyond that. Puerto Rico, Guam, and the Philippines were ceded to the United States; in return for the Philippines Spain received a compensation of $20 million. Antiimperialists, horrified at the thought of the United States's acquiring overseas possessions, were divided in counsel and ineffective in opposition. The Senate ratified the treaty in 1899, evidently persuaded that the colonies would safeguard American interests in the Western Hemisphere and open up new commercial opportunities in Asia. When William Jennings Bryan, running for the second time as the Democratic party's candidate for president, tried to make imperialism a campaign issue in 1900, he found that he could arouse little enthusiasm for granting the Filipinos their independence. Voters refused to express themselves on foreign policy, an indication that they had no strenuous objections to the direction it had taken under McKinley. "The Philippines are ours forever. . . . And just beyond the Philippines are China's illimitable markets," Albert J. Beveridge thundered in his maiden speech as a senator. The president was less flamboyant but no less candid: "It is no longer a question of expansion with us; we have expanded. If there is any question at all it is a question of contraction; and who is going to contract?"

The acquisition of colonies as a result of intervention in the struggle for Cuban independence raised some important questions about the relationship between those colonies and the United States. Did Puerto Ricans and Filipinos have the rights of American citizens? Did American tariffs apply to goods imported from Puerto Rico and the Philippines? What powers could the president and Congress legitimately exercise in colonial affairs? Did the Constitution follow the flag? In the so-called "Insular Cases" of the years 1901–1905, the Supreme Court established principles for answering such queries. Its decision in *Downes v. Bidwell* drew a distinction between "incorporated" and "unincorporated" territories. Puerto Rico was unincorporated; it was neither a foreign country nor an integral part of the United States. That ambiguous position, the Court held, did not permit exemption from payment of American tariffs. Unincorporated territories were subject to other, more indefinite restrictions. While the Constitution limited Congress in its treatment of all territories, the "procedural rights" of people living in unincorporated territories were not protected. Such rulings obviously allowed for ad hoc and sometimes makeshift policy decisions. Hawaii and Alaska were the only territories granted incorporated status and would become the only territories outside the continental limits of the United States eventually to achieve statehood.

For all the expansionism of the nineties, Americans after the turn of the

The Treaty of Paris, which ended the Spanish-American War, ceded the Philippines to the United States. Signing the treaty was easy; securing the cooperation of seven million Filipinos, who sought independence from colonial controls, proved far more difficult. In suppressing the Philippine independence movement—the action in which these troops were engaged—the United States Army lost more men than it had lost during the Spanish-American War (Oregon Historical Society).

century seemed remarkably diffident about either extending their colonial empire or creating institutions to govern the one they had acquired. After the outburst of 1898, the zeal for colonial acquisitions declined markedly. From ratification of the Treaty of Paris to American entry into World War I, the United States gained control of only two new areas, the Canal Zone and the Danish West Indies. The Canal Zone, obtained in 1903, was necessary for construction of an isthmian canal; the Danish West Indies were taken over in 1916 to keep them from falling into German hands. What caused the sputtering of colonial enthusiasm was a growing conviction—by no means peculiar to the United States—that the game was not worth the candle. A Philippine insurrection lasting from 1899 to 1902 brought headaches to colonial administrators. Troops sent to the islands to put it down eventually succeeded in doing so, but they found there none of the glory that had exhilirated Theodore Roosevelt at San Juan. What they discovered instead was that American soldiers were capable of atrocities no less brutal than those of the Spanish in Cuba. Small wonder, then, that many Americans—including bankers and businessmen—began to ask if colonial dependencies were really necessary for trade expansion and overseas investment.

Such questioning helps to account for the failure to create a central colonial office charged with comprehensive supervision of colonial possessions. Administration of overseas territories remained a patchwork of divided authority. The Navy Department assumed responsibility for the smaller islands such as Guam and Tutuila. Hawaii, with its preferred status as an incorporated territory, came under the Department of Interior. The War Department had direct supervision of the Canal Zone; but with the Philippines and, after 1909 with Puerto Rico, it dealt through its Bureau of Insular Affairs. Although the bureau might have developed into a colonial office, it never gained the influence to generate a movement toward more comprehensive authority. After 1902, with pacification of the Philippines, Congress displayed marked lack of interest in colonial problems.

Nor did Congress show much greater enthusiasm for building up the military and naval strength that might have made for more efficient colonial management. When Elihu Root became Secretary of War under Roosevelt, he instituted a number of reforms in the Army: an increase in the authorized strength of ground forces, a new emphasis on special-service schools, creation of an Army War College, changes in the militia system, and establishment of a general staff corps. But the reforms did not go as far as they should have if the Army was to operate effectively within an imperial structure. As for the Navy, its Spanish-American War record seemed to obviate the need for reform. Nevertheless, until Congress passed legislation creating an Office of the Chief of Naval Operations in 1915 and 1916, the Navy wobbled along with a loose, disjointed command structure. Furthermore, the fleet was never large enough to control sea lanes stretch-

Opposition to annexation of the Philippines was strong, even in 1898, when the New York *World* printed a cartoon depicting the archipelago as a white elephant. By 1902, when Filipino resistance to American control came to an end, anticolonial sentiment had grown. Impatience with colonies elicited a rhymed response to the paternalism that Rudyard Kipling had urged on civilized nations:

> We've taken up the white man's burden
>   Of ebony and brown;
> Now will you kindly tell us, Rudyard,
>   How we may put it down?

(The New York *Herald,* June 3, 1898)

ing from the Caribbean to the Philippines. Even if it had been, there were not enough anchorages in outlying possessions to care for such a fleet.

What, then, might be said about the imperialistic thrust of the nineties? The Spanish-American War had provided glory, colonies, confidence in an American ability to shape world affairs. And the greatest of these was confidence. The war seemed glorious and splendid, a victory for righteousness and humanity; in it Americans found confirmation of the civilizing mission of the United States. Colonial commitments, to be sure, demanded more money and effort than disappointing returns appeared to justify. Yet the advocates of expansion never threw up their hands in dismay. They formulated a new policy instead, one that would secure the rewards of empire and the benefits of vigorous international activity without the problems and frustrations of additional colonial possessions. It was a policy of confidence, for only a nation with effective power in international relations could have hoped to bring it off successfully. The men responsible for this new, noncolonial expansion of American influence in world affairs no more doubted its ultimate success than they did its salutary interim results.

**The Open Door**      Disenchantment with colonialism left two congeries of ideas as twin props of the new foreign policy worked out after 1898. The first centered on the theory that limited home markets demanded overseas commerce if the nation was to avoid a recurrence of depressions such as those of the seventies and nineties. The second clustered around the belief that, in a world of competing power blocs, the United States would run great risks in neglecting to provide for the nation's security. The first set of ideas received expression in the Open Door formula, first applied in China and then extended to other parts of the world. The second appeared most vividly in relations between the United States and other countries of the Western Hemisphere. The ideas that served as basing points for American policy were simple ones, but the realities with which that policy had to contend were exceedingly complex. Policy never precisely met need; its failure to do so would eventually—though not immediately—engender disillusionment, a hankering for the good old days of nineteenth-century isolationism, and a search for scapegoats. The United States came of age slowly in the twentieth century, the pains of adolescence revealing themselves in the process.

The Open Door policy was a response to conditions prevailing within China at the close of the Spanish-American War and to events that took place there in the two years following American acquisition of the Philippines. At the time the United States gained its Philippine foothold in the Far East, the great powers were busy establishing spheres of influence for themselves in a China weakened by internal divisions and by defeat at the hands of the Japanese in the Sino-Japanese War of 1894–1895. Japan had extended her control over Formosa and the nearby Pescadores after that conflict, and other nations were attracted by the fabled markets of China itself. In 1897–1898 Russia, taking over Port Arthur, obtained special rights in the Liaotung Peninsula; France staked out a sphere on Kwangchow Bay, conveniently located near her Indochinese colony; Germany secured a leasehold on the Shantung Peninsula; and Britain leased territory on the mainland opposite the crown colony of Hong Kong.

American expansionists who had rhapsodized about opportunities for trade in the Far East were understandably perturbed by the commercial partitioning of China. In September 1898 President McKinley issued instructions to the peace commission charged with drafting a treaty to end the Spanish-American War. Pointing out that American negotiators could not be indifferent to commercial opportunities in Asia, he added that "we seek no advantages in the Orient which are not common to all. Asking only the open door for ourselves, we are ready to accord the open door to others." Precisely what McKinley meant when he referred to an open door did not become clear until after Secretary of State John Hay had sent two sets of notes to the great powers. The first set, drafted in September 1899, requested that each recipient (1) avoid interfering with the commercial rights of other nations within its sphere of influence in China, (2) permit Chinese officials their right to collect existing tariffs without fear or favor, and (3) eschew railroad rate and port dues discriminations against the nationals of any country operating within Chinese leaseholds. Receiving what could at best be termed an indifferent response, Hay bluffed. In March 1900 he announced that, since none of the powers had raised strenuous objection to his note, he considered their approval "final and definitive."

So far so good. But Hay had reckoned only with the great powers, and a society of Chinese nationalists known as the Boxers had other ideas about Chinese affairs. Launching a drive to rid their land of all foreigners, they killed three hundred of them, occupied the capital city of Peking, cut telegraph lines, and laid siege to the British compound where members of foreign legations had taken refuge. An international force of 18,000 men, including 2,500 Americans, managed to rescue the beleaguered diplomats, but the disturbance increased the possibility that China would be carved up by powers determined to secure broader and more binding commitments than they already had. To avert that possibility Hay issued the second set of "open door" notes. In July 1900 he instructed American envoys in foreign capitals that the United States would adhere to a course of peace with China, that the Boxers would be held accountable for injuries to American citizens, and that in the future the United States would seek to "preserve Chinese territorial and administrative entity, protect all rights guaranteed to friendly powers by treaty and international law, and safeguard for the world the principle of equal and impartial trade with all parts of the Chinese Empire." The Open Door, in other words, meant equal commercial opportunity for all nations in a China whose territorial integrity the United States pledged itself to maintain.

The United States might abandon the quest for colonies, but policy makers were reluctant to withdraw from all foreign involvement. These American troops were part of an international rescue force dispatched to liberate the diplomats who took refuge in the British compound, Peking, during the Boxer uprising of 1900 (The National Archives).

To make a formal announcement of American intentions was easy; implementing American policy in its entirety proved impossible. Russia posed the principal initial threat to the Open Door. Having secured from China the right to build two railroads in Manchuria, the Russians took full advantage of the Boxer uprising to extend their influence there. Both Britain and Japan refused to countenance the Russian moves. The United States also had objections, for American investors claimed an interest in Manchuria that was no less important than that of the Russians. Indeed, they urged that the Open Door principle be applied to investments as well as to trade. No policy could have been more unrealistic, and Secretary Hay knew it. The United States would not even enforce a more limited interpretation of the Open Door. In the spring of 1903 President Roosevelt received a letter from Hay in which the secretary candidly observed that "Russia knows as we do that we will not fight for Manchuria, for the simple reason that we cannot." American interests in the region were not vital ones, no matter what investors thought of them, and neither Hay nor Roosevelt was inclined to wage war, no matter how high-minded the justification might be made to appear.

Japanese interests in Manchuria, however, were vital to the Japanese. In 1902 they concluded an alliance with Britain and proceeded to demand Russian withdrawal from the region. While negotiations were under way, the Japanese (on February 8, 1904) launched a surprise attack on the Russian squadron at Port Arthur. The Russo-Japanese War dragged on for eighteen months; Japan won the major victories but found the war an exhausting enterprise. With both sides ready for peace, Roosevelt saw an opportunity to preserve the Open Door by bringing the conflict to an end. Serving as mediator, he secured agreement to a peace treaty concluded at Portsmouth, New Hampshire, in September 1905. The Japanese obtained the southern half of Sakhalin, a sphere of influence in Manchuria, and dominant rights in Korea. TR, for his efforts, won the Nobel Peace Prize, but more important to him was the hope that Japan would support the Open Door policy that Russia had challenged.

It was a vain hope. Japan now became the principal power in Manchuria; and, while the Japanese never questioned the American right to equal commercial privileges, they did demand special investment rights in regions under their control. In the meantime a crisis over the segregation policies of California schools (policies directed against Japanese children) threatened American relations with the one Far Eastern nation with claims to great power status. A 1907 gentlemen's agreement—California rescinded its segregation law and Tokyo promised to deny passports to Japanese laborers bound for the United States—resolved the crisis but did not eliminate Japanese resentments. An anti-Japanese clique in the State Department did much to keep those resentments alive by its continuing pressure for use of American financial resources to force the Japanese out of China altogether. Fearing that Japan would be driven to assume political and administrative authority in Manchuria and knowing full well

These women, residents of a small midwestern town, enjoyed a Japanese tea party at the turn of the century. American involvement in the Far East unquestionably aroused popular interest in Oriental cultures. California's hostility to immigrants from Asia, reflected in the state's segregationist policies, was by no means a national phenomenon. In areas where Orientals were so few in number as to pose no economic threat, the interest in Asia might be appreciative rather than hostile (State Historical Society of Wisconsin).

that the United States would not go to war to preserve the Open Door there, Secretary of State Elihu Root attempted to ease tensions by signing the Root-Takahira Agreement of November 1908. The agreement pledged both countries to maintain the territorial integrity of China and the territorial status quo in the Pacific.

In 1910, after TR had moved out of the White House, he wrote President Taft a letter of admonition about the limits on American freedom of choice in the Far East. Roosevelt warned:

The "open-door" policy in China was an excellent thing, and will I hope be a good thing in the future, so far as it can be maintained by general diplomatic agreement; but as has been proved by the whole history of Manchuria, alike under Russia and under Japan, the "open-door" policy, as a matter of fact, completely disappears as soon as a powerful nation determines to disregard it, and is willing to run the risk of war rather than forego its intention.

Neither Taft nor his Secretary of State, Philander C. Knox, were of a mind to heed the voice of experience in 1910. They attempted, instead, to use American investment as a lever to force Japan out of Manchuria. And they failed.

Either the Open Door meant a readiness to fight or it meant very little. Few Americans were willing to face that unpleasant fact, and fewer still acted on lessons they might have learned from Far Eastern experiences of the years 1898 to 1914. Rather than confronting the limitations of policy, as Roosevelt urged Taft to do, most American leaders proclaimed its success. Minimizing the degree to which Chinese territorial integrity depended not on the open door but on power relationships, they exaggerated the economic benefits of trade with countries outside Europe. Thus they perpetuated a belief in the moral superiority of the American position in world affairs. They reinforced the conviction that righteousness in international relations was consistent, indeed synonymous, with expansion of foreign investment and commerce.

## Security, Economics, and Moralism in the Western Hemisphere

American interests in the Western Hemisphere, particularly in the Caribbean area, were more obvious than American interests in Asia. Relations with countries close to home had greater bearing on the security concerns of the United States than did relations with Japan or China. For that reason the McKinley, Roosevelt, Taft, and Wilson administrations found forceful intervention in Latin America acceptable policy while at the same time they displayed reluctance to deploy military contingents for the sake of an Open Door in China. This is not to suggest that economic interests had no influence in the shaping of Latin American policy, but that security interests strengthened the determination to support hemispheric programs with force if need be.

Security was a dominant note of the Platt Amendment to the Army Appropriations Act of 1901. Although the Teller Resolution (passed along with the resolution for war against Spain in 1898) had renounced annexation of Cuba as an American objective, troops remained there long after the peace treaty had been signed. They did not leave until after the Platt Amendment, establishing a special Cuban-American relationship, had been written into the Cuban constitution. The United States in effect assumed control over the island's external relations, for Cuba agreed not to impair her independence through negotiations with another foreign power. In addition, the United States received the right to establish naval bases, the right to protect "life, property, and individual liberty," and the right to assure political stability. The Platt Amendment remained in force for more than thirty years; it provided justification for setting up a provisional government with the support of American Marines in 1906, the use of Marines to crush a black rebellion in 1911, and a third intervention to put down uprisings brought on by a disputed election in 1917.

Cuban and American perspectives differed, of course, and such interventions were viewed differently in Cuba and the United States. On the

and of well-nigh incalculable possibilities for the good of this country and the nations of mankind. By the provisions of the treaty the United States guarantees and will maintain the independence of the republic of Panama. etc., etc.,

*Theodore Roosevelt*

White House Dec. 7th 1903

COLOMBIA

EXTRA INDELIBLE INK

Convinced that he was acting in the national interest, Theodore Roosevelt intervened in Panama to assure completion of the interoceanic canal. As one might infer from this cartoon, however, the president's forcefulness produced a flawed treaty, regardless of how cogently he defended his policies (Chicago *Daily News*, December 14, 1903).

one hand, many Cubans resented Yankee domination. The United States became the principal market for Cuban sugar, but economic benefits were never equally distributed. The idea that political interference and economic exploitation were inseparable was an idea that became generally accepted in Cuban thought. On the other hand, Mahan's argument for protecting approaches to the isthmian canal was one that political leaders in the United States found compelling. They hoped for commerce and amicable relations with Cubans; but, with or without trade and Cuban good will, they would pursue policies they thought vital to American security.

The interoceanic canal was indeed a central concern of United States policy makers. During the war against Spain, when the battleship *Oregon* had required ninety-eight days to make the journey from Juan de Fuca Strait around Cape Horn to Cuba, the security-conscious advocates of military and naval preparedness were provided with a dramatic demonstration of the canal's importance. After he became president, Roosevelt bent every effort—as well as several moral principles—to assure American control of the canal zone and American completion of the project. Having determined that the most feasible route was the one across Panama, TR opened negotiations with the French New Panama Canal Company to buy its franchise. To prevent the United States from building along another route across Nicaragua, the company lowered its asking price from $109 million to $40 million. But there were complications. Panama was a part of Colombia, the French lease would run out in 1904, and, if Colombia could withhold its consent to the transaction until that date, it stood a good chance of securing the full price for itself. The Colombian government therefore rejected the proposed treaty of purchase.

Roosevelt, eager to win election to the presidency in his own right in 1904, was certainly one to recognize a popular cause when he saw it. He refused to deal further with Colombia. And he let it be known, without saying so explicitly, that the United States would look with favor on a Panamanian independence movement. It was all the encouragement that Philippe Bunau-Varilla and other agents of the French company needed. Through a series of devious and complicated maneuvers, they engineered the desired revolution. When it occurred on November 3, 1903, an American cruiser prevented Colombian troops from reinforcing their garrison in Panama; three days later the United States extended recognition to the new republic of Panama. The way having been cleared for a treaty, it was promptly drawn up. The United States received perpetual rights to the Canal Zone in exchange for $10 million and a $250,000 annuity. An additional expenditure of $40 million paid for the New Panama Canal Company's assets. Builders resumed work on the waterway in 1904, completing their labors during the summer of 1914. If Roosevelt had any

Undertaken in the interest of national security, construction of the Panama Canal became a government project, not a private one. In 1904, Colonel George W. Goethals assumed supervisory responsibility over the work, which was completed ten years later. Hailed as one of the engineering wonders of the century, the canal brought commercial as well as security benefits (Panama Canal Company).

qualms about his part in the acquisition of the Canal Zone, he managed to suppress them. Justifying what had occurred in 1903, he wrote that he had carried out every action "in accordance with the highest, finest and nicest standards of public and governmental ethics."

To do him justice (a labor not to be lightly undertaken), Roosevelt perceived far more realistically than did most of his contemporaries the vital interests of the United States. Equally skilled in the arts of diplomacy and moralistic rhetoric, he frequently announced diplomatic moves with a fanfare of ethical exculpation. TR's moralism was convincing to others because he found it convincing himself. American security was, to him, a moral obligation; and, though his rhetoric abounded in priggish self-justification, it should not be allowed to obscure the fact that he had a firm grasp of what security demanded.

Nowhere was the combination of realism and moralism more evident than in TR's formulation of his famous Corollary to the Monroe Doctrine. The Roosevelt Corollary came in response to an incident that occurred in Venezuela in 1902–1903 and the threat of a similar disturbance a year later in the Dominican Republic. General Cipriano Castro's Venezuelan dictatorship (1899–1908) was notoriously lax in meeting its financial obligations. Nor was the credit rating of the revolution-torn Dominican Republic any better. When warships of Britain, Germany, and Italy blockaded Venezuelan ports and bombarded Venezuelan forts in an effort to compel payment of debts and claims, Roosevelt urged arbitration. What haunted TR, whose disdain for Castro's government led him to characterize the dictator as an "unspeakably villainous little monkey," was the threat to American security inherent in any European show of force. The Hague Tribunal eventually settled the dispute, but settlement did not guarantee that it would never recur. In fact, it was the possibility of another display of European power in 1904, directed this time against the Dominican Republic, that provoked Roosevelt into issuing a statement of policy. "Chronic wrongdoing, or an impotence which results in general loosening of the ties of civilized society, may in America, as elsewhere, ultimately require intervention by some civilized nation," he warned in his annual message to Congress in December. And he added pointedly that "in the Western Hemisphere the adherence of the United States to the Monroe Doctrine may force the United States, however reluctantly, in flagrant cases of such wrongdoing or impotence, to the exercise of an international police power."

In this case, TR concluded an executive agreement with the Dominican Republic, its terms setting up a customs receivership to collect tariffs and distribute revenues to both the Dominican government and its creditors. But what really mattered was that policy squared with an interest in security that the United States was willing to defend. Because American intervention reduced the chances of European intervention, TR's diplomacy in the Western Hemisphere did not consist of empty threats. To make satellites out of the smaller Caribbean nations was, from the United States's point of view, to assure the stability on which American security in some measure rested. Profits to be made from investment and commerce in Latin America provided an added fillip.

Roosevelt's successors were never so clearly identified with the maintenance of American security. President Taft became known for his "dollar diplomacy," while President Wilson surrounded himself with an aura of idealism. Yet in the Western Hemisphere the policies of both Taft and Wilson reveal a fundamental concern with security. Taft's dollar diplomacy was, to be sure, an effort to encourage American investment overseas; more specifically, however, it was directed toward encouraging investments that would increase the political stability of Latin America. Like the Open Door principle in that it envisioned overseas economic activities but not the acquisition of colonies, dollar diplomacy exerted a more powerful influence in Latin America than the Open Door ever did in China. What lay behind that larger influence was the conviction that in a world of great power rivalries the nation's security depended on United States domination of the Western Hemisphere.

Woodrow Wilson rejected dollar diplomacy on grounds of principle; in a typical utterance he expressed the hope that he might replace it with "a system more in harmony with our nation's traditions and ideals." If Wilson's moralism stirred in him a philosophical opposition to Taft's program for Latin America, however, it did not take him back to the position of that other moralist, TR. Roosevelt used ethical terminology to justify actions that, in his view, served the national interest. Wilson moved in the opposite direction. For him, principle came before policy; international application of his moral convictions, he believed, would automatically be in the national interest.

Although Wilson continued to profess that belief until the end of his days, his conduct of foreign affairs did not always seem consistent with it. He was not blind to international realities, and his way of dealing with them sometimes appeared to involve a denial of his professed beliefs. Thus there was irony in the fact that Wilson, an ardent antiimperialist, would intervene in the affairs of other Western Hemisphere countries to a greater degree than either Roosevelt or Taft. By ignoring the influence of World War I on the United States's foreign relations, critics of his administration could find abundant evidence of hypocrisy in American occupation of Haiti after 1915, extension of American control over the Dominican Republic in 1916, and American military intervention in Cuba in 1917. And there was something peculiarly gratifying in pointing out the inconsistency of thought and action; the discovery of hypocrisy in a moralist offers the great satisfaction of knowing that he, too, is tainted with original sin. What is remarkable about Wilson, however, is that while he and Secretary of State William Jennings Bryan carried "missionary diplomacy" as far as it could be taken, he remained fully aware of a mundane but powerful American interest in the security and stability of the Western Hemisphere.

Much that was confusing in the Wilson administration's Latin American policy becomes comprehensible once one recognizes that Wilson was not just a moralist even though his natural inclination was to move from principle to policy. His dealings with Mexico reveal moral concerns, to be sure; they also reveal concerns that were more directly related to hemispheric stability. During the first decade of the twentieth century, Mexican-American relations had been exceptionally cordial. The government of Porfirio Diaz had encouraged American investment in mining, smelting, and oil; by 1908 United States citizens controlled nearly half of Mexico's wealth and more than three-fourths of its railroad transportation. But Diaz had ignored the needs of middle classes, peasants, and workers. A social upheaval brought about his overthrow in May 1911. When Francisco Madero won election to the presidency, Taft promptly recognized the new government. The election, unfortunately, did not end Mexico's troubles. Early in 1913 a counterrevolution led by General Victoriano Huerta deposed the liberal Madero and four days later murdered him. This was where matters stood when Wilson assumed office.

Shocked by Madero's assassination and disturbed by the destruction of American property interests in Mexico, Wilson deliberated. Before long he had found a way to blend his own moral concern with the nation's economic and security interests. Having achieved that, he was ready to enunciate policy. Labeling the Huertista regime "a government of butchers," he told British diplomat Sir William Tyrrell that "the United States Government intends not merely to force Huerta from power, but also to exert every influence it can to secure Mexico a better government under which all contracts and business concessions will be safer than they have ever been."

Convinced that extending recognition to Huerta would encourage assassination in other Latin American countries, Wilson had further reasons for opposing the general. In the first place, Huerta had by no means established his authority in the country as a whole even though he did control Mexico City. Calling themselves Constitutionalists, his opponents organized under the leadership of Venustiano Carranza, the Maderista Governor of Coahuila. Second, with effective political power over all of Mexico in the balance, both Britain and Germany hoped to gain commercial and other privileges by supporting Huerta. Wilson was furious. In a famous speech at Mobile on October 27, 1913, he excoriated foreign concessionaires and hailed the day when Latin America would be free of them. The president had already encouraged the sale of arms and munitions to followers of Carranza, but now he sought direct intervention to insure constitutional government. He therefore seized upon an incident at Tampico, in which several American sailors had been arrested, to request congressional approval of his contemplated action. Before Congress could consider his proposal, the State Department received word that a German ship, loaded with ammunition for the Huerta government, was approaching Vera Cruz. At daybreak on April 21, 1914, the president ordered the Navy to occupy the port city. By the following day the order had been

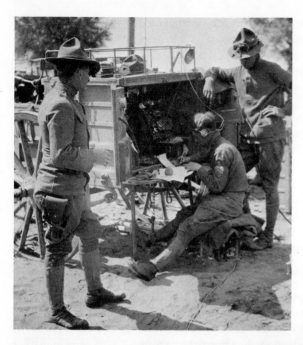

Military operations have always changed with the development of technology, and among the twentieth century's most important technical innovations was the radio. In 1916, when General Pershing's expeditionary force moved into Mexico to capture Francisco Villa, it used the wireless (photographed here at Casas Grandes) to maintain communications. That the American cavalry failed in its mission, despite the wireless, is evidence of Villa's popular support among the Mexican people (Underwood & Underwood).

Mexican revolutionists Francisco Villa (center) and Emiliano Zapata (at Villa's left) were photographed with some of their followers in the Presidential Palace, Mexico City, in 1914. Although his influence deteriorated during the troubled course of events in Mexico, Villa nevertheless remained a charismatic figure with enormous popular appeal (Culver Pictures).

carried out, but Wilson was disappointed if he expected gratitude from Carranza. Invasion of Vera Cruz, warned the First Chief of the Constitutionalists, was a violation of Mexican sovereignty.

Carranza's attitude indicated that the revolution Wilson had encouraged by his opposition to Huerta was now moving beyond his control. Nevertheless, for all the turmoil and confusion, at least one of Wilson's objectives was achieved. On July 15, 1914, Huerta abdicated and fled to Spain. Wilson recognized the triumphant Carranza regime as the de facto government of Mexico, hoping that this would be the end of friction between two neighbors. It was not. Further difficulty arose when Francisco Villa, the most spectacular of Constitutionalist generals, turned on his First Chief in an effort to gain power himself. Hoping to discredit Carranza by provoking a war with the United States, Villa began a campaign of raiding and killing that culminated in an attack on Columbus, New Mexico, in March 1916. Villistas burned the town and killed nineteen Americans. Wilson thereupon ordered General John J. Pershing to lead a punitive expedition into Mexico to capture Villa. To Carranza's dismay and Pershing's chagrin, American cavalrymen rode some three hundred miles south of the border without achieving their objective. But they did incur Mexican resentment that more than matched American resentment of Villa.

Fortunately, neither Carranza nor Wilson wanted the war that would have been popular in both countries. Slowly, but nonetheless certainly, the United States had become more and more deeply involved in the great conflict raging in Europe. American interest clearly demanded reestablishment of friendly relations with Mexico. Wilson therefore ordered the withdrawal of Pershing's forces. Finally, after the adoption of a new Mexican constitution and the election of Carranza as president under its provisions, Wilson took the further step of extending de jure recognition. On March 13, 1917, he sent Henry P. Fletcher as ambassador to Mexico. The action came none too soon. On April 2 the President called Congress into special session to ask for a declaration of war on Germany.

# 5

# War and Peace:
# The Quest for Order
# in a Troubled World

Geographically and militarily the Great War of 1914–1918 was never actually a world war. What precipitated the conflict was neither a grand plan for global hegemony nor a movement toward world liberation from European imperialism. Once war came, furthermore, it was remarkably static. Most of the fighting took place on the European continent—especially along a line across northeastern France from Belgium to Switzerland—and it involved few sweeping military maneuvers and conquests. Yet contemporaries were justified in calling it the Great War, for it brought death to nearly ten million people and marked the beginning of a new era of economic reorganization, political revolution, and international tension. A struggle between two power blocs with worldwide interests, it turned out to be so debilitating that at the close of hostilities European nations found themselves unable to dominate world affairs as they had dominated them in the nineteenth century.

The four-year struggle that produced such momentous consequences burgeoned out of a Balkan rivalry that in retrospect seems as trivial as it was banal. Austria-Hungary, one of the weakest (and because of that weakness one of the most irresponsible) of the great powers, sought to expand its influence over the Balkan states in general and over Serbia in particular. But the dual monarchy of the Habsburgs encountered opposition from Serbs, Croats, Slovenes, and Bosnians eager to unite and form a single south Slavic state. Russia, hoping to gain access to the Mediterranean through the Sea of Marmara and the Dardanelles, also had an interest in the Balkans. So did the Ottoman Empire. In 1908 the Young Turk Revolution, a nationalist movement opposed to surrendering Turkish territory in the Balkans, succeeded in gaining control of the Ottoman government. The rivalry that resulted from these disparate interests brought on three Balkan crises in the years 1908–1914, the third crisis leading directly to the Great War.

In the summer of 1914, Archduke Francis Ferdinand, heir apparent to the Austro-Hungarian throne, left Vienna with his wife for a royal visit to the province of Bosnia. They never returned. Touring the city of Sarajevo on Sunday, June 28, they met death at the hands of a Serbian nationalist. To Habsburg officials back home, the assassination justified severe retaliatory measures, and Germany's Kaiser Wilhelm II agreed to support the dual monarchy in whatever action it chose to take. Assured of German backing, Austria-Hungary sent off an ultimatum so harsh that no reply short of total surrender could have prevented a declaration of war on Serbia. Unlike earlier crises in the Balkans, this one could not be contained. Russia, relying on its alliance with France, sent troops to the Austrian border and prepared to aid Serbia. Germany, threatened by Russian mobilization, declared war on Russia and—after the French government issued general mobilization orders—on France as well. Kaiser Wilhelm's troops attacked France through Belgium and Luxembourg, and the violation of their neutrality brought England into the conflict on the side of France. By August 4, then, Europe had become embroiled in a general war, with the Central Powers (Germany, Austria-Hungary, and Turkey) fighting the Allies (England, France, and Russia). Japan and Italy joined the Allies in 1914 and 1915, and Bulgaria cast its lot with the Central Powers in 1915.

The United States struggled to remain neutral, and for a time it seemed that efforts to avoid involvement might succeed. As the war gradually widened to include issues that concerned far more than conflicting ambitions in the Balkans, however, American interests seemed increasingly threatened. Finally, on April 2, 1917, President Wilson asked Congress for a declaration of war against Germany and her allies. This chapter considers, first, American reactions to the coming of war and efforts to bring hostilities to an end by peaceful means; second, the developments that led to American entry into the conflict and the meaning of war for American society; third, Wilson's diplomacy and his efforts to secure a lasting peace; and, finally, United States rejection of the League of Nations.

**The Peace Movement**

Few people in the United States understood the full implications of events that led to the outbreak of hostilities in Europe. Like their European contemporaries, most Americans expected a short war. And while their cousins across the Atlantic marched off with misguided confidence in their capacity to force a settlement within a matter of months, Americans rested in the complacent confidence that they would not become involved. As the war quickly settled down to dreary stalemate, however, men and women on both sides of the Atlantic experienced shock and revulsion. How profoundly disturbing it was to contemplate the great power struggle cannot be fully appreciated unless one recognizes that on the very eve of Francis Ferdinand's assassination wise and good folk the world over were predicting an end to the horrors of war.

Those who looked forward to a new era in international relations had good reason to hope that the world might outgrow war. Never had the sense of international community been more pervasive or supported by sturdier props. Industrial technology and business practice had compelled nations to recognize the impossibility of maintaining themselves as isolated economic units. A communication revolution marked by the increased use of interoceanic cables and the expanded publication of books, magazines, and newspapers allowed people to become well informed about developments in other countries. The great universities of the world took on an international character with the exchange of students and professors. Various organizations sought to exercise international influence. In 1881 Catholic Christians began meeting in a series of eucharistic congresses. In 1889 Socialists organized the Second International to strengthen the common ties among laboring classes of all nationalities. Rotary was an international organization; the Boy Scout movement spread across national frontiers. Nations, it seemed, were beginning to understand the importance of cooperation; that understanding led to establishment of the Universal Telegraph Union, the Universal Postal Union, and conventions on patent and copyright laws.

To further the cause of world peace and international community, several groups had begun to organize in the mid-nineteenth century; by 1914, according to one estimate, 160 significant international peace organizations had formed. Seventeen of them had their headquarters in the United States, and they found Americans of the progressive years unusually hospitable to their cause. Progressives placed great emphasis on social harmony; and, among people who worked against a fragmentation of American society, the preservation of cordial international relations seemed a logical extension of national solidarity. Furthermore, as Professor Merle Curti has pointed out, no reform of the progressive period demanded less sacrifice on the part of middle-class Americans than did the cause of peace. Businessmen in particular stood to gain rather than lose from peaceful international relations (unless, of course, they specialized in one of the armaments industries). So it was, then, that Edward Ginn, a publisher of textbooks and an idealist with philanthropic impulses, became the first to endow the cause of world peace. He gave a million dollars, one-third of his wealth, to the World Peace Foundation. Andrew Carnegie, not to be outdone, in 1910 established the Carnegie Endowment for International Peace.

The endowed foundations joined other associations already at work. Venerable organizations such as the American Peace Society, taking advantage of a new interest, broadened their programs and increased their membership. Churches and religious groups urged active participation in the peace movement. The Federation of the Churches of Christ in America created a department of peace, and the Church Peace Union included Protestants, Catholics, and Jews on its board of trustees. Lawyers of peaceful persuasion found themselves attracted to the American Society for the Judicial Settlement of International Disputes, which looked toward crea-

Andrew Carnegie greeted French diplomat and
parliamentarian Paul Balluat, Baron d'Estournelles de
Constant, at a New York peace conference in 1907.
Men and women of various nations, political persua-
sions, and economic interest groups made common
cause in the peace movement before 1914. Seated on
the dais behind the baron was psychologist Hugo
Münsterberg, who had received his training in Germany
and had taught at the University of Freiburg before
going to Harvard; to Carnegie's left sat labor leader
Samuel Gompers (Underwood & Underwood).

tion of an international tribunal with judicial functions. The American
School Peace League sought to direct the feet of children into the paths of
peace. More than a hundred colleges and universities affiliated with the
Intercollegiate Peace Association (formed at the Mennonite Goshen College) to sponsor oratorical and essay contests in the interests of peace.

Peace organizations received encouragement from public officials, who
voiced approval of their efforts and fashioned policies to promote their
movement. The United States participated in two international conferences that met at the Hague in 1899 and 1907. Neither achieved a hoped-
for reduction of national armaments, but they did establish a Permanent
Court of Arbitration and an International Prize Court of Appeals. The
Roosevelt, Taft, and Wilson administrations all considered arbitration a
promising alternative to war, though Roosevelt was less enthusiastic about
submitting to arbitrated decisions than were either Taft or Wilson. In
1910 Taft announced that he thought the time had come when even questions of national honor might safely be submitted to agencies such as the
Hague Court, and by midsummer of 1911 his Secretary of State had signed
general arbitrations treaties with both France and England. The Senate
insisted on ruinous amendments, however; and the troubled Taft, his days
in the White House numbered, gave up attempts to renegotiate the agreements. Although the peace societies were disappointed, their hopes revived when the Wilson administration succeeded where Taft had failed.

Secretary of State William Jennings Bryan procured thirty bilateral conciliation treaties (twenty-one of them were ratified and proclaimed) binding the nations to a "cooling off" period before resort to arms. In celebration of his achievements, Bryan distributed paperweights representing
ploughshares beaten out of swords.

He was not the only one to rejoice. Events of the years between 1898
and 1914, many of them pointing up the common interests of people in all
countries, led the opponents of war to believe that permanent peace was
not only possible but probable. In 1912 Frederick Lynch of the Church
Peace Union ventured a prediction that the twentieth century would be
"an age of treaties rather than an age of wars." Others in the peace movement took a similar view. "The age is ready for peace," announced *The
Peace Forum.* "The world is weary of war." And taking up the argument
cogently presented by Sir Norman Angell in *The Great Illusion,* a persuasive and popular book first published in England in 1909, the *Forum*
went on to add that "statesmen realize how ruinous it would be for them to
fight."

Unfortunately, the lovers of peace did not understand that their optimism could contribute to the likelihood of war by raising standards of
acceptable performance for statesmen without providing adequate means for
meeting those standards. In his study of the 1914 crisis, Professor Robert
C. North has shown that perceptions of inferior capability and premoni-
tions of disaster do not deter nations from going to war. A national leader
under severe stress may find any action, even a ruinous war, preferable to
the intolerable burden of continued tension. The peace movement may
have led people on both sides of the Atlantic to expect too much of their
leaders; to have anticipated a peaceful resolution of the Balkan conflict
was not unrealistic, but knowing that many people would condemn using
force, statesmen may have been more sensitive to the *pressures* of possible
condemnation than they were to the *reasons* for it. It is a perverse logic
that would blame the pacifists for World War I, but insofar as their high
expectations made the tensions of 1914 unbearable, they helped to make
war possible.

**From Peace to
Preparedness**

That most Americans were confident of their ability to avoid involvement
did not preclude their having strong opinions about the European conflict. To the advocates of peace, it represented a return to barbarism, and
many of them worked feverishly to find a means of ending the carnage.
Others, convinced that the privileged economic interests of Europe were
out to enlarge markets and profits, thought of the war as a culmination of
class and economic rivalries. Some people were partisan to the Central
Powers either because of ethnic ties with Germany or because they had
come to think of British imperialism as the most vicious form of economic
exploitation. A much larger number, including most members of the
Wilson administration and even the president himself, leaned toward the

Allied cause, for they believed that American interests were more directly bound to the interests of England than to those of any other country.

Those who had been active in the peace movement before the declarations of war did not suddenly call a halt to their labors after 1914. Indeed, some of them became more active than ever before. A particularly noteworthy effort to bring the war to an end came with the formation of a Women's Peace Party in January 1915. Inspired by such notable American women as Jane Addams, Carrie Chapman Catt, and Charlotte Perkins Gilman, the party did not limit itself to activities in the United States. It sent forty-five delegates to an International Congress of Women at the Hague in the spring of 1915. When the congress formed the Women's International Committee for Permanent Peace, Miss Addams, becoming its chairman, worked to gain acceptance of a peace plan that had originated with Julia Grace Wales, an instructor in English at the University of Wisconsin. The plan called for the neutral nations to meet and offer continuous mediation, inviting suggestions from belligerents and revising proposals until an agreement for peace had been reached.

President Wilson listened to the proposals of the Women's Peace Party and its supporters, but he did not act on them. One reason for his reluctance to move in the direction of mediation was that the Allied position

When German U-boat 20 torpedoed the *Lusitania,* with the loss of 128 American lives, the sentiment for war against such barbarism began to build up in the United States. The Women's Peace Party, however, did not succumb to hysteria. These women demonstrated with a banner pleading for rationality and neutrality during the European conflict.

was not particularly strong in 1915, and Wilson was more sympathetic to the Allies than he ever really cared to admit. Furthermore, the peace societies and their members did not all follow the lead of the Women's Peace Party. Almost from the outbreak of war, the Carnegie Endowment took the position that German militarism must be crushed before lasting peace could be secured; the endowment withdrew support from organizations that favored mediation. Sharing that view, many of the prewar peace workers joined in the so-called preparedness movement on the assumption that American strength might be needed to achieve the conditions necessary for peace.

Activities of ethnic associations such as the German-American Alliance provided justification for the preparedness movement. Founded at Philadelphia in 1901 as a federation of German-American organizations, the alliance claimed a national membership of some two million by 1914. During the first dozen years of its existence, the alliance had vigorously promoted German culture, emphasizing the teaching of German in public schools, studying the distinctive German contributions to American history, and organizing *Turnvereine,* athletic clubs that carried on social functions along with physical culture programs. With the coming of war the German-American Alliance launched a campaign to raise funds for relief work in Germany. It sold pictures of Kaiser Wilhelm II and Emperor Francis Joseph, and it encouraged German-Americans to turn over jewelry and other valuables as a mark of their sympathy for the fatherland.

To Americans of other backgrounds, such activities seemed to skirt the fringes of acceptable behavior. Men and women already beginning to question the benefits of German culture were easily persuaded that partisan sentiments of the German-American Alliance provided justification enough for preparedness. Gradually anti-German sentiment began to build; and, as it strengthened, it received additional impetus from the reaction to assaults of German submarines on Allied shipping. After the sinking of the *Lusitania* in May 1915, fifteen young Harvard graduates meeting in New York sent a telegram to the president. They demanded adequate military measures, "however serious." Wilson demurred, for he was determined to avoid involvement. There was such a thing, he said, as being "too proud to fight." That position, in the minds of men such as Theodore Roosevelt and his friend General Leonard Wood, the Army's senior general, smacked of weak-kneed cowardice. Wood organized a military training camp at Plattsburg, New York, as a school for businessmen and other civilians who wished to become familiar with the arts of war. The Plattsburg encampment receiving wide publicity, similar camps sprouted up across the country. Participants in the Plattsburg movement lost no opportunity to plump for preparedness.

The president, under pressure of events abroad and at home, began to shift his ground. By November 1915 he was ready to announce a new military program calling for an expenditure of $500 million in ship construction and an increase in the size of the Regular Army. Aware of the opposition to such moves, Wilson went out on a speaking tour to win support. "All the world was on fire," he told a Milwaukee audience, "and our house was not fireproof." Building up military strength somehow seemed a sensible way to avoid conflagration. After a bitter struggle in which the opponents of preparedness fought a desperate but losing battle, Congress passed a measure incorporating much of what the president wanted. More than doubling the size of the Regular Army, the National Defense Act of May 1916 also authorized a gradual increase in the strength of the National Guard to 17,000 officers and 440,000 men. The Naval Appropriations Act of the following August was a victory for big Navy enthusiasts; Congress approved $313 million for the construction of four battleships, four battle cruisers, and several small craft including destroyers and submarines.

**Neutrality, U-Boats, Diplomacy, and Involvement**

The position in which the United States found itself as the richest and most powerful neutral nation helps to explain the shifting American attitudes toward the conflict in Europe. Initially the war had an adverse effect on the American economy. Foreign purchases of unnecessary items ceased, the British navy closed off German ports, and Allied shipping abandoned customary routes. Within a few weeks, however, orders for munitions and other war materiel began to come in from England and France. By the end of 1915 the nation was enjoying a new-found prosperity.

The prosperity was welcome; but, since it was based in large part on trade with the Allies, it gave rise to questions about the rights and obligations of neutral powers. *The Fatherland,* the most important German language newspaper in the United States, took a dim view of the increase in Allied trade. "We prattle about humanity, while we manufacture poisoned shrapnel and picric acid for profit," charged its editors. Other German sympathizers echoed the criticism, repeating the refrain that selling munitions and supplies to the Allies constituted an unneutral act. American officials replied, insisting that no breach of neutrality had occurred. State Department counselor Robert Lansing argued that "if one belligerent has by good fortune a superiority in the matter of geographical location or of military or naval power, the rules of neutral conduct cannot be varied so as to favor the less fortunate combatant." What really gave rise to trade differentials, in other words, was British control of the sea, and the United States could not be expected to place an embargo on items in demand merely because German ships were denied access to American markets.

Criticism of American trade policies did not lack cogency, however, for the Allies could not have continued their purchases without financial help. Responding to an inquiry from J. P. Morgan and Company, Secretary Bryan insisted in 1914 that the Department of State would not approve loans by bankers to powers at war. Money, Bryan pointed out, was "the worst of all contrabands because it commands everything else." Yet he found the policy impossible to maintain. For one thing, it had no acceptance in international law; neutral bankers had long been more than willing to help finance wars, and no international convention had stipulated against doing so. The State Department therefore saved face by permitting bankers to extend "credits" rather than loans, and by 1917 the Allies had received more than $2 billion. A change in terminology does not change facts, though it may certainly change the way in which people think about facts. And, since credits assured the continuation of prosperity, few Americans raised objections.

Trade with belligerents, irrespective of the way in which it was financed, posed other problems. The London Naval Conference of 1908–1909 had attempted to define the rights of neutral carriers and the categories of goods that might be considered contraband. But the British government never accepted the Declaration of London that issued from the naval conference. Controlling the sea, British men-of-war stopped ships bound for German ports; the Royal Navy searched them and confiscated cargoes. Although the American government objected to such procedures, British Foreign Secretary Sir Edward Grey managed to prevent resentments from getting out of hand. Modern war, he contended, involves entire populations, thus justifying departure from traditional courtesies. If the rifle a soldier carried with him to the trenches was contraband, then so was food that fed workers in a munitions plant.

Given the increase in American trade with the Allies and the British navy's success in imposing its will in matters of stoppage and seizure, the German government felt compelled to employ a recently developed instrument of naval warfare, the submarine. In February 1915 the announcement went out from Berlin: Germany would consider waters around the British Isles a part of the war zone; German submarines would sink at sight any enemy merchant vessel they encountered there. Furthermore, because British vessels sometimes flew neutral flags as a disguise, the U-boats would be under no compulsion to respect neutral ships. The statement of German policy brought immediate objections from the United States. Using submarines against navy ships was one thing, but to direct attacks on merchant vessels was quite another. Germany would be held to "a strict accountability" for any loss of American ships, and steps would be taken "to safeguard American lives and property and to secure to American citizens the full enjoyment of their acknowledged rights on the high seas."

The American reaction had the effect of tempering German policy. Until 1917 no ship of United States registry underwent attack. But did American rights include the right to travel on ships of belligerent nations? The question became more than an academic query on May 7, 1915, when a German submarine torpedoed the British Cunard liner *Lusitania* off the Irish coast. The ship sank in eighteen minutes, and 1,198 persons (including 128 Americans) went down with it.

The *Lusitania* incident aroused the righteous indignation of great numbers of Americans and provided, as already noted, an impetus to the pre-

An advertisement for the *Lusitania* and a warning from the Imperial German embassy appeared side by side in the New York *World* on May 1, 1915. Despite the fact that such warnings had no standing in international law— and despite spelling errors in the embassy's notice—the risks of sailing on the Cunard liner were obvious. More than half the passengers (1198 of the 1959 on board) did not live to regret taking their chances.

paredness movement. But opinions were far from unanimous; even the president's advisers differed in their reactions. Arguing that an American who lost his life while traveling on a British ship was actually guilty of contributory negligence, Secretary Bryan became chief spokesman for the minority view within the Administration. There was, in fact, negligence enough to go around. The *Lusitania's* officers had failed to take the most elementary precautions, even though the ship carried 4,200 cases of car-tridges and 1,250 cases of shrapnel. But what most impressed the American public was the unavoidable negligence of submarine warfare. Depending as it did on avoiding detection, the U-boat necessarily attacked without warning; and, of course, it was far too small a vessel to permit caring for passengers of ships it destroyed. The best the German government could do was to caution against traveling on ships bound for the war zone, but such admonitions did little to redeem Germany's reputation. The *Nation* expressed a commonly held view in observing, "The torpedo that sank the *Lusitania* also sank Germany in the opinion of mankind."

The furor over the *Lusitania* incident put Wilson to the test. Desiring to protect American lives, he could not condone submarine attacks; de-siring to avoid a rupture with Germany, he could not treat the *Lusitania* sinking as a cause for war. The position he finally took was as stern as he could make it without actually declaring war. "Once accept a single abatement of right," he later observed, "and many other humiliations would certainly follow." Bryan, preferring humiliation to war, resigned from his position when the president sent a strongly worded note of protest to Berlin. Robert Lansing, far more willing than Bryan to use force in defending American rights, became Secretary of State as the nation seemed to move closer to war. Other sinkings occurred, and, in April 1916 the president finally went before Congress to read an ultimatum. Unless Germany abandoned submarine warfare against all vessels including armed belligerents, he warned, the United States would sever diplomatic relations.

The ultimatum seemed to succeed. The German government replied on May 4, pledging that U-boats would sink no more merchant ships without warning and without caring for passengers and crew. But the pledge was qualified. The United States, for its part, would have to persuade the Allies to give up their blockade of German ports. Wilson scored a diplomatic victory when he accepted the German pledge but ignored the qualification. In 1916 the German government was not disposed to insist on American pressure to remove the blockade; for the time being, her submarines avoided hostile action against Allied shipping. The *Lusitania* negotiations, heralded as a triumph by Democratic partisans, were nevertheless sadly flawed. Should the time ever come when Germany could find advantages in removal of restrictions on U-boats, the United States would certainly be drawn into war.

Yet the settlement, however temporary, did have an influence on domestic politics. Republican critics attempted to defeat Wilson in the presidential election of 1916 by arguing that he had sacrificed the national honor in his efforts to avoid intervention. In so doing, they miscalculated. Although sentiment for perparedness was growing rapidly, Americans were still hopeful of maintaining their neutrality. "HE KEPT US OUT OF WAR" became, unexpectedly, a popular and persuasive campaign slogan. Wilson himself was uneasy about exploiting the peace issue during the summer of 1916. "Any little German lieutenant can put us into the war at any time by some calculated outrage," he confessed to Josephus Daniels, his Secretary of the Navy. Yet far more than Charles Evans Hughes, the Republican presidential nominee, Wilson was identified in the popular mind with the cause of peace. His advocacy of neutrality, combined with the appeal of progressivism and prosperity, gave Wilson an electoral victory by the narrowest of margins.

Interpreting his reelection as a mandate for peace, Wilson initiated new moves to bring the war to an end. In December 1916, despite the failure of earlier attempts to negotiate a settlement, he sent identical notes to the governments of warring nations asking them to indicate peace terms they would find acceptable. The effort proved fruitless. Wilhelm II and his advisers were themselves talking about peace, but were using peace proposals as a wedge to split the Allies. Britain therefore looked upon Wilson's note as a threat to Allied unity. The Allied response was a list of

**163**
*War and Peace: The Quest for
Order in a Troubled World*

In 1916 a Democratic party campaign truck provided a succinct summary of President Wilson's domestic achievements and a promise of continued neutrality in foreign policy. On November 4, just before voters went to the polls, leading newspapers across the country carried an advertisement that emphasized peace: "The Lesson Is Plain," was its message. "If You Want WAR, vote for HUGHES! If You Want Peace with Honor VOTE FOR WILSON!" (United Press International Photo).

terms so extravagant that they could not have received serious consideration in Berlin even if German armies had been losing ground.

But German armies were hardly on the run. Although they had been turned back at Verdun the previous summer, they could still realistically hope for victory. Or so German strategists believed. In their minds, however, the triumph of German arms in the field required the use of submarines on the seas. Realizing that sending U-boats back into action against ships bound for Allied ports would certainly mean an American declaration of war, the German High Command staked everything on the chance that victory might be won before the United States could mobilize effectively. On January 31, 1917, the German ambassador in Washington informed Secretary of State Lansing that his Fatherland would resume freedom of action on the high seas. Three days later he was handed his passports, while American ambassador James Gerard was called home from Berlin.

Americans waited in a state of dreadful anxiety. For some the horrors of war were too awful to contemplate; for others war promised a welcome and even exhilarating release from the terrible pressures of neutrality. Gradually, during February and March, events reduced the number of alternatives open to the president. Late in February, British Naval Intelligence turned over to the State Department a note intercepted on its way from German Foreign Minister Alfred Zimmerman to the German minister in Mexico. Its contents revealed a scheme to form an alliance with Mexico in the event of war with the United States. When released for publication on March 1, it naturally aroused bellicose instincts, particularly in the southwestern states. Two weeks later Wilson announced that

American merchant ships would be supplied with guns and gun crews. Two American women had already lost their lives when a U-boat sank the British liner *Laconia*. And by March 18, when submarines torpedoed three American merchant ships, it was apparent to all that the alternatives had been reduced to two: humiliating submission or war. Addressing Congress, the president asked for a declaration of war, and on April 6, 1917, both House and Senate complied.

| | |
|---|---|
| **A New Kind of Warfare** | Even though Americans of 1917 were conscious of something unusual about the war on which they had embarked, they were but vaguely aware of all the influences that made it significantly different from previous military involvements. As World War I receded into the past, however, its singular features began to stand out more clearly than they ever did for the men who fought it. Professor Quincy Wright, a member of the Law School faculty at the University of Chicago, was one of the first to explore the phenomenon of international warfare from a post-1918 perspective. Completing his massive *Study of War* in 1942, when the nation was involved in another conflict even more terrible and far-reaching than that of 1914–1918, Wright identified six characteristics that placed the world wars of the twentieth century in a class apart from all other international conflicts. A survey of those characteristics helps make comprehensible the popular response to Wilson's call to arms. |

The most obvious feature of the twentieth century's world wars was the degree to which mechanization and technology shaped both battlefield and home-front conduct. The Great War that began in 1914 was the first major international conflict to arise after all the great powers had begun programs of industrial development. Science and industry provided new weapons and new instruments of warfare. Machine guns, poison gases, and improvements in rifles and artillery greatly increased the long-range striking power that generals could command. Railroads and motor trucks facilitated the movement of troops and supplies. Armor plate provided more efficient protective covering than any ever before used. And when innovations in weaponry, transportation, and protection were combined—as they were in the submarine or the tank—the tactical implications were enormous. Equally significant was the way in which military technology affected the home front. Gone were the days when a soldier provided his own equipment. Now, with the techniques of warfare dependent upon industrial plant and transportation, placing one soldier in the field required the services of perhaps as many as a dozen workers at home.

Mechanization did not mean that the size of armed forces could be reduced, however, and Wright found a second notable characteristic of the two world wars in the fact that armies grew both absolutely and in proportion to population. Improvements in communication and transportation made possible a central control of mobilization, and calling as much as 10 per cent of the population into active military duty became feasible. In earlier wars, a 1 per cent mobilization had resulted in armies that were almost too large for existing transportation systems to supply. But in neither world war was it possible for 99 per cent of a warring power's citizens to engage in normal pursuits while a mere 1 per cent did all the fighting. Any nation that trains one-tenth of its people for battle is a nation that must require direct or indirect war service from its entire working population.

A third change noted by Professor Wright followed naturally from the second. Increasing the number of men called into the army made standards of selection essential. Physical fitness was, of course, a requirement for military duty, yet there were others less frequently noted. The prospective soldier's civilian occupation, for example, had to be one that could be carried on by others, either by men judged incapable of standing up under battlefield pressures or by women, children, and the aged. Men who held civilian positions essential to the war effort had to be exempted from active service. Since older men were those most likely to have essential jobs and since they were generally less physically fit than young men, mobilization placed a premium on youth. But the very process by which service was made selective had the effect of militarizing the entire population. When industrial, agricultural, and professional activities were geared into the war effort, all citizens became subject to a type of military organization.

Carrying his analysis further, Wright identified the extension of government into control over public opinion and the economy as the fourth characteristic of the twentieth century's two great wars. New weapons systems made entire populations vulnerable to attack. To sustain morale, belligerent nations initiated wide-ranging propaganda and civil defense programs. War needs, compelling as they were, required stringent economic controls as well as information and news controls. A free market system, depending on profits, could not be expected to operate effectively when necessity demanded increased production of war goods and reduction in private consumption. The hazards of war affected the economies of all countries. Trade, as Americans learned in the years 1914–1917, became hazardous when men-of-war roamed the sea lanes, and self-sufficiency, once the goal of mercantilists, now became an objective of belligerent nations. The two world wars therefore encouraged autarchic or totalitarian tendencies, while at the same time they impaired free economies and free speech.

Duress of military necessity also helped to account for the fifth characteristic on Wright's list. The increased range and destructiveness of modern weapons reduced the distinction between military and civilian pursuits, for manufacturing, transportation, and population centers became military targets. When civilian industry and morale became essential to a working out of the national will, then national purposes gained priority over more general humanitarian considerations. For belligerents, the entire life of an enemy state became an object of attack through starvation, bombardment, confiscation of property, terrorization—any technique that might reduce the capacity to wage war. And to citizens of nations at war, securing the home front seemed as important as winning battles in more traditional military encounters.

Fighting the world wars, finally, meant increasing the intensity of military action over time and extending simultaneous military operations over space. In earlier conflicts between nations, fighting had concentrated on specific strategic locations; and, in part because of the difficulties presented by winter storms, it had been seasonal. Warfare had characteristically consisted of distinct battles and campaigns separated by long periods of relative quiet. But modern military techniques drastically changed that pattern. Military strategists still stuck pins in maps, but the mechanization of warfare, the organization of entire populations, and the increased number of important targets brought to military operations a new fluidity that left little time or place for respite. The Great War of 1914–1918 was not a war of sporadic fighting. Indeed, the actions of belligerents appear in retrospect to merge into one long, continuous campaign made up of a series of battles so overlapping that none stands out as did Agincourt, Lützen and Blenheim, or—more recently—Austerlitz, Waterloo, and Gettysburg. Warfare had become more intense, more relentless, more all-encompassing than it had ever been.

What Wright's description of the world wars adds up to is that industrial development and technological innovation had destroyed man's ability to wage war as he had in the past. During World War I the generals could

The development of technology brought new means of waging war to battlefields and zones of combat. With submarines, tanks, airplanes, poison gas, and improved artillery, armies and navies greatly increased their capacity for destruction. Yet in part because commanders trained in traditional warfare did not always understand how to take full advantage of military innovations, the Great War was reduced to a sordid confrontation across the "No Man's Land" on the western front (Signal Corps, U.S. Army).

find no flanks to be turned and no way to achieve major breakthroughs. Barbed wire prevented surprise attacks and deft maneuvers. Courage, bravery, *élan* were of small consequence when men charged machine-gun emplacements. Technology brought stalemate, and infantry battalions— mired in mud—faced each other across a devastated no man's land along the western front. Technology had converted entire nations into fortresses. The nation had become a twentieth-century equivalent of the medieval castle, the objective around which a war of attrition was fought. The difference between the nation of 1917 and the castle of the Middle Ages was that now "walls (trenches) were dug, not raised, and moats (barbed wire) were raised, not dug."

As armies are no less subject to bureaucratic inertia than are other institutions, military traditions die hard. For centuries warfare had served, among other ends, purposes similar to those of the Olympic games; it had been a kind of sport. Titles of nobility, medals of honor, iron crosses, and the like were the laurel wreaths of battle. And, ever since the Middle Ages, men had thought of war as romantic adventure. Thus the generals of World War I had little understanding of the changes wrought by technology. Their system of values was one that retained the monocle, the shako, the lance, and the swagger stick as jaunty symbols of a devil-may-care military courage. But those very symbols obscured the sordid, squalid, demeaning business that war had become. No one ever explained how the spit and polish of training camps enabled troops to deal effectively with the lice and vermin of the trenches.

The romantic view of war helps to explain the remarkably ineffective way that armies made use of the new military technology during World War I. Few commanders ever really believed that modern weapons would work; so, unwilling to take risks, they employed them tentatively. Thus the Germans first released poison gas in April and May of 1915, but German troops were not prepared to exploit its devastating effect on Allied lines. When they did make full preparations in December, they found the Allies ready with gas masks and poisons of their own. The British committed tanks to battle in the fall of 1916, and again in great number at Cambrai the following year, but British officers had little idea of how tanks should be employed. Out of an ignorance that derived from inexperience, they vacillated and in the end sacrificed immense tactical advantage. Later, during World War II, tactics caught up with technology as commanders learned to use tanks and airplanes, and mobility returned to the battlefield. Such adaptation was itself a commitment, of course, and changing world conditions could make any commitment obsolete. Americans would eventually have to face the disconcerting fact that lessons of the two World Wars had limited applicability in Cold War conflicts of the years after 1945. Meanwhile, in offering unprecedented challenges to the imagination of both strategists and field commanders, World War I provided supporting evidence for George Bernard Shaw's dictum that some generals win victories only because other generals are stupider.

**Mobilizing the
Nation for War**

The popular reaction to American entry into the Great War was reflected, though not always perfectly, in the songs that document Tin Pan Alley's contribution to the Allied cause. The mood varied from exuberance ("Good Morning, Mr. Zip, Zip, Zip!") to calm confidence ("Liberty Bell, it's time to ring again. . . . Tho' you're old and there's a crack in you, Don't forget Old Glory's backin' you. . . ."). Even ignorance of the national purpose could not destroy the certainty of an American triumph:

> Good-by, Ma!  Good-bye, Pa!
> Good-bye, Mule, with yer old hee-haw!
> I may not know what this war's about,
> But you bet, by gosh, I'll soon find out;
> And, O my sweetheart, don't you fear,
> I'll bring you a king for a souvenir,
> I'll get you a Turk an' a Kaiser too—
> An' that's about all one feller can do!*

Preparations for war had already begun, but molding an effective fighting force and organizing its support was not as easy as song writers made it out to be. Marshal Joseph Joffre, who commanded the French army in 1916, had estimated that half a million American troops would be necessary for an Allied victory. His estimate was low, as time would tell; but, whatever the number, the demand for American manpower in the lines was pressing. By April 1917, in fact, Allied prospects would have seemed very dim indeed had the United States not intervened. German forces having turned back a massive French offensive on the Aisne River, the French people were beginning to talk of surrender. Ten French divisions had actually mutinied. An Allied offensive in the Balkans was faltering, and on the Italian front the Austrians were moving toward their stunning victory at Caporetto in the fall. In Russia, opposition to the Czarist regime had already forced the abdication of Nicholas II; the successful Bolshevik revolution in October would take Russia out of the war within a few months. And the U-boats—the seemingly ubiquitous U-boats—posed a constant threat on the seas as they sank one out of every four ships using British ports.

America's declaration of war had no immediate discernible effect on the battlefields of Europe, though it did boost Allied morale. The Regular Army and the National Guard could muster a combined total of less than 380,000 men at the time, and it was clear both to the president and to his Secretary of War, Newton D. Baker, that efficiency and effectiveness required a draft law. Despite considerable congressional opposition to conscription, the need was obvious enough to bring about passage of the Selective Service Act on May 18. The legislation required registration of

---

* "Long Boy." Copyright 1917 by William Herschell and Barclay Walker. Copyright assigned 1917 to Shapiro, Bernstein & Co., Inc. Copyright renewed. Used by permission.

The United States financed the war in part through government bonds, and parades
in support of Liberty Loans brought the war effort to Main Street. The four wartime
bond drives, along with the Victory Loan campaign of 1918, stirred patriotic
enthusiasm and encouraged civilian participation in the struggle to defeat the Hun
(State Historical Society of Wisconsin).

all men between the ages of twenty-one and thirty—the age limits were
later extended to eighteen and forty-five—and local draft boards assumed
the responsibility of granting exemptions to men who had dependents,
essential positions, physical disabilities or religious convictions inconsistent
with military service. Nearly 700,000 persons answered the first call in
June, and by the end of the war 2,810,000 men had been drafted into the
Army. By that time, too, enlistments had raised the total number of men
and women in the Army, Navy and Marines to 4,800,000.

Mobilizing and training men for military duty posed enormous organizational problems, but they were no more exacting than the task of mobilizing the entire national economy to support Allied forces in Europe.
About half the war costs, which came to nearly $33 billion in the months
from April 1917 to June 1920, was financed by means of "Liberty Loans."
Instead of selling bonds through bankers as it did during the Civil War,
the government marketed them directly to small investors in four nationwide Liberty Loan drives and a final Victory Loan campaign. Selling
bonds became a community enterprise in cities and towns across the land.
The technique encouraged use of coercive and intimidating sales practices;
but, perhaps because of them, the bond drives proved a great money-
raising success. All five loans were oversubscribed as 21 million people invested in government bonds.

Additional funds came from taxation, and here, too, extraordinary needs justified new practices. Congress enacted a series of special excise taxes on luxury items, but most of the wartime revenue came from income taxes. The number of individuals paying income taxes doubled between 1917 and 1920. What was even more impressive, however, was the amount of revenue raised through a 6 per cent tax on corporate income and additional excess profits taxes. Firms that earned a profit of more than 15 per cent paid an excess profits tax of 20 per cent, while those earning more than 33 per cent paid 60 per cent. Wartime exigencies provided sufficient arguments to overcome an opposition that in peacetime might well have defeated such a tax program.

The major responsibility for coordinating economic activities and organizing the nation's resources belonged to the Council of National Defense, a planning board composed of six cabinet members and seven civilian advisers. Agencies operating under general direction from the Council exerted more influence on both personal and public affairs than even the most ardent nationalist could have imagined in the years before 1917. The War Industries Board, charged with supervision of production, interpreted its powers broadly. Chaired by Bernard Baruch after March 1918, it regulated the flow of materials to manufacturers, issued directives on what products might be turned out, supervised pricing, established transportation priorities, and imposed innumerable regulations to achieve economies through standardization of products. The government-owned Emergency Fleet Corporation, created by the United States Shipping Board, took on the task of building up a fleet adequate to transport troops and supplies. It constructed four enormous shipyards, confiscated German ships interned in American ports, bought vessels from neutral countries, and contracted for millions of tons of new shipping. Although its four dockyards did not begin delivering ships until the close of the war, the corporation in one way or another gained control of ships displacing a total of more than 8,500,000 tons. This, together with the British merchant fleet, resolved the problem of logistics and troop transport.

Other government agencies worked vigorously to meet other needs. Under authority granted by the Lever Food and Fuel Control Act of 1917, the Food Administration, headed by Herbert Hoover, initiated a broad program that regulated imports and exports, fixed prices, initiated meatless and wheatless days as a food-conserving measure, and encouraged the planting of gardens as well as land hitherto untilled. The government, leasing the nation's railroads from their owners, created a Railroad Administration to operate them as a unified system. The Fuel Administration severely restricted the domestic use of fuel, imposing "coal holidays" on certain areas and introducing daylight saving time to minimize use of electrical power. The War Trade Board licensed imports and exports. The Capital Issues Committee regulated investments. A National War Labor Board was created in 1918 to mediate labor disputes, and a War Labor Policies Board concerned itself with working conditions and hours of labor. In all,

**171**
*War and Peace: The Quest for*
*Order in a Troubled World*

the activities of such agencies and many others provide ample evidence for the suggestion that World War I marked a bold new departure in the expansion of powers exercised by the federal government.

**The War and**
**American Opinion**

To many Americans the control of public opinion seemed as important as control of the economy. When the war impinged upon the daily lives of ordinary citizens as no previous international crisis ever had, attitudes of the man on the street—however mundane or unsophisticated—necessarily bore a direct relationship to the war effort. Even before it passed the Selective Service Act, Congress established a Committee on Public Information. George Creel, who had made a name for himself as a muckraking journalist, assumed direction of the committee's activities. Taking a broad view of his responsibilities, he saw them as extending far beyond the negative duties of censorship. The war, in his opinion, was "a plain publicity proposition, a vast enterprise in salesmanship, the world's greatest adventure in advertising." Recruiting scholars, artists, journalists, ministers, and others skilled in the arts of persuasion, Creel set to work on a vigorous campaign to keep the fires of patriotism burning brightly.

Propaganda of the Committee on Public Information took the form of a morality play. The image of the German as "blond beast" or "Hun" had begun to form at the outset of the war when Kaiser Wilhelm's troops invaded Belgium. Creel made the most of it, and to that image the CPI added the heroic figure of the doughboy fighting, as the president put it, "to make the world safe for democracy." Creel and his collaborators concentrated on current events, but their theme was the eternal struggle between good and evil. They wrote a series, of *Red, White and Blue* pamphlets elaborating on the American mission and recounting in detail the atrocities that threatened human decency. "Before them," Guy Stanton Ford wrote of German war leaders, "is the war god to whom they have offered up their reason and their humanity; behind them the misshapen image they have made of the German people, leering with bloodstained visage over the ruins of civilization."

The Creel Committee distributed 75 million copies of the *Red, White and Blue* pamphlets, with telling effect. But it did not rest content with that effort alone. Lecturers were also employed to stimulate the flow of patriotic juices. Seventy-five thousand "Four Minute Men" (the name derived from the approximate length of the speeches they were prepared to deliver on any occasion) instructed their fellow countrymen on "Why We Are Fighting," "What Our Enemy Really Is," and similar subjects. Creel also organized a Division of Pictorial Publicity under the direction of Charles Dana Gibson, creator of the insouciant Gibson Girl that had long been a model of feminine charm and beauty. The war crisis changed both model and painter. "Draw till it hurts," Gibson told his artists, and they produced such posters as James Montgomery Flagg's classic portrait of Uncle Sam with its caption "I WANT YOU."

Uncle Sam did, indeed, seem to want anyone who came within range of

# THE HOME FRONT DURING WORLD WAR I

The Great War of 1914–1918 imposed heavier responsibilities on the populations of belligerent powers than did any previous international conflict. The American Civil War had perhaps demanded as much, but even the severity of that struggle had not subjected citizens to the same kinds of pressures they experienced before 1917. During more than two and a half years of neutrality, Americans grew increasingly frustrated with inaction, with U-boat attacks on merchant ships, and with Allied inability (despite U.S. loans and supplies) to bring the conflict to an end.

By April 1917, when the United States finally declared war, the American people were ready to assume novel obligations in furthering the military effort. Because the demands of Mars seemed clear and unambiguous, the declaration of war brought macabre relief from mounting frustrations. One great objective, victory over the Central Powers, subsumed nearly all civilian activities. Patriotic fervor might at times be misdirected, but it burned hotly enough to melt away doubts expressed by the minority that had misgivings.

For nineteen months the American home front remained, in the popular mind, a major theater of war against the Hun. Journalist Randolph Bourne, a perceptive critic who died during the flu epidemic of 1918, left an unfinished essay in which he commented upon the tendency of individuals to identify themselves with the national purpose. "War—or at least modern war waged by a democratic republic against a powerful enemy—seems to achieve for a nation almost all that the most inflamed political idealist could desire," wrote Bourne. "Citizens are no longer indifferent to their Government, but each cell of the body politic is brimming with life and activity." By associating himself with the war effort, a person might experience a sense of power and self-assurance. Indeed, "the individual as social being in war seems to have achieved almost his apotheosis."

The threat of direct attack on the United States was slight, but few Americans wished to minimize U-boat capabilities as some of them had done in 1915 when the *Lusitania* left New York on her last voyage. Policemen, paramilitary home guard units, and citizen volunteers therefore helped out by mounting guard at strategic points. This police detail stood watch over the East River to protect New York's Williamsburg Bridge. Their demeanor suggests that through long hours of watchfulness patriotic exaltation might give way to ennui, yet with exemplary determination they remained at the post (State Historical Society of Wisconsin).

High schools began military training programs that frequently appealed to youthful
competitive instincts. The students of New York's Stuyvesant High School won
a replica of the Minuteman statue for their excellence in military drill (State
Historical Society of Wisconsin).

Among the important curricular changes war brought to the public schools was the
elimination of courses in the German language. Citizens of Baraboo, Wisconsin, in
an excess of zeal, even burned the books that students had used. "Here lie the
remains of German in B.H.S." read the inscription that identified the ashes. Later in
the 1930s, Americans regarded book burning in Nazi Germany as a repressive act
characteristic of totalitarian dictatorships (State Historical Society of Wisconsin).

Teams of both major leagues secured army sergeants to conduct drill for an hour each day, substituting bats for rifles. This Yankee squad did not display the precision needed to win a $500 prize offered by the American League president, Ban Johnson. Drill team honors went instead to the St. Louis Browns, who seldom won baseball games and whose only pennant came in 1944, when the nation was again at war (State Historical Society of Wisconsin).

A concern for physical fitness extended to all segments of government and society. Here members of the Wilson administration exercise to get in shape (for some of them a belated effort). They doubtless believed that their example would inspire others and thus serve to raise the fitness level of the entire population. From left to right: Secretary of the Treasury William Gibbs McAdoo, Attorney General Thomas W. Gregory, Assistant Secretary of Labor Louis F. Post, and Secretary of Labor William B. Wilson (State Historical Society of Wisconsin).

For
EVERY
FIGHTER
a
WOMAN
WORKER

UNITED
WAR
WORK
CAMPAIGN

CARE
for
HER
through *The* YWCA

Involvement in World War I created new job opportunities for women, as factory managers sought to replace men who left for military service. More than 100,000 women found work in munitions industries, for example, and feminist leaders hailed such employment as the harbinger of broader advancement to come. "Service to their country in this crisis," suggested Harriet Stanton Blatch, "may lead women to that economic freedom which will change a political possession into a political power." In the meantime, organizations such as the YWCA provided aid to those who entered the wartime work force (State Historical Society of Wisconsin).

Food conservation was a major concern on the home front. Women, wearing uniforms of the Food Administration, gave demonstrations in canning and preserving. They also taught cooking classes to prepare dishes that would reduce consumption of wheat and other foodstuffs needed by the armed forces (State Historical Society of Wisconsin).

# U. S. PICTORIAL SERVICE

*Courtesy New Orleans Daily States.*

## RUTH LAW WANTS TO FLY WITH U. S. MARINE

NEW ORLEANS.—Noted aviatrix, holder of the non-stop record, would like to fly with the non-stop Soldie
the Navy. She's now in Washington trying to get a commission in the aviation corps of the army or navy.
maybe you didn't know that the Marine Corps has aviators. Yes indeed, they fly as well as fight on land o
And please remember this: The only way you can distinguish a Soldier of the Navy from a Soldier of the A
is by the Globe, Anchor and Eagle the U. S. Marine wears on his hat, cap or helmet.

This Photo Furnished by
U. S. MARINE CORPS RECRUITING STATION

Some women, not satisfied with food conservation and other war work on the home front, aspired to more glamorous service in the armed forces. Ruth Law never received a commission in the Marine Corps, but recruiters exploited her effort in order to stimulate the enlistment of men with an interest in aviation. The incident suggests a persistent assumption of male superiority despite female participation in the war effort. In 1920, after the crisis had passed, there was a relative decline in female employment, and women made up a smaller percentage of the work force than they had a decade before. With the armistice, as one disappointed feminist lamented, "prejudices came to life once more" (State Historical Society of Wisconsin).

The Army provided no haven for bibliophiles, but the "Books for Soldiers" campaign attracted widespread support from public-spirited citizens (State Historical Society of Wisconsin).

People who were not otherwise involved in the war effort could at least buy liberty bonds. The noble appeal of this poster contrasted sharply with the high pressure salesmanship to which bond drive chairmen were prone.

The incipient movie industry also engaged in war work, and no actor displayed more enthusiasm for it than did Douglas Fairbanks. His unflagging athleticism on the silver screen seemed an expression of the strenuous life Theodore Roosevelt had urged, and later—during the 1920s—his aggressive style comported well with the "zip" and "pep" so admired in the culture of George F. Babbitt. During the Great War, Fairbanks's verve contributed enormously to the success of liberty bond drives. Here, boxing with liberty bond gloves, he delivers a knockout blow to Prussianism (State Historical Society of Wisconsin).

his pointing finger. Most people responded with enthusiasm: they flew flags, marched in parades, subscribed to government bonds, rolled bandages for the Red Cross, or planted vegetable gardens. Some who seem to have been particularly impressionable worried about Prussian influences in American life, searching for evidence of disloyalty in their communities and among their associates. Creel Committee propaganda aroused fears of spies and traitors, and passage of the Espionage Act in June 1917 and the Sedition Act a year later persuaded many citizens that the danger of subversive activity was no figment of a patriotic imagination. Under the Espionage Act courts could impose a fine of up to $10,000 and a prison sentence of up to twenty years for interfering with the draft or in other ways encouraging disloyalty. The Sedition Act prescribed similar punishment for anyone who in wartime "shall willfully utter, print, write, or publish any disloyal, profane, scurrilous, or abusive language about the form of government of the United States, or the Constitution of the United States, or the military or naval forces of the United States, or the flag of the United States, or the uniform of the Army or Navy."

The zeal with which self-appointed defenders of the national interest pursued spies and traitors sometimes amounted to hysteria; lynching bees, tar-and-feather parties, and instances of kangaroo justice were all too common. The Liberty Loan drives provided a convenient litmus test of loyalty. In some communities people who failed to subscribe all that was expected found themselves subjected to cruel and unusual pressures. Houses—and sometimes the householders as well—were smeared with yellow paint, names were posted on "slacker lists," and offending citizens were carried off to be tried in extralegal "slacker courts." Socialists and members of the IWW were automatically suspect. An incident in Butte, Montana, during the summer of 1917 provided a notorious example of hostility to radicals. Masked men seized Frank Little, an IWW organizer, tied him to the bumper of a car, and dragged him through town to a railroad trestle, where they hanged him. But persons with no radical affiliations also suffered at the hands of hyperpatriots. The Washburn, Wisconsin, German Lutheran Church received a notice from the Bayfield County council of defense that typified attitudes toward all Germanic influence: "The holding of services in which the German language is spoken exclusively tends to engender hate and enmity in the hearts and minds of true loyal Americans." Similar sentiment brought the cancellation of German language courses in public schools throughout the country. Various religious groups of pacifist persuasion—Molokans, Dukhobors, Dunkards, Seventh Day Adventists, Christadelphians, Russellites, Hutterite Brethren, Plymouth Brethren, River Brethren, and, of course, Quakers and Mennonites—all suffered indignities at the hands of hyperpatriots.

Much better publicized, however, were actions taken against prominent Americans, most notably Robert M. La Follette, for their opposition to the war. The senior senator from Wisconsin had assumed a leading role in the antiwar movement and had voted against declaring war in 1917. That

"He stood on a step cut out of the earth, his belly against the oozing trench-wall," reported James Hopper of one such soldier as this. "Thus silent and immobile, he waited; wrapped in the soil of France as if in the folds of a flag." Americans at home talked of patriotism and loyalty, but perhaps the infantryman's thoughts were less inspired:

Oh ashes to ashes,
And dust to dust.
If the shrapnel don't get you,
Then the eighty-eights must.

Imperial War Museum

stance irritated Wisconsinites who opposed La Follette's progressivism and who chafed at being thought traitorous because of the state's large population of German origin. When La Follette addressed a St. Paul meeting of the Non-Partisan League in September 1917, he urged speedy termination of the war. But the Associated Press erroneously reported him as saying that "we had no grievances" against Germany. The report, in combination with the senator's record, was enough to bring about an investigation of La Follette's loyalty. Although the Senate voted to dismiss charges against him, the hyperpatriots at home continued their efforts to remove him from office. The Madison chapter of the Wisconsin Loyalty Legion, for example, condemned "the war attitudes of Robert M. La Follette as being against the best interests of our country" and pledged itself "to work against La Folletteism in all its anti-war forms." While the senator weathered the storm, his troubles provided a telling illustration of the way modern warfare could stimulate pressures against nonconformity and diversity of opinion.

**Progressives and the
War Crisis**

La Follette's association with progressivism, together with his habit of using progressive phraseology to describe his antiwar position, raises some important questions about the relationship between reform activities of the progressive period and wartime activities of reformers. Without engaging in an exasperating and, on the whole, fruitless effort to determine the response to American intervention that was most typical of the progressives, it is an easy matter to show that the war frustrated many causes to which reformers had devoted great time and energy. The peace movement lost coherence as its organizations disintegrated or fell out among themselves over how to end the war and lay the foundations for permanent peace. The antitrust movement seemed irrelevant—if not unpatriotic—as wartime needs made efficiency of production more important than the elimination of economic privilege. The conservation movement could not be permitted to limit the agricultural expansion that would produce more food, even though such expansion might eventually prove an ecological disaster. In short, objectives considered desirable in peacetime lost their appeal in wartime. Some of them even appeared to be dangerously contrary to the national interest.

Progressive emphasis on the regulatory powers of government had grown out of a concern for the way in which industrialization had divided Americans. The transition from a rural, small-town society to an urban, industrial society was disruptive in itself; it was complicated, moreover, by the ethnic diversity of new immigration patterns. Progressives had worried about social fragmentation as well as economic injustice; their reforms had looked toward social control as well as economic equity. The powers of government, wielded by men who stood above class and interest and who made full use of unbiased experts, would be used to hasten progress toward the good life for all. Such was the progressive hope. Many progressives, particularly those oriented more toward domestic than toward international problems, saw the Great War as a threat to that hope.

Distrustful of power in itself, such progressives had acquiesced in the effort to neutralize private power with public power because they believed that in the hands of democratically elected reformers the public power would not be abused. But during the preparedness period, as the nation moved gradually toward intervention, they experienced a crisis of confidence. Republicans of progressive persuasion (men such as Senators George Norris of Nebraska, Asle Gronna of North Dakota, Charles Curtis of Kansas, Moses Clapp of Minnesota, Albert Cummins of Iowa, William E. Borah of Idaho, John D. Works of California, and, of course, La Follette) joined Bryan Democrats in resisting the armaments buildup. Opponents of preparedness did not have identical motives; neither did they have identical progressive credentials. Yet most of them could agree with Works when he charged that "the influence of plutocracy, wealth, big business" was behind the preparedness agitation. The "concordant and congenial evils" of plutocracy and militarism, if unopposed, would "pervert and sooner or later destroy our free republican institutions." With the coming of war, Works, La Follette, Norris, and other progressives saw prominent industrial leaders flocking to Washington as dollar-a-year men, they watched industrial profits mount despite excess-profits taxes, and they found some of their favorite programs giving way to military demands. That they developed misgivings about expanded government powers should have occasioned no surprise, for their doubts were consistent with their understanding of progressive principles.

Not all progressives shared such misgivings, however, for the wartime spirit of cooperation enhanced opportunities for planners, industrial management experts, social workers, and intellectuals. Back in 1909 when he published *The Promise of American Life,* Herbert Croly had argued that in modern times reform required a new sense of national purpose to unify a society whose agricultural homogeneity had been destroyed by industrial development. "In this country," he had written, "the solution of the social problem demands the substitution of a conscious social ideal for the earlier instinctive homogeneity of the American nation." Like nothing else since the beginnings of industrialization, the war effort united Americans in common cause. It overcame the greed and selfishness that progressives had identified with social sin—or so it seemed—and progressives who did not share the views of La Follette and his associates moved to take advantage of war-induced unity of purpose.

Many progressives, who saw the war crisis as one in which opportunity predominated over peril, believed that the United States had arrived at one of the great moments in her history in 1917. "I shall never forget the exaltation which then moved the soul of America," remembered Ray Stannard Baker in a speech delivered after the peace treaties had been drawn up. "You will recall it well. You felt it. We all felt it. Here was a vast evil threatening the world. We wanted to give everything we had to beat it down." Willingness to give everything they had took many progressives to Washington, where they used their expertise in advising administrators of wartime programs and often in serving as administrators themselves. The nation's capital, as William E. Leuchtenburg has noted, "swarmed with professors" and with university-trained intellectuals. Eager to strike a blow against the vast evil threatening the world, they also began to enthuse over what philosopher John Dewey called "the social possibilities of war."

In the War Industries Board, the Railroad Administration, the Food Administration, the War Labor Board, and other agencies, progressives found opportunities for social and economic planning on a scale that few had thought possible before 1917. The War Industries Board, for example, issued detailed directives on a variety of matters: the number of trunks a traveling salesman could carry, the number of stops elevators could make, the styles and sizes of plows, the color of ink used in typewriter ribbons. The primary object of such regulation was to improve efficiency through standardization and to reduce the waste of undisciplined production. But the wartime experience of the experts confirmed their belief in the social advantages of careful planning. In their view, the economies of standardization would benefit everyone, reducing differences in living conditions of the rich and the poor.

The war experience that aroused the ardor of planners and industrial managers elicited an equally enthusiastic response from social workers who had taken an active part in the progressive drive for melioration of social ills. Vice peddlers and prostitutes who clustered around newly established Army camps presented, to be sure, a formidable challenge to progressives concerned with moral uplift. But now, more than ever before, moral uplift could be related to the national interest, and government agencies proved unusually responsive to the appeals of reformers. Frances Kellor, who for years had been working with immigrant groups, became head of the New York Committee for Immigrants during the war. She found greater support for programs of Americanization—holding classes in the English language and instructing newcomers in American customs—than all her vigorous efforts had developed before 1917. And, for the first time, government administrators seemed to understand her argument that immigrant skills could be more effectively used. "We shall exchange our material thinking for something quite different," suggested an editorial in the General Federation of Women's Clubs *Magazine* in June 1917, "and we shall all be kin." The writer went on to add that "many wrongs will be righted, vampires and grafters and slackers will be relegated to a class by themselves, stiff necks will limber up, hearts of stone will be changed to hearts of flesh, and little by little we shall begin to understand each other." Mobilization, Boston social worker Robert Woods noted more specifically, was "the occasion of a new and better order of things affecting the restraint of the liquor trade and of prostitution, and the promotion of . . . health-giving community recreation."

Concern for the community—the sentiment reappears again and again in the writings of progressive reformers—could express itself in humanitarian activities and campaigns for moral improvement as well as in Liberty Loan drives and loyalty crusades. Nowhere did it appear more logically or clearly than in the construction of government-sponsored housing projects for war workers. Two agencies, the Emergency Fleet Corporation and the United States Housing Corporation, assumed major responsibility for administering the $175,000,000 that Congress appropriated for housing. Architects and planners, led by reformers such as Lawrence Veiller and Frederick Ackerman, took pains to avoid throwing up clusters of barracks that would soon deteriorate into blighted areas and add to the problems of already overcrowded industrial communities. Under the influence of "Garden City" concepts used in the construction of new communities in Britain, they exercised great care in house designs. They conducted elaborate field investigations to make sure that sites were suitable for new communities and located near adequate transportation facilities. They experimented with attractive row houses that were inexpensive to build. They concerned themselves with traffic patterns within the communities to keep the curved streets of residential neighborhoods from being heavily traveled. They planned, too, for open spaces, parks, squares, schools, and community buildings. And their efforts brought notable results. The best of the wartime housing projects, such as Yorkship Village at Camden, New Jersey, became models of community design.

As innovative and excellent as many of the new communities were, however, the government programs did not even come close to meeting needs. Wartime stringencies brought to a standstill the construction of houses by private builders. The resultant housing shortage continued into the early twenties, when high building costs prevented private enterprise from carrying on where government programs left off. Advocates of better community design and planning always regretted that the promise of wartime housing projects was never fully realized. It might have been, they argued, had the close of the war not brought a relaxation of the crisis that made government projects acceptable. But community planners were not alone in their mixed feelings about the armistice of 1918. A decade later Columbia University professor Rexford G. Tugwell, who would become an important member of Franklin D. Roosevelt's "Brain Trust" during the depression of the 1930s, wrote an article in praise of what he called "America's wartime socialism." The Great War had, in fact, been "an industrial engineer's utopia." But then the war ended, and "the Armistice prevented a great experiment in control of production, control of price, and control of consumption." Tugwell and others who had made the most of the 1917–1918 crisis did not regret the conclusion of war so much as they regretted the passing of wartime opportunities. They looked forward to the day when government planning could be carried on in peacetime too, although they were not optimistic about when the day would arrive. Tugwell could not have foreseen that within the next decade economic depression would bring another crisis and another expansion of government activities.

**The AEF in Europe**

The elaborate American mobilization effort was appropriate for a war lasting much longer than the Great War actually did. Several of the president's advisers believed that peace could not be won until 1919 or 1920, though Wilson himself seems to have thought that the conflict could be terminated within a few months and that naval forces would represent the primary U.S. commitment. Whatever American expectations might have been, the armistice occurred at a time when much of the war materiel produced in the United States was just beginning to appear on the battlefields of Europe. The first ship constructed at Hog Island, the largest of the Emergency Fleet Corporation's dockyards, was not ready for service until after the war had ended. Production of heavy guns did not reach significant proportions until the autumn of 1918, and the French supplied most of the artillery pieces used by the American Expeditionary Force. The number of tanks to come out of American plants was inconsequential. American aviators flew French and British planes.

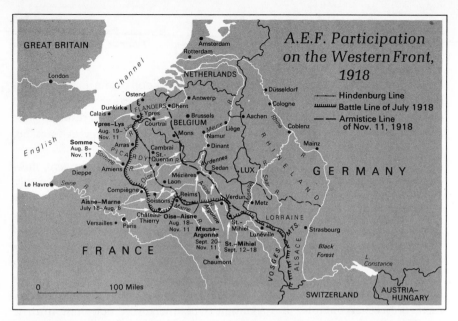

The ruins of a church in Neuilly, near the Argonne Forest, furnished a temporary shelter for wounded Americans and the setting for a photograph of war's profanity. "I was always embarrassed by the words sacred, glorious, and sacrifice, and the expression in vain," comments Lieutenant Henry, hero of Ernest Hemingway's *A Farewell to Arms*. ". . . I had seen nothing sacred, and the things that were glorious had no glory, and the sacrifices were like the stockyards at Chicago if nothing was done with the meat except to bury it . . ." (State Historical Society of Wisconsin).

Yet American troops did exercise an important influence in military operations, particularly during the summer and fall of 1918. The first contingents to reach France arrived in June 1917, but they were token forces, intended to bolster Allied morale. More would be sent overseas as they completed their training; 300,000 men were in France when German armies launched their spring offensive in 1918, and by the end of the war more than 2 million had reached Europe. The German numerical superiority of over 320,000 infantrymen on the western front had been converted to an Allied superiority of more than 600,000. That achievement was in large part the result of a new tactic, the convoy system, employed by Allied fleets to counteract the U-boat menace. The success of the convoy was remarkable. In April 1918 German submarines had destroyed 881,000 tons of shipping, but, after that, the convoy system dramatically reduced the hazards of transporting troops and supplies. Losses dropped to 289,000 tons in November; the U-boats turned out to be significantly less effective than German strategists had anticipated. Although two British transports went down with American doughboys, not a single American troop ship was sunk during the nineteen months of American belligerency.

The growing size of the American Expeditionary Force in Europe gave rise to discussions of the Allied command structure. British and French generals had hoped to use American troops as replacements, fitting them in wherever they were needed. But General John J. Pershing, who commanded the United States forces in Europe, insisted that his men would function more effectively if they fought together in their own units. Before the issue could be settled, the Germans launched a major offensive in March 1918. Coordination of Allied operations became a pressing necessity, and in April General Ferdinand Foch of France assumed command of Allied forces. Pershing agreed to deploy American troops in segments along the entire line from Ypres to the Swiss border. Late in May, when it captured Cantigny, the American First Division overcame the hardened skepticism of British and French veterans who doubted the doughboy's fighting abilities. Then in June the Second and Third Divisions halted the German drive at Château Thierry, forced the Germans back across the Marne, and went on to clear Belleau Wood of enemy forces. By mid-July, the massive German offensive having stalled, Foch ordered a series of counterattacks. Finally, on August 30, Pershing secured approval of what he had long urged, and he fielded the First American Army.

The general could not have his way entirely, however. The American army occupied territory between Verdun and the Moselle River, and Pershing contemplated a drive to the east. Contrary to the wishes of Foch, he carried out an independent operation against the German salient at St. Mihiel. It was a complete success; but, to Foch's way of thinking, the American army would serve more effectively further west. Thus there was no real followup on the St. Mihiel success. Pershing had little choice but to send his troops into the region of the Argonne and the Meuse, where they contributed to a general offensive that broke German lines and forced

Doughboys of the American Expeditionary Force advanced on the road to Grand Pre during the Meuse-Argonne offensive that finally forced a German capitulation on November 11, 1918. Extended over a period of forty days, the offensive engaged 1,200,000 troops and cost 117,000 American casualties (State Historical Society of Wisconsin).

a German surrender by the second week of November. Despite disagreements among Allied commanders, they had achieved enough unity to bring the Great War to an end. Now it remained for the statesmen and diplomats to work out a peace settlement that might prevent a repetition of the holocaust.

**Wilson and the Lost Peace**

When the statesmen and diplomats gathered in Paris to work out a peace settlement during the early months of 1919, they did so in sober awareness of what the war had cost. The conflict had mobilized 65 million men and women; nearly 10 million had lost their lives, and 22 million had been wounded. Taken together, German, Russian, and French battle casualties accounted for half of the dead. Although France had fewer total losses than either Germany or Russia, they were particularly heavy in the age group that had been between eighteen and forty-five in 1914. One out of every three men had been killed, and one of every three had been wounded. British deaths came to nearly a million, slightly less than the figure for Austria. American deaths exceeded 100,000, an unexpectedly large number considering the length of time the AEF had been actively involved in combat. The price of the Great War in life, health, and happiness was staggering, and so was the direct economic cost: a total of nearly $170 billion. The American contribution of almost $33 billion represented, according to the statistical summary of the United States General Staff, a sum large enough to pay the entire cost of running the national government from 1791 to 1914.

Whatever opportunities the war crisis had presented for planners and rationalizers, no one would argue in 1919 that the war itself had been a positive good. Woodrow Wilson was as determined as anyone to prevent a recurrence of the struggle that had cost so dearly. More inclined to employ moral rhetoric than were other negotiators at Paris, laboring under a greater sense of guilt for allowing his nation to become involved, and puritanically confident that the righteousness of his cause would prevail over lesser ambitions and self-serving interests, Wilson became the chief architect of the treaties drawn up at the peace conference. His biographer, Arthur Link, has pointed out that few American presidents have been more severely tested than Wilson was in the years between 1918 and 1920. That he failed to pass the test physically was his personal misfortune; that he failed to achieve his lofty objective of making the world safe for democracy was a global misfortune. In the lessons that world leaders and populations drew from Wilson's failure rests an explanation for much of the history of our time.

Before the peacemakers assembled in Paris, Wilson made three moves that in retrospect seem to have been tactical errors. In the political campaign of 1918, waged at a time when the war was nearing its end, he urged voters to return a Democratic Congress so that he might "continue to be your unembarrassed spokesman in affairs at home and abroad." Since

Paul Nash (1889–1946) was a British painter who enlisted in the artists' rifles at the outbreak of war in 1914. His war paintings of shattered landscapes were done with abstract detachment. This one, "We are Making a New World," offered a commentary on the disjunction between rhetorical idealism and military realities (Imperial War Museum).

Republicans had supported the war effort as loyally as the Democrats, such an appeal was either nonsensical or the tocsin of a return to partisan politics. Either way, Wilson was the loser, as Republicans won majorities in both houses. In the new Senate, which would have to ratify any treaty drafted in Paris, the GOP held forty-nine seats as opposed to forty-seven for the president's party. That majority gave the opposition control of the Foreign Relations Committee; and Henry Cabot Lodge, one of the president's most outspoken critics, became its chairman.

The president increased the possibility of difficulty with the Senate when he made his appointments to the peace commission. He almost completely ignored the Republicans, whose election victory had made recognition of their wishes a practical necessity. Of the delegates Wilson selected, only Henry White identified himself as a Republican, and he was a career diplomat with small influence in higher councils of the party. The others —Secretary of State Robert Lansing, presidential adviser Edward M. House, General Tasker H. Bliss—were so closely associated with the Wilson administration that they could scarcely be considered representative of the variety of opinion in the United States. That Wilson should avoid consultation with Lodge was understandable, but his passing over more tractable Republicans such as former Secretary of State Elihu Root or the former president, William Howard Taft, betrayed his intolerance of diversity and his dependence on sycophants.

Wilson's decision to lead the American delegation, as it turned out, also served to sharpen the conflict taking shape in Washington. The president thought he detected "a great wind of moral force moving through the world," and yet he saw himself as the only statesman who could harness that force and make it effective. Standing amid the ruins of war, the leaders of other great powers were intent upon salvaging what they could for themselves and their people. Vittorio Orlando of Italy was a determined though unsuccessful pleader for territorial gains. Baron Shinken Makino sought to obtain German holdings in the Far East for Japan. Lloyd George, who had just won a national election by promising to squeeze the German orange until the pips squeaked, labored to strengthen the British Empire and improve its trade advantages. France's Tiger, Georges Clemenceau, tenaciously held to two objectives: revenge against Germany and security for France. The Americans, thought Wilson, were "the only disinterested people at the Peace Conference." As leader of the American delegation, he engaged in some very hard bargaining. When it was over, he felt a deep personal commitment to the treaties that had been hammered out. To him they were an expression of the moral force moving the world; and, having labored mightily to obtain them, he could not bring himself to think of changing a line.

Wilson's perception of himself as agent of the world's moral force was consistent with the character traits he had developed when growing up in a Presbyterian manse. Admiring his father profoundly, he had accepted the obligation to strive incessantly for the fulfillment of God's purposes in a sinful world. But the president, it now appears, was also laboring under physical disabilities that affected his ideas and his behavior just as powerfully as did his upbringing. In an analysis of available medical evidence, Dr. Edwin A. Weinstein has shown that, at the time he went to Paris, Wilson had a long history of cerebral vascular disease. Signs of the trouble first appeared in 1896, when he suddenly experienced pain in his right arm and numbness in his right hand. Then, one spring morning in 1906, he awoke to find himself completely blind in his left eye. "The sequence of episodes of parasthesia [abnormal sensation] in one hand and blindness in the opposite eye," writes Dr. Weinstein, "is characteristic of occlusive disease of the internal carotid artery, the major supplier of blood to the brain."

Although Wilson had made a good clinical recovery by 1912, when he won election to the presidency, his ailment brought marked changes in behavior. After the 1896 attack he relaxed less and, in an effort that was consistent with the values of his Presbyterian rearing, attempted to overcome disabilities with hard work. He taught himself to write with his left hand, and he gave up the long bicycle rides that had been one of his favorite forms of recreation. His manner changed, too, especially after the 1906 attack. He became more irritable and aggressive and less able to contend with criticism and opposition. Perhaps, as would have been natural for a man of his religious convictions, he persuaded himself that his life had been spared because he was destined to perform some great, cosmic purpose. If such was the case, then Wilson's appeal for a Democratic Congress, his slighting of Republicans in forming the American delegation, and his determination to play a leading role in the negotiations himself become more understandable. He was convinced that any man who opposed the great wind of moral force would "go down in disgrace." At the same time, his actions suggest the importance of Wilson's limitations as a negotiator and the extent to which those limitations could prevent accomplishment of major objectives. It was Wilson, himself, who would go down in disgrace—not because his ideas were wrong, but because of his difficulty in making accommodations and compromises.

**The President's
Peace Program**

The program that Wilson took with him to Paris was one that developed out of fourteen points he had discussed in a speech delivered to Congress on January 8, 1918. Because its substance became in effect an agenda for the conference, the speech bears close examination. That Wilson made the address several months before the conclusion of the war is significant, however; its full meaning becomes clear only when set in the context of international affairs at the time Wilson delivered it.

By far the most important events during the year prior to the fourteen-points address were those taking place within Russia. Unrest and dissatisfaction had forced the abdication of Czar Nicholas II in March 1917, and a provisional government had taken control. When that government found itself incapable of stabilizing the situation, a second revolution in

November brought the more radical Bolsheviks to power. Russia was still technically at war with Germany, but Lenin and other Bolshevik leaders recognized the importance of peace to the success of their revolution. Early in December they arranged an armistice with Germany, and peace negotiations began at Brest-Litovsk. It was before the conclusion of those negotiations that Wilson addressed Congress.

Like Lenin, the President had long believed that an exploitative imperialism was one of the major causes of war. "We can have no sympathy with those who seek to seize the power of government to advance their own personal interests or ambition," he had announced in 1913 when he repudiated dollar diplomacy. And he made clear his determination to cut government support of American investors in foreign fields. In his speech accepting renomination for the presidency in September 1916, Wilson developed the idea that international reform could be brought about through government supervision to insure free trade and legitimate commercial expansion. "The field will be free, the instrumentalities at hand," he predicted. "It will only remain for the masters of enterprise amongst us to act in energetic concert, and for the Government of the United States to insist upon the maintenance throughout the world of those conditions of fairness and of even-handed justice in the commercial dealings of the nations with one another upon which, after all, in the last analysis, the peace and ordered life of the world must ultimately depend." What the president hoped to achieve, then, was a moderate and rational reform of the international political and economic system. He did not wish to destroy capitalism, or the nation-state as an institution, or even the commercial and political domination of the world by Western powers. But, just as the worst evils of industrial expansion could be eliminated at home through progressive reform, so could the iniquities of international exploitation be overcome by replacing the old balance-of-power system with one that would assure fairness and even-handed justice in the relations of one nation with another.

Ever since the Great War began, Wilson had been thinking about the conditions necessary for peace. Having led the United States into the conflict, he identified Germany with the international exploitation he hoped to prevent in the future. To his mind, Russian withdrawal from the struggle against the Central Powers not only would strengthen the enemy but would also represent a capitulation to evil. Wilson saw an opportunity to suggest an alternative, however, when the talks at Brest-Litovsk were recessed following presentation of the harsh German demands. Perhaps, if Bolshevik leaders understood what his program entailed, they would associate themselves with an international reform movement to insure lasting peace. And that, of course, would mean remaining with the Allies in the fight against Germany.

"What we demand in this war," the president told the world in his address to Congress, ". . . is nothing peculiar to ourselves. It is that the world be made fit and safe to live in; and particularly that it be made safe for every peace-loving nation which, like our own, wishes to live its own life, determine its own institutions, be assured of justice and fair dealing by the other peoples of the world as against force and selfish aggression." The conditions he thought necessary for the creation of such a world were those embodied in the fourteen points:

1. "Open covenants of peace, openly arrived at."
2. "Absolute freedom of navigation upon the seas, outside territorial waters, alike in peace and in war."
3. "The removal, so far as possible, of all economic barriers and the establishment of an equality of trade conditions among all the nations."
4. Reduction of national armaments "to the lowest point consistent with domestic safety."
5. Adjustment of all colonial claims, giving fair consideration to "the interests of the population concerned" as well as to "the equitable claims of the government whose title is to be determined."
6. "The evacuation of all Russian territory and such a settlement of all questions affecting Russia as will secure the best and freest co-operation of the other nations of the world in obtaining for her an unhampered and unembarrassed opportunity for the independent determination of her own political development and national policy."
7. The evacuation and restoration of Belgium.
8. The evacuation and restoration of French territory, with correction of "the wrong done to France by Prussia in 1871 in the matter of Alsace-Lorraine."
9. An adjustment of Italian frontiers "along clearly recognizable lines of nationality."
10. "The freest opportunity of autonomous development" for the peoples of Austria-Hungary.
11. The evacuation and restoration of Rumania, Serbia, and Montenegro, with access to the sea for Serbia.
12. A secure sovereignty for "Turkish portions" of the Ottoman Empire and "an absolutely unmolested opportunity of autonomous development" for "other nationalities which are now under Turkish rule."
13. Creation of an independent Polish state with "free and secure access to the sea."
14. The formation of "a general association of nations . . . for the purpose of affording mutual guarantees of political independence and territorial integrity to great and small states alike."

Although the president's program won widespread support throughout the world, Lenin and other Bolshevik leaders remained singularly unimpressed. In Lenin's view, no reform of the capitalist system was really possible. War and imperialism were characteristic of the last stage of capitalist development. They could not be eliminated by liberal capitalism, however enlightened; they could be eliminated only by socialist revolution. Inasmuch as Wilsonian reforms might delay the day of revolution, they were measures to be opposed rather than supported. Perceiving no advantage in a continuation of the war against Germany, then, the Bolshevik government proceeded to the conclusion of negotiations at Brest-Litovsk. The terms of the treaty were indeed harsh—Russia surrendered all claims to vast territories in eastern Europe—but at least the peace would permit the Bolsheviks to concentrate on strengthening their position at home and putting their program into operation within Russia.

Wilson's failure either to win Bolshevik support or to prevent Russian withdrawal from the war gradually led him to the conviction that the baneful results of revolutionary disruption were no less a part of the world's evil than the pernicious consequences of imperialistic exploitation. But the principles of his fourteen-point address remained principles worth fighting to uphold, for they would serve as well to prevent disruptive revolution as to eliminate exploitative imperialism. Convinced that the "great wind of moral force moving through the world" blew in the direction of change, he feared the possibility of revolution if the statesmen in Paris did not effect change along the lines he had suggested. On board the ship that took him to France for the Peace Conference, the president spoke of creating a new world order. He feared that, should the conference fail to create it, the people of many nations would drink the "poison of Bolshevism" as a "protest against the way in which the world has worked."

## The Peace Conference

The strains and tensions of the Paris conference were enough to break a man in better health than Wilson. That the president eventually suffered physical collapse is less surprising than his capacity to carry on as well as he did the fight to secure peace through a program based on national self-determination, free trade, and a League of Nations to handle necessary international adjustments. In a careful study of the Wilson administration's response to problems of war, revolution, and peace, N. Gordon Levin, Jr., suggests that an ambivalent attitude toward Germany increased the president's difficulties at the peace conference and eventually resulted in ambiguous policy. On the one hand, Wilson leaned toward the view that a purged and democratic Germany should assume an important position in a new nonrevolutionary community of nations. With the collapse of Wilhelm II's empire and his departure for exile in the Netherlands, the Majority Socialists became the dominant power within Germany. The promise of a new democratic nation carried with it the hope of German participation in Wilson's new world order, for Wilson believed that such participation would prevent the momentum of change from carrying the German people too far down a revolutionary course. On the other hand, the American peace delegation was never completely convinced that the proponents of German militarism and imperialism had lost all their influence to the advocates of moderation. The president's fear that a revival of Teutonic imperialism might again disrupt the peace of the world led him to sympathize with French demands for security and revenge. Thus, toward the close of the peace conference, Wilson could tell the American delegation that Germany "should learn once and for all what an unjust war means in itself."

With the idea that a reformed Germany would become a useful member of the international community, the president tried to soften Allied vindictiveness. Nowhere was his moderation more evident than in discussions of reparations and other economic questions. He had already made arrangements to provide food and other relief for needy Germans when the subject of reparations came up for discussion. The British and French delegates insisted that Germany should pay all war costs, contending that only full payment would insure a just settlement. Wilson and other Americans argued that the demand ran counter to promises made prior to the armistice and that reparations should cover only damages. Other members of the conference reluctantly agreed, but how were damages to be defined? After much discussion, thirty-one different categories of damages were reduced to ten on which there was consensus. Americans boggled at including pensions and separation allowances, but the argument that "a destroyed chimney was not to be placed above compensation for a lost life or a pension for a blinded or wounded soldier" eventually prevailed.

Finally, there was the question of amounts, periods, and method of payment. Wilson and the American delegation pleaded for a fixed and reasonable sum. They thought that rehabilitation would be easier to achieve if the Allies knew exactly how much they were to receive; but, more importantly, they did not wish to reduce Germany to economic shambles. Representatives of the Allied powers, determined to go after all they could get, were far less concerned with Germany's economic condition. In the end, the Big Four (Lloyd George, Clemenceau, Orlando, and Wilson) decided not to include a specific amount in the peace treaty because to do so seemed politically unwise. Clemenceau thought that any stated amount would fall so far short of expectations that any French government agreeing to it would be placing itself in jeopardy. Lloyd George, recalling his recent election campaign, readily agreed. The treaty therefore included a compromise solution. Germany would pay an immediate sum of $5 billion to meet expenses of the Allied armies of occupation, and another amount to be set later by a reparations commission. Presumably the unspecified amount would be a fair one.

In discussions of political and territorial questions, as on economic issues, the United States delegation took a moderate position to soften the severity of French demands. Gallic proposals were indeed severe. Having fallen behind Germany in population and industrial development before the war began, having been humiliated by German armies in 1870–1871, and having lost one-third of their young men in the Great War, the French were understandably anxious to secure their eastern frontier and to prevent another German encroachment. Clemenceau therefore demanded that Germany's western frontier be fixed at the Rhine, that a ten-thousand square mile area on the left bank of the Rhine be detached from Germany and set up as a neutral state, and that the Saar Basin with its rich coal deposits be turned over to France. With the help of Lloyd George, who shared his conviction that a new and different Germany could contribute to world peace rather than threaten it, Wilson managed to secure modification of the French proposals. But he had to bend some of his own ideas to do it. Although Clemenceau surrendered his demand for the creation of a separate buffer state, Wilson and Lloyd George agreed to occupation of the territory by an interallied force for a period of at least fifteen years. In addition, the left bank of the Rhine was to be permanently demilitarized along with a strip of territory fifty kilometers wide on the right bank. As for the Saarland, France would gain control of its coal mines, and the League of Nations would govern it until a plebiscite determined sovereignty in the territory after fifteen years.

The French obviously viewed with skepticism the Wilsonian idea that Germany might one day take her place as an equal in the family of nations.

On May 7, 1919, four years after the sinking of the *Lusitania*, Allied representatives handed the peace treaty to German delegates assembled at the Trianon Palace, Versailles. Military personnel stood on tables and chairs for a view of the proceedings, staged with dramatic finesse. Inside the room, George Clemenceau ("The Tiger") minced no words in addressing the Germans. "You have asked for peace," he snapped. "We are ready to give you peace" (State Historical Society of Wisconsin).

They doubted that the new German government would be able to control German militarism. And Wilson, too, seemed to have his doubts. Having supported the moderate socialists in their efforts to secure constitutional democracy, he could go no further for fear of encouraging disruptive revolution such as the Bolshevik revolution in Russia. At the same time, the very moderation of the new German government could limit its effective domination over the still powerful elements that had supported German militarism and imperialism. The idea that revolution posed a serious threat to international stability made Wilson sympathetic to peace terms that would make possible the full recovery of a reformed Germany. But the idea that traditional German militarism must be crushed made him equally sympathetic to terms that were punitive and—in the eyes of many Germans, at least—contrary to the generous promises Wilson had made before the armistice.

Without understanding the dilemma in which Wilson found himself at Paris, and with little knowledge of the way in which he had exercised a moderating influence, many observers were struck by the shortcomings as well as the harshness of the Versailles Treaty. Germany was forced to acknowledge responsibility for the outbreak of the war. It lost Alsace-Lorraine, Schleswig, German Poland, Danzig (the corridor that provided Poland with access to the sea), and (temporarily at least) the Saar Basin. Former German colonies were placed under the direct control of various powers as mandates of the League of Nations. The armaments provisions reduced the German army to 100,000 men, abolished the general staff, forbade the manufacture or importation of munitions, restricted the fleet to six battleships, six light cruisers, twelve destroyers, and twelve torpedo boats. And the reparations provisions—perhaps most galling of all to German minds—left open the question of how much Germany would be expected to pay her conquerors.

To some contemporaries, what the treaty left out was even more important than the severity of provisions included. British economist John Maynard Keynes criticized the negotiators for not giving due consideration to the economic problems that postwar Europe was sure to confront. American economist Thorstein Veblen thought that the treaty failed to change in any fundamental way the international commercial relationships that had helped to bring on the war in the first place. Germany, the economic as well as the geographic center of Europe, had been deprived of areas that were vitally important to industrial strength; the most prosperous European nation of 1914 had become an economic cripple. The principle of national self-determination did not seem to apply to German-speaking peoples—a discrimination that Adolph Hitler would later exploit—but putting it into effect in other areas changed the map of Europe. A large number of small, independent states came into being; and, with the drawing of new boundaries and frontiers, came new possibilities for the interruption of trade through tariff restrictions. For his part, Wilson understood some of the treaty's economic shortcomings. "How can your experts or ours be

After the Germans had been given the treaty, Woodrow Wilson and David Lloyd George paused briefly in the palace hallway. Behind them stood Wilson's advisers: Colonel Edward M. House, General Tasker H. Bliss, and Henry White. On June 28, after futile German protests against a punitive peace—and after Wilson had returned home to wage a futile fight for ratification—diplomats signed the treaty in the Hall of Mirrors, Versailles (State Historical Society of Wisconsin).

expected to work out a *new* plan to furnish working capital to Germany," he queried Lloyd George in the spring of 1919, "when we deliberately start out by taking away all Germany's *present* capital?" But, believing that the settlement was as good as any that could be obtained, Wilson placed his hope in the League of Nations. If economic and other adjustments proved necessary in the future—and the president never doubted that they would become necessary—the league was the agency to make them.

**The Fight for the League**

When Wilson returned from Paris during the summer of 1919, he had good reason to expect Senate ratification of the treaty he carried with him. There was, to be sure, a group of "irreconcilables" (led by Senators William E. Borah of Idaho, Hiram Johnson of California, James A. Reed of Missouri, Robert M. La Follette of Wisconsin, Philander C. Knox of Pennsylvania, and George H. Moses of New Hampshire) who for various reasons had pledged themselves to vote against the treaty. But the irreconcilables were few in number, their voting strength balanced by the president's loyal followers, who were prepared to support the treaty without qualification. Between those two committed blocs stood a much larger group made up of men disposed to cast their votes for ratification but only with reservations either clarifying or limiting American participation in procedures and actions of the League of Nations. In the United States, then, and more specifically in the Senate, the fate of the treaty hinged upon attitudes toward the league and the extent to which those attitudes could be reconciled with the President's view of what American membership demanded.

The Covenant, or the constitution, of the League of Nations provided that membership would include signatories to the treaty, thirteen other

states named in an annex, and any other "fully self-governing State, Do-
minion or Colony" that received a two-thirds vote of the assembly. The
assembly, in which each member nation had one vote, was set up as a
representative body. Empowered to "deal at its meetings with any matter
within the sphere of action of the League or affecting the peace of the
world," it also controlled the league budget and selected nonpermanent
members of the council. The Covenant originally provided for a council
of nine members, five of them permanent, and assigned it certain specific
tasks. It was responsible for developing plans to reduce armaments, protecting member states victimized by foreign aggressors, mediating international disputes, and receiving reports of mandatory powers. The scope of
its activities, however, was the same as that of the assembly. In addition
to the assembly and the council, the Covenant set up a third agency, the
permanent secretariat, to handle the civil-service functions of the league.

The heart of the Covenant, in Wilson's view, was Article X, which
provided that all member nations would "undertake to respect and preserve as against external aggression the territorial integrity and existing
political independence of all Members of the League." Any nation agreeing to the Covenant would not only abjure war with another member state
but would also subject any violator of the agreement "to the severance of

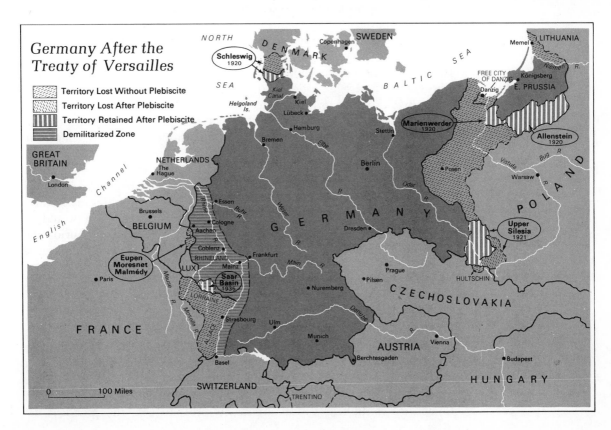

*Germany After the Treaty of Versailles*

all trade or financial relations, the prohibition of all intercourse between [its] nationals and the nationals of the covenant-breaking State, and the prevention of all financial, commercial or personal intercourse between the nationals of the covenant-breaking State and the nationals of any other State." In other words, a league member that made war in violation of its promises would be subject to complete blockade in trade, finance, and communications. In addition, the council might recommend that military action be taken against an aggressor.

Once the president had submitted the treaty, and once the Senate Foreign Relations Committee started its hearings, opposition to the League of Nations began to build. Article X became a major question of debates both in the Senate and throughout the country. Senator Borah spoke for large numbers of Americans when he said that he wanted no part of an international organization that would deprive the United States of its freedom to pursue whatever foreign policy it chose. He also expressed a commonly held opinion when he said that with Article X in its Covenant the League of Nations was actually nothing more than an agency to preserve the international status quo for the benefit of privileged economic interests. Unhappily for Wilson, committee chairman Henry Cabot Lodge, his old enemy, was not disposed to rush into a vote on the treaty; and, as the hearings dragged on, other voices began to speak out in opposition. Some senators believed that Clemenceau's demand for French security was not merely an expression of vindictiveness but was based upon a hard-headed assessment of international realities. Others listened to ethnic groups—to German-Americans who thought the treaty too harsh, or to Irish-Americans who saw in the league a device through which Britain might continue to tyrannize Ireland, or to Italian-Americans who vented their disappointment at Italy's failure to secure Fiume. Others, sharing Lodge's deep personal animosity toward Wilson, resented the possibility that a Democratic president might claim victory if the treaty were approved.

At several points during the summer of 1919 the president might have won support for ratification had he been willing to negotiate with key senators on a few mild reservations. But while he made significant gestures of conciliation, even going so far as to write out reservations he would be willing to accept, he was in no frame of mind to compromise. During the Paris negotiations he had suffered what now appears to have been a cerebral vascular occlusion that produced the symptoms of a minor stroke. Now, even more than after earlier illnesses, Wilson sought to cope with his infirmities by unrelenting labor and by single-minded pursuit of his goals. His behavior suggests that although he sensed the seriousness of his illness, he could not admit to himself that he was a sick man. He acted as though he believed that, by forcing his will, he could resolve his own inner doubts; he could prove to himself that he was sound in mind and in body. In such a state, negotiations with wavering senators were, of course, out of the question. But, as the summer wore on, and as the Foreign Relations Committee continued to hear arguments pro and con, the president de-

**199**
*War and Peace: The Quest for
Order in a Troubled World*

This cartoon, by the Chicago *Tribune's*
John T. McCutcheon, aptly summarized the
reasons for many Americans turning against
the League of Nations. "It seemed to me,"
McCutcheon himself later recalled, "that the
League, far from being an impartial body of
cold justice, was to be a manipulated device
designed to secure to Britain and France the
immense advantages they had gained by the
treaty." (Reprinted courtesy of the Chicago
*Tribune.*)

cided to pursue the one other alternative he was able to perceive. He
would bypass the Senate and take his case to the people.

On September 3, 1919, against the advice of his cabinet and his personal
physician, the president set out on an extensive tour of the American
heartland. In twenty-two days he traveled more than eight thousand miles,
delivering thirty-seven lengthy speeches calling for ratification without
reservations. He had never been more eloquent as he attempted to meet
every argument against the League of Nations. Would joining the League
commit the American people to a course of action contrary to the national
interest? Wilson pointed out that the United States would become a
permanent member of the council, the council was "the source of every
active policy of the league," and adoption of any proposal by the council
required unanimous vote. It was clear enough, therefore, that "the League
of Nations can adopt no policy whatever without the consent of the
United States." Would joining the league mean repudiation of the Monroe Doctrine? The Covenant itself made specific mention of the Monroe
Doctrine as one of the regional understandings with which the league
would not interfere. Would joining the league make the United States an
appendage of the British Empire? True, the four British Dominions
(Australia, Canada, New Zealand, and South Africa) held, along with
India, separate membership in the league assembly. But no assembly vote
would count unless the council concurred, "so that there is no validity to
any vote of the assembly unless in that vote also the representative of the
United States concurs." In sum, the choice came down to accepting the

treaty or going it alone in world affairs. "It is either this treaty or a lone hand, and the lone hand must have a weapon in it."

In using the figure, imperfect as it was, Wilson might have thought about his own lonely fight for the treaty. His weapon was his persuasive rhetoric, but neither the president nor his rhetoric was equal to the task. On September 25 he delivered a long and physically taxing speech at Pueblo, Colorado. Early the next morning his left side was paralyzed, and he had difficulty in articulating. His physician canceled the remainder of the tour, and the presidential train returned to Washington. A week later Wilson suffered a massive stroke. His hemiplegia became permanent; his left arm remained powerless, and loss of vision in the left eye made reading a difficult chore. The strong-willed chief executive had become a helpless invalid, isolated in the White House from almost all contact with the outside world.

The drama on Capitol Hill, in the meantime, was approaching its denouement. On November 6 Lodge reported out of committee advising a resolution of advice and consent to ratification of the treaty subject to fourteen reservations. The second, dealing with Article X, Wilson had denounced as tantamount to "a rejection of the covenant." Under the terms of that reservation, the United States would assume "no obligation to preserve the territorial integrity or political independence of any other country or to interfere in controversies between nations" according to the provisions of Article X. The other reservations—concerning such matters as the Monroe Doctrine and the Shantung settlement—were, the president had been at some pains to show, gratuitous. Since they did seem unnecessary, supporters of the treaty continued to believe compromise possible. But when Nebraska's Gilbert M. Hitchcock, the Democratic leader in the Senate and a member of the Foreign Relations Committee, called at the White House to urge accommodation, he met a cold rebuff. Glaring at Hitchcock, the president rose slowly from his sickbed and delivered a sepulchral ultimatum: "Let Lodge compromise!" Then, when Wilson urged "all true friends of the treaty" to withhold support from the Lodge reservations, the issue was no longer in doubt, for ratification, of course, required a two-thirds vote.

On November 19, 1919, all but four Democrats joined the irreconcilables to defeat the amended treaty, thirty-nine senators voting for and fifty-five against ratification. A resolution to approve the treaty without reservations went down 38 to 53. In March 1920 a third and final vote showed that several Democratic senators preferred an amended treaty to none at all. They defied the president, but still fell seven votes short of the necessary two-thirds. By that time public interest in the League of Nations had declined. Americans were turning their attention to the problems of living in a world that was—as they would discover—far different from the world of 1914.

# PART THREE

A Time of Prosperity
and Depression

# 6

## The New Era of
## the Nineteen Twenties

The postwar decade was one in which the American people came to grips with far-reaching changes in technology, the organization of their institutions, and the environment in which they lived.  Those changes did not occur only in the twenties, for many of them had been developing gradually over the previous century; but the Great War seemed to bring several disparate developments to a point of convergence in time.  By 1920, for example, the automobile had become a feasible means of transportation for a great many families; motorcars shaped patterns of urban growth as well as relationships within the families that owned them. Specific stars in the constellation of the twenties might not be new; but the constellation was new, and old horoscopes provided unreliable guides to conduct.

A period of rapid change can be an exciting time in which to live, and the twenties were certainly exciting.  Making adjustments to new conditions inevitably creates tensions and uncertainties, but the challenge of new problems provides opportunities for purposeful action.  Because the postwar decade was one of unparalleled prosperity, many Americans believed that they were living in an emerging utopia where all problems would be overcome.  They were sadly mistaken.  Looking backward, one is tempted to see in the twenties a demonstration of a classical theme: good fortune gives rise to hubris; hubris leads to disaster.  But in this case the classical theme is only partially true, and it can easily distort judgment of the period.  After all, other Americans were less certain that prosperity assured happy resolution of conflict, elimination of social injustice, and the good life for everyone.  And the depression that followed the stock market crash of 1929 was no respecter of opinion.  Booster and critic alike suffered from its effects.  In the meantime, however, technology continued to evolve, institutions continued to adapt, and the environment continued to be transformed.  In many ways, the twenties marked the beginning of modern America.

**The Methods of a
New Technology**

The demands of World War I had the effect of accelerating changes in the organization, methods, and scope of technological activity in the United States. During the nineteenth century the inventors whose cleverness contributed to the building of a vast industrial structure were, for the most part, craftsmen and artisans rather than scientists. Although they borrowed ideas from one another, they usually worked individually and never in research teams. Their methods were empirical as well as individualistic; while they developed remarkable understanding of scientific principles, their achievements were more the result of practical common sense and experimentation than a consequence of theoretical training in the sciences. Men such as Thomas A. Edison, Henry Ford, and the Wright brothers carried the momentum of technical progress into the twentieth century, but none of the four had ever gone to college.

One reason for the practical rather than theoretical emphasis in nineteenth-century technology is that only a small minority of young people received college degrees. Another is that colleges and universities stressed the liberal arts and provided a better education in Greek and Latin than in the sciences. Scientific training therefore came with apprenticeship or work experience, and, of course, it was applied in commonsense solutions to practical problems. Yet nineteenth-century Americans did not scorn the sciences entirely. Even before the Civil War, the demands for education in technical fields had brought about the establishment of several schools that offered courses in science and technology. In 1835 Rensselaer Polytechnic Institute began conferring degrees in engineering; by the time Abraham Lincoln became president, students with scientific proclivities could pursue their interests at Harvard, Yale, the University of Michigan, or the Polytechnic Institute of Brooklyn as well as at Rensselaer. In 1862 Congress passed the Morrill Land Grant Act, which set aside public lands for the support of education in "such branches of learning as are related to agriculture and the mechanic arts." A great boon to the state university system, the act led to the founding of many colleges that offered courses in science and technology. By 1901, when the California Institute of Technology admitted its first class, nearly all of today's major technical colleges and universities were in operation.

The spread of scientific and technical education came as a result of new demands and opportunities associated with the developing sophistication of industrial processes. Coping with the greater complexity of industrial plants and products required more thorough training in the sciences, which universities and technological institutes increasingly sought to provide. As progress in industrialization came to depend more on scientifically trained people than it did on mechanics, engineers gained new status as professionals. The developing complexity of industrial processes had other effects, too. New processes required not only broad understanding of scientific principles but also the ability to make specific application of scientific principles. With formal education in the sciences, professional engineers thus became specialists; cultivating their own particular skills, they pursued carefully defined and limited objectives.

Such specialization obviously required planning and coordination. As professional engineers gained access to industrial plants, the research laboratory replaced the craftsman's workbench as the source of technological innovation. It was there that specialists could coordinate their efforts and through cooperative investigation develop a new technology that was to shape the lives of twentieth-century Americans. The industrial research laboratory, with its characteristic pattern of team investigation, was a new phenomenon in 1900. Earlier industrial laboratories had concerned themselves primarily with testing of established processes and products, much like the government's own Bureau of Standards. Now, staffed with scientists and engineers, they began to turn their attention to the development of new processes and products.

The modern research laboratory was not an exclusively American adaptation to industrial needs. Indeed, it evolved from its late nineteenth century origins in the German organic chemical industry, an industry that owed its rapid growth to the application of science to industrial production. The value of team research techniques in making such application was dramatically demonstrated when the laboratory of Adolf von Baeyer developed aspirin, the first purely synthetic drug, in 1899. With the success of aspirin, the German chemical industry went on to construct laboratories that before World War I made Germany the major producer of dyestuffs, pharmaceuticals, explosives, and other organic chemicals. The German government early recognized the industrial importance of scientific research; shortly after the turn of the century it founded the great laboratories of the Kaiser Wilhelm Society (later the Max Planck Society), where teams of scientists made research a cooperative enterprise.

In the United States before 1900 the institution that most nearly resembled such laboratories was Edison's research laboratory in Menlo Park, New Jersey. But while Edison was deeply committed to research, he did not employ the team research with which German chemists achieved their great success. Important as Menlo Park was, therefore, methods of the new technology in the United States did not really originate there. Charles P. Steinmetz, who established the first modern American research laboratory at the research center of the General Electric Company in Schenectady, New York, made a far greater organizational contribution than did Edison. And Steinmetz clearly understood what he was about. The General Electric Research Laboratory, which he organized, became the prototype for all the major industrial and government laboratories of the twentieth century.

Set up to develop new products through cooperative investigation, the research laboratories were a mark of the growing influence exercised by men with formal training in the sciences. At the turn of the century professional engineers also began a new kind of systematic and detailed study of manufacturing processes and procedures. Directing their efforts toward im-

Thomas A. Edison, here photographed in his laboratory, assiduously cultivated a good press in the 1920s, and he received it. "It is the fashion to call this the age of industry," observed Henry Ford. "Rather, we should call it the age of Edison. For he is the founder of modern industry in this country." Associated as he was with the development of electric lighting, phonographs, radios, and motion pictures, the Wizard of Menlo Park enjoyed a secure reputation during the New Era (National Park Service).

provement of plant efficiency, they contributed to what became known as the "scientific management" movement. Discussions of how to measure efficiency and how to increase productivity attracted the attention of manufacturers and the public alike as the movement gathered momentum. The war crisis of 1917–1918 demonstrated the importance of efficiency in industrial operations, and by the decade of the twenties the place of management experts was secure.

The engineer most responsible for stimulating the enthusiasm in scientific management was Frederick W. Taylor, the son of a wealthy Philadelphia lawyer who dabbled in poetry and philanthropies. Unlike his father, the young Taylor was far more interested in the mechanical arts than in either law or literature. Although he took the entrance examination for Harvard and passed it with honors, he could not bring himself to pursue an academic career leading to the study of law. At the age of nineteen, therefore, he became an apprentice pattern maker at the Midvale Steel Company. Working full time, he also attended classes at the Stevens Institute of Technology; within six years he earned a degree in mechanical engineering and became chief engineer at Midvale. Like Theodore Roosevelt, Taylor both preached and practiced the strenuous life. Taking up work as an independent consultant, he interested himself in a wide variety of projects, acquired a reputation and a following, and was elected president of the American Society of Mechanical Engineers.

At the 1895 convention of the ASME, Taylor read a paper entitled, "A

Piece-Rate System, Being a Step toward a Partial Solution of the Labor Problem." The paper described a "differential piece rate," an incentive system of payment that the young engineer thought would increase production and reduce labor costs. It involved setting the shortest possible time for a job. If a worker completed the job within that time, he would be given a high price per piece; if he took longer than the allotted time, his piece rate would be cut drastically. Taylor's rate-fixing proposal initiated a twenty-year investigation into means of improving the efficiency of industrial operations. His basic approach to the problem was that of time study and job analysis. Arguing that the principles of efficiency applying to machines could also be applied to the hands and muscles of workers, he broke a job down into its "elementary operations" and conducted experiments to time each operation by use of a stopwatch. By determining which elements were essential and which were superfluous, and after rearranging the essential elements into time-saving patterns, Taylor hoped to improve the efficiency of workers.

Taylor's ideas and experiments struck a responsive chord. He soon acquired a following among people for whom industrial efficiency represented a means of achieving the good life through maximum productivity. Some of those attracted to Taylorism, most notably Frank and Lillian Gilbreth, proceeded to refine the techniques of job analysis. The Gilbreths used movies as well as stop watches. They also isolated sixteen basic elements of hand motion that they called Therbligs (a phonetic backward spelling of Gilbreth). By adopting more general units than Taylor's elements, they hoped to develop principles applicable to different kinds of work. Taylor himself was less than enthusiastic about such refinements, but the movement that he did so much to launch could not be confined to his disciples. Nor could scientific management be limited to industrial operations alone. In the decade of the twenties, efficiency came to be regarded as a worthy objective in many fields of endeavor.

One reason for extension of the scientific management thrust into the 1920s is that Americans were concerned with adjustment to prewar and wartime technological accomplishments. The postwar decade was one in which the United States began to absorb the more abundant goods and services made possible by technological breakthroughs of the previous century. The major achievements of the thirty years before 1917 cannot be viewed as isolated phenomena with consequences that were limited in time and restricted to the new industries they created. Indeed, their influences proved more far-reaching and profound than even sophisticated contemporary observers suspected they might be. Experiments and discoveries relating to electricity and to the internal combustion engine, especially, brought revolutionary changes in manufacturing processes and transportation. The electric power and automobile industries, which grew out of those experiments and discoveries, had enormous impact not only on the economy but also on the whole of American society. During the postwar

The crowded main street of Bingham, Utah (with its power lines, electric signs, and automobiles) displayed in microcosm the results of technological innovation during the twenties. Although such scenes were characteristic of small towns everywhere in 1927, when this photograph was taken, Bingham was not a typical community. Site of the largest open pit copper mine in the world, it produced a sizable amount of the copper used in electrical wiring (Utah State Historical Society).

decade they generated new products, new demands, new methods of doing business, and new ways of life. The magnitude of their influence justifies an excursion into the nature and significance of their development.

**Electricity and Industrial Growth**

Before 1880, the electrical industry had concerned itself primarily with communication, that is, with development of the telegraph and telephone. But incandescent lighting and the application of electrical power to transportation and manufacturing greatly increased the industry's importance. Edison, famous as the inventor of a practical electric lamp, established the first central power station on New York City's Pearl Street in 1882. Of equal industrial significance were the activities of George Westinghouse. Unlike Edison, who dealt in short-range direct current, Westinghouse built generators and transformers that made possible the transmission of alternating current over great distances. He also secured patent rights to a reliable motor using alternating current.

With the improvement of such motors, manufacturers saw important advantages in their use. They could now obtain the exact power necessary for each machine; they could turn motors on and cut them off as required; they could dispense with a heavy and dangerous clutter of shafting and belts. In short, the dependability of electricity, along with its ease of distribution, freed American manufacturers from reliance on water or steam power. Small wonder that industry's consumption of electrical energy multiplied rapidly. From the turn of the century to the outbreak of war in 1914, the total horsepower of electric motors used in manufacturing increased from half a million to 8.8 million; by the time of the stock-market crash in 1929, it had passed 30 million. In 1899, electric motors supplied only 5 per cent of the total primary factory power, but by 1929 they supplied more than 80 per cent.

Unlike steam power, which required placing engines close to furnaces and boilers for efficient production, electric power could travel hundreds of miles. Manufacturers no longer had to concern themselves with the construction of power plants to run their machines, for they could buy the necessary electrical power from central stations. The extensive development of hydroelectric power, beginning at Niagara Falls in 1895, the increased use of steam turbines after Westinghouse secured American rights to the English invention in 1896, and the perfection of transformers making possible the transmission of electric current over high voltage lines all contributed to the growth of central power stations. And, after the turn of the century, utility companies supplied an increasing proportion of the industrial demands. Of the total power required by manufacturers in 1899, less than 2 per cent was purchased electric power. By 1929, however, more than 50 per cent of the total was purchased electric power.

Because it was almost infinitely divisible as well as transmissible, electric power could be used in the home as readily as in the factory. Electricity did not discriminate against the more limited power needs of home owners, and most of them did not have to be convinced of its advantages. "Let there be light," power companies proclaimed in their advertisements, but in the beginning there was not electric light for everyone. Until development of the tungsten filament, electric lighting was confined to homes of the wealthy; working-class families continued to use kerosene or gas. Tungsten lamps used far less current than did older ones with carbon filaments, however; and, when General Electric began marketing its Mazda lamps, the cost of electric lighting came within range of smaller budgets.

Home uses for electrical power were by no means confined to lighting. With the spread of household electrification came a spectacular increase in production and sales of consumer durables such as mechanical refrigerators, washing machines, flatirons, vacuum cleaners, toasters, ·waffle irons, heating pads and—after World War I—radios. When sociologist William F. Ogburn wrote his chapter on the American family for *Recent Social Trends* (published in 1933), he emphasized the importance that electricity had assumed in American homes. He found that, during the years between 1920 and 1930, the number of domestic users of electricity had increased 135 per cent. The production of electric washing machines

Make entertaining a simple, joyous job

GENERAL ELECTRIC
**Refrigerator**

Because household refrigerators improved food preservation, they helped make possible better, healthier diets. Yet this 1928 advertisement (promising ice cubes for drinks and ease in serving "smart delicacies") emphasized General Electric's contribution to entertainment rather than health. Concentrating on luxury benefits of the refrigerator, its message was directed to a prosperous society that had learned to place a high value on gracious living (General Electric Co.).

per capita had increased 65 per cent; the production of electric irons, 50 per cent; and the production of vacuum cleaners, 20 per cent. Another scholar, Solomon Fabricant, reported in a 1940 study of changes in manufacturing output that increases in the production of radios and mechanical refrigerators were particularly striking. In 1923, radio manufacturers produced 190 thousand receiving sets; by 1929, output had reached nearly 5 million sets, an increase of 2,500 per cent. The rise in production of mechanical refrigerators was nearly as remarkable. From the 5,000 units of 1921, production increased to 900,000 units in 1929.

**The Automobile**

Electrical innovations obviously had great potential for modifying the way people lived; so, too, did improvement of the internal combustion engine. Fabricant found that during the years 1899 to 1937 the increase in manufacture of automobiles far surpassed the growth of industrial ouput in any other product. The production of 1937 represented a whopping 180,100 per cent increase over the production of 1899. American plants turned out less than 1.6 million passenger cars in 1919, but ten years later nearly 4.4 million rolled off the assembly lines. In 1931, when Frederick Lewis Allen surveyed the decade in his witty and perceptive book, *Only Yesterday,* he ventured the suggestion that "the most potent statistic" of the decade was this: "in 1919 there had been 6,771,000 passenger cars in service in the United States; by 1929 there were no less than 23,121,000."

The statistic was indeed potent, and the automobile industry grew rapidly. Like the electrical industries, it had its origins in nineteenth-century experimentation. After development of the internal combustion engine in the 1860s, European inventors such as Gottlieb Daimler and Karl Friedrich Benz led the way in creating practical motorcars. By the 1890s Americans had also entered the field; Charles Duryea built his first car in 1892, and a year later Henry Ford put one together from bicycle wheels, a piece of gas pipe, and other odds and ends.

The gains in automobile productivity were only partially attributable to the intrinsic appeal of the horseless carriage. The first motorcar factories built cars to order from parts manufactured elsewhere and were essentially assembly centers. Then Ford had an idea. He would make a cheap car for the average man rather than a plaything for the rich, and he would use mass-production techniques to lower his prices. The ungainly but serviceable Model T went into production in 1907. Five years later Ford began to experiment with a moving assembly—a system of conveyors and chutes—to

The assembly line at Henry Ford's Highland Park plant, shown here in 1913, demonstrated the benefits of efficiency in production. "I will build a motor car for the great multitude," Ford had announced four years earlier, and by introducing moving for stationary assembly he achieved his objective. Speeding up production cut unit costs, and the retail price of a Model T touring car dropped from $850 in 1908 to $360 in 1916 (Ford Motor Co.).

deliver work to his employees at predetermined speed. Workers along the line, specializing in the tasks they performed, reduced the time required for chassis assembly from 12½ to 1½ hours. By 1920, half the motor vehicles in the world were Model T Fords.

Ford's use of mass-production techniques represented one way to achieve the scale of organization necessary for rising above the competition of small-factory, individualized production. William C. Durant took another approach when he put together the General Motors Company in 1908. A salesman and promoter rather than an engineer, Durant had the wit to see a brilliant future for the automobile industry; he sought to capture that future through consolidation of companies producing automobiles to meet a variety of tastes and needs. Working with the Buick firm as his base, Durant used General Motors stock to acquire control of Oldsmobile, Cadillac, Oakland (later Pontiac), and several ancillary concerns. His limited technical understanding and his propensity for taking risks soon plunged the new company into a morass of difficulties from which it emerged only with the help of a bankers' syndicate headed by James J. Storrow of Lee, Higginson and Company. Bringing Charles W. Nash and Walter P. Chrysler into the top echelons of General Motors, the Storrow regime managed to effect a thorough reorganization.

Durant, in the meantime, had joined forces with Louis Chevrolet to produce a car designed to capture part of the market from Ford's Model T. His considerable success won him valuable support from the Du Pont family. When the bankers' trust expired at General Motors in 1916, Durant returned to power in a Chevrolet; that is, he regained control of the company and made Chevrolet a General Motors automobile. For his part, Nash was distressed by this turn of events. Too cautious and conservative to work well with Durant, he left General Motors, bought the Thomas B. Jeffery Company of Kenosha, Wisconsin, and formed the Nash Motor Car Company. Chrysler, too, eventually quarreled with Durant and departed. In 1925 he organized the Chrysler Corporation and took over the Maxwell firm. Then, three years later, when he added a company originally formed by the Dodge brothers, he immediately joined General Motors and Ford as one of the nation's major producers of automobiles.

Fortunately for General Motors, the firm did not lose the services of Alfred P. Sloan, Jr., who, after some reshuffling of personnel became president in 1923. Moving on the assumption that GM was too large and unwieldy to be controlled by a single person, Sloan introduced the organizational plan that allowed General Motors to more than hold its own against Ford and Chrysler. In accordance with Sloan's ideas, the individual companies that made up General Motors were transformed into operating divisions with independent management. Coordination came through central policy making, planning, research, and sales bodies that made their advice and services available to the operating divisions. General Motors was revitalized as Sloan built a well-coordinated business structure from the bits and pieces of a heterogeneous combination of automotive and other enterprises. It was a structure that survived and prospered. The present General Motors Corporation is essentially that structure.

Sloan's reorganization of General Motors served to emphasize the differences between his company and that of Henry Ford. Ford had approached the goal of consolidation through technical proficiency; he had gained control of a large market by using mass-production techniques to lower the price of his automobile. Yet Ford was no economist. He did not understand that considerations other than price might influence a customer's decision to buy. At the same time that Sloan was infusing General Motors with new vigor, Ford stubbornly insisted on continuing the Model T. When car buyers found that for only a slightly higher price they could have a more colorful and comfortable automobile, Model T sales declined. Ford deferred to popular demand in 1928 when he began production of the Model A, but by that time Sloan's General Motors had overtaken the Ford Motor Company in production and sales.

Thus did the basic pattern of the automobile industry take form in the decade of the twenties. When the nation entered the depression years of the thirties, General Motors and Ford together produced more automobiles than all other car makers combined. Ranking third, but well above the rest of the field, was the Chrysler Corporation. Smaller firms such as Hudson, Nash, Packard, Studebaker, and Willys-Overland managed nicely in the twenties, survived the thirties, and then were absorbed or consolidated after World War II. Some of the famous names of the twenties—the Marmon, the Duesenberg, and the Stutz "Bearcat," for example—disappeared much earlier with the passing of prosperity after 1929. Associated as they are with the twenties, but not later years, such names call to mind the decade when motor vehicles captured first place among American industries in the value of product manufactured.

Significant as its own growth certainly was, the automobile industry also provided a powerful impetus to growth in other sectors of the American economy. The increased demand for automobiles and trucks gave rise to increased demand for petroleum, glass, rubber, steel, and innumerable products derived from such raw materials. The industries most obviously influenced by growth in motor vehicle production and use were petroleum and rubber. Oil production—not all of it, of course, used by motor vehicles—increased from 443 million to more than a billion barrels between 1920 and 1929. Gasoline, which had been considered of little worth before the widespread use of internal combustion engines, replaced kerosene as the petroleum industry's most valuable product. Census Bureau estimates indicate that consumption of motor fuel went from less than 3 billion gallons in 1919 to more than 15 billion gallons in 1929. The expansion of rubber manufacturing also ran parallel to expansion of automobile production. The 1919 output of rubber tires and inner tubes was almost four times the 1914 output, while production in 1929 was more than twice as great as production in 1919.

Of the many consequences of automotive development, none was more

Touring by automobile in its early days seldom meant a carefree lark, as these travelers in Texas had good reason to know. Rutted roads and flat tires were, however, relatively minor inconveniences on a sunny day. In a heavy downpour this road—like other dirt roads across the land—was well-nigh impassable. Small wonder that highway construction became a principal demand of automobile owners! (State Historical Society of Wisconsin).

important than construction of highways capable of carrying motor vehicle traffic. Interest in good roads began to build up in the 1890s, before anyone could be certain that the automobile would ever replace the horse and buggy. Supported by railroads hoping to construct feeders for their lines and by farmers hoping to overcome their isolation, good roads promotion formed an important part of a more general movement for the betterment of rural life. The boom in motor vehicle production, of course, greatly increased demands for improved roads; it also led to new methods of constructing, administering, and financing highways.

The speed and weight of motor vehicles, especially after trucks began to appear, made the old dirt and gravel roads unserviceable. Experimenting with bituminous macadam and Portland cement mixed in rotating kilns, engineers were soon prepared to construct roads that would serve the motor age. Technical capability was not enough in itself, however, for there remained the matter of paying for the new highways. State-supported road-building programs were under way in New York and New Jersey before the turn of the century; and, with needs becoming increasingly obvious, other states followed suit. Such programs sometimes became political issues. Farmers and railroads favored using appropriations for secondary roads leading to market centers, while city dwellers preferred interstate connecting highways. As most motorists saw it, the states needed help.

Federal aid finally came when Congress passed the Highway Act of 1916. Justified on grounds that it would promote general commerce, the act would have far-reaching consequences for the American economy after World War I. By 1930 nearly 200,000 miles of a Federal-aid primary system had been completed.

**The Prosperity of
the Twenties**

Expansion of the automobile industry was an important factor in the economic prosperity associated with the twenties. At the beginning of the decade, however, the nation experienced a recession that was both sharp and severe. During the months following the Peace Conference, as might have been expected after a period of wartime stringency, the demand for capital and consumer goods had been high. Accumulation of liquid assets (government bonds and deposits), combined with a relatively high income level, had helped to make that demand effective. Even more important were national fiscal policies. Continuing to spend more than it collected in taxes, the United States government had also loaned to wartime allies substantial sums that were used largely for the purchase of American goods. The boom brought about by such influences had been characterized by rapid price inflation and a tendency on the part of businessmen to build inventories in anticipation of further price increases. Just as national fiscal policy had fed the boom, a change in that policy brought an economic reaction. From a deficit of nearly $9 billion at the close of 1919, the government moved to a Treasury surplus of $831 million by mid-1920.

In the first six months of 1920, the Federal Reserve Bank of New York raised its rediscount rates. A depression was not long in arriving as credit dried up, prices fell, businessmen liquidated inventories, and industries reduced the manufacturing work force by nearly one-fourth. Happily, the depression was as brief as it was severe. The Federal Reserve Board adhered to its deflationary policies through the summer of 1921, but then in the early fall the New York bank adjusted its rediscount rate. By that time inventories were down, and lower prices reduced speculative excesses. The essentials for long-term economic growth were still at hand, as they had been in 1919; now they could take effect. The automobile industry entered a golden era, the electric power and electric equipment producers could count on increasing demand, and the need for commercial and residential buildings of all kinds brought boom times to the construction industries.

Statistics on income and gross national product, which are summarized in Table 6.1, provide a basis for assessment of the nation's well-being during the years between 1922 and 1929. Recovery from the depression of 1920–1921 was marked by a 5.9 per cent increase in per capita income during 1922; over the next seven years per capita income increased 29.5 per cent despite minor recessions in 1924 and 1927. Among men and women who were gainfully employed, the percentage increase in income was 26.9 in the years from 1922 to 1929.

Students of the twenties, often pointing out the considerable inequities in the distribution of income per capita, have most frequently cited the disparity between farm and nonfarm income. In 1929, for example, the average per capita income of people on farms was only $273 compared with $908 for the nonfarm population. Yet such disparities were not peculiar to the twenties, and comparing increases reveals that per capita farm income rose at a more rapid rate than did nonfarm income. During the years from 1922 to 1929 the farm population registered a 45.6 per cent increase in per capita income, a much greater increase than that enjoyed by the population as a whole.

More important, perhaps, than disparities between farm and nonfarm income was the slower rate of increase in low incomes compared with high incomes. In 1929 the top 5 per cent of income recipients took 26.1 per cent of the national income; this was an increase of 19 per cent in their share of the total since 1923. In other words, the poor did not grow poorer, but the very rich increased their incomes at a more rapid rate than did the rest of the population. Unequal rates of increase could spell difficulties for the nation's economy, but—until 1929 at least—prosperity appeared to be widespread if not universal.

Annual figures for gross national product reinforce the statistics on national income. According to the estimates in Tables 6.1 and 6.2, the most rapid increases occurred in 1921–1923 and in 1928–1929. During the years of the middle twenties there was steady expansion, but the rate of increase was not so marked. GNP, of course, includes several components as indicated in Table 6.2, and inspection of the figures leads to some revealing conclusions about the prosperity of the twenties. More than four-fifths of

TABLE 6.1    Economic Growth, 1919–1929

| Year | National Income (billions of current dollars) | Income in 1929 Dollars per Capita | Income in 1929 Dollars per Gainfully Occupied | Gross National Product[1] (billions of 1929 dollars) |
|---|---|---|---|---|
| 1919 | $64.2 | $543 | $1,380 | $67.8 |
| 1920 | 74.2 | 548 | 1,380 | 68.5 |
| 1921 | 59.4 | 522 | 1,308 | 65.5 |
| 1922 | 60.7 | 553 | 1,388 | 70.4 |
| 1923 | 71.6 | 634 | 1,582 | 80.0 |
| 1924 | 72.1 | 633 | 1,569 | 81.6 |
| 1925 | 76.0 | 644 | 1,592 | 84.3 |
| 1926 | 81.6 | 678 | 1,675 | 89.8 |
| 1927 | 80.1 | 674 | 1,661 | 90.6 |
| 1928 | 81.7 | 676 | 1,665 | 91.9 |
| 1929 | 87.2 | 716 | 1,761 | 98.0 |

Sources: Simon Kuznets, *National Income and Its Composition, 1919–1938* (New York: National Bureau of Economic Research, 1941), pp. 137, 153; Robert A. Gordon, *Business Fluctuations*, 2nd ed. (New York: Harper & Brothers, 1961), p. 402.

[1] Adjusted Kuznets concept, peacetime version.

TABLE 6.2 Gross National Product and Its Chief Components, 1919–1929 (Billions of 1929 Dollars)

| | 1919 | 1920 | 1921 | 1922 | 1923 | 1924 | 1925 | 1926 | 1927 | 1928 | 1929 |
|---|---|---|---|---|---|---|---|---|---|---|---|
| Gross national product | 67.8 | 68.5 | 65.5 | 70.4 | 80.0 | 81.6 | 84.3 | 89.8 | 90.6 | 91.9 | 98.0 |
| Flow to consumers | 49.7 | 51.3 | 54.1 | 56.5 | 61.2 | 65.3 | 64.0 | 68.9 | 70.7 | 72.5 | 76.9 |
| Perishable | 19.9 | 21.0 | 21.8 | 22.6 | 23.5 | 25.3 | 25.1 | 26.3 | 26.8 | 26.7 | 28.0 |
| Semidurable | 7.5 | 6.5 | 7.8 | 8.9 | 9.8 | 9.0 | 10.0 | 10.0 | 11.2 | 11.2 | 11.8 |
| Durable | 5.0 | 4.9 | 4.0 | 5.1 | 6.6 | 6.9 | 7.8 | 8.6 | 8.2 | 8.4 | 8.8 |
| Services | 17.3 | 18.9 | 20.4 | 19.9 | 21.3 | 24.1 | 21.2 | 24.0 | 24.5 | 26.2 | 28.4 |
| Gross capital formation | 18.1 | 17.2 | 11.4 | 13.9 | 18.7 | 16.2 | 20.3 | 20.9 | 19.9 | 19.4 | 21.1 |
| Producers' durables | 5.5 | 5.3 | 3.6 | 4.2 | 5.8 | 5.4 | 6.0 | 6.5 | 6.1 | 6.5 | 7.5 |
| Construction | 6.3 | 5.4 | 6.3 | 8.8 | 9.7 | 10.8 | 12.1 | 12.8 | 12.7 | 12.3 | 11.2 |
| Residential nonfarm | 1.5 | 1.0 | 2.1 | 3.6 | 4.2 | 5.0 | 5.4 | 5.4 | 5.1 | 4.7 | 3.4 |
| Nonresidential | 4.8 | 4.4 | 4.2 | 5.2 | 5.5 | 5.8 | 6.7 | 7.4 | 7.6 | 7.6 | 7.8 |
| Change in inventories | 2.8 | 4.2 | 0.0 | 0.3 | 2.8 | −0.9 | 1.6 | 1.2 | 0.4 | −0.4 | 1.7 |
| Foreign investment | 3.5 | 2.3 | 1.5 | 0.7 | 0.5 | 1.0 | 0.7 | 0.4 | 0.7 | 1.0 | 0.8 |

SOURCE: (After Simon Kuznets, *Supplement to Summary Volume on Capital Formation and Financing*, Pt. A, National Bureau of Economic Research), Table 23 in Robert A. Gordon, *Business Fluctuations*, 2nd ed. (New York: Harper & Brothers, 1961), p. 407.

the increase in GNP between 1919 and 1929 resulted from the flow of goods and services to consumers. The consumer component accounted for 73.3 per cent of the gross national product in 1919, and for 78.5 per cent in 1929. The notable feature in movements of total capital formation in the twenties is the high level reached by 1923 and the maintenance of that level through 1929. During those seven years of heavy investment in producers' durable goods and construction, total capital formation averaged about 19.5 billion dollars in 1929 prices. Inventory accumulation and foreign investments were less important after 1922 than they had been in 1919–1920. Both producers' and consumers' durables contributed more to GNP than they had during any year before World War I.

## Metropolitan Growth in the New Era

Consequences of the new technology—and of the prosperity that accompanied its development—were profound. Although Americans in the twenties may not have been sensitive to all the implications of technological innovation, they were certainly conscious of an extraordinary transformation in their lives. They found novelty on every hand, while the prosperity of the decade encouraged them to equate change with progress. The period after World War I acquired several labels: "The Era of Wonderful Nonsense," "The Jazz Age," "The Roaring Twenties," "The New Era." Most of them suggest both an awareness of change and a positive reaction to it; but, better than the others, the "New Era" designation summed up attitudes of the postwar decade. There were, to be sure, skeptics who doubted the benefits of changes taking place about them. Some people, imbued with the values of an older America, found indications of decadence in a way of life to which they had difficulty in adjusting. Even the most enthusiastic boosters of the New Era had their moments of dissatisfaction and discontent. Yet, whatever the response to them, social changes occurred.

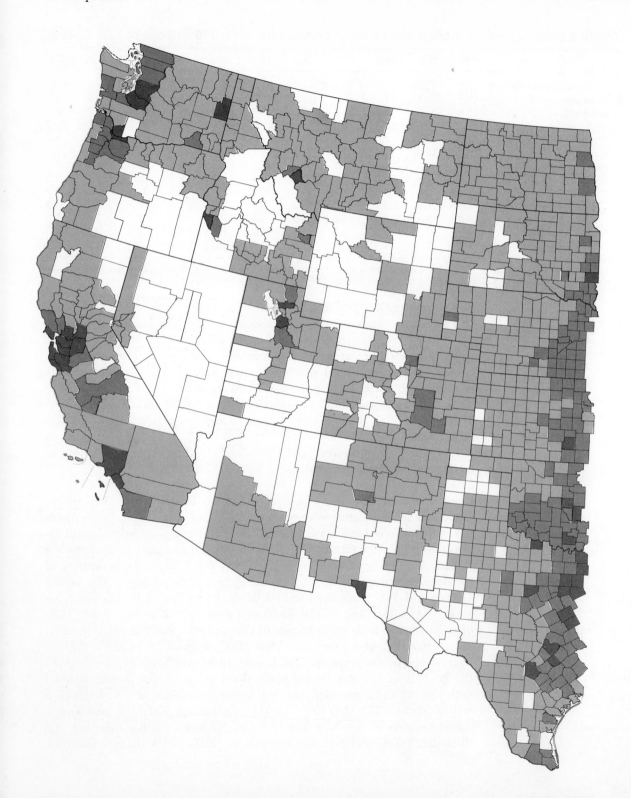

# Density of U.S. Population by Counties, 1920

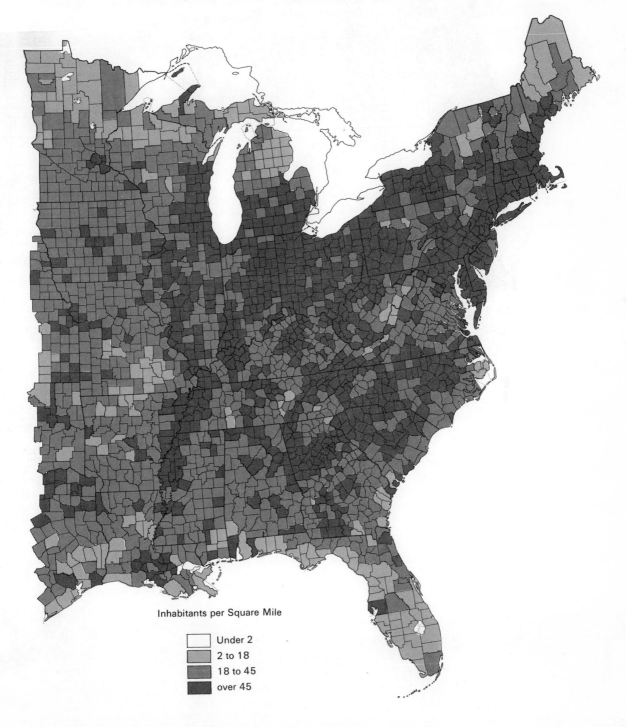

Inhabitants per Square Mile

- Under 2
- 2 to 18
- 18 to 45
- over 45

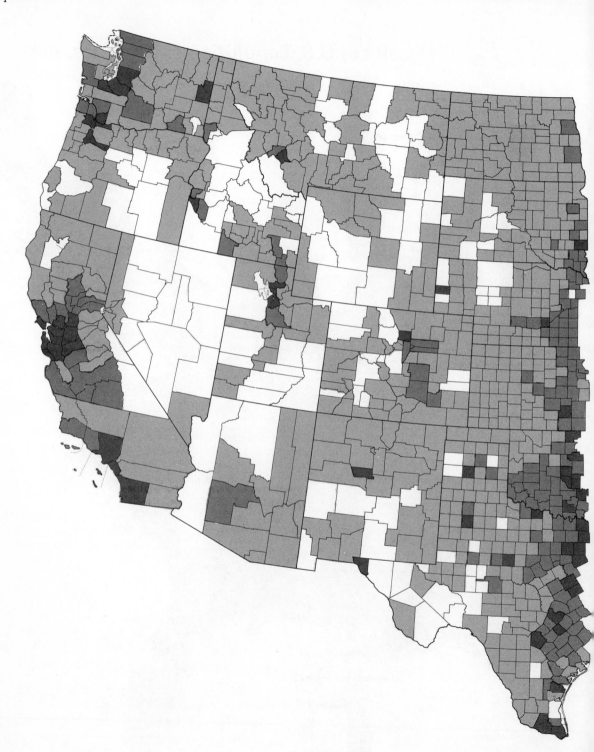

# Density of U.S. Population by Counties, 1940

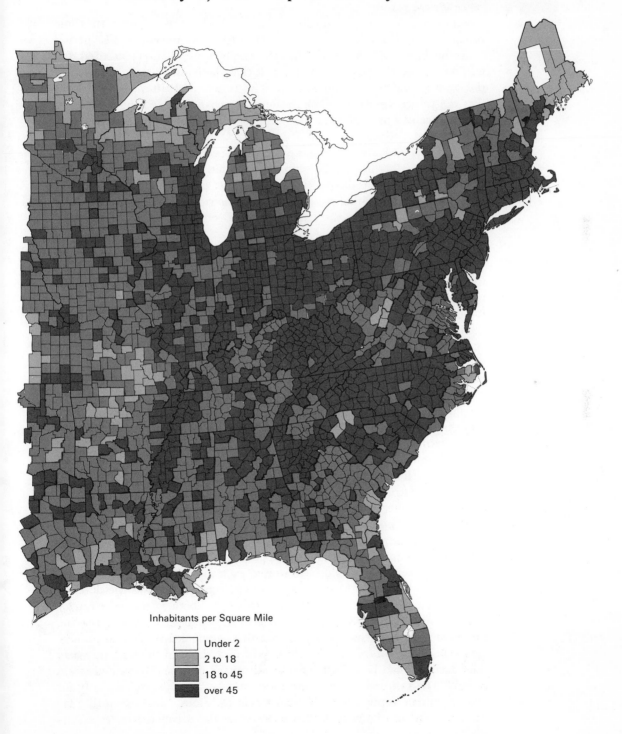

Inhabitants per Square Mile

Under 2
2 to 18
18 to 45
over 45

And the patterns of life that took shape in the twenties had great significance for the future.

Among the most important influences on the postwar decade were those revealed in the census returns from 1900 to 1920. By the end of that period —the beginning of the New Era—the nation's population exceeded 100 million. A familiar generalization has it that the United States was born in the country and moved to the city. The census of 1910, making it clear that the future direction of the nation was urban, justified the generalization; the census of 1920, showing more than half the population living in urban places, validated it.

As the United States entered the twentieth century, the typical American city under 100,000 in population was still relatively compact and self-contained. Most of its residents lived as close as possible to their places of work and business, either walking to work or riding on municipal public conveyances. Ever since the late nineteenth century, however, larger and older cities had been growing over broad areas. It was in such cities (primarily those that had attained metropolitan size of 50,000 or more prior to 1870) that a pattern of population deconcentration was most conspicuous from the 1890s on through the 1920s. In other words, the rate of population growth declined in the central city, while the rate of growth increased rapidly in the fringe areas that encircled the city. The contrasting growth rates suggest a combination of migration trends: residents of the central cities tended to move out to adjacent ring areas, while migrants from outside the region tended to settle in the outskirts of cities rather than in the metropolitan nucleus.

Urban sociologist Leo F. Schnore has discerned two fundamental reasons for the growth characteristics of metropolitan areas in the twentieth century. In the first place, the coming of international tensions and world war in the second decade greatly reduced migrations from abroad. The war therefore tended to slow down the overall growth of American cities, for it was to the cities that a majority of immigrants had come. And after passage of the restrictive legislation that established quotas for immigrants in the twenties, international migration never reached its prewar level. Had southern blacks not begun to move northward—had they not left the peonage and sharecropping of southern agriculture to take up a new life in what they thought was a land of opportunity in the urban North—the growth of inner cities would have slowed even more.

The second influence that shaped metropolitan growth was the development of new means of transportation. Railroads (both steam and electric) had, of course, already shaped the patterns of urban settlement. Spreading out from large cities in radial patterns, they channeled traffic and population into the urban center. Freight moved in and out of the nucleus where most factories had been built to take advantage of centrally located steam power. The railroad system encouraged suburban residence, but only for those fortunate enough to build homes near rail lines. Most towns that lay beyond a radius of ten or fifteen miles from the urban center, especially those that had no rail connections to the central city, maintained an independent existence.

The increased use of motor vehicles brought about spatial changes in the settlement and activities of metropolitan areas. Manufacturers and distributors, who had employed motor trucks to meet local hauling needs within cities, first began using them extensively in interurban transport during World War I. And with subsequent construction of an elaborate system of hard-surfaced roads, the urban economy began to exhibit a tendency toward decentralization. Several considerations—zoning regulations, topography, space requirements for particular enterprises, previous plant investment, availability of utilities or fire and police protection—influenced decisions on the location of manufacturing facilities. Whatever the prevailing considerations in individual cases, development of highways and motor trucks provided some industries with an opportunity to locate plants and factories in peripheral areas where land prices were lower than in the city itself.

The network of roads in metropolitan regions facilitated the movement of people as well as of the transportation of goods. Widespread ownership of passenger cars, bringing a new mobility to the labor force, greatly increased the number of residential alternatives for many people. The fringe areas proved as attractive to home buyers as they often were to manufacturers; builders began new construction on the periphery of both large and middle-sized cities. When residential population reached sufficient density, particularly at intersections of the expanding highway network, entrepreneurs moved in to provide suburbanites with the services and retail goods that were available in the city.

Urban subcenters thus experienced significant transformation. The increased ease of travel and transportation did not, however, increase the independence that had characterized urban subcenters in the railroad era. Indeed, the metropolis dominated them as never before. The purveyors of luxury goods and of infrequently needed services gravitated to the central city in order to secure access to a larger potential metropolitan market. At the same time, mass distribution techniques gave rise to chains of retail outlets, particularly for foods and convenience goods. Chain stores, operating under single ownership and directed from centrally located offices, offered merchandise at competitive prices because they were able to take advantage of economies resulting from standardization and mass buying. But the very techniques that assured success for the chains left the residents of suburban areas with little direct influence in determining what items would be offered for sale. They became, in other words, part of a larger metropolitan market.

**Mass Media and
Mass Culture**
Changes in communication that accompanied changes in transportation during the twenties also tended to reduce the independence of urban subcenters—and of rural villages too, for that matter. The telephone permitted instantaneous contact with a broad area, but even more important

was the radio. Historians of mass communications generally agree that commercial broadcasting began on the night of November 2, 1920, when Pittsburgh station KDKA reported the presidential election returns. By 1922, more than five hundred stations were sending out broadcasts to some three million homes. In the early days of radio, programs had no advertising sponsorship. Stations were operated mainly by radio equipment companies with a view toward profits to be made from the sale of sets. But in 1922 the American Telephone and Telegraph Company, which owned station WEAF in New York, initiated a policy of selling time on the air to commercial enterprises with other products for the public to buy. Radio advertising became common and provided subsidies that assured the expansion of broadcasting. Organization of the National Broadcasting Company in 1926, along with formation of the Columbia Broadcasting System a year later, guaranteed enormous network audiences. With rates as high as $5,000 an hour for network programs, revenues from radio advertising came to an estimated $7 million in 1927. By means of the air waves, then,

This sound effects man at station WMAQ in Chicago ingeniously manipulated a variety of devices to increase the verisimilitude of radio programs in the twenties. Radio was, as Robert and Helen Lynd observed, a stimulus to the imagination that enabled listeners to "call the life of the rest of the world from the air." But stimulating the imagination of listeners could also present a challenge to the imagination of the sound effects man (Chicago Historical Society).

the Clicquot Club Eskimos, the Ipana Troubadours, or the A & P Gypsies became figures of national reputation.

Such developments helped to usher in an era of mass culture. Radio diffused urban attitudes and urban tastes far beyond the limits of metropolitan areas. Residents of all but the most isolated agricultural regions were assured by popular vocalists that Chicago was indeed a wonderful town, that Manhattan was worthy of a serenade, or that exotic events transpired down yonder in New Orleans. With a triphammer intensity that reinforced a sense of immediacy, newscasters such as Floyd Gibbons described world happenings in regular daily programs. And when stations gave live coverage to political conventions or sporting events, the imagination of listeners could transform an ordinary living room into a convention hall or a stadium.

Completing the field work for *Middletown,* their intensive study of Muncie, Indiana, in 1925, sociologists Robert and Helen Lynd described radio as a new tool that was "rolling back the horizons of Middletown for the bank clerk or the mechanic sitting at home and listening to a Philharmonic concert or a sermon by Dr. [Harry Emerson] Fosdick, or to President Coolidge bidding his father good night on the eve of election." Once popular interest in the gadgetry of broadcasting had been satisfied, radio tended to concentrate on the mundane with daytime serials that traded in the dilemmas of everyday life. Yet, in spite of all the soap operas that became common fare in the depression thirties, radio continued to expand the horizons of Middletown.

In the meantime a slightly older medium, the motion picture, also served interests and needs of the New Era. Various experiments with photographic equipment in the nineteenth century had looked toward creating an illusion of movement, but once again Thomas Edison's genius succeeded in perfecting the work of others. In 1888 the Wizard of Menlo Park and his assistants constructed a cylinder that revolved to make figures "move" for the person squinting at them through a peephole. The next year, he bought fifty feet of a new cellulose nitrate film developed by George Eastman. The film could be fed first into a camera taking pictures in rapid succession, and then into a viewing machine. William Dickson, an assistant in Edison's laboratory, devised the necessary technique and had himself filmed. In a private demonstration during the fall of 1889 he appeared on a screen to greet Edison and express hope that he would be satisfied with the "kinetophonograph." The first movie was also a talkie, but Edison seemed less than satisfied. As his phonograph business was a lucrative one, he decided against continuing the combination of sight and sound for fear of phasing out the phonograph. The movies would remain silent until 1927. Yet with the first public film showing at a Broadway penny arcade in 1894, the motion picture industry began its spectacular rise.

By 1907 some five thousand nickelodeons had opened to run one-reel films for packed houses. After a series of patent squabbles, Adolph Zukor and others began to produce feature films. At the same time, movie makers

With his unusual ability to discern what the movie-going public wanted to see, Cecil B. De Mille turned out a series of films that celebrated a new morality in the post-World War I years. In 1921, appropriately garbed in the style affected by Hollywood directors, he worked on *Fool's Paradise* with Karl Struss and Alvin Wyckoff at the cameras. "Undressing was not just the taking off of clothes," wrote his brother in describing such films; "it was a progressive revelation of entrancing beauty; a study in diminishing draperies" (Wisconsin Center for Theatre Research).

In 1919, film stars Mary Pickford, Douglas Fairbanks, and Charles Chaplin joined D. W. Griffith in forming the United Artists studio. An aerial photograph of its lot at the end of the New Era indicates that the venture was a success. Yet even in its early days United Artists could afford to engage William Gibbs McAdoo (Woodrow Wilson's secretary of the treasury) at $100,000 a year (Wisconsin Center for Theatre Research).

organized the companies that were to grow, combine, compete, and dominate the industry for years: Paramount Pictures, Metro Pictures, the Goldwyn Company, the Fox Company, the Universal Company, and United Artists. Others, most notably Warner Brothers, RKO, and Columbia, would form and come into their own during the twenties. The Strand Theatre, the first large theatre devoted to cinema, opened on Broadway in 1914; a year later D. W. Griffith made *Birth of a Nation,* the first major American production. The motion picture was on the threshold of its golden age.

Not all Americans greeted the age with enthusiasm. From the very beginning many of them found the films morally deficient and sadly lacking in either aesthetic or intellectual interest. Then, too, during the first few years after the war, Hollywood produced scandals enough to make comparisons with Babylon seem justified. Moral outrage might well have resulted in government censorship of films had movie makers not shrewdly adopted a policy of self-regulation. They organized the Motion Picture Producers and Distributors of America, appointing Will Hays, who left his office as Postmaster General in the Harding administration, to direct its operations. Whether the Hays Office, as it came to be called, actually did more to improve taste or to institutionalize banality is open to question. There can be little doubt, however, that the moralists were correct in assuming an association between the content of films and the direction of social trends; where they erred was in advancing a simple cause-and-effect relationship that implied the decay of American civilization.

Motion pictures did, in fact, come to serve many of the same functions that myths have served in all societies. Myths give meaning to life's complexities; they provide a plausible frame of reference, a construct by which individual persons can comprehend what might otherwise be meaningless and confusing. So it was with the cinema in the New Era after World War I, when technological innovations brought about puzzling changes in the ways people lived and when old codes of conduct seemed irrelevant to new conditions of life. The films did not offer patterns of behavior to be slavishly emulated, but they did convey some vivid suggestions about the modernity that Americans were trying to understand.

The motion pictures produced in the twenties are easy to classify because most of them fall into well-defined categories. To describe a movie as a western, for example, tells a student of the period a great deal about the film's plot, its characters, and its message. Moviegoers of the New Era, like their ancestors who had listened to the myths spun by bards and storytellers, cared little for surprises that upset their view of a world in which they were attempting to find an identity for themselves.

A practical reason for the development of formula pictures was the investment in film companies by men who were more interested in profits than in art. The ubiquitous William C. Durant became a director of Loew's, as did Harvey Gibson, president of the Liberty National Bank.

Kuhn, Loeb and Company had already invested in Famous Players, an important prewar company; and in the postwar period Samuel Goldwyn received financial backing from the Du Ponts and the Chase National Bank. Loew, Pathé, Fox, Universal, and Metro-Goldwyn (after merger in the midtwenties) all listed stock on the New York Exchange. Of course, movie makers wanted to produce pictures that would attract large audiences, and one way to get them was to imitate a box-office success with films that developed similar themes.

The quickening business interest in film making influenced content in other ways too. Businessmen, along with other Americans, shared Woodrow Wilson's antipathy to revolutionary ferment. In the years immediately after the war, labor unrest and a series of mysterious bombings fed the fear of Bolshevism engendered during the war years. With a "Red Scare" sweeping the country, suspected radicals and agitators were apprehended; eventually more than six hundred aliens were deported. Following Warren Harding's election in 1920 the hysteria abated, and by the time he entered the White House the scare was all but over. Nevertheless the New Era was never very kind to radicals, and the cinema never placed them in a favorable light.

Several films in 1919—*The Right to Happiness* and *Bolshevism on Trial* were typical—made an explicitly anticommunist statement. Far more subtle, whether intentionally so or not, were the movies produced after the Red Scare had passed. Unlike prewar films, which had provided cheap entertainment in the tradition of nineteenth-century melodrama, those of the twenties made their strongest appeal to an upwardly mobile class. As critic David Robinson has put it, they portrayed a "leisured class, with lovely homes and lovely clothes and lovely cars and lovely lives." They seemed to urge consumption, luxury, and frenetic amusement as desirable norms; they offered a hard-boiled but insouciant materialism as an alternative to anxious brooding about the class struggle. In a period when prosperity was very real for many people, the films depicted a way of life that might be possible for any American were he lucky enough.

The familiar images of the New Era—silk stockings and short skirts, cocktail parties and country clubs, roadsters and raccoon coats—appeared with opulent profusion in movies such as *Brown of Harvard, Gimme, A Slave of Fashion, The Miracle of Money,* and *Money, Money, Money.* Affluence, or the appearance of it, seemed highly desirable in the twenties; many films implied that it was worth any price. Thus the "kept" woman, once regarded as shameful, emerged as an attractive character in films titled *Rouged Lips, Pretty Ladies, Lilies of the Field, The Joy Girl, A Woman of Affairs,* and the like.

Such films lent credibility to the charge that the motion-picture industry was obsessed with sex. And it is true that even after establishment of the Hays Office the flapper wriggled and fluttered her way through hundreds of pictures. *Male and Female, It, Adam's Rib, Our Dancing Daughters, Flaming Youth, Manhandled, Kiss Me Again,* and *Darling of the Rich* were char-

A typical film of the sort that led to establishment of the Hays Office was *Pleasure Mad,* a Louis B. Mayer production released in 1923. According to an advertising poster, " 'Tis no longer the wandering boy—but the PLEASURE MAD GIRL—who tears at the heart strings of a mother!" (Wisconsin Center for Theatre Research).

acteristic of the genre. Yet it is easy to misconstrue the meaning of these films about flappers, just as it is easy to misunderstand the flapper herself. The technology that shaped American life in the twenties probably had a more disruptive effect on women than it did on men. Refrigerators, washing machines, vacuum cleaners, and a host of other products greatly modified the way households functioned and the way families were organized. Compared with their Victorian mothers, women seemed to have been liberated; but the sweeping changes that came in the postwar period were also traumatic ones. While many people believed that Victorian standards of behavior were obsolescent, appropriate norms for the New Era were not so obvious. Insofar as the films explored alternative norms, they allowed moviegoers to experiment in fantasy with new roles and attitudes appropriate to changes in real life.

**Family Functions
and the Tensions
of the Twenties**

To view motion pictures as historical documents of the New Era is to become aware of complexities in the social behavior of Americans during the postwar decade. Without changing fundamental human needs, technological innovation created a synthetic environment for institutions that had traditionally met such needs. As the new environment changed the way that social institutions functioned, out of necessity people began to change the way they lived. Those who adapted gracefully to shifting modes of behavior had little difficulty in satisfying their basic needs. For others, adjustment was more difficult, their problems contributing to the tensions that gave the New Era some of its frenetic character.

Of all social institutions the family was the one most profoundly affected by technological changes that converged in the twenties. When sociologist William F. Ogburn wrote his analysis of the American family for the 1933 anthology, *Recent Social Trends,* he reached two significant conclusions. On the one hand, he found that the economic, educational, and recreational functions of the family had decreased greatly since colonial times; on the other, he saw the personality functions of the family as relatively more important than they had once been.

Producing most of what they consumed, many early American families had operated largely as independent economic organizations. Selecting a mate then involved choosing a business partner as well as a companion, while children were regarded as productive agents. Training in agricultural and domestic skills was an important part of child rearing in a predominantly rural setting; children were, in effect, laborers in the family enterprise. Although the work to be performed imposed limits on family activities, opportunities for religious expression and recreation were not totally ignored. The creeds of churches may have seemed less important than the socialization that accompanied religious observance, but a point of emphasis in all churches was that children should honor their parents and that parents should faithfully keep their marriage vows. The most favored forms of recreation—reading aloud, singing, parlor games, taffy pulls, picnics, spelling bees, and the like—usually took place in or near the home and included a limited number of participants.

Even after the expansion of manufacturing had provided an impetus to the growth of cities and after the expansion of transportation facilities had encouraged the growth of trade, the family remained a basic institution of American society. Gradually, however, factories and other enterprises began to take over productive operations that had centered in the home. Fewer and fewer housewives continued to bake their own bread or can their own fruits and vegetables. Public schools assumed a larger share of the responsibility for educating and training children, and the average number of years spent in school rose steadily: in 1900 there were 630,048 pupils in secondary schools, but by 1930 there were 4,740,580. As the nation entered the twentieth century, increasing numbers of people associated recreation with theaters, ball parks, circus and Chautauqua grounds, and, in some localities, dance halls. Ogburn was clearly justified in arguing that by the decade of the twenties the American family no longer functioned, except in a limited way, as an economic, educational, or recreational institution.

Changes in function brought changes in family structure. There was, for example, good reason for the gradual reduction in family size that had worried some observers of demographic trends since the turn of the century. During the New Era children imposed an economic burden for a longer time—and could be considered an economic asset for a shorter time—than had ever been the case with their parents or grandparents. Changes in function also brought changes in family responsibilities. Although many occupations disappeared from the home while electrical appliances and other conveniences were making household chores less onerous, Hildegarde Kneeland of the U.S. Bureau of Home Economics found that the average married woman in the postwar decade still spent more than sixty hours a week on her housework. The technology of the New Era was generally supposed to have had a liberating influence—and it did indeed open up new possibilities for the employment of women—but it also tended to deprive housewives of the productive work essential for achievement of personal identity. Even though they, too, worked long hours at domestic chores, married women without jobs outside the home found themselves contributing less to family support than had the wives and mothers of an earlier day.

A subtle transition in domestic relationships had taken place. Ogburn suggested that the American family of the twenties was regarded "less as an economic institution than as an organization for rearing children and providing happiness." How well did families of the New Era carry out personality functions without the cohesion that resulted from performance of economic, recreational, and other institutional functions? The answer to such questions is elusive, for measuring happiness in any period poses nearly insurmountable difficulties for historians. Considerable evidence exists, however, and it suggests—perhaps surprisingly—that wife-husband relationships were relatively pleasant in the twenties. Contemporary polls indicate that more than 70 per cent of the couples questioned thought of their marriages as happy ones. Polling techniques, of course, were not very sophisticated, and the results are ambiguous. Yet divorce rates tend to corroborate the findings of pollsters. It is true that from 1880 to 1930 the number of divorces increased at an average rate of about 3 per cent per year, but in the postwar decade alone the rate of increase was only about 1.5 per cent annually.

When tensions entered the home, they were more likely to appear in relationships between parents and children than between husband and wife. Some of the reasons for increasing tensions between parents and children can be attributed to changes occurring in education during the twenties. From 1900 to 1930 the nation's population increased 62 per cent, but the number of students enrolled in secondary schools rose by more than 652 per cent and the number in colleges by 314 per cent. The generation that grew up in the twenties obviously spent more years in school or college than did the parental generation. As schools and colleges faced the task of educating growing numbers of students, curricula were broadened to satisfy demands that had earlier been met by families. In 1890, when the United States

Bureau of Education began to collect secondary school statistics, it classified the courses offered in public high schools under nine headings: Latin, French, German, Greek, algebra, geometry, physics, chemistry, and history. By 1930 schools had added courses in the biological sciences and in such subjects as government, economics, art, music, home economics, bookkeeping, shorthand, and typing. Enrollments in the classical curriculum declined, while those in the new more vocational offerings mounted. Concurrently, increasing numbers of students engaged in expanded extracurricular activities: team sports, the programs of school music organizations, and the projects of school-sponsored clubs. Whether or not the new content of education represented an improvement in quality, the trend was one that encouraged young people to take behavioral cues from their peers rather than from their parents.

If fiction of the Jazz Age, most notably the novels and stories of F. Scott Fitzgerald, accurately reflects a prevailing mood, the twenties were surely

The balloons of this movie poster traced a flapper's progress from her first cigarette to her achievements as "an accomplished necker." The Lynds believed that young Middletown shared her experiences vicariously (and sometimes, perhaps, actually) "under the spell of the powerful conditioning medium of pictures presented with music and all possible heightening of the emotional content, and the added factor of sharing this experience with a 'date' in a darkened room" (Wisconsin Center for Theatre Research).

a period in which young Americans set the standards of taste and style. Young writers, many of them veterans of the Great War, portrayed a glittering but disillusioned society in which cynicism replaced idealism and madcap escapades mocked the pursuit of happiness. The flapper became a symbol of youth in such a society. Parents had always allowed less freedom to daughters than to sons; but now daughters shared in educational and recreational activities outside the home. The flapper cut loose from restrictions and, in the way she dressed, emphasized her freedom and her power. Largely through her influence the sweeping gowns and matronly silhouettes of the prewar era went out of style. A modish young woman of the twenties was likely to bob her hair, shorten her hemline, roll her silk stockings, clap a cloche on her head, and go out (sans corset or other foundation garment) to dance in fascinating rhythm. And, trying to emulate Zelda Fitzgerald, she was capable of risqué remarks ("My hips are going wild; you don't mind, do you?") to her partner on the dance floor.

The flapper represented youthful rejection of a morality that modern technology had made anachronistic and that war-engendered cynicism had made absurd. How far the revolt extended may be inferred from the findings of Lewis Terman and Alfred Kinsey, who in the thirties and forties conducted elaborate surveys of sexual behavior. The results of both investigations indicate significant differences between women born before 1900 and women born in the first decade of the twentieth century. In 1938 Terman reported that of the females born between 1890 and 1899, 74 per cent had had no premarital intercourse; among those born between 1900 and 1909, however, the percentage of virgin brides had declined to 51.2. Kinsey's statistics, published in 1953, corroborated the results that Terman had obtained fifteen years earlier. Kinsey found that 73.4 per cent of the married women born before 1900 had been virgin brides, while only 48.7 per cent of those born in the 1900–1909 decade had had no premarital coitus. The data reinforce the impression that a major change in sexual practice occurred during World War I and the decade following, after the girls born between 1900 and 1909 became women.

Critics of youthful behavior, while not having statistics at hand, did have their suspicions, and they made no secret of their disapproval. Dr. Francis E. Clark, president of the Christian Endeavor Society, condemned new dance styles as "an offense against womanly purity, the very fountainhead of our family and civil life." Wilfred O. Cross informed readers of the *Literary Digest* that co-eds were corrupting the morals of college men. Conditions were such, he warned, "that even St. Anthony might renounce his hermitage for the flesh-pots of the campus." Such caveats, if parents read them, only told some of them what they already knew. "It's the girls' clothing," was the comment of one Middletown mother; "we can't keep our boys decent when girls dress that way." A Middletown father was similarly troubled. His attempt to discourage his daughter from going out with a fledgling sport for a night of joy riding in a snappy car met with an angry retort: "What on earth *do* you want me to do? Just sit around home all evening!" Home fires might be kept burning, but young people of the New Era often found other flames more compelling.

**Critics of the
New Era**

The actions of young people were in themselves a commentary on traditional American society, but they did not constitute an explicit criticism comparable to that running through the pages of journals such as *The American Mercury, The Liberator,* or *The New Masses.* Attacking the assumptions of society was left to writers such as those represented in a remarkable symposium, edited by Harold Stearns, published in 1922 under the title *Civilization in the United States.* The essays of the Stearns volume constitute a sweeping indictment of American culture and institutions: a condemnation of the barrenness and intellectual sterility of American society. The book was, in the phrase of Frederick J. Hoffman, a "document of disaffection" that brought a response from people who wanted more out of life than automobiles and refrigerators.

Through essay after essay the details of the indictment mounted. Lewis Mumford deplored the undisciplined growth of metropolitan areas; the modern city, he thought, stood as a monument to material success and spiritual failure. John Macy was horrified by the public's uncritical acceptance of what it read in newspapers that had been corrupted by advertisers. The nation's universities, thought Robert Morss Lovett, had encouraged students to become specialists in the obvious. Garet Garrett saw businessmen as moral eunuchs, for American economic processes encouraged "man's acquisitive instinct acting outside of humanistic motives." In Alfred Booth Kuttner's analysis, the deplorable state of the American family was in part attributable to the typical husband's having been overcome by mother worship; he "becomes everything in his business and nothing in his home, with an ultimate neurotic breakdown or a belated plunge into promiscuity."

Scores of commentators in the twenties completed the sketches of American life outlined in Stearns's book. Perhaps because of their close association with New Era prosperity, middle-class businessmen in particular came in for their share of abuse. The businessman, noted Stuart Chase, had become "the dictator of our destinies," and "the final authority on the conduct of American society." He had, thought the author, ousted "the statesman, the priest, the philosopher, as the creator of standards of ethics and behavior." It was a minor-league businessman that Sinclair Lewis sought to portray when he wrote *Babbitt,* a novel that for all its structural weakness effectively lampooned the platitudes of booster rhetoric. Seldom reluctant to declare his opinions, realtor George F. Babbitt extravagantly admires "the Solid American Citizen" who "makes the wheels of progress go round!" He pictures his ideal American as being "busier than a bird-dog, not wasting a lot of good time in day-dreaming or going to sassiety teas." It is such men ("with hair on their chests and smiles in their eyes and adding machines in their offices") who support art and literature that have "zip" and "pep." They have little use for the creative efforts of "a lot of shabby bums living in attics and feeding on booze and spaghetti." After all, "the ideal of American manhood and culture isn't a lot of cranks sitting around chewing the rag about their Rights and Wrongs, but a God-fearing, hustling, successful, two-fisted Regular Guy . . . whose answer to his critics is a square toed boot that'll teach the grouches and smart alecks to respect the He-man and get out and root for Uncle Samuel, U.S.A!"

Lewis did not characterize Babbitt as an evil or despicable man. Nor did he accord him much personal power or influence. In that respect *Babbitt* was a business novel that differed from earlier works by William Dean Howells, Frank Norris, Theodore Dreiser, and others who featured tycoons and captains of industry. But the ideas and values that Babbitt represented were in a cultural sense powerful indeed. They gave a certain materialistic tone to American life that sanctioned governmental policies ardently desired by larger and more powerful business organizations. "To a greater degree than ever before . . . ," wrote journalist William Hard, "small businessmen have identified their interests with the interests of great corporate wealth. To put it lightly but precisely, they think now that the granting of a Rolls-Royce to others is a small price to pay for the getting of a Buick for themselves."

Criticism of American society by the intellectuals was not just a phenomenon of the twenties, of course, for writers in the United States have always been conscious of its shortcomings. A "revolt from the village" occurred in the prewar period as men such as Sherwood Anderson, Floyd Dell, Carl Van Vechten, Edgar Lee Masters, Theodore Dreiser, and others painted depressing pictures of small-town drabness, violence, hypocrisy, and hardship. For many writers the city offered an escape from the stultifying conformity of village life; only there could a person of sensitivity and intellect feel comfortable in the company of kindred spirits and so overcome his sense of alienation. With the influx of such literati Chicago had experienced a "renaissance" before the war, and Greenwich Village had become a center of creative activity in New York. In the words of Hugo Bamman, hero of Edmund Wilson's novel *I Thought of Daisy*, the bohemian life they found in the metropolis allowed writers and artists "to leave behind them the constraints and self-consciousness of their homes, the shame of not making money."

For similar reasons many of the persons who were to become prominent in the arts and literature after the war found Paris attractive. On the Left Bank one could find an atmosphere even more exciting and open than in Greenwich Village; and hotels on the little streets off the Boulevard Saint Michel or the Boulevard Saint Germain provided adequate accommodations at low prices. To the expatriates of the twenties, as Professor Warren Susman has suggested, Paris encouraged in its own unique way the artistic freedom necessary for creative achievement. It was "the laboratory of ideas," thought Ezra Pound: "it is there the poisons can be tested, new modes of sanity discovered."

For all the criticism and rejection of American society, however, what cannot fail to impress a student of the twenties is the absence of certainty in the minds of contemporaries. Neither the expatriates in Paris nor the writers who stuck it out back home ever claimed to have a firm grasp on the truth; they were seekers, not zealots. One of the nation's severest and wittiest critics, H. L. Mencken, believed that democracy had had a debilitating influence on American culture. "What ails America," he informed Kansas editor William Allen White in 1922, "is simply the fact that it has yet to develop a secure aristocracy." But Mencken had no formula for developing an aristocracy. In response to the question, "If you find so much to complain of in the United States, why do you live here?" he merely replied, "Why do men go to zoos?" White himself admitted that he was "unsure of so vast a number of things." Even Babbitt had his moments of doubt—and so did the Babbitts of real life. Another of White's correspondents was a Florida real-estate promoter who boasted in 1925 that he was "entirely surrounded by HE-MEN who know exactly what they want. They want money and want it bad and now!" But in six months the promoter wrote again to confess that he was "the funniest thing selling Florida land you ever saw."

The causes of such uncertainty are not easy to discern. The war experience doubtless had something to do with bringing it on; the brutal realities of war were difficult to square with the high ideals for which President Wilson had said the United States was fighting. Just as important was rapid scientific and technological development, for it required adjustments and accommodations that were difficult to make with confidence. What had once seemed categorical and unimpeachable no longer went without question.

In this context the "noble experiment" with prohibition is instructive. The nineteenth-century temperance movement, aimed at curbing the consumption of alcohol, gradually gave way in the twentieth century to sentiment that favored doing away with alcoholic beverages altogether. Advocates of the Eighteenth Amendment, ratified in January 1919, were confident that it would help to eliminate poverty, vice, and crime. Their arguments were logical enough if one could accept the premise that social iniquities were the result of drinking and that an abstinent society would be just. While prohibition did greatly reduce the consumption of alcohol in the twenties, enforcement of the law proved impossible. Since the demand for liquor was more an effect than a cause of social malaise, and since uncertainty and discontent did not disappear during the New Era, the market for alcohol remained as great as it had ever been. And it assured the success of bootleggers who, with automobiles and trucks for transportation and elaborate organizations for efficient operation, were able to make enormous profits. Thus the confident assurances of prohibitionists turned out to be hopelessly wrong. The Eighteenth Amendment did not reduce crime; on the contrary, by making crime profitable and criminal organization feasible, it made law-breaking more difficult than ever to combat.

When prohibition agents such as these confiscated kegs of liquor from speakeasies, they perhaps encouraged some people to believe that the Volstead Act was being enforced. Yet federal agents were poorly paid and few in number (by 1930 there were only 2,836 of them). Such raids might have served to intimidate purveyors of illicit alcohol, but the proprietor of a "speak" was more likely to respond by handing over protection money than by reforming his operations and obeying the law (Keystone View Co.).

In the eyes of the New Era's critics, then, prohibitionists and their ilk appeared ridiculous. The prohibitionists' ilk included members of the Ku Klux Klan, religious fundamentalists, and anyone else who traded in what right-thinking people of the prewar period had accepted as eternal verities. The last great spokesman for those apparent truths and for the agrarian culture that had spawned them was William Jennings Bryan, who got his comeuppance at Dayton, Tennessee, in 1925, when he joined the prosecution in the trial of John Thomas Scopes. A high school biology teacher, Scopes had deliberately violated Tennessee's Butler Law, which forbade the teaching of "any theory that denies the story of Divine creation of man as taught in the Bible, and to teach instead that man has descended from a lower order of animals." The American Civil Liberties Union having come to Scopes's defense, it was under ACLU auspices that Clarence Darrow, one of the nation's leading criminal lawyers, appeared in Dayton to assume a major role in the proceedings.

The "Monkey Trial" was more than just one of those curious incidents

—like the funeral of Rudolph Valentino or the abortive effort to rescue Floyd Collins from entrapment in a Kentucky cave—that periodically attracted the nation's attention. There were cosmic issues involved. The war period had seen a revival of religious fundamentalism, a simplistic reaction by unsophisticated people against the scientism, Nietzschean superman theories, and barbarism associated with Germany. In the fundamentalist view, the difficulties of modern times were caused by a failure to recognize biblical truth; Darwinian theory had called into question the idea that man had been created but a little lower than the angels. It had glorified, not man, but struggle; it had therefore contributed to an intellectual configuration of which war was an expression. Bryan, more knowledgeable than many of his fundamentalist followers, had long ago rejected the idea that struggle and conflict lead to progress. "How can hatred be the law of development," he had asked in one of his Chautauqua lectures, "when nations have advanced in proportion as they have departed from that law and adopted the law of love?"

Thus the issues were drawn. Scopes, Darrow, and the ACLU, on the one hand, represented academic freedom and a willingness to follow scientific inquiry wherever it might lead; Bryan and the prosecution, on the other, saw the central issue as a contest between force and love. Convinced that the doctrine of evolution paralyzed the hope of social reform, Bryan became a prisoner of fundamentalist biblicism and an easy target for Darrow's sharp questioning. The trial turned into a farce as Bryan made a fool of himself in testifying as an expert witness on the Bible. Although Scopes was convicted, the Tennessee Supreme Court later reversed the decision on technical grounds. It rendered no opinion on the constitutionality of the Butler Law, however, and the law remained on the books until 1966.

Five days after the Dayton episode, Bryan died in his sleep while taking a Sunday afternoon nap. In his own antiquated way, he had posed basic questions about the ultimate source of human value, but he had only made himself seem absurd in the opinion of his critics. They were for human dignity, too, but they opposed what seemed to them influences that would degrade man by curbing his quest for understanding: the old-time religion of people H. L. Mencken called "gaping primates from the upland valleys of the Cumberland Range"; the small-town insistence on conformity; limitations on what might or might not be discussed in the schools. But they did not offer clear-cut moral imperatives after the manner of the late "Great Commoner."

"In a material world we are worshipping material things," wrote William Allen White to Ray Stannard Baker in the year of the Scopes trial. "With ideals junked and vision smashed, the people are perishing." Science could provide no substitute for the old absolutes, and uncertainties of the New Era aroused nagging anxieties in the American mind. At the end of the decade Newton D. Baker, who had been Woodrow Wilson's Secretary of War, confessed his perplexity to Walter Lippmann. "If one compares the formal authoritative Newtonian system with the Darwinian evolutionary system from the point of view of mere certainty," he wrote, "it is easy to see what the loss has been. Then when one takes the next step into Einstein's relativity, whatever was material or real or certain seems to have dissolved so far as the physical universe is concerned." Science and technology had dissolved much that had seemed real and certain in social relationships, too.

## Black Migration and the Jazz Age

Augmenting the social changes brought about by science and technology—and interacting with them—was the migration of southern blacks to northern cities. In 1910 more than 40 per cent of the total American population of nearly 92.5 million lived in the northeastern portion of the United States, that is, in the area east of the Mississippi River and north of a line running along the Pennsylvania-Maryland boundary and the Ohio River. Of the northeastern residents, 8 million (20 per cent) were foreign born, and 719,000 (less than 2 per cent) were Negro. During the decade 1900–1910, the foreign-born population had risen by 2 million, while the black population had gone up by only 135,000. The Northeast, in other words, had added fifteen foreign-born persons for every additional black person. During the next intercensus decade, from 1910 to 1920, the proportions shifted. The number of Negroes rose by nearly 400,000, half again as great an increase as among the foreign born. The 1920s increase was even more marked: by 1930 nearly two million Negroes lived in the Northeast, most of them in urban areas. More than 90 per cent of the northeastern blacks were urban residents, and nearly 70 per cent lived in the principal cities of the region.

Several influences explain the black migration. To some extent it was a part of the general movement from rural to urban areas, but there were also specific forces at work. The development of a caste system in the South during the late nineteenth century made life miserable for blacks who had to put up with it, but until World War I few of them moved. New job opportunities in other sections were not much more plentiful than they were in the South, in part because northern industries could rely on immigration to supply needed labor. Then came the war; with immigration reduced to a trickle, northern employers turned to blacks. When they did, they found that the boll weevil had made the task of recruitment easy. The weevil entered the United States from Mexico in 1892, and by 1915 it was destroying thousands of acres of cotton in Mississippi, Alabama, and southwestern Georgia. Planters cut their losses by turning to the production of food crops and livestock, but more diversified operations required fewer hands. Croppers and tenants, their livelihood threatened, listened eagerly to the blandishments of labor agents from the North. Beset by other troubles, especially a series of floods in 1915 and 1916, many of them decided to move north.

Once under way, the black migration developed internal dynamics similar to those that had operated with European immigrant groups. Letters

This Negro family was one of many that moved to Chicago during the World War I
migration. Like black author Richard Wright, who came later, they were "taking a
part of the South to transplant in alien soil, to see if it could grow differently,
if it could drink of new and cool rains, bend in strange winds, respond to the
warmth of other suns, and, perhaps, to bloom. . . ." (State Historical Society of
Wisconsin)

from Chicago, Cleveland, or Detroit painted glowing pictures of conditions in the North: "Tell your husband work is plentiful here and he wont have to loaf if he want work"; "I do not see how they pay such wages the way they work labors. they do not hurry or drive you." The *Chicago Defender,* a weekly newspaper begun by Robert S. Abbott in 1905, had revolutionized Negro journalism with its hard-hitting attacks on racism and the philosophy of accommodation that allowed racism to continue. When the *Defender* added its encouragement to that of personal letters, it became the most widely read black newspaper in the country. The weekly publication reflected Abbott's belief that leaving the South was at once an effective protest against injustice and a way of strengthening black solidarity in the North.

In 1930 nearly 80 per cent of the 12 million American Negroes still lived in southern states, but over the past twenty years the net loss from migration to the North had been 1.4 million. A population movement of such proportions was in itself an influence making for cohesion among up-rooted blacks. As Professor Allan Spear has suggested, it was infused with religious imagery. Migrants talked about fleeing Egypt and going over into Canaan or the Promised Land. They were not just ordinary rural Americans seeking jobs in the city. They were also black people in search of a new freedom and enthralled by the thought that their children might have educational and other advantages in the North that were denied them in the South.

Their hopes remained largely unfulfilled, though for a time jobs seemed plentiful. Before the great migration most northern blacks had held positions in domestic service or as janitors, porters, and the like. Migrants, on the other hand, found employment in factories that had previously avoided hiring blacks. But opportunities in the North were more limited than they at first appeared to be, for few black workers were able to break out of the unskilled category. The Bureau of the Census found that in 1930 less than 5 per cent of all black males in the country held positions as skilled workers and foremen, while 9 per cent were classified as semiskilled. Nearly one-third of all black males were unskilled, however, and more than 40 per cent remained agricultural laborers. Black women did slightly better in semiskilled jobs than did men, but in 1930 more than 56 per cent of them were still engaged as service workers. The figures include blacks who did not migrate as well as those who did, but it is clear that blacks who obtained jobs in factories worked at the low end of the industrial scale.

A large part of the black workers' difficulty grew out of their relationship with organized labor. Unions had shown little inclination to accept Negro members in the past, and employers had often used Negroes as strike-breakers. The mutual antagonisms that developed were not resolved during the New Era, and by the end of the decade twenty-four international unions had discriminatory clauses in their constitutions or their rituals. Others opposed black membership more informally. Negroes were therefore forced into the open-shop industries, especially automobiles, steel, and meat packing. Without organization, and holding the most menial positions, they were obviously vulnerable to economic fluctuations. Workers who moved north with high hopes, then, encountered the "last hired, first fired" formula that would frustrate their ambitions.

Job discrimination and opposition from the unions were not the only disappointments that migrants confronted. Like immigrant groups, blacks tended to cluster in urban ghettoes. Already in the process of formation when the migration began, the "black belts" and "darktowns" of northern cities increased in population density as the newcomers arrived. Municipal policy usually operated to make conditions in black ghettoes even worse than in the areas where immigrant ethnic groups congregated. In Chicago, for example, the police winked at prostitution, confining their efforts to keeping vice districts away from commercial and white residential sections. The result, to the dismay of many Negro families, was that the red light burned shamelessly in or near the black belt. Ethnic ghettoes, to be sure, also suffered at the hands of city officials. Immigrant groups could never-theless escape the slums; that possibility was a powerful stimulus to the culture of upward mobility that characterized most ethnic associations. Black people did not have a similar alternative, for the racial ghetto was one from which few escaped simply by moving to better neighborhoods. Negative racial stereotypes, arising from conditions created more by white policies than by black desires, kept Negroes confined to the ghetto and continuously exposed to its problems. Escape, when that became an ob-jective, had to take forms other than packing up and leaving.

Many residents of racial ghettoes took refuge in alcohol or drugs, while others turned to religion. A few "passed" as whites, often without intend-ing to do so and usually with a sense of guilt or betrayal. That many more sought to face their problems and to overcome them through or-ganized effort is eloquent testimony to the resiliency of the human spirit under stress. With the leadership of people who had achieved some success in life (W. E. B. DuBois emphasized the key position of the "talented tenth" in black communities) , various groups had already formed prior to the great migration. They were soon joined by others. By 1920 the NAACP, the National Urban League, the National Federation of Colored Women's Clubs, the National Negro Business League, and the Association for the Study of Negro Life and History were all emphasizing black unity and achievement, albeit in different ways.

The most exciting and controversial new organization was the Universal Negro Improvement Association. While it flourished only briefly during the postwar years, the ideas advanced by its founder, Marcus Garvey, have had a lasting influence on American blacks. Garvey was a Jamaican by birth; he traveled widely, however, and finally arrived in Harlem in 1916. There he began to promote the UNIA cause, arguing that blacks must preserve their racial purity and their cultural heritage. Emphasizing Negro support of Negro business, Garvey established a UNIA chain of groceries, restaurants, laundries, and other enterprises including a hotel, a doll fac-tory, and a printing plant. His ideas soon expanded to include a nation-alist plan for the redemption of Africa under UNIA auspices, and his first move in that direction was the formation of a Negro merchant marine known as the Black Star Line.

Garvey was a brilliant showman, his campaign for the UNIA revealing a profound understanding of the prevailing psychology in racial ghettoes. His African Legion accoutered in plumed hats and handsome uniforms, his Black Cross nurses, his distribution of "African Redemption" medals, his African Orthodox Church (which glorified the "Black Man of Sorrows") all served to accentuate Garvey's fundamental point. Blacks, he reiterated, should be proud of their race; they should support black institutions through which the black genius might express itself without distortion and without risk of annihilation.

Few other Negro organizations aroused the enthusiasm that Garvey's UNIA generated among the ghetto masses, yet in 1923 it encountered

Lynching, the ultimate means of maintaining white supremacy in the South during the years after Reconstruction, was by no means confined to the South after the black migration northward. The Ku Klux Klan came to life during the New Era, won adherents in all sections of the country, and clouded the hopes of black migrants. Marcus Garvey, emphasizing racial pride, helped to restore a sense of dignity to a people that suffered countless indignities (Culver Pictures).

difficulties from which it never fully recovered. Accused of mail fraud in marketing stock of the Black Star Line, Garvey was tried, convicted, and sent to prison. Although President Coolidge pardoned him in 1927, U.S. immigration authorities deported him as an undesirable alien, and the UNIA lost its institutional coherence.

Despite the UNIA's failure, however, Garvey's celebration of the African heritage reinforced a new consciousness of strength in black tradition. Writers and artists gave expression to the soul of that tradition and made Harlem, among other things, the equivalent of Greenwich Village in creative energy. In part because entertainers encountered fewer obstacles than did Negroes in other occupations, it was through music that blacks could best identify with their African past. White Americans readily accepted the stereotype of the rhythmic Negro; the Sambo image began to change. The new image could also be demeaning, of course, for it stood in the way of perceiving any black as an individual with distinctive character. Yet the stereotype had some foundation in the African musical tradition.

As Gunther Schuller has observed in his excellent study, *Early Jazz,* African music is based upon rhythm rather than harmony, and in rhythmic structure it is the most complex music in the world. Through the long years before emancipation in the United States, the music that people brought over on slave ships underwent gradual transformation. Change occurred primarily because European conventions acted as a filter to eliminate some of the unique character of African music; but, despite that,

Edward Kennedy (Duke) Ellington, the most innovative composer to come out of the Jazz Age, is pictured here with the band he formed when he began playing at Harlem's Cotton Club in 1927. His recordings from the late twenties, with their experimental probing, led jazz historian Gunther Schuller to observe that "it was in these years that the personalities of his individual musicians and the sonorities of his orchestra became the instrument upon which the Duke learned to play" (Mills Arts Co.).

several of its strongest features found their way into the American musical idiom. The exceedingly complicated polyrhythmic structures of Africa, for example, survived in the syncopated rhythms of jazz. So also did formal elements such as the call-and-response pattern, the repeated refrain, and the chorus format of cult dances. The blues preserved improvisational and melodic patterns characteristic of Africa. Thus, even though Garvey endured prison and exile, the extraordinary appeal of African music manifested itself during the twenties. That the New Era was also the Jazz Age suggested a cultural symbiosis within American society that could be ignored or threatened only to the peril of that society itself.

**The Politics of
the Twenties**

The postwar decade was a period of Republican ascendancy in national politics. From 1920 through 1928, it seemed, any Republican presidential candidate would have had to make the most stupendous campaign blunders in American political history to avoid winning. In 1920 *The Nation* lampooned a tendency of the Republican press to read great significance into the everyday acts of candidate Warren G. Harding. From its "Special Correspondent at the Front (Porch)" came this dispatch:

Senator Harding rose early this morning and displayed his stalwart Americanism by washing, shaving, and putting on his clothes. He then sat down to breakfast, which he ate in true democratic fashion with knife, fork, and spoon. It is little touches like this which reveal the Senator's kinship with the common people and endear him to the masses. [Then came the first of the day's visiting delegations, the Dairyman's Association from Hokamazoo.] "I feel like one of you," the Senator said gracefully. "All my life I have eaten butter and drunk milk, and thus have gained a close personal insight into your problems and needs."

Calvin Coolidge did—and said—even less in 1924 than Harding had in 1920. "I don't think I have ever known a man so highly endowed with negative virtues," Ray Stannard Baker later recalled. "No one was ever able to get hold of anything he had said or done to use against him in a campaign. He seemed never identified with any important movement or measure."

Why did Americans of the New Era elect the likes of Harding and Coolidge? No doubt it was in part because during a period of rapid social change and adjustment the Republican party seemed cautiously stable, reliable, and sane. Republicans might not always be honest (the Teapot Dome scandal put that notion to rest), yet they were not the sort of men to tilt with windmills or to lead the nation on a chimerical quest for noble but unrealizable objectives. They were not likely to take on such tasks as making the world safe for democracy; they also seemed unlikely to jeopardize American economic well-being, and a majority of voters asked for little more than that. "Republicans," thought William Hard, were "realistic, hard-boiled, matter-of-fact" in contrast to Democrats who were "imagina-

Although this photograph of Calvin Coolidge was taken after he left the White House, it suggests a common assessment of his presidency: leaving the nation's affairs in the hands of others (particularly the leaders of business), he went off fishing. One critic, Fremont Older of the San Francisco *Call,* found little to admire in Coolidge because "I can't see anything noble in making a shrine out of a cash register." To him, the president seemed pathetic. Yet that quality made Coolidge a perfect representative of the American people, for "we, too, are pathetic figures" (Wide World photo).

tive, warm-hearted, matter-of-fancy, and matter-of-castles-in-Spain." The Republican party, then, went into every presidential campaign in the twenties knowing that it could count on enough Republican voters to provide victory. The party did not have to convert anybody; it had only to keep a few insurgents from deserting the ranks. Identified with prosperity as Republicans were, party loyalty was easy to maintain.

Democrats faced a very different set of problems. If Republican voters were in a majority, it follows, of course, that Democrats were in a minority. Walter Lippmann wrote in 1927 that he had "never met a professional Democratic politician who could deny this fact nor one who could remember it." The harmony that was essential for Republican victory was useless for the Democrats. As Lippmann put it, the Democrats "can't unite and stand pat. If they do they generally carry the Confederate States." In one way or another Democratic leaders had to raid, divide, and seduce Republicans. They could not appeal only to Democrats because there were not enough of them.

Only in state or local races did Democrats sometimes win. And because Democratic strength was local, Lippmann found the Democratic mind local. While Republicans learned to compromise to keep their national majority together, the Democrats mounted the barricades, "not for abstract principles, but for the things which [had] enabled them to win their local victories." Thus Lippmann could point to Democrats who were wetter than Republicans and Democrats who were dryer than Republicans. Some were more enthusiastic in their support of the League of Nations; some were more passionately opposed to it. Some were more dedicated to the public regulation of business; some were more ardent champions of laissez-faire. "Having become accustomed to playing successfully to their own gallery at home, having nothing to gain and much to lose by merely being harmonious," concluded the journalist, "the Democrats are what everyone knows them to be—masters in the art of quarreling among themselves."

Lacking national unity, the Democratic party was not in a good position to offer criticism of the Republicans in power. The political circumstances seemed made to order for a strong third-party movement, and there were several attempts at party realignment in the twenties. Efforts to change party structure were usually carried out under the auspices of an interest-group coalition that flew the banner of progressivism. In 1920 an organization that called itself the Committee of 48 (because it hoped to establish progressive connections in all forty-eight states) assumed responsibility for organizing a third party. Searching for common ground among dissident groups, the Forty-Eighters called for a convention to meet in Chicago. Nothing worked out the way they thought it might. Instead of creating a new party with broad appeal, the convention organized a Farmer-Labor party in an attempt to make political capital out of class differences. As disappointed Forty-Eighters predicted, the Farmer-Labor organization had little influence on the campaign.

Coalition-minded third-party advocates were not prepared to strike their colors, however; in 1922 they formed a new organization, the Conference for Progressive Political Action. The CPPA became a clearing house for various cooperative societies, the Socialist party, the Farmer-Labor party, the Non-Partisan League, the League for Industrial Democracy, the Single Tax party, and other independent groups. Although the CPPA managed to bring about enough of an organization to get a Progressive party formed and Robert M. La Follette nominated as its presidential candidate in 1924, the old difficulties with the platform persisted. And again third-party influence on the election seemed negligible. After La Follette's futile effort, and after his death in 1925, progressive forces disintegrated almost completely. Some third-party men gave up on politics, at least temporarily, while others returned to one of the two major parties in 1928.

The election of Herbert Hoover and the defeat of Al Smith nevertheless did little to satisfy the most devoted of third-party progressives. After the 1928 returns were in, George Record, an influential New Jersey progressive, composed a long memorandum. Assuming that another third-party effort would emerge, and wishing it every possible success, he probed for explanation of failure in other elections. He was sharply critical of efforts to create a new party by appealing to specific groups and organizations, for each of them was interested "only in their particular pet idea." If an organization could get its pet idea into a platform, then it seemed to care little about what other planks were included. Concerning this log-rolling process, Record believed that "the only thing certain about the platform thus constructed is that there is not a single individual in America to whom it will appeal as a whole."

Would the supporters of realignment try again in view of their past failures to develop a coherent program? A University of Wisconsin sociologist, Edward Alsworth Ross, advising against it, urged waiting until the time was more favorable. "You are liable to find yourselves a band of officers without soldiers," he wrote, "unless there is a widespread disgust with the old parties and I see few signs of such disgust." Political disgust appeared, of course, sooner than Ross anticipated, and with it came a deep depression-born anxiety. But even before the stock-market crash signaled the arrival of depression, a number of third-party advocates led by philosopher John Dewey had formed the League for Independent Political Action. The new organization hoped to build third-party progressive sentiment from the grass roots up and then enter a contender in the election of 1936. When depression ended the period of Republican ascendancy, therefore, progressives were as persistent, though perhaps not as hopeful, as they had been in 1920. Conditions of the postwar decade had at every turn worked against the formation of a third party. The most that could be said for independent political activities is that they served to define political choices—and they provided an object lesson—when Franklin D. Roosevelt took the oath of office as president in 1933.

**The Great Engineer**     The White House during the twenties was hardly a beehive of activity. President Coolidge usually slept ten hours a night and took an afternoon nap daily. The entire executive branch of the Federal government was not so quiescent, however, and programs of administrators in the various departments provided the New Era with much of its character. Harding's political appointments were particularly important, for he became president after eight years of a Democratic administration, and his election initiated twelve years of Republican domination in the executive branch. After several officeholders under Harding had become implicated in corruption and scandal—and even more after the coming of economic depression at the end of the decade—ridicule of New Era administrators became fashionable. Harding's pledge to surround himself with the nation's "best minds" drew bitter laughter during the thirties. Yet Wilson's successor had nevertheless taken the pledge seriously, and in retrospect his administrators appear to have been as well qualified, at least in education and training, as any who held office during the first half of the twentieth century. A comparative study reveals that more than 80 per cent of Harding's top administrators graduated from college, while in a comparable group of New Dealers only 75 per cent had baccalaureate degrees.

One of the most active and important members of the Harding and Coolidge administrations was Secretary of Commerce Herbert Clark Hoover. His career brought to mind familiar images of the self-made man, and he represented a congeries of ideas treasured by Americans of the New Era. Beginning with the publication of his little book, *American Individualism,* in 1922, and continuing through speeches, press releases, popular magazine articles, and messages to Congress, Hoover labored diligently in the twenties and thirties to make his position clear. And that position did seem reasonably clear as long as prosperity remained; only with the depression did disappointed citizens disparage the man they had venerated in the New Era as a great engineer, efficiency expert, public servant, and humanitarian.

Born in 1874 to Quaker parents living in tiny West Branch, Iowa, Hoover had been orphaned at the age of ten and had gone to live with an uncle in Willamette, Oregon. Developing his ambition to become a mining engineer, he took qualifying examinations for the new Stanford University, where he enrolled in 1891. Shortly after graduating in 1895, he obtained a position with Louis Janin, a prominent San Francisco engineer. Then began his meteoric rise to prominence in the profession. In the years before the outbreak of war in 1914, he supervised a variety of operations all over the world, acquiring global interests that yielded a fortune. In London when war came, he accepted President Wilson's appointment as chairman of the Committee for the Relief of Belgium. He carried on the work with such efficiency that in 1917 Wilson named him head of the wartime Food Administration. After the war, he assumed responsibility for the economic restoration of Europe. Throughout the years of international turmoil, Hoover's performance was consistently impressive. And, in 1921, having proven beyond cavil his right to be included among Harding's "best minds," he entered office as Secretary of Commerce. Once considered a relatively minor department, Commerce expanded rapidly under Hoover's direction; by 1928 the secretary had made it one of the most important departments in Washington while he himself had become an influential figure in New Era prosperity.

The ideas that formed the basis for Hoover's activities represented a synthesis of various strains in American thought. A central concept in his thinking was the notion of a concert of interests. The United States had managed to avoid the class conflicts that plagued Europe, he said, because capital and labor worked hand-in-hand to produce more, distribute more, and raise the standard of living for everyone. Hoover's emphasis on a concert of interests places him in the tradition shaped by prewar progressives. Worried about the fragmentation of society that seemed to come with industrialization, they had sought to develop means of resolving conflict. Hoover did not, however, find himself in agreement with those progressives who had argued that the state should function as a neutral arbiter of class and interest group differences. From the libertarian tradition he borrowed the idea that harmony could be achieved by providing equality of opportunity and freedom for individual initiative. Far from insuring social harmony, state intervention undermined it. "You cannot extend the mastery of the government over the daily working life of a people," he argued,

As secretary of commerce during the New Era, Herbert Hoover (right) constantly emphasized cooperative or associational activities. "Such cooperation," he said in 1928 during his presidential campaign, "strengthens the whole foundation of self-government and serves to maintain equality of opportunity and constructive leadership." The Hoover formula made better sense during the prosperous twenties, however, than it did after economic collapse in 1929 gave way to the great depression of the thirties. Shown with him here is his running mate, Charles H. Curtis (United Press International photo).

"without at the same time making it the master of the people's souls and thoughts." Discontent, not harmony, was likely to be the result of such mastery.

Hoover was not, of course, advocating anything like anarchy. He believed that government could properly take action in areas where individuals or local governments could not operate without assistance. He frequently urged public works projects (flood control, highway construction, public building programs) , especially in times of economic stagnation. He also believed that education, public health, scientific research, and conservation of natural resources were responsibilities of the State. For Hoover, the basic problem of government was to wield the power of the State so as to further desirable objectives without destroying individual freedom and equality of opportunity for every citizen.

Hoover thought the problem close to being solved during the New Era; his key to the solution was cooperation. Avoiding coercion, the State might assist people who were trying to cope with modern problems. Through temporary committees, conferences, and commissions, the national government could make use of experts to study those problems. Committees and commissions could gather, sift, and weigh the facts, then making them available to the public. Expert analysis need not be made the basis for executive action, however, for citizens could be trusted to judge and act for themselves. And, in helping themselves, they would strengthen the American system. Cooperation through voluntary organizations assisted by government-sponsored experts would, thought Hoover, eliminate social ills and assure continued progress. "What Government can do best," he insisted, "is to encourage and assist in the creation and development of institutions controlled by our citizens and evolved by themselves from their own needs and their own experience and directed in a sense of trusteeship of public interest. . . ."

More than most men Hoover acted upon his ideas; under his direction the Department of Commerce engaged in a variety of programs to promote cooperation. The secretary enthusiastically encouraged trade associations to organize for the welfare of manufacturers, merchants, and corporations engaged in related productive and business activities. Through central facilities such associations could distribute information on a host of vital concerns: prices, techniques of production, standard weights and measures, cost accounting procedures, insurance, employee relations, and the like. Hoover recognized that cooperative business activity might well lead to collusion constituting violation of antitrust laws, and he admitted the need for rules and regulations to maintain human rights. As he put it in a speech of 1924, however, "the question we need to consider is whether these rules and regulations are to be developed solely by government or whether they cannot be in some large part developed out of voluntary forces in the nation." In Hoover's view, "when legislation penetrates the business world it is because there is an abuse somewhere." Yet legislative regulation was clumsy and incapable of adjustment to changing needs.

The business world should therefore set its house in order, develop and enforce its own ethical standards, and thus "stem the tide of government regulation."

Hoover saw trade associations as serving an invaluable function in helping to set the American economic house in order. He created a division in the Department of Commerce to assist trade associations in preparing codes of business practice and ethics, codes intended to eliminate unfair competition and other abuses within each of the particular trades. Before promulgation a code had to be approved by the Department of Justice and the Federal Trade Commission. Business self-regulation, with Department of Commerce cooperation, in practice no doubt benefited large firms more than it did small ones. In 1932 two Columbia University professors, Adolf A. Berle and Gardiner C. Means, published *The Modern Corporation and Private Property*, a book that provided statistical documentation on the magnitude and extent of corporate concentration as of the year 1929. The authors showed that the two hundred largest nonfinancial corporations in the country owned $81 billion in assets; according to their estimates, that amount represented 49 per cent of all corporate wealth, approximately 38 per cent of all business wealth, and 22 per cent of all wealth in the United States. The American Telephone and Telegraph Company, they pointed out, was the equivalent of more than eight thousand average-sized corporations, controlling more wealth than was contained within the borders of twenty-one of the states.

While business in general and large corporations in particular profited from the cooperative activities encouraged by the Department of Commerce, it was not Hoover's intention to play favorites among the nation's economic interest groups. He pressed for the same cooperative enterprise in agriculture, for example, that he urged on businessmen. A plan proposed by George Peek (an executive of the Moline Illinois Plow Company) and embodied in the McNary-Haugen bill, first presented to Congress in 1924, persuaded Hoover that American farmers were threatened by misguided supporters. The bill went through several versions, but an essential idea behind it was that the Federal government would purchase farm commodities at good prices, sell surpluses abroad for whatever they would bring, and then make up losses with an "equalization fee" levied on commodities sold by producers. Essentially a system of price support, the bill was twice passed by Congress and twice vetoed by Coolidge. Hoover vehemently opposed the measure. "No governmental agency," he warned, "should engage in the buying and selling and price fixing of products, for such courses can lead only to bureaucracy and domination." Price supports, he thought, would also result in disastrous increases of agricultural surpluses.

The best agricultural system, Hoover believed, was "one controlled by its own members, organized to fight its own economic battles and to determine its own destinies." What American farmers needed was not equalization fees and McNary-Haugenism, but organization. He thought that the national government could appropriately, and with great rewards to the farmer, encourage agricultural associations just as it encouraged trade associations. As Secretary of Commerce, Hoover frequently urged farmers to work for cooperative marketing and cooperative buying. By the time of his presidental campaign in 1928, he had developed the idea of a Federal farm board to help farmers establish marketing cooperatives and farmer-controlled stabilization corporations. The farm board concept was, thought Hoover, consistent with American ideals: it kept government out of agricultural operations and made farmers responsible for solving their own problems. "It puts the government in its real relation to the citizen—that of cooperation," commented the Republican candidate in one of his campaign speeches. "Its object is to give equality of opportunity to the farmer."

The election of 1928 was the culminating political event of the New Era: Hoover's victory over New York Governor Alfred E. Smith represented popular enthusiasm for New Era prosperity. But it represented more than that, for Al Smith's political career made him seem, compared with Hoover, a man of very different kidney. The son of Irish-American parents, Smith was born (1873) in a tenement house below the Brooklyn Bridge and grew up on the sidewalks of New York. After the death of his father in 1886, he left school, taking a series of jobs to help support the family. Befriended by Tom Foley, a Tammany Hall boss in the Fourth Ward, he drifted into politics. In 1903 he won election to the state legislature, and over the years he grew into one of the ablest political leaders in the country. His four terms as governor of New York gave ample proof of his administrative abilities.

In several respects Herbert Hoover and Al Smith were similar: both believed in the soundness of the American economic system; both had demonstrated what could be achieved by men of ability under a system that provided—so each of them believed—equality of opportunity. Yet voters could detect what they thought were important differences, too. The Democratic candidate was city born and city bred; beyond that he identified himself with ethnic groups that clustered in urban ghettoes, and the position he took on issues of the day made him seem almost an alien to middle America. He was a Catholic, a Tammany Hall politician, and in favor of repeal of prohibition. In contrast to Smith, Hoover had grown up in a rural environment and, like most Horatio Alger heroes, had achieved success on a cosmopolitan scale. He had, furthermore, first made a name for himself in business rather than in politics. He was a Protestant, and he favored prohibition. In supporting Hoover a voter could endorse the accomplishments of American society during the New Era without rejecting a tradition that no longer dominated American behavior. Most citizens who helped to elect Hoover had little inkling that the Hoover synthesis would soon be put to a critical test—and that it would fail.

# 7

## Adversity and Aspiration:
## Years of the Great Depression

The New Era came to an end with the stock-market crash of 1929. More than a decade would pass before the American economy emerged from the worst depression in the nation's history. The anxieties and sufferings of those years affected the thought and behavior of people who lived through them in ways that later generations could not comprehend and sometimes appeared to resent. No one who bears the scars of depression voluntarily opens old wounds, yet the scars have never been considered a mark of shame or disgrace. Indeed, they are now and again exhibited as a mark of honor in the same way that the markings of primitive puberty rites are proudly displayed by those who bear them. There is much unconscious cruelty here. The exhibition implies that anyone born after that time of great trial can never prove himself mature, at least not in so convincing a way. Whatever annoyance it causes later generations is thus understandable.

The decade of the thirties was one of those periods that the indiscriminate often refer to as "historic," as though all periods are not equally historic. What the usage suggests is that the 1930s, like the 1890s, was a decade of acute historical awareness. Men and women, wrote Charles C. Alexander in his perceptive study of depression era nationalism, were "cognizant of having reached a turning point in their lives and in the evolution of their country, of having closed one era and begun another." Yet historical awareness does not imply historical accuracy. Transition from the New Era to the New Deal seemed more abrupt at the time than it actually was. Conditions of life during the thirties were of course far different from conditions of life in the twenties, but there were also striking continuities from one period to the other. No revolution occurred. And just as impressive as the profound impact of the depression on the thoughts and actions of individuals is that the crisis, for all its severity, brought so few basic changes to American institutions.

**The Great Crash**     Technological achievements of the New Era were so impressive—and the prosperity they helped to bring about was so widespread—that Americans of the twenties developed great confidence in the future. Their optimism was not entirely misplaced; but, in concentrating their energies on making adaptations to changes taking place in their lives, these Americans tended to ignore fundamental weaknesses in the nation's economy. The few Cassandras who warned of troubles ahead found themselves snubbed and disregarded. To most people, Herbert Hoover made far more sense with his repeated assurance that "our system is responsive enough to meet any new and intricate development in our economic and business life." Ringing the changes on virtues of the American system could not, however, eliminate some persistent problems.

One of the most serious problems of the postwar decade grew out of the uneven distribution of gains resulting from a rising capacity to produce in several industries. As John W. Kendrick has shown in his important study, *Productivity Trends in the United States,* percentage increases in productivity per unit of capital input and per unit of labor were indeed striking after 1919. During the decade 1909–1919 the annual rate of change in manufacturing output per unit of capital input was −1.9, while in the decade 1919–1929 it was 4.3. The increase in manufacturing output per unit of labor jumped from 0.8 per cent annually before 1919 to 5.6 per cent annually after 1919. The figures suggest that manufacturing industries were much more efficient in the postwar period than they had been before the war, and the improved efficiency points to a lowering of labor costs. Yet the reduction in labor costs did not result in proportionately higher wages. Between 1923 and 1929, for example, average hourly earnings in manufacturing increased 8 per cent, while the gain in product per man-hour was 32 per cent. Hourly earnings in railroad transportation increased 8 per cent as compared with a 15 per cent gain in productivity. The average hourly earnings of coal miners fell 14 per cent, while output per man-hour increased 4 per cent. Wage earners in general failed to achieve percentage increases in income that came anywhere near the percentage increases in productivity.

Consumers benefited no more than wage earners from the gains in productivity during the New Era. Wholesale prices of all commodities declined 5 per cent in the years from 1923 to 1929, but the cost of living was slightly higher in 1929 than it was in 1923. The great gains in productivity, then, served to increase corporate profits. Manufacturing profits went up 38 per cent from 1923 to 1929, construction profits increased 56 per cent, and profits in the electric light and power industry rose 179 per cent. Statistics for all corporations show that total corporate profits increased 62 per cent. In 1929 dividends were 65 per cent higher than they had been in 1923, while depreciation and depletion allowances were 67 per cent higher. Toward the end of the New Era some of the large corporations retained sizable funds that were not distributed in dividends or in new investments. Those amounts, supplemented by new security issues, freed corporations from dependence on commercial loans from banks. Banks did not have the power to control inflationary tendencies, and money from interest-bearing time deposits could be used in stock speculation.

Increases in property income served to aggravate inequalities in the distribution of productivity gains. Property income includes dividends, interest, rent, and remuneration to enterprisers beyond what they are paid for their services. Farmers receive property income, but aggregate farm income did not rise significantly and, in any case, the number of farmers declined in the twenties. Thus a limited number of people bene-fited from the disproportionate increase in property income. Approxi-mately 80 per cent of dividends paid during the period went to 5 per cent of the population. While 40 per cent of the nation's income went to 10 per cent of the American people in 1929, an estimated 60 per cent of the fami-lies received incomes of less than $2,000 a year. Such distribution meant, as economist John Kenneth Galbraith has observed, that "the economy was heavily and increasingly dependent on the luxury consumption of the well-to-do and on their willingness to reinvest what they did not or could not spend on themselves." Surplus funds of the prosperous flowed into the stock market, where they served to create conditions of overcapacity in certain industries and where they contributed to the increased prices of available securities. At the same time, the market for most capital goods tapered off noticeably.

Surplus funds also flowed into foreign investments—some of them ill-advised—and the movement helped to perpetuate a war-induced revision in the foreign economic position of the United States. During World War I the nation had made a rapid transition from its ranking as the world's greatest debtor country to an unaccustomed place as the world's greatest creditor. As a debtor country, the United States could advantageously export a greater value of goods than it imported; in effect, it could use the surplus of exports over imports to pay the interest and principal on loans from abroad. After the war the American position was reversed. As a creditor country, the nation had three alternatives: it could begin import-ing more than it exported so that other countries might secure the means to meet their obligations; it could forgive the debts, as some wartime allies urged; or it could make new loans to pay off the old.

American tariff policy in the twenties foreclosed the possibility of sig-nificantly increasing imports, and few people (least of all, Calvin Coolidge, whose Yankee sensibilities were offended by the suggestion) could develop any enthusiasm for debt cancellation. That left foreign investment as the principal means of maintaining an international economic balance. Ex-cept for 1923, every year of the postwar decade saw an increase in new foreign issues, and between 1925 and 1929 some $5.1 billion in foreign loans found an American market. Adding significantly to the outflow of capital were direct investments by such American corporations as the Standard Oil Company of New Jersey, the Ford Motor Company, General Motors, and International Business Machines. By 1929 direct investments reached a total of approximately $3 billion. The system seemed to function reasonably well, but any reduction in the movement of capital to other countries could spell disaster. And after the first part of 1928 the flow was sharply reduced. A boom in the stock market and rising interest rates were enough to persuade many American investors that they would do well to keep their capital at home.

Stock-market prices began to soar toward the end of the New Era in part because of a mounting credit inflation brought about by the willingness of bankers to lend money with common stocks as security. Easy money proved an irresistible temptation to operators who developed ingenious schemes for marketing securities. Not that the public needed much persuading. Small investors were all too willing to buy the stocks and bonds of pyramided holding companies, especially in the utilities field. The pyramid structure—brought about by the organization of corporations to hold stock in other corporations, which in turn held stock in yet other corporations— allowed thimbleriggers of high finance to control, with negligible investments of their own, operating properties worth hundreds of millions of dollars. The pattern was not confined to utilities, but investors had confidence in the ultimate earning power of operating units in that field, and it was there that pyramiding occurred most extensively. The popularity of stock in Middle West Utilities or Electric Bond and Share was based upon its presumed safety and its value as a speculative security. Yet that very popularity caused such stock to rise far beyond the capabilities of operating companies to keep pace. Utility stocks, in other words, became grossly inflated; even so, they could for a time be used as security for loans with which to buy other properties. By 1929, pyramided empires such as that of Samuel Insull had become incredible tangles of intercompany obligations.

Another sort of company that appealed to small investors was the investment trust. Those who had insufficient capital to diversify their holdings could do so by purchasing shares in a trust that would use accumulated funds to buy a range of securities. The principle made sense; by 1929 nearly four hundred investment trusts were in operation. Because of certain practices all too common in the New Era, however, the investment trusts were not always reliable. Officers frequently used funds not to make diversified investments but to gain control over companies in which they were interested. They also took to using trusts as dumping grounds for stocks they no longer wanted. When a Senate Committee on Banking and Currency later investigated stock-exchange practice, it found that "conflicts of duty and interest existing between the managers of the investment trusts and the investing public were resolved against the investor." The committee could not escape an obvious conclusion: "the operations of these management trusts have been calamitous to the Nation."

After the mild recession of 1927, then, various influences and practices brought about a runaway bull market even though there had been no general increase in wages, no general reduction in prices, no general continuation of demand for capital goods. Average citizens in growing num-

October 24, 1929 was a dismal day for the somber crowds that gathered on Wall Street as orders to unload reached the Stock Exchange in unprecedented volume. Thomas W. Lamont of J. P. Morgan & Company held an anxious conference with other bankers in an effort to reverse the trend. Emerging from his offices, he met reporters and delivered an understatement that became a classic. "There has been," he said, "a little distress selling on the Stock Exchange" (Wide World photo).

The concussion of the Wall Street crash closed the doors of banks across the land and brought calamity even to Americans who had not invested in stocks. Few could remain unconcerned. "People everywhere, rich and poor," John Kenneth Galbraith has observed, "were made aware of the disaster by the persuasive intelligence that their savings had been destroyed" (N.Y. Daily News photo).

ber began to dream about making a killing, and some of them were easy marks for salesmen trained to peddle securities. John J. Raskob, a director of General Motors, an ally of the Du Ponts, and chairman of the Democratic National Committee in 1928, published an article in the *Ladies Home Journal* under the alluring title "Everybody Ought to Be Rich," and such sentiment contributed to the widespread frenzy for easy profits.

The market nevertheless had its limits as a source of wealth. Consumers could not continue installment buying indefinitely. Real estate promoters could not continue to sell houses after most housing needs had been met. By the late summer of 1929, sensitive and cautious Wall Street observers noted a decline in new housing and in automobile sales, and some of them concluded that high security prices could not continue. But collapse of the speculative structure did not begin until mid-October. A series of shocks reached devastating proportions on October 24, the "Black Thursday" when nearly 13 million shares changed hands, and prices underwent the most rapid decline in stock-market history. Investment houses, private bankers, and the Federal Reserve all sought to reverse the downward plunge, but their efforts ultimately proved unavailing. Although few people at the time fully comprehended the fact, the New Era had come to an end and the Great Depression had begun.

## The Impact of the Depression

Statistical series provide an indication of how deeply the post-1929 depression cut into the American economy. The Federal Reserve Board index of economic activity, which averaged 100 for the years 1923–1925, showed industrial production at 119 in 1929. By 1930 it had fallen to 96; and, by March 1933, when Herbert Hoover relinquished presidential responsibilities to Franklin D. Roosevelt, it had dropped to 60. Construction fell from its peak of 135 in 1928 to a low of 14 in March 1933. Production of automobiles and trucks declined from 5,358,000 vehicles in 1929 to 2,389,000 in 1931.

As Table 7.1 reveals, gross national product declined more than 30 per cent between 1929 and 1933, and recovery was both slow and irregular. In 1937 real output finally equaled the 1929 level, but then the sharp recession of that year reduced GNP in 1938. Only after 1939 were economists safe in saying that recovery had arrived, for during the years of World War II, GNP continued to advance beyond its 1929 level. Serious as were the losses reflected in figures for actual output, GNP for the thirties represents an understatement of the economic calamity that had befallen the American people. Economic historian Lester V. Chandler has shown that during those grim years huge amounts were lost through underutilization of labor and other productive resources. Assuming a 3 per cent compound annual increase in the productive potential of the economy, he arrived at the figures for potential GNP presented in Table 7.1. During 1932 and 1933, the potential GNP column would suggest, the economy was performing at more than 35 per cent below capacity; during the entire period from

TABLE 7.1    Gross National Product, Actual and Potential,
1929–1941 (Billions of 1929 Dollars)

| Year | Actual GNP | Potential GNP | Lost Output (Potential GNP Minus Actual) |
|------|------------|---------------|------------------------------------------|
| 1929 | $ 104.4 | $ 104.4 | $  — |
| 1930 | 94.4 | 107.5 | 13.1 |
| 1931 | 87.8 | 110.7 | 22.9 |
| 1932 | 74.8 | 114.0 | 39.2 |
| 1933 | 72.7 | 117.4 | 44.7 |
| 1934 | 79.5 | 120.9 | 41.4 |
| 1935 | 87.8 | 124.5 | 36.7 |
| 1936 | 99.5 | 128.2 | 28.7 |
| 1937 | 105.3 | 132.0 | 26.7 |
| 1938 | 100.5 | 136.0 | 35.5 |
| 1939 | 108.7 | 140.1 | 31.4 |
| 1940 | 118.1 | 144.3 | 26.2 |
| 1941 | 136.4 | 148.6 | 12.2 |
| Total* | $1,165.5 | $1,524.2 | $358.7 |

SOURCE:    Table 1–1 from *America's Greatest Depression, 1929–1941*, by Lester V. Chandler, Harper & Row, 1970, p. 4.    (Computed from various tables in U.S. Dept. of Commerce, U.S. Income and Output, 1958.)

* Excluding 1929.

1930 through 1941, it was nearly 25 per cent below its potential. Table 7.1 indicates that the output sacrificed during the depression was more than three times the total GNP in 1929. As Chandler vividly expresses it, the lost potential "would have bought 716,000 schools, each costing $500,000; or 35,800,000 homes, each costing $10,000; or 179,000,000 automobiles, each costing $2,000; or 3,580,000 miles of highway at $100,000 a mile." To put it more personally, the lost sum would have supported 3,580,000 people at an annual consumption level of $10,000 for an entire decade.

For millions of jobless men and women, such was the stuff of which dreams were made. Unemployment grew by the month and by the year until, as Table 7.2 shows, nearly one-fourth of the labor force found itself without work in 1933. With slightly more than 1.5 million jobless in 1929, the unemployment rate had been only 3.2 per cent of the labor force. During the eleven years from 1930 through 1940, however, the average rate of unemployment was 17.1 per cent, and the average number of jobless was nearly 9.5 million. Not all of those fortunate enough to be working held positions for which they had been trained, and many of those who wanted to work full time had to be satisfied with part-time employment. In all manufacturing industries combined, according to figures compiled by the Bureau of Labor Statistics, reduced work weeks were the rule. The average number of working hours per week per wage earner went from 45.7 in 1929 to 34.5 in 1934. Only after the coming of World War II did the average worker in manufacturing begin to clock more than forty hours per week.

TABLE 7.2   Labor Force, Employment, and Unemployment in the
United States, 1929–1941 (Millions of Persons)

| Year | Labor Force | Employed | Unemployment | |
|------|-------------|----------|--------------|--------------------------|
| | | | *Number* | *Per Cent of Labor Force* |
| 1929 | 49,180 | 47,630 | 1,550 | 3.2 |
| 1930 | 49,820 | 45,480 | 4,340 | 8.7 |
| 1931 | 50,420 | 42,400 | 8,020 | 15.9 |
| 1932 | 51,000 | 38,940 | 12,060 | 23.6 |
| 1933 | 51,590 | 38,760 | 12,830 | 24.9 |
| 1934 | 52,230 | 40,890 | 11,340 | 21.7 |
| 1935 | 52,870 | 42,260 | 10,610 | 20.1 |
| 1936 | 53,440 | 44,410 | 9,030 | 16.9 |
| 1937 | 54,000 | 46,300 | 7,700 | 14.3 |
| 1938 | 54,610 | 44,220 | 10,390 | 19.0 |
| 1939 | 55,230 | 45,750 | 9,480 | 17.2 |
| 1940 | 55,640 | 47,520 | 8,120 | 14.6 |
| 1941 | 55,910 | 50,350 | 5,560 | 9.9 |

SOURCE:   U.S. Bureau of the Census, *Historical Statistics of the United States, Colonial Times to 1957* (Washington, D.C.: U.S. Government Printing Office, 1960), p. 70.

In the meantime, men and women who had grown accustomed to prosperity during the New Era engaged in a bitter and disheartening struggle with adversity. Evidences of distress began to multiply. A bumper apple crop in Oregon and Washington during the summer of 1930 led the International Apple Shippers' Association to market the abundant supply through street vendors. By October, shipments of apples began arriving in eastern cities, and from apple wholesalers the jobless picked up boxes, each containing seventy-two apples, and a printed sign reading "UNEMPLOYED . . . BUY APPLES . . . 5¢ EACH." Paying $1.75 to $2.25 for the crate, a vendor could make from $1.35 to $1.85—if he had the good fortune to sell all his apples. Few were so lucky, but for a time at least large numbers of people were willing to have a go at it. They had no other prospects. Throughout November, therefore, some six thousand apple peddlers hawked their wares on the sidewalks of New York. As Manhattan reporter Gene Fowler observed, they "crouched at the street corners like half-remembered sins sitting upon the conscience of the town." More than that, the apple seller became a symbol of the depression's most exasperating irony: the development of want in the midst of plenty.

The apple trade soon declined, but other street merchandising did not. Shoe shiners became legion in every major city. "To the streets, too," reported the *New York Times* in the summer of 1932, "has turned an army of new salesmen, peddling everything from large rubber balls to cheap neckties." And where did the shoe shiners and vendors live? Some of them slept in flophouses, subways, train stations, abandoned factories, and even phone booths. Many of them occupied makeshift quarters in the shantytowns—Hoovervilles, the residents called them—that began popping up

The apple vendors who took to the streets in the fall of 1930 were, for the most part, unemployed men hoping to make enough money to keep going. Increased competition led to price cutting, however, and damaged produce further reduced profits. A reporter who investigated the apple trade concluded that a vendor putting in a twelve-hour day might earn—if he were fortunate—95 cents (Brown Brothers).

The depression had many visible effects, none more disturbing than the shantytowns such as this one in Seattle. "Hoovervilles" appeared wherever the homeless could find a convenient plot of unoccupied land: along a railroad right of way, in a city dump, near a municipal incinerator. City refuse provided food and clothing as well as shelter (Wide World photo).

across the country. The clusters of dwellings constructed of waste lumber, cartons, and flattened tin cans housed the superfluous people of the depression. "It was as if the law of supply and demand was being applied to human beings," writes Caroline Bird in *The Invisible Scar*. "The unemployed treated themselves as a glut on the market and tried to get rid of themselves. There was something 'dead' about them."

The lassitude of the jobless was perhaps as much a consequence of inadequate diet as it was a result of lost self-respect. Municipalities and private agencies such as the YMCA, the Red Cross, and the Salvation Army opened up soup kitchens, and breadlines became a familiar mark of the depression. There was never enough to eat, however, and the jobless frequently went foraging for food in garbage cans and city dumps. "You can't imagine how we feel; you can't understand," one homeless man in a breadline remarked to a California social worker. "You have to be down and out for months, feel the pangs of hunger, the sting of charity, the shame of begging, the discomfort of a flophouse, the resentment following the receipt of a meal ticket issued to you without mercy or charity." Malnutrition and shame were linked to despair. Thousands of people took flight, hoping to better their lot elsewhere. But across the country they witnessed the same dreary sights: breadlines; Hoovervilles; job applicants huddled in gunny sacks all night while waiting for factories to open their doors in the morning; the pinched faces, distended bellies, and warped legs of starving children with dysentery and rickets; the sickening squalor of vagabond encampments.

Not everyone, not even some of those who were jobless, gave way to despair. The most cheery pronouncements, however, came from men of affluence who had grown used to having their comments received as oracular wisdom during the New Era. Charles M. Schwab, chairman of the board at Bethlehem Steel, noted in December 1929 that "never before has American business been as firmly entrenched for prosperity"; the following spring he predicted "that 1930, in broad perspective, will prove to be a year of normal business progress." Fluctuations in business, thought most such men of affairs, were unavoidable. "So long as we live under a system of individual liberty," commented Charles E. Mitchell of the National City Bank, "we are bound to have fluctuations in business." Recessions, ran the argument, were inherent in the system; but, so long as the system was preserved, recovery would always follow economic setbacks.

The best way to lick the depression, therefore, was to avoid doing anything that might inhibit recovery. Private charity was commendable, and many businessmen contributed to the relief of the needy, but government relief programs were anathema. "Many of those who are most boisterous now in clamor for work," argued NAM president John E. Edgerton, "have either struck on the jobs they had or don't want to work at all, and are utilizing the occasion to swell the communistic chorus." People should just grin, keep on as best they can, and stop worrying about the future,

In his painting, *Home Relief Station,* Louis Ribak emphasized the ennui of waiting for charity and the humiliation of having to demonstrate one's need for it. "If every mill and factory in the land should begin to hum with prosperity tomorrow morning," warned Youngstown mayor Joseph L. Heffernan in 1932, "the destructive effect of our haphazard relief measures would not work itself out of the nation's blood until the sons of our sons had expiated the sins of our neglect" (Collection of the Whitney Museum of American Art, New York).

A year after the stock market crash, unemployed men wolfed down a charity dinner in the basement of Emmanuel Baptist Church, Chicago. In providing food for the hungry the congregation acted on humanitarian impulses consistent with its faith, but private resources were clearly inadequate to meet growing needs (Chicago Historical Society).

advised Schwab. Government interference would, in the long run, prove detrimental to the general welfare.

However opinions of the Schwabs, Mitchells, and Edgertons might have been received in the twenties, they seemed far less authoritative after arrival of the depression. No longer did ordinary Americans—to say nothing of those who sold apples and lived in Hoovervilles—look up with awe to the high and the mighty. "It will be many a long day before Americans of the middle class will listen with anything approaching the reverence they felt in 1928 whenever a magnate of business speaks," wrote Gerald Johnson in *Current History*. "We now know they are not magicians. When it comes to a real crisis they are as helpless as the rest of us, and as bewildered."

Disillusionment with the wisdom of businessmen led observers of the American scene to look about for evidence of revolutionary ferment. "The depression," as Arthur Schlesinger, Jr., has put it, "was offering radicalism its long awaited chance." The radicals did their best, organizing hunger marches and demonstrations; but their efforts did little to bring on the structural change that revolutionaries sought. During February 1930 Communist speakers in Cleveland urged a crowd of 3,000 unemployed men to storm the city hall; in Philadelphia, police drove off 250 demonstrators who demanded to see the mayor; in Chicago, mounted police dispersed 1,200 demonstrators who marched through the Loop; and in Los Angeles, tear gas repelled a crowd of 3,000. Communists, designating March 6 as International Unemployment Day, staged further demonstrations in nearly every major city. These, along with subsequent hunger marches and agitation, badly misfired. As Irving Bernstein suggests in his history of American labor, they made unemployment a major concern of moderates and conservatives. Columbia University President Nicholas Murray Butler, a staunch friend of business, threw his influence into the movement for better planning. "Gentlemen, if we wait too long," he warned, "somebody will come forward with a solution that we may not like." Stirring the likes of Butler into reform activity was scarcely what the Communists had in mind, but that was nevertheless a major result of their campaign.

Radical activities in rural areas were more direct, but no more successful. Aggregate net income in agriculture declined from $7.7 billion in 1929 to $2.8 billion in 1932, while taxes and debts of farmers remained relatively constant. Thousands of farmers either lost their land for failure to meet tax payments and other obligations or lived with the fear of losing it. Perhaps even more than others, rural people were conscious of poverty in the midst of plenty; driven by their ardor for equity, they organized to subvert tax auctions and foreclosures. They also devised schemes to raise agricultural prices. During the summer of 1932, Milo Reno, leader of the Iowa Farmers' Union, organized the Farm Holiday Association. Its purpose was to withhold shipments of agricultural products until prices at least equaled the cost of production. When they had to, farmers could use force. In Iowa and neighboring states they blocked roads, used their pitch-

Farmers suffering from the effects of depression turned to direct action, as did these men in dumping confiscated milk. If such tactics succeeded, reasoned the Farm Holiday Association, scarcity would raise prices; as a result, farm incomes would increase (State Historical Society of Wisconsin).

forks to puncture truck tires, dumped milk on the roadsides, and in some localities fought pitched battles with sheriffs' deputies. Although prices did not respond to such tactics, most farmers remained unwilling to cast their lot with advocates of even more radical solutions. For all their dissatisfaction, they rejected programs that contemplated a thorough transformation of the American agricultural system. The depression aroused as little revolutionary sentiment in rural areas as it did in cities. In both town and country attitudes of despair overcame the hope of change.

**Hoover and the Depression**
At the time Herbert Hoover took the oath of office as president, he was deeply concerned with the problems of farmers. Rejecting any form of McNary-Haugenism, he supported instead the Agricultural Marketing Act that Congress passed in June 1929. The act created a Federal Farm Board —made up of the Secretary of Agriculture and eight other members appointed by the president—that controlled a $500 million revolving fund with which to improve and stabilize agricultural prices. The board was also authorized to coordinate the activities of various agricultural cooperatives. The program had hardly gotten under way when the market collapsed; thus it accomplished little. Exhausting its funds in a vain effort to halt the drop in prices, the board attempted to encourage cutbacks in agricultural production. Since it could neither impose sanctions nor offer inducements, efforts to reduce production also came to naught. By 1932

farmers had lost confidence in both the president and his Farm Board. Activities of the Farm Holiday Association were a measure of their discontent.

Hoover had initiated his agricultural program before the onset of the depression. After the crash on Wall Street, he, of course, felt obliged to meet the problems that multiplied as economic shock waves were felt throughout the country. During the first months of depression Hoover sought to restore confidence and prosperity through the cooperation of business and political leaders—much as he had sought, while Secretary of Commerce, to extend New Era programs through cooperative associations. In White House meetings with business leaders as early as November 1929, he emphasized the serious implications of recent events and extracted pledges to maintain current wages and hours. He also urged states and municipalities to increase their appropriations for public works projects. In the spring of 1930 he approved congressional action that authorized expenditure of some $750 million for public buildings, highways, and river and harbor improvements.

Hoover's actions seemed to have some effect, but then a financial panic in Europe increased the tensions that already existed in international

The president's name, associated with efficiency and prosperity during the New Era, gave rise to bitter puns during the early years of the depression. Vacuum cleaner jokes ("Hoover cleaned us out!") were not very funny, and neither were jokes about "hoovering" clouds of economic gloom. They were, nevertheless, an indication of increasing acerbity directed toward the Great Engineer who had spoken so reverently about the "American System" (The Bettmann Archive, Inc.).

finance; these in turn increased the severity of problems in the United States. In June 1931, hoping to stabilize the European economy, the president called for a one-year moratorium on all international debt and reparations payments. He also prepared to expand his program of countercyclical measures at home. When Congress convened in early December, Hoover outlined his plans. He proposed reduction of administrative expenditures in government and further expansion of Federal public works. To prevent foreclosure of mortgages he urged creation of a system of home-loan banks and an increase in the lending powers of Federal Farm banks. He also advocated, under pressure from several large banking houses, a reconstruction agency to help put business organizations back on their feet.

Seven months of wrangling in Congress finally produced a set of recovery measures the president could accept. Patterned after the old War Finance Corporation, the Reconstruction Finance Corporation became the principal agency of the entire program. The RFC received its charter from Congress in January 1932, with a capital stock of $500 million to be subscribed by the Treasury and with authority to borrow three times that amount in tax-exempt obligations. Six months later Congress passed the Emergency Relief and Construction Act, which more than doubled the private funds the RFC could raise; it also appropriated $322 million for specified Federal projects and another $300 million for loans to states in need of money for relief of the unemployed. Before Hoover's term in office expired, the agency had loaned out more than $1.5 billion. Banks and trust companies, mortgage loan companies, railroads, insurance companies, and agricultural credit corporations all received help from the RFC, but notwithstanding whatever good it did, criticism of its operations could not be silenced. And charges of favoritism did begin to seem plausible in 1932. Charles G. Dawes resigned his position as head of the agency, and shortly thereafter his bank in Chicago received a $90 million loan. The sum was three times what needy states obtained for relief in 1932, and it provided substance for Will Rogers's ironic observation that "the bankers were the first to go on the 'dole.' "

The remark touched upon what many observers considered the most serious inadequacy in the president's response to the depression: his refusal to mount a relief program sufficient to meet the needs of the unemployed. Hoover worried a great deal about the jobless, but his thoughts kept turning away from their physical well-being and toward the conditions necessary for retaining strength of character. He could not believe that direct government relief would in the long run prove beneficial; he had never relinquished the idea that extending government influence over the working life of a people would make government the master of the people's souls and thoughts. Like many of the nation's business leaders, he encouraged neighborly assistance and private charity. "My own conviction," the president remarked in a press release early in 1931, "is strongly that if we break down this sense of responsibility of individual generosity to individual and mutual self help in the country in times of national difficulty and if we start [direct relief] appropriations . . . we have not only impaired something infinitely valuable in the life of the American people but have struck at the roots of self-government." The residents of Hoovervilles may have taken satisfaction in governing themselves, but they may also have wondered what else of infinite value remained unimpaired.

As he did in other matters, Hoover used a voluntary, cooperative approach to the problem of relief for the jobless. In October 1931 he created an Emergency Committee for Employment charged with developing ideas to alleviate the distress of the needy. The committee carried on an active publicity campaign, providing information on how communities and industries were spreading available work and caring for the transient unemployed. It also offered suggestions on growing home gardens and buying low-cost foods. But it made little headway in proposing a substantial increase in appropriations for public construction. When Allen T. Burns, executive director of the Association of Community Chests and Councils, assured him that private and local agencies could handle relief during the coming winter, Hoover was delighted. Reorganizing his committee and renaming it the President's Organization on Unemployment Relief, he encouraged it to cooperate with Burns and the community chests. Like its predecessor, POUR carried on a vigorous publicity campaign, but its chairman, Walter S. Gifford, was blessed with so little insight that he could not imagine how the organization could do more. Gifford revealed the depth of his wisdom when he announced that "what we need is that everybody go back to work and have full pay for all jobs."

Genuine though Hoover's concern for the jobless was, then, it expressed itself in ways that were woefully inadequate for the times. During the summer of 1932, as the presidential election campaign began to get under way, the nation received a dramatic exhibition of the Administration's ineptness in coping with problems of relief. The demonstration grew out of demands for early payment of bonus certificates granted to World War I veterans after the armistice and scheduled to mature in 1945. During the depression crisis unemployed veterans were not sure they could wait. Walter W. Waters, an ex-sergeant from Portland, Oregon, therefore won a sizable following when he organized a "Bonus Expeditionary Force" to march on Washington and pressure Congress into authorizing bonus payments immediately. By June, some fifteen thousand bonus marchers had congregated in the nation's capital, taking up quarters in unoccupied government buildings on Pennsylvania Avenue and constructing a makeshift encampment on mud flats near the Anacostia River. Congressman Wright Patman of Texas introduced a bill embodying the veterans' demands, and the House passed it on June 15. Two days later, however, with thousands of veterans holding gravely hopeful vigil on the Capitol grounds, the Senate killed the bill. The disappointment of the veterans was intense. Nevertheless, in what was surely one of the most heartrending expressions of the national temper in 1932, they joined in singing "America" and then quietly dispersed.

In 1932, Americans sang a popular song entitled "Brother, Can You Spare a Dime?" The question was one that veterans were asking Congress on the night of June 16, 1932, when Bonus Marchers sat on the Capitol Plaza waiting for action on the Patman bill. The Senate turned them down the following day (Underwood & Underwood).

With no better place to go, the marchers stayed on in their encampments and provided, as Professor Walter Johnson has put it, "a hateful, daily reminder of the ferment of dissatisfaction, bitterness, and distress that was abroad in the nation." The president refused to receive a delegation of BEF leaders, but he did help to secure passage of a bill appropriating funds to pay the veterans' transportation home. Many of them had no homes and so were still on hand on the afternoon of July 28, when trouble broke out as police were clearing buildings scheduled for demolition. After the riot began, the District of Columbia commissioners sent the president an urgent request for troops to disperse the veterans and return them to their camps until a full-scale investigation could be conducted. Hoover responded by directing his secretary of war, Patrick J. Hurley, to assemble the necessary forces; Hurley in turn relayed the message to Army Chief of Staff Douglas MacArthur. Upon receipt of the request for troops, MacArthur took the initiative away from Hoover so that the president lost the power to influence the course of subsequent events. Down Pennsylvania Avenue the general sent more than six hundred battle-equipped troops: the

16th Brigade of the 3rd Cavalry, the 1st Tank Regiment, and the 12th Infantry Regiment. By 8 o'clock that evening, the marchers had withdrawn to the main BEF encampment across the Anacostia River, but the Army did not simply contain them there. It, too, crossed the bridge and by midnight the encampment had been burned to the ground, fired by fleeing marchers and by their pursuers.

General MacArthur seemed well pleased with the day's action. "That mob was a bad looking mob," he later remarked. "It was animated by the essence of revolution." He insisted that American political institutions would have been "severely threatened" had the BEF not been run out of Washington. Hoover, too, attempted to defend the action, even though he was not directly responsible for what had taken place. In so doing, he left himself open to the criticism that he knew was certain to come. William R. Rice, commander of the American Legion, congratulated him for giving the nation a demonstration of his "sadistic principles of government." And novelist Sherwood Anderson expressed the feelings of millions of citizens when he wrote the president a meditative letter. Calling attention to the people who searched garbage cans for food by day and slept on park benches at night, he articulated the thoughts that crossed his mind: "I am wondering, Mr. President, if men like you, men now high in our public life, captains of industry, financiers—the kind of men who seem always to be closest now to our public men—I am wondering if all of you are not nowadays too much separated from the actuality of life. Everything has been very highly organized and centralized in America. Perhaps you have been organized and centralized out of our common lives."

## A Perspective on Depression Psychology

In 1941, when the depression had all but ended, German-born psychologist Erich Fromm published a thoughtful book to which he gave the title *Escape from Freedom.* Familiar with both European and American culture and trained in psychoanalysis, the author provided an explanation not only for the emergence of National Socialism in Germany but also for dominant behavior patterns in the United States. Expanding on his opening discussion of difficulties that individuals meet in growing from childhood to maturity, Fromm was able to suggest that historical forces have moved Western society in a manner similar to that in which psychological and biological forces shape individual growth.

To begin with, the psychologist pointed out that birth means biological, but not functional, separation of a baby from its mother. For several years the child and the mother (or the family) are bound by what Fromm called "primary ties." So long as the ties remain, the child lacks freedom; on the other hand, so long as they remain, the child experiences security and a sense of belonging. Once the primary ties begin to dissolve, a youngster faces the task of rooting himself in the world, the task of finding security in ways other than those he has experienced in his family relationships.

This process of "individuation," suggested Fromm, has two aspects. In the first place, as the child grows, his will and reason guide the development of his "self," which is the organized and integrated whole of his personality. Even though social conditions impose limitations on the development of personality (every society has its definitions of what is "normal" behavior), "one side of the growing process of individuation is the growth of self-strength." In the second place, however, individuation inevitably means separation and isolation. Dissolution of the primary ties that offer a basic unity with the world outside himself leaves the individual standing alone and facing "the world in all its perilous and overpowering aspects."

The process of individuation and the growth of the self, though related, are not the same. While individuation takes place automatically as the child matures, the growth of the self may be hampered for various individual and social reasons. When growth of the self is thwarted, the freedom that comes with individuation produces a sense of desperate desolation. Desolation, in turn, produces mechanisms of escape that often take the form of submission. That is, as the individual finds himself threatened by forces over which he has no control, he may attempt to find a substitute for the primary ties that have broken in the process of growth. But the price he pays in submitting to a new authority is the strength and integrity of his "self." Perhaps only dimly aware of what he has sacrificed, the individual in his dependency on authority becomes hostile, rebellious, and capable of intense hatred. His contempt for himself leads him to despise others. In such a state he cannot establish a "spontaneous relationship to man and nature," which expresses itself in love and productive work.

Fromm argued that phylogenetically, too, the history of man can be viewed as a process of individuation and growing freedom. Human existence began with emergence from instinctual determination of behavior, and Fromm saw the biblical myth of Adam and Eve's expulsion from Eden as symbolizing this emergence. In breaking God's command and in eating the forbidden fruit, the first man and woman became aliens. They freed themselves from the pleasant bondage of the garden, but their act left them naked and ashamed. In traditional religious interpretation their act was a sin, for it resulted in separation from God. In Fromm's interpretation, however, Adam and Eve's defiance of authority meant that they had freed themselves from coercion and emerged from the unconscious existence of prehuman life to the level of man. They had cut the primary ties of the garden and liberated themselves from its regulations. But "freedom from" is not the same thing as "freedom to." Man was not yet free "to govern himself, to realize his individuality."

Thus the great psychological truth of the biblical myth, as Fromm saw it, was its insight into the human condition throughout historic time. From the beginning of human existence men and women had struggled to realize their individuality in society. And through historic ages the process of growing human freedom had exhibited the same dialectical character as did the process of individual growth. "On the one hand it is a process of growing strength and integration, mastery of nature, growing power of human reason, and growing solidarity with other human beings," wrote

Fromm. "But on the other hand this growing individuation means growing isolation, insecurity, and thereby growing doubt concerning one's own role in the universe, the meaning of one's life, and with all that a growing feeling of one's own powerlessness and insignificance as an individual."

Much of the historical analysis of *Escape from Freedom* concentrated on the transition from medieval to modern times. The author believed that what characterized medieval, in contrast to modern, society was its lack of individual freedom. In the medieval period a person was identical with his social role. He was a peasant, an artisan, a knight, or a priest; he was not an individual who had a particular occupation. Although a person might not be free in the modern sense, he held "a distinct, unchangeable, and unquestionable place in the social world from the moment of birth." He was not alone and isolated, but "rooted in a structuralized whole." For various reasons, the structure of society and the personality of man began to undergo transformation during the late Middle Ages. The unity of medieval society gradually disintegrated as "capital, individual economic initiative and competition grew in importance." The individualism that increased with the rise of capitalism had a profound effect on all spheres of human activity: "taste, fashion, art, philosophy, and theology." It shaped the culture of the Renaissance and the ideas of the Reformation. Capitalism freed man from the limitations of a highly structured society. At the same time it made everyone a potential competitor and so threatened all persons with "powerful suprapersonal forces, capital and the market."

Fromm seemed to suggest, then, that the trauma of the Great Depression was but a particularly intense phase in a long period during which men had freed themselves from rigid social restrictions and yet isolated themselves from one another in meeting problems of life. During the Reformation, he argued, Luther and Calvin had sought to relieve their anxiety and uncertainty by total submission to the authority of an all-powerful God. Response to the terrors of freedom during the depression was not so much the religious response of a Luther or a Calvin, but many people did seek to relieve their anxieties by surrender to authority. For some of them the authority was Huey Long, Father Coughlin, or one of many prophets of salvation who came to life during the thirties. For most Americans, however, the benevolent authority of Franklin D. Roosevelt was far more compelling; and (though Fromm did not make the point), because of the benign leadership FDR offered, submission to his authority involved relatively small psychological risk.

This is not to say, of course, that the cry for a leader can be heard only during periods of depression, nor is it to say that submission to a dominant personality was the only escape resorted to during the thirties. The depression intensified the isolation that modern man feels in his confrontation with the world and its problems, and it therefore intensified a longing for security. In the process of submission, the self—the integrated whole of the personality—is denied. While many Americans during the thirties did not deny themselves in order to follow a leader, they did sacrifice development of the self to the demands of their jobs. Unemployment is difficult to bear psychologically as well as economically, and during the depression the dread of unemployment overshadowed the lives of people fortunate enough to have work. As Fromm put it, "to have a job—regardless of what kind of a job it is—seems to many all they could want of life and something they should be grateful for." In so elevating the job, many workers subjected themselves to forces they could not control; they thus compounded their sense of powerlessness and their sense of isolation.

To deny one's self is to deny the capacity for love, for a person who does not approve of himself is incapable of generous impulses toward others. Selfishness arises not from self-love, but from self-abasement, and it finds extreme expression in masochism and sadism. Adolph Hitler's *Mein Kampf* provides abundant evidence of a sadistic craving for power, and incredibly sadistic persecutions resulted from the triumph of National Socialism in Germany. If Hitler could seize control of Germany, why did the United States produce nothing comparable to the Nazi movement? Fromm took pains to point out that "in our own society we are faced with the same phenomenon that is fertile soil for the rise of fascism anywhere: the insignificance and powerlessness of the individual." Why, then, was there no significant American Nazi party?

Fromm suggested that the American response to anxieties of the depression thirties was not so much submission to a leader like Hitler, as what he called "automaton conformity." In employing this mechanism, the individual "adopts entirely the kind of personality offered to him by cultural patterns; and he therefore becomes exactly as all others are and as they expect him to be." The conforming person need not feel isolated, for he has destroyed the discrepancy between himself and millions of other automatons. What he has given up in his conformity, however, is his self. In adopting a kind of protective coloration he loses his distinctive identity.

Observers other than Fromm noted the phenomenon of conformity in American life during the thirties. When Robert and Helen Lynd returned to Middletown (Muncie) in 1936, they found that people were reluctant to let their opinions become sharp. They believed in "peace, but—" or in "fairness to labor, but—" or in "freedom of speech, but." In other words, Middletowners of the thirties tried to avoid placing themselves outside the community consensus.

To sum up, Fromm believed that the style of the whole period corresponded to the picture of American society he sketched: "Vastness of cities in which the individual is lost, buildings that are as high as mountains, constant acoustic bombardment by the radio, big headlines changing three times a day and leaving one no choice to decide what is important, shows in which one hundred girls demonstrate their ability with clocklike precision to eliminate the individual and act like a powerful though smooth machine, the beating rhythm of jazz—these and many other details are expressions of a constellation in which the individual is confronted by uncontrollable dimensions in comparison with which he is a small particle.

These black people, lined up to obtain relief supplies in 1937, seem unaware of anomalies in the picture the photographer was taking. The depression gave rise to various forms of radicalism, but even more remarkable was the quiet passivity of large numbers of citizens. The incantation of traditional shibboleths reinforced social conformity (M. Bourke-White, Time-Life Picture Agency).

All he can do is to fall in step like a marching soldier or a worker on an endless belt. He can act; but the sense of independence, significance, has gone."

In a period such as the depression thirties, conformity runs few risks and avoids the big chance. To change Fromm's metaphor, it takes up a safe position on the rock of orthodoxy to feed on a diet of conventional ideas, hoping that the deluge will soon pass. A few desperate or ingenious souls may devise novel ways to escape both the deluge and the rock's discomfort, but conformity sits on, masticating triteness.

**FDR and the Resurgence of Hope**

Fromm and the Lynds were perceptive in detecting evidences of conformity during the thirties. Like authoritarianism, however, conformity could be found in other periods, too, as Fromm himself well knew. Furthermore, while conformity served some of the same purposes as submission to a leader, it does not fully explain the absence of an effective fascist movement in the United States during the depression. Another reason for American reluctance to support such a movement derives from the character of Franklin D. Roosevelt and from the sort of program he provided after he succeeded Hoover as president. Self-confident and imperturbable, FDR exuded optimism in a time of trouble. As chief executive, Professor Paul Conkin has remarked, he "gave millions of Americans a transfusion of courage," an accomplishment that stands out as his "only unalloyed success." The New Deal program he espoused was neither internally consistent nor consistently successful, but it did support an illusion of success in meeting the problems of depression without actually venturing far from the rock of orthodoxy.

Roosevelt's remarkable self-assurance developed early and naturally in the environment of his youth. A child of fortune, he was born in 1882, the only son of James and Sara Delano Roosevelt. His father had speculated in a variety of enterprises, particularly railroads; but, by the time of his son's birth, he had become more interested in his Hudson Valley estate. Sara, his second wife, was half his age, and she was fully prepared to spend long hours in rearing her child. Young Franklin enjoyed a secure, happy boyhood at Hyde Park. "It was not a world of envy, ambition, or power," biographer James M. Burns has written. "It was a world of benevolent authority, with class lines separating the close little family of three at the top from the nurses and governesses, and these in turn from the maids and cooks indoors, and these in turn from the stableboys and farm hands outside." In that setting, the boy began to develop the vigorous and commanding—but not arrogant—presence that would serve him well as an adult.

At the time of FDR's inauguration in 1933, a fatigued and embittered Herbert Hoover saw no reason for pleasantries. Toward the close of the election campaign, he had identified Democratic pledges with "the same philosophy of government which has poisoned all of Europe." And when he rode with his successor from the White House to the Capitol he appeared to be sniffing "the fumes of the witch's cauldron which boiled in Russia" (United Press International photo).

Tutored at home until he was fourteen, Franklin was then enrolled at Groton School, which had been modeled after the great public schools of England. Groton, according to Rector Endicott Peabody, stood for "everything that is true, beautiful, and of good report," and during his years there Franklin saw no reason to question the verities that Peabody dispensed. In 1900 the young Roosevelt entered Harvard, where for the first time he became enormously popular among his classmates and a leader in extracurricular activities. He held memberships in more than a half-dozen campus clubs; during his senior year he became chief editor of the *Harvard Crimson,* a position that enhanced his campus reputation and brought him great personal satisfaction. Inside the classroom he was less successful. Bored by abstractions and formalities, he once complained that his program was "like an electric lamp that hasn't any wire." But he did not often complain. He crammed for his examinations and managed to get by with a mediocre grade point average.

From Harvard, Roosevelt went on to the Columbia University Law School, where he remained long enough to pass the New York state bar examinations but not long enough to obtain his LL.B. degree. While a law student he married Eleanor Roosevelt, his distant cousin and a niece of Theodore Roosevelt. Although Franklin probably thought he loved Eleanor, his relationship with her was only slightly more intimate than his relationships with other people. For all of his desire to win acceptance— by the social clubs at Harvard and then, later on, in politics—Roosevelt was never one to reveal the inner man. His warmth and friendliness were largely superficial, although Eleanor was one of the few people in a position to know that. And her love for Franklin was always too great to admit it. Bearing five children in rapid succession, she remained for years in the curiously public obscurity that the families of prominent men frequently suffer.

Within a few years after his marriage FDR did become prominent. Upon passing his bar examinations in 1907, he joined the Wall Street firm of Carter, Ledyard and Milburn as a junior clerk, but he did not remain long in the practice of law. Like his cousin Theodore, he sought a career in politics, and in 1910 he was given his chance. Hudson Valley counties consistently voted Republican, and, because their resources were needed elsewhere, Democrats usually supported candidates who could pay their own expenses. Roosevelt thus ran for the state senate from Dutchess County, where in the previous half-century only one Democrat had managed to win. He waged a vigorous campaign, denouncing bossism, avoiding partisan labels, and exploiting the family name. Winning election, he soon became a leader of the reform faction in the state legislature.

Roosevelt's support of Woodrow Wilson in the campaign of 1912 earned him an appointment as Assistant Secretary of the Navy, a post that Theodore Roosevelt had once held. As a member of the Wilson administration, Roosevelt learned a great many things about politics. He learned to accommodate both the admirals and Secretary of the Navy Josephus Daniels (no small accomplishment, since they were often at odds). He learned to cut through bureaucratic red tape to achieve his ends. On leave of absence to run for the United States Senate in 1914, he also learned to take defeat. Returning to the Department of the Navy, he demonstrated administrative techniques that he later used as president. "He was a great trial and error guy," Emory S. Land would recall, "but he did have some good ideas."

In 1920, the Democratic party named Roosevelt as its vice-presidential candidate, and again he tasted defeat. Worse than that was the illness he contracted in the summer of 1921. Vacationing at Campobello Island, New Brunswick, where his family had a summer home, he was stricken with poliomyelitis so severely that for some time he was almost completely paralyzed. Despite intense suffering, he refused to give way to despair or despondency. From the beginning—and for many years after—he insisted that he would recover full use of his legs. Hours of hard work and therapeutic treatments availed little, however, and he would never walk again without heavy braces. Neither would he retreat from political activity; within two weeks after the initial attack he was writing letters to political associates. Soon he was sending Eleanor as his surrogate to conferences and gatherings he could not attend himself.

In at least two ways, as it worked out, Roosevelt's illness proved a political blessing. His unquenchable spirit appealed to all who admired courage in adversity. More important, he could avoid the defeats that dogged other Democratic politicians in the twenties without disassociating himself from politics. When he once again became a candidate for office in 1928, he campaigned vigorously and, in so doing, demolished suggestions that polio had rendered him unfit to carry official responsibilities. He also brought into his campaign for governor of New York a buoyancy and freshness that made him appear as an exciting successor to Al Smith at a time when many Democrats had grown sullen in defeat. Of course he won.

Considering the fact that he had to work with a legislature unsympathetic to his program and the fact that Smith's accomplishments were difficult to match, Roosevelt compiled an impressive record as governor. He centered his program on tax relief for farmers and lower utility rates for consumers. He managed to secure legislative approval of a power authority that would exploit the tremendous power potential of the St. Lawrence River. It was a program that upstate New Yorkers found extraordinarily attractive; combined with reactions to the depression, it provided him with a plurality of 725,000 votes when he sought reelection in 1930.

As the depression following the market crash deepened, Roosevelt revealed no more profound economic insight than did Hoover. He did reveal more compassion, however. Like the president, he talked about the fundamental soundness of the American system; but, unlike him, he took positive action for relief of the jobless. He assumed the initiative in calling for a conference of governors to discuss unemployment, and the New York Temporary Emergency Relief Administration was the first state relief agency to begin operations. To be sure, FDR worried about interference by the national government, for as long as he was governor he wished to concentrate as much power as possible in Albany. Yet he demonstrated his willingness to use his powers as governor, and the power of the state he headed, to serve social ends.

Burns has made an apt comparison of Roosevelt and Hoover. The governor's response to the depression, wrote FDR's biographer, did not differ significantly from that of the president. Both rejected either a dole or national appropriations for relief; both argued for relying on state and private agencies; both thought that government expenses should be cut and the national budget balanced. "Yet each presented a different image to the public—Roosevelt, that of a man in motion, Hoover, a man stuck fast." It was the man in motion who appealed to Democrats when they met in national convention at Chicago during the summer of 1932. Roosevelt reinforced that image when he flew to the convention to make his acceptance speech instead of following hoary tradition by waiting for a delegation to inform him of his nomination. His flight, he said, was symbolic of his determination to avoid hypocrisy and sham. "Let it be from now on the task of our Party to break foolish traditions," he told the cheering delegates, "and leave it to the Republican leadership, far more skilled in that art, to break promises."

## The Hundred Days

FDR was not a man gnawed by dogmas or ideals, but he was eager to go into action if Americans were willing to follow his leadership. That they were willing became abundantly clear shortly after his inauguration on March 4, 1933. Not so evident at the time was that beyond providing relief for the distressed and bringing about recovery, the president had little sense of where he wanted to take them. Originally intending to prepare carefully the program he would submit to Congress, his first moves were in areas where the need for action was obvious. On March 6, his first Monday in office, FDR declared a "bank holiday," suspending banking operations until Congress met in special session four days later to consider emergency legislation. The Emergency Banking Act, passed in a matter of hours, certainly represented no sharp break with tradition. It simply authorized the Federal Reserve Board to issue currency against bank assets, empowered the Secretary of the Treasury to take over gold bullion in exchange for paper, provided for supervision of bank reopenings, and permitted the Reconstruction Finance Corporation to make loans to banks. On March 12 the president delivered his first fireside chat to assure his listeners that the crisis had passed; and, by March 15, three-fourths of the banks in the Federal Reserve System had reopened their doors. FDR had taken a subject like banking, commented Will Rogers, and made everybody understand it—even the bankers.

While citizens watched the new administration meet the banking emergency, Roosevelt called for further legislation that would introduce stringent economy in government and legalize the sale of 3.2 beer. Economy, he said, would serve to balance the budget, and beverage taxes would increase Federal revenues. The two measures hardly represented a drastic departure from Hoover's approach to the problems of depression; it was the speed with which Roosevelt acted that distinguished him from his predecessor. FDR's swift moves created an illusion of purpose in the exercise of presidential power; but, for the time being at least, Americans cared less about what Roosevelt did than his manner of doing it. Again it was Will Rogers who best expressed the national mood. "The whole country is with him, just so he does something," he wrote of the president. "If he burned down the Capitol we would cheer and say 'well, we at least got a fire started anyhow.'"

FDR was too canny a politician to sacrifice the momentum that his first measures had stimulated. Instead of retreating to the drawing boards for painstaking development of his program, he pressed on with further recommendations. His advisers, the "brain trust" led by former Columbia University professors Rexford Guy Tugwell, Adolph A. Berle, and Raymond Moley, worked feverishly to get a variety of proposals into shape; so did department heads and members of Congress. For the next three months legislation was enacted with such unprecedented dispatch and in such unprecedented volume that for years New Dealers would speak with awe about accomplishments of the "hundred days."

During the early months of the New Deal the principal emphasis was on recovery, but the Administration concerned itself with relief too. From the outset Roosevelt was responsive to the needs of the unemployed, and throughout the thirties he consistently supported the conservation of resources and planned land use. Those two interests brought about establishment of the Civilian Conservation Corps, authorized by Congress in March and put into operation in April 1933. With an initial grant of $300 million, the CCC enrolled 250,000 young men and sent them to some 1,500 camps. There, under direction of the War Department, they worked at programs of flood control, soil conservation, and reforestation. By 1935 a half-million young men from all over the country were involved in the "C's"; by 1942, when the corps was dissolved, more than 2.5 million had served in the camps. Their comments attest to the value of the experience: "I feel almost as if I owned that land"; "if a boy wants to go and get a job after he's been in the C's, he'll know how to work"; "it made a man of me all right."

For all its accomplishments the CCC could not meet every relief need, and in May 1933 Congress passed the Federal Emergency Relief Act. Admittedly a stopgap measure, it provided a half billion dollars to be granted to the states and to municipalities. The president named Harry Hopkins as administrator of Federal relief activities, and under his direction they were later refined and expanded. A series of acts also provided assistance to millions of persons in need of mortgage relief. Under authority of the Emergency Farm Mortgage Act and the Farm Credit Act, FDR consolidated several bureaus into a single Farm Credit Administration

In August 1933, several prominent New Dealers accompanied FDR on a visit to the CCC camp at Big Meadows in the Shenandoah Valley, Virginia. Lunching with the president at the camp were (from left to right) Louis Howe, Harold Ickes, Robert W. Fechner, Henry A. Wallace, and Rexford G. Tugwell. Fechner, director of the CCC, was an old-time trade unionist and a former vice president of the Machinists. He received his appointment in part because Roosevelt wished to overcome criticism from union leaders who thought that the "C's" might bring about a militarization of labor (Associated Press photo).

that extended and administered loan programs for farmers. A Home Owners Loan Corporation, created at the end of the hundred days, refinanced home mortgages and provided for deferring or spreading out payments. Later, in 1934, Congress created the Federal Housing Administration to insure mortgages. Finally, under Roosevelt the Reconstruction Finance Corporation began to broaden the scope of its activities; between 1932 and 1941 it loaned a total of $15 billion to farmers, small businessmen, and even some home owners.

FDR's interest in reform matched his interest in relief, and the speculative disaster of 1929 made financial institutions a prime target for New Deal reformers. They did not rest content with inspection provisions of the Emergency Banking Act; on the contrary, they hoped to prevent some of the worst Wall Street malpractices with enactment of the Glass-Steagall Banking Act in mid-June 1933. This legislation, requiring separation of investment from commercial banking, made each Federal Reserve bank responsible for the investments of its member banks. No longer could speculators secure bank loans to purchase stocks and bonds. And small depositors received the additional security provided by the Federal Deposits Insurance Corporation, which insured deposits up to $2,500 (later raised to $5,000 in 1935, and then, incrementally, after World War II to $20,000). The Securities Act of 1933, supplemented by the Securities Exchange Act a year later, brought the possibility of regulating the securities market closer to realization. A five-man Securities and Exchange Commission received power to regulate trading practices and to demand information on the soundness of companies under scrutiny.

As echoes of prewar progressivism resonated in efforts to control stock-market practices, echoes of the greenback and populist movements reverberated in pleas for currency reform. Among many advisers who argued for raising prices through devaluation of the dollar was Professor George F. Warren of Cornell University; to the president, Warren's charts and graphs were convincing. As the Thomas Amendment to the Agricultural Adjustment Act provided the necessary authorization, Roosevelt proceeded to take the United States off the gold standard and raise the dollar price of gold (that is, he allowed the dollar to depreciate relative to foreign currencies). The president also undermined efforts of the World Monetary and Economic Conference, then meeting in London, to stabilize foreign exchange arrangements. He sent a message to disassociate the United States from what he termed the "specious fallacy" of attempting a "temporary and probably an artificial stability in foreign exchange on the part of a few large countries." Eventually, in January 1934, the President set the price of gold at $35 an ounce, thereby reducing the dollar to 59.06 per cent of its pre-1933 value in gold. Monetary reform, however, produced none of the consequences that Warren and others predicted. Prices did not rise, debtors were not benefited, and the new rate of exchange in effect increased the tariff by nearly 50 per cent.

**Efforts to Achieve Recovery: AAA and NRA**

Despite the failure of monetary manipulation, FDR remained optimistic, for he was not one to place exclusive reliance on dollar devaluation to bring about recovery. Indeed, the key recovery measures enacted during the hundred days were the Agricultural Adjustment Act and the National Industrial Recovery Act. A major difficulty in procuring farm legislation was the lack of cohesion among farmers and agricultural experts on what sort of legislation was required. During his first week in office, Secretary of Agriculture Henry A. Wallace met with farm leaders under orders from Roosevelt to lock themselves in a room and not come out until they had agreed on a program. The memorandum adopted by the conference contained a potpourri of ideas, many of them vintage suggestions that agriculturalists had long advocated; they formed a basis for the proposal drafted almost immediately and sent to Congress on March 16, 1933.

Enacted on May 12, the Agricultural Adjustment Act recognized the need for higher agricultural prices and aimed at increasing the farmers' share of the national income. An omnibus measure, the law provided the Administration with several options in its handling of farm problems. The Secretary of Agriculture secured power to reduce production of seven (later nine) basic products through acreage and other controls; in return, farmers would receive "fair and reasonable" rental or benefit payments. To raise funds necessary for such payments, the act imposed a tax on the processing of agricultural commodities. Crop reduction, thought the act's sponsors, would raise agricultural prices to parity (to the point, that is, where they would be comparable to prices of the 1909–1914 period).

Triple-A principles—acreage limitations, price supports, and land retirement—were to remain central in later agricultural programs. Nevertheless, the Agricultural Adjustment Administration, a new agency created to carry out provisions of the act, got off to a shaky start. With crops already in the ground, cotton farmers were looking forward to a banner production year. To meet the effect that an abundance of cotton would have on prices, AAA officials toured the South persuading farmers to plow up cotton in return for immediate payments. Hogs, too, threatened to overwhelm markets, so the AAA bought some six million pigs. Most of the animals were butchered and processed, with much of the pork going to relief agencies. But what most impressed New Deal critics was the

As if the depression were not already serious enough, dust storms compounded the problems of farmers on the Great Plains. "Wearing our shade hats, with handkerchiefs tied over our faces and Vaseline in our nostrils," wrote a woman from Eva, Oklahoma, in 1935, "we have been trying to rescue our home from the accumulations of wind-blown dust which penetrates wherever air can go" (Culver Pictures).

This couple, having lost a farm in Missouri, joined the legions of migratory workers who trekked to California during the years of drought and depression. Traveling from job to job when crops ripened and orchards came into bearing, they scratched out a meager existence, as did the Joads of John Steinbeck's novel, *Grapes of Wrath* (Library of Congress).

destruction of thousands of pigs and the dumping of edible meat. Socialist Norman Thomas remarked caustically that Henry Wallace was trying to solve the problem of poverty in the midst of plenty by eliminating the plenty.

The Supreme Court later invalidated portions of the Agricultural Adjustment Act, but the most trenchant criticism of its provisions had little to do with their constitutionality or with the awkwardness of early efforts to cut production. The fact is that the AAA followed more closely the wishes of large operators such as those identified with the Farm Bureau Federation than it did recommendations of small producers such as those identified with the Farmers' Union. Acreage reductions encouraged agricultural technology by stimulating a desire for higher yields, and it was farmers already relatively well off who could best afford to improve their methods.

In his excellent synthesis of the thirties, *The Age of the Great Depression,* Dixon Wecter concluded that the Triple-A had operated according to dubious principle: "to him that hath it shall be given." Marginal farmers, sharecroppers, and growers of crops not covered by the Agricultural Adjustment Act found themselves at least as bad off as they had been before the New Deal. "In '34 I had I reckon four renters and I didn't make anything," recalled an Oklahoma landlord. "I bought tractors on the money the government give me and got shet o' my renters." What happened to his renters he did not say; but, like other marginal farmers tractored off the land, they may well have packed up their flivvers and become migrant workers drifting from job to job. During the depression crisis American agriculture came to terms with limited markets and modern technology, but at horrendous cost to those forced off the land. For all its considerable achievements, the AAA did less than it could have to revitalize the nation's economy.

The National Recovery Administration, created by FDR to carry out provisions of the National Industrial Recovery Act, was even less successful. While divided counsel and interests characterized agriculture, trade and manufacturing were even less harmonious. Since 1931 the United States Chamber of Commerce had been developing a plan to control production and raise prices through a national council of industrialists working with trade associations. Like Hoover, the Chamber emphasized cooperative action and self-regulation. In the meantime, shortly after the election of 1932, Senator Hugo Black introduced a bill to prohibit interstate shipment of goods produced by labor working more than thirty hours a week. Intended to spread available work, the bill drew criticism from the president. It was rigid, said FDR, and contained no provision for minimum wages. When he asked Secretary of Labor Frances Perkins to develop an alternative, she produced amendments calling for minimum wages and supervision by industrial boards made up of representatives from labor, industry, and government. Business leaders balked at the secretary's amendments, which seemed to involve far more government regulation than they were ready to accept. While businessmen and New Dealers debated recovery, Raymond Moley, Rexford Tugwell, and Hugh S. Johnson managed to work out a compromise that would reconcile the principle of Federal control with the Chamber of Commerce idea of self-regulation. The chamber approved the compromise as an acceptable alternative to the Black bill, and in late May 1933 Congress passed the measure by an overwhelming margin.

The National Industrial Recovery Act harnessed two agencies in tandem to pull the nation out of the quagmire of depression. One of them, the Public Works Administration, received an appropriation of $3.3 billion for a variety of projects such as highways, courthouses, and public housing developments. Hitched to the faithful old mare of public works was Roosevelt's frisky colt, the National Recovery Administration. The act had given the president broad powers to draft industrial codes as a means of bringing about recovery, and the NRA assumed responsibility for the code-writing process. Professor Ellis Hawley has shown that under the law the agency might move in one of three directions: it could proceed to the creation of a government-protected, cartelized business commonwealth in line with Chamber of Commerce proposals; it could impose a collectivist economic system upon private corporations; or it could encourage a return to the old ideal of competition in an economy untrammeled by monopoly privilege. The vision of a business commonwealth was a refinement of the associational approach that businessmen had found so seductive in the twenties. The collectivist goal appealed to planners who favored controls over profits and investments as well as over prices and production; in the end, thought the planners, integrated groups of enterprises should operate to benefit consumers rather than owners. The competitive model attracted those who believed that large business agglomerations had helped to bring on the depression and that a restoration of small business would foster recovery.

Conflicts of vision within the agency prevented the NRA from carrying out an effective program. Of the three groups that sought to direct policy, advocates of a business commonwealth enjoyed the greatest influence both in the writing of codes and in the activities of code enforcement authorities. Business domination meant that the NRA came close to industrial self-government with all its tendencies toward cartelization; it meant, too, that wages and hours provisions of the codes were riddled with exceptions and loopholes. The turn that the NRA took aroused considerable criticism after the hundred days' euphoria had passed. Labor leaders pointed out that prices were rising more rapidly than wages and that collective bargaining provisions of the Recovery statute were being circumvented by company unions. Farm spokesmen complained that rising industrial prices threatened the Triple-A program. Even businessmen—always uncomfortable with official scrutiny, however sympathetic it might be—expressed annoyance with the red tape and administrative tangles of a complicated code structure.

The criticism provided advocates of competition with an opportunity to force changes in NRA policy, in part by exerting pressure on FDR. During its first months of operation the agency had received little direction from the president, but early in 1934 he issued an executive order permitting direct appeal to the Federal Trade Commission if small businessmen complained about NRA policy. He also named trial lawyer Clarence

"That Ought to Jolt Him" shows the Blue Eagle stinging the depression in 1933.

In 1933, when the National Industrial Recovery Act brought the NRA into being, director Hugh S. Johnson chose the blue eagle as its symbol. Like many New Dealers, the New York *World Telegram's* political cartoonist (Talburt) was optimistic about what results the bird might produce. Far from wiping out Old Man Depression, however, the blue eagle was itself wiped out by 1935 (Harold M. Talburt, N.Y. *World Telegram*).

Darrow to head a review board charged with the task of investigating the effect of NRA codes on small business. Hugh Johnson, who as chief administrator of the agency had shown a marked preference for business commonwealth objectives, eventually resigned his post in August. The way had been cleared for reorganization, but the work of reconstituting the NRA had scarcely begun when the Supreme Court rendered a decision invalidating the legislation on which it had been based.

The brief history of the first AAA and the NRA yields evidence of Roosevelt's limitations as chief executive; it also provides a partial explanation for the depression's lasting so long. Lacking a satisfactory theory to determine the causes of economic crisis, FDR could not act decisively to bring about recovery. Telling disputing advisers to lock themselves in a room until they could agree was a politically cautious but economically ineffective substitute for unambiguous commitment to a discriminating recovery program. Yet, in surrounding himself with men of diverging viewpoints, Roosevelt acted as though a patchwork New Deal would produce the needed economic stimulus. Perhaps he deluded himself as well as others. Certainly he seemed never to understand that elements of his New Deal might be contradictory and might therefore cancel each other in their effects. The AAA at least benefited large farmers and established a basis for future agricultural policy. The NRA, however, was driven by men of such contrary opinion that the once frisky colt began to behave as though it had been browsing in locoweed. Had the Supreme Court not put it out of its misery, New Dealers themselves might have shot it down. FDR was not himself blamed for the NRA's failure to pull its share of the recovery load, but the fact remains that he never did devise a way to restore prosperity.

## The Politics of the New Deal

However limited he may have been in his economic vision, FDR was a skilled politician, and the early New Deal was an enormous political success. A majority of Americans who lived through the thirties saw no anomaly here; they were aware of no incongruity that demanded explanation. One reason for their satisfaction was the considerable achievement of several New Deal programs. Especially noteworthy were the accomplishments of the Tennessee Valley Authority, which demonstrated that, given the right conditions, multiple-purpose agencies could function effectively despite internal disagreement.

The origins of TVA lay in the location of Wilson Dam and two government-owned nitrate plants at Muscle Shoals, Alabama, during World War I. In the postwar period several industries had cast covetous eyes on the installations; and, when Henry Ford offered to lease them for a hundred years at an annual rental of $1.5 million, President Harding had been disposed to accept the proposal. George Norris, progressive senator from Nebraska, could not agree. Convinced that the tremendous hydroelectric potential of the valley should not be bartered away to private interests, he successfully opposed the Ford lease, battling throughout the twenties for public development of the region. With Roosevelt's election in 1932, Norris and others who had joined his crusade rejoiced at the prospect of victory. They were not disappointed, for on May 18, 1933, Congress passed the necessary legislation.

Under a three-man board of directors, TVA first concentrated on mastering the Tennessee River and improving its 40,000 square-mile basin. Engineers and workers set about constructing dams for flood control and clearing a channel for navigation. They did not stop there. Arthur Morgan, first chairman of the TVA board, envisioned a regional utopia, and his influence was evident in a variety of projects. Experts went out to organize rural communities, set up demonstration farms using fertilizer produced at Muscle Shoals, establish recreation areas near newly created lakes, and supervise the planting of trees in areas vulnerable to soil erosion. But Morgan's plans for transforming the lives of valley residents encountered opposition from his fellow board member, David Lilienthal, who argued that the production of cheap electric power should be the authority's principal concern.

Lilienthal won his battle for control of TVA policy. He also won his battle with private utility companies worried about government competition in the electric power field. In *Ashwander v. TVA,* the Supreme Court ruled that the private companies had no legitimate complaint against TVA power production. By the time World War II brought an end to the depression, the authority was providing electric power for seventy-six municipalities and thirty-eight rural cooperatives. The valley ranked far above the rest of the nation in per capita use of electricity, and residents paid lower rates. Cheap electric power had also helped attract industries to the area; these in turn served to improve the region's economic condition. By 1940 per capita income in the valley had increased 73 per cent over that of 1933, as compared with a 56 per cent increase for the nation as a whole. Back in 1933 Senator Norris had asked the president what he would tell people who were curious about the political philosophy of TVA. "I'll tell them it's neither fish nor fowl," FDR replied with characteristic disdain for theoretical distinctions, "but, whatever it is, it will taste awfully good to the people of the Tennessee Valley."

TVA proved the prediction correct, but just as significant was the way Roosevelt stated it. His response to Norris was the response of a politician, not that of an economist. Happy to try within limits almost any proposal for overcoming the depression, the president tended to judge programs not by their effectiveness in the cause of recovery but by their capacity to please. FDR was intrigued with the ideas of planners; and, as might be expected of one who grew up on a well-managed Hudson Valley estate, he was fascinated by the promise of ecological programs—by agricultural experimentation, soil conservation, reforestation, and the like. He valued the advice of Tugwell, whose ideas about planning, if carried out, would have brought thorough regimentation of the entire economy with positive controls for every major economic activity. Yet Roosevelt probably never

A North Carolina hillside provided a convincing demonstration of how effective the
Tennessee Valley Authority's agricultural program could be. Before the program
went into effect, the two fields were equally eroded. Fertilization and planting
of ground cover restored the pasture on the left, thus permitting increased
livestock production (Tennessee Valley Authority).

really understood the full implications of Tugwell's ideas. If he did understand them, he was not prepared to run the political risk of acting upon
them. As Tugwell conceded and as Paul Conkin has observed, "Roosevelt
could not be induced to think and act outside of a political context."

If New Deal programs such as TVA achieved positive economic results,
then, it was because they were both economically sound *and* politically
popular. FDR was not one to adhere to an enterprise, however economically beneficial it might be, if its benefits were not readily understood and
as readily accepted. But as a political leader he was responsive both to
human need and to the interests of particular groups. His awareness of
political realities helps to explain his great popularity at a time when people experienced anxiety and loneliness in facing the terrors of life. A
White House secretary collected salutations of letters addressed to him,
and they indicate how the anxious and lonely reacted to the man who had
brought them a New Deal. Some correspondents addressed him with
cumbersome formality ("Dear humanitarian friend of the people") and
others with poignant familiarity ("My Pal!" and "Dear Buddy"), but most
of them saw the president as a good friend who stood ready to provide help
when they needed it.

All this is not to suggest, of course, that Americans unanimously supported Roosevelt. The American Liberty League was one of several organizations that consistently opposed nearly all his works. Made up largely

of disgruntled Democratic politicians (Al Smith, Jouett Shouse, John W. Davis) and disaffected businessmen (the Du Ponts, Sewell Avery of Montgomery Ward, J. Howard Pew of Sun Oil), the organization attacked the New Deal from either a conservative or a libertarian position. It was especially noisy in its hostility to anything that smacked of the welfare state. Yet the Roosevelt administration had little cause for concern about the carping of Liberty Leaguers; in a period when welfare meant survival for many people, FDR may actually have gained in popularity because of the enemies he made.

Far more threatening to the president were peddlers of patent economic remedies who, along with camp followers of the depression, solicited on the borders of discontent. In California, novelist-reformer Upton Sinclair developed a plan under the acronym EPIC (End Poverty in California). His central concept was a "production for use" system in which the state would buy or lease land and factories so that the unemployed could grow their own food and produce items to meet their own needs. Sinclair's victory in the Democratic gubernatorial primary of 1934 was a measure of EPIC's appeal, but his triumph also united the opposition in the November election. Receiving no assistance from FDR, Sinclair went down to defeat. But California was fertile with ideas, and the state produced the Townsend Plan as well as EPIC. Dr. Francis E. Townsend, a retired Long Beach physician, proposed that every unemployed person over the age of sixty receive a pension of $200 a month. The idea, attractive as it obviously was to oldsters, gave rise to Townsend Clubs that began to form all over the nation.

California did not stand alone in generating novel proposals. The governors of several states were candid in expressing doubts about the New Deal and in suggesting alternatives. In Minnesota, Floyd B. Olson, proclaiming himself a radical, announced a "Cooperative Commonwealth" as his ultimate goal. Under the leadership of Governor Philip F. La Follette, the Wisconsin Farmer–Labor Political Federation organized itself in 1935; the son of "Old Bob" was beginning to think about national political realignment to unite the progressives in both major parties. The most ambitious of state leaders, however, was Senator Huey Long of Louisiana. As governor during the twenties, Long had been a champion of the Louisiana back-country, working with a good-humored disregard for constitutional niceties to provide better schools, roads, and hospitals for the state. After his election to the Senate, and after the coming of depression, Long formulated what he called the Share Our Wealth plan. He promised every family a homestead and an annual income of $5,000; the program was to be funded by confiscating great fortunes. Every man would be a king, promised Long, and he presented his arguments so persuasively that even FDR began to worry. Only Long's assassination in 1935 removed what the President considered a real threat from "the Kingfish."

Others—including Gerald L. K. Smith, the Shreveport minister who had been active in developing Long's Share Our Wealth movement; and Father

Charles Coughlin, the "radio priest" whose weekly broadcasts from Royal Oak, Michigan, grew increasingly vitriolic—added to the spirit of discontent. FDR knew he could not rest on laurels he had accumulated during his first months in office; thus in 1935 he moved to secure new reforms. The most important measures (the Social Security Act, the Wagner Act, and the Emergency Relief Appropriation Act) allowed Roosevelt to maintain New Deal momentum and thus helped to thwart the ambitions of his rivals.

Yet there were ironies aplenty in the activities of 1935. Under the Social Security Act the Federal government assumed new responsibilities for the welfare of American citizens after retirement; in so doing, it took initiative from the Townsend movement. Yet the law was a far cry from enlightened welfare legislation. It made inadequate provision for unemployment or for illness prior to retirement; and it denied coverage to various classes of workers, most notably farm laborers and domestics. Worst of all, it was supported by a system of regressive taxation that withdrew vast sums of money from circulation, paying benefits on the basis of past earnings rather than of current needs.

Students of the period—at least those sympathetic to labor—have found less to criticize in the Wagner Act. The measure strengthened the National Labor Relations Board, giving it power to recognize appropriate bargaining agents and to restrain management from such unfair labor practices as company unions, blacklists, and yellow dog contracts. But it was New York Senator Robert F. Wagner, not FDR, who deserved credit for the act. Indeed, Roosevelt opposed it until after it had passed the Senate; and, while his eleventh-hour support allowed the bill to breeze through the House, it was never really his measure.

Again it was Roosevelt's identification with relief rather than with reform or recovery that serves to explain the New Deal's continuing popularity despite mounting criticism from the radicals and the Liberty League. The Emergency Relief Appropriation Act, which FDR worked out with the help of Harold Ickes and Harry Hopkins, provided an appropriation of $5 billion—the largest in American history—to create jobs for 3.5 million unemployed. Hopkins took the lead in developing the program once Congress had authorized it, approaching the task with energy and imagination. Always opposed to make-work projects such as leaf raking, Hopkins took the Works Progress Administration into several activities from mosquito control and the beautification of cemeteries to adult education classes and symphony orchestra performances.

Several lesser agencies developed as subsidiaries of the WPA. The National Youth Administration, set up to aid young people, provided part-time jobs for more than two million high school and college students. It also aided those who were not in school. The Federal Theatre Project employed actors, directors, and craftsmen to produce plays, circuses, and vaudeville shows; in four years it staged performances for audiences totaling at least thirty million people. The Federal Writers' Project turned out

Roosevelt was the first president effectively to communicate with American citizens via the air waves, and he has never been surpassed in the art. "As he talked his head would nod and his hands would move in simple, natural, comfortable gestures," recalled Frances Perkins when she described the fireside chats. "His face would smile and light up as though he were actually sitting on the front porch or in the parlor with them. People felt this, and it bound them to him in affection" (Brown Brothers).

a thousand publications, including fifty-one excellent state and territorial guides and twenty regional guides. The Federal Arts Project sponsored classes in arts and crafts and published an *Index of American Design*. More visible were the murals that the Arts Project placed in post offices and other public buildings. FDR never displayed more sensitivity than he revealed in his comment on the work of WPA muralists. He found "some of it good, some of it not so good, but all of it native, human, eager, and alive—all of it painted by their own kind in their own country, and painted about things that they know and look at often and have touched and loved." When relief took such forms, the grounds for FDR's political popularity were well established.

## A Succession of Difficulties

Frances Perkins's reminiscent biography, *The Roosevelt I Knew,* contains a revealing account of the president's response to the probing questions of a young reporter. Was Roosevelt a Communist? A capitalist? A Socialist? To each query the reply was negative.

"Well," the reporter burst out, "what is your philosophy then?"

The President seemed puzzled. "Philosophy?" he asked. "Philosophy? I am a Christian and a Democrat—that's all."

The Secretary of Labor was doubtless correct in assuming that Roosevelt referred to his party affiliation, but he was a democrat also in his belief that the majority should rule. FDR habitually thought of himself as an agent of the popular will, and his triumph over Alfred M. Landon in the presidential election of 1936 reinforced that perception of his role. Some 27 million voters cast their ballots for FDR, and he carried forty-six states; Landon polled 16 million popular votes, winning the electoral votes only of Maine and Vermont. After such a victory few would fault the president for identifying his actions with the will of the people.

Over the past two years, however, the Supreme Court had offended the democratic instincts of Roosevelt and his supporters. The New Deal had vastly increased the range of the Federal government's activities, and state governments had also enlarged their powers through "little New Deal" measures. From the beginning four of the nine justices—James Mc-Reynolds, Willis Van Devanter, George Sutherland, and Pierce Butler—took a dim view of expanding government activities. Three of their colleagues—Louis Brandeis, Benjamin Cardozo, and Harlan Fiske Stone—were far more amenable to New Deal innovations. That left Owen Roberts and Chief Justice Charles Evans Hughes in key positions at the center of the Court. The "Steady Four" needed only one recruit to dominate, and in the spring of 1935 Roberts began siding with the advocates of limited government and the rule of law.

The sessions of 1935 and 1936 were thus exceedingly painful ones for Roosevelt as the Supreme Court invalidated no less than twelve acts of Congress along with state legislation that harmonized with New Deal objectives. If a majority of the justices believed that the New Deal had broken precedent, they certainly retaliated in kind. Never before had the Court found an act of Congress unconstitutional because it delegated legislative power to the executive branch of the government. Three times in little more than a year the majority opinion employed the argument, most notably in the Schechter Case that brought on the demise of the NRA. The majority had other weapons in its arsenal, some of them archaic but still serviceable. The regulatory power of the government, argued Justice Sutherland in *Carter v. Carter Coal Company,* had to be based on the commerce power, and mining coal was not interstate commerce. Working conditions in the mines were therefore local conditions over which the Federal government had no control. In *United States v. Butler,* Justice Roberts took a limited view of congressional power to tax and spend. The processing tax of the Agricultural Adjustment Act, he argued, was actually a device to control production rather than a means of raising revenue, and Congress had therefore exceeded the powers delegated to it by the Constitution. Of the major New Deal programs that were subjected to judicial scrutiny, only the TVA survived. The Wagner Act and the Social Security Act were not reviewed, but New Dealers had reason to fear how the Court might deal with them if the opportunity arose.

With his astounding victory in 1936, Roosevelt was understandably eager to put the Court in its place. For once, however, his political finesse left him. Instead of securing reform through constitutional amendment (he thought the process too time-consuming), he called congressional leaders to the White House in February 1937, asking them to introduce a bill that he hoped would produce a Court more sympathetic to the New Deal. The president proposed that he be given power to appoint a new justice for every justice who failed to quit the bench within six months after reaching the age of seventy. The bill provided that he might appoint a total of six new justices and thus conceivably increase the Court to fifteen members.

The proposal brought a quick reaction. Several congressmen who were not opposed to its substance were offended by FDR's tactics. He had not mentioned Supreme Court reform during the campaign, and after the

When Roosevelt pressed for congressional action on a bill that would permit him to increase the size of the Supreme Court, his proposal brought a mixed reaction. Cartoonist Fred O. Seibel of the Richmond *Times-Despatch* was one of those who sided with the president against the "nine old men." Congressmen were not as cooperative as the cartoon made them out to be, however, and the court-packing bill came to naught (Richmond *Times-Despatch*).

election he had taken few people into his confidence. His professed concern for an overburdened Court was a transparent subterfuge and easily met by an open letter from Hughes showing that the justices were, in fact, abreast of their work. What ultimately frustrated the president's plan, however, was a shift in the nature of decisions rendered after the bill had been introduced. Late in March 1937, with Justice Roberts reversing his position, the Court upheld a state of Washington minimum wage law similar to a New York law it had struck down ten months earlier. "A switch in time saves nine," remarked a legal wit, not yet aware of the fact that his comment would apply to more than one case. In short order the Court sustained the Administration in five important cases involving the National Labor Relations Act, and in May it upheld the Social Security Act. When Justice Van Devanter announced his retirement, the need for changes in the Court seemed even less compelling. "Why run for a train after you've caught it?" asked Senator James F. Byrnes.

FDR could take small satisfaction in results of the Court fight, however, even though he tried to claim victory. In the anticlimactic conclusion of the struggle, his bill was pared down to inconsequential reforms that received the president's signature. More important were other results of the struggle. For the first time, influential and sympathetic members of his own party questioned Roosevelt's judgment. His reputation for political insight beginning to tarnish, he did little to refurbish it when, in the elections of 1938, he sought without success to "purge" from the party several Democrats of doubtful loyalty. The breezy confidence of 1933 had blown away, and it was a sobered president who turned his attention to other problems.

Some of these, too, were his own making. Running against Hoover in 1932, FDR had said that he regarded "reduction in Federal spending as one of the most important issues of this campaign." In subsequent years he ran heavy deficits as a temporary expedient, but he never gave up the notion that balanced budgets would inspire the confidence necessary for complete recovery. By 1937 the worst of the depression had passed. More than 46 million people were gainfully employed, as compared with less than 39 million in 1933. National income, in 1929 prices, had risen from $56.7 billion to $80.8 billion, and GNP had gone from $72.7 billion to $105.3 billion. Early in 1937, then, FDR and his advisers believed the time had come to turn over to private business the responsibility for achieving full recovery. The national budget for the fiscal year 1938 reduced by one-third the government expenditures for relief and recovery. The Federal deficit dropped from $3.6 billion in 1936 to $400 million in 1937, so sharp was the cutback. With the surpluses of state and local jurisdictions, the combined budgets of all governmental units went from a 1936 deficit of $3.1 billion to a 1937 surplus of $300 million. Other restrictive influences accompanied the turn from deficit to surplus financing. Among the most important were the new Social Security taxes (which removed $1.3 billion from the national income) and the Federal Reserve Board's decision to double the reserve requirements of member banks (which checked the expansion of bank credit and the money supply).

Roosevelt's new fiscal policy, along with other deflationary pressures, soon produced horrors that threatened to match those of 1929–1933. GNP declined to $100.5 billion in 1938. The number of unemployed persons increased from an estimated 7.7 million in 1937 to 10.4 million in 1938. The index of manufacturing output (1929 = 100) fell from 103.3 to 80.9, lower than it had been in 1930, 1935, or 1936. Residential construction was hard hit, and private investment dropped by almost one-half. Americans began to talk about the "Roosevelt recession."

Liberty Leaguers, Republicans, and others of classical economic persuasion held the New Deal responsible for the crisis because it had coddled labor, undermined the free enterprise system, and destroyed business confidence. For their part, New Deal partisans countered with equally irrelevant arguments and actions. Capital had gone on strike to embarrass the president, charged some, including Roosevelt. Monopoly, they added, had produced high prices, which in turn had reduced consumption. FDR secured congressional approval for a Temporary National Economic Committee to scrutinize the nation's economy, while Thurman Arnold, who headed the Antitrust Division of the Justice Department, launched a full-scale attack on monopoly. Valuable as the voluminous TNEC reports proved to be, and effective though Arnold's trust-busting might have been, they did not bring about recovery. They were, indeed, evidences of means unsuited to the end that FDR and the nation sought.

## The Advent of Keynesian Economics

In December 1933 a Cambridge don by the name of John Maynard Keynes wrote an open letter to the President of the United States. He urged upon Roosevelt the importance of increasing public expenditures rather than increasing taxes. Taxation would merely transfer buying power from one group to another, but government spending would create new aggregate demand and serve to bring on recovery. Six months later Keynes visited Washington, calling at the White House to elaborate on the argument of his letter. His conference with Roosevelt was as disappointing to the don as it was confusing for the president. Shortly afterward, when visiting Frances Perkins, Keynes expressed admiration for some of the New Deal's content, but he added wistfully that he had "supposed the President was more literate, economically speaking." The Secretary of Labor also received a report from FDR. "I saw your friend Keynes," remarked the president. "He left a whole rigmarole of figures. He must be a mathematician rather than a political economist."

Roosevelt correctly sensed that his visitor was a man whose interests extended beyond political economy. In addition to lecturing on economics, Keynes patronized the ballet (his wife was a ballerina), collected modern art and rare books, ran a theater and a farm, advised His Majesty's Government from time to time, wrote books and articles, held a variety of positions including the chairmanship of a life insurance company and a directorship of the Bank of England, played bridge daringly, and was a star of the Bloomsbury cluster that dazzled Britain with its intellectual brilliance. He claimed to have but one regret: that he had not drunk more champagne. Unlike Karl Marx, who died in penury the year of Keynes's birth, he had a golden touch that brought him great wealth. If Marx was "the draftsman of Capitalism Doomed," as Robert L. Heilbroner has suggested, then Keynes was to become "the architect of Capitalism Viable."

The author of several highly acclaimed books (including a polemic on the peace treaties of 1919 and a mathematical *Treatise on Probability*), Keynes had not yet published his major work at the time he first met Roosevelt in 1934. But the central ideas of *The General Theory of Employment, Interest, and Money* had already formed; after its publication in 1936 it would bring about—in combination with events—a transformation of economic thought in the Western world. *The General Theory* annihilated old orthodoxies that did not square with realities of the thirties. It built a new theoretical structure to explain economic stagnation. It recommended recovery measures that proved effective in 1938. The war years provided further validation of Keynesian ideas, and in the postwar period they gained general acceptance among academicians and policy makers alike.

Even a sketchy discussion of Keynes must begin with the pre-1929 economic orthodoxy that he attacked. Jean-Baptiste Say, a nineteenth-century French economist, had formulated a "Law of Markets" so simply and persuasively that most economists still accepted its basic principle. Succinctly put, Say's law held that "supply creates its own demand." Men produce goods only in order to make possible their consumption of other goods, the argument ran; and, since increased production means increased capacity to consume, demand will always keep pace with production. The law implied, as Keynes pointed out, that full employment was always possible, and orthodox theory held that all unemployment was either frictional (that is, seasonal) or voluntary. Workers, according to theory, functioned on a pleasure-pain principle. That is, since work was painful but wages brought pleasure, the decision to work involved a judgment that the pleasure of wages would be greater than the pain of work. If wages were not sufficient reward for the pain of labor, then workers would remain idle.

All this struck Keynes as nonsense. For one thing, he could easily demonstrate that involuntary unemployment in the thirties was extensive. Orthodox analysis was obviously faulty; Keynes argued that what it lacked was a theory of aggregate demand. The development of that theory was, according to economist Robert Lekachman, the "highest distinction" of Keynes's book. Reduction of wages by a single businessman would, all other things being equal, result in greater profits. But, as Keynes pointed out, other things could never remain equal if *all* businessmen reduced wages and costs. If the total of all wages fell, then the demand for goods would fall proportionately. Aggregate demand for goods depends upon aggregate income. Thus, while one employer might increase his profits by reducing wages, all employers would suffer from a general decline in income.

Entrepreneurs anticipate selling goods at prices that at least equal the costs of production (which include wages and normal profits). A stable economy is one in which the aggregate costs of production of all entrepreneurs exactly equals the volume of sales they expect to make. Since, however, economic equilibrium does not always prevail, Keynes believed that entrepreneurial desire to expand or reduce employment, wages, and output is related to what he called the aggregate demand function. If actual demand for goods exceeds expectations, inventories decline, retailers and wholesalers increase orders to manufacturers, and manufacturers increase production. On the other hand, if demand does not meet expectations, then inventories mount, orders are canceled, and manufacturers reduce production.

The level of employment that actually prevails is determined "by the point of intersection between the aggregate demand function and the aggregate supply function," for it is there that the entrepreneur finds his greatest possible profit. Say's law—contentedly assuming that demand follows supply—is simply invalid. Furthermore, the assumed wage bargain between employer and employee is a fiction. Employment is related to aggregate demand for the goods and services of the entire economy, not to the operation of a pleasure-pain principle among workers, and equilibrium can be reached at any level between zero and full employment.

Because aggregate demand is crucial to all economic activity, Keynes turned his attention to its sources. In other words, assuming that government taxes as much out of the income stream as it contributes in the form of expenditures, he focused his attention on consumers and investors. Decisions of consumers are influenced by three considerations: the amount of income they have to spend, objective factors such as the cost of living, and subjective factors such as the desire to save money for a college education or for some other personal purpose. Subjective factors have little short-term importance, and objective factors other than the cost of living are either trivial or tend to counterbalance each other. But the amount of income available to the consumer is of prime importance. Keynes called it a "fundamental psychological law" that people are inclined "to increase their consumption as their income increases but not by as much as the increase in their income."

The consumption function, depending as it does on income, could never explain the size of either the national income or employment. Only investment, the other component of aggregate demand, can explain national income. No other variable in the Keynesian system is more important than investment. As it increases or decreases, it produces multiplied effects on national income and employment. In good times savings tend to increase, and they are put to work in "real" investments (that is, new machines, factories, and enlarged inventories, not stocks and bonds). In such times business expectations, interest rates, and profits all favor producers. Increased investment brings higher incomes and fuller employment. On downward swings of the business cycle, however, the expectations of investors are reduced; the rate of investment thus falls off. Declining investment diminishes national income, consumption shrinks, savings are dissipated, and employment declines.

A fundamental problem that Keynes discerned in an unregulated capitalist economy is that it could reach equilibrium at any point short of full employment. Aggregate demand would be insufficient to create jobs, and equilibrium could extend a depression for a very long period of time. The task of policy makers, then, was to find some way of increasing aggregate demand. Throughout *The General Theory* Keynes scattered several suggestions for achieving that objective. Coercing interest rates so as to encourage optimum investment offered some possibilities, but Keynes himself doubted that it would revive the economy. What remained as a logical alternative was for the government itself to become an investor. All the favorable multiplier effects of private investment could just as easily be achieved through government investment. Even ridiculous projects—building pyramids or filling coal mines with rubbish—could produce beneficial economic results if government expenditures were large enough. But if government spending was to be socially as well as economically beneficial, Keynes believed, it should be devoted to public works projects of greater utility. Tax reductions might also achieve recovery, though reducing taxes would enlarge the area of private control over spending.

To its critics, *The General Theory* seemed nothing more than an apology for what the Roosevelt administration was already doing, and they pointed out that the New Deal had not achieved full recovery. Furthermore, charged some of them, New Deal deficits imposed an untold burden on future generations of Americans. Both points deserve comment. In the

At 12:01 on the morning of April 7, 1933, engine number 8027 began moving beer out of the Schlitz Brewery in Milwaukee. Prohibition was coming to an end, and in cities such as Milwaukee, St. Louis, and Baltimore celebrants greeted the resurrection of John Barleycorn with sirens, steam whistles, and cheers. Nevertheless, as John Maynard Keynes knew, it would take far more than measures such as modification of the Volstead Act and passage of the Twenty-first Amendment to pull the nation out of depression (State Historical Society of Wisconsin).

Keynes certainly did not disapprove of prohibition repeal, but of far greater economic importance were measures to increase aggregate demand. New Deal work relief programs, such as this road-building project, were a means of providing assistance to the jobless. Had the government investment in roads and other improvements been more massive, however, it might have been correspondingly more potent in stimulating recovery (State Historical Society of Wisconsin).

first place, government investments that seemed gigantic during the thirties were never large enough to increase aggregate demand to a point where full employment was possible. Then, too, the New Deal was not a coherent set of agencies and operations; Keynes could approve parts of it, but other parts ran counter to his ideas. Social Security taxes, for example, withdrew funds from the national income stream and therefore counteracted the effects of welfare appropriations.

Although some of his advisers were advocates of massive spending, FDR never believed that Americans could spend their way out of the depression. His effort to balance the budget in 1937, an indication of how little he understood Keynes's thesis, brought about a recession precisely because it cut back government investments sharply. Ironically, Roosevelt retained along with others an almost superstitious fear of budgetary deficits. Critics of government spending (especially Liberty Leaguers) never could comprehend that a depression is the worst time to be puritanical—that houses, schools, roads, and dams cannot be considered a burden to people they benefit, or that a public debt is an asset to those who hold it. Roosevelt's attempt to balance the budget suggests that he in part shared the economic misconceptions of his most vociferous opponents.

Even though Roosevelt never grasped the argument of Keynes, he did accede to a more thoroughly Keynesian program in 1938 than he had ever before accepted. In April he sent Congress a series of "Recommendations Designed to Stimulate Further Recovery." Both houses responded and in June passed a $3.75 billion omnibus measure. The PWA, which had been liquidated only a few months before, came to life with nearly a billion dollars' worth of the appropriation. Harry Hopkins's WPA did even better, receiving $1.4 billion. FDR and his advisers parceled out lesser amounts for low-cost housing, parity payments to farmers, the Farm Security Administration, and the National Youth Administration.

The spending program had the effect that Keynes predicted. In 1939, GNP rose above its 1937 level, private investment picked up, and—more slowly—unemployment declined. If FDR learned anything from the recession experience, however, he showed little indication of having been educated. In private he continued to hanker for a balanced budget; in his speeches he deplored deficits and promised a return to fiscal orthodoxy as soon as possible. He never returned, of course, for the outbreak of World War II necessitated a massive investment in the tools of war that would never have been approved had it been proposed for tools of peace. Nevertheless, the spending for national security provided even more convincing validation of Keynesian theory than did the spending of 1938. After all, Keynes had pointed out that the nature of the investment had little to do with its economic consequences. Thus the huge wartime investments of the forties brought a prosperity that no one in the depression thirties had dreamed possible.

# 8

# Prosperity, Depression, and the World: American Foreign Policy, 1919-1941

Although the United States spurned the League of Nations in 1920, Americans entered the postwar decade with confidence in their ability to preserve essential national interests. Never questioning their power, they questioned only the uses to which President Wilson had put it. A perceptive British critic suggested that allied vindictiveness made the peace treaties all but unworkable, and the investigations of American historians in the twenties stripped away the moral justification for so harsh a settlement. The conclusion that the nation had made a ghastly blunder in 1917 gained common currency; so, too, did the supposition that league membership would have compounded the error. Their prosperity was not dependent on international organizations, most Americans believed, for American power was sufficient to take whatever action was necessary to preserve it. The United States would not shut itself off from the rest of the world, but neither would citizens repeat the mistake of 1917 by sanctioning the gratuitous assumption of international responsibilities. During the postwar decade, then, American diplomats labored for reductions in national armaments so as to prevent another outbreak of military madness and for international economic well-being so as to promote the foreign markets that would advance prosperity at home.

The depression of the thirties taught a very different lesson. Not just an American phenomenon, it profoundly altered the character of international relations. It placed Japan under even greater economic stress than it did the United States, and it exacerbated within Germany the intense dissatisfactions that assured the rise to power of Adolf Hitler and National Socialism. Neither League of Nations mechanisms nor American policies were adequate to cope with the international problems that multiplied as Japan out of perceived economic necessity adopted a program of expansion, and as Nazi Germany (acting in concert with Fascist Italy) began its drive for the domination of Europe.

Few Americans—not even the president—had any clear or positive idea of what direction United States foreign policy should take during the years of economic uncertainty. With their understanding of the recent past, however, most Americans formed some very clear ideas about the direction it should not take. Time and again in the thirties the newly developed public opinion polls indicated that respondents thought Wilson's policies in 1917 unsound, and time and again the polls reflected a deep-seated preference for the position taken by isolationists who wanted no part in foreign quarrels. Isolationism won easy victories in the passage of neutrality acts and partial victories in forcing the Roosevelt administration to at least take isolationist arguments into account. Yet war came once more to the United States, and this time the opponents of American involvement would have to share blame for the suffering it brought.

**Economic
Consequences of
the Peace**

In 1919 Maynard Keynes served as financial representative of the British Treasury at the Paris Peace Conference. As one who believed that Europeans had always formed a cultural entity, he hoped that the treaty concluding the Great War would be written in a spirit of reconciliation. If the nations that had "flourished together" and "rocked together in a war" could reach a mutually satisfactory agreement, they might return to prewar amity; if not, they would have to face the consequences in "the bankruptcy and decay of Europe" that would inevitably affect victor and vanquished alike. In short order the young economist came to a depressing assessment of the prospects for a peace of reconciliation; but, thinking he might temper the spirit of vindictiveness, he stayed on in Paris through May. Finally, he informed Lloyd George of his intention to resign. "I can do no more good here," he wrote to the prime minister. "I've gone on hoping even through these last dreadful weeks that you'd find some way to make of the Treaty a just and expedient document. But now it's apparently too late. The battle is lost." Returning to Britain, Keynes spent the summer of 1919 writing a bitter denunciation of the treaties the diplomats had drafted.

Passion and intelligence produced *The Economic Consequences of the Peace,* a document as penetrating in its analysis of the settlement's shortcomings as it was caustic in its description of negotiators. Central to its argument was the contention that reparations provisions of the treaty were unrealistic and, beyond that, destructive. As Keynes saw it, the German economic system before the war had relied on three supports: overseas commerce involving the German merchant marine, colonies, foreign investments, exports and trading connections; German coal and iron resources, along with the industries that developed out of their exploitation; and the German transport and tariff system. He charged that the Versailles Treaty deprived Germany of all these supports while it also imposed enormous (though as yet not specified) reparations obligations on the German people.

Keynes hammered away at the point that war guilt, wherever it rested, had nothing to do with postwar economic realities. Germany did not have the means to make payments such as the Allies were likely to demand. Liquidation of remaining German assets (a $300 million stock of gold, a depleted merchant marine, and foreign securities) would have raised only a fraction of the total amount required. Only by maintaining a highly favorable balance of payments—which would require Spartan living conditions and extraordinary effort—could Germany raise as much as half a billion dollars a year. That even this amount would be insufficient became evident in the spring of 1921, when the Reparations Commission finally decided on the extent of German obligations. The reparations total was fixed at $33 billion in addition to Belgium's war debt; payments were to be made in fixed annuities of $500 million and in variable annuities equal to a tax of 26 per cent on German exports. Even if Germans had been convinced that the payments were just, they might have been unable to meet them. In any case, no one who read *The Economic Consequences of the Peace* should have been surprised that Germany defaulted.

Determined to have reparations in one way if not another, the French and Belgian governments sent troops into the Ruhr in January 1923. Germans countered with passive resistance, but they faced economic disaster as the deutschmark became worthless and industry came to a standstill. At this point a new German government under Gustav Stresemann sent word to the Reparations Commission indicating a willingness to resume payments and requesting a review of German economic capabilities. The United States took an active part in the review. In fact, President Coolidge appointed Charles G. Dawes as chairman of the committee charged with the responsibility of making recommendations.

The Dawes Plan, submitted to the Reparations Commission on April 9, 1924, contained several proposals. It did not modify the total German obligation, but it did set up a new schedule of reparations discharge. Under the Dawes schedule, payments would start at $250 million, rising gradually over a four-year period to $625 million. Future payments might be adjusted upward or downward according to an index of German prosperity. The Dawes Plan also proposed stabilizing German currency by reorganizing the Reichsbank under an international board of supervisors and providing it with exclusive control over paper money for a fifty-year period. In addition, the Dawes Committee suggested a loan of $200 million to assure the fiscal soundness of the German economy. Both the Reparations Commission and the Stresemann government accepted the plan; by September 1924 it was in operation. During the following July the last of the French and Belgian troops departed the Ruhr.

The Dawes Committee did not bring to an end American involvement in the affairs of Europe. Eventually, in 1929, further revision of the reparations schedule was entrusted to another committee of experts in international finance. Owen D. Young, chairman of the board of directors of General Electric and an organizer of the Radio Corporation of America, assumed leadership of the committee, which came up with recommendations

Few international problems produced more misunderstanding than did the debt-reparations tangle. Many Americans, refusing to acknowledge any benefit from loans to other countries, viewed "Uncle Samaritan" as did cartoonist John T. McCutcheon. Hence their vexation when all debtor nations, except Finland, defaulted during the early years of the Great Depression. (Reprinted courtesy of the Chicago *Tribune*.)

even more favorable to Germany than the Dawes Committee had produced. The Young Plan reduced the total German liability to $8 billion and cut the "unconditional" annual payments back to $165 million. Other payments, scaled to German prosperity, were secured by a mortgage on that country's railroads. To handle the necessary transactions, the Young Plan called for creation of a new Bank of International Settlements to be set up in Basel, Switzerland. The Young proposals went before a diplomatic conference at the Hague, where they were approved in January 1930.

Why should the United States, rejecting membership in the League of Nations, demonstrate such interest in the reparations problem during the decade of the twenties? A partial answer to that question lies in the fact that, although the American government consistently denied it, there was a close relationship between reparations and war debts. After entry into the Great War, the United States had loaned more than $10.3 billion to American allies. When British negotiators at the Peace Conference proposed a general cancellation of all inter-Allied war debts, Wilson rejected the suggestion; his successors continued to insist that the money be returned with interest. During the postwar period debtor nations attempted to persuade the United States that repayment was contingent upon Germany's meeting its reparations agreements, but the American government stood firm. Refusing to concede any connection between debt and reparations payments, it demanded in 1922 that the debts be funded. The funding was accomplished, interest rates being reduced in the process; but it was clear that some means of easing the reparations problem had to be found. The Dawes and Young plans were responses to that need.

Another justification for the United States's involvement in German economic problems rested on the conviction that European well-being and American prosperity were bound by commercial ties. Secretary of Commerce Hoover, whose interest in foreign trade led him to establish a Bureau of Foreign and Domestic Commerce within his department, reasoned that a depressed Europe would provide a poor market for American goods. In part to assure European prosperity, then, Hoover and others encouraged loans to European countries including Germany. Thus there developed the anomalous condition referred to in chapter 7. American money, privately loaned to other countries, helped to pay for exports—particularly agricultural exports—from the United States. American loans also helped Germany meet reparations payments, which in turn improved overseas markets as well as the chances for payment of inter-Allied war debts.

**American
Revisionism**
The American interest in commercial expansion abroad was not confined to Europe, and one may well wonder how the United States acquired a reputation for being "isolationist" in the years after World War I. The variance between action and reputation, however, may be more apparent than real. Slipperiness of definition (a common problem with words employed as epithets) has produced enough ambiguity to reduce many a discussion to the point of futility. If isolationism implies a total lack of interest in other countries, then, of course, the United States has never been isolationist. But for only a few people has the term ever carried such implication. In its most common usage it suggests a desire to avoid the quarrels of other countries and a reluctance to assume responsibility for policing the world. Isolationism, historian John Cooper has argued, is a political position, not a pattern of economic behavior. Its essence is "refusal to commit force beyond hemispheric bounds, or absolute avoidance of overseas military alliances." Isolationists, in other words, adopted unilateralist and noninterventionist attitudes; they opposed alliances with other powers because they thought that foreign entanglements might lead to involvement in war, and they opposed using American power to resolve conflicts when other nations allowed themselves to drift into war. Viewing isolationism as a political position with programmatic and ideological dimensions permits recognizing the importance both of the drive to expand overseas markets and of the retreat from overseas alliances and commitments.

Isolationism began to emerge during the Great War that ended nearly a hundred years of international stability. Throughout most of its history the United States had enjoyed, as Professor C. Vann Woodward has observed, a remarkable "physical security from hostile attack and invasion." That security was not a result of policy, but a gift of nature. Protected by the Atlantic Ocean to the east, the Pacific in the west, and the polar icecap in the north, the North American continent required no great fleets or armies to discourage interference or invasions. And in the Atlantic, where danger was remotely possible, British national interest maintained a fleet from which the United States benefited. Only during the Civil War, then, did Americans raise armies of significant size, but the Civil War was a domestic rather than a foreign conflict. With imperialist ventures of the late nineteenth century and with deepening involvement in the struggles of Europe after 1914, however, free security began to erode. Surveying such erosion with dismay, many Americans cast about for a means of reversing the process they saw taking place in international affairs. Woodrow Wilson rested his hopes in the League of Nations. Others, with less confidence in the league, tended to favor rejection of any foreign commitment however well intentioned.

In 1917 the isolationist forces had succumbed to the pressures for war, but they did not disintegrate, and with the coming of peace they began to reassert themselves. They collaborated in the fight against Wilson and the league, and throughout the twenties they labored to refine arguments against international obligations that could lead to a second involvement of American troops on foreign soil. During the years after 1919 the isolationists found reinforcement in the researches of historians. Before war's end the new Bolshevik government of the USSR opened up state archives to reveal prewar secret treaties to which the Czarist regime had been a party; and, after peace had been negotiated, archives of the Central Powers added to the flow of documents. With source materials in abundance, historians on both sides of the Atlantic turned their attention to determination of responsibility for the war.

During the summer of 1920 Sidney Bradshaw Fay published in the *American Historical Review* the first of a series of articles on the origins of the war. Relying on German and Austrian sources, Fay demonstrated conclusively that, while the German government might not have acted with wisdom, it had certainly not engaged in a plot to set off a holocaust. The war guilt clause of the peace settlement, which placed responsibility for the war on governments of the Central Powers, obviously gave treaty sanction to an oversimplification if not an untruth.

Fay's articles provided substance for an acrimonious debate among historians, with the discussion of war guilt then producing a school of "revisionists" who began to investigate Allied complicity in the events leading to conflict. Before long the historical debate expanded into media with broader appeal than the *American Historical Review*. Oswald Garrison Villard, who in 1918 had taken over editorial responsibilities for *The Nation,* vigorously supported historical revision in articles and reviews. The editor encountered no dearth of literature critical of the Allies. Widely read books such as Frederick Bausman's *Let France Explain* and John Kenneth Turner's *Shall It Be Again?* spread doubts that the treaty's war guilt clause was justified. Kansas editor William Allen White, among others, began to ask questions about what good the war had accomplished. "Every new book destroys some further illusion," observed Reinhold Niebuhr, then a young clergyman in Detroit. "How can we ever again believe anything when we compare the solemn pretensions of statesmen with the cynically conceived secret treaties?"

The most strident of the revisionists was Harry Elmer Barnes, professor of historical sociology at Smith College. His propensity for stirring controversy assured him an audience beyond the campus, and he made the most of his opportunities. Beginning with a review article, "Seven Books of History against the Germans," published in the *New Republic* early in 1924, Barnes spent several years writing and lecturing on the origins of the Great War. Few would quarrel with his generalization that the "wrong-headed and savage European system of nationalism, imperialism, secret diplomacy and militarism" provided the context for conflict. Yet he also offered listings of the nations most culpable, listings he revised from time to time. Never did Germany rank number one, and by 1925 Barnes was contending that France and Russia were solely responsible for the hostilities that broke out in 1914.

Revisionism in the twenties naturally raised the question of why the United States had taken part in the conflict that shook the foundations of European civilization. American intervention, argued Barnes, had not been a response to the threat of invasion; neither was it undertaken to make the world safe for democracy. The United States had gone to war "to protect our investment in Allied bonds, to insure a more extensive development of the manufacture of war materials and to make it possible to deliver our munitions to Allied ports." American industry and finance clearly had good reason to throw their "enormous power" to the Allied cause. In *Why We Fought,* a book published in 1929, C. Hartley Grattan provided support for the thesis that economic ties had drawn the United States into war. Germany's interest demanded destruction of Allied shipping, while American economic interest required shipment of goods to the Allies. It was the clash of those two interests, Grattan argued, that brought about American intervention. Neither propaganda nor principle had much to do with Wilson's request for a declaration of war; trade and investment predisposed the United States government to favor the Allies over Germany.

The revisionists were not necessarily isolationists in the twenties. Grattan quite simply believed that few interests were worth the price of a war. Barnes called for an international organization to enforce peace; in so doing, he revealed his affinity for Wilsonian ideas about the institutional basis for world harmony. The trouble with the League of Nations, he observed in 1928, was that it was a league of victors. If it could be transformed into a league of all nations ("into an organization honestly devoted to undoing the injustices of the past and to promoting fair-dealing in the future"), then there was yet hope for international tranquility. Even though many revisionists of the decade after World War I felt uncomfortable with the isolationist label, however, their interpretations of the

To Rollin Kirby of the New York *World Journal Tribune*, the brightest light in the firmament was the star of disarmament. His concern was not with the efficacy of disarmament, but with the willingness of statesmen to pursue it (Kirby, *World Journal Tribune*).

1914–1918 crisis provided the isolationists with cogent raisons d'être. And several of the arguments that would become commonplace for isolationists in the thirties appeared in revisionist writings of the twenties.

**The Washington Conference**

American foreign policy took shape during the postwar decade under the pressure of forces that were sometimes in basic conflict. Overseas investments and the desire for trade moved the nation toward a growing involvement in the financial agonies of war-torn Europe, a continuation of the Open Door policy in Asia, and an effort to expand economic opportunities in Latin America. At the same time, disillusionment with American participation in the Great War—expressed in revisionist analyses of that conflict—severely limited the kinds of foreign commitments the United States could enter. In general, the Republican administrations of the New Era resolved the problem of policy formation by responding to both pressures. They vigorously pursued multilateral agreements to reduce armaments and to avoid war as a means of settling international disputes; they also pursued programs intended to assure international prosperity through trade and economic development.

The Washington Conference of 1921–1922 established a pattern for American foreign policy during the twenties and early thirties. Several considerations led Charles Evans Hughes, then Secretary of State in the Harding Administration, to call for a meeting of the great powers along with the nations that had territorial interests in the Pacific. Key developments leading to the conference were those affecting power relationships in the Far East, developments that had brought about a deterioration of Japanese-American amity. The trouble increased shortly after the election of 1912, when the California legislature enacted a law intended to prevent Japanese people from owning land in the state. Although President Wilson adopted a conciliatory attitude, thus managing to avert conflict with Japan, the Japanese were still seething when World War I broke out.

Wilson had no desire to become involved in Asian troubles; and, for a brief period after assuming office, he appeared to be withdrawing from aggressive pursuit of Open Door objectives. At his insistence, Americans abandoned a consortium of international bankers organized for the purpose of arranging loans to China. After 1914, however, the expansion of conflict into the Far East persuaded Wilson that American interests there must not be abandoned. Entering the Great War on the side of the Allies, Japan made the most of Germany's preoccupation with the European struggle, seizing the German naval base and concession in Shantung Province. When Japan took further steps toward domination of China by attempting to impose "twenty-one demands" on the Chinese, the Wilson administration reversed its earlier position on the consortium loan project. In the fall of 1917, Secretary of State Robert Lansing and Japanese envoy Kikujiro Ishii worked out an ambiguous agreement that recognized both the Open Door and Japan's special interests in China.

In 1918, after the Allied decision to send an expeditionary force to Russia, Japanese and American troops came face to face in Siberia. There was some justification for Wilson's belief that Japan had determined to fill the northeast Asian power vacuum created by the turmoil within Russia. The Japanese did, in fact, have designs on the Chinese Eastern Railway running westward from Vladivostok through Manchuria. To block action that might upset the tenuous Far Eastern equilibrium, therefore, the President dispatched nine thousand troops to Vladivostok. His move was at least partially successful. The Allied command thwarted Japanese efforts to gain control of the Chinese Eastern when it placed the line under supervision of the Inter-Allied Railway Commission.

To the Japanese, American policy suggested both an ignorance of overcrowded Japan's territorial needs and a determination to frustrate its attempts to meet them. The coming of peace did not bring a resolution of Japanese-American problems. Indeed, negotiations at the peace conference in 1919 actually increased tensions that had been building up during the war. Japanese delegates went to Paris with three objectives in mind: the assumption of control over former German interests in Shantung, the acquisition of German possessions in the Pacific (the Marshall Islands, the Marianas, and the Carolines), and recognition of racial equality for Orientals. They believed that Shantung and the Pacific islands were Japan's by right of conquest. The third demand was important, as a member of Japan's house of representatives put it, because of the need "to obtain freedom of residence for [Japanese] people in all and any territory in and on the Pacific."

At the Paris conference Wilson found himself in the position of opposing all three objectives. Largely through his influence, the Covenant of the League of Nations included no statement on racial equality. In the Pacific, American naval advisers strongly opposed Japanese acquisitions that might some day threaten the line of communication between Hawaii and the Philippines, and Japan had to be satisfied with mandates over the three island groups. The settlement, though advantageous to the Land of the Rising Sun, was less than Japanese delegates had hoped to secure, for in no mandated territory was construction of military or naval bases permitted. The agreement on Shantung satisfied no one. Wilson opposed Japanese claims because he thought recognizing them would lead to another partition of China. He finally gave in, much to the annoyance of American missionaries and their supporters; but Japan had to promise that it would retain only economic privileges and would restore full sovereignty to China.

Adding to Japanese irritation with the United States after the peace conference was the American navy's insistence on carrying out plans for a new fleet under the authority of an act passed by Congress in 1916. At the time of planning—before the United States had entered the war—the Navy Department had reasoned that the nation required a balanced fleet equal to that of Britain. Wartime exigencies had forced a concentration on small craft such as destroyers and submarines, but at war's end the Navy was ready to return to its earlier plans. The building program alarmed both Britain and Japan. The Japanese countered by authorizing a construction program of their own, while the British urged convening a conference to discuss the situation and to find a way of ending the armaments race. Hughes's call for delegates from various interested powers to meet in Washington was a response to Britain's suggestion.

The Secretary of State came straight to the point in his welcoming speech to the delegates. He called for a ten-year holiday in capital ship construction and the scrapping of ships by Britain, the United States, and Japan. What he had in mind was establishment of a tonnage ratio of 5–5–3 respectively among the three powers. Surprised that Hughes offered specific suggestions so early in the conference, the delegates nevertheless settled down to discuss his proposals. By February 1922 they had drafted three major treaties and settled a number of problems in several lesser agreements.

The Five Power Naval Treaty, the best publicized of the Washington accords, carried out Hughes's suggestion that fleets of the major powers be limited by a ratio formula. The treaty provided that a ratio of 5–5–3–1.7–1.7 be established for the capital ship tonnage of Britain, the United States, Japan, France, and Italy. It limited Britain and the United States to 525,000 tons, Japan to 315,000, and France and Italy to 175,000. The nations also agreed to restrict the size and armaments of capital ships; battleships, for example, had to be no more than 35,000 tons burden. Smaller craft were not in any way restricted by the treaty, an omission that drew increasing criticism in the year following the conference; but the signatory nations did include a provision against improving fortifications on island possessions in the Pacific west of Hawaii.

A second treaty resulting from the Washington Conference was signed by Japan, Great Britain, France, and the United States. It pledged the four powers to respect one another's rights in the Pacific and to meet in consultation should any controversy arise. This Four Power Treaty superseded an Anglo-Japanese alliance that had been formed in 1902 and renewed in 1905 and 1911. It also provided formal recognition of American agreement that encountered significant opposition in the United States Senate. William E. Borah of Idaho, Hiram Johnson of California, and other "irreconcilables" suspected that the treaty came dangerously close to the sort of alliance that isolationists always found offensive. The Senate eventually approved the treaty, but only after passing a qualifying reservation to the effect that approval involved "no commitment to use armed force, no alliance, no obligation to join any defense."

The third major treaty to come out of the Washington Conference—one to which all nine delegations affixed their signatures—gave treaty form to the basic Far Eastern policy that the United States had followed since the days of William McKinley and John Hay. The powers agreed "to respect the sovereignty, the independence, and the territorial integrity of China" while allowing that country the fullest opportunity "to develop and maintain for herself an effective and stable government." They also pledged themselves to refrain from seeking "special privileges which would abridge the rights of subjects or citizens of friendly states." In other words, the powers would avoid creating spheres of influence and would aid in keeping the Chinese door open to all nations. For its part, China would not discriminate among the nationals of other countries seeking commercial relations.

## Disarmament and Trade

Reaction to the various Washington agreements was overwhelmingly positive. Opponents of war, most of whom believed that militarism was a major cause of international hostility, rejoiced at the drafting of the first major disarmament agreement of modern times. To be sure, Oswald Garrison Villard's *Nation* viewed with skepticism a treaty that did not totally abolish armaments, but most American publications were not so finicky. The *New York Times* looked forward to the day when sea power would cease to be a consideration in international relations and when merchant ships would not require navies for protection. "We are taking perhaps the greatest forward step in history to establish the reign of peace," Hughes had said in his congratulatory speech at the close of the conference. And in a *New York World* editorial, Walter Lippmann praised him for reversing the drift toward war. As Robert E. Osgood put it in a later study of foreign policy, Americans were enormously pleased that the Secretary of State had "elevated the United States to the active role of missionary among heathen."

Statements in support of the treaties commonly employed the language of altruism, contributing to an impression of righteousness emanating from Washington. Revisionists were beginning to suggest that American investments had been a major influence pressing the United States toward intervention in World War I; thus, for many people, the treaties represented a victory for humanity over the sort of crass economic power that had, they thought, sent American doughboys into Allied trenches. Yet profit-minded businessmen approved the Washington Conference as enthusiastically as did high-minded pacifists. Speaking at a meeting of the Iron and Steel Institute in November 1921, Charles M. Schwab announced that for the sake of a permanent peace he would gladly see "the war-making machinery of the Bethlehem Steel Corporation sunk to the bottom of the ocean." And in the same month the National Association of Manufacturers devoted an entire issue of *American Industries* to a symposium on the virtues of disarmament.

Although they sometimes expressed themselves in idealistic rhetoric, businessmen were not thinking pacifist thoughts. They simply believed that they stood to gain from disarmament, and they said so. "Forgetting all about humanity," remarked an official of the American Hoist and Derrick Company, "war is bad business and bad for business." In his opinion, disarmament would "relieve the world from the burden of taxation and apprehension which modern war entails." Like him, most businessmen were convinced that heavy taxation stifled business; and, like him, they expected a reduction in taxes to follow closely upon a reduction in armaments. Beyond the stimulating effect of lower taxes, however, New Era businessmen saw other advantages in disarmament. A powerful Navy was obviously desirable in wartime, but John Hays Hammond was not alone in deploring the "economic waste involved in 'armed peace.'" Money squandered on shipbuilding after the war, thought Secretary of Commerce Hoover, "would have contributed materially to the entire economic rehabilitation of the world."

While businessmen contemplated the economic benefits of disarmament, they also approved writing Open Door provisions into the Nine Power Treaty, even though few of them knew what the Open Door entailed. Those who did have some expertise in Chinese affairs were the bankers (especially Thomas W. Lamont of the House of Morgan) associated with the Second China Consortium finally established in 1920. Yet the Second Consortium brought few tangible rewards either to China or to American commercial interests. Refusing to support large, long-term loans on the grounds that China was a poor credit risk, it succeeded only in demonstrating that the Open Door was a delusion. The American government, nevertheless, refused to abandon the policy. Various China Trade Acts passed between 1921 and 1933 and intended to encourage trade and investment in China were consistent with the Open Door, but they, too, failed. The fabled China market never lived up to the expectations of economic expansionists.

However favorable their pronouncements on the Open Door may have been, American businessmen acted on the belief that Japan provided a greater source of profits than did China. Trade statistics show that in the years from 1923 to 1931 less than 3 per cent of all exports from the United

Disarmament was a popular cause in the early 1920s. It appealed to businessmen and industrialists as well as to people in other walks of life. Indeed, few citizens disagreed with Nelson Harding's cartoon attributing "Our Greatest Naval Victory" to the Washington Conference of 1921–1922 (Harding, *Brooklyn Eagle*).

States went to China, while more than twice that amount went to Japan. By 1932 Japan was the fourth largest purchaser of American goods, absorbing 8 per cent of all U.S. exports. The Japanese, in the same period, sent an average 22 per cent of their exports to China and more than 40 per cent of their exports to the United States. Between 16 and 18 per cent of China's imports came from the United States, but some 27 per cent came from Japan. Using trade as a yardstick, then, Japan was far more important to American commerce than was China; and the China market was far more important to Japan than it was to the United States. Investments reveal a similar pattern. Of the $3.5 billion invested in China by 1932, 7 per cent came from the United States while 33 per cent came from Japan. Only slightly more than 1 per cent of American foreign investments went to China, but more than 80 per cent of Japan's foreign investments went to that country. In the meantime, Americans had invested $466 million in Japan as compared with $250 million in China. During the decade after the Washington Conference, developing economic relationships in the Far East made the United States Japan's best customer; at the same time, Japan rather than the United States became China's best customer. Comparing the heavy concentration of Japanese investment in China with the trivial American investment suggests the relative importance of China to each of the two powers.

Because they relied on the Open Door formula, American policy makers in the twenties could not readily accommodate themselves to economic developments in the Far East. As a result, policy and commercial practice began to diverge in a cluster of ironies. The Open Door was supposed to maintain peace through equality of opportunity for all nations in China, but in reality it meant that the United States demanded equality with the Japanese when American interests were in no way equal to those of Japan. Businessmen, who were among the intended beneficiaries of the policy, were ready to abandon it in practice when doing so might bring commercial advantage and greater profits. This was something that policy makers were unwilling to approve, for they were convinced that the peace of the world depended on equality of opportunity. Economic trends in the Far East thus imposing on the American government an obligation to find other ways of maintaining world peace, it turned to disarmament as a coordinate of the Open Door. The reduction of naval forces, however, threatened to deprive the United States of effective means of supporting not only the policy to which it was committed but also the commerce that businessmen were seeking to expand.

Nevertheless, the United States continued to urge disarmament after the Washington Treaties had been ratified. The Five Power Treaty, as already noted, had not imposed limitations on the construction of auxiliary naval vessels such as cruisers, destroyers, and submarines. Under no treaty restraint, Britain and Japan proceeded to construct smaller craft rather than battleships, and eventually American shipbuilders also began to lay keels for auxiliary ships. Naval expansion in such form could increase the likelihood of war as much as if the powers had been engaged in battleship construction; thus, early in 1927, President Coolidge called for a conference to work out a formula for limiting auxiliary vessels.

Delegates and naval advisers of the three powers met at Geneva the following summer, but they found negotiations almost impossible to conduct. Though both the British and the American delegations feared growing Japanese naval power in the Pacific, they could not agree on the best way to counterbalance it. The most important differences between the two centered on cruiser limitation. The United States, with few naval bases outside home waters, favored heavy cruisers with long-range capabilities. The British, on the other hand, with their network of strategically placed naval bases, preferred a larger number of light cruisers. The Anglo-American differences could not be resolved; after six weeks of futile discussion the conference adjourned without an agreement.

Failure at Geneva led to the completion of plans for increasing American cruiser strength, but it did not put an end to hopes for an eventual naval agreement. The efforts of idealistic advocates of peace, though directed toward the abolition of war rather than the limitation of armaments, improved the chances of a naval treaty that would satisfy both Britain and the United States. Professor James T. Shotwell of Columbia University, in an interview with French Foreign Minister Aristide Briand, suggested that Briand propose a bilateral treaty that would renounce war between France and the United States. The foreign minister, seeing in the suggestion an opportunity to associate American power with the system of alliances he was building against Germany, followed through on Shotwell's advice. But Frank B. Kellogg, who had succeeded Hughes as Secretary of State in 1925, was less than enthusiastic about a treaty that implied even so negative a commitment to French security and delayed his response. Finally, after consulting the Senate Foreign Relations Committee, he countered by suggesting a multilateral treaty that would renounce war as an instrument of national policy. A treaty condemning "recourse to war for the solution of international controversies" was accordingly drafted at Paris in August 1928; its signers included Britain, Germany, Italy, Japan, and the Soviet Union as well as France and the United States. The Pact of Paris (or Kellogg-Briand Pact) was not what Briand had in mind, and all signers had their doubts about how effective it might be. It did, nevertheless, pave the way for agreements on other matters.

During the fall of 1929 British Prime Minister Ramsay MacDonald visited the United States, calling on President Hoover. In a spirit of good will the two statesmen discussed issues that had aborted the Geneva Conference, reached an understanding on naval limitation, and called for another disarmament conference to meet in London the following year. When it convened, Anglo-American compatibility on major objectives

Frank B. Kellogg tipped his hat to photographers when he became Secretary of State in 1925. Although he generally scorned peace societies, he also bowed in their direction when he proposed a multilateral treaty rejecting war as an instrument of national policy. Kellogg won the Nobel Peace Prize for his efforts but the Kellogg-Briand Pact of 1928 proved unavailing in the international crises of the 1930s (Minnesota Historical Society).

conquered differences over specific application of the disarmament principle. The United States, dropping its earlier demand for twenty-one heavy cruisers, accepted a flexible provision that would allow either eighteen such vessels and less cruiser tonnage than the British navy maintained or fifteen heavy cruisers and tonnage equality with Britain. Japan's cruiser strength, according to the London agreements, might be 70 per cent of Britain's. Japan also agreed to a 7–10 ratio in destroyers but received equality in submarines. The London Conference extended the prohibition of capital ship construction to 1936, with delegates working out a formula for destroying capital ships then in commission. The resulting ratio of capital ship strength for Britain, the United States, and Japan would be 15–15–9. France and Italy, unable to agree on cruiser ratios, accepted only specified sections of the treaty.

The London Naval Conference was the last disarmament conference to produce substantial agreement among the major powers. In September 1931, Japanese troops seized the Manchurian city of Mukden, setting off a chain reaction that eventually led to the second great war of the twentieth century. Sensitive observers of international relations had never been unrealistically sanguine about the chances of saving the world from war through agreements such as those worked out at the Peace Conference of 1919, the Washington Conference of 1921–1922, or the London Conference of 1930. Nor did they believe that the Kellogg-Briand Pact was in itself sufficient to outlaw international conflict. Furthermore, by the end of the New Era many Americans had begun to have second thoughts about disarmament. Some businessmen, for example, became increasingly disenchanted with naval limitation treaties in the years following the Washington Conference, for a weak Navy seemed unlikely to encourage expansion of foreign commerce. In 1927, the *Coast Banker* put the case succinctly: "We owe a duty to ourselves and the world to safeguard our prosperity [from even] partial disarmament." Americans were beginning to prepare arguments for a great debate over the nation's proper position in world affairs, a debate that would become increasingly clamorous during the depression thirties.

| | |
|---|---|
| **Testing the Instruments of Peace: The Manchurian Crisis** | International arrangements that defined the global position of the United States during the New Era were viable only so long as the nation remained economically prosperous. Arrival of the depression after 1929 sharply reduced the American investor's ability to support the European economy by exporting American capital. With interruption of the movement of capital from the United States, the circular flow of reparations-debt payments dried to a trickle and then evaporated. The Hoover Moratorium of 1931, which suspended for one year all debt and reparations payments, was in effect a recognition of the need to evaluate and revise American relationships with Europe. Because the moratorium did not succeed in restoring prosperity to central Europe, however, it did little to alter conditions that |

made possible the emergence of National Socialism in Germany. And dealing with Hitler, as Americans would discover, revealed the inadequacies of a foreign policy limited by principles of unilateralism, noninterventionism, and commercial expansion.

In the Far East, too, the depression brought changes that significantly altered relationships among the powers with interests there. The most obvious change was a disruption of the trade pattern that had taken shape during the New Era. Falling commodity prices and a diminished capacity to consume greatly contracted the American market for Japanese goods. Silk had been the most important Japanese export to the United States during the twenties, but the price and demand for silk fell sharply as under duress of economic necessity women began wearing hose and dresses made from cotton and other less exotic fabrics. In 1930, for the first time in a decade, the American share of Japan's export trade fell below 40 per cent, and the Smoot-Hawley tariff of that year compounded Japan's already serious commercial problem. Raising the duties on Japanese goods by an average of 23 per cent, the tariff seriously reduced the importation of such products as chinaware, canned goods, and cultured pearls. In the meantime, American exports to Japan dropped 30 per cent during the first year of the depression and another 20 per cent between 1930 and 1931.

These developments coincided with events in China that threatened to close Chinese markets to Japan. Since the end of World War I the Kuomintang party, under the leadership of Sun Yat-sen and Chiang Kai-shek, had worked to overcome particularistic "warlords" and to bring political unity to China. To further Chinese nationalism Sun Yat-sen had accepted aid from the USSR; but, two years after his death in 1925, Chiang Kai-shek, renouncing Communist support, sought to establish his control over North China. His bid for power in Manchuria appeared to succeed in the winter of 1929–1930, when Manchurian leaders acknowledged his authority. At the same time the Nationalists organized for a boycott of Japanese goods. The growing strength of Chiang Kai-shek and the success of Chinese nationalism produced yet another menace to the Japanese economy. Japan's moderate government, headed by Kijuro Shidehara, began to face sharp criticism from belligerent expansionists who favored restoration of prosperity through military conquest.

An opportunity for the expansionists presented itself on the night of September 18, 1931, when an alleged explosion on the South Manchuria Railroad served as a pretext for Japanese seizure of the Chinese garrison at Mukden as well as several other important points along the right of way. The army acted without approval from Shidehara's government, but the popular reaction throughout Japan was one of satisfaction that the Rising Sun's interests would be protected against Chinese incursions. With such support at home, Japanese troops extended their occupation of Manchurian cities, and in short order all of Manchuria came under their control.

Whatever Japan's rights and interests in the region may have been, using military force to protect them constituted a violation of the Kellogg-Briand

Philadelphia *Record* cartoonist Jerry Doyle expressed a popular attitude toward the Japanese conquest of Manchuria in 1931–1932. Although the Lytton Report recognized Japanese economic interests, it did not approve the use of force. American distrust of Japan was to increase during the 1930s, reaching its apogee after Pearl Harbor (Doyle, Philadelphia *Record*).

Pact, and the conquest of Manchuria thus presented Hoover with new diplomatic and moral problems at a time when he was already preoccupied with economic problems. The president turned the matter over to his Secretary of State, Henry L. Stimson, whose initial response was to avoid extreme action in hopes that American restraint would set an example for the Japanese. The tactic proved ineffective. Then, on January 7, 1932, the Secretary sent identical notes to Japan and China setting forth the position eventually designated the "Stimson Doctrine." Quite simply, the doctrine stated that the United States would recognize neither Japanese conquests in Manchuria nor any other changes brought about in violation of existing treaties.

The implications of nonrecognition were ambiguous, however, and Hoover's understanding of it differed from Stimson's. The Secretary of State looked upon nonrecognition as a first step in what might become a series of increasingly firm coercive moves undertaken in cooperation with the other great powers and perhaps even with the League of Nations. Hoover, however, refused to consider intensifying the pressure on Japan. For him, nonrecognition expressed American opposition to Japanese expansionism; he could not bring himself to consider further sanctions for fear that they would lead to war. Collective action, furthermore, seemed to call for just the sort of entangling alliance that had made American entry into World War I possible. Hoover was determined to avoid the errors of 1917; so were the American people. Nonrecognition was as far as they would go in 1931–1932.

European powers were equally averse to the exercise of further sanctions in the Far East. When Japan began the conquest of Manchuria, China appealed to the League of Nations, whose council appointed a Commission of Inquiry headed by the British Earl of Lytton. The Lytton Report, published in October 1932, recognized Japan's legitimate economic interest in

Manchuria, but it called for an autonomous government there. Dissatisfied with any such arrangement, the Japanese withdrew from the league and set up their own new state of Manchukuo in the conquered territory.

Yosuke Matsuoka, who had been Japan's chief delegate to the league, passed through the United States on his way home from Geneva. Interviewed by reporters, he employed a metaphor that tellingly expressed the deep resentment motivating Japan's policy of aggressive expansion. Western powers had taught Japan to play poker, he observed; but, after winning most of the chips for themselves, they decided that the game was immoral and demanded that everyone play contract bridge instead. Justified or not, the Manchurian invasion made clear Japan's intention to withdraw from quiet diplomatic games. When the League of Nations followed the American lead in adopting a policy of nonrecognition, Japan paid little attention, having already thrown in its hand. Measures far greater than nonrecognition would have been needed to force Japan back to the card table; and, faced with problems of the depression, statesmen of the world were not in a position to exert the necessary pressure.

## Genesis of the Rome-Berlin-Tokyo Axis

In the meantime, events in Europe diverted American attention from Manchuria to Germany. During the years of world depression after 1929 the Weimar Republic's parliamentary structure had gradually eroded. Between 1929 and 1932, Germany's national income dropped by 20 per cent, while unemployment spread to 43 per cent of the work force. As businesses went bankrupt and breadlines formed, confidence in the postwar republican constitution evaporated. The so-called Weimar parties (the moderate Socialists, Centrists, Bavarian People's party, Democrats, and German People's party) lost popular support to the Communist party on the left and various anti-Weimar parties on the right (particularly the German National People's party, the National Socialists, and the Economic party). In 1932 the aging Paul von Hindenburg, a tottering relic of Kaiser Wilhelm's Reich, won reelection as president of Germany; but, so unstable was the Reichstag, he had difficulty in finding a chancellor who could command sufficient support. Finally, on January 30, 1933, he turned to Adolf Hitler, whose National Socialist German Workers (Nazi) party had six months earlier captured 230 seats in a Reichstag of 608 members. During the next few weeks Hitler employed strong-arm methods and scare tactics to win dictatorial powers for himself. A rule of terror began.

The Nazi revolution in Germany coincided with a general disarmament conference that had opened in Geneva on February 2, 1932. Sixty nations had sent delegates, so, of course, differences of opinion were many. France, insisting that disarmament without security was futile, proposed that an international force be placed at the disposal of the League of Nations. Germany demanded recognition of its right to possess the same armaments as other countries. The Soviet Union urged proportional and progressive reduction of armaments leading to their eventual abolition. The United

States suggested the division of land forces into "police components" and "defense components" with a drastic reduction of the latter. For months the discussions dragged on. Finally, in June 1933, the conference adjourned until the following October on the assumption that the powers might reach agreement through informal discussions. Two days before the conference was scheduled to reconvene, the German foreign minister announced that his government would take no more part in the disarmament talks and that, going even further, it would withdraw from the League of Nations itself. The German move sabotaged the conference. More than two years of effort had not reduced national armaments by as much as a single rifle.

With good reason the political leaders of Europe began to fear Hitler's intentions. Anyone who took the trouble to read *Mein Kampf* knew that what he had in mind was nothing less than German domination of the entire continent. Failure of the disarmament conference therefore brought a flurry of activity as the nations sought security for themselves. The Locarno treaties of 1925 had already pledged Italy and Great Britain to guarantee the Franco-German and Belgo-German frontiers and to maintain a demilitarized zone in the Rhineland as stipulated in the Versailles Treaty.

The old Germany gave way to a new force in 1933, when Adolf Hitler became chancellor. President Paul von Hindenburg, approaching his death the following year, delivered an old soldier's salute; Hitler and his Nazis, making the most of Hindenburg's prestige, advanced to assume a power they were to make absolute in the Third Reich (Wide World photo).

To supplement the Locarno agreements, French diplomats began negotiations with Italy in 1934 to work out a series of pacts that would remove causes of friction between the two Latin countries. In eastern Europe the Soviet Union, Poland, and Rumania signed a treaty pledging mutual respect for their existing borders, and in the fall of 1934 the USSR joined the League of Nations.

Yet Hitler did not move immediately to rearm Germany—at least openly. The Treaty of Versailles had placed the Saar Basin under a League of Nations commission for a period of fifteen years, at the end of which time a plebiscite would determine whether the territory would be ruled by France or by Germany. The Nazi Fuehrer did not want to risk antagonizing the league until after the Saarland's future had been decided. Following his overwhelming victory in the January 1935 plebescite, however, Hitler was under no compulsion to restrain himself. An interested observer of the great powers' pusillanimity at the time of Japan's seizure of Manchuria, he had accurately discerned how far he might go without fear of opposition. With the Saar once more under German rule, therefore, Hitler acted swiftly. He proclaimed a return to compulsory military service and increased the size of the German army to more than 500,000 men. The League of Nations condemned his unilateral repudiation of the disarmament sections of the Versailles Treaty, but none of the powers was prepared to confront Germany with force. A year later the Fuehrer contemptuously violated both the Treaty of Versailles and the Locarno Pact when he sent twenty thousand German troops into the demilitarized zone along the Rhine River.

Hitler shrewdly timed his move into the Rhineland to coincide with a tense moment in international relations. Italy had long coveted Ethiopia as a colonial possession; and, after signing of the pacts with France in 1935, Italian dictator Benito Mussolini felt free to take over control of Emperor Haile Selassie's landlocked kingdom. On October 3, without a declaration of war, Italian troops launched simultaneous attacks from Eritrea in the north and Italian Somaliland in the south. Moving with unaccustomed speed to meet this new crisis, the League of Nations immediately declared Italy to be the aggressor. It voted to impose economic sanctions but did not restrict shipments of oil. When limited sanctions seemed to produce negligible results, several member nations urged an embargo on oil to Italy. While the proposal was under discussion, Hitler sent his troops into the Rhineland, and harried statesmen gave up the effort to preserve Ethiopian independence. On May 5, 1936, Italian forces hoisted their flag over Addis Ababa, and on June 1 Mussolini decreed that Eritrea, Italian Somaliland, and Ethiopia would be consolidated into a single colony known as Italian East Africa. The conquest of Ethiopia had demonstrated that the league was as ineffective when it imposed sanctions as it was when it followed a policy of nonrecognition.

Nevertheless, Hitler's remilitarization of the Rhineland did prompt another round of agreements to counteract the threat of German aggression.

The stiff-armed Nazi salute was a signal of approbation, loyalty, and obedience when the Fuehrer addressed the *Reichstag*. "You cannot establish a dictatorship in a vacuum," Hitler once remarked to American newsman H. V. Kaltenborn. "A government that does not derive its strength from the people will fail in a foreign crisis. . . . Yet dictatorship is justified if the people declare their confidence in one man and ask him to lead" (Imperial War Museum).

Britain at once made a commitment to aid Belgium and France in case of an attack; in April 1936 military commanders of the three countries met to plan defensive strategy. In June, Rumania, Yugoslavia, and Czechoslovakia renewed an earlier agreement to oppose unification of Austria and Germany. Rumania also arranged to construct a railroad to facilitate the movement of Russian troops should German armies attempt the conquest of eastern Europe. And an exchange of visits by the chiefs-of-staff of Poland and France strengthened defense agreements that had been worked out between the two nations at Locarno in 1925.

Germany, it seemed, had managed to bring about her own isolation; but, if that made neighboring nations euphoric, Hitler soon snatched away their illusions. Beginning with a promise to respect Austrian sovereignty in July 1936, the Fuehrer took several steps to gain support for himself outside Germany. He joined Mussolini in sending aid to General Francisco Franco when civil war broke out in Spain, and in October he formed a more definitive alliance that pledged collaboration between Germany and Italy in all matters affecting their parallel interests. Among those interests was the defense of European civilization against Communism. To assure the Reich's success in that struggle, the Nazi leader made overtures to Japan on the other side of the Soviet Union.

In November, Germany and Japan signed a pact pledging mutual cooperation against the Communist International (also known as the Comintern, or Third International) and its effort to achieve world Communist federation. A year later, Italy joined the anti-Comintern pact, and the Rome-Berlin-Tokyo Axis was consummated. Mussolini gave notice that he would not oppose unification of Austria and Germany, and that Italy would withdraw from the League of Nations. To confirm their new relationship with Japan, both Germany and Italy recognized Manchukuo. Then Hitler ordered out of China all German military advisers to Chiang Kai-shek. By 1938 the nations of the world were once again well on the way to the formation of two hostile alignments.

**The New Neutrality**

To many people in the United States and elsewhere, the events following Japan's conquest of Manchuria seemed disquietingly like a replay of events leading up to the outbreak of war in 1914. Disturbing similarities between the two periods encouraged continued examination of American involvement in the Great War. Yet books and articles on the subject began to sound warnings that made them quite different from writings of the twenties. During the postwar decade the war guilt question had been a major preoccupation of scholars, but after 1931 the emphasis shifted to problems of neutrality. Students of the Great War emphasized the idea that the past contains lessons for the present, and much historical analysis in the thirties sought to supply perspectives on how to escape involvement in the war that appeared imminent.

In the spring of 1932 the Social Science Research Council awarded a grant of $25,000 to Charles A. Beard, who had first made a name for himself as a historian with the publication of *An Economic Interpretation of the Constitution* in 1913. The grant was to be used for investigations directed toward a definition of the "national interest." Before the year 1934 came to an end, Beard had published two books from his research. The first volume, *The Idea of National Interest,* reviewed the thought of various national leaders and how they had given particular shape to the concept. Beard was especially interested in the way expansion of foreign commerce had been justified as a pursuit of the national interest when in reality it had benefited only specific interest groups. More important than the distribution of rewards, however, was the fact that the rationale for commercial expansion required a national commitment to protect special interests in a time of crisis such as World War I. Some American business firms had been trading with the Allies, but the entire nation had gone to war. In his more prescriptive companion volume, *The Open Door at Home,* Beard contended that pursuit of a truly national interest required giving top priority to "the creation and maintenance of a high standard of life for all [the American] people." In other words, any foreign involvement of the United States should further rather than hinder reconstruction at home. Since foreign commerce benefited the few rather than the many, it was a hindrance to the national housecleaning that Beard thought necessary. And imposing strict limitations on external commerce would make possible both reform and avoidance of military entanglements.

In the same year that Beard produced his two volumes on the national interest, Charles Warren published a widely read article, "The Troubles of a Neutral," in *Foreign Affairs.* The burden of his argument was that maintaining neutral rights in wartime was a matter of expediency rather than law, and that, if the United States wanted to remain neutral, it would have to impose severe restrictions on the activities of its own citizens. To defend neutral rights against a belligerent government determined to violate them would, of course, mean war for the United States. Since Americans would therefore have to practice self-denial, Warren suggested several measures to make self-denial effective. The most important of his suggestions was a law imposing an automatic and impartial arms embargo against all belligerents should war break out.

The same idea had occurred to a number of political leaders, their enthusiasm for it helping bring about creation of a Senate Special Committee Investigating the Munitions Industry in 1934. North Dakota Senator Gerald P. Nye assumed chairmanship of the committee, and for two years he led an extensive probe into the post-1914 activities of armaments manufacturers, shipbuilders, and other "merchants of death." The Nye Committee did not adopt the thesis that economic interests were solely responsible for American entry into war in 1917; but, since it had been appointed to investigate economic influences, its findings buttressed revisionist interpretations. After listening to the testimony of J. P. Morgan, Nye conceded that it would be unfair to say that the House of Morgan "took us into war" to safeguard investments in the Allied cause. Nevertheless, the senator believed that "these bankers were in the heart and center of a system that made our going to war inevitable." After President Wilson permitted them to extend credit to the Allies, "the road to war was paved and greased for us."

Over the months from April 1, 1935, to June 19, 1936, the Munitions Investigating Committee submitted seven long reports and several legislative proposals to the Senate. Among its many recommendations were suggestions for taking the profits out of war through price controls and taxation, regulating the shipbuilding industry to prevent profiteering, establishing government ownership of the munitions industry, and restricting American loans and exports to belligerents. Most of the committee's recommendations failed to gain support sufficient for enactment, but its findings did aid the senatorial isolationists and their colleagues who fought for passage of the Neutrality Act of 1935.

Signed reluctantly by Roosevelt at the end of August, the Neutrality Act reflected a desire to avoid the mistakes that had led to American military commitments in 1917. It required the president to impose an arms embargo on all belligerents should war occur, it set up a special board to regulate the export of munitions to any country, and it prohibited American ships from carrying arms to or for a nation at war. When the law expired

On April 22, 1937, while Congress debated the American role in world affairs, students at the University of Chicago prepared to stride out on a peace march. "If we would really undertake to stay out of other people's wars in the future, we must deny ourselves any taste of the profit from other people's wars," Gerald P. Nye was telling his colleagues in the Senate. In passing the Neutrality Act of 1937, Congress responded to isolationist sentiment, if not to all of Nye's recommendations (Wide World photo).

after a year, Congress enacted a new one that not only extended the embargo provision but also forbade either the extension of credit to a belligerent or the sale of its securities in the United States. A third Neutrality Act in 1937 reenacted the main provisions of the 1935–1936 legislation, including the arms embargo, but it added some refinements. It stipulated that nations at war might buy goods in the United States, but they could not use American ships to carry such goods and could export them only after American citizens had surrendered all right, title, and interest. This "cash and carry" provision was to last for two years. In addition, the Neutrality Act of 1937 forbade American citizens to travel on belligerent ships and gave the president power to restrict the use of American ports by nations involved in armed conflict. The act, as Professor Donald F. Drummond has suggested, represented "the most complete program of isolation to which the country had ever been committed."

The "new neutrality" of the thirties rested on a venerable assumption: that the size, strength, and geographical position of the United States rendered it immune to the consequences of wars fought by other countries. That was the essential reason for isolationist opposition to any commitment that might draw the American people into international conflict. Isolationists believed that, whatever happened in the rest of the world, the United States could take care of itself; furthermore, they believed that the nation could best avoid involvement in other nations' troubles if it prohibited the export of arms and munitions and the extension of loans to belligerent states. That the new neutrality had considerable popular support was indicated by a series of public opinion polls in the years 1936–1937. In March 1936 some 82 per cent of the people questioned favored prohibiting the manufacture of munitions for profit. A September survey indicated that 71 per cent approved of a national referendum before war could be declared. Two months later 95 per cent registered their opposition to American participation in another world conflict, and in April 1937 70 per cent thought that the United States had blundered in going to war in 1917.

## Roosevelt and Foreign Affairs: The Good Neighbor

After the election of 1932 President Roosevelt, focusing his attention on the depression, seemed determined to prescribe narrow, nationalistic remedies for overcoming it. Isolationists and revisionists were pleased with his initial actions. They comforted themselves with the thought that, unlike Wilson, this Democratic president would not sacrifice domestic well-being to dangerous foreign commitments. During his campaign FDR had specifically rejected any suggestion that the United States join the League of Nations, and following his inauguration he refused to go along with the London Economic Conference effort to stabilize currency exchange rates. Charles A. Beard did not lack company in detecting evidence of economic doors opening at home. When he congratulated the president for recognizing that recovery would come not from international conferences but from the "collaboration of domestic interests," millions of Americans echoed his sentiments.

Yet Roosevelt was not a narrow nationalist, and he always considered a renewal of foreign trade essential to the restoration of prosperity. It was in large part the desire for new markets overseas that led to American recognition of the Soviet Union in November 1933. And under authority of the National Industrial Recovery Act, FDR created the Export-Import Bank, establishing what would eventually become a permanent agency to facilitate foreign commerce and open up new markets. Secretary of State Cordell Hull also contributed to the New Deal's effort to overcome the depression by expanding foreign trade. Urging bilateral commercial understandings, he was influential in persuading Congress to pass the Reciprocal Trade Agreements Act of 1934. The act permitted the executive branch to negotiate with another country agreements that might reduce import duties by as much as one-half if the other nation would make similar reductions for American products. During the next five years the State Department concluded twenty-one such agreements. While the specific results of New Deal trade policies are difficult to determine, FDR clearly did not wish to lock himself into a Beardian formula. Maintaining flexibility in international relations, he would not commit the Administration to a firm position on the isolationist-internationalist spectrum.

Roosevelt was no more inclined to be doctrinaire in foreign policy than he was disposed to be dogmatic in domestic policy. Above all, he was concerned in both areas with popular support. That was one reason for FDR's working as hard as he did to develop better relations with Latin American countries. His "Good Neighbor" policy was one with which both isolationists and internationalists could in large measure agree. Actually, Roosevelt did not originate the idea of winning friends south of the Rio Grande, for Herbert Hoover had long sought to reverse attitudes and practices that had given the United States a bad name in Latin America. In endorsing a memorandum against using the Roosevelt Corollary of 1905 to justify intervention, in adopting a policy of recognizing de facto governments, and in removing the Marines from Nicaragua, Hoover laid a foundation on which his successor was able to build a structure of hemispheric solidarity.

FDR's Good Neighbor policy sought first the elimination of all actions that suggested Big Stick coercion. In December 1933 Secretary Hull headed the American delegation to the Seventh Pan-American Conference at Montevideo, Uruguay; there—to the pleased surprise of delegates from other countries—he supported a Convention on Rights and Duties of States. The convention included a clause denying any state the privilege of intervening "in the internal or external affairs of another," and in subsequent bilateral agreements the United States made clear its intention to withdraw from interventionist practices. In 1934 American Marines were pulled out of Haiti, and the Roosevelt administration signed a treaty surrendering United States controls over Cuban sovereignty. At the Buenos Aires Inter-American Conference in 1936, Hull signed a protocol that in forbidding intervention "directly or indirectly, and for whatever reason" went even further than the convention of 1934.

Did the Roosevelt administration act in good faith? In 1938, when it expropriated foreign oil holdings, the Mexican government put the president to the test; he passed it with credits to spare. He demonstrated his sincerity in rejecting, despite pressure from oil companies, a suggestion that troops be dispatched to prevent the takeover by the Mexican government. And when the matter reached final settlement in 1941, the United States accepted a payment that came to only one-tenth of what the companies sought in reimbursement.

By the end of the decade, then, Roosevelt's policies toward Latin America had gone a long way toward reversing earlier interventionist tendencies on the part of the United States. But that was not all that FDR had in mind. As Hitler began to move toward formation of the Axis alliance, New Deal diplomats began to worry about security in the Western Hemisphere. To counteract the threat of penetration by an unfriendly power, Roosevelt and Hull sought to make the Monroe Doctrine multilateral. That is, they sought to unite all American nations in opposition to intervention from Germany, Japan, or Italy. At the Buenos Aires Conference of 1936, delegates agreed that their nations would consult with one another should a war threaten their security. Two years later, the Eighth Pan-American Conference meeting in Lima, Peru, adopted a declaration that enabled any American state to call a conference of foreign ministers. The machinery for consultation had been built, and the Americas would—with the exception of Argentina—stand united in opposition to the Axis powers.

**New Arguments for Intervention—and Their Rejection**

Isolationists had always made allowances for hemispheric solidarity: the Good Neighbor policy was one that most of them could support while continuing to oppose a more aggressive policy in Europe. Yet isolationism had never completely dominated American opinion; now, as Hitler, Mussolini, and the Japanese began to appear more menacing, increasing numbers of citizens saw a need for the United States to exert more influence in world affairs. Some of them became skeptical of the philosophical and moral assumptions of revisionist critics who condemned American participation in World War I. A bellwether of the new strain in national thought was Reinhold Niebuhr, who in 1928 had left his Detroit pastorate to join the faculty at Union Theological Seminary in New York.

During the twenties Niebuhr had gradually moved away from disillusionment with war-induced idealism and into contemplative appreciation of ethical complexities in modern life. In 1932 he published *Moral Man and Immoral Society,* which posed somber questions about the efficacy of love and reason in politics or international relations. "The limitations of the human mind and imagination, the inability of human beings to transcend their own interest sufficiently to envisage the interests of their fellowmen as they do their own," he wrote, "makes force an inevitable part of the process of social cohesion." Social justice, he concluded, required the use of power to combat group egoism. By 1940 Niebuhr was attacking Christian pacifism in *Christianity and Social Power.* Advocates of neutrality and pacifism, he charged, had brought about a moral paralysis in the name of moral purity. In measuring political realities by their own ideal standard, they had encouraged cynicism and irresponsibility in the face of dangers that might prove fatal.

Urging Americans to face the implications of Axis ideologies and power, Niebuhr won a reputation for realism and a following. Meanwhile, others were beginning to express similar concerns. In 1937 Hamilton Fish Armstrong, editor of *Foreign Affairs,* published *We or They,* which argued that American security depended upon the security of other democracies. The following year Max Lerner contributed *It Is Later Than You Think.* Democratic power was clearly necessary to overcome nondemocratic power, thought Lerner, calling for a "militant democracy" to replace a "mortal fear of fascism." The idea that the United States could not survive if similar systems of life succumbed to authoritarian control also found support in Lewis Mumford's 1939 book, *Men Must Act.*

These and other expressions of concern about the drift of events formed part of the intellectual milieu of the Popular Front, a new policy adopted by the Seventh World Congress of the Communist International in the summer of 1935. Worried about Hitler's rearming of Germany, Mussolini's designs on Ethiopia, the activities of Rightist parties in Spain, and Japan's conquest of Manchuria, the Communists called for all progressives to join in a united effort to thwart the rise of fascism. The new line brought a marked change in the attitudes of American Communists. Before 1935, they had professed to see no difference between the programs of Roosevelt and those of Hitler and had accused FDR of "waving the U.S. swastika." After adoption of the Popular Front strategy, however, New Deal iniquities suddenly became less apparent. The great issue of the day, announced party leader Earl Browder, was not socialism or capitalism, but "progress or reaction, democracy or fascism." In the United States the New Deal was the party of progress and democracy, and Browder pledged Communist support to FDR in his struggle against reactionaries. The *Daily Worker* took to printing Roosevelt's picture with laudatory comment, while the party adopted the slogan "Communism Is Twentieth Century Americanism."

The Popular Front was important neither because American Communists were numerous (which they were not), nor even because it served to mute radical criticism of the New Deal after 1935 (which it did). It was important because, by temporarily forsaking nice ideological distinctions, it was able to appeal to liberals for whom sectarian squabbling had seemed futile as well as divisive. Now, working through various "front" organizations such as the American League against War and Fascism, Communists were able to attract support beyond the limits of party membership. Popular Front concerns became respectable as many of the nation's ablest writers and commentators—Archibald MacLeish, Max Lerner, Bruce Bliven, John Dos Passos, Ernest Hemingway, Freda Kirchwey, and Van Wyck Brooks among them—participated in the effort to organize an effective anti-fascist alliance. For a time the effort seemed to be succeeding. During the Spanish Civil War that began in 1936 Popular Front activists organized the Abraham Lincoln Brigade to fight in the Loyalist cause, and some three thousand Americans enlisted in the "little world war" against Spanish fascism.

Yet Popular Front unity was not destined to survive a succession of crises in the late thirties. Democratic powers were slow to join the struggle against fascism in so direct a way. Haunted by the specter of a general war rising from Spanish battlefields, they sought, above all, to contain the conflict. They therefore followed a policy of nonintervention, as the United States declared a "moral embargo" on shipments of goods to either side. Results of nonintervention were mixed. World War II did not begin in Spain, but close collaboration between Mussolini and Hitler did begin there with the military assistance they provided General Francisco Franco. Eventually, in 1939, the Spanish Loyalists succumbed to the forces of Franco, who established himself as *Caudillo* with dictatorial powers.

By that time, however, the Axis nations had aroused such consternation throughout the world that Franco's triumph went almost unnoticed. In July 1937 Japan began a second phase of military action in China with a full-scale attack resulting, by the end of 1938, in control of Chinese coastal cities and connecting rail lines. Meanwhile, Hitler proceeded with Mussolini's blessing to complete the unification of Germany and Austria. In mid-March 1938, hailing Austria as a state of the German Reich, he entered Vienna amid a show of great enthusiasm for *Anschluss* (union) and *Gleichshaltung* (elimination of political dissent). Having achieved that long-sought objective, the Fuehrer next turned his attention to Czechoslovakia and the 3.5 million Germans living there. The "tortured and oppressed" Germans of the Sudeten district, he announced, would have to be saved from Czechoslovakian misrule.

To Americans associated with the Popular Front, and to individuals such as Niebuhr, Armstrong, Lerner, and Mumford, Axis activities called for an unambiguous response from the United States and other democratic nations. In any case, Roosevelt took his first tentative steps toward a more active opposition to the policies of Japan, Italy, and Germany. After the

Reporting of international crises became increasingly sophisticated with improvements in radio and in news analysis. From the roof of a hotel on the French border, H. V. Kaltenborn made one of the first battle broadcasts in August, 1936, a month after civil war broke out in Spain (State Historical Society of Wisconsin).

Japanese attack on China in 1937, he refused to invoke the Neutrality Act on the grounds that war had not been declared. Since the act's provisions would have prohibited shipments of arms and the use of American ships (which China needed and Japan did not), the president's refusal represented a diffident but unmistakable proffer of aid to China. Then, in October, the United States sided with the League of Nations in expressing moral support for China, and Roosevelt delivered a speech in which he suggested that an "epidemic of world lawlessness" called for a "quarantine" of aggressor nations.

The reaction to FDR's quarantine suggestion was not what he hoped it would be. Whatever the cogency of Popular Front and interventionist arguments—and whatever imposing a quarantine meant in Japan's case—popular response clearly indicated that isolationism still had a powerful hold over American minds. Roosevelt therefore cautiously stopped from further advances toward an interventionist position. When a league-sponsored conference met in Brussels to consider the problems of China, American delegate Norman Davis carried instructions to avoid any mention of sanctions against Japan. Not even Japanese bombing of the *Panay,* an American gunboat that had escorted American tankers to China, was enough to rouse more vigorous opposition to Japanese maneuvers in China. In November 1938 the Japanese Foreign Office issued a proclamation announcing a "new order" founded on "a tripartite relationship of mutual aid and cooperation between Japan, Manchukuo, and China in political, economic, cultural, and other fields." Because the new order would in effect close the door that American policy makers had long insisted on keeping open, the United States refused to recognize it. But, for the time being, FDR could do little more without the risk of antagonizing determined isolationists.

Meanwhile, the president had turned his attention to Europe, where he encountered a desire to avoid provoking Hitler that was at least as strong as American reluctance to become involved in Sino-Japanese hostilities. After the domestic crisis precipitated by the abdication of Edward VIII in 1936, Neville Chamberlain, who succeeded Stanley Baldwin as Prime Minister of Great Britain, initiated a five-year rearmament plan. British rearmament came nowhere near matching that of Germany, however, so Chamberlain devoted far greater effort to resolving international crises through other means. The means he settled upon involved approving the demands of Hitler and Mussolini on the theory that, having won what they sought, the two dictators would be appeased. The prime minister thus accepted the unification of Germany and Austria, but he rejected a Soviet suggestion that the governments of the USSR, Britain, France, and the United States make plans for collective action against fascist aggression.

France was even less prepared to confront Hitler. Industrial unrest and cabinet instability resulting from conflicts between parties of the left and the right had focused attention on domestic problems to such a degree that many Frenchmen failed to appreciate the significance of Hitler's rise to

Hitler greeted Neville Chamberlain at Godesberg in the Rhineland on September 22, 1938. At this conference the Fuehrer rejected the prime minister's proposals for dismemberment of Czechoslovakia, charging that they were too dilatory. He thus set the stage for Chamberlain's capitulation at Munich a week later (Imperial War Museum).

power in Germany. Since 1930, to be sure, military engineers had been busy constructing fortifications along the Franco-German border, and after the *Anschluss* the government of Edouard Daladier employed patriotic appeals to increase industrial production. Yet the Maginot Line implied a defensive military strategy, and in any case the Daladier government could not persuade Chamberlain of the need for collective action against the Axis.

Even had he wanted to do so, therefore, Roosevelt would no doubt have had difficulty in promoting resistance to Hitler's demand for cession of the Sudetenland to Germany. And there is no evidence to indicate that FDR ever contemplated collective resistance. Thus with Hitler flexing his military muscles, with Sudeten Germans agitating for reunion with the fatherland, and with international anxieties mounting, Chamberlain flew to confer with the Fuehrer. Two meetings in September 1938 resulted in impasse. Germany might have the Sudetenland, Chamberlain agreed, but Hitler rejected the plans for withdrawal of Czechoslovakian military and official personnel as too dilatory. Possession, he said, must be immediate. The Czechoslovakian government resisting, war seemed imminent. Then, with Roosevelt joining Chamberlain and Daladier in an appeal for another conference, Hitler appeared to relent. At Munich on September 29 Chamberlain and Daladier arranged for the dismemberment of Czechoslovakia under the delusion that they were securing "peace in our time." If the Popular Front or any other coalition ever had a chance of forcing Germany, Italy, or Japan to meliorate Axis foreign policies, the chance went aglimmer at Munich.

**Nonbelligerency in a War-Torn World**

The months after Munich were a sobering time, a time for the nonfascist nations to come to terms with realities. Hitler broke promises made at Munich and began to talk of annexing the free city of Danzig as well as parts of Poland. France and Britain belatedly recognized the futility of appeasement, extended promises of assistance to Poland, Rumania, and Greece, and sought to have the Soviet government guarantee the western borders of Poland and Rumania. Russian diplomats were also reassessing foreign policy, however; they would not make such guarantee without firm commitments of support from Britain and France. Suspecting that Chamberlain was capable of selling them out, too, they began to consider a deal with Hitler. In the United States Roosevelt and his advisers felt themselves hamstrung by neutrality legislation, but the president took what action he could. Perhaps aware that his gesture was hopeless, he sent a communiqué to Hitler and Mussolini urging a multilateral nonaggression agreement. Il Duce never deigned to respond, but the Fuehrer made a speech in which he said that he had received no information to indicate that other nations feared Germany. Roosevelt was unduly alarmed, he told the Reichstag, and he ridiculed the president's effort.

The charade of 1939 fooled no one, but nations worried about Axis maneuvering proved themselves unable to take the diplomatic initiative to promote cooperation with one another. Chamberlain distrusted the Russians as much as they did him, and in both the U.S. and the USSR the Popular Front was losing its credibility. Stalin's bloody purge of party dissidents in 1936–1938, thought many Americans, made a mockery of the

**"COME ON IN. I'LL TREAT YOU RIGHT.
I USED TO KNOW YOUR DADDY."**

Whatever war's seductive charms for some of Europe's leaders and nations, her victims in both world struggles of the twentieth century were the young and the innocent. Convinced that the nation's involvement with war had been a gross mistake in 1917, American isolationists vigorously opposed all further trafficking with the sleazy prostitute (Batchelor, New York *Daily News*).

idea that the two countries occupied common ground. For their part, Americans had amply demonstrated a determination to shun foreign entanglements. To the USSR, the message was clear: a Popular Front strategy was not worth the candle. For all the mutual suspicion, however, few people in Britain, France, or the United States were prepared for the Nazi-Soviet Pact that Vyacheslav Molotov and Joachim von Ribbentrop signed in Moscow on August 23, 1939. Openly guaranteeing Russian neutrality should Hitler send troops into Poland, the agreement also secretly provided for the partition of eastern Europe between the two powers. War, now inevitable, was not long in coming. On September 1 German armies swept across the Polish frontier.

Roosevelt's response to the invasion of Poland, outlined in a fireside chat on the evening of September 3, contemplated neither American belligerency nor American impartiality. "I hope the United States will keep out of this war," said the president, but he added that "even a neutral cannot be asked to close his mind or his conscience." Two days later he officially proclaimed American neutrality, invoking the 1937 Neutrality Act. The cash and carry provision of the law had expired in April, however, and FDR now moved swiftly to secure new legislation that would repeal the arms embargo and permit a flow of supplies to Britain and France under a revised cash and carry formula. Three weeks after the *Wehrmacht* began its lightning thrust into Poland, the president appeared before Congress to deliver a carefully prepared address. Though he made no mention of assistance to the nations opposing Hitler, he argued that cash and carry would keep American merchantmen out of hostile waters and thus help to preserve neutrality.

The president's proposal once again stirred debate about the American role in world affairs. The machinations of Hitler and the Axis powers were enough to persuade many citizens and members of Congress that American security required, at the very least, repeal of the arms embargo. Pacifists, revisionists, and isolationists, on the other hand, revived and reiterated arguments that had become familiar in the two decades after World War I. With a second conflict already under way, a new sense of urgency surrounded the discussion; the foreign policy debate captured popular attention as never before.

Several major ethnic groups, especially those of German, Irish, Italian, and Scandinavian origin, supported the advocates of strict neutrality. American fascists dominated none of these groups (even the pro-German *Amerika-Deutsche Volksbund* could claim no more than 230,000 Nazi sympathizers), yet each of them had its reasons for favoring neutrality and nonintervention. Germans and Italians were naturally reluctant to wage war on the homeland, but more importantly they feared being singled out as traitors should such a war occur. The Irish opposed any support of Britain, the ancient oppressor of Ireland. Scandinavians reflected their traditional preferences for pacifism and neutralism that had grown out of conditions characteristic of northern Europe. All the ethnic groups favoring neutrality could sympathize with the comment of Theodore Hoffman, chairman of the anti-Nazi Steuben Society: "Americans of Germanic extraction do not want Communism, Nazism, or Fascism and they do not want British imperialism. They want Americanism." The Anglophobic character of Hoffman's remark harmonized with a familiar theme of agrarian radicalism. That agrarian tradition, along with the strength of neutralist ethnic groups in the central portions of the United States, served to give the Middle West a reputation for being the most isolationist section of the country. It was there that the American First Committee, most prominent of the noninterventionist organizations, experienced its greatest success in recruiting members.

Roosevelt and others who urged repeal of the arms embargo and revision of the neutrality law could muster support of their own, some of it no less ethnic in character than that of the isolationists. Anglo-Saxon conformity had long been a central idea in predominant theories of immigrant assimilation, and Anglophilia had given rise to organizations such as the English-Speaking Union. A large reservoir of friendship for Britain survived revisionist efforts, especially along the Atlantic seaboard, and supporters of the president drew heavily from it. American Jews were also nearly unanimous in favoring revised neutrality laws, for anti-Semitism had become national policy in the Third Reich. And the heavy concentration of Jews in the New York metropolitan area reinforced eastern attitudes sustaining the president.

In addition to such backing, FDR received significant help from the effective organization of citizens who saw repeal of the arms embargo as essential to the national interest. Prominent Republicans—especially Alfred M. Landon, Henry Knox, and Henry L. Stimson—all came out for repeal. Clark Eichelberger, director of the American Union for Concerted Peace Efforts, worked in collaboration with the Administration to form a new organization, the Non-Partisan Committee for Peace through Revision of the Neutrality Act. At the urging of Cordell Hull, Kansas Republican William Allen White accepted the committee chairmanship, lining up some two hundred famous Americans to hold rallies and deliver radio addresses in support of neutrality law revision.

Newspapers and magazines began to take editorial positions, and letters and telegrams began to flow into Washington. If those expressions could be taken as a reflection of popular attitudes, they suggested a national trend toward the president's position. In a series of conferences with doubtful senators and congressmen, FDR used all his persuasive skills to convince them that the trend was significant. In the end he and his coadjutors were successful. The Senate passed his neutrality bill on October 27, the House accepted it on November 3, and it went into effect on November 4, 1939. Belligerents could now purchase anything they wanted in the United States provided they paid cash and supplied their own transportation. The legislation would not in itself defeat the Axis, but the nation had set a new course away from neutrality and isolationism.

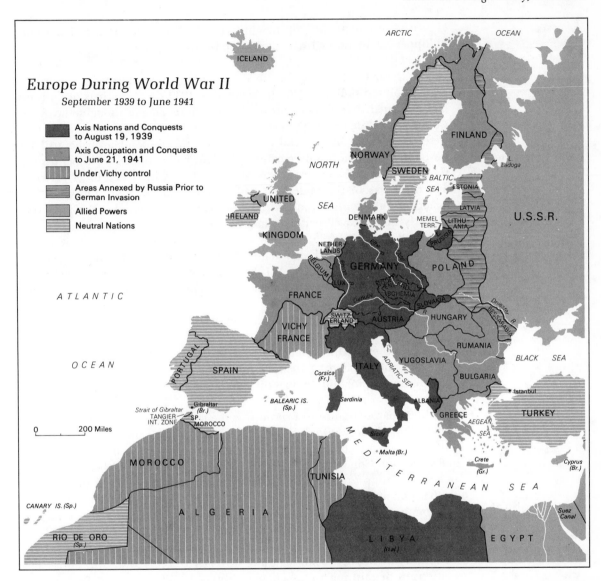

Europe During World War II

September 1939 to June 1941

A lull in the fighting after Germany's conquest of Poland rendered ineffective the arguments of interventionists who continued to urge more aid to Britain and France. But then in April 1940 German troops smashed into Denmark and Norway; on May 10 Hitler sent his divisions into the Low Countries and mounted a massive offensive against Allied lines. *Blitzkrieg* tactics forced the surrender of Belgium and the evacuation of British forces at Dunkirk. French forces, plagued by inefficiency and puzzled by tactical innovations, could not halt the German advance. On June 17 French leaders requested armistice terms, five days later agreeing to German occupation of more than half of France including Paris. The

French government took up new quarters at Vichy, where Marshal Henri Philippe Pétain headed a regime friendly to Germany.

The fall of France brought about a significant shift in American attitudes toward the conflict in Europe, a shift that found expression in the public opinion polls of 1940. In September 1939 the soundings of pollsters had indicated that 82 per cent of the American people thought the Allies would win, while only 7 per cent thought Germany would win; 11 per cent were undecided. By the end of July 1940, the respondents who still believed that England would emerge victorious had dropped to 43 per cent of the total, those who expected a Nazi triumph had increased to 24 per cent, and the ranks of the undecided had arisen to 27 per cent. Opponents of American intervention took satisfaction in pointing out that the polls consistently indicated 80 per cent against direct military involvement. Yet in May and June 1940 36 per cent of the respondents believed that aid to Britain, even at the risk of war for the United States, was more important than preserving neutrality. A July poll suggested that 73 per cent of the nation wanted to do everything possible, short of war, to help Britain defeat Hitler.

Roosevelt's policies and the activities of independent interventionist groups were carefully orchestrated to harmonize with the findings of opinion researchers. During May, Eichelberger and White set about reorganizing and expanding their Nonpartisan Committee to provide coordinated support for aid to Britain and France. The new association, the Committee to Defend America by Aiding the Allies, effectively publicized the idea that assistance to Britain was the surest way to preserve American neutrality. A more informal association, calling itself the "Century Group" after the private club where many of its meetings were held, reinforced the efforts of the Committee to Defend America. Francis P. Miller, one of the Century Group organizers, moved from the premise that "the problems of either one of the continents which frame the Western World are problems of common concern" to the conclusion that "the keystone of our foreign policy must be close collaboration with the British Commonwealth of Nations." The argument gained plausibility in August as Hitler's *Luftwaffe* began nightly bombing raids to destroy the Royal Air Force and soften up Britain for a cross-channel invasion. The Battle of Britain convinced most Americans that Hitler's appetite for conquest was insatiable and that a victory over British forces would mean a direct attack on the United States.

Yet Roosevelt hesitated. Isolationists were by no means subdued, and 1940 was an election year in which FDR sought an unprecedented third term. On June 28 Republicans nominated Wendell Willkie, a vigorous and affable businessman whose approval of many New Deal measures made him a champion of the party's progressive wing. Willkie was no isolationist, and he at first pitched his campaign to win the votes of citizens who doubted the wisdom of electing anyone to a third term in the White House. Failing to arouse enthusiasm with that tactic, however, he began

Herman Goering's *Luftwaffe* made many mistakes during the Battle of Britain in 1940–1941; not the least was the decision to bomb London and other industrial cities rather than British airfields. Thus, while the area around St. Paul's was reduced to rubble, RAF fighter planes continued to fly. In 1941, the *Luftwaffe* defeated, Hitler cancelled his planned invasion of Britain (Wide World photo).

to attack the president as a warmonger. More than ever, then, FDR had to persuade Americans that his foreign policy was a cautious policy of defense and not one of reckless interventionism.

Concern for his chances in the election of 1940 helps to account for FDR's boggling response to an unusual request from Britain's new prime minister, Winston Churchill. Shortly after taking office in May, Churchill asked that the United States transfer several destroyers to the Royal Navy to assist in convoy duty and help protect England against invasion. With the Battle of Britain under way the need was obvious, yet Roosevelt demurred, for he had no desire to weaken American defensive capabilities and so intensify isolationist opposition. In the end, after receiving assurances that the Navy could spare fifty destroyers and after securing Willkie's pledge to keep the deal out of the campaign, FDR concluded negotiations for the transfer. In September Britain obtained fifty destroyers of World War I vintage, in return leasing locations for American bases in Newfoundland, Bermuda, the Bahamas, Jamaica, St. Lucia, Antigua, Trinidad, and British Guiana. Advantages of the exchange were enough to spike isolationist criticism that it was an unneutral act, yet the isolationists were correct in seeing the destroyer deal as marking an end to American neutrality.

Their fears mounted when, following the election, Roosevelt proposed that the United States go even further and lend armaments to Britain. When a neighbor's house was on fire, he observed in one of his celebrated analogies, one did not haggle over the price of a garden hose to help quench it. Responsible behavior called for putting out the fire and getting the hose back when the crisis had passed. With that homely parable FDR made his case for the Lend-Lease bill (H.R. 1776!) then pending in Congress. The bill would authorize Roosevelt to assist any nation "whose defense the President deems vital to the defense of the United States."

In vain the isolationists argued that Lend-Lease would surely mean war. Montana's Burton K. Wheeler attacked FDR's "triple-A foreign policy" because it would "plough under every fourth American boy." But Wheeler's testiness was really an evidence of isolationist defeat. Even George Norris, whose noninterventionist credentials were impeccable, supported Lend-Lease on the grounds that aid to Britain might bring about Hitler's defeat and thus prevent attacks on the United States that would follow an Axis victory. Historians and moralists might later question the rationale, for it suggested that, as Stephen Ambrose has put it, the United States would "pay others to do the fighting that had to be done." Yet given the national and congressional state of mind at the beginning of the new year, 1941, that line of thinking was probably the only one that could have won sufficient support for Lend-Lease. With the bill's passage by Congress on March 8, American commitment to an Allied victory became unequivocal.

Events following enactment of Lend-Lease gradually moved the United

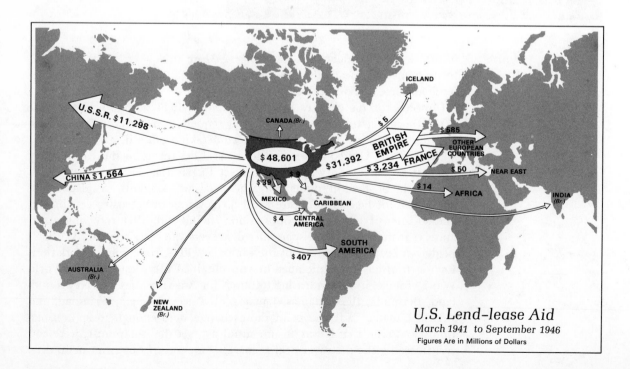

## U.S. Lend–lease Aid
*March 1941 to September 1946*
Figures Are in Millions of Dollars

States to the point of belligerency. Abandoning "Operation Sea Lion" (the planned invasion of Britain), Hitler sent troops to bolster faltering Italian forces in the Balkans and North Africa. Then, to everyone's amazement, he suddenly repudiated his Soviet alliance and initiated "Operation Barbarossa"—a furious attack on the USSR—in June 1941. From the German point of view, Barbarossa was a monumental blunder. It made Stalin's 1939 participation in the division of Poland and his 1940 "Winter War" on Finland seem the essence of oracular wisdom, for German divisions now had to subdue extensive territories before they even reached the Russian frontier. The attack also brought an extension of Lend-Lease assistance to the USSR. Though American aid was not sufficient immediately to turn back Nazi forces, Hitler's invasion had compelled a cooperation that the Popular Front had sought but never achieved.

More important, perhaps, than aid that went to Russia was the fact that Nazi preoccupation with the eastern front allowed the United States to become deeply involved in convoying supplies to Britain without fear of full-scale German retaliation. American ships and planes were already patrolling the western Atlantic; and, by agreement with Denmark, Greenland had been placed under the temporary protection of the United States. Now, after Barbarossa, a brigade of American marines went to Iceland for protection of the island nation, and American ships began to serve convoy duty to that point in the North Atlantic. With such activities under way, brushes with Nazi U-boats were unavoidable. In September the U.S.S. *Greer* sustained fire from a German submarine, on October 17, 1941, torpedoes damaged the destroyer *Kearney,* and on October 31 U-boats sank the *Reuben James.* With the United States in fact if not in international law at war on the sea, the Neutrality Act had clearly become obsolete. On November 7 a somber Senate voted 50–37 to remove all restrictions on trade with the Allies; six days later, by a vote of 212–194, the House concurred. Americans had less than a month in which to think of themselves as nonbelligerents.

**Collision Course in the Pacific**

One reason for American naval activity in the North Atlantic was Roosevelt's belief that Nazi Germany and Fascist Italy posed a greater threat in Europe than did Japan in the Far East. After Germany's invasion of Poland FDR sought to ward off a conflict in Asia lest it interfere with the more important task of aiding the Allies in Europe. During the troubled months from September 1939 to December 1941, however, the United States proceeded incrementally to frustrate specific Japanese ambitions in China and broader Japanese aspirations in the Far East. Unavoidable and perhaps irreconcilable differences with Japan culminated in the Japanese attack on Pearl Harbor that brought unqualified entry of American forces into war against the Axis powers.

American policy in Asia and the Pacific took shape within a traditional Open Door framework and found expression in a series of limited maneuvers. No single move was sufficiently drastic either to provoke a Japanese

With their attack on Manchuria in 1931, the Japanese began a protracted struggle for control of China. By 1938, when these troops were photographed in action near Hankow, Japan had developed the concept of a "New Order" for Asia. Despite tactical military successes, however, the Rising Sun shed—at best—a flickering light over the Chinese people (Wide World photo).

attack on the United States or to provide Chiang Kai-shek and the Nationalists with support adequate to drive Japanese forces out of China. Overwhelmingly important, however, was the cumulative effect of American actions. Along with fascist successes in Europe and unexpected difficulties that Japanese troops encountered in China, it led militant Japanese political factions to the conclusion that their country had nothing to lose in a war with the United States.

The Roosevelt administration took its first important step against Japan's "New Order" in Asia in July 1939, when Hitler was preparing to negotiate his nonaggression pact with the USSR. Secretary of State Hull announced that the United States would terminate its trade treaty with Japan on January 1940. Abrogation of the treaty would not in itself halt trade, but it would permit the president to impose limits on commerce with Japan. FDR, of course, knew that Japanese control over China depended upon shipments of American oil and scrap metal; he hoped that under the threat of economic sanctions Japan would meliorate her China policies. During the gloomy autumn of 1939, however, the threat produced nothing but soothing words from the Japanese Foreign Office to the effect that, once the Greater East Asia Co-Prosperity Sphere had been established, trade would be resumed to everyone's benefit.

For the time being, Roosevelt avoided further action, but then in the spring of 1940 Nazi forces swept into the Low Countries on their way to the conquest of France. With Hitler's occupation of the Netherlands, Japanese leaders began to cast longing glances at the Dutch East Indies, an area rich in oil, rubber, tin, bauxite, nickel, and manganese. Temporarily satisfied with a Dutch pledge to keep trade routes open, the Japanese were nevertheless impressed by the argument that Europe's trouble was the Rising Sun's opportunity. With the fall of France Japanese forces began the occupation of Indochina, and Japanese diplomats began to look toward closer cooperation with Hitler. In September Japanese representatives journeyed to Berlin, there signing a Tripartite Pact with Germany and Italy. The Axis powers recognized Japanese dominance in East Asia and German-Italian supremacy in Europe; each of the three also pledged to support either of the others should it come under attack.

Alarmed by Japanese diplomacy—which they could only see as a threat to the security of American interests in Asia—Roosevelt and his advisers executed bolder moves than they had heretofore. After ordering the Pacific fleet from San Diego to Pearl Harbor, the Administration made exports of aviation fuel and high-grade scrap metal subject to Federal control. Then, in September, the president announced an embargo on all scrap metal exports to Japan. By April 1941 the United States had extended Lend-Lease aid to China, and FDR had signed an executive order that permitted volunteers to join Colonel Claire L. Chennault's "Flying Tigers," an organization that gave direct military assistance to Chiang Kai-shek. Finally, on July 25, Roosevelt played one of his highest cards when he froze all Japanese assets in the United States. Britain and the Dutch government-in-exile followed suit. The freezing order placed trade relations under presidential control, for only a special license from the United States government would release Japanese funds to pay for goods purchased on the American market.

Two weeks after announcement of the freeze, FDR and Churchill met in a secret conference at sea off the coast of Newfoundland. Best remembered because it produced the Atlantic Charter, a formulation of principles in support of popular sovereignty and cooperation for international justice and welfare, the conference also provided an opportunity to discuss problems of the Far East. Churchill urged an American commitment to war if Japan invaded Malaya or the Dutch East Indies. FDR saw no advantage in a formal declaration at that time; but, after his return to Washington, he did warn the Japanese ambassador that persistence in a program of aggression would place the United States under obligation to take "any and all steps" necessary for the protection of American interests.

Roosevelt did not merely threaten and bluster (nothing would have been more out of character), and not all Japanese leaders believed that their nation should ignore American protests. The government of Premier Fumimaro Konoye struggled with proponents of war to keep open the lines of diplomatic communication. Indeed, through September 1941, he had a ship standing by in Yokohama harbor ready to take him to a rendezvous with Roosevelt if the president would only give his assent to a meeting. FDR seemed interested, but Hull dissuaded him. After all, the secretary had already held several futile conferences with Ambassador Kichisaburo Nomura, and it seemed to him that a top-level discussion could only raise false hopes. Given the growing strength of Japanese militants, Prince Konoye could offer no new concessions. Either that meant Roosevelt's withdrawal from the position he had already taken, or it meant failure of the proposed talks and the criticism that failure would bring.

China was the great stumbling block on the pathway to an agreement with Japan. All political factions under the Rising Sun had committed themselves to the achievement of announced objectives in China, though there was some hope for compromise on other questions. Roosevelt and Hull would not consider other questions, however, if doing so required American abandonment of Chiang Kai-shek, that is, abandonment of the Open Door. Japanese-American differences had become irreconcilable. With Japan experiencing the effects of American embargo policies, and with needed supplies lying close at hand in Southeast Asia and the East Indies, Konoye suffered the consequences of his failure to find a way out of the diplomatic impasse with the United States. His government fell from power. On October 16 Emperor Hirohito summoned General Hideki Tojo—known to the Japanese as "Razor Brain" because of his quick, tough-minded advocacy of more forceful policies—and asked him to assume office as Japan's prime minister.

Unlike Konoye, Tojo was not one to be diverted from the policy adopted by his government back in July. The cabinet had at that time decided to take advantage of Soviet preoccupation with Hitler's advancing armies in Europe, which left Japan free to extend her control into Southeast Asia without fear of a Russian attack on Manchukuo. Concerned about American naval power, Konoye had instead attempted a diplomatic solution to Japanese problems. Tojo could now point to the miscarriage of that effort and insist upon a return to the July policy. In a portentous meeting with the Emperor on November 5, civil and military leaders agreed to continue diplomatic efforts until November 25; if the United States had not by that time made an appropriate response, Japan would resort to war and would urge Germany and Italy to join the Rising Sun in its ascendancy over American arms.

In Washington, American leaders were not ignorant of Japanese plans. American cryptanalysts, having broken the Purple Cipher, Japan's highest diplomatic code, had set up machines (given the name Magic) to decode intercepted messages. From Magic the Roosevelt administration learned that November 25 was the deadline for American acceptance of Japanese demands. Shortly thereafter Ambassador Nomura presented "Plan A," the first of two sets of proposals. It called for restoration of trade with Japan and cessation of American aid to China. In return, the Japanese promised an open door to commerce in their empire when the rest of the world

This photograph is one of many that document the destruction wrought by Japanese planes at Pearl Harbor on December 7, 1941. It was, President Roosevelt told the Congress and the American people, "a date which will live in infamy." Nevertheless he was coldly and indignantly confident that "the American people in their righteous might will win through to absolute victory" (United Press International photo).

accepted the principle, withdrawal of troops from China after "the lapse of a suitable interval" following the conclusion of peace, and eventual evacuation of Indochina. The American government, as Tokyo assumed it would, rejected Plan A out of hand. Saburo Kurusu then arrived in Washington to help with negotiations. Acting without authority, he tried to arrange a truce that would remove trade restrictions and secure withdrawal of Japanese troops from southern Indochina. For his pains, as Magic revealed, he received a rebuke from his government.

Nomura, aware that time was running out, handed "Plan B" to Secretary Hull on November 20. Under its terms Japan would undertake no new action and would withdraw from Indochina with the conclusion of a general Southeast Asian settlement. The United States, for its part, would be expected to release Japanese assets, supply Japan with oil, put pressure on the Dutch to reopen trade with Japan, and withdraw support from Chiang Kai-shek. With the knowledge that his efforts would probably fail to produce results, Hull nevertheless set about drafting a reply.

The Secretary of State was justified in his pessimism. Although Tokyo had extended the deadline to November 29, Tojo's government would not yield elsewhere. The prime minister had learned that his European partners would declare war if Japan's actions brought it about, and that knowledge made him even more unreceptive to Hull's response than he otherwise might have been. On December 1 he and other Japanese leaders meeting with the emperor reached a final decision for war. A week earlier, Admiral Isoroku Yamamoto had ordered a well-trained task force to leave its base in the Kuril Islands and to proceed on an eastward course toward a point 230 miles north of Hawaii. When the carrier based planes of the task force had completed their mission on December 7, they left Pearl Harbor a smoking shambles, the United States Pacific fleet in ruin, and 3,500 American servicemen dead.

# PART FOUR

A Time of War,
Affluence, Disruption,
and Judgment

# 9

# Global War
# and the Limits of Power

The Japanese attack on Pearl Harbor brought the United States formally into war, and in many ways the four years after December 7, 1941, were cathartic. The economic sluggishness of the thirties gave way under pressure of new demands for the products of American industry. Abundant employment opportunities had a rehabilitating effect on people grown accustomed to job scarcity. A cleansing vitality replaced the despair of depression, and after initial setbacks the nation's military success restored confidence in the institutions of government and society. Citizens suffered few doubts about the legitimacy of American involvement in the struggle against Axis powers, and Roosevelt nourished the social cohesion that began to appear as the war effort got under way.

Yet the unity that characterized the months after Pearl Harbor was not complete. Minority groups denied a proportionate share in the great national cause became embittered, and Japanese-Americans herded into relocation camps felt keenly the sting of discrimination. In a powerful way the war presented a challenge to fervent rhetoric that took American righteousness as its premise. Did people of the United States really believe what they said about freedom and equality of opportunity? Were American institutions really superior to those of Nazi Germany? If so, the point required more concrete demonstration than it had yet received, and the war years provided an impetus to action. The crisis of war thus produced a movement to improve American institutions at the same time that their soundness was vigorously affirmed.

Perhaps even more important than economic and social effects of World War II was the way that it altered the American position in world affairs. Before 1939 the nation enjoyed the luxury of a ranking among the great powers without always feeling a need to assume the responsibilities of power. After 1945 the United States headed one of the two major alignments in a bipolar world. The Soviet Union headed the other. The attainment of coequal eminence was a consequence of the manner in which nations of the Grand Alliance against Hitler formulated strategy and conducted their operations. Rivalries and tensions that characterized the postwar period and produced a Cold War thus had their roots in the Grand Alliance that achieved victory over the Axis. One result of those Cold War tensions was a new anxiety about the security of American institutions. The national unity of the World War II period then gave way to an angry partisanship that tended to distort perceptions of international realities. Distorted perceptions, in turn, led to policy decisions that increased antagonisms both at home and abroad.

The American
Economy in
Wartime

Entry into war presented new challenges to the American economy after Pearl Harbor. The heavy demand for war materiel overcame economic depression as the organization of productive efforts became a primary concern. Under duress of military necessity the national government had to provide incentives for civilian industries to retool and expand plant facilities; beyond that, it had to undertake and encourage the construction of new plants designed for fabricating needed goods. Improving manufacturing capabilities was, however, only a part of the wartime economic problem. The expansion of agricultural production, the acquisition and allocation of raw materials, the scheduling of processes and deliveries, the provision of adequate transportation, and the recruitment of a trained labor force all required careful planning and supervision. And, as the economy moved toward full employment during a period of shortages in consumers' goods, the threat of inflation demanded additional regulatory measures. Going beyond New Deal precedents that had once aroused libertarian fears of regulation, the national government became more deeply involved in economic planning and control than ever before. Justified by wartime necessities, that involvement would outlive its justification, working a permanent transformation in American life.

Whatever its long-range influence, economic mobilization for war advanced haltingly. The process actually began in the months before Pearl Harbor when the United States became, in Roosevelt's phrase, "the arsenal of democracy." The president took a first tentative step in August 1939, when he approved a War Department recommendation urging the creation of a War Resources Board. Yet, fearful that the Board would usurp executive power, he quickly replaced it with several more limited agencies such as the National Defense Advisory Commission, the Office of Production Management, the Office of Price Administration and Civilian Supply, and the Supply Priorities and Allocations Board. Because authority was divided, the plethora of offices permitted FDR to exercise effective control over mobilization, and—for all the accumulation of red tape—munitions production increased 225 per cent during 1941.

After American entry into war, Congress granted the president broader powers than he had previously held; and, in response to demands for greater administrative efficiency, he created the War Production Board in January 1942. Still reluctant to encourage a power play, FDR selected the politically unambitious and sometimes indecisive Donald Nelson to head up the board. Under Nelson the WPB acceded to a dilution of its authority: private industries retained considerable autonomy, military procurement remained with the Army and Navy, and independent administrations were created to deal with special problems (distributing petroleum supplies, allocating rubber and developing a synthetic substitute, attracting manpower to essential industries, and the like). Dispersion of responsibility, particularly when its outer limits were left undefined, naturally caused bureaucratic improvisation, rivalry, and friction. To settle disputes over rationing, pricing, and supply, the president asked James F. Byrnes to take charge of an Office of Economic Stabilization in October 1942. The former South Carolina senator and Supreme Court justice soon established himself as FDR's right-hand man in all economic matters, and in May 1943 he assumed control of the newly created Office of War Mobilization. His job, chiefly one of coordination, was performed well. In large part through his influence, the sometimes chaotic system of controls began to develop consistency and coherence.

Among the problems that caused difficulties for government administrators was conversion of the nation's industry from peacetime to wartime production. Many industrialists resisted the suggestion that they reorganize their operations to produce goods for which there would be little demand after the war. Others were leery of engaging in activities that might warrant a "merchant of death" label. The chance of quick wartime profits did not seem worth the possible loss of gradual, long-term growth. Had the War Production Board not limited production of nonessentials and forbidden use of raw materials in short supply, some industries would never have converted. Nevertheless, by the summer of 1942 the production of consumer durables had been severely curtailed. The wartime importance of major industries—especially the automobile industry—is obvious. Yet as Professor Richard Polenberg has noted, small manufacturers also converted their plants to meet military needs: they "switched from making shirts to mosquito netting, from model trains to bomb fuses, from metal weatherstripping to mortar shells, and from kitchen sinks to cartridge cases."

To encourage production of needed goods and supplies, the government offered attractive inducements to manufacturers who would expand their operations. Early in the war Nelson introduced a plan whereby the cost of expansion could be amortized over a short five-year period, drastically reducing taxable income. If a firm showed a loss at the end of the war, the government promised to allow a refund. "Cost-plus" contracts, by which the government agreed to meet all costs to manufacturers and to pay a guaranteed fee as well, reduced risks and assured profits. Finally, by granting exemption from antitrust laws to companies demonstrating that cooperation would aid the war effort, the Administration provided yet another incentive to expansion.

Farmers, too, received encouragement to increase production. During

I'm proud of YOU FOLKS too!

The war effort imposed heavy demands on American industry and on the industrial work force. Under the pressure of those demands serious morale problems could easily develop at any time. Posters such as this one were designed to stimulate pride among war workers and thus prevent flagging enthusiasm (State Historical Society of Wisconsin).

the depression thirties the Department of Agriculture had sought to maintain prices by curbing farm output, but mounting military and Lend-Lease demands after 1939 made possible the lifting of restrictions. In 1941 Secretary of Agriculture Claude Wickard raised production goals in most commodities (except for wheat, cotton, tobacco, and others available in surplus), and, until October 1942, ceilings on farm prices were set at 110 per cent of parity. When the resulting high cost of food brought complaints from consumers and from the Office of Price Administration, Congress responded by passing a Stabilization Act that would restrict agricultural prices to 100 per cent of parity. Yet at the same time farmers won an important legislative concession: prices in basic commodities would be maintained at 90 per cent of parity for two years after the return of peace. Agricultural producers were thus relieved of anxieties about a possible collapse of markets such as the one they had met after World War I.

With the government backing production increases and developing a comprehensive system of controls, the economy soon worked its way out of the doldrums of depression. During the last three years of the war, annual agricultural productivity was 20 per cent greater than it had been in 1939, and net income per farm (measured in constant dollars) was double that of 1939. Even more noteworthy was the "miracle" of war materiel production. During 1941 the United States accounted for 12.5 per cent of the estimated world production of munitions, with the Allied and Axis powers dividing the remainder almost equally. By 1943, American munitions production was 40 per cent of the world total, exceeding by one-third the output of all Axis nations combined. American industry accounted for nearly half of the combined Allied production of munitions during the war. Home-front achievements, of course, worked significant changes in the economy. In 1939 war production had accounted for only 1 per cent of the gross national product, but by 1943 about 40 per cent of GNP was attributable to war production. Table 9.1, indicating impressive

TABLE 9.1    Total Gross National Product and Industrial Production in the United States, 1939–1945

| Year | GNP (in billions of dollars) | Industrial Production (F.R. Board Index, 1957–1959 = 100) |
|------|------------------------------|-----------------------------------------------------------|
| 1939 | $ 90.5 | 38.3 |
| 1940 | 99.7 | 43.9 |
| 1941 | 124.5 | 56.4 |
| 1942 | 157.9 | 69.3 |
| 1943 | 191.6 | 82.9 |
| 1944 | 210.1 | 81.7 |
| 1945 | 211.9 | 70.5 |

SOURCE: *Economic Report of the President*, January 1967 (Washington, D.C.: U.S. Government Printing Office, 1967), pp. 213, 250.

increases in GNP and industrial production during the war years, reflects the influence of military concerns in the achievement of recovery.

Economic recovery implied a return to full employment, but recovery under conditions of total war also implied government regulation and control of manpower. The armed forces had begun drafting men between the ages of twenty-one and thirty-six after passage of a selective service law in September 1940. Age limits were later extended to eighteen and thirty-eight, and draftees were sworn in for the duration of the war and six months thereafter. By mid-1945 more than fifteen million men and women had seen active service. The Army and Navy encountered only limited problems in meeting their manpower needs, but providing the workers for war industries posed greater difficulties. The War Manpower Commission created in the spring of 1942 had few coercive powers, for FDR preferred to rely on voluntary cooperation. The failure of that approach was all too obvious; absenteeism, rapid turnover, and "manpower pirating" hampered industrial efficiency. The War Manpower Commission received additional responsibility in 1943, when Roosevelt placed the selective service system under its supervision, and it experimented briefly with a tough "work or fight" policy. But coercion was no more effective than voluntarism. Eventually wartime agencies found a way to resolve manpower problems by a method of balancing production needs and labor supply. Local committees first estimated the number of available workers in a given locality; then firms in the area could obtain government contracts only if assured of the labor sufficient to meet them. Thus the government turned away from conscription of civilian workers, nevertheless exercising important controls through its balancing of interests.

As national mobilization got under way with the outbreak of war in Europe, economists and consumers worried about effects of the inflation that appeared to be in the making. Wholesale prices rose at a rate of 2 per cent a month during the summer of 1941, and the newly created Office of Price Administration seemed powerless to halt an increase in the cost of living. After American entry into war, Congress passed the Emergency Price Control Act (which granted the OPA statutory power to control prices and rents) ; but, despite the legislation, prices continued to move upward by as much as 4 per cent between October 1942, and April 1943. FDR finally issued a "hold the line" directive imposing ceilings on wages and prices. Workers resented controls on hourly wages, but with overtime they were able to extend their total earnings. While wage rates rose only 24 per cent during the war, weekly earnings increased 70 per cent. At the same time, the freeze on prices proved remarkably effective. In the war months after the president's announcement of his hold-the-line order, both consumer and wholesale prices remained surprisingly stable in view of increases that had occurred during World War I.

These women workers were photographed at the Douglas Aircraft plant, Long Beach, California, in November 1942. Serious as wartime labor shortages were, the problem might have been worse. Necessity overcame objections to the employment of women in certain positions, and female war workers demonstrated their competence in all industrial activities (Wide World photo).

The success of price control was attributable to fiscal policies that skimmed off excess purchasing power. The war effort justified government deficits of a magnitude that Roosevelt had never dared contemplate during the depression. The deficit rose from less than $4 billion in 1939 to more than $57 billion in 1943, and during the war years the public debt increased from less than $46 billion to nearly $260 billion. Government spending had the multiplier effect that Keynes had predicted; the booming war economy required a broadly based tax system as well as price controls to check inflation. Beginning with the Revenue Act of 1940 Congress raised rates, extended the tax base, and eventually increased tax receipts to ten times what they had been before the war. The practice of withholding at the source taxes on wages and salaries began in 1943, but even in the previous year 42 million people had paid income taxes as compared with only 4 million in 1939.

Some economists argued that the mounting national debt as well as the threat of inflation called for heavier tax rates than those actually imposed. Others contended that too extreme a burden of taxation would impair morale, an argument that FDR found convincing. Thus, instead of raising tax rates, the government placed greater reliance on other antiinflation measures such as rationing and the sale of war bonds. Rationing was, of course, primarily a device for making the best use of scarce products and commodities. Restriction of gasoline purchases, for example, helped to conserve rubber, and the food stamp program made possible an equitable distribution of sugar, coffee, and other items in short supply. Black markets developed, to be sure; but, insofar as rationing limited consumption, it automatically reduced consumer spending.

At the beginning of the war several experts in public finance (Keynes among them) urged the imposition of a forced savings program. Fearful of citizen responses to such a program, the Administration sought achievement of the same end through less coercive means. Thus, with the help of advertising agencies willing to contribute their expertise and celebrities happy to lend their names to the cause, the government launched a vigorous campaign to sell war bonds. Although they were not so effective in cutting back on consumer spending as forced savings might have been, the bond drives did register at least some successes. Corporations, insurance companies, and banks bought more than two-thirds of the $156.9 billion in national securities sold by the Treasury during the war. Yet some 25 million workers made good use of payroll bond purchasing plans to build up nest eggs for themselves while—unconsciously perhaps—helping to combat inflation. In 1944 more than 7 per cent of personal income after taxes went toward the purchase of Series E bonds.

Whatever economic problems accompanied it, the war effort provided a convincing demonstration of the economy's productive capacity. The flow of supplies from farm and factory helped submerge the Axis; beyond that, expanded production marked the restoration of economic prosperity. The need for war materiel in effect greatly increased aggregate demand for the products of American industry, and military involvement thus lent great plausibility to Keynesian theory. With the Allied victory of 1945, Keynesian economics entered a period of nearly universal acceptance. Yet the war did more than restore prosperity and validate the ideas of Keynes. The association between economic recovery and mobilization also helped to bring about a noticeable shift in American attitudes toward the rest of the world. The obvious benefits of wartime prosperity to some degree moderated resistance to military intervention outside the Western Hemisphere.

**Cracks in the American Armor**

Economic prosperity was only one of several unifying forces that World War II insinuated into American society. Few people questioned the war's legitimacy after Pearl Harbor, and a preponderant majority of citizens shared a common animus toward the Axis powers. Concentrating on the nation's enemies abroad, Americans found less time for promoting antagonisms at home. Mobilization created a vast number of job opportunities that reduced psychological causes of tension as men and women gained the self-respect that derives from employment in socially approved occupations. Furthermore, while the rewards of a common effort required minimum sacrifice, wartime slogans invested routine activities with greater than routine significance. Sharing in a car pool, for example, would help win the war by conserving rubber; members of a pool knew that "the empty seat is a gift to Hitler," and that "Hitler smiles when you waste miles." This is not to minimize the dreadful losses of war. Nearly a million servicemen were killed, wounded, or lost in action. Yet American casualties represented less than 1 per cent of the population, a small number compared with an 8 per cent loss for the Russian people. Contributing to victory thus conferred enormous psychic satisfaction at low cost, and the bargain price for so great a benefit reinforced popular commitment to the war effort.

For all its obvious manifestations, however, wartime unity of purpose did not prevail throughout all segments of society. Racial minorities had suffered greater hardships during the depression than had a majority of Americans; and, with increases in industrial production for military needs, they shared with the economically disadvantaged a hope for better times. Yet when blacks and other racial minorities sought jobs with companies advertising for workers, they usually encountered discriminatory hiring policies. "The Negro will be considered only as janitors and in other similar capacities," announced North American Aviation with ungrammatical bluntness. "Regardless of their training as aircraft workers, we will not employ them." North American may have been more candid than most firms, but others adopted similar practices. In 1940 the aircraft industry employed some 100,000 workers, and only 0.25 per cent of them were black. Less than 1 per cent of the electrical machinery industry's work force was black; in the rubber industry the percentage was less than 3. The propor-

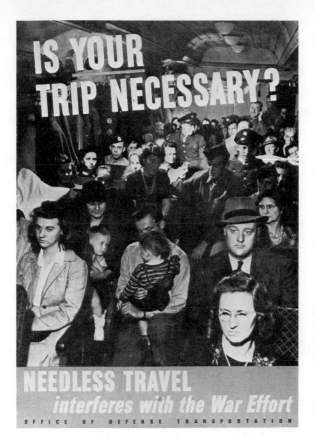

IS YOUR TRIP NECESSARY?

NEEDLESS TRAVEL
*interferes with the War Effort*
OFFICE OF DEFENSE TRANSPORTATION

With gasoline rationed and automobile usage greatly reduced, the nation's railroads bore the major responsibility for passenger transportation. Overcrowded facilities led the office of Defense Transportation to encourage voluntary reduction of travel, and most citizens probably logged fewer unnecessary miles than in peacetime. Even so, the ODT photograph of a crowded railway coach did not exaggerate (State Historical Society of Wisconsin).

tion of blacks working in all branches of manufacturing in 1940 was less than it had been a decade earlier, and at the end of the year one out of five black workers was unemployed. Those who did have jobs commonly held menial positions vacated by whites who took advantage of better opportunities in war-related industries.

During the early months of the war, government agencies and the armed forces were nearly as discriminatory as private companies. Blacks encountered unusual obstacles in government training programs even when the heads of agencies attempted to prevent unfair treatment. The armed services were rigidly segregated at the time of Pearl Harbor. A black who wanted to enlist in the Navy could enter only as a messman, while both the Air Corps and the Marines refused to consider black applicants. The Army restricted black enlistment to four regular Army units that had been created after the Civil War. On every hand racial minorities met rejection and disdain when they responded to appeals for support of the nation's war effort. The Red Cross went so far as to reject blood from black donors on the grounds that haphazard mixing of Caucasian and Negro blood might repel a majority of whites. The passage of two decades, in short, seemed to have brought few changes in the social or economic position of blacks; their status at the beginning of World War II did not appear significantly different from their status at the time of World War I.

The frustration experienced by black people led many of them to view the second great conflict of the twentieth century as no less a white man's war than the first. Before Pearl Harbor Negro newspapers such as the Pittsburgh *Courier* and the Chicago *Defender* advocated a form of racial isolationism. "Our war is not against Hitler in Europe," declared *Courier* columnist George Schuyler, "but against the Hitlers in America." Various organizations—the Ethiopian Pacific Movement, the World Wide Friends of Africa, and the Brotherhood of Liberty for the Black People of America were among the most prominent—anticipated cooperation among dark-skinned populations of the world, including the Japanese. And after Pearl Harbor members of several cults identified themselves with the Rising Sun. It is true that pro-Japanese sentiment among American blacks never amounted to much, but it is also true that for blacks in the United States the war meant a struggle for democracy at home as well as abroad. Thus the *Crisis,* a publication of the National Association for the Advancement of Colored People, saw little to choose between doctrines of white supremacy in the United States and Nazi attitudes toward the Negro. At the same time, a majority of American blacks believed that war presented an unusual opportunity. Negroes should use the national crisis, proclaimed the Pittsburgh *Courier,* "to persuade, embarrass, compel and shame our government and our nation . . . into a more enlightened attitude toward a tenth of its people."

Early in 1941 A. Philip Randolph, president of the Brotherhood of Sleeping Car Porters, carried out the suggestion that black people exert pressure on the nation's government when he issued a call for a mass demonstration in Washington. Demanding "the right to work and fight for our country," the March on Washington Movement (MOWM) aroused great enthusiasm among black citizens; by mid-summer some fifty thousand of them were preparing to join the march. Fearing possible consequences of a mass demonstration, the president conferred with Randolph; he agreed to issue an executive order prohibiting racial or religious discrimination in defense industries and creating a Committee on Fair Employment Practices. Randolph canceled the march even though FDR's order failed to meet all black demands, but he would not cancel (even had he been able to) the rising militancy to which the MOWM had given expression. Throughout the war racial tensions increased in every section of the country as Negroes struggled against the prejudices that denied them not only the rights of citizens but also a chance to meet the obligations of citizens.

Sociologist Robert E. Park, sensitive to the new black militancy, thought he saw a "cracking" of the racial accommodation that since Reconstruction had shaped white attitudes toward the nation's largest minority. White supremacy, he thought, was being attacked "at a time and under conditions when it is particularly difficult to defend it." War needs also served to provide black people with unaccustomed opportunities that reinforced their hope for equality. By the fall of 1944, some 700,000 black soldiers were serving in the Army as compared with 97,000 at the time of Pearl

# Pvt. Joe Louis says_

## "We're going to do our part ... and we'll win because we're on God's side"

World heavyweight boxing champion Joe Louis, one of the great heroes of American sport in the late thirties, drew attention to the role of black soldiers during the war. Louis was neither theologian nor social reformer. Yet his celebrated remark, the caption of this poster, provided a text for countless sermons and a poignant commentary on the need for improved race relations in the United States (State Historical Society of Wisconsin).

Harbor. And when James Forrestal became Secretary of the Navy in 1944, that branch of the armed forces began to move rapidly toward integration. In the summer of 1942 blacks comprised only 3 per cent of all war workers, but by the end of the conflict 8 per cent of the work force in defense plants was black. The War Labor Board had outlawed wage differentials between whites and racial minorities, and the National Labor Relations Board had refused to certify unions that would not admit to membership people from minority groups.

Yet Federal agencies did not resolve all racial tension. The President's Committee on Fair Employment Practices lacked the power to enforce compliance with its regulations; although it might request cancellation of a defense contract, the Administration was always reluctant to jeopardize production by meeting such a request. The Army adhered to segregationist policies; even Secretary of War Henry L. Stimson complained that "what these foolish leaders of the colored race are seeking is at the bottom social equality." A half-hearted attempt to integrate training camps in 1944 accomplished little. On the battlefield, black troops fought in their own combat units except in unusual circumstances. During the Battle of the Bulge, for example, 2,500 black volunteers served as infantry replacements in platoons assigned to white companies.

Thus, despite some progress toward the end that Stimson scorned, appropriate targets for black militancy remained in abundance. During the summer of 1943 racial frustrations and antagonisms led to outbursts of violence in nine military training camps and in several cities where the exigencies of war had disrupted traditional social relationships. Perhaps the worst of the riots occurred in Detroit, where a racial conflict in June left twenty-five blacks and nine whites dead, nearly seven hundred people of both races injured, and some $2 million in property destroyed. In the Southwest, Mexican-Americans suffered as much from discrimination as did blacks, and a flare-up in Los Angeles (involving servicemen and zoot-suited Mexican-Americans) added another racial note to wartime social discord. All the disturbances unmistakably pointed toward the need for thorough social reconstruction at home if the war against fascism was in fact to have the moral justification that patriotism accorded it.

The prevailing wartime attitude of black Americans was one of cynicism toward moralistic rhetoric, militancy growing out of heightened racial consciousness, and hope for a better future; the dominant outlook among Japanese-Americans was closer to despair. Like the First World War, the Second aroused suspicion of people whose ancestry might have stirred sympathy for enemy powers. By 1941, however, German and Italian Americans had lost much of their ethnic identity, encountering little of the hostility that German groups had suffered during World War I. With the Japanese it was different. The Issei, or foreign born who had migrated to the United States before 1924, could not qualify for citizenship; the Nisei, or those born in the United States and therefore citizens, were for the most part too young to vote. Lacking political power and poorly assimilated—few of them were employed as professionals, and most of them worked as domestics or on small vegetable farms—the Japanese were readily identified. A relatively small group, they would have to bear the burden of public anger aroused by the attack on Pearl Harbor.

In February 1942 President Roosevelt issued an executive order directing the Secretary of War to delineate sensitive military areas that would be off-limits to Japanese-Americans. Representatives of the departments of Justice and the Army agreed to clear the entire west coast, and in March the removal process began. By June more than 100,000 people of Japanese ancestry had been taken to assembly centers preparatory to relocation. The War Relocation Authority (WRA) hastily constructed ten camps in isolated areas of the West, and it was to those camps that the uprooted were assigned. Resembling CCC work camps of the thirties, they provided few comforts and much regimentation. Eventually the WRA tempered its evacuation policy by allowing camp residents to take permanent leave provided they could prove that they had jobs waiting for them on the outside and that they would gain acceptance in the community. By 1945 some 35,000 had managed to secure such leave, but others were not so fortunate. Uncharged with any crime, they remained behind barbed wire throughout the war. The internment of American citizens and their parents solely because of ancestry should not be equated with imprisonments at Buchenwald or Dachau, tempting though such comparisons might be, but it does represent one of the most infamous violations of constitutional guarantees in American history.

The statistic of this Southern Pacific billboard advertisement was intended to emphasize the military importance of railway freight. When juxtaposed with the photograph of a little girl who was sent with her family to one of the War Relocation Camps, its racist overtones seem to become more shrill. Fear of Japanese-American treachery of course activated maggots on the xenophobic brain. After the shock of Pearl Harbor, however, less excitable citizens also worried about Japanese spies; detention camps then came to be regarded as a reasonable precaution, set up in the national interest. It was certainly not the only occasion in world history when anxiety combined with patriotic zeal distorted judgment and produced injustice (above, Dorothea Lange Collection, The Oakland Museum; below, War Relocation Authority photo, National Archives).

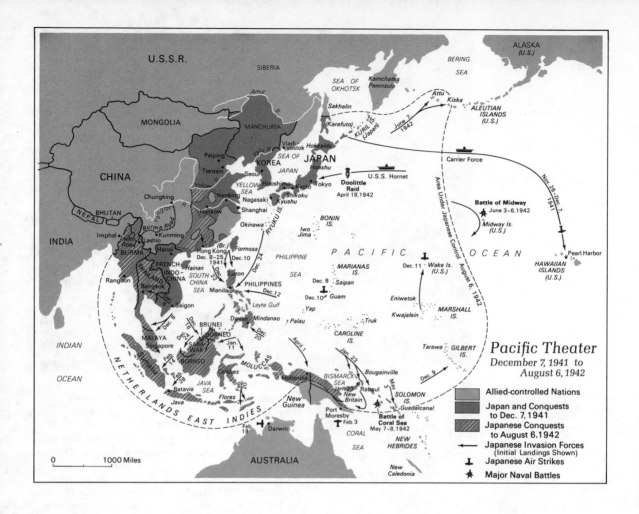

**Pacific Theater**
December 7, 1941 to
August 6, 1942

Allied-controlled Nations
Japan and Conquests to Dec. 7, 1941
Japanese Conquests to August 6, 1942
→ Japanese Invasion Forces (Initial Landings Shown)
⊥ Japanese Air Strikes
★ Major Naval Battles

**Strategic Interests of the Allied Powers**

The treatment of minority groups in the United States reflected a popular belief that winning the war must take priority over all other matters. President Roosevelt, with his compelling interest in military and naval problems, shared the popular view; until his death in April 1945, he exerted a dominating personal influence over American foreign and military policies. The cheery optimism and good humor that had served him well during the dark years of depression served him equally well during the trying years of conflict. But, important as that optimism was in maintaining American morale, it encouraged avoidance of basic difficulties in international relations. Capable of ranging widely through a variety of interests and concerns, FDR was never one to concentrate his attention on particular detail. Thus he exuded confidence in the ultimate triumph of Allied arms without ever thinking very deeply about how the victory should be achieved or about how the means of achieving it would affect power relationships in the postwar world. His superficial comprehension of the fundamental interests of other nations led him to an excessive reliance on his ability to work out understandings with the leaders of those nations. It led, also, to a postponement of efforts to resolve intricate international problems until after victory had been assured.

Winning the war obviously required a coordinated effort of the Big Three powers: Britain, the USSR, and the United States. On the basic strategic decision—that the Allied effort should be directed first toward the defeat of Germany—there was little disagreement, for the logic behind it was clear and sound. Germany might carry on the war without Japan, but Japan would surely fall without German assistance. Roosevelt considered Hitler's surrender so important, in fact, that he had committed himself to forcing it even before the United States declared war. After Pearl Harbor the decision received confirmation at a conference of British and American leaders held in Washington under the code name ARCADIA in December 1941. Accord on defeating Germany first did not, however, imply consensus in subsequent deliberations of the Allied leaders. Divergent traditions, institutions, objectives, and experiences in World War I all helped to shape three distinct perspectives and three discrepant lines of policy.

The American experience reinforced Roosevelt's optimism and his tendency to minimize differences of opinion that struck Winston Churchill and Josef Stalin as well-nigh antithetical. Because of its geographical position, the United States had seldom taken more than an indirect part in European power struggles; and, in any case, Americans could not fully appreciate the day-by-day complexities of international issues on the continent of Europe. The extension of those issues to global scale, a development that reached fulfillment during the war, would forever reduce the luxury of free choice in matters of international involvement and would leave the nation full-freighted with international responsibilities. At the war's beginning, however, neither FDR nor the American people were sensitive to the nuances and imperatives of problems that did not lie close to home.

Lessons that Americans learned from their study of history also tended to produce a simplistic world view. Since achieving independence the United States had never been required to engage in long-sustained military action against another power. School textbooks could therefore emphasize the superior fighting qualities of American soldiers and their quick, easy success on the field of battle. People who remembered World War I saw no reason to quarrel with that assessment of American military prowess, for the armistice had come within a few months after the commitment of American troops in sizable number. The nation had been reluctant to enter World War II, to be sure, but once in it citizens recalled their history and confidently looked forward to their triumph over evil. Singing "Praise the Lord, and pass the ammunition," they pressed for victory by the most expeditious means. FDR's military advisers shared popular convictions and desires, as did the president himself; they favored a strategy of direct attack, a strategy formulated to accomplish Hitler's defeat in the shortest possible time.

British experience taught lessons that suggested a very different strategy. Sea power, combined with a policy of maintaining a balance of power on the Continent, had long formed the basis of British influence in international affairs. In the twentieth century, however, that influence had begun to erode at the same time that costs of maintaining the Continental balance mounted. During World War I Britain had paid an extraordinarily high price to sustain France as a counterweight to German industrial and military might. In the four years after 1914, the British people had seen an entire generation decimated in the squalid horror of the western front. Now, despite Neville Chamberlain's efforts to avert another such conflict by appeasing Hitler, the *Wehrmacht* had overrun Britain's World War I ally, British forces had considered themselves fortunate to escape at Dunkirk, and Britain had stood alone against the Nazi terror until Hitler's invasion of the USSR.

The United Kingdom contained no statesmen who were ready to advocate an immediate, direct attack upon Germany. Almost to a man, British leaders found the risks both appalling and unnecessary. It made no sense to chance another devastating Continental commitment when German troops were too preoccupied with Operation Barbarossa to constitute an immediate threat to the British Isles. But even without the risks, prudent diplomatic tradition called for a policy that would allow Germany and the USSR to continue their struggle. Defeating Hitler too quickly might leave the Russians in a position of such strength as to threaten the United Kingdom from another quarter. Prime Minister Winston Churchill therefore argued against a premature frontal attack, proposing instead a series of shifting operations on the periphery of Europe. It was a strategy that would provide minimum assistance to Russian forces while maintaining British forces at maximum strength. Peripheral action, followed by an invasion of Germany when the risks had been reduced, would grant His Majesty's government its best opportunity to influence the postwar course of events.

If the United States enjoyed greater freedom of choice among strategic alternatives than did the United Kingdom, British leaders could choose from among a larger number of options than could Russian leaders. Indeed, for the USSR there were no strategic choices at all during the first two years of the war against Germany. With Hitler's divisions almost completely surrounding Leningrad and pressing toward the capture of Moscow and Stalingrad, the Russians could only resist the German advance, hope that Japan would not attack Siberia, and urge their Western allies to open a second front as soon as possible. In their defensive maneuvers the Russians had exploitable advantages, and, of course, they made the most of them. The Red Army could retreat over a vast territory without sacrificing major sources of supply and could thereby compound the German logistics problem. It could also rely upon fierce winter blasts to sweep across east European plains and stall the unprepared *Wehrmacht* in frozen immobility. Beyond enlisting space and weather as well as people in defense of the USSR, however, Russian leaders could do little.

Not until Nazi forces began to retreat did strategic alternatives present themselves to Stalin, his generals, and his diplomats. Beginning in the fall of 1943, then, Russian representatives joined their British and American counterparts to plan both the final campaigns against the Axis and a settlement for the postwar world. By that time the experiences of war had worked changes in the thinking of British and American strategists, but strategy had become a multilateral concern. The prospect of victory thus brought greater complexity to relations between the United States and its allies, and out of that new welter of conflicting interests and choices a new sort of war—a Cold War—was eventually to emerge.

**From TORCH to Teheran: Strategy and Compromise**

The ARCADIA conference of December 1941 created a structure for Anglo-American cooperation, developed goals for the production of ships and armaments, and made tentative plans for military operations. Seldom have two heads of government hit it off so well as did FDR and Churchill, and never has the cooperation of two sovereign nations been more complete than the Anglo-American collaboration of 1941–1945. The institutional apparatus for a unified effort was largely military in character. The British came to Washington with an established command structure in the form of a Chiefs of Staff Committee (COS). American leaders immediately set up a parallel organization, the Joint Chiefs of Staff (JCS), chaired by Admiral William D. Leahy and made up of the heads of the Army, Navy, and Army Air Corps (General George C. Marshall, Admiral Ernest King, and General Henry H. Arnold). At the ARCADIA conference the two bodies merged to form the Combined Chiefs of Staff (CCS), which functioned in the manner of a war cabinet for the two governments. When disagreements arose, Roosevelt and Churchill compromised differences, setting forth policies that were usually satisfactory to both leaders.

The ARCADIA conference produced a formal agreement—signed by Roosevelt, Churchill, Maxim Litvinov of the USSR, and representatives of twenty-three other nations fighting the Axis—pledging mutual support during the war and continued adherence to principles of international decency after peace had been won. However broad the commitment to victory, military reverses during the early months of the conflict nevertheless brought into bold relief Anglo-American differences over strategy. Japanese successes required sending more men and supplies to the Pacific than the CCS at first contemplated, and German U-boat attacks on Allied shipping aggravated logistical problems. Thus, when General Marshall argued for a major cross-channel thrust in 1942 or at the latest by 1943, British military leaders could counter the proposal by reading him chapter and verse on why Allied setbacks made so early a date unrealistic.

Although Churchill had no desire to risk British forces in a second-front operation just to aid beleaguered Russians, he did have the wisdom to understand Roosevelt's political position in the United States. In the absence of any significant Anglo-American offensive in Europe, popular pressure to concentrate on defeating Japan would become irresistible. At least some action in the European theater was essential to sustain American morale and the ARCADIA agreements. The prime minister therefore proposed a campaign to drive German forces out of North Africa. Such a campaign would, he promised, provide indirect aid to the Russians, clear the Mediterranean for Allied shipping, open the Suez Canal, and greatly increase strategic alternatives in southern Europe. FDR was convinced. Overruling Marshall and other American advocates of a cross-channel invasion, he ordered them to begin planning for landings in North Africa. TORCH, the code name of the operation, was set for no later than October 30, 1942.

British forces initiated the North African campaign on October 24, when General Sir Bernard Montgomery's Eighth Army attacked German lines in the East at El Alamein. Two weeks later, British and American troops landed at Casablanca, Oran, and Algiers in the West. U.S. forces followed the outmoded practice of carrying the Stars and Stripes into battle on the theory that French defenders would not wish to fire on attackers who identified themselves as Americans. Yet the theory did not fit the facts, especially at Casablanca, and American operations in North Africa brought new uncertainties into the already tangled relationship between the United States and the French government at Vichy. Marshal Pétain, who headed the Vichy regime, cut diplomatic relations with the United States on

In the fall of 1942 the Allied campaign in North Africa began turning the tide against German forces under the command of Field Marshal Erwin Rommel. Withdrawing across northern Libya, the retreating *Afrika Korps* left behind shattered remnants of its once powerful air support (Imperial War Museum).

Campaigns in North Africa
October 1942 to May 1943

November 9 and urged French forces to resist the Allied invasion of Morocco and Algeria. Within forty-eight hours, however, German troops invaded unoccupied France, and the French in North Africa were left without a home government to direct them. The ranking official on the scene was Pétain's deputy, Admiral Jean François Darlan, a man of proven anti-Semitic and pro-Nazi credentials.

Could Anglo-American commanders deal with Darlan? Churchill thought not, for Darlan was an Anglophobe whose collaboration with Hitler contrasted with Charles de Gaulle's sturdy opposition to Vichy. The prime minister described the Free French movement, with which de Gaulle was identified, as "the core of French resistance and the flame of French honour." Roosevelt had never found de Gaulle so attractive; the Frenchman's hauteur suggested to him the attitude of a man eager to assume dictatorial powers should an opportunity present itself. The president, seeing no reason to create such an opportunity, therefore extended qualified sanction to a deal that American negotiators worked out with Darlan. In return for recognizing the admiral's authority over French forces, they would gain Darlan's support of the Anglo-American effort against Germany. The agreement was an ethical embarrassment. It horrified all who found Nazism morally reprehensible. Fortunately for the sake of Allied unity, however, little came of it; a young French anti-Nazi assassinated the admiral on Christmas Eve, 1942. Yet the episode did raise questions about American fidelity to principles endorsed at the ARCADIA conference, questions that were more difficult to kill than was a Vichy admiral.

In the meantime, with Anglo-American forces moving toward control of Tunisia from both east and west, Churchill and Roosevelt met with their strategists at Casablanca in mid-January 1943. American leaders agreed to support the British plan for a Mediterranean offensive that would include an invasion of Sicily after the Germans had been driven from North Africa. The United States, the British conceded, might proceed to carry out plans for offensive operations in the Pacific. Strategists accorded top priority to eliminating the U-boat threat in the Atlantic and to supplying the USSR with needed materiel. They also made arrangements to have the U.S. Air Force join the RAF in heavy bombardment of Germany, but they equivocated on a decision to launch the cross-channel invasion that Stalin urged.

The Casablanca Conference clearly pointed toward operations in the central Mediterranean as the major thrust of Anglo-American forces in 1943. Yet the conference concerned itself with political as well as military matters. With Darlan eliminated, Roosevelt turned to General Henri Giraud as one who might serve as spokesman for the French people. The British continued to prefer de Gaulle, however, persuading him to attend the conference in order to work out an agreement. Eventually he and Giraud became co-presidents of the French Committee of National Liberation, but the sagacious and forceful de Gaulle soon emerged as the more effective commander. FDR then accepted de Gaulle because he had no other choice. It was a political marriage of convenience, which never blossomed into love. Indeed, American interference in the selection of a leader for Frenchmen working toward liberation, like American relations with Vichy, produced resentments that fostered a continuing distrust of American purposes.

Roosevelt's desire to alleviate Russian anxieties about the strength of American commitment to the Allied cause—anxieties that the Darlan deal had stirred—was one of the considerations that led to the most controversial decision of the conference. Before going to Casablanca, the president had been thinking about "unconditional surrender" as the basis for a peace settlement with the Axis. Although he took the matter up with Churchill early in the conference, he did not insist upon a joint proclamation. Instead, he proceeded to make his own announcement: "The elimination of German, Japanese, and Italian war power means the unconditional surrender by Germany, Italy, and Japan." Churchill was displeased, for he thought that such terms might strengthen the determination of German and Italian populations to continue the war. He did not publicly dissent, however, and eventually he approved the statement.

The prime minister may have been correct in thinking that the unconditional surrender slogan would prolong the war, but in Roosevelt's mind there were compensating advantages. Unconditional surrender contained no hint of generous promises such as Wilson had made in 1918; FDR would not, therefore, provide some future demagogue with a chance to argue that Germany had been stabbed in the back. On the other hand, he would be giving Russian leaders reassurance that the United States contemplated no deal with Hitler and that Americans would maintain their resolve to the end. The unconditional surrender policy was nevertheless flawed. While it had very little real meaning—a peace settlement always involves conditions—it encouraged a mode of thought that tended to view all struggle as a conflict between good and evil. Narrowly concentrating on military victory, and too readily assuming that defeat of the Nazi evil would resolve all major international tensions, many Americans were unprepared to cope with more subtle problems of the postwar years.

Whatever its long-range influence, the Casablanca Conference coincided with an improvement in Allied military fortunes. Having held firm under devastating assault at Stalingrad, the Red Army mounted a counteroffensive against German forces in February 1943. By October it had driven into the Ukraine and was preparing for a winter push into Rumania. Allied destroyers and destroyer escorts, with the help of air patrols and sonar, were able significantly to reduce the effectiveness of U-boats. Allied forces under the command of General Douglas MacArthur and Admiral Chester Nimitz began to turn the tide in the Pacific. Anglo-American armies closed in on German-held Tunisia, forcing a surrender in May. Pressing the attack, they made the crossing to Sicily and by mid-August gained control of the island. The series of victories during 1943 called for further conferences of Allied leaders. Roosevelt welcomed Churchill to Washington in May, and with their advisers the two heads of state made plans for

American troops entering Cologne in March 1945 found a metropolis in ruins. The ancient city on the Rhine had been a target of the war's first saturation bombing in May 1942, and in all it suffered more than 250 air raids. Although "around the clock" bombing was intended to reduce German resistance to Allied advance once a second front had been opened up, its military effectiveness remains doubtful.

invading Italy that fall. They also set May 1, 1944, as the date for OVER-LORD, the long-awaited cross-channel assault.

Two months after the conference, the Fascist Grand Council ousted Mus-solini as head of the Italian government, replacing him with Marshal Pietro Badoglio. The marshal was no democrat, but faced with defeat he was ready to change sides. Should the Allies respond to his overtures? Again Roosevelt and Churchill conferred, this time in Quebec, and decided to accept the new Italian government's surrender. The decision did not mean that Anglo-American forces could immediately take over all of Italy, however, because Hitler moved eighteen divisions down into the Italian peninsula. In fact, some of the most difficult fighting of the war took place there after Anglo-American forces landed in September, and not until June 4, 1944, did Allied troops occupy Rome.

At the conference in Quebec, and during a three-week period of consulta-tion in Washington after the conference, the president and the prime min-ister discussed plans for postwar Germany and for an international organi-zation to secure the peace of the world. Such deliberations obviously required more than bilateral participation, for Russian cooperation would be essential to preserving peace after the guns had ceased firing. Stalin was already miffed at having been virtually ignored when negotiations with Badoglio were under way, and some diplomats were worried lest he use the Italian precedent to justify imposing his own peace on eastern Europe without consulting Britain or the United States.

Two important conferences in 1943 served to shore up the Grand Alli-ance against the Axis. The first was a meeting of foreign ministers in Mos-cow during the last two weeks in October. Secretary of State Cordell Hull held lengthy discussions with Anthony Eden and Vyasheslav Molotov on a variety of problems both immediate and foreseeable. Molotov's principal concern, as it had been since 1941, was the second front, and the assurances he received from Hull and Eden set a tone of cordiality for the discussion of other questions. The British, however, were more concerned with spe-cific provisions of a postwar settlement than were either Hull or Molotov. Hull, urging the formation of an international organization, agreed to the creation of a European Advisory Commission to work out problems result-ing from the liberation of the Continent. Yet he did not wish to make com-mitments on specific arrangements. The Russians, too, seemed inclined to avoid particulars. Where Hull and Molotov differed was on the recogni-tion of China as one of the dominant powers in the alliance. The Russians were reluctant to risk their neutral position in the Far East, but Hull was insistent. In the end the Chinese ambassador in Moscow joined in signing the Four Power Declaration drafted by the conference. As the war entered its final stage, Allied unity seemed assured; all that remained was for the heads of state to seal the bargain.

The second important conference of 1943, at Teheran, brought Roose-velt, Churchill, and Stalin together for the first time. Although Churchill urged an expansion of Mediterranean operations by Anglo-American forces, the Big Three encountered little difficulty in agreeing on a strategy for the final phase of the war in Europe. With Roosevelt and Stalin both backing a cross-channel attack, the plans for OVERLORD were quickly approved. Stalin promised to coordinate the Red Army's spring offensive with the Normandy landings. He also committed the USSR to a declaration of war on Japan after the Allies had defeated Germany. More important than military planning, however, were the political discussions at Teheran. Roosevelt, it is true, made no firm political commitments; but, in playing the role of an affable mediator between Churchill and Stalin, he profoundly influenced the course of events.

On the most important topic taken up at the conference, the future of central Europe, Churchill took a moderate position. He favored detachment of Prussia from Germany and a confederation of the other German states. International stability, thought the prime minister, could not be achieved by creating a power vacuum on the Continent; the same reasoning led him to favor the reestablishment of a viable French state. To FDR, restoring a balance of power offered little hope for future peace. His wartime experience had led him to believe that great-power unity would triumph over Hitler and that great-power cooperation would assure international tranquility in the years ahead. He was not so naive as to think that harmony would always characterize relationships of the Big Three, but he acted as though it might be either coaxed or coerced. In his conversations with Stalin the president coaxed. Thus he sided with the Russians in favoring political dismemberment of the Reich and an international trusteeship over the Ruhr and Saar industrial areas. Also agreeing that the French must pay for their collaboration with Hitler, he joined Stalin in opposition to a restoration of French influence.

Roosevelt was delighted with the results of Teheran. Victory over the Axis was still a long way off; but the president believed that, by expanding the Anglo-American strategic partnership to include the Russians, the conference had done much to bring victory closer. He did not share Churchill's anxieties about moving toward a peace settlement that would leave the Soviet Union as the only significant power on the continent of Europe. Confident of Russian good sense and of his own ability in the arts of persuasion, he seems to have thought that skillful diplomacy would resolve whatever differences might arise to hamper great power cooperation. Teheran thus marked a high point of Allied unity in the war effort, but at the same time Roosevelt's negotiations with Stalin exacerbated conditions in Europe that proved troublesome for the Atlantic powers during the postwar years.

**Planning for Victory
and Peace**

In January 1944 General Dwight D. Eisenhower, taking command of the Allied Expeditionary Force in Britain, began working on the final plans for OVERLORD. He encountered few obstacles, although bad weather and a shortage of landing craft forced a postponement of action until June 6. When it finally came off, the amphibious operation was a smashing success.

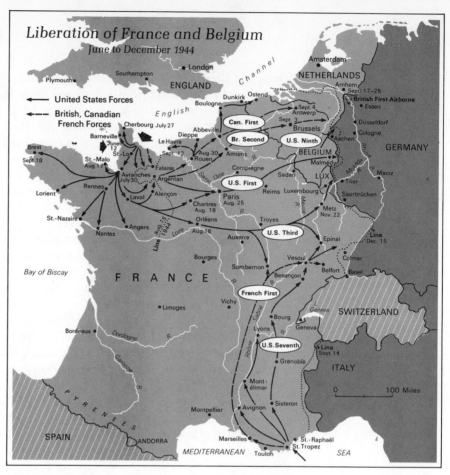

Liberation of France and Belgium
June to December 1944

Hitting the beaches of Normandy rather than those at Pas de Calais as the Germans expected, Allied forces moved rapidly inland. They captured Cherbourg, Caen, and St. Lô, and within two weeks stood ready for a drive through France and Belgium toward Berlin. The breakthrough began when General George S. Patton's Third Army swept across Brittany to surround German forces near Falaise. As the *Wehrmacht* pulled back toward the Siegfried Line, the Allies struck again, on August 15, in southern France. Landing near St. Tropez, the French First Army and the American Seventh Army moved northward up the Rhone Valley toward a rendezvous with the American Third Army. In the meantime, French troops under the command of General Jacques Leclerc marched into Paris on August 25, and the following day General de Gaulle led a triumphal procession down the Champs-Élysées.

By mid-December the Allies had liberated most of France and had reached Germany's West Wall. Facing certain defeat, the Fuehrer ordered a final desperate counterattack on December 16. Crashing into the Ardennes Forest in southern Belgium, panzer divisions and infantry began a massive effort to pierce the Allied front. The month-long Battle of the Bulge was by all odds the most confused action involving American troops in Europe. More than a million soldiers took part, and the fighting was so furious that lines dissolved in chaos. Both sides captured prisoners only to lose them, and lost them only to retake them. Wounded men froze to death when the weather turned bitter cold. But, for all the viciousness of the assault, it did nothing to preserve Hitler's Reich. Indeed, the Battle of the Bulge hastened deterioration of German defenses; after the front lines were restored at the end of January 1945, the war in Europe had only three months to go.

True to his promise at Teheran, Stalin had ordered a general offensive in the spring of 1944. While his western allies were clearing German troops out of the Ardennes, the Red Army captured Warsaw and moved on toward the Oder River. Allied military successes on both fronts called for the Big Three to reach final agreement on a postwar settlement before the great jaws of a continental vise squeezed the Wehrmacht to extinction. Evidences of dissension in the Grand Alliance had already begun to appear; and, without an understanding on crucial matters (reparations, the place and future of Germany, the role of France, the government of Poland, and the charter of the United Nations), military victory could prove illusory. Roosevelt, Churchill, Stalin, and a full complement of military and diplomatic advisers therefore met at Yalta in the Crimea from February 4 through 11 in what was to be their last, their most important, and—especially in the foreign policy debates of later years—their most controversial parley.

Each of the three principal negotiators had definite objectives in mind, and each of them arrived at the conference prepared to make whatever

Generals Omar Bradley, Dwight Eisenhower, and George Patton conferred in Bastogne, Belgium, in January 1945. American troops in the city had been surrounded by German forces during the Battle of the Bulge, but they had rejected surrender. Holding out, they emphasized the futility of Hitler's final *blitzkrieg.* "Those bottom-of-the-barrel reserves that might have slowed the Russian onslaught," wrote Bradley, "had been squandered against us in the Ardennes" (The Bettman Archive).

compromises were necessary for their achievement. The immediate concerns of American representatives centered on plans for the invasion of Germany and for concluding the war on Japan. British and American commanders had been feuding over invasion plans: Montgomery was urging a dramatic, concentrated thrust to Berlin, while Eisenhower was insisting upon a more cautious eastward movement along a broad front. American strategists sought British acquiescence in the broad-front offensive. As for the Far East, Roosevelt was eager to obtain unambiguous Russian commitment to a declaration of war against Japan. Beyond such immediate concerns, Roosevelt attached great importance to formation of a new international organization, the United Nations. Since August 1944, when representatives of the Big Three powers and China had met at Dumbarton Oaks in Washington to discuss a structure for international cooperation, the president had turned his mind increasingly to problems of collective security. He never gave up on the idea that great powers should act in harmony to preserve peace, but he believed that the UN would provide an instrument through which they might operate effectively.

Because he looked forward to rapid withdrawal of American troops from Europe, the President demonstrated little interest in details of territorial agreements or political implications of the settlement. The British, however, exhibited a lively concern for such problems. Geographical proximity and traditional attitudes toward nations of the Continent led them to place emphasis on Allied policies in Germany and eastern Europe, the rehabilitation of France, and the need to exercise influence in the Balkans and Iran. Churchill was especially firm in his support of France, his opposition to the dismemberment of Germany, and his determination to prevent Russian domination of Poland.

If the Russians had been severely limited by military imperatives early in the war, the approach of victory increased their diplomatic options. Yet neither Stalin nor his advisers could forget that twice within a span of twenty-five years Germany had attacked Russia through Poland; their concern for security led them to stress the political and territorial settlement in eastern Europe. Especially important in their view was the creation of a Polish government that would be friendly to the USSR. Stalin had, in addition, two other principal interests. Having paid dearly for victory, he wanted reparations from Germany; and having promised to declare war on Japan, he wanted to recover Asian territories lost by the Czarist government in the Russo-Japanese War of 1904–1905.

In the intricate negotiations at Yalta, each of the Big Three leaders gained at least qualified acceptance of his principal objectives while giving way on other matters that seemed to him of lesser importance. When Stalin and Churchill were in fundamental disagreement on the dismemberment of Germany, Roosevelt at first tended to side with Stalin. Since the plenary session could reach no common ground, however, the Big Three decided to rely on a meeting of foreign ministers to resolve differences. The result was a statement pledging the Allies to take such action "in-

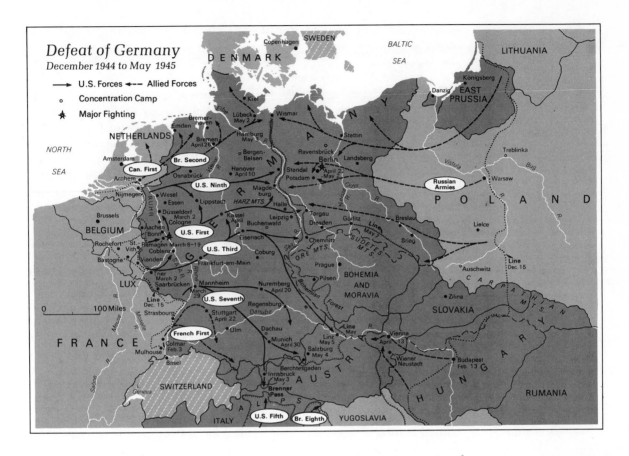

**Defeat of Germany**
December 1944 to May 1945

→ U.S. Forces ←-- Allied Forces

○ Concentration Camp

★ Major Fighting

cluding the complete disarmament, demilitarization and the dismemberment of Germany as they deem requisite for future peace and security."

Hailed as a compromise, the formula was actually a victory for Churchill. Stalin agreed to accept French participation in the occupation of Germany and Austria, and zones of occupation for the four powers were confirmed. Berlin and Vienna, lying within territory controlled by the USSR, were each partitioned into four sectors under respective supervision of the occupying powers. Dividing Germany and Austria in this manner, the statesmen at Yalta deferred consideration of permanent dismemberment. Yet they left the way open for pursuit of independent policies by the occupying powers, and in so doing they made possible the perpetuation of a divided Germany. During the postwar period, when rivalry between the USSR and the West increased, the occupation took on a new character and significance. While Russian control remained firm in the eastern zone, the United States acted to rebuild West German economic and military strength. Thus a Continental power vacuum never developed as Churchill feared it might; instead, divided Germany became a focus of conflict in the Cold War.

In working toward a balance on the Continent, the prime minister achieved much of what he sought—but not all. For months he had been struggling without success to assure anticommunist members of the London-based Polish government-in-exile a voice in ruling their homeland. At Yalta he and Roosevelt concerned themselves with both the government and the boundaries of postwar Poland. Since Russian troops had already occupied the country, and since the USSR had already recognized the pro-Russian Lublin committee as the provisional government of Poland, FDR and Churchill were in the awkward position of trying to modify a *fait accompli*. They agreed to draw the Russian-Polish border at the Curzon Line, a boundary that lay some 150 miles to the west of the pre-1939 boundary; but they boggled at accepting the Oder and Neisse rivers for the Polish-German frontier. They did grant that Poland should receive "substantial accessions of territory in the North and West," however, and eventually the Oder-Neisse line became the accepted frontier. Stalin also won out in discussions of the Polish government, although for a time the victory was obscured by diplomatic rhetoric. He accepted a Provisional Government of National Unity that would include Poles returning home from abroad. He also agreed that there should be "free and unfettered elections" to establish a permanent Polish government. Given the Russian insistence upon a friendly neighbor, the chances for controversy over what constituted free elections were endless. But the Yalta discussions on Poland never left much doubt that Russian national interest would dominate the politics of eastern Europe.

While Stalin would concede very little to Churchill and Roosevelt in Poland, he proved willing to go along with American proposals for the United Nations. The basic issue calling for resolution was the nature of the veto power to be exercised by members of the Security Council. At Dumbarton Oaks the Russians had demanded the right to veto discussion of any dispute in which the USSR was involved, but at Yalta they agreed that a permanent member of the Security Council might not veto consideration of a dispute in which it was a party although it might veto sanctions against itself. With Russian acceptance of the American voting formula, all other differences over the UN were quickly resolved. The USSR accepted three votes in the Assembly and did not insist upon the sixteen votes originally requested. The Russians also agreed to send representatives to a San Francisco conference charged with responsibility for drafting a United Nations charter.

In a separate bargain, one that was not made public, the USSR pledged entry into the war against Japan within three months after Germany's defeat. In return for that pledge Stalin received assurance of Russian control in Outer Mongolia, transfer of the Kuril Islands from Japan, and the restoration of rights and territories lost in the Russo-Japanese War. While the losses of that earlier war were now to be restored, the Russians gained no firm accord on reparations from Germany. Roosevelt and Churchill would only agree to establish a Reparations Commission with headquarters

Central and Eastern Europe:
Territorial Changes, 1939–1947

Annexed by Russia

Formerly German–Under Soviet
and Polish Administration

Divided and Occupied by
Russia and U.S.

Churchill, Roosevelt, and Stalin sat for an official portrait at the Yalta Conference
in February 1945. The pressures of thirteen years in the White House—years of
depression and war—were visible in the lines on FDR's face and in the fatigue of
his gestures. He had little more than two months to live (Ewing Galloway).

in Moscow and to use the Russian demand as a basis for discussion of the
amount to be paid.

In later years, after the emergence of Cold War resentments between the
USSR and the United States, the Yalta Conference received bitter criticism
from people who believed that Roosevelt had sacrificed more than was necessary. Yet the Cold War was not a consequence of Yalta; it developed out
of events that transpired after the conference had adjourned. On the afternoon of April 12, 1945, as Allied armies advanced toward a jubilant meeting in central Germany, President Roosevelt died at Warm Springs, Georgia, of a massive cerebral hemorrhage. With his passing the balanced
diplomatic interaction that had characterized Yalta gave way to growing
suspicion and skepticism among the Allies. This is not to say that, had he
lived, Roosevelt would have been able to dispel tensions between East and
West, for his successor faced new problems of even greater complexity than
those with which FDR had contended. The point is that Roosevelt operated in a world where balanced interaction could still take place within a
traditional diplomatic framework. The successful development of an
atomic bomb altered that world so profoundly that the Yalta agreements
came to seem misguided if not divorced from realities.

**The Pacific War and
the Atomic Bomb**

On August 6, 1945, an American B-29 dropped an atomic bomb on Hiroshima, an urban concentration of some 343,000 inhabitants. The explosion wiped out four square miles and destroyed two-thirds of the city's buildings. Perhaps a hundred thousand people died instantly; for another hundred thousand death came more slowly from burns, injuries, and radiation sickness. The Hiroshima bomb (along with another dropped on Nagasaki three days later) brought to an end the second great war of the twentieth century, and the return of peace stirred a series of celebrations across the United States. Then Americans began to have second thoughts. Some of them saw the weapon as an effective instrument of American policy. Others believed that the decision to release atomic energy for destructive purposes raised serious moral questions. Whatever the reaction to it, the new weapon initiated an uncommonly jittery period in world history. Why did the new president, Harry S Truman, decide to use the bomb against Japan? The answer to that question may be forever concealed in the rapid flow of events after Yalta. Perceived imperatives of the Pacific war nevertheless provide a partial explanation of the Hiroshima hecatomb, and the

The first atomic bomb employed in warfare exploded two thousand feet above the center of Hiroshima. Heat from the fireball was intense enough to melt granite within a thousand yards of the hypocenter. "My God!" exclaimed the B-29 co-pilot, looking down on the inferno. "What have we done?" This photograph, taken some time later, provided only a partial answer (US Air Force photo).

strategy of American operations in the Pacific theater thus requires scrutiny.

Two features of the war against Japan made it very different from the war in Europe. In the first place, operations in the Pacific, carried out over a vast expanse of territory, were largely naval or amphibious. After Pearl Harbor Japanese forces rapidly conquered the Philippines, Malaya, and Burma; by the end of March 1942, they could claim control over an enormous area from the Gilbert Islands in the Central Pacific through the Solomons and New Guinea to Burma. Then a pair of naval engagements —the Battle of the Coral Sea in May and the Battle of Midway in June— brought a reversal of Japanese fortunes and deprived Japan of air superiority. Allied strategists could begin planning a counteroffensive; but, in doing so, they had to take distance into account. For one thing, distance made logistics a greater problem in the Pacific than in Europe. Less than 3,400 nautical miles separate New York from London or Le Havre, but San Francisco is more than 6,300 miles from Sydney or Manila. In effect, one ship sailing to Europe was the equivalent of two ships bound for the South Pacific. The supply problem alone dictated the peripheral strategy of an island-hopping counteroffensive. To attempt an engagement of the main Japanese forces in China or elsewhere was out of the question.

Another distinguishing feature of the war against Japan was its relegation to secondary consideration in the overall planning of Allied leaders. If Hitler was to be defeated first, then obviously a full-scale attack on Japan had to await his demise. Although two distinct plans of operation emerged, neither one contemplated a massive assault on Japan itself until after an Allied victory in Europe. General Douglas MacArthur, in command of the Army and responsible for operations in the Southwest Pacific, favored moving up on Japan through the East Indies, the Philippines, and Formosa. Admiral Chester Nimitz, refusing to subordinate himself to MacArthur and jealous of his position as commander of naval forces in the Central Pacific, preferred a westward advance by the Navy from Hawaii. Both operations were employed, but neither one placed American forces in control of a staging area for the invasion of Japanese home islands after victory in Europe.

Because military priorities, distance, and other considerations made American action on the mainland of Asia unfeasible, the United States sought to strengthen the forces of Chiang Kai-shek and the Kuomintang. If successful, the expedient would produce effective combat units to counteract Japanese armies within China during the war and a power to help stabilize international relations in Asia after the war. The general purpose of American policy thus bore a resemblance to British objectives in Europe. While Churchill sought to elevate de Gaulle to a position of influence, Roosevelt attempted to elevate Chiang Kai-shek. Although the policy perhaps made sense in the abstract, it did not work in practice, for the Kuomintang displayed far more interest in securing American aid than in fighting the Japanese. When General Joseph W. Stilwell went to China as

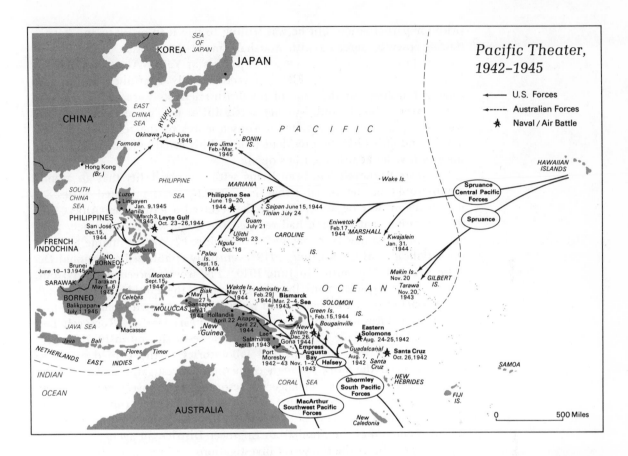

an adviser in 1942 with modernization of the Chinese army as his objective, he encountered a mare's nest of greed, corruption, and repression that led him to despair of completing his assignment. Frustrated in his efforts to bring about Chinese unity through a working relationship between the Kuomintang and the Communists led by Mao Tse-tung, "Vinegar Joe" grew bitter. In September 1943, after months of effort, he charged that Chiang Kai-shek would "go on milking the United States for money and munitions," not to carry on the war against Japan, but "for the purpose of maintaining his present position, based on one-party government, a reactionary policy, or the suppression of democratic ideas with the active aid of his gestapo."

Stilwell remained in China until late 1944, despite his sense of futility, because no other alternative offered a reasonable chance of success. Nevertheless, during the closing months of the war, another approach to the Far Eastern problem began to seem advantageous. If the USSR could be persuaded to enter the struggle against Japan, then the United States would have less need to depend on the unreliable Kuomintang. General Marshall, in particular, urged an agreement that would extend the Russian-American alliance into the Far East. He knew that Stalin would have his price for participation, but he was willing to pay it in order to end hostilities. Roosevelt, agreeing with Marshall, made the Russian declaration of war on Japan one of his principal objectives at Yalta. Always inclined to hedge his bets, however, FDR characteristically continued to support Chiang Kai-shek. At the time of his death scientists were nearly ready to test an atomic bomb; and, whether successful or not, no one could predict what the political and diplomatic consequences of the testing might be. To the end of his life the president followed his usual practice when facing uncertainty: he kept his options open.

For years Roosevelt had been living with the possibility that an atomic bomb would be developed either in Germany or the United States. A month before war began in Europe, he received a letter from Albert Einstein warning that research had reached the point where "extremely powerful bombs of a new type may be . . . produced." At first unable to grasp the significance of the warning, FDR eventually established a National Defense Research Committee in June 1940. The work proceeded slowly; but, after exchanging ideas with British researchers, the President's science advisers concluded that a bomb could indeed be constructed from U-235 produced by a diffusion plant. By the time of Pearl Harbor, Roosevelt had recognized the supreme importance of atomic research, and in 1942 Churchill agreed to transfer scientists and laboratories to the United States in order to speed the work through cooperative investigation. Because the project required greater managerial resources and government funding than the scientists could assemble, Roosevelt ordered the Army to supervise the program. At the end of August 1942, General Leslie R. Groves assumed command of the Manhattan Engineer District, an agency created to organize and direct the top-secret investigations of three major installations (Oak Ridge, Tennessee; Hanford, Washington; and Los Alamos, New Mexico).

As intelligence reports indicated that German scientists were already at work on atomic investigations of their own, no one involved in planning the Manhattan Project questioned the need for either speed or secrecy. Yet the elaborate security precautions that were taken (the Army and the FBI, for example, maintained continuous surveillance of J. Robert Oppenheimer, director at Los Alamos) greatly increased tensions among the nations of the Grand Alliance. The Quebec Conference of August 1943 set up a committee to supervise the joint investigations of Britain, Canada, and the United States, but Roosevelt and Churchill refused to consider sharing atomic energy information with the Russians. Niels Bohr, the eminent Danish physicist who came to the United States early in 1944 as a consultant for the Manhattan Project, did his best to assure international control of atomic energy. He thought that before using the bomb—an action he did not oppose—Britain and the United States should reach an agreement with the USSR to prevent a potentially calamitous nuclear arms race from developing after the war. Churchill vehemently opposed surrendering the diplomatic advantages conferred by an atomic monopoly; at a second Quebec conference in September 1944, he persuaded a sympathetic Roosevelt that sharing atomic secrets with the Russians would be a mortal crime.

Activities of the Manhattan Project thus remained a closely guarded secret. Although Russian leaders did have some indication of what British and American scientists were up to—for atomic research antedated wartime security regulations—they were in no position to make formal inquiry. Yet Anglo-American secrecy forced them to take a strong stance on all questions relating to security for the USSR. At Yalta, therefore, Stalin refused to give much ground on eastern European issues, and he drove a hard bargain with Roosevelt on the agreement to fight Japan. For his part, the president could not be sure that scientists would actually produce the new weapon on which they had been working; prudence required a conciliatory approach on diplomatic questions if not on those relating to atomic energy. Nevertheless, within three months after Roosevelt's death, the first atomic bomb was ready for testing. Detonated on July 16, 1945, at Alamogordo Air Force Base in New Mexico, it awesomely met every expectation of its most confident builders. It also provided a means of ending the war against Japan—without the aid of either Chiang Kai-shek or the Russians.

**Origins of the
Cold War**

On the afternoon of April 12, 1945, Harry S Truman went to the White House, where Eleanor Roosevelt told him that her husband was dead. Stunned by the news at this critical point in American history, he later recalled that "the moon, the stars, and all the planets fell on me." Sadly uninformed and struggling with a sense of his own inadequacy for the tasks

On April 12, 1945, Harry Truman was visiting with Speaker Sam Rayburn when he was called to the White House and informed of Roosevelt's death. That evening Chief Justice Harlan Fiske Stone administered the oath of office. Too nervous to trust himself to speak, Truman held with his Bible a slip of paper on which he had written the words of his oath. One phrase the new president did speak clearly and firmly: "So help me God!" (Wide World photo).

he now faced, he nevertheless relied upon a strong combative instinct. Unlike FDR, who never seemed troubled by uncertainty and often encouraged it as an operational technique, Truman was too blunt and candid to stand for any more uncertainty than was unavoidable. The former senator from Missouri had entered politics under the aegis of Thomas Pendergast's Kansas City machine and had later served on Capitol Hill without distinction, except during the war, when he had chaired a committee to head off profiteering and mismanagement in the defense program. Throughout a long political career his most notable characteristic had been his unswerving loyalty to the Democratic party. Though plain-spoken himself, he could tolerate friends and associates who were not. One thing he could not tolerate was ambiguity. Harry Truman would, if he could, master the situation in which he found himself.

FDR's successor came into office at a time when the Grand Alliance was beginning to show signs of rupture. In order to maintain Allied unity of action against the Axis, the Big Three had generally postponed discussion of specific arrangements that were potentially divisive. Now, in the full flush of triumph over Hitler, Allied expectations had mounted. Reaching a settlement that would meet all those expectations was impossible, for some of them were contradictory. Yet in his first White House press release Truman struck an optimistic note. He announced that the San Francisco Conference, scheduled to begin drafting a charter for the United Nations on April 25, would proceed as planned. In two months the conference completed its work, and the Senate ratified the charter on July 28, 1945. Whatever problems the future might bring, the United States would at least hold membership in an international organization with an obligation to find solutions for them.

Americans greeted formation of the United Nations with an enthusiasm that turned out to be unwarranted. The new organization, modeled on Woodrow Wilson's League of Nations, could not resolve every difficulty resulting from a war that reduced the relative strength of all but two great powers. Truman was quick to accept rivalry with the USSR as a stark fact of the postwar period; his foreign policy took shape under the influence of that rivalry rather than under the influence of international cooperation within the UN. Even before the San Francisco Conference met, Ambassador Averell Harriman—just home from Moscow—warned the president that Soviet intentions were far from honorable and that a policy of firmness was the only way to meet Russian aggression in eastern Europe. The USSR, he suggested, needed American economic aid, a need that would provide Truman with a lever to force Russian cooperation. The president agreed. He was "not afraid of the Russians," he told the Ambassador, and he promised to stand firm.

Shortly after his meeting with Harriman, Truman left for Potsdam (a suburb of Berlin), to confer with Churchill and Stalin on the occupation of Germany, the procedures to be employed in drafting peace treaties, the settlement of political questions in eastern Europe, and the payment of reparations to the Allies. For nearly two weeks—from July 17 to August 2 —representatives of the Big Three powers bickered over these and other matters. In the midst of the discussions Clement Attlee succeeded Churchill as Prime Minister of the United Kingdom, and FDR's old comrade in arms returned home. Churchill's departure had symbolic significance. With his leaving, the conference took on the character of a confrontation between Truman and Stalin, and in that stand-off were intimations of the difficulties that were to characterize U.S.-Soviet relationships during the postwar period. Truman was disturbed by Russian moves to gain domination over eastern Europe, moves that he thought were in violation of agreements made at Yalta. While he could do little to prevent creation of a Russian sphere of influence in Poland, Rumania, or Bulgaria, he could see to it that Germany was not reduced to impotence by means of a heavy reparations formula. As for the peace treaties, they could be referred to the Council of Foreign Ministers. Potsdam thus became a holding action that settled little of consequence in Europe.

Truman's attitude toward the Russians at Potsdam perhaps derived in part from the successful atomic test at Alamogordo the day before discussions began. Control of an atomic bomb meant not only that the United States could do very well without Russian help against the Japanese, but also that the president now had a means to bend Stalin to his will—or so he thought. Some historians, most notably Gar Alperovitz, have in fact argued that dropping "Lean Boy" on Hiroshima was ordered more to intimidate Stalin than to defeat Japan. Conclusions on the point must remain tentative—for a weighting of the many considerations that influenced Truman's decision to drop the bomb is clearly unattainable—but it is certainly true that, as Secretary of War Henry L. Stimson reported, the Alamogordo test gave the president "an entirely new feeling of confidence."

Yet the bomb did not produce results that Truman might have expected. For one thing, its usefulness as a coercive weapon was severely limited. People do not use sledgehammers to set carpet tacks, and atomic retaliation would certainly have been an inappropriate response to Russian intransigence on Polish elections or to other Russian moves in eastern Europe. Furthermore, the United States had no stockpile of bombs, and those produced in the immediate postwar period were in any case not powerful enough to wreak total destruction on the USSR. The trouble with employing the bomb as a diplomatic lever, Professor Stephen E. Ambrose has remarked, "was that even as early as 1945 it bore little relation to reality." The atomic threat nevertheless did have an effect. The secrecy that surrounded the Manhattan Project tended to increase Russian suspicions of the United States. Those suspicions made Russians more than ever concerned with security matters and more than ever determined to expand their sphere of influence.

The actions that Soviet leaders justified on grounds of security took on a very different character when viewed from the West. A week after Germany surrendered, Acting Secretary of State Joseph C. Grew elaborated on

Garbed in academic regalia, President Truman presented Winston Churchill to an
expectant audience at Westminster College. The former prime minister did not
disappoint his listeners. His call for Anglo-American military cooperation
emphasized the threat of a common danger from behind the "iron curtain"
(United Press International photo).

a theme that would become dominant in the United States during the postwar period. The Allied victory, he remarked, meant "the transfer of totalitarian dictatorship and power from Germany and Japan to Soviet Russia
which will constitute in the future as grave a danger to us as did the Axis."
Confident of having learned a lesson from Munich, American leaders readily assumed that "appeasement" would only whet Russian appetites for
more territory and more power. Truman would not play the part of an
American Neville Chamberlain.

In the closing months of World War II, then, mutual distrust, suspicion,
and fear fostered tensions that produced the Cold War. Hardly had fighting men begun to return home from the battlefields of Europe and atolls
of the Pacific before older citizens began to think that their post-1917 fears
of international Bolshevism were well founded. In the spring of 1946
Winston Churchill paid a visit to the United States, delivering a powerful
address at tiny Westminster College in Fulton, Missouri. "From Stettin in
the Baltic to Trieste in the Adriatic," he intoned, "an iron curtain has descended across the continent." The tough old fighter went on to add that
"from what I have seen of our Russian friends and allies during the war, I
am convinced that there is nothing they admire so much as strength, and

there is nothing for which they have less respect than for military weakness." Churchill's counsel of firmness called to mind that dark day after Dunkirk when he had spoken defiantly of a German invasion: ". . . we shall fight on the beaches, we shall fight on the landing-grounds, we shall fight in the fields and in the streets, we shall fight in the hills; we shall never surrender. . . ." Truman could not be so eloquent, but he could be just as stubborn.

Churchill was not the only one to offer advice. Although the proponents of a hard line predominated within the Truman administration, Secretary of Commerce Henry A. Wallace spoke out in favor of greater patience and cooperation with the Soviet Union. He made little headway either within official circles or outside them. At a dinner party early in 1946 newspaper columnist Joseph Alsop called his opinions "a barrel of horse-shit." When Wallace persisted in expressing his ideas, Secretary of State James F. Byrnes, along with others in both the Administration and Congress, complained that the Secretary of Commerce was interfering with the conduct of foreign policy. By September, Wallace had made such a nuisance of himself that the president requested his resignation.

The ouster of Wallace marked the victory of a policy of firmness over a policy of conciliation, and during the following year firmness found a formulation under the rubric of "containment." The progenitor of the containment idea was George F. Kennan. A career foreign service officer attached to the American embassy in Moscow at the time of Wallace's resignation, he had summarized his ideas in a long cable to the State Department. When George C. Marshall succeeded Byrnes as Secretary of State in January 1947, he made Kennan his Policy Planning Adviser. The approach that Kennan urged was outlined publicly in an article, "The Sources of Soviet Conduct," published in *Foreign Affairs* in July and mysteriously signed "X."

Kennan's thesis was that, on the basis of both Russian experience and Communist ideology, Soviet leaders were committed to the idea that communism and capitalism were incompatible and that coexistence between East and West was impossible. Given such an attitude, the principal element in American policy "must be that of a long-term, patient but firm and vigilant containment of Russian expansive tendencies." The containment of the USSR did not, for Kennan, necessarily involve exerting military pressure, for he believed that skillful diplomatic pressure would be more flexible and would work just as well. And what would be the results? The thwarting of expansionist tendencies would presumably aggravate tensions within the Soviet system; therefore, if they wanted to remain in power, Soviet leaders would have to meliorate their foreign policies in order to placate domestic dissatisfactions. The Kremlin would have no choice but to surrender its world revolutionary aims and to arrange a modus vivendi with the United States.

As the Truman administration sought to implement a containment policy, it gradually moved away from the subtle diplomatic pressures that

Kennan advocated and toward the kinds of military alliances and other agreements that he wanted to avoid. Containment at first took the form of foreign economic aid, in part because postwar needs of European countries were so obvious and in part because Truman himself had already employed American economic influence to thwart Soviet expansion. In 1946 the United States had loaned $3.75 billion to prevent Britain's economic collapse and to help maintain British strength in Europe. Yet despite that aid the British government had early in 1947 informed the United States that it could no longer continue to assist Greece and Turkey as it was doing. With the notification had come a warning that without help the two nations might well find themselves unable to prevent a Communist takeover. The president's response was to ask Congress for $400 million in aid to Greece and Turkey. His rationale, dubbed the "Truman Doctrine," called for "the United States to support free peoples who are resisting attempted subjugation by armed minorities or by outside pressures."

When Marshall became Secretary of State, the principle of the Truman Doctrine received broader application, albeit without the anticommunist strings that Truman had attached to it. At the Harvard University commencement exercises in June 1947, the secretary announced his plan, which he said was "directed not against any country or doctrine, but against hunger, poverty, desperation and chaos." Congress reacted positively, passing the Economic Cooperation Act in the spring of 1948 and eventually appropriating some $17 billion over a four-year period. The Marshall Plan (or European Recovery Program) appealed to humanitarian strains in American thought, but it also attracted support because congressmen and citizens alike believed that a restoration of European prosperity would preserve the independence of European nations from Communism. In 1949, with adoption of the "Point IV" program, economic assistance was extended to developing nations in Asia, Africa, and Latin America. Later, during the 1950s and 1960s, critics of such assistance would contend that the Marshall Plan and Point IV were not so altruistic as they had been made to appear and that too much aid took the form of military subsidies. Nevertheless, American foreign policy continued to make full use of the nation's economic power during the Cold War years.

Justified or not, the United States also sought to implement containment through the formation of regional alliances. The United Nations structure rested on the sort of great-power cooperation that had prevailed among the Allies during the war. Its effective operation as an agency for maintaining international harmony depended upon the continuation of amicable relations between the United States and the Soviet Union. As Cold War tensions increased, the United Nations began to reflect them rather than to resolve them, and American policy makers believed themselves compelled to operate outside the UN framework. In 1948, therefore, the Truman administration modified Kennan's ideas about the instruments of containment so as to utilize military alliances along with economic assistance. The

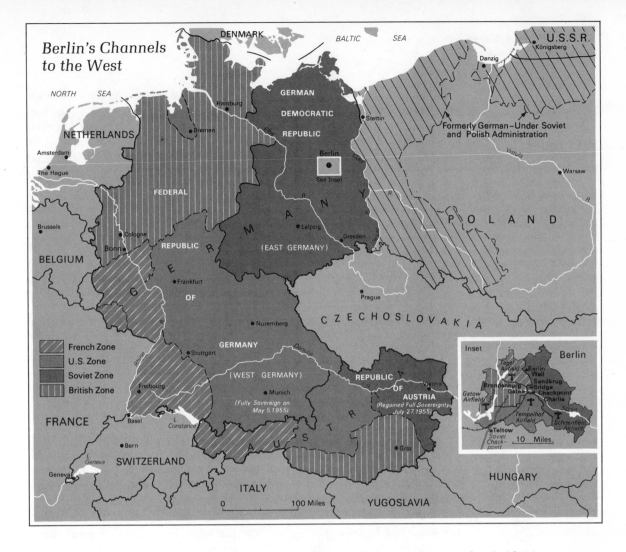

**Berlin's Channels to the West**

most important of the alliances that took shape under Cold War pressures
was the North Atlantic Treaty Organization.

The nucleus of NATO was the Brussels Pact, a fifty-year agreement binding Britain, France, and the Benelux countries to mutual assistance should
any of the five come under attack. Secretary Marshall had encouraged the
arrangement; now with its formation he moved to broaden its provisions to
include the United States, Canada, Norway, Denmark, Iceland, Italy, and
Portugal. Representatives of the twelve nations thus met in Washington to
sign the NATO pact in April 1949. Greece and Turkey joined the alliance
later, in 1951, and West Germany was included in 1955. At its inception
the NATO idea did not incorporate plans for rearmament through a program of American military assistance. As the alliance took shape, however,
Russian anxiety about American intentions began to grow.

The USSR had already intervened in Czechoslovakia to assure Communist control over that country, but was the Russian sphere of influence in
eastern Europe sufficient protection? Was it not possible that the NATO

alliance would pose a further threat to Soviet security? Stalin's reaction was to impose a blockade on all traffic to Berlin; if the United States had given up the idea of German reunification, he reasoned, then the Western powers should be forced to pull out of the eastern zone. The process of escalation that began so ominously in 1948 did not bring on the full-scale war that many international observers feared, for the U.S. Air Force and the RAF managed to airlift needed supplies into the city. But the Berlin blockade did change the character of NATO. In the face of what the United States perceived as a military threat, NATO countries received aid for rearmament, while American forces secured bases in Europe. The implementation of containment through NATO seemed greatly to increase the chances of the Cold War becoming a hot war—hardly the objective that Kennan had had in mind in 1947. Furthermore, the Administration's foreign policy soon met resistance at home; in the face of increasing criticism, the president began to encounter difficulties in justifying the position he had taken in foreign affairs.

**Domestic
Dissatisfaction**
Paradoxically, Truman's foreign policy troubles began at the time of his greatest political triumph. On assuming presidential responsibilities he had encouraged the idea that his experience was inadequate to the tasks at hand, and during much of his first term Democrats and Republicans alike looked upon him as a caretaker president. In that role, Truman enjoyed widespread bipartisan support for his foreign, if not for his domestic, program. Republicans, hoping to rid themselves of a reputation for surly contrariety (a reputation they had acquired as a result of knee-jerk opposition to FDR during the New Deal era), could demonstrate a sense of national responsibility by cooperating with the president in an hour of great international tension. Bipartisanship in foreign affairs seemed not only safe but, given the circumstances, politically sound. Republican leaders were convinced that Truman posed no serious threat in 1948; they believed that their record on foreign policy would deprive the Democrats of any effective issues in the campaign. The GOP allowed itself to dream of a grateful citizenry returning the party to power by an overwhelming majority.

The difficulty with Republican reasoning was that with obstinate scorn for expectations and predictions, Truman determined to retain his hold on the presidency. He worked out a broad program of social legislation—including provisions for housing, unemployment, the development of natural resources, and the protection of civil rights for minorities—and attacked the Republican-controlled Eightieth Congress for its failure to respond to the concerns of citizens. Republicans made the mistake of underestimating the political appeal of a plucky underdog president. The GOP nominee in 1948, New York Governor Thomas E. Dewey, campaigned as though victory were already in the bag. Looking beyond the election, he avoided partisan polemic so as to assure himself of the broadest possible support when he took office. In the end, however, Dewey's bland campaign provided

The presidential canvass of 1948 was one of
the last extensively to employ the campaign
train. Far better than did Dewey, Truman
understood how to talk with the folks down
at the station. Indeed, in the tactics of a
whistle-stop appeal the president had no
peer (Courtesy the Washington (D.C.)
*Star-News*).

"Give 'em Hell Harry" the chance he needed to register one of the most
startling electoral upsets in American history.

Truman's unexpected victory made the GOP gorge rise. Aside from
their distaste for a diet of crow, Republicans resented the president's vitu-
perative attacks upon them during his whistle-stop campaign. After the
presidential billingsgate of 1948 there would be no more nonsense about a
bipartisan foreign policy, no more kid-gloved politeness about the Administration's domestic program. The GOP began casting about for issues on
which to counterattack and thereby gain control of the White House in
1952.

Republicans soon identified areas where the Truman administration
seemed particularly vulnerable. With a diligence inspired by righteous resentment toward what they saw as Truman's fluke victory, they took up the
political offensive. Many people had their doubts about the president's
early association with Boss Pendergast (who, after all, had served time at
Leavenworth Penitentiary for income tax evasion), and congressional investigations after 1948 did little to enhance Truman's reputation for pro-
bity. A Senate Committee on Executive Expenditures began conducting
well-publicized hearings that exposed the activities of "five percenters" who
used their influence—especially in military procurement sections—to line
their own pockets. By 1952 reports of scandal had multiplied. Revelations
exposed the fact that Truman's military aide, Major General Harry
Vaughan, had received a $500 deep-freeze as a gratuity, and that a White
House stenographer was given a $9,540 mink coat because her husband had
made the most of his connections to obtain an RFC loan for an applicant.
With the deep-freeze and the mink coat serving as symbols of corruption in

**LESS DANGEROUS**

**THAN CARELESS TALK**

World War II aroused and kept active a general fear of sabotage. Defense workers wore identification badges, were checked by security guards at plant entrances, and read everywhere posters such as this one warning against careless talk. Few Americans doubted that "a slip of the lip may sink a ship." The security slogans that gained currency during the crusade against the Axis served to prepare the public mind for a Cold War crusade against communist subversion. (State Historical Society of Wisconsin).

Washington, Republicans won popular support when they promised to clean up the "mess."

Even more important than the charge of corruption was the allegation that Truman had been "soft on Communism." Using Communism as a political weapon was scarcely an innovation—Communists had been bogeymen for some politicians ever since the nineteenth century—but, as Cold War pressures mounted, so did a tendency to associate Communism with subversion. In 1946 Truman himself appointed a Temporary Commission on Employee Loyalty; the following year he issued an executive order establishing boards and procedures for loyalty checks in all executive departments of the government. When the president had so demonstrated his sensitivity to the threat of Communist subversion, how was it that he could be attacked for softness? And why did the attack seem plausible to millions of citizens? Several developments help to explain Republican success with the Communist scare tactic.

In the first place, if the United States were really as powerful as Americans had been told, then for many of them the only comprehensible explanation for difficulties abroad was subversion at home. Truman's own loyalty program fostered doubts about the patriotism of government officials and civil servants. So, too, did a series of sensational trials involving charges of espionage. The most prominent case was that of Alger Hiss, a former State Department official who was alleged to have provided former

Communist party member Whittaker Chambers with secret information back in the 1930s. Hiss denied the charge; but, in January 1950, after eighteen months of legal wrangling and two trials, a Federal court sentenced him to five years in prison for perjury. During the second Hiss trial, on November 22, 1949, Truman announced that the Soviet Union had detonated an atomic bomb. For many Americans the timing was more than coincidental and its significance obvious: the mess in Washington had become threatening. For Republicans the threat of Communist subversion provided an effective theme for campaign rhetoric, none using it more dramatically than Wisconsin Senator Joseph R. McCarthy. Early in 1950, in a speech at Wheeling, West Virginia, he assumed his role as a Republican Hercules who would clean Communists and left-wing subversives out of the Augean stables on the banks of the Potomac.

In "rooting out the skunks" (to use his own phrase), McCarthy employed tactics that were crude, sometimes in violation of civil liberties and generally outrageous, yet there was something in McCarthyism that appealed to solid citizens. Truman's courting of the common man with his "Fair Deal" program was an obvious effort to tap the residual strength of FDR's New Deal coalition, and in 1948 he was successful. Yet in order to deliver on his promises, the president believed that a trimming of expenditures abroad was essential. That meant defense cutbacks, and defense cutbacks involved the Administration in some hard choices. Like his predecessor, Truman gave Europe priority over Asia; if reductions in American aid had to be made, it would be far better to reduce aid to Chiang Kai-shek (especially in view of the Kuomintang's wartime performance) than to reduce aid to European allies. In any case, Mao Tse-tung's forces were already in control of Manchuria and gaining strength almost daily.

Senator Joseph R. McCarthy made much of the "documents" he habitually fished out of his briefcase during public addresses. Whether or not they proved what the Senator said they did, he used them effectively to suggest that his investigation of subversion was worthy of support. Until he finally overreached himself and became an embarrassment to his own party, McCarthy wielded enormous power (Brown Brothers).

Truman therefore decided against trying to prop up Chiang Kai-shek's
dead horse. In August 1949 the State Department halted arms shipments to
the Nationalists; a few weeks later Mao sealed their fate. He proclaimed
the formation of the People's Republic of China while Chiang Kai-shek
escaped to Formosa with the remnants of his army. Critics held the president and his Secretary of State, Dean Acheson, largely responsible for the
"loss" of China. Truman, thought many of them, had come under the influence of effete "eastern establishment" intellectuals who had always
turned toward Europe; McCarthyism appealed to people who had always
been suspicious of a Europe-first emphasis. Solid citizens of Main Street
disliked Acheson's aristocratic demeanor and broad "a" nearly as much as
they disliked Communist subversion.

**The Korean War
and Triumphant
Republicanism**

In the meantime, as part of the Administration's decision to emphasize containment of Russian influence in Europe, the State Department had been
planning to raise no strenuous objection should Mao Tse-tung's armies
proceed to the conquest of Formosa. The United States would then recognize the People's Republic of China, and American policy would be directed toward augmenting a hoped-for division in the Communist bloc. Although the idea appealed to Acheson and others, it would clearly lend
credence to the charge that Truman was soft on Communism. The President therefore ordered a top-secret review of American foreign policy to
supplement his decision to develop a hydrogen bomb. By the early spring
of 1950, a blue-ribbon committee of Defense and State Department officials
had produced the document that came to be known as National Security
Council Paper No. 68 (NSC-68). The paper, exploring several alternatives
(including the reduction of defense budgets, withdrawal into "fortress
America," and "preventive war"), rejected all but one: "rebuilding the
West's defensive potential to surpass that of the Soviet world, and . . .
meeting each fresh challenge promptly and unequivocally."

Within two months a development that might be construed as a challenge took place in Korea, which had been a divided nation since the close
of World War II. After the defeat of Japan, American troops had occupied the area south of the 38th parallel and Russian troops the area
north of it. Neither force expected to remain there for long; but, with the
increase in Soviet-American rivalry, efforts to unify Korea came to nought.
When, in 1947, the United States placed the issue before the United Nations General Assembly, that body appointed a commission to hold elections for a constitutional assembly. The Russians—reasoning that if Korea
could be united by such means, then Germany could also—refused to
allow the UN Commission entry into the North. Elections therefore took
place only in the South. The Republic of Korea, formed by this process
and recognized by the United Nations, included all the Korean peninsula
south of the 38th parallel. The Democratic People's Republic of Korea,
set up at the same time but under Russian supervision, controlled all ter-

ritory to the North. Korea thus had two republics, one recognized by the Soviet Union and one by the United States.

Few American policy makers considered Korea of any strategic significance in the Cold War. Indeed, in January 1950, Acheson had made a speech before the National Press Club in which he described the American "defensive perimeter" as running through the Aleutians, Japan, the Ryukyus, and the Philippines. Korea lay outside that perimeter. Although Acheson's speech accurately reflected the Truman administration's foreign policy preferences, it was not consistent with the recommendations of NSC-68. Thus on the morning of June 25, when North Korean troops crossed the 38th parallel in a drive to unite all of Korea, the Truman administration had to decide whether to follow its Europe-first strategy or the new program of resistance at any point threatened by the Soviets or their allies.

Smarting under charges that he had been soft on Communism, Truman did not hesitate. He immediately requested a UN Security Council resolution labeling the attack as an act of aggression and calling for the North Koreans to withdraw. Because the Russians were then boycotting the UN in protest against its refusal to seat delegates from the People's Republic of China, the Security Council acted with dispatch in approving the resolution. Under United Nations authority, therefore, the president proceeded to name General Douglas MacArthur as commander of UN forces and to throw American troops into the struggle. He also reversed earlier policy by ordering the United States Seventh Fleet to protect Formosa, and—in a move with ominous implications for the future—he increased American aid to the French in their effort to maintain imperial control over Indochina.

For three anxious and angry years the conflict in Korea dominated the news and aggravated political discord within the United States. The fighting shifted from South to North and North to South in seesaw swings that frustrated American military forces and exasperated the civilian population at home. The president, seeming to waver with the movement of troops, shifted military objectives as circumstances changed.

Having crossed the 38th parallel initially in June, North Korean forces moved rapidly southward toward Pusan. Meanwhile, MacArthur was planning a countermove: on September 15 his UN troops successfully carried out an amphibious landing at Inchon, far behind North Korean lines. The action, combined with a UN offensive in the South, forced the North Koreans to retreat. By the end of September MacArthur's armies were once again at the 38th parallel. At that point Truman and his advisers decided to continue into the North so as to bring about Korean unification under United Nations supervision. But, as should have been expected inasmuch as Peking had issued a warning, the advance of UN troops toward the Yalu River brought Chinese forces into the war.

Inexplicably, MacArthur had divided his command on assuming the offensive in the North, and the Chinese took advantage of his blunder.

Conflict in Korea, 1950–1953

Pouring through the gap in the center, they compelled the Eighth Army to retreat in the eastern sector and forced troops on the right flank to evacuate by sea at Hungnam. The Chinese–North Korean armies pressed on beyond the border parallel and beyond Seoul. Lines stabilized by the end of January 1951, however, and UN forces counterattacked in March. They recaptured Seoul for the second time, once again reaching the 38th parallel. The United Nations and the United States thereupon reverted to their pre-Inchon objectives. The president had not counted on having to fight the Chinese. After their involvement, the Truman administration was ready to settle for restoration of the prewar dividing line between North and South.

Truman's restriction of military operations and abandonment of the effort to force unification of Korea struck MacArthur as contrary to American interest. He began to issue statements challenging both the Truman policy and the president's authority to make it. In a letter that GOP minority leader Joseph W. Martin, Jr., read on the floor of the House of Representatives, the general expressed his resentment in no uncertain terms: "It seems strangely difficult for some to realize that here in Asia is where the Communist conspirators have elected to make their play for global conquest, and that we have joined the issue thus raised on the battlefield; that here we fight Europe's war with arms while the diplomats there still fight it with words, that if we lose the war to Communism in Asia the fall of Europe is inevitable, win it and Europe most probably would avoid war and yet preserve freedom." Six days after Martin made MacArthur's letter public, Truman dismissed the recalcitrant general.

A conquering hero could not have been greeted with more emotional enthusiasm than was MacArthur when he returned to the United States for the first time in sixteen years. The near-hysteria of his reception was a measure of the frustration that Americans felt, and Republicans stood ready to take advantage of it. MacArthur would have liked to also, no doubt, but the GOP in 1952 gave its nomination to Dwight D. Eisenhower. The party proceeded to build its campaign on the formula $C_2K_1$: Communism, corruption, and Korea. Voters whose' anxieties about subversion had greatly increased as a result of the Hiss case and McCarthy's charges were assured that proper security measures would be enforced by a Republican administration. Those who found influence peddling distasteful were promised that Eisenhower would put an end to it. To those who were frustrated by the sporadic fighting and seemingly interminable negotiations in the area of the 38th parallel, Eisenhower pledged that he would "go to Korea" for the purpose of restoring peace. The 1952 campaign, then,

The death of a friend always brings grief, as it did for this infantryman during the early weeks of the Korean War. That seesaw conflict was neither the longest nor the bloodiest test of American arms, but it was surely one of the most frustrating. It provided more than a taste of the bitterness that was to grow as Cold War strategies led to involvement in limited hot war hostilities (US Army photo).

produced a result far different from the results of the 1948 campaign. Eisenhower easily defeated Adlai Stevenson, former Democratic governor of Illinois. Americans, trusting that the Allied commander of World War II would now somehow make Korea go away, settled down to enjoy in peace the fruits of economic prosperity that had returned during the years of war.

Yet in another sense—a more important and less intentional sense— Harry Truman predominated over his opponents. After MacArthur's dismissal, the Senate Armed Forces and Foreign Relations committees held combined hearings that provided a forum for discussion of differing strategic concepts. In his testimony MacArthur questioned the Administration's emphasis on Europe, its reluctance to remove restrictions on American forces in Korea, and its sensitivity to criticism from European allies. The general wanted to blockade the Chinese coast, send U.S. bombers on missions into the Chinese interior, and encourage Chiang Kai-shek to launch an attack on the mainland. Administration spokesmen, on the other hand, argued for collective security, containment of Communist expansion, and limitation of the Korean conflict to objectives sanctioned by the United Nations. Secretary Acheson suggested that the MacArthur plan would run the risk of war with both China and the Soviet Union, and that other respected military strategists were less convinced than MacArthur that his proposals would achieve the results he predicted. General Omar Bradley summarized the case for the Administration. The MacArthur proposal, he asserted, "would involve us in the wrong war, at the wrong place, at the wrong time, and with the wrong enemy." By the time the hearings came to an end on June 27, 1951, it was clear that the United States would continue Truman's foreign policy in its essentials. In other words, implementing recommendations of NSC-68, the United States would become involved in peripheral wars of containment but never in wars with the USSR or the People's Republic of China. By the time he turned the White House over to Eisenhower in 1953, then, Truman had defined the character of the Cold War.

# 10

# The Affluent Society

In April 1944 Montana Senator Burton K. Wheeler dictated a long letter to Charles E. ("Red Flag Charlie") Taylor, a fellow veteran of his state's political battles. The senator, peering into the future, had little liking for what he saw: "I am very much afraid that after this war is over and the boys who are fighting become disillusioned and back here looking for jobs, and the men in the war plants are thrown out of work, that we are more than likely to have Fascism." Throughout his long political career Wheeler had always been his own man. La Follette's running mate on the Progressive ticket of 1924, he never hesitated to express his independent judgment; during the thirties he opposed FDR's court-packing proposal and the Administration's interventionist foreign policies. Seen from the White House, Wheeler had all the markings of a maverick. Yet he did not stand alone in anticipating hard times after peace had been restored. His gloomy foreboding of postwar economic disruption and political unrest was an apprehension he shared with many of the nation's economists and political leaders.

Maintaining economic prosperity after 1945 was a major concern of the American people. So, too, was preserving the peace in a world of bipolar power relationships. The achievement of both peace and prosperity inevitably required some hard choices and some trade-offs that were properly subjects of discussion and debate. But in a period of Cold War tension, debate seemed risky and sometimes even disloyal. Thus Americans were inclined to lay great stress on social harmony, extending the reach of what one popular magazine called "togetherness." With prosperity and harmony achieved, and with the return of peace after the Korean conflict, why, then, did so many Americans appear to find their lives dull and uninteresting? In part it was because a new technology emerged from the stress of war to impose subtle stresses on the society. With the new technology Americans surpassed many of the economic goals that Wheeler plainly thought would not even be approached. In surpassing them they encountered new problems that the senator could not have anticipated.

**Economic
Performance and
the Springs of
Affluence**

Anxieties about another depression arriving on the wings of a dove proved to be unwarranted. Americans made the transition from war to peace with little difficulty and then—after 1949—entered a period of sustained economic growth that was to last more than twenty years. As Table 10.1 indicates, total gross national product (measured in 1958 dollars) went from $323.7 billion in 1948 to $452.5 in 1957. At that point a recession brought reversal of the upward trend, but the recession was short-lived. During the sixties GNP advanced to more than $725 billion. Statistics on disposable personal income and personal consumption expenditures provide equally dramatic documentation of American well-being. People of the United States enjoyed a prosperity after World War II that was far greater than the prosperity of the twenties; indeed, they achieved an affluence hitherto unknown in any society at any time. Again using 1958 dollars, disposable personal income (see Table 10.2) rose from $1,642 per capita in 1945 to more than $2,500 by the end of the sixties. Consumption expenditures went from $1,308 per capita to more than $2,300 during the same period. Per capita consumption expenditures in 1970 were double what they had been in 1929, and total consumption expenditures were nearly 3.5 times as great.

The high level of disposable income per capita was consistent with a high level of employment. During the depression thirties between 15 and 25 per cent of the labor force had been jobless, but the manpower demands of World War II ended that distressing state of affairs. Although unemployment rates fluctuated from year to year, they never rose above the 6.8

TABLE 10.1 GROSS NATIONAL PRODUCT, 1929–1972 (Billions of 1958 Dollars)

| Year | Total GNP | Year | Total GNP | Year | Total GNP |
|------|-----------|------|-----------|------|-----------|
| 1929 | 203.6 | 1948 | 323.7 | 1960 | 487.7 |
|      |       | 1949 | 324.1 | 1961 | 497.2 |
| 1933 | 141.5 |      |       | 1962 | 529.8 |
|      |       | 1950 | 355.3 | 1963 | 551.0 |
| 1939 | 209.4 | 1951 | 383.4 | 1964 | 581.0 |
|      |       | 1952 | 395.1 | 1965 | 617.8 |
| 1940 | 227.2 | 1953 | 412.8 | 1966 | 658.1 |
| 1941 | 263.7 | 1954 | 407.0 | 1967 | 675.2 |
| 1942 | 297.8 | 1955 | 438.0 | 1968 | 706.6 |
| 1943 | 337.1 | 1956 | 446.1 | 1969 | 725.6 |
| 1944 | 361.3 | 1957 | 452.5 |      |       |
| 1945 | 355.2 | 1958 | 447.3 | 1970 | 722.1 |
| 1946 | 312.6 | 1959 | 475.9 | 1971 | 741.7 |
| 1947 | 309.9 |      |       | 1972ᵖ | 789.7 |

SOURCE: *Economic Report of the President*, January 1973 (Washington, D.C.: U.S. Government Printing Office, 1973), p. 194.

ᵖ Preliminary.

TABLE 10.2    Total and Per Capita Personal Income and Personal Consumption Expenditures, 1929–1972 (Current and 1958 Dollars)

| | Disposable Personal Income | | | | Personal Consumption Expenditures | | | | |
| | Total (billions of dollars) | | Per capita (dollars) | | Total (billions of dollars) | | Per capita (dollars) | | Population (thousands)[1] |
| Year or Quarter | Current dollars | 1958 dollars | Current dollars | 1958 dollars | Current dollars | 1958 dollars | Current dollars | 1958 dollars | |
|---|---|---|---|---|---|---|---|---|---|
| 1929.......... | 83.3 | 150.6 | 683 | 1,236 | 77.2 | 139.6 | 634 | 1,145 | 121,875 |
| 1933.......... | 45.5 | 112.2 | 362 | 893 | 45.8 | 112.8 | 364 | 897 | 125,690 |
| 1939.......... | 70.3 | 155.9 | 537 | 1,190 | 66.8 | 148.2 | 510 | 1,131 | 131,028 |
| 1940.......... | 75.7 | 166.3 | 573 | 1,259 | 70.8 | 155.7 | 536 | 1,178 | 132,122 |
| 1941.......... | 92.7 | 190.3 | 695 | 1,427 | 80.6 | 165.4 | 604 | 1,240 | 133,402 |
| 1942.......... | 116.9 | 213.4 | 867 | 1,582 | 88.5 | 161.4 | 656 | 1,197 | 134,860 |
| 1943.......... | 133.5 | 222.8 | 976 | 1,629 | 99.3 | 165.8 | 726 | 1,213 | 136,739 |
| 1944.......... | 146.3 | 231.6 | 1,057 | 1,673 | 108.3 | 171.4 | 782 | 1,238 | 138,397 |
| 1945.......... | 150.2 | 229.7 | 1,074 | 1,642 | 119.7 | 183.0 | 855 | 1,308 | 139,928 |
| 1946.......... | 160.0 | 227.0 | 1,132 | 1,606 | 143.4 | 203.5 | 1,014 | 1,439 | 141,389 |
| 1947.......... | 169.8 | 218.0 | 1,178 | 1,513 | 160.7 | 206.3 | 1,115 | 1,431 | 144,126 |
| 1948.......... | 189.1 | 229.8 | 1,290 | 1,567 | 173.6 | 210.8 | 1,184 | 1,438 | 146,631 |
| 1949.......... | 188.6 | 230.8 | 1,264 | 1,547 | 176.8 | 216.5 | 1,185 | 1,451 | 149,188 |
| 1950.......... | 206.9 | 249.6 | 1,364 | 1,646 | 191.0 | 230.5 | 1,259 | 1,520 | 151,684 |
| 1951.......... | 226.6 | 255.7 | 1,469 | 1,657 | 206.3 | 232.8 | 1,337 | 1,509 | 154,287 |
| 1952.......... | 238.3 | 263.3 | 1,518 | 1,678 | 216.7 | 239.4 | 1,381 | 1,525 | 156,954 |
| 1953.......... | 252.6 | 275.4 | 1,583 | 1,726 | 230.0 | 250.8 | 1,441 | 1,572 | 159,565 |
| 1954.......... | 257.4 | 278.3 | 1,585 | 1,714 | 236.5 | 255.7 | 1,456 | 1,575 | 162,391 |
| 1955.......... | 275.3 | 296.7 | 1,666 | 1,795 | 254.4 | 274.2 | 1,539 | 1,659 | 165,275 |
| 1956.......... | 293.2 | 309.3 | 1,743 | 1,839 | 266.7 | 281.4 | 1,585 | 1,673 | 168,221 |
| 1957.......... | 308.5 | 315.8 | 1,801 | 1,844 | 281.4 | 288.2 | 1,643 | 1,683 | 171,274 |
| 1958.......... | 318.8 | 318.8 | 1,831 | 1,831 | 290.1 | 290.1 | 1,666 | 1,666 | 174,141 |
| 1959.......... | 337.3 | 333.0 | 1,905 | 1,881 | 311.2 | 307.3 | 1,758 | 1,735 | 177,073 |
| 1960.......... | 350.0 | 340.2 | 1,937 | 1,883 | 325.2 | 316.1 | 1,800 | 1,749 | 180,671 |
| 1961.......... | 364.4 | 350.7 | 1,984 | 1,909 | 335.2 | 322.5 | 1,825 | 1,756 | 183,691 |
| 1962.......... | 385.3 | 367.3 | 2,065 | 1,969 | 355.1 | 338.4 | 1,903 | 1,814 | 186,538 |
| 1963.......... | 404.6 | 381.3 | 2,138 | 2,015 | 375.0 | 353.3 | 1,981 | 1,867 | 189,242 |
| 1964.......... | 438.1 | 407.9 | 2,283 | 2,126 | 401.2 | 373.7 | 2,091 | 1,943 | 191,889 |
| 1965.......... | 473.2 | 435.0 | 2,436 | 2,239 | 432.8 | 397.7 | 2,228 | 2,047 | 194,303 |
| 1966.......... | 511.9 | 458.9 | 2,604 | 2,335 | 466.3 | 418.1 | 2,372 | 2,127 | 196,560 |
| 1967.......... | 546.3 | 477.5 | 2,749 | 2,403 | 492.1 | 430.1 | 2,476 | 2,164 | 198,712 |
| 1968.......... | 591.0 | 499.0 | 2,945 | 2,486 | 536.2 | 452.7 | 2,671 | 2,256 | 200,706 |
| 1969.......... | 634.4 | 513.6 | 3,130 | 2,534 | 579.5 | 469.1 | 2,859 | 2,315 | 202,677 |
| 1970.......... | 689.5 | 533.2 | 3,366 | 2,603 | 616.8 | 477.0 | 3,010 | 2,328 | 204,879 |
| 1971.......... | 744.4 | 554.7 | 3,595 | 2,679 | 664.9 | 495.4 | 3,211 | 2,393 | 207,049 |
| 1972.......... | 795.1 | 578.7 | 3,807 | 2,771 | 721.1 | 524.8 | 3,453 | 2,513 | 208,837 |

SOURCE: *Economic Report of the President,* January 1973 (Washington, D.C.: U.S. Government Printing Office, 1973), p. 213.

[1] Population of the United States including Armed Forces overseas; includes Alaska and Hawaii beginning 1960. Annual data are for July 1.

per cent recorded during the recession of 1957–1958. For the decade of the fifties the average was 4.6 per cent, and during the four years from 1966 through 1969 the rate dropped to below 4 per cent. It is true that such figures can be misleading. They do not distinguish among workers in various occupations, age or ethnic groups, geographical areas, or full- and part-time employees. They do not show, for example, that in some cities the unemployment rate among black adolescents reached a shameful 25 to 30 per cent during the high employment years of the sixties. Nevertheless, despite pockets of distress, Americans of the postwar period did not have to face the mass unemployment that Wheeler feared.

The interaction of various concurrent forces serves to explain the American economy's impressive performance in the quarter-century after Hiroshima. The drive to victory over the Axis powers produced a series of technological breakthroughs into a new age of nuclear power, electronics, and space flight. Cumulative technological growth gave rise to new industries, while products of those industries helped bring about economies of large-scale production. The increase in Cold War tensions during the late forties reinforced tendencies already set in motion by World War II. Continued rivalry with the Soviet Union in the production of atomic weapons, in the development of delivery systems, and in the space race made the United States government an important sponsor of scientific and technical research. Military expenditures during the Korean and Vietnam wars, as well as defense spending to meet the threat of attack, had a significant economic impact.

The most important growth industries after 1945 based their expansion on defense contracts and on a rapidly burgeoning technology. Those that at least doubled their total production during the 1950s included the gas and electric utilities, electric machinery, aircraft, chemicals, instruments, rubber and plastic products, and natural gas and gas liquids industries. In 1957 aircraft plants, which had taken on particular importance after American involvement in the Korean War, quadrupled their output of ten years before. During that same decade the chemical industries began a rapid expansion with the production of new synthetics, plastics, drugs, and a variety of other goods. Increased use of electricity in both town and country helped to stimulate rapid growth in the utilities field; by 1959 more than 90 per cent of wired homes in the United States had radios, television sets, refrigerators, and electric washers.

More important than the increased number of appliances was the application of theoretical principles to the production of goods in common use. "The history of science demonstrates beyond a doubt," observed James B. Conant in 1952, "that the really revolutionary and significant advances come not from empiricism but from new theories." New theoretical departures in the physical sciences had made possible the harnessing of atomic energy; they also formed the basis for a revolutionary postwar technology in electronics. Thus in the years after 1945 the principles of quantum mechanics and solid-state physics found application in the development of computers, industrial control equipment, microwave communications systems, television sets, tape recorders, and high-fidelity phonographs. Such products strikingly altered the techniques of industrial production, methods of doing business, the character of the labor force, and indeed the whole of American life.

A basic instrument of the postwar technological revolution was the electronic computer, and it is not too much to say that in the thirty years after World War II its influence was even more far-reaching and profound than the influence of atomic energy development. Although punched card machinery had been employed in weaving cloth during the eighteenth century and mechanical calculators had come into use during the nineteenth, the day of the computer did not dawn until 1944, when Harvard University's Howard Aiken completed the "Automatic Sequence Controlled Calculator" (or Mark I) in cooperation with the International Business Machines Corporation. Aiken's machine contained 78 devices, 500 miles of wiring and 3,304 electromechanical relays. In comparison with today's refined computers the Mark I was cumbersome—it required three seconds to multiply two eleven-place numbers—and it was not electronic. But it worked, and it marked an important beginning.

The first electronic computer was ENIAC (Electronic Numerical Integrator and Computer), designed and constructed for the U.S. Army by scientists at the University of Pennsylvania. Completed in 1946, ENIAC employed a binary mode of calculation that eliminated mechanically moving parts and thus made possible more rapid operations. The new machine required less than three-thousandths of a second to multiply two ten-place numbers. An astounding achievement, it was followed by others equally astounding. John von Neumann of Princeton University developed methods by which operating instructions, or programs, could be stored inside the computer memory and means by which the computer could be made to modify instructions. Other important developments included replacing radio tubes with transistors (first produced at the Bell Telephone Laboratories in 1947) and substituting printed circuits for wired circuits.

Perfection of computers in the fifties helped bring about significant changes in operations of both the economy and the society. Brokers used computers to analyze market portfolios. Hospitals used them to diagnose and treat diseases. Highway builders and city planners employed them in designing angles, grades, and traffic interchanges. Engineers in the aerospace industry found that computers could be employed to "fly" rockets and airplanes while they were still on the drawing board. Government agencies such as the Bureau of the Census, the Internal Revenue Service, and the Weather Bureau found computers indispensable; computer games provided useful exercises for Pentagon strategists. Computers were called into the service of nearly every occupation and institution to sort, grade, or record everything from apples and oranges to bank checks and college student registrations.

Development of computers also made possible significant changes in methods of the mass production industries, for computers provided a means of controlling automatic processes. The novelty of those changes in production processes is implied in the formation of a new vocabulary to describe them. In 1948 Professor Norbert Wiener of the Massachusetts Institute of Technology published *Cybernetics;* two years later he came

The technician laboring on the console of this IBM computer appears to have become a part of the machine. Development of the computer aroused fears that it would have a dehumanizing influence; it therefore met opposition from the people C. P. Snow called "natural Luddites." Advantages of the new machines were so obvious, however, that the opposition had little effect (State Historical Society of Wisconsin).

out with *The Human Use of Human Beings.* In coining the term *cybernetics* Wiener supplied a word meant to suggest processes of communication and control in men and machines. His books argued that electronic controls would take over important decision-making functions in business and society, and that automatic factories would reduce the need to employ human brains, just as machines had reduced the need for human muscle. Some of Wiener's predictions were unduly alarming, especially to labor unions. Nevertheless automation, or the automatic handling of parts in the manufacturing process, did become increasingly important. In 1968 at the Cleveland engine plant of the Ford Motor Company, for example, forty-eight men using automated machinery could produce an engine block in twenty minutes; in 1958 twice as many workers had taken twice as long. To many observers automation appeared to be only the latest stage in an effort that began in prehistoric times—the effort to remove burdens of work by mechanical means. Yet technological wonders of the fifties and sixties were so sweeping and brought changes of such magnitude that they were, in fact, different in kind from innovations of the earlier industrial revolutions upon which they built.

Technological innovation after 1945 combined with sizable defense expenditures to foster modification of American industrial organization. Military procurement during World War II tended to favor with government contracts the large corporations that had facilities for production of necessary hardware, and defense spending during the Cold War followed a similar pattern. At the same time, general prosperity encouraged a corporate liquidity that made possible the mergers, acquisitions, and restructuring of enterprises characteristic of the period. The result was the creation of a great many new multinational, multiproduct corporations of colossal size. The nation's largest industrial firm was General Motors, which had in the 1920s adopted a decentralized corporate design that would serve as a model for the post-World War II years. In 1972 GM's $30,352.2 million in revenues exceeded the gross national product of all but fourteen noncommunist countries.

Other companies—many of them engaged in broadly diversified activities—also bulked large. By the end of the sixties, according to *Fortune,* the five largest industrial corporations had nearly 11 per cent of all assets used in manufacturing, the fifty largest had 38 per cent, and the five hundred largest had 74 per cent. In 1967, when military commitments in Vietnam accounted for most of the $12 billion increase in defense expenditures over the previous year, two-thirds of all prime defense contracts went to only a hundred firms. In the same year, 21 per cent of all research and development expenditure was associated with but four corporations. Companies that employed ten thousand or more people (there were 274 of them) accounted for 84 per cent of R & D spending, while those with fewer than a thousand employees accounted for only 4 per cent.

The United States government was in large measure responsible for the nation's economic growth after 1945. During the years of affluence it became more than a regulator of the economy such as the pre-World War I progressives had envisioned, more than a promoter of individual enterprise as in the New Era, and more than an agency for administering recovery, relief, and welfare programs as in the depression thirties. After Pearl Harbor the Federal government necessarily became an involved participant in economic activities, and the Cold War made government policies a bubbling force in the springs of affluence. State and local governments also enlarged their programs and expenditures: indeed, except during years of military activity or the threat of it, total state and local government spending kept pace with Federal spending.

Table 10.3 provides indications of the economic influence that accrued to government departments and agencies with the enlargement of their programs. In 1929 government purchases had accounted for less than one dollar in ten of the national output; before the decade of the fifties ended, government purchases regularly made up more than one dollar in five of all the goods and services that were sold. The largest government outlays were for national defense. In 1947 military expenditures dropped to $9.1 billion from a World War II high of $87.4 billion. Then conflict in Korea greatly stimulated defense spending, and only once after 1951 did it drop

TABLE 10.3    Growth of the Public Sector in the United States (Selected Years, in Current Dollars)

| Year | GNP (billions) | Government Purchases of Goods and Services (billions of dollars) Federal | State and Local | All Government Purchases as % of GNP |
|---|---|---|---|---|
| 1929 | $ 103.1 | $ 1.3 | $ 7.2 | 8.2% |
| 1933 | 55.6 | 2.0 | 6.0 | 12.6 |
| 1939 | 90.5 | 5.1 | 8.2 | 14.7 |
| 1944 | 210.1 | 89.0 | 7.5 | 45.9 |
| 1950 | 284.8 | 18.4 | 19.5 | 13.3 |
| 1956 | 419.2 | 45.6 | 33.0 | 18.7 |
| 1962 | 560.3 | 63.4 | 53.7 | 20.9 |
| 1968 | 864.2 | 98.8 | 100.8 | 23.1 |
| 1972ᵖ | 1,152.1 | 105.9 | 148.9 | 22.1 |

SOURCES:   Charles H. Hession and Hyman Sardy, *Ascent to Affluence* (Boston: Allyn and Bacon, 1969), p. 795; *Economic Report of the President*, January 1973 (Washington, D.C.: U.S. Government Printing Office, 1973), p. 193.

ᵖ Preliminary

below $40 billion. In 1947 less than 4 per cent of GNP was attributable to national defense; in the peak years 1968 and 1969, however, defense expenditures accounted for 9.1 and 8.4 per cent of GNP. When economist John K. Galbraith published his important study *The New Industrial State* (1967), he emphasized the economic impact of Cold War policies. "If a large public sector of the economy, supported by personal and corporate income taxation, is the fulcrum for the regulation of demand," he wrote, "plainly military expenditures are the pivot on which the fulcrum rests."

**The Affluent Society**    The "knowledge revolution," for which the electronic computer serves as an appropriate symbol, was a powerful force behind economic performance after World War II. It did more than merely help to maintain prosperity, however, for it effected profound qualitative changes in American society. Traditional ways of earning a living beginning to give way to new occupations, people found themselves working at jobs they could not even have dreamed about in the years before Pearl Harbor. While the new technology brought unprecedented career opportunities, it also brought more leisure time and, particularly through television, novel ways of spending it. The knowledge revolution not only accelerated the growth of metropolitan areas, but it also just as thoroughly altered the demographic features of every section and region of the country. In countless ways— some deliberate and some inadvertent—leaders of the revolution changed the environment in which the American people lived.

The transformation of agriculture has been in process from the very beginning of American settlement, characterized chiefly by a remarkable growth in productivity. The principal sources of increased output in the nineteenth century were three: the introduction and improvement of farm machinery, the development of railroad transportation, and regional crop and livestock specialization. Farmers reduced the man-hours required for a given unit of production by using mechanical processes. In giving them access to markets, railroads stimulated agricultural expansion. By a process of experimentation, agriculturalists learned what crops and livestock would flourish in particular localities. They discovered, for example, that the hard red winter wheat of eastern Europe would do better than would other, softer varieties in the western plains. Throughout most of American history, in other words, agricultural progress was associated with improving machinery and adapting to the climatic and soil conditions of various regions.

Changes that took place in agriculture after 1945 were of a different order from those that preceded World War II, for they depended as much on understanding of chemistry and genetics as they did upon adaptation and mechanical efficiency. Development of hybrid corn during the 1930s marked the beginning of genetic manipulation, and after 1945 plant breeding became an even more important means of increasing yields. Extensive use of chemicals—synthetic fertilizers, herbicides, and insecticides—was also a phenomenon of the postwar years. The new approach to agriculture aimed at producing higher yields per acre and greater, more rapid growth in livestock. It succeeded. In combination with continued progress in the effort to achieve greater productivity per man-hour (a long-standing objective), it brought an astonishing rate of increase in the output of American farms. Never before had people been able to eat as well or as cheaply. During the years of affluence the average family in the United States spent about one-fifth of its income for food, far less than families anywhere else in the world.

Effects of the remarkable increase in agricultural productivity went beyond relative reduction in food costs. Total farm output in 1972 was more than 62 per cent higher than in 1945, output per man-hour was 352 per cent greater, and output per acre was 73 per cent higher. American agriculture provided an example of what could happen when productivity moved in an upward direction while man-hours moved in a downward direction. More than ever before, farm workers became marginal men, gravitating to towns and urban areas where job opportunities were more abundant. Small farmers, too, began to seek employment in cities, for they encountered great difficulty in competing with large-scale agribusiness organizations that had the means to engage in extensive operations. The achievement of productivity increases in agriculture thus exerted pressures to force farmers off the land; during the post-World War II period farm population declined rapidly. At the time of Pearl Harbor, the number of people living on farms was more than 30 million, approximately what it had been in 1929. When World War II ended, the number was still high (about 24.5 million) compared with what it would be after the passage of three decades. As the nation prepared to celebrate its bicentennial, farm population was down to less than 10 million, or 4.5 per cent of the total American population.

The new technology also brought about a significant transformation in occupations not related to agriculture: the American work force gradually changed its character. Particularly noteworthy was an increase in the number of white-collar workers, especially when compared with a decline in the number of persons engaged in certain types of blue-collar and service occupations. At the turn of the century less than one-fifth of the employed population could be classified as holding white-collar jobs, but by the end of the sixties nearly half of all employed persons held such positions. While the proportion of employees in blue-collar jobs remained stable— fluctuating slightly from year to year between 36 and 40 per cent—there were important changes within the blue-collar category. In general, craftsmen and skilled workers became relatively more numerous, while unskilled laborers were displaced by machines.

Because of the increase in its relative importance after World War II, the white-collar group merits closer examination. In 1956 white-collar workers outnumbered blue-collar workers for the first time since industrialization gave rise to distinctions between the two kinds of occupation, and the white-collar group continued to widen its numerical lead in subsequent years. The United States, noted Seymour Wolfbein in his suggestive *Work in America* (1971), is the only nation in the world that has an occupational profile of this kind, "with so marked a white-collar bent and

In 1970 the farm population of the United States was less than a third of what it had been at the time of Pearl Harbor. Abandoned farm houses that dotted the countryside stood as monuments to a sophisticated agriculture, rather than as symbols of failure. Yet the dreams that shaped such structures had desiccated and blown away, leaving only a husk of wistful memory.

with so rapid an acceleration in white-collar employment." The group includes professional workers; clerical workers; sales workers; and proprietors, managers, and officials. Of those four categories, two have been almost entirely responsible for the growing relative importance of white-collar occupations as a whole. In 1947 skilled craftsmen had outnumbered professional workers two to one, but in the next twenty years the professionals advanced to the point where they constituted 14 per cent of the work force, passing the craftsmen in total number. Professional personnel, of course, included teachers and professors, engineers and technicians, doctors and nurses, scientists and mathematicians, architects and lawyers, social workers and librarians. The second category responsible for increases in the number of white-collar workers is that made up of clerical personnel. Back at the turn of the century clerical workers constituted only 3 per cent of the labor force. By 1947 they made up 12 per cent, and by the end of the sixties 17 per cent of all employed people were clerical workers. The category includes not only secretaries and stenographers, but also bookkeepers, bank tellers, office-machine operators, and electronic computer personnel (key-punch operators and the like).

The other two classifications in the white-collar group—sales workers; proprietors, managers, and officials—did not register significant increases after World War II. Throughout the twentieth century some 6 per cent of employed people have been engaged in sales of all kinds. Unlike the stability of sales workers, however, that of proprietors, managers, and officials has been more apparent than real. Increase in the number of salaried managers and officials of business enterprise (about 60 per cent during the 1960s) was not enough to overcome reductions in the number of independent proprietors or small businessmen. Yet shifts within the proprietor-manager-official category were highly significant, for they reflected the development of a corporate economy with its large-scale organizations.

With such occupational shifts taking place, social and geographic mobility became a characteristic feature of the years after World War II. Americans coming out of the depression thirties and the war crisis were ready to equate mobility of both kinds with national progress and personal satisfaction. People flocked to cities and to the suburban fringes surrounding them because it was there that opportunities created by the new technology were most abundant. With good reason, geographic moves came to be associated with professional advancement and upward social mobility. The migration rate for men with at least one year of college was more than double the migration rate for men with only a grade school education, it was 60 to 70 per cent higher for whites than for nonwhites, and it was far higher for professionals of the white-collar group than it was for any of the blue-collar categories. Geographic movement, in other words, was more characteristic of those people likely to achieve job promotions and higher social position than it was of people with relatively fixed social and economic status. Some corporations, in fact, linked the advancement of

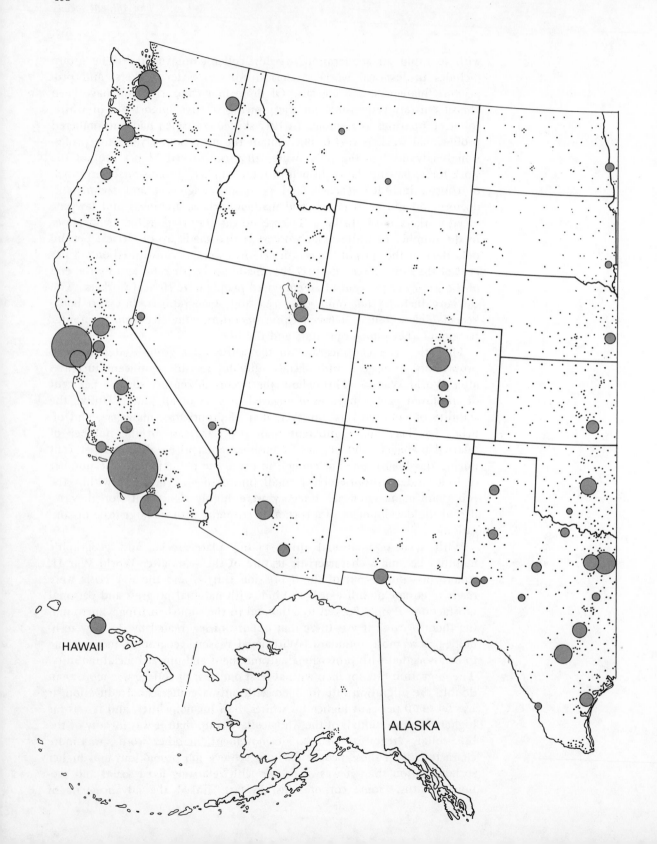

HAWAII

ALASKA

# U.S. Population Distribution, 1970

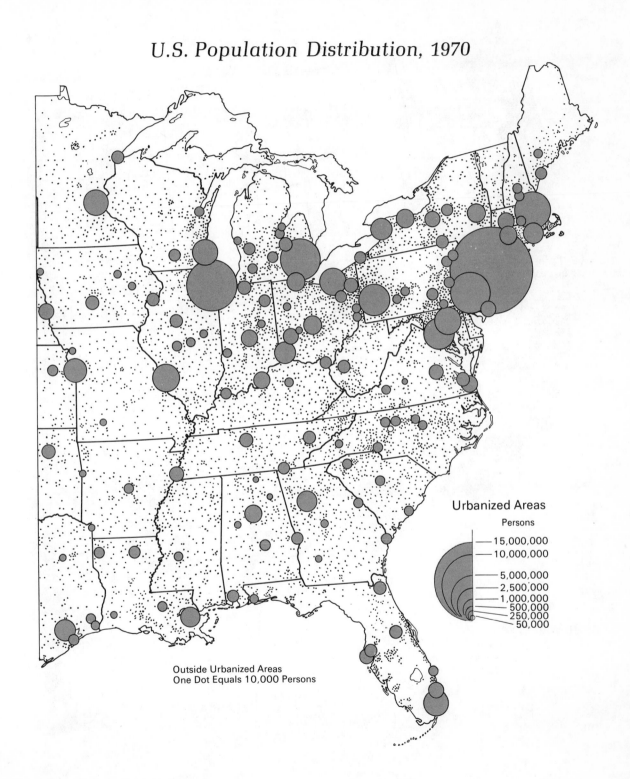

Urbanized Areas

Persons

— 15,000,000
— 10,000,000

— 5,000,000
— 2,500,000
— 1,000,000
— 500,000
— 250,000
— 50,000

Outside Urbanized Areas
One Dot Equals 10,000 Persons

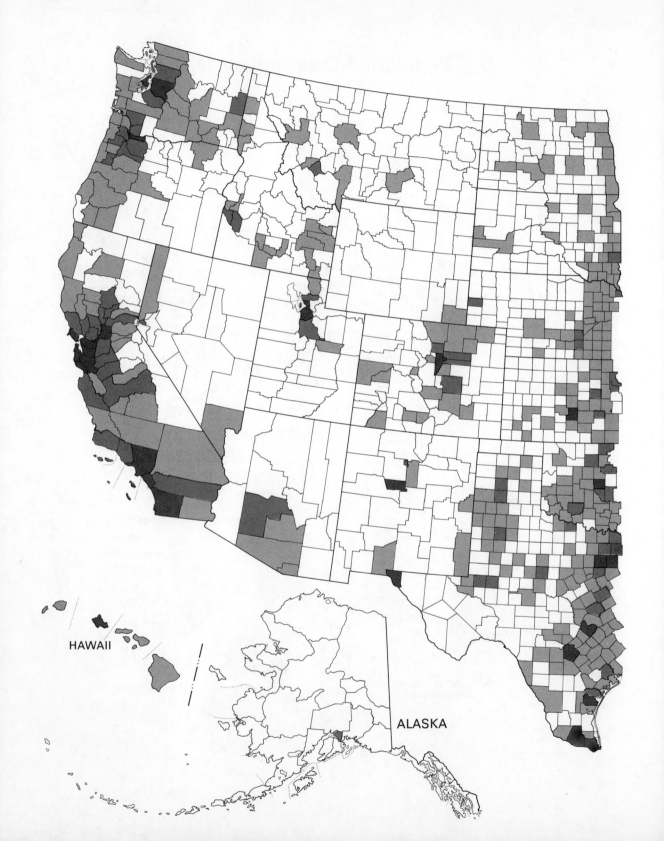

HAWAII

ALASKA

# U.S. Population Density by Counties, 1970

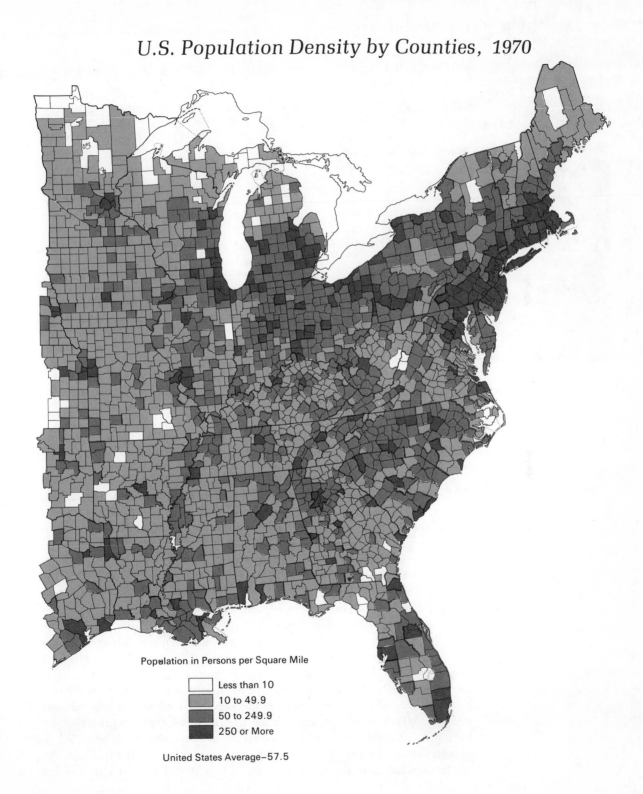

Population in Persons per Square Mile

- Less than 10
- 10 to 49.9
- 50 to 249.9
- 250 or More

United States Average—57.5

U.S. SAVINGS BONDS
will help get you there!

SECURITY

We Are Saving Through
PAYROLL SAVINGS

The wartime savings bond campaign was part of an anti-inflation program. A system of voluntary investment seemed preferable to a system of forced saving. Because it was voluntary, however, bond-buying had to be made attractive. The most common sales pitch emphasized home, family, and security; it thus reinforced conditions that made for a postwar baby boom (State Historical Society of Wisconsin).

managers and executives with transfers from one city to another; a lateral physical move became an upward social and economic move. This is not to say that economically disadvantaged groups remained immobile during the years after 1945. It is only to suggest that they moved less often.

**Suburban America**

While the American population steadily increased throughout the nation's history, the long-range trend in fertility was downward. At its low point during the depression thirties, when economic conditions forced reductions in family size, the rate of births per woman in the United States was 2.2. Then, after World War II had come to an end, fertility took a sharp upward turn. During the fruitful fifties, years of an unprecedented "baby boom," American women bore children at a rate of 3.51 per woman. Causes of the baby boom were legion: Many couples who had deferred marriage during depression and war began to have families at the same time that younger people were marrying and producing children. Incomes were on the increase, and prosperity encouraged larger families. Housing costs were kept to a minimum with government loans and the GI Bill; increased family size did not necessarily imply overcrowding of homes. Young adults who had experienced the privations of depression and war came to have a new appreciation for life; some of them expressed it by having more children than their parents had been able to afford. Whatever its causes, the baby boom helps to explain a remarkably rapid upsurge in the population of the United States. When World War II ended, there were 139.9 million Americans; twenty-five years later, there were 204.9 million, an increase of 46.4 per cent.

Metropolitan areas, and more specifically the suburban portions of metropolitan areas, absorbed much of that population growth. In 1920, as noted in chapter 6, the American population had for the first time exceeded 100 million; and, while more than half of it was classified as urban, only 17 per cent of it was suburban. In 1950 35 per cent of the American people lived in the central cities, while 27 per cent lived in the suburbs of standard metropolitan areas. By 1970, two out of every three Americans were metropolitan residents; but the number living in central cities had dropped to 31 per cent, while the number on the suburban fringe had risen to 37 per cent of the national total. Perhaps because such rapid expansion of suburbs was a recent phenomenon, they attracted considerable attention during the 1950s. And perhaps because of the sweeping changes taking place in American life, misconceptions about suburbia multiplied.

Best-selling books—from Max Schulman's witty novel *Rally Round the Flag* to more serious popular studies such as William H. Whyte's *The Organization Man*—fed the misconceptions by spooning out a broth of pejorative and overgeneralization. So, too, did a spate of popular magazine articles and other reports. Thus the word *suburban* itself became a pejorative. Its *au courant* meaning took in a set of axioms summarized by William M. Dobriner in *Class in Suburbia* (1963). In the popular mind, he noted, suburbs were pictured as "warrens of young executives on the way up; uniformly middle class; 'homogeneous'; hotbeds of participation; child centered and female dominated; transient; wellsprings of outgoing life; arenas of adjustment; Beulah Lands of return to religion; political Jordans from which Democrats emerge Republicans."

As with all myths, the myth of suburbia had enough solid substance to make it plausible. Many suburbs were, in fact, attractive to young executives on the way up (as was Park Forest, Illinois, the community from which Whyte drew most of his inferences). Commuting to the central city was indeed an important daily exercise for many heads of households in suburbia; if they did well at their jobs, they were happy to accept promotions, pull up stakes, and drive them down again in another, more exclusive tract. Many suburban housewives harbored secret resentments at being left with child-care and chauffeuring responsibilities. The houses of some suburban tracts resembled "little boxes made of ticky-tacky," and the imagery of Malvina Reynolds's song struck a responsive chord. A few suburban churches were like the one Peter De Vries described in his novel *Mackerel Plaza:* a split-level structure that had a small worship center off in one corner of its gymnasium and a flourishing psychiatric counseling service on its lower level. In the elections of 1952 and 1956, Republican nominee Dwight D. Eisenhower captured a heavy proportion of the suburban vote.

The trouble with the journalistic and literary description of suburbia in the fifties is that it was a caricature drawn from limited observation and

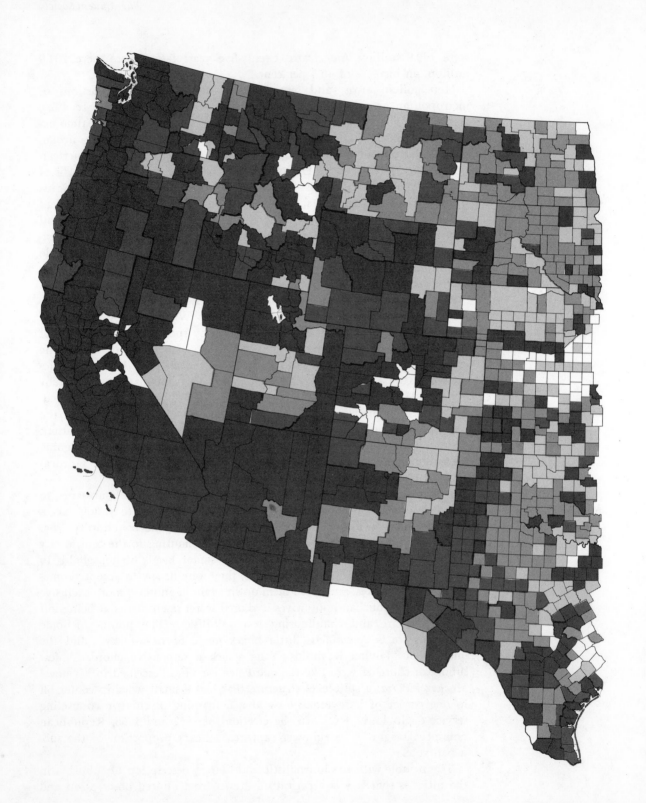

# Year of Maximum U.S. Population by Counties

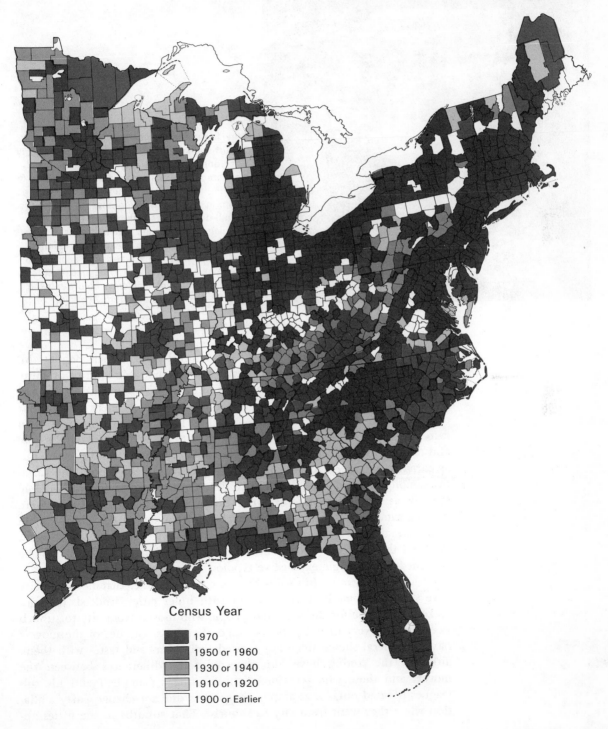

Census Year

- 1970
- 1950 or 1960
- 1930 or 1940
- 1910 or 1920
- 1900 or Earlier

May 1 was the favored moving day for suburbanites, and on that day in 1954 nearly everyone in this Los Angeles neighborhood appeared to be pulling up stakes. Accompanying the postwar population explosion, a boom in low-cost housing covered thousands of bull-dozed acres with houses of undistinguished design and slipshod construction. Grown accustomed to dreary Army camps during the war, many Americans seemed to have been anaesthetized to ugliness—at least for a brief time of residence before moving elsewhere (Time-Life Picture Agency).

analysis. Not all suburbs developed in identical ways. When Bennett M. Berger investigated Milpitas, California, a suburban community of automobile assembly line workers, he was impressed with how little they had in common with residents of the stereotypical suburb. There 81 per cent of the workers voted Democratic, more than half went to church only on rare occasions, few had given much thought to getting ahead on the job, and most regarded their new homes "not as a temporary resting place, but as paradise permanently gained." Yet Milpitas represented only one variation among many. New tract suburbs differed from old towns that became suburbs as a result of metropolitan expansion; residential suburbs were not the same as suburbs with industrial or commercial complexes; some suburbs maintained ethnic homogeneity while others did not. So it went. With all their diversity, communities of the suburban fringe could not be crammed into a single exhaustive typology.

If the differences within suburbia were considerable, that heterogeneity gave suburbia something in common with inner cities. Indeed, one can make a good case for the idea that people who moved from city to suburb were changed very little by their change of address. Studies of the movers have in general shown that they carried their ideas and tastes with them, although the studies have also detected some differences between the movers and those who remained behind. Angus Campbell and his colleagues pointed out, for example, that voters did not change party affiliation when they went from city to suburb. That suburbs in the fifties appeared to be more Republican than Democratic may have been the result of a greater willingness to move on the part of Republicans as well as the result of President Eisenhower's popularity. A more significant difference between residents of suburbia and residents of inner cities was a racial difference. By 1970 only 40 per cent of the metropolitan white population remained in the central city, while 80 per cent of the metropolitan blacks lived there; 20 per cent of the nation's inner-city residents were black, but less than 5 per cent of suburban residents were black. From the concentration of racial minorities in the inner cities and the concurrent movement of whites to the suburbs derived many of the antagonisms and fears threatening domestic tranquility at the same time that citizens worried about threats from abroad.

According to the suburban myth, denizens of the metropolitan fringe were young adults who looked toward a future bright with hope. In 1959, when Robert C. Wood published *Suburbia: Its People and Their Politics,* he challenged the idea that suburban residents faced the future rather than the past. The new technology and its appurtenants, he argued, justified "a single gigantic metropolitan region under one government and socially conscious of itself as one community." But that is not the way American metropolises were constructed; old ideas, shaped by historical experience, emphasized the value of local autonomy and worked against the organization of urban areas on a grand scale. Popular moralistic rhetoric had long paid homage to the neighborliness and sense of community associated with political jurisdictions of limited size. Depression and war had expanded the role of government, and the knowledge revolution provided technical means for making governments effective in meeting enlarged responsibilities. Nevertheless, a conviction that the small society was the natural home of democracy remained an article of faith for many people. Whatever their character or composition, the suburbs resisted annexation, consolidation, and merger that would threaten local autonomy. Thus, in Wood's view, they defied the trends of modern life; they rejected large-scale organization, efficiency, economy, and rationalization. Wary of concentrated political power, suburbanites preferred the multiplication of local governments to the creation of a grand metropolitan government, however efficient or economical it might be.

Homogenizing influences nevertheless had as great an effect on suburbia as they did on the rest of the country. Television serves as the prime example of a force great enough to threaten the cultural, if not the political, autonomy of any community. The technical development of TV was completed in the 1930s, but its commercial expansion did not begin until after the war. As late as 1948 only 172,000 families had receiving sets; these were served by fewer than twenty stations. Then the boom began. The Census Bureau found that in 1950 five million families owned television sets; during the years thereafter ownership increased at a rate of more than four million receivers a year. By 1972 there were some 95 million TV sets in the United States, and more than 95 per cent of all households had at least one of them. Television had long since become, in Max Lerner's phrase, "one of the great tying mechanisms of American culture." Never merely a plaything of the rich, its enchantments were accessible to every American. With its capacity instantaneously to focus the attention of millions of people on the same thing at the same time, television was for good or ill the single most powerful homogenizing force in Western cultural history. Sitting before the tube, there was neither suburbanite nor urbanite, neither white collar nor blue, for TV's vast audiences were unseen participants in a common experience.

**Truman and the
Fair Deal**

Despite the forces moving Americans toward uniformity and cohesion, the immediate post-World War II period was one of political controversy and discord. The years of controversy were the years of Truman's presidency; fighter that he was, his gamecock character may have contributed to the dissension. Yet the president's partisan combativeness was only one of a combination of stresses producing tensions at home to match the Cold War tensions increasing abroad. Most Americans remember the 1950s as a placid decade, a decade of international peace after the Korean War and domestic tranquility after Eisenhower's election. But the fifties may have seemed calmer than they actually were, if only because of the turbulence that characterized the years before 1952.

A month after Hiroshima, Truman appeared before Congress to present a twenty-one point program to redeem pledges that the Democrats had made during the campaign of 1944. Following it up with further recommendations, the Man from Missouri seemed determined to show that reform and welfare programs of the thirties had been only temporarily diverted by war. Included in his messages to Congress were proposals for full employment legislation, expanded unemployment compensation, a permanent Fair Employment Practices Commission, an increased minimum wage, a program to facilitate construction of housing and hospitals, a National Science Foundation, a comprehensive health program, assistance to farmers and small businessmen, nationalization of atomic energy, and development of the St. Lawrence seaway. In time the entire package of proposals would be known as the "Fair Deal." Though Truman was not able to secure all the legislation he sought, he did achieve some of his objectives.

Critics of the president thought his request for such a comprehensive program indicative of his political naiveté. An innocent in politics or not —and he most certainly was not—Truman gave the impression of having a deeper commitment to the Fair Deal than FDR ever had to the New. If he experienced greater difficulties with Congress than did his predecessor, it was because he faced a different set of alignments and a different sort of public pressure. The circumstances of the late forties could hardly be compared with the circumstances that Roosevelt had faced in 1933.

The initial reaction of Congress was all that Truman could reasonably have expected. The Maximum Employment Act of February 1946 established a three-member Council of Economic Advisers to study economic trends and suggest appropriate policies. The Atomic Energy Act, approved in August of the same year, placed control of nuclear research and production in the hands of an Atomic Energy Commission, composed of five civilian members, and required presidential authorization of atomic bombing in wartime. The Veterans Emergency Housing Act and the Hospital Construction Act also received congressional approval. Though in implementation they were not as effective as the president wished, that was neither the fault of Truman nor of Congress. Additional appropriations went to reclamation, flood control, public power projects, and soil conservation. Objectively it was not a bad record, even though the performance of Congress had been obscured by a struggle over continuation of the Office of Price Administration. The president's veto of a bill extending OPA was based upon his conviction that stronger controls were necessary, but the result of his action was the beginning of an inflationary spiral.

Other controversies—a quarrel with John L. Lewis of the United Mine Workers, government seizure of railroads after the Engineers and Trainmen went on strike, and the dismissal of Henry Wallace were the most important—aided Republicans in the congressional elections of 1946. With Democrats suffering their worst defeat in eighteen years, almost everyone assumed that it marked the beginning of a triumphant campaign to place a Republican in the White House. Almost everyone, except Truman, misinterpreted the returns. And even he seemed temporarily subdued. Then the former captain of Battery D launched an offensive against the Eightieth Congress.

Truman began by rejecting two bills that would have reduced taxes. Arguing that the measures were inflationary and would provide more tax relief for the wealthy than for middle and lower income groups, he managed to make his vetoes stick. A few days later he also returned the Taft-Hartley bill with his veto attached. Although this time Congress overrode it, the president won back some of the points he had lost with labor during the strikes of 1946. The act outlawed the closed shop and specified certain unfair union practices. It allowed management to sue unions for breach of contract and gave the president power to use injunctions during strikes that threatened national security. It forbade political contributions from unions, and it required union officials to file affidavits that they were not Communists before a union could receive certification. With good reason organized labor opposed the measure as one that would deprive workers of all they had won in the Wagner Act of 1935. When Truman joined in attacking the Taft-Hartley Act as "a clear threat to the successful working of our democratic society," he evoked a warm response from labor union members and their leaders.

The president's attack on the Eightieth Congress picked up momentum after passage of the Taft-Hartley Act. Flaying legislators for their nonperformance, he did not mince words. In February 1948 he sent over to Capitol Hill a vigorously phrased message on civil rights. Although prompted by Henry Wallace's move to the Progressive party and concern lest he attract liberal support from the Democrats, the message nevertheless reflected Truman's convictions. The president's position provoked a revolt in the southern wing of the Democratic party, but precisely what he might lose from the Dixiecrat rebellion was difficult to determine. And he had gained further evidence to support his charge that the Eightieth Congress was a "do-nothing Congress."

Truman's tactics were, of course, spectacularly successful during the campaign of 1948. His support from the old Roosevelt coalition and from northern blacks and civil-rights advocates—combined with the fact that Wallace and not Truman was tarred with Communist associations—helps to explain the shocking upset of 1948. The way Truman campaigned also serves to explain some of the difficulties he encountered after his reelection. There was a great deal of difference between challenging the Eightieth Congress with a legislative program it would never approve, and developing one that might be passed by the Eighty-first. Action on the scale that Truman had been urging was difficult to achieve, and failure to carry his proposals through to enactment inevitably brought disappointment and calumny.

Some Fair Deal measures did win the approval of Congress. Most noteworthy was its passage of legislation to increase the minimum wage; extend Social Security coverage to an additional ten million people; begin a six-year program for the clearance of slums and the construction of 810,000

Faced with an uncooperative Congress after the 1946 elections, Truman at first attempted to placate the opponents of his legislative program. By the summer of 1947, however, he began to sense the political utility of a vigorous fight for civil rights, housing, anti-inflation, and other measures. As the 1948 presidential contest moved into full swing, Truman emphasized his differences with Congress, lambasting its "do-nothing" record at every whistlestop. As a gritty though unprepossessing tribune of the people against the interests, he gained the support he needed to push his self-assured opponent, New York governor Thomas E. Dewey, into the sidelines (courtesy the Washington (D.C.) *Star-News*).

new houses; double hospital construction; and expand flood control, reclamation, rural electrification, and public power programs. But measures that many of the Fair Deal's supporters thought even more important were allowed to languish or die. A Senate bill providing for aid to education never cleared the House committee. Truman's proposal for a national health insurance plan ran afoul of a vigorous campaign that the American Medical Association launched against "socialized medicine," and the insurance proposal did not even come up for a vote. Neither did the civil rights program; it, too, was buried, although Truman did desegregate the armed forces by executive order. The Brannan Plan, or the program of price supports for agriculture, was too controversial to attract the votes necessary for passage. As for the Taft-Hartley law, the thorn in labor's side, nothing came of efforts to repeal or revise it. Other measures also failed to make much headway. Then came the war in Korea, with attention shifting to foreign affairs and to the threat of Communist subversion. Thus the Fair Deal program never fully materialized during the troubled years that Truman lived in the White House.

## Modern Republicanism

The acrimony that became characteristic of political discourse during Truman's seven years as president soon dissipated after the election of 1952. The victory of 1948 had been won on traditional party lines, and the shock of "defeat snatched from the jaws of victory" had shaken the Republican party. At the next GOP national convention in 1952, therefore, delegates rejected the partisan favorite, Robert A. Taft. Instead, they nominated Eisenhower, a national hero in the war against Hitler, a man of good will who would neither cut back on New Deal–Fair Deal welfare programs nor extend them, a peacemaker who would end Truman's folly in Korea— in short, the one candidate with qualifications for serving as president of all the people. As mass communications, the expansion of business organizations, certain demands of the Cold War, and other influences tended to make American society more homogeneous, General Eisenhower's enormous popular following may well have derived from his projection of a nonpartisan image. When he sought reelection in 1956, one team of researchers found that voters were attracted by "his sincerity, his integrity and sense of duty, his virtue as a family man, his religious devotion, and his sheer likeableness." Qualities such as these ranked high in the scale of values of a society threatened by sweeping transition and yet hoping to benefit from it.

The characteristics that voters found attractive were not characteristics usually associated with strong presidents. Having made a successful career for himself in the Army, Eisenhower was, of course, influenced by military procedure and organization. He was certainly not a martinet, nor was he rigidly insistent upon a chain of command, but he did exhibit a tendency to delegate responsibility. Thus he relied heavily on Secretary of the Treasury George Humphrey to formulate fiscal policy and even more heavily on

These campaign posters proclaim an attraction to Dwight D. Eisenhower that
broke down traditional party allegiances and helped assure his election in 1952.
Eisenhower's sincerity and good will did not fully compensate for political naivete,
but his circumspection and judgment (especially in foreign affairs) protected him
against gross miscalculation (United Press International photo).

Secretary of State John Foster Dulles to develop foreign policy. The sub-
tleties of political relationships that FDR had understood and used to his
advantage were beyond Eisenhower's textbook comprehension of federalism
or the separation of powers.

All this is not to suggest, however, that Eisenhower had no ideas of his
own. Early in his first term he took pains to outline the "dynamic conservatism" that would shape his economic and social policies. He proposed,
first of all, to abandon programs calling for heavy Federal expenditures
and "planned deficits." He would rely on "the natural workings of economic law" to assure continued prosperity, and he would therefore be in a
position to balance the budget and reduce the burdens of taxation. On the
other hand, he pledged his support of aid to public schools, an expanded
Social Security program, and equal employment opportunities for all citizens. In sum, the new president would find "a middle way between un-
trammeled freedom of the individual and the demands for the welfare of
the whole Nation." He would neglect neither the underprivileged nor the
helpless, but at the same time he would avoid "government by bureaucracy."

The fiscal policies of what some Eisenhower supporters called "modern

Republicanism" were never very successful, and indeed may have contributed to the recessions of 1954 and 1957–1958. During his first year in office, Eisenhower recommended smaller reductions in Federal expenditures than some fiscal conservatives had been led to expect. The president argued that national security required avoidance of "penny-wise, pound-foolish" cutbacks in defense spending, but he and Secretary Humphrey tried to do better in 1954. They reduced expenditures by almost 10 per cent, and Humphrey also adopted a tight-money policy in a move against inflation. The result of such measures was that investments, employment, production, and corporate profits all declined. Eisenhower's ardently sought balanced budget went aglimmering in the recession of 1954, and he abandoned the quest. Adopting a more flexible policy, he sanctioned countercyclical measures when necessary. The Administration therefore achieved budgetary surpluses only in 1956, 1957, and 1960. There was cold comfort in the surplus of 1957, for with it came another brief recession.

Modern Republicanism had other faces; one of them looked toward the states as jurisdictions that might be accorded greater influence so as to avoid too heavy a concentration of power in Washington. It was the suburban mentality writ large; but, with considerable justification, critics of the Administration saw more to it than that. Modern Republicanism also looked toward a strengthening of business and industry through their participation in programs that New Dealers had been only too willing to turn over to government control. Like specters from the 1920s, the two faces appeared in the tidelands oil, Hell's Canyon, and Dixon-Yates controversies. In 1953 the president signed the Submerged Lands Act, which granted various states title to the oil-rich lands that lay beneath the sea off their respective coastlines. In 1955 a private power company secured approval for the construction of three dams on the Snake River in Idaho, a concession that precluded a public power project similar to TVA. The Dixon-Yates story broke during the same year. So as to avoid expansion of TVA, it developed, Eisenhower had approved a contract giving private interests the right to construct a power plant for the city of Memphis. Under the fire of critics the president canceled the contract, and Memphis constructed a municipal plant. Along with the tidelands oil measure and the Idaho Power Company license, however, the Dixon-Yates controversy took some of the luster off modern Republicanism.

The President's personal popularity nevertheless remained high. One reason for this was his refusal completely to reverse programs and policies begun during the New Deal. Agricultural legislation in 1956 and 1958 introduced a "soil bank" plan to reduce the farm surplus and substituted flexible for inflexible price supports, but the new farm program by no means abandoned the principle behind assistance for farmers. The Federal Aid Highway Act of 1956, requiring the national government to pay 90 per cent of the cost for a vast network of interstate highways, was consistent with the public works tradition. Housing, too, received government support. The National Defense Education Act of 1958 and the Civil Rights

Act of the previous year even went beyond anything contemplated by Eisenhower's predecessors, albeit for reasons that had more to do with Cold War rivalry and domestic dissatisfaction than with public philosophy.

In retrospect the Eisenhower years appear to have been years of marking time. Although there were occasional crises in international relations, the domestic scene was calm to the point of being dull. So, at least, did a great many critics of the American culture find it. Princeton historian Eric Goldman, for example, expressed his disdain in January 1960, when he published an article in *Harper's* under the title, "Good-by to the 'Fifties— and Good Riddance." Conceding that the age of Eisenhower was one in which the American people had grown prosperous, he remained unimpressed with postwar economic achievement, for "we maunder along in a stupor of fat." In the suffocating affluence of American society he could find little *joi de vivre:* "We live in a heavy, humorless, sanctimonious, stultifying atmosphere, singularly lacking in the self-mockery that is self-criticism." In short, he concluded, "the climate of the late 'Fifties was the dullest and dreariest in all our history." Journalist William V. Shannon was even more contemptuous. The Eisenhower fifties, he suggested, had been "years of flabbiness and self-satisfaction and gross materialism." That "age of the slob" had few redeeming qualities, and the "loudest sound in the land has been the oink-and-grunt of private hoggishness."

**Critics and Classes**

Goldman and Shannon objected to the greed that accompanied the achievement of prosperity. American society had become acquisitive, far more interested in accumulating material things than in developing the taste to choose wisely among the things available to it. But such attacks formed only a part of the general assault on American culture that characterized the 1950s. Not since the muckrakers wrote their articles of exposure had journalists and scholars been so ready to heap scorn on ways of life in the United States. Unlike the muckrakers, however, the critics of the fifties seldom identified specific targets. They more often than not condemned abstractions: Madison Avenue, the exurbanites, the man in the gray flannel suit, or the organization man.

Sociologists David Riesman, Nathan Glazer, and Reuel Denney set the tone for such criticism when they published *The Lonely Crowd* in 1950. The book described three types of society characterized by distinctive configurations of behavior labeled as tradition-directed, inner-directed, and other-directed. The first was a primitive or tribal society and did not figure prominently in the analysis. The second was one that had presumably existed in the United States during the nineteenth century. The third was the type that Riesman and his collaborators saw developing after World War II. The image used to explain inner-direction was the gyroscope. Inculcated with moral principles and behavioral absolutes from childhood, the nineteenth-century American was sure of his direction; his inner gyroscope kept him on even keel whatever storms he encountered. By the decade of the fifties, however, the gyroscope had been replaced by a radar set. Modern man had become other-directed, sending out constant impulses and governing his behavior by the patterns he detected in the crowd.

The typical American had become a conformist, according to popular sociological studies of the fifties, and the attacks on conformity multiplied. In many ways the best of them was *The Organization Man,* written by *Fortune* editor William H. Whyte and published in 1956. The argument Whyte advanced was that the institutions of business, government, and education were producing a common type, a person who not only worked for the organization but belonged to it as well. Upon taking the vows of organization life, he managed to subdue every creative instinct and subordinate every original impulse for the good of the larger group.

Whyte cited Herman Wouk's best-selling novel *The Caine Mutiny* as a parable of the time. In the novel the psychopathic Captain Queeg, commander of a mine sweeper, is relieved by the executive officer, Maryk, when the ship is threatened by a typhoon. The executive officer saves the ship, but he must face court-martial for countermanding the captain's orders. He is exonerated when Captain Queeg is revealed as a craven neurotic. Then, in an astonishing conclusion, Maryk and the other officers are made to appear morally reprehensible for relieving Queeg. "I see that we were in the wrong," one of them writes later. "The idea is, once you get an incompetent ass of a skipper . . . there's nothing to do but serve him as though he were the wisest and the best, cover his mistakes, keep the ship going, and bear up." For Whyte, this was a distillation of the thinking that had begun to dominate life in the United States.

On every hand Americans met criticism of values that organization men were supposed to have held dear. Findings of popular periodicals conducting surveys of college students revealed that young people were less interested in achieving excellence than in finding security and comfort. Russell Lynes, for example, reported in *Mademoiselle* in 1954 that undergraduate women associated professional achievement with ruined health and broken friendships. They conceived of the successful person as "a combination of a bore, a bastard and a battered and broken adventurer." In 1956 *The American Scholar* presented Riesman's interpretation of student responses to an opinion survey. Members of the class of 1955, he concluded, cherished few lofty aspirations, but they did look forward to comfortable lives in suburban ranch houses, lives made possible by employment as junior executives in large corporations. They were not drifters, but neither were they consumed by driving ambition. They wanted escalators, not ladders, and they expected to maintain pleasant associations with their friends while they enjoyed the benefits of American affluence. They would, in other words, do nothing to distinguish themselves; they would remain in the crowd (the suburban community, the neighborhood church, the PTA, the corporation), taking satisfaction in their civic-mindedness and in living exactly as their friends and neighbors lived.

The volume of such criticism was so enormous that, if one took it seriously, it could lead only to the conclusion that affluent Americans of the fifties were uniformly dull. Prominent historians of the decade contributed to notions about the uniformity of American society if not to impressions of its dullness. They did so by emphasizing the uniqueness of the "American character" and by minimizing conflicts in the American past. An important member of the so-called "consensus school" was Louis Hartz, whose *Liberal Tradition in America* came out in 1955. The book's thesis was a negative one: American society did not develop out of feudal institutions, and this absence of feudalism in the beginning had profound and lasting consequences. Without feudalism the United States had never had an *ancien régime* resistant to change; therefore no pressure for the adoption of radical change had ever developed. Having neither a landed aristocracy to destroy nor a landless rabble to put down, the United States had always shown a remarkable consistency in social philosophy. With an abundance of land for all, citizens readily accepted a Lockean idea that the acquisition

In the affluent fifties and sixties prosperous Americans took to the wilderness as a way of recharging spiritual batteries. Loaded down with all the equipment they could pack in their trailers, some of them established temporary weekend residence on the barren ground of much-used campsites. Perhaps they returned home refreshed; perhaps, on the other hand, they returned with a vague sense of never having been away (Bruce Davidson, Magnum Photos).

of property was equivalent to the pursuit of happiness. The liberal Lockean consensus thus tended to turn revolutionaries into conservatives and conservatives into cautious liberals. The only significant social stratification was based upon wealth, but in a dynamic economy wealth could change and bring about changes in social status.

Though *Liberalism in America* was a brilliant book, it grossly exaggerated—as did much popular commentary of the fifties—the uniformity of thought and the homogeneity of American society. Class structure in the United States had, to be sure, always seemed fluid. But classes had existed in the American past, and they continued to exercise an important influence during the 1950s. Indeed, the popular criticism of American conformity, acquisitiveness, and love of comfort was lacking in sophistication and depth when it did not come to grips with the reality of class differences. Max Lerner's willingness to recognize the existence of classes, as well as his effort to understand their dynamics, made his ambitious *America as a Civilization,* published in 1957, one of the important books of the decade.

Lerner began his discussion of classes by citing several studies showing that the class structure was becoming more rigid. C. Wright Mills, for example, had emphasized the difficulties confronting a wage worker who hoped to improve his position. Statistically, the son of an unskilled laborer had only 6 chances in 100 of ever getting into college but 58 chances in 100 of becoming either a semiskilled worker or an unskilled laborer like his father. Lerner contended, however, that the United States had never been a classless society; to imply that opportunities were disappearing was therefore misleading. The real change that was taking place in the post-World War II period, in his view, was from a class structure with relatively clear divisions and modes of life to one in which divisions became blurred and modes of life converged in a middle-class style. He elaborated the point in concentrating on three segments of the society: the wealthy and powerful elite, the new middle class, and the workers.

Examining first the elites of top wealth and corporate position, Lerner concluded that they did indeed show evidences of rigidity. It was difficult—almost impossible—for anyone to move all the way from the bottom of the social and economic pyramid to its peak. Yet movement from the middle ranks to the upper ones did occur. Children of the wealthy had an easier time remaining among the elite than did middle-class persons in gaining access to it, but movement was possible. An important influence here was the "GI Bill," which made government subsidies available to veterans who wanted to obtain college educations. Education was, in general, the most important avenue from the middle to upper class.

Powerful though the elites of business, education, government, and the military might be, Lerner did not consider them the pivot class of American culture. That distinction belonged to a new and evolving middle class. Farmers, shopkeepers, and small businessmen made up a relatively less important proportion of the middle class than they had before World War II; technicians, managers, government bureaucrats, salesmen, advertisers, office, and other white-collar workers were relatively more important than they had been. Members of the middle class had become, for the most part, salaried employees.

What held such a loose collection together closely enough to justify thinking of it as a class? For one thing, most middle Americans did not own the businesses or institutions for which they worked. Middle-class salaried employees were as much without a property stake in their working positions as were industrial laboring men. Another cohesive influence derived from the kinds of work the middle classes performed; they did not do manual labor, and they could wear street clothes on the job. Because they were salaried, they did not consider themselves members of the working class.

This, then, was the middle class: "a formless cluster of groups, torn from the land and from productive property, with nothing to sell except their skills, their personality, their eagerness to be secure, their subservience and silence." They held neither the reins of government nor power over economic decisions of the corporations; but, as Lerner viewed them, they did rule the culture. It was the middle classes that set patterns of consumption and formed the largest and most important part of television audiences. They were modest folk with modest goals, looking "up to the high places of big business that they hope to reach and down to the lowly places of the workers that they wish to avoid."

The working class, standing apart from the Middle Americans, was neither so revolutionary as some of its leaders hoped it would be, nor so docile as some of its opponents expected it to be. Laborers were not ashamed to identify themselves as workers when they thought of the jobs they performed, but at the same time they refused to isolate themselves from the mainstream of American culture. The class militancy of workers was channeled through job-conscious unions toward the achievement of better wages and working conditions; it was not directed toward the achievement of broad social change. Off the job, workers developed consumer tastes that made them indistinguishable from members of the middle class.

Why had workers not become more self-consciously proletarian? Robert and Helen Lynd suggested that one reason for their lack of strong class identity was that the media, in combination with business interests, had beguiled them into accepting the "Middletown spirit." Lerner believed that three other influences were equally powerful. One was the availability of education through high school. In the past, children had often been forced to quit school to help support their families, but that occurred with decreasing frequency throughout the twentieth century. In the post-World War II period, more and more young people from working-class families were able to attend college. The second influence was the democratizing effect of mass consumption. With the higher wages that came after World War II, workers had nearly as much access to consumers goods as did most members of the middle class. Third, there was the persistent hope of upward mobility for the children of workers.

Housing projects mushroomed on the fringes of metropolitan areas after World War II. Here one might find a new beginning, form new friendships, and share in community experience. Here one might belong, and in belonging establish an identity for oneself and for the neighborhood. With a mobile population, the process might repeat itself many times over (State Historical Society of Wisconsin).

Using the three principal indices of class—power, income, and status—Lerner saw workers occupying a stronger position during the 1950s than they had held in earlier periods. Individually, of course, workingmen had little power, but through their unions they could collectively exercise vast power over the nation's economic destiny. The knowledge that they could, if they wished, have such influence gave them assurance and confidence. In income, too, workers had fared better since the beginning of World War II than they had in previous decades. To be sure, they had not gained at the same rate as members of the business elite, but there was considerable overlap between the lower income echelons of the middle class and the upper income groups among workers. Finally, in the area of status and prestige, workers sought to imitate the standards and style of the middle classes, not the living standards of the powerful elites. And they had progressed significantly if not satisfactorily. They could belong to the same churches and clubs with little sense of being discriminated against. Joining the middle class in status became, in other words, a compassable goal.

Among all classes and groups within classes, except possibly for the elites, much energy was directed toward gaining social acceptance either within the class or by the next one up. Lerner saw the burden of class watchfulness as a demanding one regardless of status. Indeed, the psychic tension it could create often proved destructive, for mobility could occur in a downward as well as an upward direction. The badges of class membership—education, marriage alliances, club associations, and the like—had assumed crucial importance. Americans, Lerner thought, did not often ask what their station in life was, but they were haunted by the question "Do I belong?" Seldom did they receive a clear, unambiguous answer. As a result, all classes were characterized by a "drive toward success, a recoil from failure, and a hunger for security."

Mobility thus became the key influence in bringing about the social phenomena that critics of the fifties found so distasteful. The qualities they attacked (conformity to behavior patterns of the crowd, an obsessive concern with status, a longing for security, a desire for consumption of the same goods enjoyed by the class above) were qualities characteristic of an open society. Critics might argue eloquently for the cultural traits and the tastes of a closed society; but, so long as mobility remained a driving force, their strictures and lamentations would have little influence. The real shortcomings of American society in the fifties, then, derived not from materialism, hoggishness, or even conformity, but from a tendency to view "every phase of life through the lenses of advancement." The intrinsic value of goods, services, and associations was often ignored; nowhere was that tendency more evident than in attitudes toward education. For many people a college degree was valued because it cleared the way for upward mobility and not because a student might deepen his sensitivity and understanding in the process of earning it.

## The New Look in American Foreign Policy

President Eisenhower came into office at a time when many Americans were more concerned about the threat of subversion in the United States than they were about social conformity. Senator Joseph R. McCarthy had not yet lost his credibility as he was to do in 1954 when he held hearings on alleged subversion in the Army. When widespread dissatisfaction with the war in Korea imposed upon the new Administration an obligation to modify American foreign policy, the task of charting a new course devolved upon Secretary of State John Foster Dulles.

A skilled diplomat himself, Dulles was the grandson of one Secretary of State (John Watson Foster) and the nephew of another (Robert Lansing). He was a legal counsel at the Versailles Conference after World War I and served as a member of the Reparations Commission. In 1945 he helped to draft the United Nations charter; a State Department consultant after 1950, he took most of the responsibility for negotiating a long-delayed peace treaty with Japan. When Dulles assumed his new duties under Eisenhower in 1953, he was fully aware of the pressure to restore confidence in his office. He also recognized the practical political need for policies that would satisfy those who believed Truman both wasteful and ineffective in his use of American power. He responded to both sets of demands, Professor Hans J. Morgenthau later suggested, by carrying on his curiously personal diplomacy to the accompaniment of ringing pronouncements (on "liberation," "agonizing reappraisal," and walking to the "brink" of war) while allowing security conscious anticommunists and economy-conscious Republicans to dominate the Department of State.

For Dulles's vigorous slogans to have an influence on foreign powers as well as on American voters, they had to be credible. A saber rattler must have a saber to rattle. In products of the new technology—rockets and nuclear weapons—the United States could boast of truly awesome engines of destruction. It was with that weaponry that the Eisenhower administration fashioned its "New Look" in military and Cold War strategy. To the delight of Secretary Humphrey, Taft, and others eager to balance the budget, the New Look promised to reduce military expenditures and produce "a bigger bang for a buck." It also placed the United States in a position to have its way in international affairs: the USSR could be forced to liberate Russian satellites, Chiang Kai-shek could be restored to power in China, the Western Hemisphere could be made secure, and revolutionary cadres in developing countries could be stopped in their tracks.

A saber rattler must be willing to use his weapon if rattling it does not produce the desired results, and limitations of the New Look became apparent when Dulles confronted that second axiom of international power relationships. While the United States would doubtless have employed what the secretary called "massive retaliation" in response to a direct attack, the use of nuclear weapons was obviously inappropriate for purposes of liberating satellite countries. Aside from moral questions that atomic attack might have raised, the Soviet Union had by 1953 developed a nuclear striking force of its own. Thus when East Berliners revolted against Communist domination in 1953 and when the Hungarian revolt took place in 1956, the United States extended expressions of sympathy but no direct assistance. Russian forces easily quashed both rebellions. In Europe, therefore, the Eisenhower administration fell back to the old Cold War policy of containment implemented through NATO, economic aid, and—after 1954 —the European Defense Community.

The death of Stalin in 1953 and the subsequent emergence of Nikita Khrushchev as Premier and First Secretary of the Party in 1958 brought a gradual relaxation of tensions in Europe. Opportunistic and clever, the new Russian leader was also a realist. Recognizing that no nation could win in a nuclear war, he announced that such a conflict was "not a fatalistic inevitability." While incidents might occur to threaten Soviet-American relations, as did the capture of U-2 pilot Gary Powers during his abortive reconnaissance mission over the USSR in 1960, the chances of nuclear war in Europe were greatly reduced. Distrust remained, to be sure, but attention shifted to other regions of the world.

Of those regions none was more important to the success of American diplomacy than the Middle East, for NATO relied on the oil with which the area was so munificently endowed. The USSR also required petroleum, however; therefore, Russians competed with Americans for the favor of Middle Eastern states. The situation was complicated by rivalry within the region itself. Arab countries had resisted the partition of Palestine and creation of the state of Israel under a United Nations resolution in 1948, and Arab-Jewish enmity would be a constant for years to come. To the Arabs, Israel stood as a reminder of European intervention and imperialism; to the Israelis, many of whom had suffered Nazi persecutions, the new state was the realization of an ancient hope. American policy in the area was circumscribed, then, by two conditions: the Arab states had an abundance of oil and Israel did not; but, on the other hand, Jewish voters exercised a powerful influence in American politics.

Tensions in the Middle East began to build up after 1953, when a revolutionary movement in Egypt succeeded in deposing King Farouk and proclaiming a republic. The following year, Colonel Gamal Abdel Nasser became premier. One of his principal objectives was to secure British withdrawal from the Suez Canal, a goal strongly approved by Egyptian nationalists. At the same time Nasser appealed to other countries for economic aid. Dulles, seeing Egyptian friendship as having some utility in Cold War rivalries, sought to tie Nasser to his kite with promises of assistance. The Egyptian premier refused to be tied. He resented Dulles's encouragement of the Baghdad Pact (which united Britain, Pakistan, Iraq, and Iran in a defensive alliance in 1955) because it smacked too much of European imperialism. And even though Dulles cut off military aid to Israel, Nasser

**CLEOPATRA**

Both the U.S. and Soviet governments courted Gamal Abdel Nasser's favor in their desire to add Egypt to the bloc of nations forming on either side of the Cold War. Nasser, a self-proclaimed neutralist, rebuffed Secretary of State Dulles's advances in a series of events that triggered the Suez crisis (King, New York *Daily News*).

concluded a trade agreement with Czechoslovakia and began negotiations for Russian assistance. For Nasser the rivalry between the United States and the Soviet Union was secondary to the achievement of his nationalist objectives; he would accept help from any source. To Dulles, on the other hand, the struggle with Communism was all important; thus, if Nasser refused to align himself with the United States, he would get no American aid. In 1956, therefore, Dulles withdrew an offer to help finance construction of the Aswan Dam on the Nile River. Nasser then promptly nationalized the Suez Canal, thereby threatening the economies of Europe. His move brought quick retaliation; in October 1956 Israel, Britain, and France attacked Egypt, and in short order Egyptian forces faced certain defeat.

Eisenhower was enraged by the combined attack on Egypt, not because he loved Nasser more than did the attackers but because they had acted without consulting the United States. When the question came before the United Nations Assembly in November, Americans joined with Russians to help pass a resolution calling for a cease-fire. By the end of 1956 French, British, and Israeli troops had withdrawn, and a United Nations Emergency Force was patrolling the border between Israel and Egypt. Conflict between Arab and Jew was to break out again in 1967 and 1973, but the Suez Crisis established the pattern of American response. Although both the United States and the Soviet Union were uncomfortable with the Middle Eastern state of affairs, neither power wanted to risk full-scale nuclear war to change it. Again, as in Europe, the Eisenhower administration had to be satisfied with containment. The New Look had proven to have very little utility in meeting Middle Eastern problems.

Meanwhile, on the other side of the globe, the New Look was proving itself equally irrelevant to actual conditions. Eisenhower's impatience with delay in Korean peace negotiations led him to announce that, if terms were not arranged, the United States might retaliate against the Communist side "under circumstances of our own choosing." Because the outstanding issues were quickly resolved, Dulles believed that the threat of force had achieved its objective. Yet intimations of massive retaliation did not produce similar results in Southeast Asia, where French forces were fighting to maintain control over Indochina. The Truman administration had been sending aid to the French, in part because of a fear that without it France would be unable to carry her share of the NATO burden. Despite that assistance, however, the Vietminh nationalist movement, led by Ho Chi Minh and supported by China and the USSR, was proving itself too strong to suppress.

With the French fortress at Dien Bien Phu under siege early in 1954, Eisenhower warned that a Vietminh victory would have grave consequences for the noncommunist world. It would produce a chain reaction like a row of falling dominoes, he suggested, and all of East Asia would be threatened. Simultaneously, the Administration gave serious consideration to direct intervention, even going so far as to contemplate using atomic weapons. For

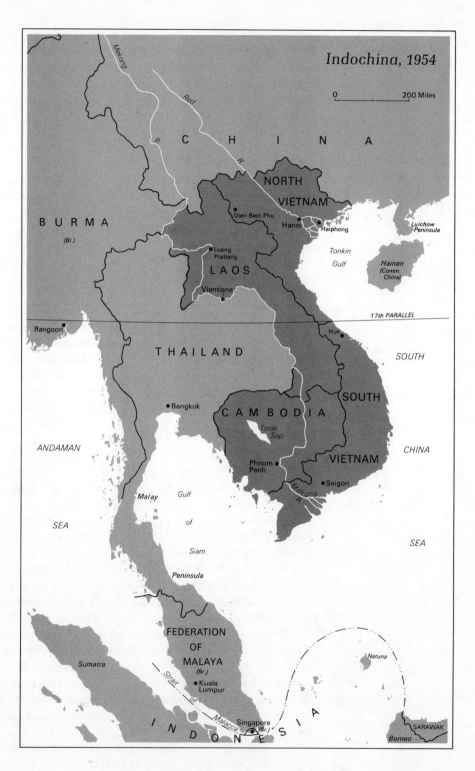

Indochina, 1954

0       200 Miles

C H I N A

BURMA
(Br.)

NORTH
VIETNAM

Dien Bien Phu

Hanoi

Haiphong

Luichow
Peninsula

Luang
Prabang

LAOS

Vientiane

Tonkin
Gulf

Hainan
(Comm.
China)

17th PARALLEL

Rangoon

THAILAND

Hué

SOUTH

Bangkok

C A M B O D I A

Tonle
Sap

SOUTH

CHINA

ANDAMAN

Phnom
Penh

VIETNAM

Saigon

SEA

Malay

Gulf

of

Siam

SEA

Peninsula

Sumatra

FEDERATION
OF
MALAYA
(Br.)

Natuna

Kuala
Lumpur

Singapore
(Br.)

I N D O N E S I A

SARAWAK

Borneo

at least two reasons, however, no such action was taken. In the first place, both sides in Indochina were ready for peace; in the second, the British government withheld its approval of American intervention. Dulles and Eisenhower thus walked to the brink of war, but they could persuade no one to walk with them.

The conference that provided for French withdrawal from Indochina opened at Geneva on April 26, 1954, only a few days before the fall of Dien Bien Phu. Dulles took no part in the negotiations, but Eisenhower's friend, Walter Bedell Smith, was present as an observer. The compromises of the Geneva Conference were calculated to please everyone involved, yet they contained so many internal contradictions that they pleased no one except perhaps the war-weary French people. Vietnam was to be neutralized and divided temporarily at the 17th parallel, but general elections were scheduled for July 1956.

The South Vietnamese representatives at Geneva, insisting upon freedom of action, would sign no agreement. Later, the Saigon regime of Ngo Dinh Diem refused to hold the elections required by the accords, for it seemed very clear in 1956 that Ho Chi Minh would have won. Because he opposed a movement with Communist ties, Diem knew that he could rely on support from the United States. With the approval of Democrats who had had enough of being labeled "soft on Communism," Eisenhower and Dulles condoned Diem's refusal. Although American policy did not produce results that the Administration had hoped to achieve, its failure could be masked for a time by organizing the Southeast Asia Treaty Organization (SEATO) and by identifying the Republic of South Vietnam with the cause of freedom and democracy.

## Eisenhower and the Search for Peace

In the mid-1960s, critics would strive to peel the layers of illusion off American foreign policy. Before he left office, however, Eisenhower had already initiated that difficult process. The old soldier's most cherished desire was to reduce the possibility of war and thus increase the chances for peace. During his second term Eisenhower repeatedly warned against engaging in an arms race with the Soviet Union or turning the American nation into a garrison state. A man of conservative economic views, he recognized that one did not have to agree with Communists in order to live with them and that negotiating with the USSR over disagreements would preserve American security more effectively than would missiles or A-bombs.

The president began haltingly to articulate these opinions in 1957, after the Russians had successfully tested the first intercontinental ballistics missile and had sent into orbit the first man-made satellite. The two achievements stirred world respect for Russian scientists, also arousing anxieties about where such accomplishments might lead. The anxieties produced an endless list of comparisons, but the Gaither Report summarized the most important of them. H. Rowan Gaither of the Ford Foundation headed a committee that had been collecting statistics; it found that, in gross national product, military expenditures, and nuclear and missile development, the USSR was more than holding its own with the United States. Within two years, according to the Gaither committee, the Russians would be capable of launching a hundred ICBMs with megaton nuclear warheads. Its report therefore recommended a significant increase in defense spending, the construction of fall-out shelters, improvement in warning systems, and a reorganization of the Pentagon.

Panic seized a great many Americans who were ready to believe that an atomic holocaust was at hand. It did not seize Eisenhower, for he knew that the report greatly exaggerated Soviet capabilities. The president's information was based upon photographs taken by high-altitude planes, known as U-2s, which had been flying reconnaissance missions over the Soviet Union since 1956. Soviet leaders were aware of the flights, but they could do little to stop them because they had no aircraft that could go as high. Intelligence operations frequently work in mysterious ways: Khrushchev knew that Eisenhower knew that Soviet missile superiority was largely imaginary; and, since the president refused to exploit the fears of American citizens, Khrushchev began to look upon him as a man to be trusted. The Russian was correct. The last thing Eisenhower wanted was increased military spending that might bankrupt the country and provoke an arms race. A new understanding at the highest levels, the president believed, might well make possible an end to the Cold War.

Khrushchev also desired an easing of tensions, but he had some unfinished business he wanted to get out of the way first. Above all, he wanted to settle the Berlin problem, an almost constant source of friction ever since 1945. Lying deep within East Germany (the DDR), Berlin was an outpost for Western propaganda and espionage as well as a convenient point of departure for escaping refugees. In November 1958, therefore, Khrushchev announced that he was ready to turn Berlin over to the East German government. That meant that he was prepared to sign a peace treaty with the DDR, which would terminate the occupation agreement of 1945. He suggested, further, that British, French, and American troops would have to be withdrawn in six months' time.

The Berlin crisis of 1958 aroused cold warriors who regarded disengagement as weakness and who pressed for increasing the size of the Army so as to deal firmly with Russian demands. Democrats, especially, resurrected the ghost of Neville Chamberlain and talked about the futility of appeasement. But the president would not succumb to their demands. He saw no need for a military buildup, he expostulated with a hint of his legendary temper, because "we are certainly not going to fight a ground war in Europe!" Khrushchev, finding the sentiment appealing—for he, too, favored arms reductions—showed signs of being mollified. He promised to visit the United States in the fall of 1959, and Eisenhower agreed to hold a summit conference in Geneva the following year.

Through talks with Premier Nikita Khrushchev, President Eisenhower hoped to attain agreement on both arms control and the prickly question of German reunification. His hopes were literally dashed to the ground with the downing and capture of an American U-2 spy plane on Russian territory. Divided over what their policy should be, Soviet leaders seized upon the U-2 incident as an excuse to cancel the Russian-American summit conference scheduled for the following year (from *Straight Herblock* [Simon & Schuster, 1964]).

All went well until the eleventh hour before the summit meeting was supposed to convene. Khrushchev's American tour was a great success, concluding with such cordial talks at the president's retreat in the Catoctin Mountains that reporters began to make references to "the spirit of Camp David." Perhaps it was all too friendly, too suggestive of détente to set very well with hard-headed intransigents of both sides. Dulles had resigned his office in April because of the illness that would take his life in May, but there were others even more critical of Communists than he. For his part, Khrushchev had to deal with a sharply negative reaction from the People's Republic of China in addition to murmurings at home. To Mao, the developing cordiality between the U.S. and the USSR suggested a rapprochement from which China could gain little. Mounting criticism led Khrushchev to renege on his promise to meet Eisenhower in Geneva. He seized upon the downing of Powers's U-2 as an excuse for canceling the talks and as a quick means of reasserting his leadership both at home and in the Communist bloc. Eisenhower's last chance to end the Cold War went down with the U-2 spy plane, but his efforts had not been without some effect. He and Khrushchev had at least begun to open lines of communication that others could extend if they chose to do so.

# 11

## The Troubled Sixties

On the morning of July 16, 1969, nearly a million people gathered at Cape Kennedy as astronauts Neil Armstrong, Edwin Aldrin, and Michael Collins boarded their Apollo 11 spacecraft. Millions more, even many who were by this time jaded with Walter Cronkite's TV reports of blast-offs into space, were transfixed by what they saw on their television screens. Propelled by an enormous Saturn 5 rocket, Apollo 11 was headed for the moon. Lift-off occurring in an ecstatic moment of fire and smoke at the end of the count-down, the three spacemen were on their way. A hundred miles or more over the earth they entered into temporary orbit to allow time for the guid-ance system to complete its computations. Then, the S-4B stage of the Saturn ignited, Apollo 11 began streaking for the moon at a speed of 24,000 miles an hour. Three days later the spacecraft went into lunar orbit, as Armstrong and Aldrin settled into *Eagle,* the module that would take them down to the Sea of Tranquility on the lunar surface. At 4:17 P.M. EDT on Sunday, July 20, came the laconic announcement: "Tranquility Base here. The *Eagle* has landed." Later that evening, Neil Armstrong emerged from the module, set foot on the moon, and delivered his epigram: "That's one small step for man, one giant leap for mankind." President Nixon has-tened to embellish the sentiment. "For one priceless moment in the whole history of man," he told Armstrong in a telephone call that broke the long-distance record, "all the people on this earth are truly one—one in their pride in what you have done and in our prayers that you will return safely to earth."

The element of show biz in the whole proceeding did not detract from its symbolic importance, but the symbolism suggested by Armstrong and the president was at once too sweeping and too simplistic. The moon land-ing, to be sure, represented an achievement for which Americans could not claim exclusive credit, and they obviously shared with the world an interest in the undertaking. But the program that developed the Apollo had grown out of rivalry with the Soviet Union. Smarting with humiliation because the Russians had been the first to send a man into space (and anxious about the implications of Soviet sophistication in space technology), the nation had received with enthusiasm President Kennedy's 1961 pledge to land a man on the moon within a decade. In the minds of many Americans, then, Armstrong's words represented the generous sharing of a great national triumph.

Not everyone sensed the exultation of the triumph, however, for while the National Aeronautics and Space Administration was perfecting Apollo and Saturn, critics of American society were growing increasingly raucous. The technology that was capable of sending men to the moon was also capable of working great changes in American customs and institutions. It served to extend World War II prosperity into an indefinite future, and with such innovations as television and the computer the postwar period took on a distinctive character. It was a time of unparalleled abundance, a time of seemingly insatiable consumption, a time of unprecedented production. Americans produced children as well as goods; some of those children joined racial minorities and the poor in criticism of the technological culture and its ways. This chapter examines the society that launched Apollo 11 and the concerns that dimmed the luster of its triumph.

## The Race to Tranquility

Scientists who worked on the atom bomb during World War II believed that their Axis counterparts were engaged in a similar undertaking. They were mistaken, for Hitler had not given high priority to atomic research. Manhattan Project personnel nevertheless drove themselves with the belief that they were in competition; the mere thought of Hitler's having atomic bombs at his disposal was a powerful incentive. The Manhattan scientists thus became—for the best of reasons—the first to race for military achievement in the new areas of atomic investigation that had opened up since the 1920s. During the years after 1945, as Soviet-American antagonism deepened, another race began. This time the scientific competition was no phantom; it was far more sophisticated than most Americans thought. One of the great ironies of the post-World War II period is that, while the USSR was conceded to have a powerful army and an effective spy network, it was thought to be backward in the sciences.

Even the testing of the first Soviet atomic bomb in August 1949 did not seem a convincing demonstration of Russian scientific understanding. Most Americans believed that, had it not been for Communist espionage agents, the USSR could not have developed the bomb this rapidly. The test therefore did much more to activate an anticommunist movement in the United States than it did to foster respect for Soviet science. The fact that the Russians had the bomb was indisputable, however; in combination with the formation of a Sino-Soviet alliance and the coming of war in Korea, it provided a justification for American development of the still more powerful hydrogen bomb.

The Cold War arms race was on. Americans produced the first thermonuclear reaction at Eniwetok in May 1951, but the first true H-bomb test did not take place until the spring of 1954 at Bikini. Russian scientists, in the meantime, were in the process of developing their own H-bomb. Testing and stockpiling, both the United States and the USSR rapidly increased their destructive capabilities. In 1950 the American program had already advanced to the point where it was capable of bringing about in a single day an amount of destruction equivalent to the total destruction of World War II. Within the next decade the strategic weapons stockpile of the United States was increased to an energy equivalent of ten thousand such wars. The USSR was determined to keep pace, and the proliferation of nuclear weapons inspired a series of doomsday forecasts that could not be dismissed as imaginative nonsense.

Awesome as nuclear destructive power always was, the attention of military planners turned increasingly to systems of delivery. That they did so was a result of the way in which Soviet-American military rivalry took shape during the years after World War II. The United States emerged from that conflict with two great strategic advantages: an atomic monopoly and an effective air force. Protecting the monopoly and improving the U.S. Air Force with the addition of B-47 and B-52 jet bombers, it was assumed, would assure American military security against threats from the USSR or anyone else. Slower to produce an atomic bomb, the Soviet Union placed greater emphasis on the development of missiles for delivery of the bombs that it began to turn out during the 1950s. The United States strategists also became interested in missile development, of course, but they were less concerned about pay load because their bombs were better engineered and therefore lighter than were those of the Russians. Thus both the USSR and the U.S. turned to missile development, but the Russians emphasized large-thrust rockets more than did the Americans.

Although Robert H. Goddard achieved the first liquid fuel rocket flight at Auburn, Massachusetts, in 1926, rocket technology reached significant practical proportions during World War II with the German development of V-1 and V-2 missiles. The V-1 was little more than a pilotless plane, an air-breathing missile with a rudimentary and unreliable control system that was preset before takeoff. The V-2, however, was a ballistic missile; shaped like a bullet, the V-2 reached a high speed from its rocket motor and then was steered to its target by a guidance system of remarkable accuracy. Both missiles were developed at the Peenemünde laboratory of General Walter Dornberger and Wernher von Braun. After the war, Operation Paper Clip took both men as well as much equipment to the United States. The USSR, too, secured equipment and personnel from the Peenemünde program and laboratory.

In June 1946, at its White Sands Proving Ground in New Mexico, the Army fired the first of the hundred V-2s it had brought over from Germany, and the Jet Propulsion Laboratory of the California Institute of Technology soon began the testing of rockets that had been developed in the United States during the war. Since the state of missile technology was still primitive, however, the United States continued to rely on aircraft for delivery of the atomic weapons it was developing. Then, beginning in 1952, a series of events brought important changes in the entire American missile development program. The hydrogen bomb, the reorganization of the executive branch of the government after Eisenhower's election, and intelligence reports confirming Soviet concentration on long-range rockets led to the burgeoning of several crash programs for the production of nuclear-tipped strategic missiles. Three of them—the Atlas, Titan, and Minuteman—were ICBMs, or intercontinental ballistics missiles. Two others—the Thor and Jupiter—were missiles of intermediate range. And a sixth, the Polaris, was intended for launching at sea from submarines.

John von Neumann, who had been a major contributor to the rapidly improving computer technology of the postwar period, assumed the chairmanship of a special committee to advise the Secretary of Defense on various military rocket programs. Early in 1954 the committee reported that an ICBM was feasible, that the Russians had already begun work on missiles and were ahead of the United States in their development, and that greater coordination of the American effort was essential for maximum efficiency. The last recommendation was ignored, for each of the six programs already under way had persuasive defenders. The result was a missile development effort that was chaotic and wasteful.

Perhaps officials relied too heavily on American efficiency and "know-how" (a term then in vogue) to develop a variety of missiles that would maintain the United States in its dominant position. In any case the effort to put a satellite into orbit received less attention than did military missile programs, even though missile technology was essential to the launching of space probes. The United States did plan to send a small satellite aloft as its contribution to the International Geophysical Year (an eighteen-month period in 1957–1958), but Eisenhower insisted that its purpose was scientific and not military. For that reason the Vanguard, or satellite program, had low-priority status.

The cracking of American complacency came in August 1957 when Russian scientists launched an ICBM on a trajectory that carried it across Siberia. When the Soviets sent Sputniks I and II into orbit in October and November, the American reaction was one of shock. The USSR had beaten the United States out of the blocks in a new race, and many Americans began hysterically to measure and judge nearly every activity of American society by "what the Russians are doing." More often than not in those post-Sputnik days of disappointment and fear, the United States came out second-best in such comparisons. The conviction that Soviet accomplishments were symptomatic of a "missile gap" brought a demand for new programs that would close the Soviet lead in space.

The president was not one to be unduly alarmed by Sputnik, which was, after all, only "one small ball in the air." Minimizing its importance, he told a restless press conference that it was "something which does not raise my apprehensions, not one iota." Yet Eisenhower did recognize that citizens were alarmed, and he took steps to meet the challenge in space that many people saw as a challenge to American security. To assure expert counsel, he established the President's Science Advisory Committee (PSAC) under the chairmanship of educator James R. Killian, head of the Massachusetts Institute of Technology. Killian actually served in a double capacity, for he also accepted appointment to a newly created position as Eisenhower's special assistant for science and technology. The PSAC was instrumental in bringing about a major administrative change when it recommended a new agency for space. In July 1958 Congress passed legislation creating the National Aeronautics and Space Administration (NASA). An independent agency, NASA assumed control over nonmilitary activities of the U.S. space program, becoming the chief guiding influence behind the many American space probes of the next decade.

For various reasons the initial ventures into space were disappointing. Public pressure forced the Department of Defense into premature attempts to launch a satellite, and only after two launching failures did an "Explorer" get into orbit. Furthermore, as critics were quick to point out, it weighed only 30 pounds as compared with 183 pounds for Sputnik I and 1,120 for Sputnik II. Clearly the Russians were using larger rockets to boost Soviet prestige as well as the Sputniks themselves. Long before the Soviet triumph in space, American planners had decided against using large ICBM boosters for the scientific IGY satellite. The United States did, in fact, have rockets adequate for much heavier payloads but was holding them in reserve for military ICBMs. Thus the charge that a "missile gap" had developed was a distortion of the facts.

If there had been a failure in the American missile program, it was more one of public relations than of rocket development. But public relations could be crucial, too. While Eisenhower might speak of Sputnik I as a small ball, the American Explorer seemed more like a small potato. A sense of shame mingled with the fear and the disappointment. Just as it would be difficult to overestimate the effect that Sputnik had on American opinion, so it would be difficult to overstress the importance that most citizens attached to catching up with the Russians and surpassing them. From the beginning the space race had a curious and grotesque dimension.

During the 1960 presidential campaign, Democratic candidate John F. Kennedy made much of the missile gap and the need to get America moving again. After his election in November not much more was heard about a missile gap, but Eisenhower's young successor saw a great many votes twinkling in the heavens. On May 25, 1961, shortly after he took office, he went before Congress to say "that this Nation should commit itself to achieving the goal, before this decade is out, of landing a man on the moon and returning him safely to earth."

Recognizing the value of the reassurance that would result from getting a man into space and then to the moon, Congress appropriated the necessary funds for the program conceived, as Oklahoma Senator Robert Kerr put it, to "enable Americans to meet their destiny." In less than a year Colonel John Glenn made his three-orbit flight that represented the turning of a corner on the way to the moon. Some allies of the United States

Charles A. Lindbergh flew the "Spirit of St. Louis" from New York to Paris in 1927, a feat that made the "Lone Eagle" a great national hero during the New Era. Achievements in space since that time are represented in the Smithsonian Institution's museum. Polaris missiles were first deployed in 1960, just three years before these pictures were taken. That the Polaris became a museum piece in so short a time is a measure of very rapid acceleration in space accomplishments during the sixties (photographs by Herbert F. Wiese).

were as relieved as citizens at home. (One small American, Steven Glad, was at the time a kindergarten pupil in Marburg, Germany. Glenn's flight provided the occasion for a classroom victory celebration and a message of felicitation: "Wir gratulieren zum Weltraumflug am 20 Februar 1962." In his own small way, Steven shared an American sense of well-being that contrasted sharply with the anxieties he had been too young to feel in 1957.)

In 1969, after the moon mission had been completed, *New York Times* columnist James Reston suggested that, to work well, the American political system seemed to need "great challenges and clear goals." The moon project had mobilized intelligence to attain a specific goal within a limited time. "The whole idea of America," he concluded, "was to create a society nobody had ever created before, and it could be that the moon-men, with their concentration, purpose and timetable have shown us the way." Perhaps. In the meantime, whatever the future in space might be, a series of problems—problems that were less ethereal but even more challenging—had for years impinged upon the American consciousness with their claims for attention.

## John F. Kennedy

The election of 1960 demonstrated that Eisenhower's victories in 1952 and 1956 did not mark a long-term movement of voters into the Republican party. With the Democratic nomination of John F. Kennedy and the Republican nomination of Richard M. Nixon, the president's personality was no longer a determinant of voting behavior. And because the Eisenhower administration had done little to change the social welfare program growing out of the New Deal, the coalition that Roosevelt had built during the 1930s remained intact. By making the most of FDR's old combination of interests, Kennedy assured his victory. The only real surprise in 1960 was that the election proved to be so close. Of the many explanations for the narrow margin, the most persuasive is that Kennedy's Catholicism reduced his vote in areas that traditionally went Democratic but were also overwhelmingly Protestant. In the two previous elections Eisenhower's personal popularity had overcome the Democratic national majority; in 1960 the religious issue reduced it to the smallest possible plurality.

Admirers of the new president would make much of the personal charm that derived from his dry wit and compelling candor, his intellectual virtuosity that found expression in the telling phrase, and the sophistication that allowed him to enjoy the company of artists as well as politicians. His youthful vigor appealed to young people who wanted to "get America moving again" after eight years of Grandfather Eisenhower, and his reputation for derring-do promised exciting times in the realization of national greatness. Yet, even if Kennedy's narrow margin of victory in 1960 had not called for caution in the development of his legislative program, he was never the sort to overturn political applecarts. His conservatism on domestic issues fell somewhere between cynicism and realism, revealing itself in a tendency to manipulate or manage the crises he faced. Confronting an unemployment level of 7.7 per cent when he took office, for example, he proposed no structural changes in the American economy; he sought a fiscal solution instead, using tax policies, defense spending, and foreign trade to stimulate economic growth. In foreign affairs, too, he seemed more adept in responding to tensions than he was in circumventing them.

Kennedy spoke often and eloquently about courage and judgment—qualities that bulked large in his own responses to overt challenge—but in situations fraught with moral ambiguities he appeared either bored or diffident. Elected to the United States House of Representatives in 1946 and to the Senate in 1952, he was active in politics during a period when McCarthyism and the civil rights movement offered abundant opportunities for the exercise of moral courage. The young congressman's father had contributed funds to McCarthy's cause, and his brother served as assistant counsel and minority counsel for the Senate Permanent Subcommittee on Investigations that McCarthy chaired. But Kennedy himself had taken no firm position. "McCarthy may have something," he had told a Harvard audience in 1950, and so he avoided challenging whatever pro-McCarthy sentiment there was both within his own family and among his constituents. As for civil rights, he extended assistance to black people after his election in 1960, but he had never identified himself with their interests in any significant way before that. In short, Kennedy's courage was real enough, but it found its best expression in situations of dramatic international confrontation rather than in the humdrum of everyday life. He generally avoided taking the high road of moral principle, for he had seen others follow that path to absurdity and oblivion. But if he saw a compelling need, as he often did in foreign affairs, he would run enormous risks in the name of freedom.

At the time of Kennedy's inauguration, foreign relations were characterized by a new fluidity. The bipolarity of the early Cold War years, when the United States and the USSR dominated international affairs, was giving way before nationalist movements in the Third World of the developing countries. The People's Republic of China had set a pattern for others to follow. Nasser, for example, had ridden the crest of a nationalist wave in Egypt; even though his armies had not distinguished themselves in the Suez crisis, he had come out of that affair as a great national hero with the Suez under his control and the Aswan Dam project under way. In Cuba, too, the forces of nationalism led by Fidel Castro had ousted the harsh dictatorship of Juan Batista. And the Castro regime initiated a program of land reform that worried foreign investors in much the same way that Nasser's movement had worried interests that controlled the Suez Canal. Because Third World nationalist leaders appeared to be increasing their ties with the USSR, it was easy to conclude that the Communist bloc was growing in strength and becoming ever more threatening to American security. In fact, however, Communism was far from monolithic, as disagreements between China and Russia demonstrated; and Khrushchev was as concerned about preserving Soviet leadership of the Communist alignment as he was about rivalry with the United States. Indeed, increased pressure from the United States could force the Russian leader into an awkward position: he might have to demonstrate Soviet strength in resisting the United States so as to counteract criticism from other Communist countries and from his allies.

The international situation, then, was one that called for sensitive appreciation of Khrushchev's position and for delicate avoidance of pressures that might bring retaliation. Eisenhower had understood that forbearance represented wisdom rather than weakness or cowardice. His young successor, on the other hand, during his first two years in office demonstrated little of the deftness that the change in international relationships required. Kennedy's first major move in foreign affairs, his support of the Bay of Pigs invasion, was a horrendous miscalculation. For some months the Central Intelligence Agency had been concerned about Castro's preferences for Communism and about what might happen in other Latin American nations if he succeeded in making Cuba a Communist state. The CIA had therefore set about organizing anti-Castro Cuban refugees and training them for an invasion of the island. Kennedy accepted the reasoning behind the project. Having long believed that Cubans would welcome

A comparative youngster amid the personae of the international scene, John Fitzgerald Kennedy played his diplomatic role with relish and a flair for the dramatic that sometimes frightened more cautious statesmen. In time, he nevertheless won the guarded admiration of world leaders. Here Kennedy poses informally for photographers with Germany's Chancellor Konrad Adenauer (Fred Ward, Black Star).

Shortly after being elected president, Kennedy met with Soviet Premier Nikita Khrushchev in Vienna on the subjects of détente and the German question. As this cartoon depicts, the two leaders seemed to be sizing one another up in a situation where the measure of the man lay more in unbending strength than in flexibility. The test of wills proved a stalemate and a waste (Parrish, Chicago Tribune–New York News Syndicate, Inc.).

an overthrow of Castro and his oppressive dictatorship, he saw in the CIA plan an opportunity to strike a blow for their freedom. He therefore approved the invasion that took place on April 17, 1961. It was, of course, a disaster, for the Cuban people did not rally round the rebel cause and Castro's troops overwhelmed the invaders within three days.

Kennedy had run great risk in order to thwart Communist penetration of the Western Hemisphere, but he came out of the affair looking both foolish and irresolute. Apologists for the president, pointing out that the invasion plans had been formulated while Eisenhower was still in office, tried to shift some of the blame to Kennedy's predecessor. But it was special pleading. The invasion had been consistent with the alarmist attitude toward Communism that the president had expressed during his campaign and at the time of his inauguration. His narrow margin of victory in the election had perhaps been a factor in his approval of the invasion, for he had seen how anticommunism could unite the American people, but the Bay of Pigs venture also represented the sort of gamble he would take to assure national greatness.

Although the president admitted his mistake with respect to the invasion, he nevertheless proceeded, with the help of Secretary of Defense Robert McNamara, to increase the strength of the armed forces. Because he did not want to be locked into dependence on atomic bombs and missiles alone, he and McNamara also planned on conventional and guerilla forces to provide the instruments of "flexible response." The military buildup had predictable effects in Moscow. Although Kennedy talked about arms limitation, the hard-liners in the Kremlin saw subterfuge in his rhetoric and demanded that Russian forces be expanded to meet the American challenge. When Kennedy met Khrushchev for bilateral talks in Vienna in the summer of 1961, the Russian gave him a stiff lecture on the attitude of the USSR toward revolutionary change in the Third World and the need for a settlement in Berlin. Détente with Eisenhower had been a possibility because Eisenhower would neither embarrass the USSR nor press Khrushchev into an arms race; but détente with Kennedy was impossible so long as he insisted upon maintaining the status quo with American military muscle.

With Kennedy's refusal to consider withdrawal from Berlin, Khrushchev finally took the action he thought necessary to stanch the flow of refugees from East Germany. On August 13, 1961, workmen hastily threw up the cinder block barrier that would divide the city indefinitely. The Berlin Wall was an ugly symbol of the *Zerrissenheit* (a torn condition or inner strife) that had been a recurring theme in German history. Marking as it did the end of their hopes for reunification, the German people found it hideous to contemplate. Nevertheless the wall did solve the refugee problem for Khrushchev, since Kennedy was willing to tolerate it so long as the western zone of the city remained under Western control.

Clever though his Berlin tactic may have been, Khrushchev continued to suffer attacks from critics at home and in other Communist countries. Even a series of atomic tests in 1961–1962 could not guarantee his remaining in power. Castro's growing dependence on the Soviet Union, however, seemed to open up new possibilities. During the summer of 1962 Soviet arms shipments and technicians began to reach Cuba in sizable number. What were the Russians up to? The president found out on October 14, when American U-2s brought back photographs of launch pads under construction. When completed they would be capable of firing missiles with a range of a thousand miles. Khrushchev was presenting a challenge to American prestige such as the nation had not known since the Cold War began: Kennedy responded with chilling determination. On October 22, informing the American people of what had occurred, he announced that he was placing Cuba under quarantine until the missile sites had been dismantled. The launching of a missile from Cuba against any nation in the Western Hemisphere, he warned, would be considered an attack on the United States "requiring a full retaliatory response on the Soviet Union."

Kennedy's reaction to the Soviet challenge may not have been a model of crisis management, for it left Khrushchev with no alternative between humiliating withdrawal and nuclear war. Yet the sequel to the missile crisis was far more satisfying than most Americans expected. The Soviet Union agreed to negotiate an atomic test ban treaty, and installation of a "hot line" between Washington and Moscow marked the beginning of détente. Kennedy delivered an address at American University calling for a reexamination of American attitudes toward the Soviet Union in June, and Averell Harriman went to Moscow to negotiate a treaty that was initialed in July 1963. Calling for the abandonment of atmospheric or underwater testing, the treaty was promptly ratified by the Senate on September 24, 1963. "I think it is a very dangerous, untidy world," Kennedy mused in his last press conference. "I think we will have to live

A black soldier stands isolated in front of the cinder block wall that cuts across the
city of Berlin. Walls are nothing new to him. Divided cities, divided societies,
divided personalities bring to mind the lines of Goethe's *Faust:*

> Two souls, alas, reside within my breast
> And each withdraws from and repels its brother
> (Leonard Freed, Magnum Photos)

with it." He was saying, in other words, that he had come around to the
view that his predecessor had reached before leaving office.

**Winds of Change
across Black
America**

While American policy makers searched for an understanding of Cold War
tensions and the means to resolve them, another kind of war was producing
its own tensions within American society. Various pressures and influences
aroused among black people a profound dissatisfaction with the second-
class citizenship they had endured since their emancipation from slavery.
The mechanization of agriculture had already uprooted millions of rural
blacks and sent them fleeing to cities before the coming of World War II.
The demand for labor after Pearl Harbor brought new job opportunities
for those not conscripted into the armed forces. The war itself also produced a new militancy in the quest for social justice, a heightened sensitivity to incongruities in the shibboleths of American democracy, and a
sharpened identification with non-Caucasian peoples of the world.

After 1945 President Truman and other leaders, moving toward desegregation of the military establishment and adoption of fair employment
practices, saw the need for recognizing the rights of black Americans. The
Supreme Court dealt a series of blows to Jim Crow custom: in *Smith v.
Allwright* (1944) the Court affirmed the right of blacks to participate in
party primaries; in *Sweatt v. Painter* (1950) it required the University of
Texas to admit a black student to its law school; and in *Brown v. Board*

*of Education of Topeka* (1954) it held that segregation in the public schools was unconstitutional under the Fourteenth Amendment. "For the first time," observed black psychologist Kenneth Clark after the Brown case, "every Negro felt he was a man in his own right and that his government would help him prove it."

The protracted struggle of black Americans to prove themselves nevertheless met continued resistance as it went through a series of painful permutations. Beginning with a succession of legal and legislative maneuvers, it gradually took the form of nonviolent direct action during the middle years of the fifties. Blacks and whites set up organizations to carry on the work, cheering themselves with the assurance that together they would overcome the prejudice that prevented Negroes from achieving their full human potential. Then, as blacks in the middle sixties improved their position over what it had been in the past but failed to make economic or social gains relative to whites, the ghettoes of American cities broke out in violence. Integration into white society no longer seemed so desirable or so promising as it had during the early years of the movement, and by the seventies black people were emphasizing racial identity and seeking to create new institutions for the realization of black aspirations.

The organization that took the lead in early legal and legislative battles for social justice was the National Association for the Advancement of Colored People. The NAACP worked quietly but persistently at all levels of government to outlaw discrimination in employment, housing, and public accommodations. The organization (along with others such as the Urban League) provided legal assistance to blacks who were ready to carry the fight against prejudice into the courts. There black people won victory after victory over restrictive covenants in housing and the discriminatory practices of buslines, railroads, swimming pools, and other public and semipublic facilities. The NAACP won its best publicized victory when its counsel, Thurgood Marshall, argued the Brown case before the Supreme Court in 1954.

While the Court's decision was widely hailed as a landmark, however, its immediate effects were negligible. Guidelines for implementing desegregation did not come until after a year had passed, and by that time opponents of the action had organized themselves. Furthermore, the guide-

A hundred years after Abraham Lincoln's Emancipation Proclamation, American negroes were still denied ordinary amenities, to say nothing of their constitutional rights. The Civil War of the 1860s had its counterpart in the civil rights movement of the 1960s.

Fusing the cadences of traditional black oratory with the ideas of nonviolent direct action, Martin Luther King's rhetorical style was a vital element in his charismatic leadership (photograph by Herbert F. Wiese).

lines charged lower courts with finding equitable means of admitting pupils "on a racially nondiscriminatory basis with all deliberate speed." Beyond the ambiguity about how fast that might be, there was the lower courts' susceptibility to pressure from local segregationist groups. The 1955 decree was, as Professor Stanley Kutler has remarked, "an invitation to evasion." After five years of deliberate speed only about 6 per cent of the South's three million black students were attending public schools with whites; most of that percentage were in the District of Columbia and the border states. Not until after the Justice Department began initiating its own suits, and after it was made clear that segregated schools risked losing Federal funds, did the process of desegregation begin to speed up.

In other ways, too, the techniques of legislative and legal action proved insufficient. Although the white primary had been declared unconstitutional, blacks were still disfranchised throughout most of the South. Decisions calling for desegregation of transportation facilities were largely ignored. And, as if the activities of White Citizens' Councils were not enough, the rate of black unemployment began to go up. In 1953 the rate among nonwhites was 4.5 per cent, but in the years from 1958 to 1964 it was over 10 per cent. Throughout the entire twenty-year period after 1953, the unemployment rate among nonwhites was more than twice the rate among whites. For many blacks, to borrow E. J. Kahn's telling metaphor, the wheel of fortune continued to be merely a treadmill.

Such was the mood of black people on December 1, 1955, when Rosa Parks wearily boarded a bus in Montgomery, Alabama. A seamstress, she had been working all day at her job and was in no mood for nonsense. She took a seat in the section reserved for whites and then refused to surrender it to a white man. Quiet Mrs. Parks had resolved never to move again. Her arrest touched off a reaction in Montgomery and across the nation. It was not the first time that a black person had resorted to direct action, but it was the incident that, more than any other, prompted black Americans to take matters into their own hands. The Reverend Dr. Martin Luther King, a disciple of Henry David Thoreau and Mahatma

Gandhi, preached nonviolent resistance to evil and organized a bus boycott among Negro citizens. The civil rights movement increasingly turned to nonviolent direct action, winning some victories that were no less important because they were largely local in character. The Montgomery bus company, for example, capitulated within the year in order to recoup losses from a 40 per cent drop in the number of paying passengers.

King organized the Southern Christian Leadership Conference (SCLC) in 1957 to coordinate direct action projects in cities of the South. His group did not carry on in isolation. Back in the war years James Farmer, who shared King's nonviolent philosophy, had formed the Congress of Racial Equality (CORE) with assistance from the pacifist Fellowship of Reconciliation. Now, with the direct action movement gaining momentum, CORE came into its own. In February 1960, when four students from the North Carolina Agricultural and Mechanical College at Greensboro staged the first "sit-in" of the sixties, it was CORE that came to their aid. The students had been refused service at a Woolworth lunch counter; but, instead of leaving, they remained in their seats. The tactic spread across the South and into some cities of the North as well. Eventually the responsibility for organizing the sit-ins came into the hands of the Student Nonviolent Coordinating Committee (SNCC), which King helped to organize in April 1960. CORE then developed the idea of "freedom rides" to challenge Jim Crow practices on bus lines and in terminals. Once they had arrived at their destinations, many of the freedom riders turned their energies to the registration of black voters.

The multiplication of organizations, all of them contributing in one way or another to the civil rights movement, struck some outsiders as an indication of cleavage in the cause. While no one would deny that organizational rivalry existed, it is also true that competition among the several groups provided a stimulus to broadening direct action tactics. Furthermore, members of each group seldom lost sight of goals that all had in common. Where their activities overlapped, cooperation was more apparent than internecine hostility. Working together with greater harmony than usually prevails among reformers, the five major organizations (the NAACP, the Urban League, SCLC, CORE, and SNCC) sang along with several smaller groups a chorus of protest that reverberated through the halls of both the White House and the Capitol.

Congress had already passed two moderate civil rights statutes, one in 1957 and the other in 1960. The first had authorized a civil rights commission and a new Assistant Attorney General to protect the voting rights of black citizens; the second granted to referees appointed by Federal courts the power to investigate violations of voting rights. During his brief months in office, President Kennedy seemed less interested in further legislation than in taking strong executive action in behalf of minorities. In 1962 he ordered Federal housing authorities to halt discriminatory practices in the financing of private homes. He exerted pressure on firms with government contracts to get them to adopt fair employment practices. The

Federal government, as the nation's largest employer, began to hire blacks at middle and higher levels in unprecedented number, and some of Kennedy's appointments drew special praise. He named Robert C. Weaver as head of the Housing and Home Finance Agency, Carl Rowan as ambassador to Finland, and Thurgood Marshall as a justice of the United States Circuit Court. The president and his brother, the Attorney General, were especially active in the field of education. By calling out hundreds of Federal marshals and the national guard, they forced the University of Mississippi to enroll James Meredith despite the state's-rights objections of Governor Ross Barnett. It was only the most dramatic of their efforts to eliminate racial discrimination from schools and colleges.

In the summer of 1963 the direct action phase of the black struggle reached an emotional climax when more than four hundred organizations united to sponsor a massive "March on Washington for Freedom and Jobs." Kennedy hailed the event as one in which Americans could take pride. He had decided to ask Congress for the most comprehensive civil rights law yet proposed, and he saw in the march on Washington an impressive demonstration of support. The bill passed both houses—after Kennedy was in his grave—and Lyndon B. Johnson promptly signed it into law on August 6, 1964. The legislation guaranteed access to public accommodations, strengthened the government's power to enforce fair employment practices, established a Community Relations Service to settle racial disputes, and authorized cutting off funds to segregated schools. Mourners of the murdered president hailed the law as a tribute to his memory; they could not have suspected that, five days after his successor signed the measure, violence would break out in the Watts section of Los Angeles.

The black struggle was taking on new character, and four successive long, hot summers of violence would blast away the smug complacency with which many white liberals contemplated all they had done for the Negro. Author James Baldwin warned that few black people ever really believed that whites would give them anything, for whites had never actually given themselves. Among white participants in the civil rights movement, he suggested, there was always the presumption that it was the Negro who had become—or would become—equal. Thus the efforts of white participants in the movement "overwhelmingly corroborate[d] the white man's sense of his own value." Black people, especially the poor of the urban ghettoes, began to turn away from integrationist efforts. They had seen at first hand what most Americans only saw on their television screens during the summer of 1963 when cameramen turned their lenses on the likes of Birmingham police commissioner Eugene "Bull" Connor using vicious police dogs, fire hoses, and cattle prods against civil rights marchers. And many of them, repelled by self-serving white integrationists and sickened by white violence, began asking the question that Baldwin had phrased in 1962: "Do I really *want* to be integrated into a burning house?"

Heeding Martin Luther King's admonition against violent action, civil rights groups staged a peaceful demonstration to climax their 1963 March on Washington. A throng of marchers assembled at the Lincoln Memorial (from the top of which this photo was taken) and around the Washington Monument's reflecting pool, where they listened to speakers proclaim equal rights for all citizens. Less than five years later, a nearby area of the city was engulfed in clouds of smoke from fires lit in rage against continued racism. After the civil rights movement reached its apex, King's assassination brought a passionate response (Wide World photo).

For Malcolm X, whose father had been a follower of Marcus Garvey and who himself had founded the Organization for Afro-American Unity, the answer was a resounding negative. He ridiculed the idea that blacks who went "tripping and swaying along arm-in-arm with the very people they were supposed to be angrily revolting against" would ever lead the way to anything but a white man's heaven that was a black man's hell. During the summer of 1966, at a meeting of several civil-rights organizations in Memphis, SNCC chairman Stokely Carmichael expressed a similar view. "What we need," he proclaimed, "is black power!" Five times he repeated the expression that would make him famous, and five times his audience echoed his cry of rage.

What Carmichael and others who used the term meant by black power never became precisely clear, and what changes they expected it to produce in black communities were never thoroughly described. Perhaps the best summary of its content was contained in the resolutions passed at the first National Conference on Black Power held at Newark, New Jersey, in 1967. Along with various stipulations and demands, the conference called for the establishment of black financial institutions such as credit unions and cooperatives, selective purchasing and boycotting of white merchants in black communities, a guaranteed annual income for all people, and boycotts of black newspapers and magazines that accepted advertisements for hair straighteners and bleaching creams. While the economic program was not thoroughly worked out and raised as many questions as it answered, black power did give an emphasis to self-respect and pride in race without which black Americans would invite white paternalism at best and sadistic persecution at worst.

The appeal of black power indicated that the nonviolent tactics of the Southern Christian Leadership Conference required an infusion of new purpose if Dr. King's organization was to remain a viable one. King himself pressed forward on several fronts, especially in a campaign to focus attention on the extent and seriousness of poverty in the United States. Problems of the nation's ghetto residents—the inadequacy of their housing, education, and job opportunities—were matters of basic concern. When the sanitation workers of Memphis, Tennessee, went on strike, King lent his support to their cause. He traveled to Memphis, where an assassin lay in wait to gun him down on April 4, 1968. Black Americans had lost their most respected leader, and white Americans had lost a better friend than many of them knew. "What did nonviolence do for *him?*" The phrasing was that of an Andrews, Texas, teenager, but it was a question many people asked. "Nonviolence is a dead philosophy," was the bitter comment of CORE's Floyd McKissick, "and it was not the black people that killed it." Events of the decade that claimed King's life appeared to validate McKissick's pronouncement. One of the rueful ironies of the period is that less than five years earlier, most Americans had hoped to eliminate the sort of violence perpetrated in Dallas.

**The Great Society
and War in Vietnam**

No man ever took the oath of office as President of the United States with more humane objectives than did Lyndon Baines Johnson after the assassination of John F. Kennedy on November 22, 1963. Texas born, he had gone to Washington in 1932 as secretary to Congressman Richard M. Kleberg and had developed an admiration for Franklin D. Roosevelt that amounted to adulation. After serving for a time in the mid-thirties as national youth administrator for Texas, he won election to the United States House of Representatives in 1937. Following World War II he moved over to the Senate—after winning a narrow primary victory in 1948—and soon made a name for himself as a persuader of wavering legislators. He became minority leader in 1953, and from 1955 to 1960 he served effectively as majority leader. Selected as Kennedy's running mate in 1960, he spent much of his time as vice-president in heading up the Committee on Equal Employment Opportunity.

In serving out the remainder of the term to which Kennedy had been elected, Johnson enhanced his reputation as a shrewd political tactician. He cleverly but sincerely invoked the memory of his predecessor to secure legislative enactment of most of Kennedy's program, including the Civil Rights Act of 1964. After his decisive victory over Republican candidate Barry Goldwater in 1964, he developed a far more comprehensive program of his own. His proposals, he observed in his State of the Union message of 1965, were measures appropriate for the "Great Society." To LBJ the Great Society would be the equivalent of FDR's New Deal. With characteristic energy he began bombarding Congress with requests in such number that veteran politicians recalled the excitement of the Hundred Days in 1933.

Most of Johnson's measures received congressional approval, and his record of success with the Great Society program would surely become the envy of his successors in the White House. A cursory discussion of his accomplishments in 1965–1966 may make them seem more impressive than they really were, but they were in fact remarkable. The Appalachian Regional Development Act provided $1.1 billion for resource development, health centers, and highways in one of the nation's most depressed areas. The Housing and Urban Development Act subsidized low-rent public housing and authorized the spending of $2.9 billion for urban renewal over a four-year period. With the passage of Medicare, the aged could receive adequate medical treatment and hospitalization through Social Security. The Elementary and Secondary Education Act, setting up a $1.3 billion program, assisted schools with large numbers of children from poor families; the Higher Education Act granted scholarships to 140,000 needy college students. The Demonstration Cities and Metropolitan Area Redevelopment Act looked toward slum clearance and toward improvement of ghettoes through construction of schools and hospitals as well as housing units. Concern for the environment had already found expression in the Land and Water Conservation Act and National Wilderness Preservation

In 1966, when Lyndon Johnson spoke at a Democratic dinner in Des Moines, Iowa, the theme of the gathering was consistent with the president's vision of a Great Society. Somehow the nation's leader missed a turn in the road; he and the American people never reached the Great Society goal, but instead became mired down in the Vietnam imbroglio (photograph by Herbert F. Wiese).

Act of 1964; these were followed by the Highway Beautification Act and other measures to protect endangered species, scenic rivers, the California redwoods, and the Indiana Dunes.

Although the president supplemented the Great Society programs during his later years in office, overseas commitments increasingly demanded his attention after 1965. The most important of those commitments was in Vietnam—the war in Southeast Asia that was to become a tragedy not only for Johnson but for all Americans. The war wasted both human and material resources; and because the president tried to fight the war and have his Great Society, both without increasing taxes, he set in motion an inflation that would plague the American people after a truce had been signed and troops brought home. What had lured the United States into the Southeast Asian quagmire? Why did Johnson escalate the conflict when so many citizens could find no real national interest in waging it? And why could he find no way to extricate himself and the American people? Such questions have confounded knowledgeable analysts, to say nothing of the man on the street.

In the first place, the logic of an American presence in Vietnam derived from the bipolarity of the early Cold War years. A world view that saw

Onward and Upward

Kennedy's successor, Lyndon Johnson, completing much of the assassinated president's unfinished program, secured as well an astonishingly comprehensive one of his own. But Johnson's hopes for a Great Society were continuously weighed down by the grim realities and increasing demands of the Vietnam war. (Reproduced by permission of the Newspaper Enterprise Association.)

the struggle between Communism and freedom as the central fact of international relations produced during the Truman years a strategy of containment. That strategy—despite Dulles's talk about liberation, the Bay of Pigs venture, and moves toward détente by both Eisenhower and Kennedy—remained the guiding principle of American foreign policy through most of the 1960s. Containment had two corollaries: one held that Communism was a monolithic force and that all Communists were equally committed to world revolution; the other held that if any part of the world moved into the Communist camp, its "fall" might produce a domino reaction that would in the end destroy American security. Thus every postwar president from Truman to Nixon justified American involvement in Indochina with the argument that while the nation had no vital interest in Vietnam itself, it did have a vital interest in preventing the reaction that would surely follow its "loss."

Events that produced the containment strategy also produced an unreasoning fear of Communist subversion within American society. And in a period of affluence, when a large number of citizens had much to lose by revolutionary upheaval, the fear of subversion could shape the outcome of elections. While some politicians, such as Joseph R. McCarthy and Richard M. Nixon, were willing to exploit anxieties in order to gain political advantage over their opponents, few candidates for public office wanted to leave themselves open to charges that they had been "soft on Communism." Political leaders were therefore placed in a position where they could not afford the sacrifice of votes that withdrawal from Vietnam might entail. The American presence there came to be associated not only with maintaining credibility for the United States in its relations with other countries, but also with maintaining a viable and prosperous free society at home.

Second, the question concerning Johnson's escalation of the Vietnam war is more complex, requiring a brief review of developments prior to his entry into the White House. None of Johnson's predecessors had sought total victory over the forces of Ho Chi Minh, and neither did Johnson seek it. While individuals and groups (the hawks) might insist upon winning a decisive victory, others (the doves) urged disengagement and withdrawal. "Our Presidents reacted to the pressures as brakemen," recalled former Defense Department official Leslie Gelb in 1971. That is to say that they pulled the switch "against both the advocates of 'decisive escalation' and the advocates of disengagement." Truman, Eisenhower, and Kennedy were not political theorists, and they were not ideologues. All of them would have been satisfied with a negotiated settlement, and all were prepared to use only the minimum necessary influence to prevent a Communist takeover.

One of the central facts of American involvement in Vietnam is that the minimum necessary influence gradually increased before Johnson took office. Truman had given aid to the French because his containment strategy seemed more important than opposition to French colonialism. With French withdrawal in 1954, Eisenhower found himself having to do more than send aid. By going along with the territorial compromise of the Geneva accords, he kept the United States out of war; but at the same time the preservation of South Vietnamese independence had become an American responsibility. Kennedy also did what was minimally necessary for the Saigon government, but Diem's political maladroitness (especially his repression of Buddhists) aroused great bitterness and eventually led to his assassination. With South Vietnam in need of a stable government, Kennedy began sending more troops. He increased their number from 685 to 16,000, adding to his speeches some rhetorical flourishes about the importance of Southeast Asia. Although he may have preferred disengagement, he could not afford the political risk of antagonizing the hawks. Like Eisenhower, he was prepared to hold on and hope for the best, but the cost of holding on was increasing.

Various developments converged in the middle sixties to make it easier for Johnson than for his predecessors to plunge the nation into massive military involvement in Vietnam. After the Cuban missile crisis had passed and the test-ban treaty had been ratified, the world seemed a safer place. At least it seemed that hostilities between the United States and the USSR were less likely. Yet, at the same time that Vietnam was becoming relatively more important, the Saigon government's position was growing more tenuous. Without increased American support it would probably have fallen to the forces of Ho Chi Minh in 1965. And unlike Eisenhower, whose Secretary of State had been forced to rely on threats of massive retaliation, Johnson had the forces to send into a limited operation. "In sum," writes Gelb, "Vietnam became relatively more important, it was in greater danger, and the U.S. was in a position to do something about it.''

Johnson therefore took the step that would make a shambles of his presidency, destroying the reputation he had hoped to build up, and very nearly destroying the society he had hoped to make great. Why did he not withdraw when he saw the effects of the war at home? There were, no doubt, many personal and other reasons for his holding to the course he had set. What is particularly important, however, is that the same considerations that led Truman, Eisenhower, and Kennedy to increase American influence in Indochina were still operative. And, as in the past, they brought an escalation of the conflict rather than withdrawal. This time it became more intense, but no less futile. The sad fact is that the struggle in Vietnam was—and remained even after American withdrawal—a civil war. The Cold War logic that justified American intervention bore little relationship to the realities of a war for Vietnamese national independence. Johnson and his predecessor knew that. Yet they also assumed that leaving Vietnam to be taken over by the Communists would produce political repercussions at least equal to those that followed Chiang Kai-shek's re-

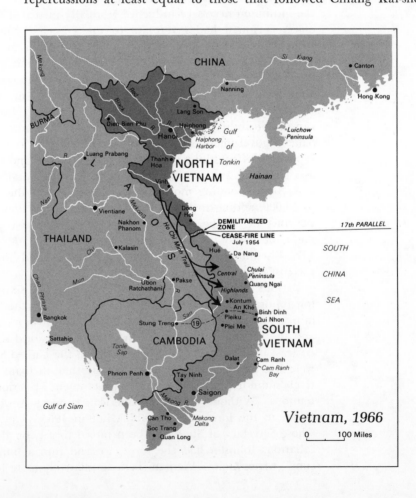

Vietnam, 1966

0    100 Miles

One of the most dramatic shots of the Vietnam or any other war, this superb photograph catches the universal horror of combat. The soldier with hands upraised was guiding a rescue helicopter. His demeanor that of a supplicant, he was, in fact, pleading for aid from on high. These men, the ambulatory wounded as well as the grimacing trooper on the ground, needed help in the Vietnam jungle. Because they did, and because they were there at all, Americans at home were also deeply troubled (Wide World photos).

treat to Taiwan. Thus Johnson pursued the strategy begun by Truman. His only contribution—perhaps inspired by overly optimistic reports he received from military commanders and diplomats as well as by the course of events—was to increase the number of troops in that small Southeast Asian country to 540,000. Otherwise he held on short of nuclear war with China or the USSR, hoping always that he would indeed see the light at the end of the tunnel. He never did see it.

**The Way Out**  Nixon fared better, at least until the spring of 1973, than did Johnson. A care-worn LBJ announced during the presidential campaign of 1968 that he would not seek reelection, but would concentrate instead on peace talks with the North Vietnamese. That left three men—Vice-President Hubert Humphrey, Senator Eugene McCarthy, and Senator Robert Kennedy—to contend for the Democratic nomination. Humphrey was an old liberal closely identified with Johnson's foreign and domestic policies; McCarthy and Kennedy sought support from doves within the party and throughout the country. Kennedy's assassination in June, after he had defeated McCarthy in the California primary, shocked the nation and reduced the Democratic campaign to chaos. With peace demonstrators roaming the streets of Chicago, site of the Democratic National Convention, delegates stolidly proceeded to nominate Humphrey. It was not a popular choice with voters, for Humphrey had antagonized the supporters of Alabama Governor George Wallace with his domestic program and the doves with his acquiescence in Johnson's Vietnam policies. Nixon could not have asked for more favorable circumstances under which to conduct his campaign. He projected an air of quiet confidence, appealing to the silent majority of Americans who were not agitators and assuring them that he had a plan to bring about peace in Southeast Asia. Humphrey made a better race of it than anyone thought he would, but Nixon had too big a lead to be overcome.

The new president's public career teemed with ironies and paradoxes. A cold warrior who had exploited the fear of left-wing subversion in the fifties, he made various agreements with Communist countries a part of his initial strategy when he began formulating foreign policy in 1969. Having established his bona fides as a staunch crusader against Communism, his move toward accommodation with the USSR and China involved few political risks. And while it was not directed toward a Vietnam settlement, it helped produce an international atmosphere conducive to a Vietnam settlement. Nixon began with disarmament. In 1969 he endorsed the Nuclear Proliferation Treaty that was an outgrowth of the 1963 test-ban treaty. He rejected the use of biological and chemical means of waging war and ordered destruction of materials already developed for that purpose. He also supported the opening of strategic arms limitation (SALT) talks in 1970. At the same time, however, he urged a new antiballistic system (Safeguard) and development of a new multiple warhead (MIRV) to defend the United States against attack.

Critics of Nixon's expanded missile program argued that it might well prevent an arms limitation treaty, but the president countered by suggesting that the United States would be negotiating from strength and would thus improve the chances for a treaty. He insisted that Safeguard and MIRV were intended purely for defensive purposes and that the United States would abandon an earlier tendency to become directly involved in the affairs of other countries. Economic and technical aid would be made available, but military aid would be withheld. As if to emphasize American partnership rather than American domination, he adopted a policy of reducing conventional military forces. Thus the SALT discussions began to move ahead rapidly, and in the spring of 1972 negotiators completed the drafting of two important arms accords. The first was a treaty that limited to two the number of ABM (antiballistic missile) sites in either the United States or the USSR; it also permitted monitoring by means of photoreconnaissance satellites. The second was an Interim Agreement that imposed a five-year ban on increasing the number of strategic offensive missiles in either nation's arsenal. Nixon flew to Moscow to join party chairman Leonid Brezhnev in signing the accords on May 26, and the two leaders used the occasion to draw up other agreements. Among them was one to improve trade and another to liquidate the World War II lend-lease obligation of the Russians.

Even more astonishing to veteran Nixon watchers was his willingness to improve relations with the People's Republic of China. Beginning with the visit of a table tennis team in the spring of 1971, a stream of Americans traveled to Peking. Chinese leaders made clear that they would welcome an official delegation—in part because of a rift with the USSR and in part because of Japan's remarkable economic growth, they were ready to emerge from relative isolation—and on July 15 Nixon announced that he would oblige. Presidential adviser Henry Kissinger arranged the details for the visit, which came off without a hitch in February 1972. Nixon and Premier Chou En-lai issued a joint communiqué in which they expressed a desire to settle differences over Taiwan, Korea, and Indochina and proposed expansion of trade and cultural associations. In the wake of the new

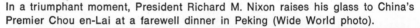

In a triumphant moment, President Richard M. Nixon raises his glass to China's Premier Chou en-Lai at a farewell dinner in Peking (Wide World photo).

Sino-American relationship came further agreements among other countries: China gained admission to the United Nations, and Japanese premier Kakuei Tanaka agreed to recognize Peking's claims on Taiwan.

The most important agreement, the one that would bring American forces home from Vietnam, remained to be worked out. Although Nixon never revealed specific details of the plan to which he referred during the campaign of 1968, he did develop a policy he called Vietnamization. The term was used to suggest that South Vietnamese units would assume more combat responsibility as they improved their military proficiency. American troops might then be withdrawn from the fighting and brought home. To speed the process of Vietnamization the President employed massive air attacks to destroy bases of supply in the North and to support ground operations wherever necessary. As a strategy of military withdrawal the policy worked, albeit with delays that seemed endless and breaks in the pattern that looked far more like escalation than withdrawal.

On at least three occasions Nixon appeared to be expanding the war. In the spring of 1970 a joint United States–South Vietnamese force invaded neutralist Cambodia after a coup led by General Lon Nol had ousted Prince Norodom Sihanouk. The invaders were to search for and destroy the bases and supply areas from which the North Vietnamese were launching attacks on the South. In late June, Nixon termed the operation a success (though what it had successfully accomplished was never very clear), and American forces returned to South Vietnam. American bombers, however, continued to attack targets in Cambodia, and also in Laos. A second operation with escalation possibilities was a South Vietnamese attack on Laos in February 1971. Unsuccessful as an offensive maneuver, it raised doubts about Vietnamization and a fear that American forces would have to rescue South Vietnamese troops. Yet intervention in the action proved unnecessary, and indeed the region near the 17th parallel grew more calm. The relative quiet came to an end in March 1972, when the North Vietnamese began a major offensive. American ground forces were not involved in the defensive action, but air raids into North Vietnam were increased. The President also ordered the mining of Haiphong harbor. The move was intended to cut off the flow of supplies from North Vietnam's supporters, but it also aroused the concern of Americans who had had their fill of war.

Doves found little to praise in Nixon's Vietnam policies during his first three years in office, but nevertheless the war was winding down for American forces. Beginning in 1969 there were periodic troop withdrawals until finally the last American soldier left for home in March 1973. What made possible his return was the conclusion of long drawn-out negotiations that had begun in Paris while Lyndon Johnson was still president. Bickering at the peace table had been enough to try the patience of all involved, not to mention the people, governments, and forces they represented. The propaganda moves, the jockeying for position, and the exaggerated demands of both sides were frustrating, sometimes obscuring the central issues under discussion: arrangements for withdrawing troops, ending the bombing, and bringing about first a truce and then a final peace settlement. The North Vietnamese negotiators argued that no meaningful terms could be drafted until American troops and planes had been pulled out of action, while the Americans refused to consider withdrawal until the release of prisoners of war.

Finally, after seemingly interminable postponements, evidences of bad faith and threats of more massive bombing, secret discussions between Kissinger and North Vietnamese diplomats Le Duc Tho and Xuan Thuy led to an agreement early in 1973. Signed in Paris on January 27, the settlement went into effect immediately. All remaining U.S. troops were to be withdrawn within sixty days, and all American military bases were to be dismantled. Mines along the North Vietnamese coast were to be deactivated and removed immediately. For their part, the North Vietnamese would release all American prisoners of war at staged intervals over the next two months. To supervise the truce there would be two teams of observers, one an international group (with members from Canada, Poland, Hungary, and Indonesia) and the other including members from the United States, North Vietnam, South Vietnam, and the Vietcong. The existing South Vietnamese government would remain in power until a council representing various Vietnamese political factions could make arrangements for a national election. The longest and most unpopular war in the nation's history had come to an end—at least for the American people.

**The Emergence of a New Left**

The struggle in Vietnam exposed fundamental disagreements about the proper organization of society at home as well as the proper role of the United States in foreign affairs, and all segments of the American population were profoundly affected by the discord. Yet the social distress and disruption of the sixties were so closely associated with the young—with the maturing children of the post-World War II baby boom—that the behavior of the nation's youth became a focus of concern. At their best many young people were astute moral critics, and they demonstrated time and again their willingness to act on the principles they professed. Others responded to the pressures of the decade, absorbing ideas that came to them from more thoughtful associates. Some "dropped out," joining the flower children and the hippies of an American counterculture. Some shared the attitudes of the society in which they grew up, and they continued to observe its conventions. Most young people who reached maturity in the sixties were neither so rebellious as their elders feared nor so revolutionary as they themselves thought they were. Their number was nevertheless great enough to compel attention (in 1963, 27 million Americans were between fifteen and twenty-four years of age), and the issues that agitated many of them were basic enough to require consideration.

The twisting intricacies of protest and the drive for social change that gave rise to what became known as "the Movement" challenged analysts of every persuasion. Although activists of the era identified themselves as radicals with left-wing views, they were a different breed from the militants of the depression thirties, the "Old Left." For one thing, the "New Left" did not develop out of a commitment to Marxist or Leninist ideology. The Movement was remarkably free of dogma, and its leaders deliberately sought to avoid the formal rigidities of any system. Theirs was a radicalism that expressed itself in deeds rather than words, in tactics rather than strategy, in moral rather than in intellectual commitment. They would not adhere to a *party* line—for they distrusted all organization—but they spoke repeatedly of putting their *bodies* on the line.

The New Left, to be sure, developed its coterie of intellectual heroes. Most of them were critics who not only attacked the conformity of the fifties à la William H. Whyte, but also urged a break from institutional controls. Paul Goodman, for example, argued against an educational system that was concerned with "fitting the man to the machine and chopping him down to fit." He encouraged a search for opportunities in the economy that might bring out the man, "and if you can't find such an opportunity, make it." Columbia University sociologist C. Wright Mills denounced "smug conservatives" and "tired liberals" for celebrating what his colleague, Daniel Bell, called "the end of ideology." Their mistake, Mills insisted, was in searching for militancy in the wrong place. Radicalism no longer drove the working classes, for prosperity had made them docile, but it did drive the young intellectuals. They were the "radical agency of change" that would bring the age of complacency to an end. Herbert Marcuse, combining the Marxian idea of alienation with the Freudian idea of repression, emphasized the power of an advanced industrial society to contain "qualitative change." But he also suggested "that forces and tendencies exist which may break this containment and explode the society."

Such ideas appealed to the New Left because they were consistent with what its adherents already believed. The ideas, in other words, did not give rise to the Movement; they reinforced it. What, then, did generate the agitation of the sixties? The young people who took part in it were not a downtrodden proletariat, but beneficiaries of the post-World War II affluence. Aside from their youth, the radicals of the sixties shared other characteristics. They were, for the most part, reared in comfortable though often sterile middle-class surroundings, and they were comparatively well educated. The fact that much of the decade's disruption centered on college campuses is an indication of the background and training of the rebels. White, laboring-class youths who did not go to college but entered the work force after high school were seldom drawn into the Movement.

The conditions that attracted the attention of protesters were ones most likely to arouse a visceral response among idealistic and informed young people. They read John Kenneth Galbraith's *The Affluent Society* (1958) or Michael Harrington's *The Other America* (1963), finding confirmation of what many of them suspected: that the post-World War II prosperity did not reach into every corner of the United States. The civil rights movement made them aware first of the disabilities experienced by blacks, and then of the discrimination practiced against Spanish-Americans, American Indians, the elderly, migrant workers, and many other groups. The same concern that made young people sensitive to the needs of underprivileged groups at home led them to search for world brotherhood. But just as their deepening understanding of the minorities' problems exposed them to the evils of racism, their quest for international good will brought them into grim contact with Cold War rivalries. And in time many of them began to believe that American policy did not square with the righteous clichés on which most of them had been weaned.

Idealism is a universal characteristic of youth. Why did the idealism of those who were young in the sixties give rise to radicalism? A partial answer to that question lies in the experience of growing up in an environment far different from that of their parents' childhood, an experience that prompted much discussion of a "generation gap." Fathers and mothers had known the privations of depression and the anxieties of war. Even though the years after 1945 had brought a change of fortune, they could not suddenly stop thinking of themselves as members of a sacrificial generation. The two searing crises of their lives had left them, as University of Michigan Professor John W. Aldridge put it, "with no resources . . . out of the past, no norms or precedents of conduct, no tradition of amenities or graces, luxuries or even comfort." Thankful that the moderate New Deal had preserved American values and that the Allies had triumphed over the Axis evil, they had "bulldozed the land into rubble . . . and laid out thousands and thousands of miles of company streets all lined with family sized barracks." There, in the now peaceful and prosperous suburbs of middle-class America, they would continue to sacrifice; they would devote themselves to their offspring and perhaps find fulfillment through them.

The children who grew up in that environment, and who bore the psychological burdens of family hopes, had no wish to duplicate the sacrifices of their parents. Furthermore, it seemed to many of them that striving for success as their elders had done only deadened the spirit, for the institutional style of life that accompanied it offered few opportunities for creativity or originality. In only one institution, the institution of higher learning, did many middle-class children see much hope of redemption. Happily, their families were as eager to send them to college as they were to go. Once there, the children of affluence would blossom, cultivate good taste, savor the ideas of important thinkers, and enjoy the varied activities of the campus. Or so they believed.

Colleges and universities, however, were rapidly filling up as a result of the postwar population explosion and the prosperity that made educational expenses relatively easy to meet. With eager young people anxiously filling out application forms and even more anxiously taking entrance and scholastic aptitude examinations, many institutions of higher learning became painstakingly selective. Some applicants were rejected by the colleges

This remarkable confrontation occurred at the 1970 Goose Lake, Michigan rock
festival. Counterculture fashion, style, and behavior were often deeply disturbing to
Americans of conventional taste. Such "straight" folk might be amused, intrigued,
shocked, or contemptuous, but they generally viewed the "hippies" as degenerates.
For their part, the children of the counterculture cared little for conventional
opinions (John Collier, Black Star).

they chose, and adjustment to the disappointment of having to settle for
a second or third alternative was sometimes difficult. Those whose grades
and test scores were good enough to merit admission were not always better
off. The competition had a way of inflating expectations; and, anticipating
greater satisfactions than any college could provide, they, too, were disappointed.

The colleges and universities were far from blameless. They seem to
have sold themselves as well as young people on the superior virtues of
academe, gradually developing a hubris that many students found intolerable. In the early fifties, when McCarthyism aroused fears of Communism on the campus, educational institutions had become defensive.
After the witch hunt subsided, some of them threw up a network of regulations to control student activity and to keep peace between town and
gown. They hoped, thereby, to allay distrust and so prevent the incursions
of patriots with little understanding of academic freedom. In 1959 the
University of California at Berkeley, for example, issued directives that
placed the student government under the chancellor's supervision and

forbade it to take positions on off-campus issues. While such regulations were disturbingly authoritarian, the universities could ignore complaints because they had such an enormous pool of qualified applicants on which to draw. Thus for many students the university that had promised so much turned out to be just another cold, repressive institution that stifled creativity and critical thinking.

The conditions they confronted led young people to consider means of changing them, and that, of course, implied organization. Already in existence were several student groups that might be used as vehicles for the discontented. The National Student Association, made up of student governments from several hundred colleges and universities, was identified with liberal causes. It had, for example, solicited the support of northern students for civil rights activities. But the NSA had little influence over ordinary undergraduates on individual campuses; it was, furthermore, secretly funded by the Central Intelligence Agency to counteract the Communist threat. The Student Peace Union, organized in 1959, was an association with particular appeal for pacifists; after a brief period of growth, however, it fell into disarray with ratification of the atomic test-ban treaty in September 1963. The Young People's Socialist League was for a time the most influential organization professing radical views, yet it lived in the past and spent much of its effort in distributing dated polemics against the class structure. Far more extremist was the Trotskyist Young Socialist Alliance, but it was too radical to attract a large following.

The limited appeal of such organizations left only the Student League for Industrial Democracy (SLID), which had been formed in 1930 under the auspices of the socialist League for Industrial Democracy. During the depression SLID had merged with another group to become the American Student Union, but then in 1945 it returned to its original name. With the campus dissatisfaction of the late fifties providing new opportunities for growth, SLID underwent another reorganization and emerged as Students for a Democratic Society (SDS). A loose coalition of various groups unhappy with their remoteness from the decision-making process, SDS sought to unite "liberals and radicals, activists and scholars, students and faculty" in a force that would preserve "maximum freedom for the individual."

The hopes of SDS leaders involved them in a dilemma that they were never able to resolve. They wanted, on the one hand, to correct the social flaws of an advanced capitalist economy, the banalities and the shortcomings they read about in the writings of Goodman, Mills, Marcuse, and others, including Marx. But, on the other hand, they wished to avoid the dangers of organization. They did not want to set SDS up as a "vanguard party" that would impose rigid discipline, become authoritarian in preserving its own ideological purity, and in the end turn out to be as repressive as the institutions they were seeking to change. Holding its annual convention at Port Huron, Michigan, in the summer of 1962, the fledgling SDS worked out a formula that seemed to offer possibilities of overcoming the dilemma. Its "Port Huron Statement" called for "the establishment of a democracy of individual participation," a kind of free-form system that was difficult to regard as a system at all.

The SDS program of participatory democracy would presumably give individual citizens a chance to make decisions in matters affecting their own lives. Far better than the prevailing institutions, thought members of the organization, it would serve the needs of minorities, the poor and underprivileged, and, of course, university students. They were also realistic enough to recognize that participatory democracy might be impossible to achieve. Thinking it worth attempting, nevertheless, they set about changing the society without exercising effective control over the forces of change. That the Movement turned out to be chaotic and disorganized was not surprising. Most of the young people who took part in it shared the SDS preference for individual choices made under an umbrella of general good will and the SDS aversion to corporate decisions made by a few and imposed on the many.

**Years of Violence and Disruption**
The children of the postwar baby boom began appearing in college classrooms in the early sixties; they were just beginning to express their dissatisfaction with the experience when John F. Kennedy made his ill-fated trip to Dallas in late November 1963. The president's assassination on the 22nd perhaps affected students even more profoundly than it did others, and two consequences of his death were particularly important. In the first place, the assassin's bullet stilled the voice of one who had spoken eloquently for involvement in great causes. In making that appeal, Kennedy had in some measure given direction to activities of the young. Later, after his death, the shining moment that was Camelot lost its brilliance for young dissidents, but in the fall of 1963 college students mourned the first president with whom many of them could closely identify. Second, a commission of inquiry, headed by Chief Justice Earl Warren, seemed careless in conducting its investigation of the tragedy. It failed to answer questions that many young people were asking. While the Warren Report gained general acceptance with its reassurance that the assassin was indeed Lee Harvey Oswald, an emotionally disturbed loner, it did not satisfy a generation that had grown up absorbed by the intricate plots of television mystery and spy dramas. To many of the young, the report was simplistic and contained special pleading; far from reassuring them, it aroused their skepticism and distrust of authority.

Following the crime in Dallas young people resolved—as did Lyndon Johnson—to work for the completion of Kennedy's civil rights program. At the close of the academic year Congress was just putting the finishing touches on the most far-reaching Civil Rights Act since Reconstruction. Filled with enthusiasm for the cause, hundreds of students headed for the Deep South to register black voters and to help out in other ways. The hostility they encountered there produced a sense of outrage at the inequities of racial discrimination, but even more painful was their failure to secure from the Justice Department the protection against harassment that they requested. Especially disturbing was the murder of three civil rights workers in Nashoba County, Mississippi, though twelve other persons were also killed in different areas. "There is a town in Mississippi named Liberty," went one bitter comment. "There is a department in Washington named Justice." The results of Freedom Summer were difficult to assess; but, by the time it was over, one effect had become obvious. Government officials had lost another large portion of their credibility, and experiences with the black struggle for equality had made civil rights workers more sympathetic to radical change.

When they returned to classes in the fall of 1964, students were in no frame of mind to put up with nonsense. The first semester had hardly opened when the news media began to carry reports of activities in Berkeley that captured the attention of young people on campuses across the country. After Freedom Summer the University of California ban on solicitation for off-campus political activity could easily be interpreted as a deliberate effort to hurt the civil rights cause. California dissidents, many of whom were eager to try out on the campus the direct action tactics they had used in the South, organized the Free Speech Movement with the help of CORE, SNCC, and national leaders such as James Farmer and John Lewis. The first of many campus demonstrations that were to follow, FSM directed attention not only to authoritarian tendencies of universities but also to their complicity in the evils of the society as a whole. Just as Freedom Summer undermined faith in public officials, the FSM greatly reduced the respect that young people had for universities. After a troubled fall, Berkeley officials lifted restrictions on student political activities, but they could do little to restore student confidence.

Shortly after the Berkeley revolt, dissidence increased. It also took a new direction. In January 1965 the Johnson administration began systematic bombing of North Vietnam and committed itself to sending the troops needed for victory in the Indochina conflict. Although whites continued to be active in civil rights efforts until the following year, the war now became a consuming interest. Again the universities and colleges were caught in the coils of recent history, and they paid dearly for policies that had seemed wise and circumspect during the early Cold War period.

At the time of the Korean conflict educators had been concerned with maintaining enrollments as manpower demands mounted. They therefore lobbied vigorously to continue the student deferments provided by the Selective Service Act of 1948. Although their arguments were not always sound (the nation, went one of the most reprehensible, should not grind up its seed corn), they succeeded. Throughout the sixties a college student could be deferred so long as he maintained a creditable record. Thus, for male students at least, the normal pressures of higher learning were increased, as was the sense of guilt that always to some extent accompanied the privilege of pursuing it. Perhaps it was the guilt, seldom openly expressed, that led many young people to question the righteousness of

American foreign policy. It may also have led them to sympathize with those revolutionary movements in the Third World that the United States seemed all too willing to oppose with armed force. In any case, few students could ever look forward with enthusiasm to spending two years in the Army after receiving their baccalaureate degrees. When the United States increased its forces in Vietnam, however, and when the war lengthened despite that increase, resistance to the draft became intense.

Opposition to the Vietnam war was by no means confined to those who were subject to conscription. For two years after the president began systematic bombing of the North, protest took the form of public demonstrations similar to those employed in the civil rights movement. SDS sponsored a March on Washington in the spring of 1965, and in the fall local demonstrations were carried out across the country under the general rubric of "International Days of Protest." Many campuses held "teach-ins" to familiarize students with the issues in Vietnam and to emphasize the domestic consequences of the American commitment. For those who took part in them, the teach-ins provided a refreshing departure from formal instruction in the classroom. Students could discuss subjects they considered "relevant," subjects such as the way a military-industrial complex ordered their lives and was attempting to bend the world to its will. By mid-1966, after black people had insisted upon taking racial concerns into their own hands and had suggested that white civil-rights workers set their own house in order, student attention began to focus more sharply on the universities. Campus dissidents organized new forms of protest such as the demonstrations against recruiters for the Dow Chemical Company, a firm that manufactured napalm used in Vietnam. The symbolism was clear. To many young people, educational institutions came to seem not just authoritarian but an integral part of military-industrial repression.

Few developments could have produced a greater sense of alienation among the young, or have been more conducive to dropping out. The bohemian cultural rebellion that began with the beatniks of the fifties attracted hippies and others with no stomach for the struggles of life in the early sixties. It set a pattern to which many young people now turned. The beats had rejected the bourgeois materialism of American society, flouted its conventions, and devoted themselves to a wandering existence that centered on sex and drugs. In the early sixties the drugs changed with the increased use of LSD. Hippies then appeared on the scene to develop a psychedelic culture featuring rock music and light shows, outlandish apparel, and a variety of cults and communal societies. For a time it all seemed a delightful alternative to the straight society with its hang-ups, but the fun and games were ephemeral. The flower children talked about peace, love, and beauty. In the Haight-Ashbury section of San Francisco or the East Village in New York, however, self-pity was more common than sensitivity, freaking out more common than fulfillment, and hepatitis more common than happiness. Death stalked the streets with the pushers and other intruders bent on destruction. Young men of the counterculture

As a candidate in the Democratic primaries of 1968, Senator Eugene McCarthy inspired support from college students that amounted to adulation. Intellectually oriented, he did not achieve sufficient political backing to win nomination at the Chicago convention (Robert Azzi, Nancy Palmer Photo Agency).

were often beaten up by the terrorist gangs such as Hell's Angels, and young women were easy marks for rapists.

To a degree the counterculture impinged upon the universities. On almost any campus one could find its symbols—the costumes and the hair, the drugs and the "grass"—but more apparent than the despair of the dropout was the anger of the activist. The anger peaked in 1968. In the spring an SDS-led uprising at Columbia brought forceful seizure of several buildings and effectively shut down the University during the last month of the semester. Confrontation became the order of the day, and other campuses experienced increasingly violent unrest in the fall. Furious polemics whipped up crowds of students to a high pitch of excitement and blasted them off to "trash" windows and wreak destruction. Police and national guardsmen attempted to keep order, but they were easy to elude and often inexperienced in crowd control.

In 1968, too, unrest and anger spread from the colleges and universities into the society. The assassination of Martin Luther King on April 4 and of Robert Kennedy on June 5, though individual acts of violence, were widely interpreted as signs of a deep and expanding social malaise. In that atmosphere Eugene McCarthy's primary campaign took on enormous importance, for his was a voice of sanity that had reached large numbers of young protesters as well as older citizens who opposed continuation of the war. His sizable vote in conservative New Hampshire was a moral victory, and his impending victory in Wisconsin had prompted the president's unexpected announcement of March 31: "I shall not seek, and I will not accept, the nomination of my party for another term as your President." Johnson's withdrawal from the campaign was testimony to the power of protest.

# Three Phases of Protest

The decade of the sixties, at once exciting and terrifying, poses problems of analysis that challenge the historical imagination. To begin with, there were conditioning influences: the depression and wartime experiences of anyone who had reached the age of thirty by 1960; the postwar prosperity that permitted both a high birth rate and a blossoming of consumer culture; the technological breakthroughs that revolutionized communications, created new products for consumers, and impelled the American people toward uniform patterns of thought and behavior.

Yet had those influences dominated absolutely, the sixties would have taken on a character very different from the one that developed. Events such as the assassination of John F. Kennedy brought imponderable and immeasurable consequences. So, too, did perceptions of events. The meaning commonly attached to construction of missile sites in Cuba, for example, forced Americans to consider nuclear war as a possible response to Soviet penetration of the Western hemisphere. Except in abstractions, the public nous may be incapable of contemplating anything so destructive. In any case, the torment of anxiety had the effect of twisting thoughts, warping minds.

Many people adopted a TV spy thriller view of life as a contest between conspirator/lover-of-justice and oppressor/upholder-of-law-and-order. It was a time of protest and demonstration, when cleavages became palpable. In the protests, to be sure, naive and stripling absurdities abounded; so also did visions of a new heaven and a new earth. During the decade of the sixties toxic lunacy and tonic sanity were never, it seemed, very far apart. Examining selected features of the protests, as recorded on film, may provide insight into a troubled time and thus deepen comprehension of the concerns that moved Americans.

National guardsmen watched as smoke from burning buildings polluted the skies over Chicago in the spring of 1968. Disillusionment with nonviolence had already become evident during the long, hot summers of the middle sixties as troubled black ghettoes broke out in flame. Now, in April, the assassination of Martin Luther King provoked multiple outbursts of passion across the land (Tom Kneebone and the Chicago Historical Society).

474

In October 1960 a hundred young blacks took seats at the "whites only" section of a Woolworth restaurant in Atlanta. Sit-ins had begun eight months earlier in Greensboro, North Carolina, when four black students were denied service at a downtown lunch counter. They had stayed put and, ignoring the taunts of white racists, had returned day after day. Their exemplary courage and dignity won support in other parts of the country, and the sit-in became an effective tactic of the civil rights movement (Wide World photo).

Black protests against segregationist policies were almost always nonviolent during the early sixties. The same could not be said for white reaction to the protesters. Firemen in Birmingham, Alabama, turned their hoses full force on a peaceful demonstration in 1963 (Wide World photo).

During the summer of 1963 various civil rights organizations united to sponsor the "March on Washington for Jobs and Freedom." Carrying signs that emphasized their goals, and led by Martin Luther King, Jr., Bayard Rustin, Roy Wilkins, A. Philip Randolph, and others, the marchers were optimistic. King closed his famous address at the Lincoln Memorial with the assertion that later became his epitaph: "Free at last, free at last, thank God Almighty I'm free at last" (United Press International photo).

This SDS poster, with its unflattering caricature of Mayor Daley, urged opponents of the Vietnam war to join a demonstration timed to coincide with the Democratic National Convention of 1968. "The majority of the American people want the United States to stop the bombing and get out of Vietnam," proclaimed a handbill of the National Mobilization Committee. "The politicians are in Chicago threatening to continue the war and to suppress opposition" (Chicago Historical Society).

As black activists became increasingly militant and increasingly aware of a need to control their own affairs, the escalating violence in Indochina represented a new affront to idealist sensibilities. Thus the middle years of the sixties—particularly after American bombers began systematic raids on North Vietnam—were years in which protest began to focus on the "dirty war" (Charles Harbutt, Magnum Photos).

Antiwar demonstrators in Chicago were far from united in tactics: the National Mobilization Committee wanted to distribute leaflets and persuade; SDS sought to recruit new members; the Youth International Party (Yippies) favored a "festival of life" and ridicule. The Chicago police seem to have been more purposeful if less cerebral. "The cops had one thing on their mind," observed Jimmy Breslin. "Club and then gas, club and then gas, club and then gas." A particularly violent confrontation occurred near "The Haymarket" restaurant (United Press International photo).

The Kent State killings brought a sense of horror to college students everywhere, but it was not only students who were shocked by the violence of war. Nor was it the first time that others expressed their concern. This father took his daughter to a 1967 Veterans' Day protest in Union Square, New York. Among the antiwar organizations none had more credibility than did the Veterans for Peace in Vietnam (Shelly Rusten).

The invasion of Cambodia on April 29, 1970 provoked protests across the country, but the most shocking development took place at Ohio's second largest university. On May 4 national guardsmen moved ominously across the campus at Kent State, firing tear gas at taunting students as they advanced. Suddenly, for no apparent reason, the guardsmen opened fire with their M-1 rifles. The body count: four students dead (two of them young women on their way to class) and nine wounded (one paralyzed with a bullet in his spine) (United Press International photo).

This march for women's liberation picked up themes that were as old as Lysistrata. Civil rights and antiwar organizations of the sixties —not distinguished for their recognition of women's rights—nevertheless served to produce an atmosphere conducive to a new feminism (Wide World photo).

Betty Friedan's book, *The Feminine Mystique* (1963) brought into focus the dissatisfaction of many women eager to abandon the housewife role. "To say that a woman is really 'happy' with her home and kids is as irrelevant as saying that the blacks were 'happy' being taken care of by Ol' Massa," was Ti-Grace Atkinson's way of putting it. "She is defined by her maintenance role. Her husband is defined by his productive role. We're saying that *all* human beings should have a productive role in society" (Burt Glinn, Magnum Photos).

Legalized abortion, most feminists insisted, was crucial to the achievement of career opportunities for women. Childbirth and child care had always imposed handicaps on employed women and had worked against on-the-job advancement. With overpopulation posing a threat to human welfare, however, traditional and moral opposition to abortion began to seem senseless. In 1970 more than 200,000 women received legal abortions, and in 1973 the United States Supreme Court struck down the antiabortion statutes of Texas and Georgia (Dennis Brack, Black Star).

Men who categorically insisted upon male superiority might have profited from this woman's warning, but if they were indeed "male chauvinists" they paid little attention. Nicolas Chauvin was a French soldier who fought in the French Revolutionary and Napoleonic wars. Pleased with his military honors and a small pension, he became famous for his simple-minded devotion to Napoleon. Thus the meaning of *chauvinism:* a blind, excessive, and unreasoning patriotism or loyalty that is amenable neither to fact nor logic (Black Star).

In 1966 Friedan and other feminists established the National Organization for Women (NOW). Concerned with enforcement of Title VII of the 1964 Civil Rights Act, which prohibits sex discrimination in employment, NOW has often been regarded as the NAACP of the feminist movement. Other organizations might be more radical, but all opposed discrimination against women in employment as well as in institutions such as bars, clubs, sporting events, or political parties (Leonard Freed, Magnum Photos).

**Passion, Violence,
and Demography**

When the Democratic National Convention met in Chicago that summer of 1968, confrontations between demonstrators and Mayor Daley's police kept the city in turmoil. Although it was not so apparent at the time, however, the demise of the radical movement was already under way. The first clear signal of New Left disarray was the breakup of SDS in the spring of 1969. The organization split into two groups, one associating itself with the Progressive Labor party, and the other—more violent—faction identifying itself as the Weathermen. Demonstrations and protests continued during Nixon's first years in the White House, to be sure, and the Cambodian invasion of 1970 produced uprisings that were even more shocking and bloody than those that had taken place in 1968. Yet in a curious way the violence of 1970 placed the violence of the decade in perspective. Far from indicating the triumph of revolution, it marked more profoundly than did the collapse of SDS the death of "the Movement."

Philosopher J. Glenn Gray was one of the few persons wise enough to grasp the meaning of disruptions in the sixties. His remarkably clear-headed 1970 essay, *On Understanding Violence Philosophically*, drew some distinctions that are important to an understanding of the era. The appeal of violence, he wrote, grows out of an inability to act effectively. Major forces in the twentieth century—industrialization, technology, overpopulation, and the like—greatly reduce the capacity to act in significant ways or to believe in the importance of one's individuality. Frustration of the power to act creates passions. Passion, a word often misused, suggests "a being acted upon from without in contrast to an action which is initiated within." It is, as properly employed by theologians when they speak of the passion of Christ, "a kind of suffering in which we are handed over to external forces, are acted upon, and are rendered unfree." A characteristic response to passion is violence, and so it was with the violence of the sixties.

In the sometimes careless diction of the decade, as Hannah Arendt wrote in another essay on the subject published in *The Journal of International Affairs* in 1969, the term *violence* was frequently used interchangeably with other terms such as *power, force, strength,* or *authority.* Force, an exercise of legitimate power and right for the achievement of societal ends, may be used to control rioting citizens. But when those who exercise force succumb to rage or resentment—that is to say, when they are seized by passion—their actions lose legitimacy and become violence. Even the most casual observer of demonstrations and disturbances in the sixties could not fail to detect evidences of violent behavior among officials who were supposed to be upholding the law.

Furthermore, if official violence could be found in the United States, it was even more common in Vietnam. All wars produce atrocities, and this one had its full share. Beyond shameful episodes such as the massacre at My Lai, the invasion of Cambodia in 1970 seemed an illegitimate exercise of power, that is, a violent move. Students at Kent State University, like students across the nation, protested the action with violence of their own.

Ohio Governor James Rhodes called out the national guard, and on May 4 the guardsmen precipitated a national crisis. Incredibly, they fired their M-1 rifles into a crowd of students, killing four and wounding nine. Kent State would serve as the best example of confusion about the difference between force and violence; it would stand as a reminder that violent behavior was not characteristic of young radicals alone.

"Power to the People!" was one of the cries that thundered from throngs of protesters during the demonstrations of the late sixties and early seventies. But who were the people? The cry was a passionate one, and those who raised it meant to include all persons who were acted upon and rendered unfree. Yet it was the young that the chanters really had in mind. It was the children of the postwar baby boom, now growing into adolescence and young adulthood, who saw themselves as being constantly tested, programmed, rejected by society, and conscripted into the Army. Adolescence is and always has been a difficult time of life, if only because of biological changes taking place. It is also then that people make tentative career decisions, develop associations outside the family, and formulate the thoughts that will give them a character of their own. All people who go through the process of developing a mature identity tend to be peculiarly sensitive to pressures they cannot control. That sensitivity was as characteristic of teenagers in 1870 as it was of teenagers in 1970, and it was characteristic of adolescents in all the intervening years as well.

What distinguished the young people born during the postwar baby boom was not so much their individual difficulties in growing to maturity and achieving a self, but their numbers. As Peter Drucker has suggested, the demographic shifts of the postwar period had much to do with violent disturbances that climaxed at the time of the Cambodian invasion and the Kent State killings. During the decade after 1945 the total number of babies born in the United States each year increased by almost 50 per cent, and total births remained at a high level (more than four million annually) until the 1960s. That astonishing increase in births meant that by 1964 the largest single age group beyond childhood was seventeen years old, and for seven years thereafter it would steadily increase in number. The most sizable age group of the 1960s was younger than at any time since the early nineteenth century. What made its ascendancy even more impressive was that in 1960 the largest age group had been composed of people in their late thirties. Even without racial conflict and a war in Vietnam, a demographic shift of such proportions would have had a profound impact on American society. Yet the war, in particular, gave them a cause, and their numbers gave them a sense of strength. They would, as some of their leaders put it, restructure American society.

But would they? Because the baby boom was followed by a baby bust after 1960, the dominant age group in the United States grew older with each passing year. Whatever the limits placed upon them, students of the sixties had at least commanded resources that allowed them to act on their convictions. They could afford to be radical. Children of prosperity, they did not expect to encounter difficulty finding places in a booming economy after they graduated; in the meantime, they would act to humanize the business and professional world they expected to enter. But in the seventies, when demonstrators of the late sixties began to think about jobs and salaries, tables and chairs and food on the tables, they were brought up short by a new reality. Numbers that had been an asset in the cause of radical change, and in the cause of peace, could place such pressure on the economy as to seem almost a liability. Furthermore, the drop in birthrate after the boom served to throw job markets severely out of line with prevailing markets of the sixties. Placing a college graduate in the job of his choice became increasingly difficult; securing a satisfactory position in the seventies proved as traumatic for the youngest of the baby-boom generation as gaining entrance into the college of preference had been for the oldest.

The situation was particularly tight for those seeking careers in the professions. The baby bust brought stable or declining enrollments in American schools and colleges, which had hired a total of more than five million teachers and administrators during the years from 1955 to 1970. The teacher shortage thus disappeared, and an overabundance of young educators already on the job effectively reduced opportunities for recent graduates. Students read the signs of the time and began preparing for careers in law and medicine, with the result that professional schools were inundated with applications. Like the undergraduate colleges of a decade earlier, those in law and medicine became highly selective under duress of necessity. During the spring of 1974, for example, the Loyola University Stritch School of Medicine in Maywood, Illinois, had 7,600 applicants for its first-year class; it could accept only one out of fifty-five who sought admission.

The professions were not alone in experiencing a tightening of career opportunities. The day when a college graduate could have his choice of several high-paying positions had faded into the past. In the seventies, as a greater number of college graduates began to contend for jobs in a shifting market, career competition had the effect of turning attention away from causes that had been important to young people in the sixties. Many undergraduates of the seventies worried about being forced into a pattern of downward mobility, a concern that had seldom crossed the mind of an undergraduate during the sixties. When protests occurred in the seventies, they often had an economic thrust, as did teacher strikes or trucker strikes, for example. Occasionally such protests provoked violence; but, if they did, they had more in common with disturbances of the late nineteenth century (which were also largely economic in character) than with those of the 1960s.

# 12

# Looking Backward—and Forward—from Watergate

On January 20, 1973, President Nixon delivered his second inaugural address. The republic had survived an unpopular war in Vietnam, a decade of social turmoil, and outbursts of pathological hatred that brought death to three prominent Americans and to many others who were not so prominent. "Above all else," observed the president, "the time has come for us to renew our faith in ourselves and in America." And he urged all citizens "to make these next four years the best four years in American history, so that on its 200th birthday America will be as young and as vital as when it began, and as bright a beacon of hope for all the world." Although the rhetoric suffers by comparison with that of Lincoln's second inaugural, the sentiment seemed appropriate. Ceremonial observance of the bicentennial might have no great significance in itself; but it would provide an opportunity for national stock-taking and would stimulate meditation about gains and losses over time.

**Nixon and Watergate**

Nixon's second inaugural address was a plea for national unity, an extension of appeals he had made during his campaign for the presidency in 1968 and during his campaign for reelection in 1972. In 1968, when demonstrations against the war in Vietnam and riots in black ghettoes threatened the disruption of American society, candidate Nixon had taken his stand with the advocates of law and order. He would, he promised, listen to "the voice of the great majority of Americans, the forgotten Americans, the nonshouters, the nondemonstrators." Electing him, he implied, would restore social harmony because he had a plan for peace with honor in Vietnam. And with harmony restored, maintaining law and order would present few problems.

Once in office, Nixon did not move so rapidly as the doves thought possible, but troop withdrawals and Vietnamization gradually reduced American participation in the Indochina conflict. By election time in 1972, Nixon's achievements in foreign affairs, his following among "forgotten

In the fall of 1973, President Nixon put in an appearance at a Realtors' Convention, where he enthusiastically acknowledged cheers. Despite his show of confidence, however, he had (as *The New Yorker* put it) "unexpected reserves of weakness to draw on." In the face of multiplying Watergate revelations, his campaign to regain public support proved abortive (*Newsweek,* Wally McNamee).

Americans," and awkward campaigning by the Democrats assured his re-election by an impressive majority that gave him 520 electoral votes as opposed to only 18 for McGovern. The political campaign concluded, the war also came to an end for American troops with the cease-fire of January 27, 1973. The President was surfing smoothly along the crest of a wave of success when suddenly, in the vernacular of the sport, he "wiped out." He was compelled to spend the remainder of his years as chief executive in trying to remount the presidential surfboard.

Nixon's troubles were in some respects similar to the troubles of Ulysses S. Grant, who had occupied the White House a century before. Both men would be remembered for the corruption of their administrations. To press the parallel too far would be to distort the truth, however, for the differences between the two presidents were more important than the similarities. Grant was a successful military commander whose tactics had brought defeat to the Confederacy and won him a devoted following in the Union he had helped to save. He was a straightforward, uncomplicated man, a neophyte in politics at the time of his election in 1868. Personally honest, he neither understood nor became involved in political maneuvering. He was a perfect dupe for the unscrupulous manipulators who took advantage of his naiveté. Nixon, on the other hand, had spent much of his life in politics, and his shrewd opportunism had always been a factor in his political success.

Intimations of disaster for the Nixon Administration began with a bungled break-in that led to investigations revealing a squalid interior behind the formal facade of the White House. On June 17, 1972, five men were arrested inside Democratic party headquarters at the Watergate office-hotel complex in Washington. Carrying electronic surveillance equipment, they may have been after information that might prove useful to the president. Or, as some evidence later suggested, they may have sought to retrieve information that would prove damaging to his cause. Because the incident at first appeared to be only a minor oddity of the campaign, and because of the time required to bring the burglars and two accomplices to trial, the Watergate affair had little effect on the outcome of the election. Bit by sordid bit, however, the facts began to come out. The burglars had received money from the Committee for the Reelection of the President (Nixon's personal campaign organization), and the "Watergate Seven" included CRP official James W. McCord, Jr., and CRP lawyer G. Gordon Liddy. By the end of January 1973, McCord and Liddy had been convicted of felonies, and the other five had pleaded guilty.

On March 23, at the time he imposed sentence, U.S. District Court Judge John J. Sirica read a letter from McCord alleging that other persons had also been involved, that perjury had been committed during the trial, and that pressure had been exerted on the defendants to persuade them to plead guilty. The letter produced a succession of bewildering moves. The Senate had already established a select committee to investigate the affair. Nixon announced on April 17 that he had ordered "intensive new inquiries" and that there had been "major new developments in the case."

'. . . The whole truth and nothing but the . . .'

As the tortuously unraveled facts of Watergate were laid one by one before a disbelieving American public, Nixon's credibility crumbled under the cumulative weight of his own deceptions. To cartoonist Haynie, Nixon's plight was like that of the fabled Pinocchio, whose every lie only brought his peccadillos more clearly to view. (Editorial cartoon by Hugh Haynie of the Louisville *Courier-Journal.* (c) Los Angeles Times Syndicate.)

Two weeks later, in a televised address, he accepted general responsibility (though he made clear that he did not accept specific responsibility). At the same time he announced the resignations of four prominent members of his Administration: H. R. Haldeman, his chief of staff in the White House; John D. Ehrlichman, his adviser for domestic affairs; John W. Dean III, a presidential counsel; and Richard Kleindienst, the Attorney General. If Nixon believed that he could restore confidence in his leadership by announcing four resignations and pledging impartial pursuit of justice, he was wrong. A Gallup Poll on May 4 revealed that half the people questioned thought the president was involved in covering up the scandal.

Meanwhile the affair was becoming Byzantine in its complexity. In 1971 a Defense Department analyst, Daniel Ellsberg, had photocopied a multivolume, classified study of American policy in Vietnam and released it to the press. When excerpts from the "Pentagon Papers" began to appear in the *New York Times* and the *Washington Post,* the government sought injunctions to halt publication of the document. The Supreme Court denied the request, and the government then brought suit against Ellsberg for theft, conspiracy, and espionage. The Ellsberg case seemed unrelated to Watergate until late April 1973, when District Judge William M. Byrne released a Department of Justice memorandum that associated Liddy and another Watergate conspirator, E. Howard Hunt, with burglary of the office of Ellsberg's psychiatrist. Plans to ransack the psychiatrist's files had developed out of a secret White House investigation undertaken by Ehrlichman at the president's request. The burglars had found no useful information, but Judge Byrne thought that disclosure of their activity had "incurably infected the prosecution" of Ellsberg, and he dismissed the case.

Every day seeemed to bring new revelations of irregularities in the presidential campaign and in White House operations. The Senate committee began its public hearings on May 17, and throughout the summer of 1973 television viewers were treated to a remarkable display of contrition and arrogance, condemnation and justification, as witness after witness told of his involvement in Watergate. (By now the name was used generically to identify all facets of the intricate puzzle.) John Dean's testimony was the most important because it implicated Nixon in the attempt to cover up the conspiracy. The former presidential counsel also sketched a picture of White House anxieties about political opponents, antiwar demonstrators, and social activists. Producing a list of "political enemies" from his files, he suggested that the people whose names appeared on it were considered fair game for White House headhunters. Several persons were involved in the coverup, he said, but the two men most responsible were Haldeman and Ehrlichman. The "Katzenjammer Kids," as they were called, also testified. Ehrlichman, questioned at length on the burglary at the office of Ellsberg's psychiatrist, showed little remorse. Covert operations of that nature, he contended, were necessary for the maintenance of national security.

WHY, IT'S
LAW-AND-ORDER-MAN

EXECUTIVE    PRIVILEGE

WATERGATE

The law-and-order plank of Nixon's
campaign platform became one of
the ironies of Watergate. Not even
the cloak of executive privilege
could conceal his participation in
the wrongdoing (Marlette-Charlotte
*Observer*).

Then Haldeman appeared. Former presidential aide Alexander Butterfield
had already testified that the White House and Executive Office Building
were bugged; and, when Haldeman told the committee about listening to
the tape of a crucial meeting, he set off a heated controversy over evidence.

If tapes of White House meetings were available, then key portions of
Dean's story could be checked; but the president refused to turn any tapes
over to the Senate select committee. The committee was not alone in want-
ing to hear them, however, for other persons also had investigative responsibilities. Back in April, Nixon had nominated Elliot Richardson to replace Kleindienst as Attorney General and had promised to give him full
responsibility for the Administration's own Watergate probe. At the time
of his confirmation, Richardson agreed to appoint a special Watergate
prosecutor, naming Archibald Cox, one of the professors under whom he
had studied law at Harvard. When Cox requested access to certain tapes,
Nixon rejected the request. Cox then went to Judge Sirica, who issued a
court order directing Nixon to show cause why he should not comply with
the Cox subpoena. Nixon claimed executive privilege, insisting on the
need to protect presidential privacy. Sirica was willing to recognize the
claim, but he said he would have to hear the tapes himself before he could
decide whether or not it was justified. The president turned to the U.S.
Court of Appeals to secure a ruling on the decision, and he lost. On October 12 the Court of Appeals ordered him to surrender the tapes to Sirica.

Instead of appealing to the Supreme Court, Nixon offered to compromise. Vice-President Spiro T. Agnew had just pleaded no contest to a

charge of falsifying his 1967 income tax return and had resigned his office. With the Administration under gathering clouds of suspicion, Nixon announced his concession. He proposed to prepare and make available a summary of the tapes, a summary to be validated by Senator John C. Stennis of Mississippi. When Cox rejected the compromise, however, the president ordered him "to make no further attempts by judicial process to obtain tapes, notes or memoranda of Presidential conversations." When the professor refused to obey the order, Nixon demanded that Richardson dismiss him. Richardson resigned. Then the president asked Deputy Attorney General William D. Ruckelshaus to discharge Cox. Ruckelshaus refused and was fired himself. The "Saturday night massacre" finally came to an end after Solicitor General Robert Bork carried out the dismissal of Cox. What the president gained by his actions was difficult to determine, for they provoked such an outcry that he felt compelled to relent and send the tapes to Sirica.

The controversy continued for many months, with the president's credibility all the time gradually diminishing. First it developed that because of a technical malfunction, two of the subpoenaed tapes were nonexistent. Then the U.S. District Court was asked to believe that Rose Mary Woods, Nixon's personal secretary, had inadvertently erased an eighteen-minute section of another on which a conversation between Nixon and Haldeman had been recorded. Skeptics suspected tampering with the tapes, and ex-

Despite Nixon's attempts to outdistance the Watergate scandal by focusing on other matters (such as this dedication ceremony for the Cedars of Lebanon Health Care Center, Miami), the spectre of impeachment continued to loom on his every horizon (United Press International photo).

perts supported that view. At any rate, Sirica upheld Nixon's claim of privilege on portions of the tapes and turned the remainder over to Leon Jaworski, who had replaced Cox as special prosecutor.

By the spring of 1974 the president was showing signs of strain. He began reiterating a line from his recent State of the Union address: "One year of Watergate is enough!" He also launched a strenuous campaign for public support. Courting sympathy, he attended the opening of a new auditorium for the Grand Ole Opry at Nashville, Tennessee, and—apparently to demonstrate his folksiness more than his soundness of mind—played with a yo-yo given him by country-music enthusiasts. But neither petulance nor plebeianism brought dispensation from the consequences of scandal.

Unfolding events and developments kept the Watergate open to controversy. Haldeman, Ehrlichman, and five other Nixon aides were indicted on charges of conspiring to obstruct justice by assisting in the coverup. To be sure, former Attorney-General John Mitchell and former Secretary of Commerce Maurice Stans were acquitted of perjury and conspiracy in a case involving illegal campaign contributions and fraud in the manipulation of investment funds. Yet their acquittal did nothing to lift the cloud of suspicion surrounding the Nixon administration, for Dwight Chapin, who had served as presidential appointments secretary, was convicted of lying to a grand jury about dirty tricks in the 1972 campaign. Furthermore, an investigation of Nixon's income tax returns revealed that he owed nearly a half million dollars to the Internal Revenue Service. In the meantime, Watergate prosecutor Jaworski was pressing forward in his investigations with a persistence that grew increasingly embarrassing to the president, and in the House of Representatives discussion of impeachment mounted in intensity.

Nixon's room for maneuver was gradually narrowing, though he did not seem fully conscious of how limited it had become. On April 30, a year after the departure of Haldeman, Ehrlichman, Dean, and Kleindienst, the president went on television again. This time he announced that he would make public the edited transcripts of certain subpoenaed conversations and that they would reveal all there was to know about his involvement in the Watergate affair. The transcripts, however, raised as many questions as they answered. Not only did portions of them appear to corroborate Dean's testimony, but *in toto* they unmasked a president who was astonishingly indecisive, preoccupied with trivia, and given to language that was offensive when it was not imprecise. In sum, the transcripts served to diminish rather than strengthen public confidence in Nixon.

Early in May, the House Judiciary Committee under the chairmanship of New Jersey Congressman Peter Rodino began its inquiry into the president's conduct. For two months it questioned witnesses and probed for information, compiling nineteen volumes of data and evidence in the process. In the meantime, with the Judiciary Committee hard at work, erstwhile Nixon aides continued to fare poorly in the courts. Kleindienst was fined

Hoping to forestall the inevitable, Nixon made a last attempt to exonerate himself from the burdens of Watergate. On April 30, 1974, he announced over nationwide television that edited transcripts of tapes revealing his entire part in Watergate were to be made public. The transcripts, however, only worsened his position (*Newsweek* Wally McNamee).

$100 and given a suspended one-month sentence for lying to the Senate at the time of his confirmation as attorney general. Former Special Counsel Charles W. Colson was fined $5,000 and sentenced to one to three years in prison for his part in the Ellsberg case. Ehrlichman, in turn, received a sentence of from twenty months to five years for his involvement in the Ellsberg caper.

At the end of July, in a somber mood that reflected the gravity of its undertaking, the Judiciary Committee wound up its inquiry with a week-long televised debate over recommending Nixon's impeachment to the full House of Representatives. Chairman Rodino was scrupulously fair in wielding his gavel; while he made no secret of his own position in favor of impeachment, he took great pains to assure a full and complete hearing. Thus the viewing public received a priceless lesson on the Constitution, as supporters of the president tussled with the majority that favored bringing him to trial. Led by the brilliant Charles E. Wiggins of California, Republican loyalists defended Nixon to the bitter end. Nevertheless, the vote to recommend impeachment was bipartisan. Several Republicans joined the Democratic majority to pass three articles charging the president with obstructing the administration of justice, interfering with the constitutional rights of citizens, and refusing to comply with duly authorized subpoenas. When the final tallies were counted on July 30, no one who had witnessed the proceedings—not even those who were still sympathetic to Nixon—could rightfully charge that the committee bore resemblance to a kangaroo court.

With the nation preparing for an agonizing and possibly divisive debate in the House and trial in the Senate, the Nixon administration entered its final hours. Speculation over strategy in that tense period turned up two major possibilities: in the House of Representatives, opponents of impeachment made plans to substitute a motion of censure for one to impeach; in the White House there was discussion of bypassing the House of Representatives by going directly to trial in the Senate, where Nixon might salvage enough votes ( he needed only 34) to avoid ultimate disgrace. When the end came, however, it arrived with surprising swiftness. On July 24, before the Judiciary Committee had voted to recommend impeachment, the Supreme Court had handed down an 8–0 ruling that rejected Nixon's claims to absolute executive privilege and that compelled him to turn over all tapes subpoenaed by Special Prosecutor Jaworski. The men who were now closest to the president—primarily his chief aide, Alexander Haig, and his attorney, James D. St. Clair—then learned what the tapes contained. For the first time they became aware of how deeply involved in the coverup Nixon had been from the very beginning. In a painful conference at Camp David they urged the president to admit his complicity and threatened to resign if he did not.

On August 5, Nixon complied. He issued a statement conceding that the tapes were "at variance with certain of my previous statements." He had, in other words, lied repeatedly for two years. The president's support collapsed, and though he desperately struggled to justify fighting his case through impeachment and trial, he finally realized that his was a lost cause. Republican leaders in Congress (the party's 1964 candidate, Senator Barry Goldwater of Arizona, Senate Minority Floor Leader Hugh Scott of Pennsylvania, and House Minority Leader John Rhodes of Arizona) met with Nixon at the eleventh hour. Their assessment confirmed the erosion of his strength: if brought to the House floor, impeachment was a certainty; if tried in the Senate, the president could count on no more than fifteen votes against conviction. On Thursday evening, August 8, Nixon appeared on television to announce his resignation. It had become evident, he said, "that I no longer have a strong enough political base in Congress to justify continuing" in office. After a tearful farewell he departed Washington the next morning. He was not on hand to watch Gerald Ford, the man he had named to replace Spiro Agnew, take the oath of office as thirty-eighth President of the United States.

Americans greeted Ford's accession to the presidency with a sense of relief and cautious optimism. Having been educated at the University of Michigan (a center on the football team, he was voted its most valuable player in 1934) and at Yale (where he graduated in the top third of his law school class in 1941), the new chief executive was a man of parts. No poetaster or intellectual, his mind had always moved instinctively toward practical affairs. After service in the Navy during World War II, he entered politics and won election to Congress as representative from Michigan's Fifth District. He remained in that office for a quarter century,

"Hi, guys! I'm Jerry Ford, the new substitute . . .
Geewhiz, how'd you fellas manage t'get so muddy?"

A momentary wave of relief washed over the country as Gerald Ford acceded to the presidency. The informality and openness of his first days, full of bustle and activity, created a welcome contrast to the somber mood just before Nixon's resignation. (Editorial cartoon by Hugh Haynie of the Louisville *Courier-Journal.* © Los Angeles Times Syndicate.)

cautiously compiling a conservative voting record that appealed to his constituency, and building a reputation for candor that appealed to his colleagues in the House.

It was his colleagues, as much as Nixon, who were responsible for Ford's elevation to the vice presidency after Agnew's disgrace. Nixon made the appointment because, with the storm of scandal breaking around his head, he needed to associate himself with the common sense and honesty that Ford's associates so much admired. Yet in making that appointment, as it turned out, Nixon was actually helping to assure his own downfall. Had a nonentity been waiting in the wings, there is some doubt that the House Judiciary Committee would have voted overwhelmingly for articles of impeachment, and there is every likelihood that the vote would have been more partisan. In any case, the assurance of Ford succeeding Nixon doubtless weakened the position of Republicans who opposed impeachment. Clearly, the party would suffer little, if at all, from Nixon's departure; and if a new Republican administration could succeed in the battle against inflation, which was becoming ominous and which Ford identified as "Public Enemy No. 1," the party might actually register some significant gains. Thus the Nixon resignation was accompanied by less Republican rancor than some people expected and more Republican optimism than they had thought possible. If a time of healing had not actually begun, it was at least conceivable.

**The Philadelphia Centennial**

Scandals of the Nixon administration were, by almost any standard of evaluation, as reprehensible as any ever perpetrated by officials of the United States government or their advisers. The bizarre occurrences of 1972 and subsequent years demanded an explanation, and few citizens were without some theory or hypothesis by which to make sense of the apparently senseless. Even fewer minimized Watergate's importance. Historical analysis of the scandals might logically begin at any of several points, but the following discussion goes back a hundred years. Its purpose is not to establish a direct causal relationship, but rather to suggest dimensions of the fundamental problem that produced the Watergate conspiracy. Comparing the state of the Union on the eve of its 200th birthday with the state of the Union at the time of its 100th birthday reveals more than obvious similarities between the anniversary celebrations and the scandals that marked both the opening and closing of the nation's second century.

On its 100th anniversary the United States had not yet fully recovered from the Civil War, and the Centennial Exhibition held in Philadelphia from May to November 1876 emphasized the themes of patriotism, union, and peace. Members of the commission that supervised the exhibition had taken their work seriously. They studied reports on previous fairs, especially the London Crystal Palace Exposition of 1851, and they carefully planned the placement and construction of 194 buildings on a 236-acre site in Fairmont Park. The many exhibits of the Philadelphia Centennial were intended to demonstrate advances made in manufacturing and transportation, engineering and architecture, the plastic and graphic arts, the diffusion of knowledge, and efforts to improve the moral condition of man. They left visitors with the impression that, as one of them remarked, "if America has not attained her highest eminence, she will attain it." A centennial hymn, written for the occasion by John Greenleaf Whittier, expressed confidence in divine guidance toward a brilliant future:

> Our fathers' God! from out whose hand
> The centuries fall like grains of sand,
> We meet today, united free,
> And loyal to our land and thee,
> To thank thee for the era done,
> And trust thee for the opening one.

Five major edifices dominated Fairmont Park. The Main Building was devoted to manufactures, and Memorial Hall to the fine arts; in addition, there were separate buildings for machinery, agriculture, and horticulture. Each of the exhibition halls differed from the others, for the guiding principle of the centennial's structures was associative or symbolic. Thus the agricultural building had the Gothic spires, buttresses, and vault of a medieval cathedral; it symbolized the close relationship between God and the farmer in the seasonal processes of planting, nurture, and harvest that were processes of creation and use. The horticultural building (a greenhouse for the display of living plants) incorporated Moorish and Turkish elements in its design because a colorful profusion of flowers brought to mind the exotic Near East. Inasmuch as the arts were supposed to have first reached a high level of refinement during the Renaissance, Memorial Hall was designed to suggest a sixteenth-century palace.

The symbolism of Machinery Hall and the Main Building was not so direct, and may even have been in part unconscious. The two structures were simple and functional in design, but fair-goers were more impressed by their size than by their ornamentation. Machinery Hall covered 558,550 square feet; the Main Building, the largest in the world at the time, was 1,880 feet long (the length of six football fields!) and 464 feet wide. Iron trusses resting on iron columns supported the roofs of both buildings, and the wall space of each frame was filled with a glass curtain. The designers could not let well enough alone, however, for the idea that a building's character derives from its function had not yet gained acceptance. Various embellishments and projections were added. The Machinery Building, for example, had a carillon with thirteen bells representing the thirteen original states, and over the clock in its central gallery perched a large American eagle.

The architecture of the Philadelphia Centennial was an accurate representation of popular American attitudes toward art and technology in 1876. In his hymn of celebration, Whittier had thanked God "for art and labor met in truce . . . beauty made the bride of use." Intimations of a functional aesthetic appeared here, to be sure, yet the poet and his contemporaries believed that beauty and use belonged in separate realms of experience. It was as though Americans had never read Emerson's essays. Form and function thus came into balance at the Centennial Exhibition by means of truce or marriage, but they did not fuse in organic unity.

The exhibits themselves maintained the distinction between use and beauty. Two gigantic Corliss engines standing in the center of Machinery Hall became the fair's most popular attraction. Each engine had a 10-foot stroke and a cylinder 44 inches in diameter. Between them a 56-ton flywheel made 36 stately revolutions per minute in transmitting power through an elaborate underground system of cogs and shafting to all the other machines in the hall. Neither the stationary engines nor the machines were encumbered with excessive ornamentation. They were, as anyone could plainly see, performing their work, and as functioning exhibits they needed no embellishment. They were in themselves symbolic of technological progress into the future.

Unlike the functioning machines, the fine arts went to decorative excess. Art, one contemporary commentator believed, was "the expression of something not taught by nature, the presentation of that ideal, the mere concep-

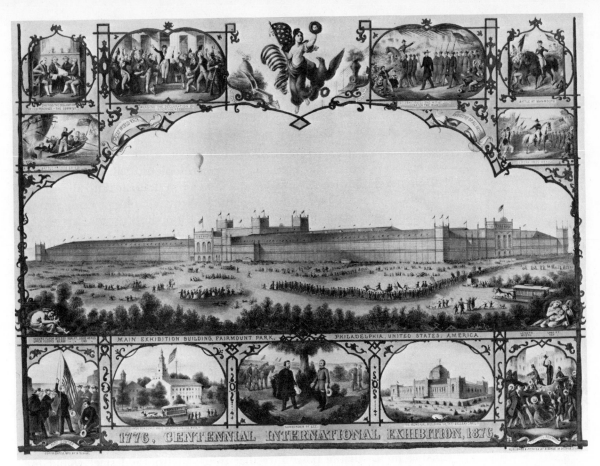

Planners of the Philadelphia Centennial Exhibition of 1876 hoped to use it as a means of re-establishing national unity and social cohesion after years of Civil War and sectional hostility. The fair's symbolism, which was supposed to have a unifying influence, could not support so heavy a burden. What emerged as the Exhibition's most impressive displays, therefore, were located in Machinery Hall and were functioning products of a technological imagination. (Courtesy of The New York Historical Society, New York City.)

tion of which raises man above the level of savagery." Sculptors and painters therefore sought to portray the American spirit in a way that would establish the superiority of American culture. They usually met aesthetic defeat in their struggles with symbolic meaning. In the rotunda of Memorial Hall stood the largest ceramic work that had ever been crafted: *America* riding a bison and guided by figures representing the United States, Canada, the Aztecs, and the Spanish conquistadors. Competing for attention was a strange assortment including a twenty-one foot Antietam soldier, a dying Cleopatra, and a colossal George Washington astride an eagle flying heavenward. Sentimental genre scenes and romantic landscapes dominated the paintings, for, like the sculptors, painters meant to glorify the historic American ethos. Some of the work was winsome (Winslow Homer's *Snap the Whip,* for example), but of fresh, new creations there was scarcely a hint. Thomas Eakins's straightforward painting of a surgical operation, *Gross Clinic,* was considered gross indeed and was hung with the medical exhibits.

Although the Centennial Exhibition achieved an uneasy truce between an uncluttered and efficient technology on the one hand and symbol-laden arts purporting to represent the American spirit on the other, the solution was neither a satisfactory synthesis nor a harmonious dualism. While symbolism and decorative extravagance continued to flourish until the turn of the century, the balance shifted rapidly toward technology. Even some of the exhibition's eight million visitors were as horrified by the arts as they were impressed by the machines. After spending a week at the fair, William Dean Howells concluded that it was "in these things of iron and steel that the national genius most freely speaks." The progress of technology, along with industrial and other influences that accompanied it, altered almost beyond recognition the society represented by Eastman Johnson's *Old Kentucky Home* or Walter Shirlaw's *Toning the Bell.*

**Twists of Time**    Howells thought the national genius benign and its expression beneficent. Yet in the way that men who controlled the things of iron and steel articulated it, the national genius struck workers, farmers, and other ordinary people as threatening rather than benign. Shortly after the Centennial Exhibition closed, the nation shook with industrial violence as Federal troops and militia were called out to counteract the forces of striking railroad workers. Periodic economic disruptions climaxing in the depression of the nineties increased the possibility that things of iron and steel would provoke enough discord to bring on the cataclysmic upheaval that Ignatius Donnelly anticipated. Yet a Brotherhood of Destruction never formed, a revolution never developed, and a Caesar Lomellini never constructed a column with the bodies of dead oligarchs. Instead, a wave of new immigrants increased the ethnic diversity of American society, discontented groups of farmers and workers focused their attention on narrow objectives, and business and industry undertook the formation of new organizations and enterprises. The return of prosperity after 1897 brought the possibility of social fragmentation and not revolution, a splintering of society that was antithetical to an organized movement of protest as well as to social cohesion.

Progressive reformers, like members of the Philadelphia Centennial Commission, were concerned with social cohesion. "The changes which have been taking place in industrial and political and social conditions have all tended to impair the consistency of feeling characteristic of the first phase of American national democracy," lamented Herbert Croly in *The Promise of American Life.* Published in 1909, the book was an important tract of the progressive period; in it, Croly urged the need for a powerful but neutral state that would act in the national interest. "The earlier homogeneity of American society has been impaired," he wrote, "and no authoritative and edifying, but conscious, social ideal has as yet taken its place." Croly's nationalism provided such an ideal; and, while other progressives developed different formulations of the concept, they all agreed that the state should take whatever action was necessary to preserve justice and promote the welfare of all Americans. The art of the Philadelphia Centennial was beginning to appear tasteless, but the manipulative approach of the artists (which they directed toward a symbolic representation of the American ethos) survived in progressivism as a function of the state.

The idea of a powerful national government, democratic in form and capable of controlling special interests for the welfare of all, gained general acceptance in the twentieth century. Through three major crises—the two world wars and an intervening depression—accretions of power made the Federal government stronger than it had ever been. Progressivism provided a moral justification for concentrated authority by associating government power with reform, efficiency, decency, prosperity, and justice. Many people, some of whom would not have identified themselves as reformers, began employing progressive rhetoric; many others, who did identify with reform causes, began calling themselves liberals. In the 1920s pundits of the New Era adopted the progressive idiom, blending it with traditional formulas to produce a rationale for prosperity. Herbert Hoover, contrary to a popular belief, did not associate that prosperity with laissez-faire but with a restrained use of government assistance. The New Deal, perhaps as different in style from the pre-World War I reform movement as it was from the New Era, drew heavily on progressive ideas in meeting economic problems that the earlier reformers had never confronted. Liberals of the thirties, unlike liberals of classical persuasion, placed unbounded confidence in the capacity of government programs to effect recovery, and FDR used his fireside chats to bring all Americans into his family circle.

Although most New Dealers abandoned claims to righteousness such as progressives had been fond of making, other features of the progressive idiom remained influential. To those Americans who remembered the earlier reform movement, World War II seemed a fulfillment of progressive hopes. More powerful than ever before, the Federal government functioned with restraint as well as efficiency. More united than ever before, citizens demonstrated their fundamental decency in a struggle against evil. More prosperous than ever before, the nation gradually began turning its attention to the achievement of justice for all segments of society. That the Axis threat had brought out the best qualities in the American character was a common belief, and the self-esteem of the American people was one reason for their willingness to accept perpetual international crisis. World War II had united them in a good cause, and during the early Cold War few citizens doubted their ability to maintain a national consensus.

There were, however, important differences between the two struggles. For one thing, Cold War dangers were far more subtle than World War II dangers had been. The anticommunism of the late forties and early fifties took the form it did in part because Americans were as uncertain about how they were being threatened as they were certain that a threat existed.

The Axis menace had been overt after Pearl Harbor, and the response it demanded was clear enough to require little reflection. But the atomic bomb made the recurrence of full-scale war unthinkable. If there was a Communist menace, therefore, it had to be subversive. And detecting it required an almost extrasensory perception of disloyal tendencies within American society.

The anticommunism of the Cold War did not directly coerce unity and homogeneity, but during the Eisenhower years its subtle influence encouraged a kind of intellectual conformity. The progressive idiom could serve that cause, too, especially in a time of great economic prosperity. American historians, for example, no longer languished like the beggar Lazarus at the gate of Dives. They had generally taken a favorable view of the progressive movement; and, while they worried about McCarthyite threats to academic freedom, they were reluctant to forego career opportunities in an affluent society. The result of such sometimes divergent concerns was "consensus history," which minimized conflict in the nation's past and cloaked the American character in progressive moralism.

Community and political leaders also saw advantages in a national consensus that would benefit the people of the world as well as American citizens. Thus in his inaugural address John F. Kennedy welcomed an opportunity to defend freedom in its hour of maximum danger, for "the energy, the faith, and the devotion which we bring to this endeavor will light our country and all who serve it, and the glow from that fire can truly light the world." Painters and sculptors who displayed their works at the Philadelphia Centennial had manipulated symbols to rebuild national unity after years of sectional cleavage and civil war. With the help of historians and other interpreters of the American character, leaders and citizens who feared the Communist threat to national solidarity were still manipulating symbols in order to preserve it a hundred years later.

In Watergate the progressive century reached its culmination. Nixon and his advisers were men of their time. They rejected neither the rhetoric of progressivism nor the social cohesion that was its principal goal. Anyone seeking to comprehend the scandal must therefore confront the difficult question of why those responsible for Watergate used odious means to achieve an end consistent with progressive values. No simple answer can suffice. At least four related influences converged in 1972: the Cold War fostered a mentality that could only regard antiwar demonstrations as weakening national solidarity and the power to do good; the president desired a reelection victory so decisive as to refute any implication of significant disagreement over American policy; electronic achievements profoundly altered the gathering and broadcasting of news, the methods of acquiring information relating to security matters, and the techniques of political campaigning; and finally, government operations had to be carried on despite insufficient precedents or standards that were applicable in the unusual circumstances faced by the White House staff.

The interrelationship of these influences was exceedingly complex. During Eisenhower's second term the crude anticommunism of Senator McCarthy and his cohorts lost much of its influence. While most Americans still believed that Communism posed a threat in international affairs, the evidence for a widespread subversive conspiracy at home was not convincing. Social conventions of the early Cold War began to encounter skepticism. The beatniks, for example, rejected nearly every one of them and became intensely introspective. President Kennedy, with his stirring calls to duty and his appeals to courage, slowed the spread of disillusionment only temporarily. Even before his assassination, the social cohesion of the early Cold War began to curdle as a result of two simultaneous developments: the United States gradually became more deeply involved in the Vietnamese war, and children of the baby boom began to enter puberty. Sharing the self-pity but not the introspection of the beatniks, teenagers of the sixties raged against a system that demanded sacrifices for causes in which they did not believe.

Richard Nixon did believe in those causes, and so did many other people whose experience included exposure to first the threat of Nazi aggression and then the threat of Communist expansion. Republican appeals to the "great majority of Americans" or to the "overwhelming majority" during political campaigns of the sixties bespoke an effort to counteract insurgent movements. But the movements lost none of their momentum. Why should they? The war went on and on. Despite promises of politicians and military commanders, no one detected a glimmer of light at the end of the tunnel. Opposition mounted, and with each passing year teenagers increased in number to provide recruits for protest organizations. After his victory in 1968 Nixon struggled to pacify both hawks and doves, but he had not yet succeeded in that effort when he found himself facing yet another political campaign. Given the social disruption and advances that had been made toward peace, a narrow victory would be inadequate; it would encourage further opposition at home and perhaps prolong the peace negotiations in Paris. As the president and his advisers viewed the election, then, his chances of ending the war and restoring domestic harmony would increase as he drew closer to winning every electoral vote. To many Republicans, and especially to those associated with the Committee for the Reelection of the President, those twin objectives justified a campaign of "dirty tricks" and acceptance of illegal contributions to finance them.

The electronic sophistication of the years after World War II greatly facilitated the playing of dirty tricks. Transistors, tape recorders, and the like did not cause the scandal, but without them any such enterprise would have had to take a different form. The use of electronic devices in the Watergate affair gave special point to a question that troubled many people before the break-in: would the new technology lead to invasions of privacy? Just as important, though less directly related to the scandal, were questions about the relationship between television and political campaigning. After the advent of TV, American political processes underwent significant change. Like television advertisers, candidates became concerned with selling themselves and their products. And there were no established procedures for television campaigning, no rules of the game. Television therefore tended to break down established practice, and it perhaps encouraged an "anything goes" approach to politics. Certainly the Committee for the Reelection of the President acknowledged few restraints in its single-minded pursuit of its objective.

Television and bugging devices were not, of course, the only technological marvels of the years after World War II. Computers, supersonic aircraft, space ships, and hundreds of lesser innovations such as heart valves and pacemakers transformed not only the way Americans lived and how long they lived, but also the institutions that gave structure to the society. Progressive behavioral norms did not always seem applicable in an age when supersonic travel had become common, when television transported viewers back and forth from the streets of Dodge City during the heyday of the cowboy to outer space in the twenty-first century, when NASA probes and moon landings reduced the cosmic significance of planet earth to that of a spaceship, and when computers brought a new sophistication to busi-

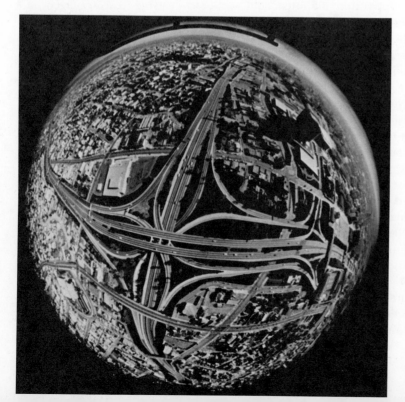

A fish-eye camera lens grossly distorts the image recorded on film. Here it distorts an environment already thoroughly modified by the machines of civilization and now dominated by urban influences. The result, in this photograph, is technological manipulation compounded (J. Eyerman, Black Star).

ness and other organizations. Inevitably in such an age, new institutions came into being as old institutions changed their modes of operation. But appropriate institutional adaptations were not self-evident, and blunders were perhaps unavoidable.

The White House, no less than other institutions, was susceptible to error. That became apparent during the summer of 1973, when the Watergate Committee hearings provided Americans with an unusual insight into procedures of the Nixon administration. One could hardly escape the conclusion that under Haldeman and Ehrlichman there were few norms for the guidance of presidential assistants. John Dean believed that a "do-it-yourself White House staff, regardless of the law," had helped to create a context for Watergate. No doubt at least some of the conspirators did what they thought was expected of them, but what they did suggested an anomie that was the negation of a rule of law and of progressive righteousness.

Thus the second century of American national existence began and ended with an effort to restore national unity after a period of disruption, war, and social disharmony. The first attempt was an aesthetic failure, the last a political calamity. Multiple consequences of the Watergate horror would surely continue to influence American life and politics long after the nation's bicentennial celebration. If that was not apparent the day Nixon departed Washington, it became distressingly evident a month later when President Ford announced his grant of "full, free, and absolute pardon unto Richard Nixon for all offenses against the United States which he, Richard Nixon, has committed or may have committed or taken part in during the period from January 20, 1969 through August 9, 1974."

The pardon was, Ford contended, an act of mercy that would serve to heal the wounds of Watergate. Yet because it was an act of mercy without justice there was no certainty that healing would follow. Indeed, if it produced cynicism about American institutions and leaders, it could have effects quite the opposite of those the new president hoped to bring about. The young men who had deserted the Army during the Vietnam conflict, along with those who had evaded the draft by escaping the country, were particularly sensitive to unfair discrimination in such matters. So, too, were their friends and families. Ford's pardon of Nixon coincided with his announcement of conditional amnesty (that is, amnesty upon completion of alternative service in place of military service) for deserters and draft evaders. Inevitably, different though the cases were, many Americans drew bitter comparisons. At any rate, whatever it implied, the pardon of Nixon presented the nation with yet another challenge as it approached the close of its second century.

**The New Feminism**    Warfare, economic prosperity, urban and suburban growth, the new technology, the baby boom, and the baby bust—all the influences that stimulated the shifting of social relationships after 1945—gave rise to Nixon's bid for national cohesion. Such asymmetrical forces also made stability and consensus difficult to achieve. No segment of the American population felt the impact of change more keenly than did women. Reviewing their accomplishments and the problems they confronted provides an invaluable perspective on social evolution in the United States after 1945. More than that, the new feminism that began taking shape in the 1960s grew to significant proportions by the mid-1970s. If Watergate was a culminating event of the progressive century, the new feminism represented a linkage with the century that lay ahead.

To begin with, one must recognize that the two decades following ratification of the Nineteenth Amendment in 1920 were disappointing ones for women who sought the same rights that men enjoyed. Behavioral freedoms achieved by flappers in the New Era brought few changes in the traditional sexual division of labor under which women assumed domestic and child-rearing responsibilities while men pursued careers outside the home. An Equal Rights Amendment proposed in 1923 by the National Women's Party made little headway, in part because it ran counter to established custom and in part because some women's organizations feared the abandonment of protective legislation for women workers. The depression years were even more discouraging than years of the prosperous twenties, for economic hardship solidified the sexual division of labor. In a period of job scarcity, according to a notion advanced by labor unions and government officials, women should not take jobs when doing so might deprive family breadwinners of employment. State legislatures passed laws limiting the employment of wives who, the reasoning ran, had husbands to support them. As the depression came to an end, therefore, the economic position of women showed no improvement over what it had been before World War I; in 1940, as in 1910, only one woman in four worked at a job for which she received income.

Then came a dramatic change. Labor scarcities and the return of prosperity during World War II brought women into the work force in unprecedented number. Holding a variety of positions from unexceptional jobs as typists and stenographers to exceptional ones as stevedores, blacksmiths, foundry helpers, welders, and drill-press operators, they demonstrated their ability to perform effectively not only in "women's work" but also in work once left exclusively to men. More than 200,000 women enlisted in the armed forces, but Rosie the Riveter became the most important symbol of women's contribution to the war effort. By 1945, when hostilities ended, 35 per cent of all civilian workers were female. Nearly 20 million women (an increase of 6.5 million over 1940) were employed in remunerative occupations. Even more significant than the higher labor force participation rate, however, was the changing profile of women wage earners. More female workers were over thirty-five than under thirty-five, and more were married than unmarried.

The war years, in other words, marked the beginning of a shift in attitudes toward the working wife. In 1940, when opposition to female employment ran high, only 15.2 per cent of all married women held paying jobs; at the war's end, the proportion had increased to 24 per cent, and it continued to rise in the postwar period. By 1973 the labor force participation rate for married women stood at 44 per cent. World War II and the continuation of prosperity beyond the war appeared to have permanently undermined the traditional idea that a woman's place was in the home and that her proper concerns were with *Küche, Kirche, Kinder*. Yet equality for women was not so easily won. Determining how well they fared in comparison with men demands consideration of the education they received, the kinds of work they did, the salary and wage levels they achieved, the time they spent on the job, the unemployment they experienced, and their chances for promotion. All available information on such matters indicates that during the postwar period women continued to encounter discrimination and other problems that proved difficult to overcome.

In the first place, whether they held jobs or not, most women were trained from infancy to have a career orientation far different from that of men. At birthday celebrations, for example, little girls customarily received dolls, tea sets, and the like, while little boys were given toy automobiles, fire trucks, and trains. Disparities in the rearing of boys and girls had always existed, of course, and they were by no means peculiar to Western civilization. The point is that increases in the number of working women after World War II did not change them. Furthermore, patterns of behavior encouraged in early childhood found reinforcement in the educational process. The vocational emphasis for girls in school was usually less than for boys; when it did exist, it tended to direct schoolgirls into secretarial and other stereotyped female occupations. In colleges and universities women were overrepresented in fields such as English, languages, and the fine arts and underrepresented in many disciplines with a strong vocational thrust. Thus in 1970 less than 10 per cent of the baccalaureate degrees in business administration went to women, and in engineering fields the proportion was even smaller. Women earned only 8.5 per cent of the M.D. degrees and 5.6 of the law degrees. On the other hand, in fields customarily thought appropriate for females, the proportions were reversed. In 1971 women received 74 per cent of the B.A. degrees in education, 82 per cent of all degrees in library science, and 98 per cent of all degrees in nursing. From the moment of birth, then, school and family functioned to give men and women very different occupational distributions.

The amount of time spent in pursuit of educational objectives was, like the content of educational programs, an important determinant of occupation. Here, too, discrepancies between male and female placed men in a favored position. While women were more likely to graduate from high school, they were less likely to complete college degrees. The number of women entering graduate programs was smaller yet, and the percentage completing graduate school was miniscule. In 1971 women received 44 per cent of all bachelor's degrees, 40 per cent of the master's degrees, and 14 per cent of the doctorates. Such disparity was one reason for fewer women than men in professional and managerial occupations such as those included in Table 12.1.

While the number of working women increased to more than 33 million by the end of 1972, that increase brought no significant change in occupational distribution. The *Economic Report of the President* transmitted to Congress in 1973 contained an occupational dissimilarity index by which the years 1960 and 1970 might be compared. The measure was based upon 197 occupations and calculated by halving the sum of absolute differences between the percentages of experienced male and female labor force in each occupation. Applying this technique to identical occupational distributions would show an index of 0. Using it with data taken from the 1960 census yielded an index of .629, while data from the 1970 census produced an index of .598. The slight difference in index numbers for the two years suggests the persistence of established occupational patterns despite profound social change during the decade.

Wage and salary differences between men and women grew, in part, out of differences in occupational distribution. In 1971 the median earnings for year-round, full-time women workers were $5,593 as compared to $9,399 for men. The income pattern, like occupational distribution, remained fairly constant during the postwar period. Indeed, the ratio of female to male income declined slightly during the late fifties before leveling off at 60 per cent. But income was not entirely a function of the job distribution pattern. It was also related to experience, for promotions and raises usually went to workers with seniority. Wives of child-bearing age, especially during the baby boom, often found that domestic responsi-

TABLE 12.1  Women as a Per Cent of Persons in Several Professional and Managerial Occupations, 1910–1970

| Occupational Group | *(Per cent)* | | | | | | |
| --- | --- | --- | --- | --- | --- | --- | --- |
| | 1910 | 1920 | 1930 | 1940 | 1950 | 1960 | 1970 |
| Clergymen.......................... | 0.6 | 1.4 | 2.2 | 2.4 | 4.0 | 2.3 | 2.9 |
| College presidents, professors, and instructors[1]...................... | 18.9 | 30.2 | 31.9 | 26.5 | 23.2 | 24.2 | 28.2 |
| Dentists............................ | 3.1 | 3.3 | 1.9 | 1.5 | 2.7 | 2.3 | 3.5 |
| Editors and reporters................. | 12.2 | 16.8 | 24.0 | 25.0 | 32.0 | 36.6 | 40.6 |
| Engineers.......................... | [2] | [2] | [2] | .4 | 1.2 | .8 | 1.6 |
| Lawyers and judges................. | .5 | 1.4 | 2.1 | 2.5 | 3.5 | 3.5 | 4.9 |
| Managers, manufacturing industries..... | 1.7 | 3.1 | 3.2 | 4.3 | 6.4 | 7.1 | 6.3 |
| Physicians......................... | 6.0 | 5.0 | 4.4 | 4.7 | 6.1 | 6.9 | 9.3 |

SOURCE: *Economic Report of the President*, January 1973 (Washington, D.C.: U.S. Government Printing Office, 1973), p. 101.

[1] Data for 1920 and 1930 probably include some teachers in schools below collegiate rank. The Office of Education estimates the 1930 figure closer to 28 per cent.

[2] Less than one tenth of 1 per cent.

Note.—Data are from the decennial censuses. Data for 1910 and 1920 include persons 10 years of age and over; data for 1930 to 1970 include persons 14 years of age and over.

Betty Friedan, leader of the women's movement of the 1960s, is shown addressing a
conference on "Women: A Political Force,"
conducted in the State Assembly Chamber
at Albany, N.Y. A group of about one
hundred persons calling themselves the
"Women Workers Protest" disrupted the
meeting (Wide World photo).

bilities forced temporary withdrawal from the labor force at a point where
men of the same age were advancing to better positions and higher pay.
By the time mothers returned to work—whether they returned in a few
months or a few years—they had fallen even further behind men.

Child-bearing, in turn, also tended to preserve the traditional outlines
of occupational distribution as women took jobs where adjustments to
pregnancy and babies were either relatively easy to make or a common
need. More importantly, high birth rates in the forties and fifties greatly
increased the demand for elementary and secondary school teachers in the
fifties and sixties. By 1970, when the five-to-fifteen-year age group began
to decrease in size, there were 1,698,100 female elementary and secondary
school teachers. The number of women teaching in schools was twice the
number of nurses, half again as large as the number of waitresses, and
nearly the same as the combined total of retail, wholesale, and manufacturing saleswomen. Only two employment categories outranked elementary and secondary school teaching in attracting women workers:
3,786,900 were employed as stenographers, typists, and secretaries, while
2,789,600 held jobs as unclassified clerical workers. Since neither type of
position had the same educational prerequisites as teaching, each had a
larger labor pool on which to draw. The significance of the teacher shortage created by the baby boom cannot be overstated. Economic demand
attracted many of the nation's ablest and best-educated women into work
that had long been considered an appropriate female calling. Without the
teacher shortage they might have pursued professional careers away from
the schoolhouse and thus greatly reduced the occupational dissimilarity
index. More widely dispersed throughout the work force, women might

have contributed far more effectively than they did to the creation of a society that recognized both the equality and the uniqueness of its members.

Such a society became the objective of a new feminism that developed during the 1960s. It was a decade in which many protest movements formed, of course, and people with grievances were not reticent about airing them. Betty Friedan led the way for an incipient feminism with her book, *The Feminine Mystique,* published in 1963. She argued that advertisers, the media, and opinion makers had victimized the American woman by portraying her domestic role as one of blissful contentment. Actually, in the author's view, a typical American home was more like a "comfortable concentration camp" that offered few opportunities for creative or intellectual development. Other articulate feminists reinforced the thesis of Friedan's book with studies of their own, and women who longed for better things out of life began to close ranks.

Varieties of opinion and degrees of dissatisfaction among women (in combination with the fact that many women expressed no dissatisfaction at all) gave the feminist movement an appearance of being inchoate and disjunctive. In 1966 Friedan formed the National Organization for Women (NOW), a reform group that attracted support from professional persons and housewives. Other groups—New York Radical Women, the Women's International Terrorist Conspiracy from Hell (WITCH), the Redstockings, the Feminists, and the Radical Feminists, for example— were doubtless inspired in part by the campus and direct action ferment of the sixties. Whatever her attitude toward the institutions of society, toward men, or toward her lot, a woman could usually find an organization that spoke to her needs. The multiplication of organizations and the disagreements that divided them should not, however, mislead anyone into believing that the feminists could never agree among themselves. They gave nearly unanimous support to the elimination of job and wage discrimination, the repeal of abortion laws, the creation of child-care centers, and to various other measures intended to promote greater freedom for women.

The feminists could not expect instantaneous success, for attitudes developed over centuries are not easily changed. But they did register some gains. Beginning with the Equal Pay Act of 1963, which required the same compensation for men and women performing work of equivalent skill and responsibility, Congress enacted a series of laws to improve the status of women. The 1964 Civil Rights Act, prohibiting discrimination in hiring, firing, and compensation, applied to women as well as to minorities. In 1972 Congress passed the Equal Employment Opportunity Act giving the Equal Employment Opportunity Commission enforcement power through the courts to deal with cases of sex discrimination. Title IX of the Education Amendments enacted in 1972 prohibited sex discrimination in educational programs and activities. During the same year the Senate voted 84 to 8 in favor of the Equal Rights Amendment that the House had passed in 1970, and by the end of 1973 it had been ratified by thirty of the thirty-eight states required for approval. Legislation accounted for many advances, but not all. In *Roe v. Wade* and *Doe v. Bolton* the Supreme Court held in 1973 that under the Fourteenth Amendment a woman may decide for herself whether or not to bear a child. In 1973, too, the President appointed a Citizens Advisory Council on the Status of Women to make legislative and other recommendations.

Even without action by the national government, it was clear by the middle seventies that ancient ideas about woman's place were crumbling at their foundation. Medical scientists, geneticists, and physiologists were suggesting that in nearly every respect the human female organism was at least equal to that of the male. Women suffered fewer genetic malformations, had fewer problems with congenital ailments and disorders such as hemophilia, deafness, or blindness, experienced fewer complications from diseases such as mumps or pneumonia, and enjoyed a greater life expectancy. Only in muscular strength did men have a physical advantage over women. In the distant past, when muscles were important for many kinds of work, that single and obvious superiority probably contributed to the notion that men were generally superior to women. Twentieth-century technology replaced muscles with machines in almost every line of work and, along with medical science, destroyed an important rationale for male domination.

Over the centuries, however, the most important reason for women being identified with hearth and home was that only females could bear children. Although medicine and technology could do little to alter female biological functions, they could reduce the birthrate through control devices, pills, and abortions. By the 1970s motherhood had become more a matter of choice than ever before in history; and, as a concern about overpopulation coincided with emergence of the feminist movement, declining birthrates became a certainty. Fewer child-care responsibilities, except for those that were sought, also foreshadowed an end to male domination outside the home.

The feminist movement had not achieved its purpose at the time of the nation's bicentennial. Controversy still surrounded some of its objectives, especially those relating to birth control and abortion, and disputes seemed likely to continue for many years. Nevertheless there was good reason to hope that women's causes might succeed. Insofar as they could achieve their goals, the feminists would move American society beyond symbolic homogeneity to a substantive unity allowing free play for individual interests and skills.

## The Consumption and Development of Energy

The outlook for the century ahead was not one to encourage unqualified optimism. The fourth Arab-Israeli war during the autumn of 1973 brought warning of a serious problem that Americans would have to face, and it is not too much to say that the way they dealt with it would shape the future. Important as Middle Eastern rivalries were, and seriously as they affected relationships between the two superpowers, the Arab-Israeli conflict had more than diplomatic significance. Oil was the crux of the matter. More than half the world's reserves are located in the Middle East, and Arab states were beginning to consider how they might use the resource to their economic as well as diplomatic advantage. As the largest oil-consuming nation, the United States felt acutely the impact of Arab policies imposed during the war.

The trouble began on October 6, when Egypt and Syria launched a surprise attack on Israel. It was Yom Kippur, the holiest of days in the Jewish calendar, and Israel took seventy-two hours to achieve full mobilization in support of her thin lines of defense. With assistance from Jordan and Iraq, Syrian columns advanced into the Golan Heights; Egyptian troops and tanks crossed the Suez Canal, broke Israel's Bar-Lev line, and penetrated the Sinai. That Arab forces were better prepared, better equipped, and far more spirited than they had been during the Six-Day War of 1967 was evident to all observers. Yet the Israeli counterattack drove the Syrians back to within artillery range of Damascus in the North and cut Egyptian lines near Ismailia in the South. The USSR had sent supplies to the Arabs, and the United States had given assistance to Israel. With the war threatening to reactivate Russian-American tensions, U.S. Secretary of State Henry Kissinger quickly negotiated cease-fire terms. In December both sides sent representatives to Geneva for discussion of a permanent settlement.

Syrian and Egyptian military power had not been impressive, but the

During the Middle Eastern crisis of 1973, the Arab nations made effective use of oil in diplomatic maneuvers. In this cartoon, world statesmen kneel in prayer as would a Moslem. They direct their petitions not to Allah, however, but to the muezzin standing on an oil pump minaret (Cummings, The Sunday Express, London).

NOVEMBER 4, 1973

Arab states made more effective use of their oil weapon than anyone had anticipated. The oil-exporting nations first announced a 5 per cent a month production cutback, and then an embargo on oil shipments to the United States and the Netherlands. Threatened with the loss of oil supplies, other countries adopted policies the Arabs could accept as friendly. Thus at the end of the conflict Israel was more isolated than it had ever been, and the United States was struggling to cope with an energy crisis. Late in November Nixon announced a 15 per cent reduction in supplies of gasoline to wholesalers, reductions in available heating oil, and a return to daylight saving time for a two-year period. He also urged service stations to close on Sundays. In December Congress passed legislation cutting off highway funds to states that did not lower maximum speed limits to 55 miles per hour.

Although it was in some respects a short-range problem (Americans were neither seriously inconvenienced nor immobilized for any length of time), the crisis was no less complicated than the Watergate scandal with which it shared newspaper headlines. To many Americans it appeared to be even more serious. Some thought that the large oil companies, more than the Arabs, had engineered the crisis. They had done so, according to a widely held belief, in order to gain approval of offshore drilling, drive independent distributors from competition, and justify an increase in gasoline prices. Whatever their manipulations, the companies were indeed concerned about the likelihood of having to pay higher prices for Arabian oil. That concern was nothing new. Indeed, it went back to 1956, when the Iranian parliament passed a law establishing the principle of joint venture between foreign-producing companies and the producing country. Recognizing the risks involved in complete dependence on Middle Eastern supplies long before the crisis of 1973, then, the companies had broadened their search for new sources of oil and had diversified their interests to include coal, uranium, and processes for the development of synthetic gas and nuclear energy.

To ask whether the oil companies were actually as altruistic as some television commercials portrayed them was to raise a legitimate question. Equally important, however, were post-World War II trends that made production and distribution of energy and energy sources enormously profitable. In 1970 the total American energy consumption (expressed in quantity of heat) was 69 quadrillion British thermal units, more than double that of 1950. Consumption in the United States far surpassed that of all western European countries, although their combined population was 75 per cent greater than the American population. The per capita U.S. consumption rose from 224.3 million BTU in 1950 to 335 million in 1970, while per capita consumption in western Europe went from 57.8 million BTU in 1950 to 118.6 million in 1968.

The four primary sources of energy during the postwar period of expansion were the same ones that had provided energy before 1940: coal, oil, natural gas, and hydro. After 1945, however, shifts took place in the

Americans, particularly the work force, confronted an added complication of life in the fall of 1973: the gasoline shortage. With heating oil also in scarce supply, the winter ahead looked bleak indeed (photo Allan Tannenbaum).

relative contribution of each primary source except the last. Coal, which had once been preeminent in all consumption sectors, lost its number one ranking. It nevertheless remained the preponderant fuel in thermal electricity generation, in 1970 supplying 20 per cent of the nation's energy needs. Oil, already important before the war, when it supplied one-third of all energy requirements, exhibited modest relative growth to 1960, then leveling off as the source of 43 to 45 per cent of energy consumed. Natural gas was the primary source that increased most rapidly in relative importance. Supplying less than 15 per cent of energy needs at the end of the war, it provided for one-third of them by 1970. Hydro remained a relatively constant source, contributing 4 to 5 per cent throughout the postwar period. The nuclear source, enormous in potential, remained insignificant in use because of widespread concern about its development.

The "energy crisis" that most Americans probably associated with the Arab oil embargo was actually a complex of crises involving multiple relationships among all the sources, uses, and consumption of energy. Coal, for example, became relatively less important than other sources not because it was in short supply, but because it lost out to natural gas in household and commercial use and to petroleum in transportation use. Natural gas was clean and cheap. Under the Natural Gas Act of 1938 the Federal government had the right to set wellhead prices; it kept them low until alleged shortages led to a doubling of natural gas prices after 1971. By that time, of course, many industries and a majority of households had converted to gas, and people felt the pinch of cold as they turned down their thermostats to keep fuel bills within reasonable limits.

In transportation the steam engine gave way to the internal combustion engine. Airplanes, automobiles, and trucks assumed a larger share of the transportation services once performed by steam locomotives and steamships. The new transportation systems were faster and more convenient. By 1970 coal was serving only 0.1 per cent of the nation's needs in transportation, while petroleum was serving 95.9 per cent. According to the Bureau of Mines, the domestic demand for motor fuel rose from less than 700 million barrels in 1945 to nearly 2.4 billion in 1972. American production of motor fuel remained greater than demand until 1960; after that, the United States depended increasingly on imports, and by 1970 had apparently exhausted its reserve production capacity. Therein lay one reason for the disturbing impact of Arabian oil policies. In 1973 the State Department estimated that the American demand for petroleum (including oil used for space heating and other purposes) at 17 million barrels per day and the domestic supply at slightly more than 11 million barrels per day. By 1980 the projected daily demand would be 24 million and the supply 12 million.

The high energy consumption growth rate was, however, nowhere more evident than in electricity. During 1945 utility companies used all the sources of energy, but primarily coal, to produce 222 billion kilowatt-hours. By 1972 the production of electricity had gone up to 1.75 trillion kilowatt-hours, an increase of nearly 700 per cent. For several reasons the influence of electricity seemed likely to increase still more in the future. Simple to transport and adaptable in application, its uses multiplied in the residential, commercial, and industrial sectors of the economy. More important in view of the search for new energy sources was the ease with which any of them—tried and untried—could be converted into electrical power.

That new sources of energy would be developed in the third American century was as certain as any prediction could be. Discussions of the energy problem during the winter of 1973–1974 made Americans aware of several possibilities, some of them in the early stages of development. Synthetic gas could be made from coal, the nation's most abundant resource, by a process (hideously) labeled "coal gasification." Solar energy offered a safe and clean solution to the problem. In 1972 a joint report of the National Science Foundation and the National Aeronautics and Space Administration suggested that power derived from the sun could, by the year 2020, provide 35 per cent of the heating and cooling of buildings and 20 per cent of all the electricity in the country. The National Science Foundation, to emphasize the abundance of solar energy, estimated that the amount falling on the surface of Lake Erie in one day is greater than the total U.S. energy consumption in a year. Another clean, safe source that came up for consideration was geothermal power, already used to generate electricity in many parts of the world. Power plants had been located over underground reservoirs of steam and hot water such as those beneath the floor

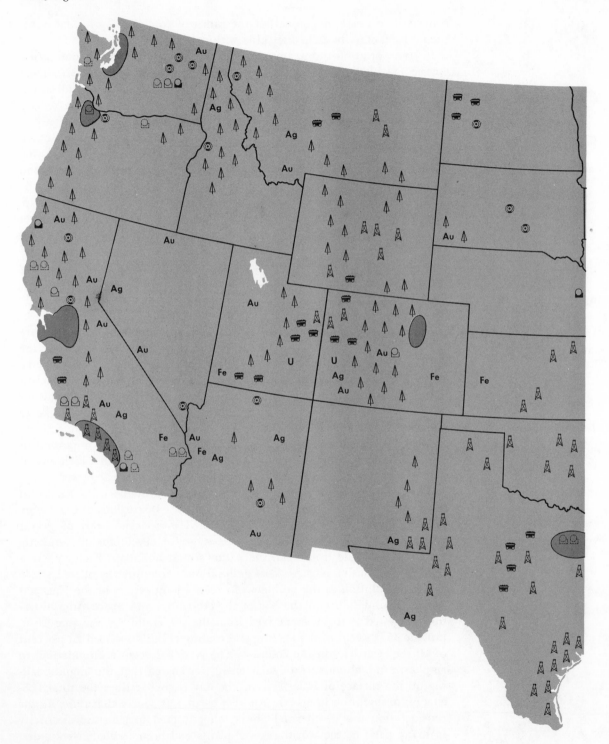

# U.S. Industry and Natural Resources, 1960's

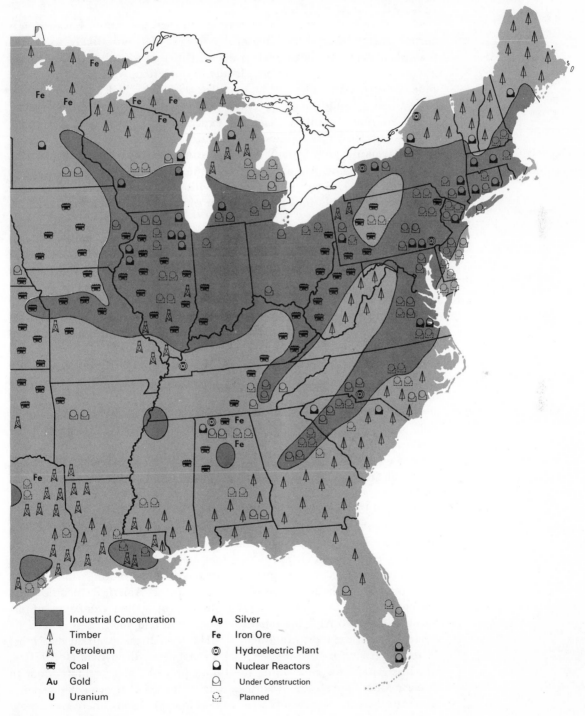

Industrial Concentration
Timber
Petroleum
Coal
**Au** Gold
**U** Uranium

**Ag** Silver
**Fe** Iron Ore
Hydroelectric Plant
Nuclear Reactors
Under Construction
Planned

of California's Imperial Valley. With improvements in deep-drilling methods there was no technical reason why geothermal energy could not be tapped almost any place.

The source that received greater attention than any other, however, was nuclear energy. For several reasons it seemed the most likely to be developed in the years ahead. When the oil embargo went into effect, thirty-seven nuclear power plants were already in operation, with fifty-seven more under construction. The technology of the industry had advanced to the point where it could make increased energy available in a relatively short period of time. Nations that had experienced energy shortages much earlier than the United States (particularly the United Kingdom, France, West Germany, and Japan) were pressing vigorously forward on the nuclear front. The Atomic Energy Commission and the president both urged that the United States proceed with equal enthusiasm toward the realization of expectations that had been common in the years immediately after World War II.

During the euphoria that followed the bombing of Hiroshima and Nagasaki, many Americans believed that the miracle of atomic energy could accomplish undreamed-of wonders at home as well as prevent aggression abroad. The peacetime development of nuclear power did not proceed as expected, however, for the anxieties of scientists and reports from Japan gradually made people aware of what horrors "radiation sickness" could bring. Atmospheric testing of bombs prior to the 1963 Limited Nuclear Test Ban Treaty created a critical fall-out problem, despite AEC denial of radioactive pollution. The United Nations Scientific Committee on the Effects of Atomic Radiation estimated that the testing before 1958 had been responsible for somewhere between 2,500 and 100,000 serious genetic defects around the world. Military planners might talk euphemistically about a clean bomb, but in fact there was no such thing. And the AEC's assurance of safety in nuclear power plants encountered the skepticism of environmentalists, scientists, and laymen. Thus the nations with energy deficits moved with greater enthusiasm in the development of nuclear energy than did the United States.

"The public," observed AEC chairman Glenn T. Seaborg, "is up-tight about the environment." But it was not just an ill-defined public that was concerned. Two scientists with the commission, J. W. Gofman and A. R. Tamplin, expressed their conviction that the radiation resulting from "the rapidly-burgeoning atomic energy programs is a far more serious hazard than previously thought possible" and that the American people were "being deceived by a clever, well-financed propaganda campaign of delusion." The two AEC opponents of nuclear development were joined by others. One of the most prominent was Hannes Alfven, awarded the Nobel Prize for physics in 1970 for his work in magnetohydrodynamics (MHD), which is critical for controlling the fusion process. In a memorandum to Senator Mike Gravel, the Swedish physicist warned that even if the pollution caused by fission reactors were kept below safe levels, there was always the chance that one of them might go out of control. In any case, "in a full-scale fission program, the radioactive waste will soon become so enormous that a total poisoning of our planet is possible." Such critics of nuclear development obviously had an influence. In 1973 Dixy Lee Ray, a zoologist with impeccable credentials as an ecologist, became head of the Atomic Energy Commission. One of her first moves was to set up an independent Division of Reactor Safety Research. Perhaps the safety of the nuclear energy program could be assured. Environmentalists continued to harbor doubts.

**No Such Thing as a Free Lunch**

The environmentalists had a point, or to be more precise, they had several interrelated ones. Economists, especially those with a healthy respect for the regulating influence of the market, had for some time been working with a similar concept they called opportunity cost. They emphasized the concept's importance with a parable about a ruler made suddenly wealthy by the production of oil within his sheikdom. Thinking to avail himself of scholarly insights, he summoned his advisers and commanded them to produce a set of volumes that would be a compendium of economic principles. The work completed, the ruler became impatient with its length and ordered it reduced to one volume. Again he was dissatisfied. Further compression pleased him no more than the one volume abstract. Finally he asked for a single sentence that would sum up all economic wisdom. His advisers fretted and labored and eventually produced a one-liner of diamond clarity: "There is no such thing as a free lunch."

An inflationary trend that began in the mid-1960s contributed a special pungency to the parable. President Johnson's determination to carry on both the Vietnam war and his Great Society program (without raising taxes) served greatly to increase aggregate demand pressures upon price stability. By the time Nixon entered the White House in 1969 the economy had become seriously distorted. Reluctant to impose higher taxes that would surely provoke a negative reaction among voters, and finding no way significantly to reduce government spending, the Nixon administration resorted to a program of income and price controls. The program failed, in part because it was poorly administered, and in part because the producers' quest for profits along with the consuming public's desire for goods exerted constant force against stable prices. Americans had grown accustomed to the abundance that came with remarkable productivity increases and to the affluence that came with nearly full employment. As efforts to halt inflation failed, however, people began to find that they would have to pay for their lunches. They found, also, that the price of a lunch was increasing every month.

The generalization was true in a literal as well as in a figurative sense, as any grocery shopper could attest. Worldwide food shortages, an increase in population, and the disappearance of reserves that had been accumulated through agricultural subsidy programs all contributed to a whopping 14.3 per cent increase in food prices during 1973. At the same time, while grocery bills were mounting more rapidly than at any point within recent memory, the Arab oil embargo provided a justification for price increases in petroleum products and products dependent on petroleum supplies and energy. Actually, the economic problem was more complex than a double-digit rate of inflation would alone suggest. That became clear during the fall of 1974, after a series of "summit" economic conferences called by President Ford to elicit advice and solicit cooperation. The conferences produced a variety of suggestions, but economists, businessmen, labor leaders, and politicians could reach consensus on few anti-inflation measures. Conference participants and observers alike could only conclude that Americans should expect neither a "quick fix" to the inflation problem nor a return to the exhilarating rate of economic growth that had brought prosperity.

The opportunity cost parable had implications for yet other developments in the United States at the close of its second century. Economic indicators by no means provided a complete picture of what had happened to the American people and the land they occupied. Barry Commoner, director of the Center for the Biology of Natural Systems at Washington University in St. Louis and one of the nation's foremost ecologists, made that point in suggesting that the "free lunch law" is as valid for the environment as for the economy. His lucid and popular 1971 study, *The Closing Circle,* presented variations on the theme. As Commoner developed them, ecological principles are in many places at odds with manipulative tendencies in the progressive approach to problems of American society. A survey of the progressive century, beginning with a dis-

As meat prices soared, grocery shoppers tried various counter-measures, including a one-week beef boycott, soybean additives, and extensive use of fish and poultry. A few even bought pet food for themselves. Some of the more affluent beef-eating families neither fought nor switched, but even they often substituted hamburger for steak. (Drawing by Modell; © 1975 The New Yorker Magazine, Inc.)

cussion of time and including in its first chapter a passage on the land as a coordinate of time, may appropriately end with a brief summary of how the American environment changed as the bicentennial approached. This conclusion therefore explores some ecological implications of the free lunch law as the United States prepares to celebrate its 200th birthday.

Although the global environment is exceedingly complex, ecological principles are simple and straightforward. The environment is made up of a thin global covering of air, water, earth, and the living things that inhabit it. This ecosphere took a long time to develop by an evolutionary process that is irreversible; once destroyed, in other words, it cannot be restored. The ecosystem by which it functions is an elaborate network of interrelated parts that follow an ecological cycle. Thus fish produce organic waste, bacteria act upon the waste and leave inorganic products, algae flourish on the inorganic products, and fish feed on the algae. The fresh-water cycle is beautifully coordinated; what is waste for the fish is essential to the bacteria, and so on around to the beginning. But the fresh-water cycle or any other cycle may be broken by the introduction or withdrawal of material that disrupts its self-governing process; when that happens, the complete cycle is eliminated. This is where human beings enter in, for though they are dependent on the ecosphere and its functioning, they are also capable of disrupting the ecosystem. Hence the application of the free lunch law. Every gain involves a cost, and the ecological cost of economic gain may be high indeed.

In the prosperous period after World War II the American people paid more dearly for their affluence than most of them thought. Technological wonders of the postwar world appeared to offer a free lunch for all. A majority of Americans gorged themselves without full knowledge of how the new technology and its products—the plastics, detergents, synthetic pesticides, and herbicides, to say nothing of man-made radioisotopes—would affect the ecosystem. During the early years of abundance, the years of the Cold War, few people understood that displacement of older processes by the newer ones might introduce products that the system was incapable of absorbing. Only a handful knew how harmful indestructible waste might be, how grave a matter it was that nothing in the ecosystem would act upon synthetic waste as bacteria act upon the waste products of fish and animals. When the knowledgeable few spoke up, they met ridicule; tagged as bird watchers and nature lovers, they were hooted out of serious consideration. Thus environmental pollution was largely a result of the new technology that sustained an affluent society whose members thought they could ignore the free lunch law.

The irony was monstrous if not tragic. Worried about Communist subversion during the McCarthy era and after, American society was itself subverting the ecosystem and calling its actions progress. Not until 1962, when Rachel Carson published her powerful and shocking polemic, *Silent Spring*, did environmental concerns begin to get a sympathetic hearing. But what was the environmental impact of economic growth? Carson responded to the question luridly because she had to in order to exert an influence; she wrote about "rivers of death," poisons that went "beyond the dreams of the Borgias," and "great reservoirs of carcinogenic agents which would continue to claim new victims faster than the as yet elusive 'cure' could allay the disease" of cancer. Yet the book was sound, and other studies could be less sensational after *Silent Spring* had made Americans conscious of the problem's seriousness. Lurid or not, the answers to questions of environmental impact must consider technological innovations and their consequences in agricultural, textile, chemical, packaging, transportation, and other industries. By the middle 1970s, ecologists had accumulated a vast store of information relating to environmental impact; only a few details must here suffice.

Although agricultural production after 1946 increased at roughly the same rate as population, the methods of production changed significantly. An indication of the change is that acreage under cultivation decreased, while the use of inorganic nitrogen fertilizer rose sharply. To be specific, in the years from 1949 to 1968 the harvested acreage declined 16 per cent, and in the same period the annual use of fertilizer nitrogen increased by 648 per cent. In effect, the fertilizer became a substitute for land as yield per acre increased 77 per cent. So far so good, but what were the costs? A clue to what they were may be found in the added amount of fertilizer used in 1968 to obtain a crop yield that was equal to the yield in 1949. Inorganic nitrogen fertilizer, quite simply, could not replace the organic nitrogen produced in humus when organic substances (plant residues, manure, garbage) were returned to the land. With reductions in the humus content of soil, plant roots did not efficiently absorb added fertilizer. Much of the inorganic nitrogen that farmers spread on their fields, then, leached out of the soil in the form of nitrate and entered surface waters to become a pollutant.

The enormous increase in nitrogen threatened the fresh-water cycle by producing algae overgrowth; moreover, it threatened human beings. Ingested into the body, nitrate from drinking water could be converted into nitrite through bacterial action, and nitrite could cause asphyxiation and death. Perhaps even more dangerous to human beings were the pesticides turned out by chemical industries primarily for use in agriculture. Between 1950 and 1967 the use of synthetic pesticides increased from 286 million pounds annually to more than a billion pounds annually. DDT, which was sprayed with reckless abandon, produced birth defects in laboratory animals and could explain some similar problems in humans.

The chemical (including petrochemical) industries brought changes in textiles also, and at equally high ecological cost. Producing fibers such as nylon contributed to the energy crisis and to air pollution because of the heat and electrical power required for their synthesis. In contrast to synthetic polymers, cotton—though it requires energy—uses the sunlight and does not pollute. Leading to the substitution of nylon for cotton, of course, were other considerations such as the fact that nylon would wear

In November 1966, New York City experienced an inversion. That is, an upper zone of warm air and a lower zone of cold air prevented vertical circulation because of the cold air's greater density. When an inversion occurs it may hold an air mass in place for several days, and pollutants may accumulate to dangerous and toxic proportions (photograph by Herbert F. Wiese).

longer. Yet it wears longer because it is an ecological waste; that is, nylon is a polymer that cannot be used in the ecosystem. It is, therefore, a pollutant. In yet another way the manufacture of synthetic fibers had a negative environmental impact. Synthesizing nylon requires the use of chlorine as a reagent. This chlorine was produced in electrolytic mercury cells by a process that (until controls were imposed on the industry) released large quantities of mercury into the ecosphere. The result was an increase in mercury poisoning among fish, and also among fishermen who caught and ate them.

The atmosphere, as well as surface water, suffered pollution as a consequence of post-1945 technological innovations. The automobile was a prime offender against that portion of the ecosphere. Population growth, patterns of settlement in metropolitan areas, displacement of railroad freight by truck freight, construction of an elaborate highway system, and other influences brought about huge increases in both freight and passenger miles. In 1973 American passenger cars were driven more than a trillion miles, an increase of 55 billion miles over the distance driven in 1971. Truck mileage went from 235 billion to 275 billion miles in the same two-year period. Vehicle-miles traveled obviously helps to account for pollution of the air by nitrogen oxides, carbon monoxide, waste fuel, and lead. The engine modifications after World War II also had an effect. Especially important were increases in horsepower and compression ratio;

the first reduced mileage per gallon of fuel, and the second increased pollutants because of the gasoline additives it made necessary. Emissions of nitrogen oxide, the central ingredient in the formation of smog, increased nearly 700 per cent between 1946 and 1970.

Enough information, perhaps, has been provided to indicate the magnitude of ecological problems facing the United States at the end of the progressive century. It is now clear that threats to the environment were principally a result of awesome changes that came with the new post-World War II technology. Gradually Americans began to develop an awareness of what the new technology had cost them. While they were unlikely to insist upon an immediate return to the industrial processes of 1945—a step that some ecologists insisted was essential to halt destruction of the ecosystem and hence assure the survival of mankind—they would not again be so blithely gluttonous at lunchtime. If they remained ignorant of the fact that they themselves would have to pay for what they ate, then there was no hope for them.

A curious mood prevailed throughout American society as preparations for the bicentennial celebration began. Citizens of the United States had lost many of their illusions. Those who still believed that the ecosystem could survive unlimited pollution were a minority. Those who maintained confidence in the general superiority of men over women and of white over black or brown were at least talking less boastfully about it. Those who thought that working in the oval office at 1600 Pennsylvania Avenue somehow conferred the infallibility of a medieval pope, or the wisdom of a Solomon, were probably less numerous than members of the Flat Earth Society. Loss of illusions need not produce despair, of course, and losing them may be a sign of maturity.

University students of the middle 1970s, following in the littered wake of campus demonstrators of the 1960s, were not inclined to wear their hearts on their sleeves and proclaim their convictions with bull horns. They had their principles, however; among them was a commitment to hard work unmatched since World War II veterans received their baccalaureate degrees. Perhaps it was the Vietnam veteran, unheralded, unsung and sometimes scorned, who made the difference. At any rate, the down-to-earth realism of students in the seventies was leavened with an idealism that represented what was best in the progressive tradition.

On the eve of the bicentennial, then, the manipulative strain in progressivism had been thoroughly discredited by Watergate and by ecological disasters. The strain that carried with it a deep social concern remained strong. The American people as a whole had lost many illusions, and few of them anticipated receiving a free lunch. On the other hand, they had survived a series of crises and had demonstrated their resilience in adapting to change. They refused to abandon hope. The toughness of the human spirit might yet see them through a difficult period and, after they had entered the third century of national existence, lead them to the discovery of hitherto unperceived bounties.

# Bibliography

PART ONE: MODERNIZING AMERICA

**Syntheses and Interpretations**
Charles A. and Mary R. Beard, *The Rise of American Civilization* (2 vols., 1927); Harold U. Faulkner, *Politics, Reform and Expansion, 1890–1900* (1959); Ralph Gabriel, *The Course of American Democratic Thought* (1956); John A. Garraty, *The New Commonwealth, 1877–1890* (1968); Ray Ginger, *Age of Excess, The United States from 1877 to 1914* (1965); Eric Goldman, *Rendezvous with Destiny* (1952); Louis Hartz, *The Liberal Tradition in America* (1955); Samuel P. Hays, *The Response to Industrialism, 1885–1914* (1957); Richard Hofstadter, *The American Political Tradition and the Men Who Made It* (1948); H. Wayne Morgan, ed., *The Gilded Age* (1970); Reinhold Niebuhr, *The Irony of American History* (1954); Gilman Ostrander, *American Civilization in the First Machine Age, 1890–1940* (1970); Vernon L. Parrington, *Main Currents in American Thought* (3 vols., 1927–1930); David M. Potter, *People of Plenty* (1954); Robert Wiebe, *The Search for Order, 1877–1920* (1967); William Appleman Williams, *The Contours of American History* (1961).

**Time and History**
Henri Bergson, *Time and Free Will* (1910); Robert F. Berkhofer, Jr., *A Behavioral Approach to Historical Analysis* (1969); Herbert Feigl and Grover Maxwell, eds., *Scientific Explanation, Space, and Time* (1962); J. T. Fraser, ed., *The Voices of Time: A Cooperative Survey of Man's View of Time as Expressed by the Sciences and by the Humanities* (1966); Edward T. Hall, *The Silent Language* (1959); John Higham with Leonard Krieger and Felix Gilbert, *History* (1965); Wilbert E. Moore, *Man, Time and Society* (1963); Nathan Rotenstreich, *Between Past and Present: An Essay on History* (1958); Pitirim Sorokin, *Socio-Cultural Causality, Space, Time* (1943); Rudolf Thiel, *And There Was Light* (1957); Stephen Toulmin and Jane Goodfield, *The Discovery of Time* (1965); G.L.S. Schackle, *Decision, Order, and Time in Human Affairs* (1961).

**Manufacturing, Transportation, and Labor**
Victor S. Clark, *History of Manufactures in the United States, 1860–1893* (1929); Thomas C. Cochran and William Miller, *The Age of Enterprise* (1961); Julius Grodzinsky, *Jay Gould* (1957); Ralph W. and Muriel Hidy, *Pioneering in Big Business, 1882–1911: History of the Standard Oil Company* (1955); William T. Hutchinson, *Cyrus Hall McCormick* (2 vols., 1930–1935); Arthur Menzies Johnson, *The Development of American Petroleum Pipelines, 1862–1906* (1956); Matthew Josephson, *The Robber Barons* (1934); Edward C. Kirkland, *Industry Comes of Age: Business, Labor and Public Policy, 1860–1897* (1961); William Miller, ed., *Men in Business* (1952); Allan Nevins, *Study in Power: John D. Rockefeller, Industrialist and Philanthropist* (2 vols., 1953); Ida Tarbell, *The Nationalizing of Business, 1878–1898* (1936); Peter Temin, *Iron and Steel in Nineteenth Century America* (1964); Joseph F. Wall, *Andrew Carnegie* (1970).

Thomas C. Cochran, *Railroad Leaders, 1845–1890* (1953) ; Robert W. Fogel, *Railroads and Economic Growth* (1964) ; Julius Grodzinsky, *Transcontinental Railway Strategy, 1869–1893* (1962) ; James B. Hedges, *Henry Villard and the Railways of the Northwest* (1930) ; Edward C. Kirkland, *Men, Cities and Transportation: A Study in New England History, 1820–1900* (1948) ; George Rogers Taylor and Irene D. Neu, *The American Railroad Network, 1861–1890* (1956).

Louis Adamic, *Dynamite: The Story of Class Violence in America* (rev. ed., 1934) ; Robert V. Bruce, *1877: Year of Violence* (1959). John R. Commons and others, *History of Labour in the United States* (4 vols., 1918–1935) ; Henry David, *History of the Haymarket Affair* (1936) ; Foster R. Dulles, *Labor in America* (1966) ; Gerald Eggert, *Railroad Labor Disputes: The Beginnings of Federal Strike Policy* (1967) ; Gerd Korman, *Industrialization, Immigrants, and Americanizers: The View from Milwaukee, 1866–1921* (1967) ; Almont Lindsay, *The Pullman Strike* (1942) ; Donald L. McMurry, *The Great Burlington Strike of 1888* (1956) ; Robert Ozanne, *A Century of Labor Management Relations at McCormick and International Harvester* (1967) ; Henry Pelling, *American Labor* (1960) ; Joseph G. Rayback, *A History of American Labor* (1959).

**Agriculture and the Farmer**

Allan Bogue, *From Prairie to Corn Belt* (1963) and *Money at Interest: The Farm Mortgage on the Middle Border* (1955) ; Margaret Beattie Bogue, *Patterns from the Sod: Land Use and Tenure in the Grand Prairie, 1850–1890* (1959) ; Solon J. Buck, *The Granger Movement* (1913) ; Hiram M. Drache, *The Day of the Bonanza: A History of Bonanza Farming in the Red River Valley of the North* (1964) ; Gilbert C. Fite, *The Farmer's Frontier, 1865–1900* (1966) ; Earl W. Hayter, *The Troubled Farmer* (1968) ; Eric E. Lampard, *The Rise of the Dairy Industry in Wisconsin* (1963) ; James C. Malin, *Winter Wheat in the Golden Belt of Kansas* (1944) ; Leo Rogin, *The Introduction of Farm Machinery in Its Relation to the Productivity of Labor in the Agriculture of the United States during the Nineteenth Century* (1931) ; Theodore Saloutos, *Farmer Movements in the South, 1865–1933* (1960) ; Fred Shannon, *The Farmer's Last Frontier: Agriculture, 1860–1897* (1945) ; Reynold Wik, *Steam Power on the American Farm* (1953).

**Economic Performance**

Arthur F. Burns and Wesley C. Mitchell, *Measuring Business Cycles* (1946) ; Rendigs Fels, *American Business Cycles, 1865–1897* (1959) ; Alvin Hansen, *Fiscal Policy and Business Cycles* (1941) ; Charles Hoffmann, *The Depression of the Nineties* (1970) ; John W. Kendrick, *Productivity Trends in the United States* (1961) ; Simon Kuznets, *Capital in the American Economy* (1961), *National Income, A Summary of Findings* (1946), and *National Product Since 1869* (1946) ; Simon Kuznets and Dorothy S. Thomas, *Population Redistribution and Economic Growth, United States, 1870–1950* (1960) ; C. D. Long, *Wages and Earnings in the United States, 1860–1890* (1960) ; Wesley C. Mitchell, *Business Cycles* (1927) ; Albert Rees, *Real Wages in Manufacturing, 1900–1914* (1961).

**Political Parties, Leaders, and Movements**

Geoffrey Blodgett, *The Gentle Reformers: Massachusetts Democrats in the Cleveland Era* (1966) ; Vincent P. De Santis, *Republicans Face the Southern Question, The New Departure Years, 1877–1897* (1959) ; Paul W. Glad, *McKinley, Bryan and the People* (1964) ; Stanley P. Hirshson, *Farewell to the Bloody Shirt: Northern Republicans and the Southern Negro, 1877–1893* (1962) ; Richard Jensen, *The Winning of the Midwest: Social and Political Conflict, 1888–1896* (1971) ; Stanley L. Jones, *The Presidential Election of 1896* (1964) ; Matthew Josephson,

*The Politicos, 1865–1896* (1938); Albert D. Kirwan, *Revolt of the Rednecks: Mississippi Politics, 1876–1925* (1951); Paul Kleppner, *The Cross of Culture, A Social Analysis of Midwestern Politics, 1850–1900* (1970); George Harmon Knoles, *The Presidential Campaign and Election of 1892* (1942); Arthur Mann, *Yankee Reformers in the Urban Age* (1954); Robert D. Marcus, *Grand Old Party, 1880–1896* (1971); George H. Mayer, *The Republican Party, 1854–1964* (1964); Samuel T. McSeveney, *The Politics of Depression, Political Behavior in the Northeast, 1893–1896* (1972); Horace S. Merrill, *Bourbon Democracy of the Middle West, 1856–1896* (1953); H. Wayne Morgan, *From Hayes to McKinley: National Party Politics, 1877–1896* (1969); David J. Rothman, *Politics and Power: The United States Senate, 1869–1901* (1966); John G. Sproat, *"The Best Men": Liberal Reformers in the Gilded Age* (1968); Leonard D. White, *The Republican Era, 1869–1901: A Study in Administrative History* (1958).

Harry Barnard, *"Eagle Forgotten": The Life of John Peter Altgeld* (1938); Thomas Beer, *Hanna* (1929); Paolo E. Coletta, *William Jennings Bryan* (3 vols., 1964–1969); Ray Ginger, *Altgeld's America: The Lincoln Ideal versus Changing Realities* (1958); Paul W. Glad, *The Trumpet Soundeth: William Jennings Bryan and His Democracy, 1896–1912* (1960); Louis W. Koenig, *Bryan: A Political Biography of William Jennings Bryan* (1971); Margaret Leech, *In the Days of McKinley* (1959); Horace S. Merrill, *Bourbon Leader: Grover Cleveland and the Democratic Party* (1957); H. Wayne Morgan, *William McKinley and His America* (1963); Allan Nevins, *Grover Cleveland: A Study in Courage* (1933); Martin Ridge, *Ignatius Donnelly, The Portrait of a Politician* (1962); Francis Butler Simkins, *Pitchfork Ben Tillman* (1944); C. Vann Woodward, *Tom Watson, Agrarian Rebel* (1938).

O. Gene Clanton, *Kansas Populism: Ideas and Men* (1969); Chester M. Destler, *American Radicalism, 1865–1901* (1946); Robert F. Durden, *The Climax of Populism: The Election of 1896* (1965); Milton Friedman and Anna Jacobson Schwartz, *A Monetary History of the United States* (1963); Joseph Gusfield, *Symbolic Crusade: Status Politics and the American Temperance Movement* (1966); John D. Hicks, *The Populist Movement* (1931); Ari Hoogenboom, *Outlawing the Spoils: A History of the Civil Service Reform Movement, 1865–1883* (1961); Walter T. K. Nugent, *Money and American Society, 1865–1880* (1968) and *The Tolerant Populists* (1963); Norman Pollock, *The Populist Response to Industrial America* (1962); William Warren Rogers, *The One-Gallused Rebellion: Agrarianism in Alabama, 1865–1896* (1970); Robert Sharkey, *Money, Class and Party: An Economic Study of Civil War and Reconstruction* (1959); Irwin Unger, *The Greenback Era: A Social and Political History of American Finance, 1865–1879* (1964); Allen Weinstein, *Prelude to Populism: Origins of the Silver Issue, 1867–1878* (1970); C. Vann Woodward, *Origins of the New South, 1877–1913* (1951).

**Immigration and Minorities** Rowland T. Berthoff, *British Immigrants in Industrial America, 1790–1950* (1953); Theodore C. Blegen, *Norwegian Migration to America* (1940); Thomas N. Brown, *Irish-American Nationalism* (1966); Alexander De Conde, *Half Bitter, Half Sweet: An Excursion into Italian-American History* (1971); Charlotte Erickson, *American Industry and European Immigration, 1860–1885* (1957) and *Invisible Immigrants: The Adaptation of English and Scottish Immigrants in Nineteenth Century America* (1972); Rudolf Glantz, *Jew and Italian: Historic Group Relations and the New Immigration* (1971); Milton Gordon, *Assimilation in American Life* (1965); Oscar Handlin, *Boston's Immigrants, 1790–1880* (1959), *Race and Nationality in*

*American Life* (1957), and *The Uprooted* (1951); Marcus Lee Hansen, *The Immigrant in American History* (1940); John Higham, *Strangers in the Land: Patterns of American Nativism 1860–1925* (1955); Luciano J. Iorizzo and Salvatore Mondello, *The Italian-American* (1971); Maldwyn A. Jones, *American Immigration* (1960); Frederic C. Luebke, *Immigrants and Politics: The Germans of Nebraska, 1880–1900* (1969); Humbert S. Nelli, *Italians in Chicago, 1880–1930: A Study in Ethnic Mobility* (1970); Barbara Solomon, *Ancestors and Immigrants: A Changing New England Tradition* (1956); Carl Wittke, *We Who Built America, The Saga of the Immigrant* (1939).

Roger D. Abrahams, *Deep Down in the Jungle* (rev. ed., 1970); Francis L. Broderick, *W.E.B. DuBois: A Negro Leader in a Time of Crisis* (1959); W.E.B. DuBois, *The Souls of Black Folk* (1903); Henry Fritz, *The Movement for Indian Assimilation, 1860–1890* (1963); W. T. Hagan, *American Indians* (1961); John S. Haller, Jr., *Outcasts from Evolution: Scientific Attitudes of Racial Inferiority, 1859–1900* (1971); Louis R. Harlan, *Booker T. Washington: The Making of a Black Leader, 1856–1901* (1972); Jack Temple Kirby, *Darkness at the Dawning: Race and Reform in the Progressive South* (1972); Rayford W. Logan, *The Negro in American Life and Thought: The Nadir, 1877–1901* (1954); August Meier, *Negro Thought in America, 1880–1915* (1963); August Meier and Elliott M. Rudwick, *From Plantation to Ghetto* (1966); H. Brett Melendy, *The Oriental Americans* (1972); Wendell H. Oswalt, *This Land Was Theirs: A Study of the North American Indian* (1966); Kenneth Wiggins Porter, *The Negro on the American Frontier* (1971); Loring B. Priest, *Uncle Sam's Step-Children: The Reformation of the United States Indian Policy, 1865–1887* (1942); Edwin S. Redkey, *Black Exodus: Black Nationalist and Back-to-Africa Movements, 1890–1910* (1969); Lawrence D. Rice, *The Negro in Texas* (1971); Elliott M. Rudwick, *W.E.B. DuBois: A Study in Minority Group Leadership* (1960); Emma Lou Thornbrough, *The Negro in Indiana: A Study of a Minority* (1957); George Brown Tindall, *South Carolina Negroes, 1877–1900* (1952); Robert M. Utley, *The Last Days of the Sioux Nation* (1963); Booker T. Washington, *Up from Slavery: An Autobiography* (1901); Vernon Lane Wharton, *The Negro in Mississippi, 1865–1890* (1947); C. Vann Woodward, *The Strange Career of Jim Crow* (third rev. ed., 1974); Charles E. Wynes, *Race Relations in Virginia, 1870–1902* (1961).

**Thought and Society**

Daniel Aaron, *Men of Good Hope: A Story of American Progressives* (1950); Henry Adams, *The Education of Henry Adams* (1918); Charles A. Barker, *Henry George* (1955); Paul F. Boller, Jr., *American Thought in Transition: The Impact of Evolutionary Naturalism, 1865–1900* (1969); Sylvia Bowman, *The Year 2000: A Critical Biography of Edward Bellamy* (1958); Wilbur J. Cash, *The Mind of the South* (1941); Joseph Dorfman, *The Economic Mind in American Civilization, 1865–1918* (1949); Daniel M. Fox, *The Discovery of Abundance: Simon Patton and the Transformation of Social Theory* (1967); Richard Hofstadter, *The Age of Reform* (1955) and *Social Darwinism in American Thought* (1949); Frederic Cople Jaher, *Doubters and Dissenters* (1964); Edward C. Kirkland, *Dream and Thought in the Business Community, 1860–1900* (1956); Arthur E. Morgan, *The Philosophy of Edward Bellamy* (1945); Lewis Mumford, *The Brown Decades: A Study of the Arts in America, 1865–1895* (1931); Arnold M. Paul, *Conservative Crisis and the Rule of Law: Attitudes of Bench and Bar, 1887–1895* (1960); Benjamin G. Rader, *The Academic Mind and Reform: The Influence of Richard T. Ely in American Life* (1966); Henry Nash Smith, *Mark Twain: The Development of a*

*Writer* (1962) and *Virgin Land: The American West as Symbol and Myth* (1950); Morton White, *Social Thought in America: The Revolt Against Formalism* (1957); Lazar Ziff, *The American 1890s* (1966).

Lewis Atherton, *Main Street on the Middle Border* (1954); Thomas Beer, *The Mauve Decade: American Life at the End of the Nineteenth Century* (1926); James Bryce, *The American Commonwealth* (2 vols., 1895); John G. Cawelti, *Apostles of the Self-Made Man in America* (1965); Earl F. Cheit, ed., *The Business Establishment* (1964); Sigmund Diamond, *The Reputation of the American Businessman* (1955); Sidney Fine, *Laissez-Faire and the General Welfare State: A Study of Conflict in American Thought, 1865–1901* (1956); Frederic Cople Jaher, ed., *The Age of Industrialism in America: Essays in Social Structure and Cultural Values* (1968); H. Wayne Morgan, *The Gilded Age* (1970); Elting E. Morison, *Men, Machines and Modern Times* (1966); John Tomsich, *A Genteel Endeavor: American Culture and Politics in the Gilded Age* (1971); Stephan Thernstrom, *Poverty and Progress: Social Mobility in a Nineteenth Century City* (1964); Richard Weiss, *The American Myth of Success: From Horatio Alger to Norman Vincent Peale* (1969); Irvin G. Wyllie, *The Self-Made Man in America* (1954).

PART TWO: A TIME OF REFORM CONSENSUS AT HOME AND CONFLICT ABROAD

**The Progressive Era and Its Issues**

John Braeman, Robert H. Bremner, and Everett Walters, eds., *Change and Continuity in Twentieth Century America* (1964); Henry Steele Commager, *The American Mind: An Interpretation of American Thought and Character Since the 1880s* (1950); John Chamberlain, *Farewell to Reform: The Rise, Life and Decay of the Progressive Mind in America* (1932); Herbert Croly, *The Promise of American Life* (1909); Benjamin P. Dewitt, *The Progressive Movement* (1915); Arthur A. Ekirch, Jr., *The Decline of American Liberalism* (1955); Harold U. Faulkner, *The Quest for Social Justice, 1898–1914* (1931); Ray Ginger, *Age of Excess, The United States from 1877–1914* (1965); Eric Goldman, *Rendezvous with Destiny* (1952); Otis L. Graham, Jr., *The Great Campaigns: War and Reform in America, 1900–1928* (1971); Richard Hofstadter, *The Age of Reform: From Bryan to F.D.R.* (1955); Gabriel Kolko, *The Triumph of Conservatism* (1963); Christopher Lasch, *The New Radicalism in America, 1889–1963* (1965); Walter Lippmann, *Drift and Mastery* (1914); Henry F. May, *The End of American Innocence* (1959); David W. Noble, *The Paradox of Progressive Thought* (1958); Jean B. Quandt, *From the Small Town to the Great Community: The Social Thought of Progressive Intellectuals* (1970); Michael Rogin, *The Intellectuals and McCarthy: The Radical Spectre* (1967); James Weinstein, *The Corporate Ideal in the Liberal State: 1900–1918* (1968); Walter Weyl, *The New Democracy* (1912); Morton White, *Social Thought in America: The Revolt Against Formalism* (1957); Robert Wiebe, *The Search for Order, 1877–1920* (1967); Norman M. Wilensky, *Conservatives in the Progressive Era: The Taft Republicans of 1912* (1965); William Appleman Williams, *The Contours of American History* (1961).

Eleanor Flexner, *Century of Struggle: The Woman's Rights Movement in the United States* (1959); Alan P. Grimes, *The Puritan Ethic and Woman Suffrage* (1967); David M. Kennedy, *Birth Control in America: The Career of Margaret Sanger* (1970); Eileen Kraditor, *The Ideas of the Woman Suffrage Movement* (1965); David Morgan, *Suffragists and Democrats: The Politics of Woman Suffrage in America* (1972); William L. O'Neill, *Divorce in the Progressive Era* (1967) and

*Everyone Was Brave: The Rise and Fall of Feminism in America* (1970) ; Robert Smuts, *Women and Work in America* (1959) .

Maxwell H. Bloomfield, *Alarms and Diversions: The American Mind Through American Magazines, 1900–1914* (1967) ; Charles Forcey, *The Crossroads of Liberalism: Croly, Weyl, Lippmann and the Progressive Era, 1900–1925* (1961) ; Frank Luther Mott, *A History of American Magazines* (1957) ; Harold S. Wilson, *McClure's Magazine and the Muckrakers* (1970) .

Jane Addams, *Twenty Years at Hull House* (1910) ; Robert H. Bremner, *From the Depths: The Discovery of Poverty in the United States* (1956) ; Allen F. Davis, *Spearheads for Reform: The Social Settlements and the Progressive Movement, 1890–1914* (1967) ; Jack M. Holl, *Juvenile Reform in the Progressive Era: William R. George and the Junior Republic Movement* (1971) ; Roy Lubove, *The Progressives and the Slums: Tenement House Reform in New York City, 1900–1917* (1962) .

Samuel P. Hays, *Conservation and the Gospel of Efficiency, 1890–1920* (1959) ; James Penick, Jr., *Progressive Politics and Conservation: The Ballinger-Pinchot Affair* (1968) ; James Timberlake, *Prohibition and the Progressive Movement* (1959) ; Hace Sorel Tishler, *Self-Reliance and Social Security 1870–1917* (1971) .

### Progressivism in Cities, States, and Regions

Richard M. Abrams, *Conservatism in a Progressive Era: Massachusetts Politics, 1900–1912* (1964) ; Walton Bean, *Boss Reuf's San Francisco* (1952) ; Stanley P. Caine, *The Myth of a Progressive Reform: Railroad Regulation in Wisconsin, 1903–1910* (1970) ; James Crooks, *Politics and Progress* (1968) ; Sheldon Hackney, *Populism to Progressivism in Alabama* (1969) ; Melvin G. Holli, *Reform in Detroit: Hazen S. Pingree and Urban Politics* (1969) ; Albert D. Kirwan, *Revolt of the Rednecks: Mississippi Politics, 1876–1925* (1951) ; Herbert Margulies, *The Decline of the Progressive Movement in Wisconsin, 1890–1920* (1968) ; Robert S. Maxwell, *La Follette and the Rise of the Progressives in Wisconsin* (1956) ; William D. Miller, *Memphis during the Progressive Era, 1900–1917* (1957) ; Zane Miller, *Boss Cox's Cincinnati: Urban Politics in the Progressive Era* (1968) ; George Mowry, *The California Progressives* (1951) ; Ransom E. Noble, Jr., *New Jersey Progressivism before Wilson* (1946) ; Russel B. Nye, *Midwestern Progressive Politics* (1959) ; Spencer C. Olin, Jr., *California's Prodigal Sons: Hiram Johnson and the Progressives, 1911–1917* (1968) ; David P. Thelen, *The New Citizenship: Origins of Progressivism in Wisconsin, 1885–1900* (1972) ; George B. Tindall, *The Emergence of the New South, 1913–1945* (1967) ; Hoyt Landon Warner, *Progressivism in Ohio* (1964) ; C. Vann Woodward, *Origins of the New South, 1877–1913* (1951) .

### Leaders of Reform

Hugh C. Bailey, *Edgar Gardner Murphy: Gentle Progressive* (1968) ; Robert C. Bannister, Jr., *Ray Stannard Baker: The Mind and Thought of a Progressive* (1966) ; Dorothy Rose Blumberg, *Florence Kelly: The Making of a Social Pioneer* (1966) ; Claude Bowers, *Beveridge and the Progressive Era* (1932) ; Clarke A. Chambers, *Paul U. Kellogg and the Survey, Voices for Social Welfare and Social Justice* (1971) ; Robert Crunden, *A Hero in Spite of Himself: Brand Whitlock in Art, Politics & War* (1969) ; John C. Farrell, *Beloved Lady: A History of Jane Addams' Ideas on Reform and Peace* (1967) ; Charles Larsen, *The Good Fight: The Life and Times of Ben B. Lindsey* (1972) ; Daniel Levine, *Jane Addams and the Liberal Tradition* (1971) and *Varieties of Reform Thought* (1964) ; Lawrence W. Levine, *Defender of the Faith: William Jennings Bryan, the Last Decade, 1915–1925* (1965) ; Richard Lowitt, *George W. Norris* (2 vols., 1963–1971) ; Alpheus T.

Mason, *Brandeis: A Free Man's Life* (1946); Ross E. Paulson, *Radicalism & Reform: The Vrooman Family and American Social Thought, 1837–1937* (1968); Harold T. Pinkett, *Gifford Pinchot: Private and Public Forester* (1970); A. Bower Sageser, *Joseph L. Bristow: Kansas Progressive* (1968); John E. Semonche, *Ray Stannard Baker: A Quest for Democracy in Modern America, 1870–1918* (1969); Lincoln Steffens, *The Autobiography of Lincoln Steffens* (1931); Jack Tager, *The Intellectual As Urban Reformer: Brand Whitlock and the Progressive Movement* (1968); Julius Weinberg, *Edward Alsworth Ross and the Sociology of Progressivism* (1972); Robert F. Wesser, *Charles Evans Hughes: Politics and Reform in New York State, 1905–1910* (1967); William Allen White, *The Autobiography of William Allen White* (1946).

**Religion in the Progressive Era**

Robert D. Cross, *The Emergence of Liberal Catholicism in America* (1958); Lawrence B. Davis, *Immigrants, Baptists, and the Protestant Mind in America* (1973); John Tracy Ellis, *American Catholicism* (1956); Louis Finkelstein, *The Jews: Their History, Culture and Religion* (1949); Nathan Glazer, *American Judaism* (1957); Arthur A. Goren, *New York Jews and the Quest for Community: The Kehillah Experiment, 1808–1922* (1970); Will Herberg, *Protestant–Catholic–Jew: An Essay in American Religious Sociology* (1955); Charles H. Hopkins, *The Rise of the Social Gospel in American Protestantism, 1865–1915* (1940); Henry F. May, *Protestant Churches and Industrial America, 1865–1915* (1949); Sidney Mead, *The Lively Experiment: The Shaping of Christianity in America* (1963); H. Richard Niebuhr, *The Social Sources of Denominationalism* (1929); Moses Rischin, *The Promised City: New York's Jews, 1870–1914* (1962); Herbert Wallace Schneider, *Religion in 20th Century America* (1952).

**The American Economy and Its Changing Structure**

Ralph Andreano, ed., *New Views on American Economic Development* (1965); Joe S. Bain, *Barriers to New Competition* (1956); Adolf A. Berle and Gardiner C. Means, *The Modern Corporation and Private Property* (1932); Louis D. Brandeis, *Other People's Money and How the Bankers Use It* (1914); Vincent P. Carosso, *Investment Banking in America: A History* (1970); Alfred D. Chandler, *Strategy and Structure: Chapters in the History of Industrial Enterprise* (1962); A. W. Coats and Ross Robertson, eds., *Essays in Economic History* (1969); Richard A. Easterlin, *Population, Labor Force and Long Swings in Economic Growth: The American Experience* (1968); Alfred E. Eichner, *The Emergence of Oligopoly: Sugar Refining as a Case Study* (1969); Solomon Fabricant, *Employment in Manufacturing, 1899–1939* (1942) and *The Output of Manufacturing Industries, 1899–1937* (1940); Harold U. Faulkner, *The Decline of Laissez-Faire, 1897–1917* (1951); C. A. E. Goodhart, *The New York Market and the Finance of Trade, 1900–1913* (1969); John W. Kendrick, *Productivity Trends in the United States* (1961); K. Austin Kerr, *American Railroad Politics, 1914–1920: Rates, Wages, and Efficiency* (1968); Gabriel Kolko, *Railroads and Regulation, 1877–1916* (1965); Simon Kuznets, *Economic Growth and Structure* (1965) and *Modern Economic Growth: Rate, Structure and Spread* (1966); Stanley Lebergott, *Manpower in Economic Growth* (1964); William Letwin, *Law and Economic Policy in America: The Evolution of the Sherman Anti-trust Act* (1965); Albro Martin, *Enterprise Denied: Origins of the Decline of American Railroads, 1897–1917* (1971); Willard F. Mueller, *A Primer on Monopoly and Competition* (1970); Gerald D. Nash, *United States Oil Policy, 1890–1964* (1968); Ralph L. Nelson, *Merger Movements in American Industry, 1895–1956* (1959); Hans B. Thorelli, *The Federal Anti-trust*

*Policy: Origination of an American Tradition* (1954) ; Melvin I. Urofsky, *Big Steel and the Wilson Administration* (1969) ; Robert Wiebe, *Businessmen and Reform* (1962) ; Clair Wilcox, *Public Policies Toward Business* (1960) .

**Farmers, Workers, and Radicals**

Harold Barger and H. H. Landsberg, *American Agriculture, 1899–1939* (1942) ; Murray Benedict, *Farm Policies in the United States, 1790–1950* (1953) ; Melvyn Dubofsky, *When Workers Organize: New York City in the Progressive Era* (1968) ; Philip S. Foner, *History of the Labor Movement in the United States* (4 vols., 1947–1965) ; Marc Karson, *American Labor Unions and Politics, 1900–1918* (1958) ; Marguerite Green, *The National Civic Federation and the American Labor Movement* (1956) ; Marc Karson, *American Labor Unions and Politics, 1900–1918* (1958) ; Lewis L. Lorwin, *The American Federation of Labor* (1933) ; Grant McConnell, *The Decline of Agrarian Democracy* (1953) ; Theodore Saloutos and John D. Hicks, *Agricultural Discontent in the Middle West, 1900–1939* (1951) ; Philip Taft, *The A.F. of L. in the Time of Gompers* (1957) ; Irwin Yellowitz, *Labor and the Progressive Movement in New York State, 1897–1916* (1965) .

Paul F. Brissenden, *The IWW: A Study of American Syndicalism* (1919) ; Joseph R. Conlin, *Big Bill Haywood and the Radical Union Movement* (1969) ; William M. Dick, *Labor and Socialism in America: The Gompers Era* (1971) ; Melvyn Dubofsky, *We Shall Be All: A History of the Industrial Workers of the World* (1969) ; Donald D. Egbert and Stow Persons, eds., *Socialism and American Life* (2 vols., 1952) ; Nathan Fine, *Labor and Farmer Parties in the United States, 1828–1928* (1928) ; Ray Ginger, *The Bending Cross: A Biography of Eugene V. Debs* (1948) ; David Herreshoff, *American Disciples of Marx: From the Age of Jackson to the Progressive Era* (1967) ; Ira A. Kipnis, *The American Socialist Movement, 1897–1912* (1952) ; John H. M. Laslett, *Labor and the Left: A Study of Socialist and Radical Influences in the American Labor Movement, 1881–1924* (1970) ; R. Laurence Moore, *European Socialists and the American Promised Land* (1970) ; Robert L. Morlan, *Political Prairie Fire: The Nonpartisan League, 1915–1922* (1955) ; Howard Quint, *The Forging of American Socialism* (1953) ; Patrick Renshaw, *The Wobblies: The Story of Syndicalism in the United States* (1967) ; David Shannon, *The Socialist Party of America: A History* (1955) ; Robert L. Tyler, *Rebels of the Woods: The I.W.W. in the Pacific Northwest* (1967) ; James Weinstein, *The Decline of Socialism in America, 1912–1925* (1967) .

**The Politics of Reform: Roosevelt and Wilson**

John Blum, *The Republican Roosevelt* (1956) ; John A. Garraty, *Right Hand Man: The Life of George W. Perkins* (1960) ; Willard B. Gatewood, Jr., *Theodore Roosevelt and the Art of Controversy: Episodes of the White House Years* (1970) ; William Harbaugh, *Power and Responsibility: The Life and Times of Theodore Roosevelt* (1961) ; George E. Mowry, *Theodore Roosevelt and the Progressive Movement* (1946) and *The Era of Theodore Roosevelt and the Birth of Modern America, 1900–1912* (1958) ; Henry F. Pringle, *The Life and Times of William Howard Taft* (2 vols., 1939) and *Theodore Roosevelt, A Biography* (1931) .

John Blum, *Joe Tumulty and the Wilson Era* (1938) and *Woodrow Wilson and the Politics of Morality* (1956) ; William Diamond, *The Economic Thought of Woodrow Wilson* (1943) ; Alexander and Juliette George, *Woodrow Wilson and Colonel House: A Personality Study* (1956) ; James Holt, *Congressional Insurgents and the Party System, 1909–1916* (1967) ; Arthur Link, *Wilson* (5 vols., 1947–1965) and *Woodrow Wilson and the Progressive Era, 1910–1917* (1954) .

| | |
|---|---|
| **International Relations and the Balance of Power** | Herbert Feis, *Europe the World's Banker, 1870–1914* (1930) ; F. H. Hinsley, ed., *The New Cambridge Modern History.* Volume XI, *Material Progress and World-Wide Problems, 1870–1898* (1962) ; F. H. Hinsley, *Power and the Pursuit of Peace: Theory and Practice in the History of Relations Between States* (1963) ; Herbert C. Kelman, ed., *International Behavior* (1965) ; William L. Langer, *The Diplomacy of Imperialism, 1890–1902* (1951) and *European Alliances and Alignments* (1950) ; John P. Lovell, *Foreign Policy in Perspective* (1970) ; R. G. Neale, *Great Britain and United States Expansion, 1898–1900* (1966) ; Robert Osgood, *Ideals and Self-Interest in America's Foreign Relations* (1953) ; Bradford Perkins, *The Great Rapprochement: England and the United States, 1895–1914* (1968) ; J. M. Roberts, *Europe, 1880–1945* (1967) ; A. J. P. Taylor, *The Struggle for Mastery in Europe, 1848–1918* (1954) ; Barbara Tuchman, *The Proud Tower: A Portrait of the World Before the War, 1890–1914* (1962) . |
| **War and Peace** | Norman Angell, *The Great Illusion* (1909) ; Leon Bramson and George W. Goethals, eds., *War: Studies from Psychology, Sociology, and Anthropology* (1968) ; Robin Clarke, *The Science of War and Peace* (1972) ; Jesse D. Clarkson and Thomas C. Cochran, *War as a Social Institution* (1941) ; Merle Curti, *Peace or War: The American Struggle, 1636–1936* (1936) ; Sylvester John Hemleben, *Plans for World Peace Through Six Centuries* (1943) ; William Livezey, *Mahan on Sea Power* (1947) ; Alfred Thayer Mahan, *The Interest of America in Sea Power* (1898) ; C. Roland Marchand, *The American Peace Movement and Social Reform, 1898–1918* (1973) ; Wilbert E. Moore, *Order and Change* (1967) ; T. H. Pear, ed., *Psychological Factors in Peace and War* (1950) ; W. D. Puleston, *Mahan* (1939) ; F. J. P. Veale, *Advance to Barbarism* (1968) ; Quincy Wright, *A Study of War* (2 vols., 1942) ; Sondra R. Herman, *Eleven Against War: Studies in American Internationalist Thought, 1898–1921* (1969) . |
| **The United States in World Affairs** | Charles H. Brown, *The Correspondents' War: Journalists in the Spanish-American War* (1967) ; Foster R. Dulles, *America's Rise to World Power, 1898–1954* (1955) ; David Healy, *U.S. Expansionism: The Imperialist Urge in the 1890s* (1970) ; Walter La Feber, *The New Empire: An Interpretation of American Expansion, 1860–1890* (1963) ; Howard K. Beale, *Theodore Roosevelt and the Rise of America to World Power* (1956) ; Robert L. Beisner, *Twelve Against Empire: The Anti-Imperialists, 1898–1900* (1968) ; William Reynolds Braisted, *The United States Navy in the Pacific, 1909–1922* (1971) ; Merle Curti, *Bryan and World Peace* (1931) ; Robert L. Daniel, *American Philanthropy in the Near East, 1820–1960* (1971) ; Tyler Dennett, *Americans in Eastern Asia* (1922) ; Raymond Esthus, *Theodore Roosevelt and Japan* (1966) ; A. Whitney Griswold, *The Far Eastern Policy of the United States* (1938) ; Richard W. Leopold, *Elihu Root and the Conservative Tradition* (1954) ; Ernest R. May, *American Imperialism: A Speculative Essay* (1968) and *Imperial Democracy: The Emergence of America as a World Power* (1961) ; Thomas J. McCormick, *China Market: America's Quest for Informal Empire, 1893–1901* (1967) ; H. Wayne Morgan, *America's Road to Empire* (1966) ; Charles D. Neu, *An Uncertain Friendship: Theodore Roosevelt and Japan, 1906–1909* (1967) ; Carl P. Parrini, *Heir to Empire: United States Economic Diplomacy, 1916–1923,* (1969) ; David M. Pletcher, *The Awkward Years: American Foreign Relations Under Garfield and Arthur* (1962) ; Julius Pratt, *Expansionists of 1898* (1936) ; Walter V. Scholes and Marie V. Scholes, *The Foreign Policies of the Taft* |

*Administration* (1970); R. W. Van Alstyne, *The Rising American Empire* (1960); Paul A. Varg, *The Making of a Myth: The United States and China, 1899–1912* (1968); Rubin F. Weston, *Racism in U.S. Imperialism: The Influence of Racial Assumptions on American Foreign Policy, 1893–1946* (1972); William Appleman Williams, *The Roots of the Modern American Empire* (1969) and *The Tragedy of American Diplomacy* (1959); Akira Iriye, *Pacific Estrangement: Japanese and American Expansion, 1897–1911* (1972); Jerry Israel, *Progressivism and the Open Door: America and China, 1905–1921* (1971).

**World War I and American Neutrality**

Edwin Borchard and W. P. Lage, *Neutrality for the United States* (1940); Edward Buehrig, *Woodrow Wilson and the Balance of Power* (1955); John Milton Cooper, Jr., *The Vanity of Power: American Isolationism and the First World War, 1914–1917* (1969); Ross Gregory, *The Origins of American Intervention in the First World War* (1971) and *Walter Hines Page: Ambassador to the Court of St. James's* (1970); George Kennan, *American Diplomacy, 1900–1950* (1950); Arthur Link, *Wilson the Diplomatist* (1957); Ernest R. May, *The World War and American Isolation, 1914–1917* (1959); Walter Millis, *The Road to War* (1935); Harley Notter, *The Origins of the Foreign Policy of Woodrow Wilson* (1937); Charles Seymour, *American Neutrality, 1914–1917* (1935) and *American Diplomacy during the World War* (1934); Daniel M. Smith, *The Great Departure* (1965); Charles C. Tansill, *America Goes to War* (1938).

**The United States, World War I, and the Peace Settlement**

Thomas A. Bailey, *Woodrow Wilson and the Lost Peace* (1944); Daniel R. Beaver, *Newton D. Baker and the American War Effort, 1917–1919* (1966); Paul Birdsall, *Versailles Twenty Years After* (1941); George T. Blakey, *Historians on the Homefront: American Propagandists for the Great War* (1970); Garry Clifford, *The Citizen Soldiers: The Plattsburg Training Camps Movement, 1913–1920* (1972); Edward M. Coffman, *The Hilt of the Sword: The Career of Peyton C. Marsh* (1966) and *The War to End All Wars: The American Military Experience in World War I* (1968); Robert D. Cuff, *The War Industries Board: Business-Government Relations during World War I* (1973); Peter G. Filene, *Americans and the Soviet Experiment, 1917–1933* (1967); Denna F. Fleming, *The Origins and Legacies of World War I* (1968) and *The United States and the League of Nations, 1918–1920* (1932); W. B. Fowler, *British-American Relations, 1917–1918: The Role of Sir William Wiseman* (1969); Lawrence E. Gelfand, *The Inquiry: American Preparations for Peace, 1917–1919* (1963); Charles Gilbert, *American Financing of World War I* (1970); Frank L. Grubbs, Jr., *The Struggle for Labor Loyalty: Gompers, the A.F. of L., and the Pacifists, 1917–1920* (1968); Joan M. Jensen, *The Price of Vigilance* (1968); George F. Kennan, *Soviet-American Relations, 1917–1920* (2 vols., 1956); John M. Keynes, *The Economic Consequences of the Peace* (1919); Warren F. Kuehl, *Seeking World Order: The United States and International Organization to 1920* (1969); N. Gordon Levin, Jr., *Woodrow Wilson and World Politics* (1968); Seward W. Livermore, *Politics Is Adjourned: Woodrow Wilson and the War Congress, 1916–1918* (1966); Arno J. Mayer, *Political Origins of the New Diplomacy, 1917–1918* (1959) and *The Politics and Diplomacy of Peacemaking* (1967); H. C. Peterson and Gilbert C. Fite, *Opponents of War, 1917–1918* (1957); William Preston, Jr., *Aliens and Dissenters, Federal Suppression of Radicals, 1903–1933* (1963); Ralph Stone, *The Irreconcilables: The Fight Against the League of Nations* (1970); William Appleman Williams, *American-Russian Relations, 1781–1947* (1952).

PART THREE: A TIME OF PROSPERITY AND DEPRESSION

**Technological Innovation**

Kendall Birr, *Pioneering in Industrial Research: The Story of the General Electric Research Laboratory* (1957); Robert Bruce, *Bell: Alexander Graham Bell and the Conquest of Solitude* (1973); Daniel H. Calhoun, *The American Civil Engineer, Origins and Conflict* (1960); Monte A. Calvert, *The Mechanical Engineer in America, 1830–1910* (1967); Frank Barkley Copley, *Frederick Winslow Taylor* (2 vols., 1923); A. Hunter Dupree, *Science in the Federal Government: A History of Policies and Activities to 1940* (1957); Henry Elsner, Jr., *The Technocrats, Prophets of Automation* (1967); James L. Flink, *America Adopts the Automobile* (1970); Siegfried Giedion, *Mechanization Takes Command* (1948); H. J. Habakkuk, *American and British Technology in the Twentieth Century* (1962); Samuel Haber, *Efficiency and Uplift* (1964); Thomas P. Hughes, *Elmer Sperry, Inventor and Engineer* (1971); John Jewkes, David Sawers, and Richard Stillerman, *The Sources of Invention* (2nd ed., 1969); Matthew Josephson, *Edison* (1959); Sudhir Kakar, *Frederick W. Taylor: A Study in Personality and Innovation* (1970); Melvin Kranzberg and Carroll W. Pursell, Jr., eds., *Technology in Western Civilization* (2 vols., 1967); Edwin T. Layton, *The Revolt of the Engineers: Social Responsibility and the American Engineering Profession* (1971); Malcolm MacLaren, *The Rise of the Electrical Industry during the Nineteenth Century* (1943); W. R. Maclaurin, *Invention and Innovation in the Radio Industry* (1949); Elting Morison, *Men, Machines, and Modern Times* (1966); Lewis Mumford, *Technics and Civilization* (1963); Milton J. Nadworny, *Scientific Management and the Unions* (1955); Harold C. Passer, *The Electrical Manufacturers, 1875–1900* (1953); John B. Rae, *The American Automobile* (1965), *American Automobile Manufacturers* (1959), *Climb to Greatness: The American Aircraft Industry, 1920–1960* (1968), and *The Road and the Car in American Life* (1971); Nathan Rosenberg, ed., *The Economics of Technological Change* (1971); Nathan Rosenberg, *Technology and Economic Growth* (1972); Jacob Schmookler, *Invention and Economic Growth* (1966); W. Paul Strassmann, *Risk and Technological Innovation: American Manufacturing Methods during the Nineteenth Century* (1959); Reynold M. Wik, *Henry Ford and Grass-Roots America* (1972).

**Prosperity and Depression**

Evan Benner Alderfer, *Economics of American Industry* (1957); Harold Barger, *The Management of Money* (1964); Thomas C. Cochran, *The American Business System, 1900–1950* (1957); Solomon Fabricant, *Employment in Manufacturing, 1899–1939* (1942) and *The Output of Manufacturing Industries, 1899–1937* (1940); Milton Friedman and Anna Jacobson Schwartz, *A Monetary History of the United States, 1867–1960* (1963); John G. Glover and Rudolph L. Lagai, *The Development of American Industries* (1959); Robert A. Gordon, *Business Fluctuations* (2nd ed., 1961); Morrell Heald, *The Social Responsibilities of Business: Company and Community, 1900–1960* (1970); Merle Fainsod and L. Gordon, *Government and the American Economy* (1959); John W. Kendrick, *Productivity Trends in the United States* (1961); Simon Kuznets, *National Income and Its Composition, 1919–1938* (1941); Cleona Lewis, *America's Stake in International Investment* (1938); Robert Sobel, *Amex: A History of the American Stock Exchange, 1921–1971* (1972); Thomas Wilson, *Fluctuations in Income and Employment* (1942).

Irving Bernstein, *The Lean Years: A History of the American Worker, 1920–1933* (1960) and *Turbulent Years: A History of the American Worker, 1933–1941* (1970); David Brody, *Labor in Crisis: The Steel Strike of 1919* (1965); Sidney

Fine, *Sit Down: The General Motors Strike of 1936–1937* (1969); Walter Galenson, *The CIO Challenge to the AFL: A History of the American Labor Movement, 1935–1941* (1960); James O. Morris, *Conflict within the AFL: A Study of Craft versus Industrial Unionism, 1901–1938* (1958); Philip Taft, *The AF of L from the Death of Gompers to the Merger* (1964); Robert Zieger, *Republicans and Labor, 1919–1929* (1969).

Adolf A. Berle and Gardiner C. Means, *The Modern Corporation and Private Property* (1932); Lester V. Chandler, *Benjamin Strong, Central Banker* (1958); President's Committee on Recent Economic Changes, *Recent Economic Changes in the United States* (1929); Louis Galambos, *Competition and Cooperation: The Emergence of a National Trade Association* (1966); Ralph L. Nelson, *Merger Movements in American Industry, 1895–1956* (1959); James W. Prothro, *The Dollar Decade: Business Ideas in the 1920s* (1954).

Lester V. Chandler, *America's Greatest Depression, 1929–1941* (1970); Sidney Fine, *The Automobile under the Blue Eagle: Labor, Management and the Automobile Manufacturing Code* (1963); John Kenneth Galbraith, *The Great Crash* (1955); John Kenneth Galbraith and G. Griffith Johnson, Jr., *The Economic Effects of the Federal Public Works Expenditure, 1933–1938* (1940); John Maynard Keynes, *The General Theory of Employment, Interest, and Money* (1936); Robert Lekachman, *The Age of Keynes* (1968); David Lynch, *The Concentration of Economic Power* (1946); Broadus Mitchell, *Depression Decade: From New Era through New Deal, 1929–1941* (1947); Goronwy Rees, *The Great Slump* (1970); James Shideler, *Farm Crisis, 1919–1923* (1957); Robert Sobel, *Panic on Wall Street* (1968); Herbert Stein, *The Fiscal Revolution in America* (1969).

**American Society in the New Era**

Frederick Lewis Allen, *Only Yesterday, An Informal History of the Nineteen-Twenties* (1931); John Braeman et al., eds., *Change and Continuity in Twentieth Century America: The 1920s* (1968); Clarke A. Chambers, *Seedtime of Reform: American Social Service and Social Action, 1918–1933* (1963); Norman H. Clark, *The Dry Years: Prohibition and Social Change in Washington* (1965); Foster R. Dulles, *A History of Recreation: America Learns to Play* (1940); Robert H. Elias, *"Entangling Alliances with None": An Essay on the Individual in the American Twenties* (1973); Norman F. Furniss, *The Fundamentalist Controversy, 1918–1931* (1954); Paul Goodman and Frank Otto Gatell, *America in the Twenties* (1972); Jerry Israel, ed., *Building the Organizational Society: Essays on Associational Activities in Modern America* (1972); John Kobler, *Capone: The Life and World of Al Capone* (1971); J. Stanley Lemons, *The Woman Citizen: Social Feminism in the 1920s* (1973); William E. Leuchtenburg, *The Perils of Prosperity, 1914–32* (1958); William G. McLoughlin, *Billy Sunday Was His Real Name* (1955) and *Modern Revivalism* (1959); Robert M. Miller, *American Protestantism and Social Issues, 1919–1937* (1958); Robert K. Murray, *Red Scare: A Study of National Hysteria, 1919–1920* (1955); George E. Mowry, *The Urban Nation, 1920–1960* (1965); Roderick Nash, *The Nervous Generation: American Thought, 1917–1930* (1970); President's Research Committee on Social Trends, *Recent Social Trends in the United States* (2 vols., 1933); Andrew Sinclair, *Prohibition: The Era of Excess* (1962); June Sochen, *The New Woman: Feminism in Greenwich Village, 1910–1920* (1972).

St. Clair Drake and Horace R. Clayton, *Black Metropolis: A Study of Negro Life in a Northern City* (1945); Charles Glaab and A. Theodore Brown, *A History of Urban America* (1967), Amos H. Hawley, *The Changing Shape of Metropolitan*

*America: Deconcentration Since 1920* (1956) and *Urban Society: An Ecological Approach* (1971); Kenneth T. Jackson, *The Ku Klux Klan in the City, 1915–1930* (1967); Louise V. Kennedy, *The Negro Peasant Turns Cityward* (1930); Don S. Kirschner, *City and Country: Rural Responses to Urbanization in the 1920s* (1970); Robert S. and Helen M. Lynd, *Middletown* (1929); Blake McKelvey, *The Urbanization of America, 1865–1915* (1963) and *The Emergence of Metropolitan America* (1966); Gilbert Osofsky, *Harlem: The Making of a Ghetto, 1890–1930* (1966); Américo Paredes and Ellen J. Stekert, *The Urban Experience and Folk Tradition* (1971); John W. Reps, *The Making of Urban America: A History of City Planning in the United States* (1965); Seth M. Scheiner, *Negro Mecca: A History of the Negro in New York City, 1865–1920* (1965); Leo Schnore, *The Urban Scene: Human Ecology and Demography* (1959); Allan H. Spear, *Black Chicago: The Making of a Negro Ghetto, 1890–1920* (1967).

Charles Alexander, *The Ku Klux Klan in the Southwest* (1965); David M. Chalmers, *Hooded Americanism: The First Century of the Ku Klux Klan, 1865–1965* (1965); E. David Cronon, *Black Moses: The Story of Marcus Garvey* (1955); Elizabeth W. Etheridge, *The Butterfly Caste: A Social History of Pellagra in the South* (1972); John Hope Franklin, *From Slavery to Freedom: A History of American Negroes* (1967); S. P. Fullinwider, *The Mind and Mood of Black America: 20th Century Thought* (1969); Nathan I. Huggins, *Harlem Renaissance* (1972); August Meier and Elliott M. Rudwick, *From Plantation to Ghetto: An Interpretive History of American Negroes* (1966); Gunnar Myrdal, *An American Dilemma* (2 vols., 1944); William M. Tuttle, Jr., *Race Riot: Chicago in the Red Summer of 1919* (1970); Theodore G. Vincent, *Black Power and the Garvey Movement* (1971).

Erik Barnouw, *A Tower in Babel: A History of Broadcasting in the United States. Volume I: to 1933* (1966); Herbert Blumer, *Movies and Conduct* (1933); Malcolm Bradbury, ed., *The American Novel: The Writers of the 1920s* (1971); James B. Gilbert, *Writers and Partisans: A History of Literary Radicalism in America* (1968); Frederick Hoffman, *The Twenties: American Writing in the Post War Decade* (1955); Alfred Kazin, *On Native Grounds: An Interpretation of Modern American Prose Literature* (1942); Lewis Jacobs, *The Rise of American Film* (1968); Arthur Knight, *The Liveliest Art* (1957); Gunther Schuller, *Early Jazz, Its Roots and Musical Development* (1968); Sigmund Spaeth, *A History of Popular Music in America* (1948); Alec Wilder, *American Popular Song: The Great Innovators, 1900–1950* (1972).

**The Politics of the Twenties**  LeRoy Ashby, *The Spearless Leader: Senator Borah and the Progressive Movement in the 1920s* (1972); David Burner, *The Politics of Provincialism: The Democratic Party in Transition, 1918–1932* (1967); Randolph C. Downes, *The Rise of Warren Gamaliel Harding, 1865–1920* (1971); Theodore Draper, *The Roots of American Communism* (1957) and *American Communism and Soviet Russia: The Formative Period* (1960); Gilbert C. Fite, *George N. Peek and the Fight for Farm Parity* (1954); John S. Gambs, *The Decline of the IWW* (1932); Oscar Handlin, *Al Smith and His America* (1958); John D. Hicks, *Republican Ascendancy, 1921–1933* (1960); Herbert Hoover, *Memoirs* (3 vols., 1951–1952); Preston J. Hubbard, *Origins of the TVA: The Muscle Shoals Controversy, 1920–1932* (1961); J. Joseph Huthmacher, *Massachusetts People and Politics, 1919–1933* (1959); Craig Lloyd, *Aggressive Introvert: A Study of Herbert Hoover and Public Relations Management, 1912–1932* (1972); Richard Lowitt, *George W. Norris: The*

*Persistence of a Progressive, 1913–1929* (1971) ; Arthur Mann, *La Guardia: A Fighter Against His Times, 1882–1933* (1959) ; Kenneth C. MacKay, *The Progressive Movement of 1924* (1947) ; Donald B. McCoy, *Calvin Coolidge: The Quiet President* (1967) ; Franklin D. Mitchell, *Embattled Democracy, Mississippi Democratic Politics, 1919–1933* (1968) ; Edmund A. Moore, *A Catholic Runs for President* (1956) ; Robert K. Murray, *The Harding Era: Warren G. Harding and His Administration* (1969) ; *The Politics of Normalcy: Governmental Theory and Practice in the Harding-Coolidge Era* (1973) ; Burl Noggle, *Teapot Dome: Oil and Politics in the 1920s* (1962) ; Arnold S. Rice, *The Ku Klux Klan in American Politics* (1962) ; Albert U. Romasco, *The Poverty of Abundance: Hoover, the Nation, the Depression* (1965) ; Francis Russell, *The Shadow of Blooming Grove: Warren G. Harding in His Times* (1968) ; Arthur M. Schlesinger, Jr., *The Crisis of the Old Order* (1957) ; Jordan A. Schwartz, *The Interregnum of Despair: Hoover, Congress, and the Depression* (1970) ; Andrew Sinclair, *Available Man: The Life Behind the Masks of Warren Gamaliel Harding* (1965) ; Gene Smith, *The Shattered Dream: Herbert Hoover and the Great Depression* (1970) ; Donald Swain, *Federal Conservation Policy, 1921–1933* (1963) ; Harris G. Warren, *Herbert Hoover and the Great Depression* (1959) ; Nancy J. Weiss, *Charles Francis Murphy, 1858–1924: Respectability and Responsibility in Tammany Politics* (1968) ; William Allen White, *A Puritan in Babylon* (1938) ; Donald L. Winters, *Henry Cantwell Wallace as Secretary of Agriculture, 1921–1924* (1970) ; Robert Zieger, *Republicans and Labor, 1919–1929* (1969) .

**The Impact of the Depression**

James Agee and Walker Evans, *Let Us Now Praise Famous Men* (1939) ; Charles C. Alexander, *Nationalism in American Thought, 1930–1945* (1969) ; Frederick Lewis Allen, *Since Yesterday: The Nineteen-Thirties in America* (1940) ; Erik Barnouw, *The Golden Web: A History of Broadcasting in the United States. Vol. II: 1933 to 1953* (1968) ; Caroline Bird, *The Invisible Scar* (1965) ; Dan Carter, *Scottsboro: A Tragedy of the American South* (1969) ; Alistair Cooke, *A Generation on Trial* (1950) ; Roger Daniels, *The Bonus March: An Episode of the Great Depression* (1971) ; Edward Robb Ellis, *A Nation in Torment: The Great American Depression, 1929–1939* (1970) ; Clarence Enzler, *Some Social Aspects of the Depression (1930–1935)* (1939) ; Leo Gurko, *The Angry Decade* (1947) ; Victor Hoar, ed., *The Great Depression* (1969) ; F. Jack Hurley, *Portrait of a Decade: Roy Stryker and the Development of Documentary Photography in the Thirties* (1972) ; Isaac L. Kandel, *The End of an Era* (1941) ; Donald J. Lisio, *The President and Protest: Hoover, Conspiracy, and the Bonus Riot* (1974) ; Robert S. and Helen M. Lynd, *Middletown in Transition* (1937) ; John L. Shover, *Cornbelt Rebellion: The Farmers' Holiday Association* (1965) ; Bernard Sternsher, ed., *Hitting Home: The Great Depression in Town and Country* (1970) ; Harvey Swados, ed., *The American Writer and the Great Depression* (1966) ; Studs Terkel, *Hard Times: An Oral History of the Great Depression* (1970) ; Dixon Wecter, *The Age of the Great Depression* (1948) ; Raymond Wolters, *Negroes and the Great Depression: The Problem of Economic Recovery* (1970) .

**FDR and the New Dealers**

Dean Albertson, *Roosevelt's Farmer: Claude Wickard in the New Deal* (1961) ; Bernard Bellush, *Franklin D. Roosevelt as Governor of New York* (1955) ; Francis L. Broderick, *Right Reverend New Dealer: John A. Ryan* (1963) ; James M. Burns, *Roosevelt: The Lion and the Fox* (1956) and *Roosevelt: The Soldier of Freedom* (1970) ; Searle F. Charles, *Minister of Relief: Harry Hopkins and the Depression*

(1963); Bernard F. Donahoe, *Private Plans and Public Dangers: The Story of FDR's Third Nomination* (1965); James A. Farley, *Behind the Ballots* (1938) and *Jim Farley's Story* (1948); Frank Freidel, *Franklin D. Roosevelt: The Apprenticeship* (1952), *Franklin D. Roosevelt: The Ordeal* (1954), and *Franklin D. Roosevelt: The Triumph* (1956); Daniel Fusfeld, *The Economic Thought of Franklin D. Roosevelt and the Origins of the New Deal* (1956); Harold F. Gosnell, *Champion Campaigner* (1952); Thomas Greer, *What Roosevelt Thought* (1958); Richard A. Henderson, *Maury Maverick: A Political Biography* (1970); Cordell Hull, *Memoirs* (2 vols., 1948); J. Joseph Huthmacher, *Senator Robert F. Wagner and the Rise of Urban Liberalism* (1968); Harold Ickes, *The Autobiography of a Curmudgeon* (1948) and *Secret Diary* (3 vols., 1953–1954); William E. Leuchtenburg, *Franklin D. Roosevelt and the New Deal, 1932–1940* (1963); Herbert S. Parmet and Marie B. Hecht, *Never Again: A President Runs for a Third Term* (1968); Frances Perkins, *The Roosevelt I Knew* (1946); Edgar E. Robinson, *The Roosevelt Leadership, 1933–1945* (1955); Alfred B. Rollins, Jr., *Roosevelt and Howe* (1962); Eleanor Roosevelt, *This Is My Story* (1937) and *This I Remember* (1949); Samuel I. Rosenman, *Working With Roosevelt* (1952); Edward L. and Frederick H. Schapsmeier, *Henry A. Wallace of Iowa: The Agrarian Years, 1910–1940* (1968); Theron F. Schlabach, *Edwin E. Witte, Cautious Reformer* (1969); Arthur M. Schlesinger, Jr., *The Age of Roosevelt: The Crisis of the Old Order, 1919–1933* (1957), *The Coming of the New Deal* (1958), and *The Politics of Upheaval* (1960); Robert E. Sherwood, *Roosevelt and Hopkins* (1948); Bernard Sternsher, *Rexford Tugwell and the New Deal* (1964); Rexford G. Tugwell, *The Democratic Roosevelt* (1957) and *FDR: Architect of an Era* (1967); Grace Tulley, *F.D.R., My Boss* (1949); Thomas E. Vadney, *The Wayward Liberal: A Political Biography of Donald Richberg* (1971); A. J. Wann, *The President as Chief Administrator: A Study of Franklin D. Roosevelt* (1968).

**The New Deal, Its Critics, and Its Interpreters**

Arthur Altmeyer, *The Formative Years of Social Security* (1966); Joseph L. Arnold, *The New Deal in the Suburbs: A History of the Greenbelt Town Program, 1935–1954* (1971); Donald C. Blaisdell, *Government and Agriculture: The Growth of Federal Aid* (1940); Sidney Baldwin, *Poverty and Politics: The Rise and Decline of the Farm Security Administration* (1968); J. Douglas Brown, *An American Philosophy of Social Security: Evolution and Issues* (1972); Josephine C. Brown, *Public Relief, 1929–1939* (1940); Paul K. Conkin, *The New Deal* (1967) and *Tomorrow a New World: The New Deal Community Program* (1959); Marriner Eccles, *Beckoning Frontiers* (1951); Clyde T. Ellis, *A Giant Step* (1966); Robert M. Fisher, *Twenty Years of Public Housing* (1959); Ellis W. Hawley, *The New Deal and the Problem of Monopoly: A Study in Economic Ambivalence* (1966); Charles O. Jackson, *Food and Drug Legislation in the New Deal* (1970); Roy Lubove, *The Struggle for Social Security, 1900–1935* (1968); Jerry Mangione, *The Dream and the Deal: The Federal Writers' Project, 1935–1943* (1972); Jane De-Hart Mathews, *The Federal Theatre, 1935–1939: Plays, Relief, and Politics* (1967); Thomas K. McCraw, *Morgan vs. Lilienthal: The Feud Within the TVA* (1970) and *TVA and the Power Fight, 1933–1939* (1971); William F. McDonald, *Federal Relief Administration and the Arts* (1969); Charles McKinley and R. W. Frase, *Launching Social Security: A Capture-and-Record Account, 1935–1937* (1971); Richard D. McKinzie, *The New Deal for Artists* (1973); Raymond Moley, *After Seven Years* (1939) and *The First New Deal* (1966); Daniel Nelson, *Unemployment Insurance: The American Experience, 1915–1935* (1969); Francis V. O'Connor, ed., *The New Deal Art Project: An Anthology of Memoirs* (1972); Van L. Perkins, *Crisis in Agriculture: The Agricultural Adjustment Administration and the New Deal, 1933* (1969); Richard Polenberg, *Reorganizing Roosevelt's Government: The Controversy over Executive Reorganization, 1936–1939* (1966); C. Herman Pritchett, *The Tennessee Valley Authority: A Study in Public Administration* (1943); Basil Rauch, *The History of the New Deal* (1944); John A. Salmond, *The Civilian Conservation Corps, 1933–1942: A New Deal Case Study* (1967); Clarence S. Stein, *The New Deal in the Suburbs: A History of the Greenbelt Town Program, 1935–1954* (1971); Edwin E. Witte, *Development of the Social Security Act* (1962).

Jerold S. Auerbach, *Labor and Liberty: The La Follette Committee and the New Deal* (1966); Leonard Baker, *Back to Back: The Duel between FDR and the Supreme Court* (1967); David E. Conrad, *Forgotten Farmers: The Story of Share-croppers in the New Deal* (1965); Arthur A. Ekirch, Jr., *Ideologies and Utopias: The Impact of the New Deal on American Thought* (1969); George Q. Flynn, *American Catholics & the Roosevelt Presidency, 1932–1936* (1968); Otis Graham, Jr., *An Encore for Reform: The Old Progressives and the New Deal* (1967); Donald H. Grubbs, *Cry from the Cotton: The Southern Tenant Farmers' Union and the New Deal* (1971); Daniel S. Hirshfield, *The Lost Reform: The Campaign for Compulsory Health Insurance in the United States from 1932 to 1943* (1970); Richard S. Kirkendall, *Social Scientists and Farm Politics in the Age of Roosevelt* (1966); Robert J. Morgan, *Governing Soil Conservation: Thirty Years of the New Decentralization* (1966); Paul L. Murphy, *The Constitution in Crisis Times, 1918–1969* (1972); James T. Patterson, *Congressional Conservatism and the New Deal: The Growth of a Conservative Coalition in Congress, 1933–1939* (1967) and *The New Deal and the States* (1969); Merlo J. Pusey, *Charles Evans Hughes* (2 vols., 1951); William D. Rowley, *M. L. Wilson and the Campaign for the Domestic Allotment* (1970); Walter I. Trattner, *Crusade for the Children: A History of the National Child Labor Committee and Child Labor Reform in America* (1970).

Daniel Aaron, *Writers on the Left* (1961); John W. Aldridge, *After the Lost Generation* (1951); Charles A. Beard, *America in Midpassage* (1939); Alfred Bingham, *Insurgent America* (1935); Maxwell Geismar, *Writers in Crisis: The American Novel, 1925–1940* (1961); Charles P. Larrowe, *Harry Bridges: The Rise and Fall of Radical Labor in the United States* (1972); R. Alan Lawson, *The Failure of Independent Liberalism, 1930–1941* (1971); Theodore Lowi, *The End of Liberalism* (1969); Samuel Lubell, *The Future of American Politics* (1952); Walter B. Rideout, *The Radical Novel in the United States, 1900–1954* (1956); Frank A. Warren III, *Liberals and Communism: The "Red Decade" Revisited* (1966).

Ellsworth Barnard, *Wendell Willkie: A Fighter for Freedom* (1966); David H. Bennett, *Demagogues in the Depression: American Radicals in the Union Party, 1932–1936* (1969); Bernard K. Johnpoll, *Pacifist's Progress: Norman Thomas and the Decline of American Socialism* (1970); Donald B. Johnson, *The Republican Party and Wendell Willkie* (1968); Morton Keller, *In Defense of Yesterday: James M. Beck and the Politics of Conservatism, 1861–1936* (1959); Sheldon Marcus, *Father Coughlin: The Tumultuous Life of the Priest of the Little Flower* (1973); Donald McCoy, *Landon* (1966); Warren Moscow, *Roosevelt and Willkie* (1968); Murray B. Seidler, *Norman Thomas: Respectable Rebel* (1967); Charles J. Tull, *Father Coughlin and the New Deal* (1965); T. Harry Williams, *Huey Long* (1969); George Wolfskill, *Revolt of the Conservatives: A History of the*

*American Liberty League, 1934–1940* (1962); George Wolfskill and John A. Hudson, *All but the People: Franklin D. Roosevelt and His Critics, 1933–39* (1969).

**Pacifism, Revisionism, and Isolationism**

Selig Adler, *The Isolationist Impulse* (1958) and *The Uncertain Giant, 1921–1941: American Foreign Policy Between the Wars* (1965); Mark L. Chadwin, *The Hawks of World War II* (1968); Charles Chatfield, *For Peace and Justice: Pacifism in America, 1914–1941* (1971); Murray I. Cohen, *The American Revisionists: The Lessons of Intervention in World War I* (1967); Wayne S. Cole, *America First: the Battle against Intervention, 1940–1941* (1953) and *Senator Gerald P. Nye and American Foreign Relations* (1962); Robert A. Divine, *The Illusion of Neutrality* (1962); Donald F. Drummond, *The Passing of American Neutrality* (1955); Denna F. Fleming, *The United States and World Organization, 1921–1933* (1968); Donald J. Friedman, *The Road from Isolation: The Campaign of the American Committee for Non-Participation in Japanese Aggression, 1938–1941* (1968); Walter Johnson, *The Battle Against Isolation* (1944); Manfred Jonas, *Isolationism in America, 1935–1941* (1966); John K. Nelson, *The Peace Prophets: American Pacifist Thought, 1919–1941* (1967); James M. Seavey, *Neutrality Legislation* (1939); John Wiltz, *In Search of Peace: The Senate Munitions Inquiry, 1934–1936* (1963).

**American Foreign Policy in the Twenties**

Dorothy Borg, *American Policy and the Chinese Revolution, 1925–1928* (1947); Thomas H. Buckley, *The United States and the Washington Conference* (1970); Richard N. Current, *Secretary Stimson* (1954); Alexander DeConde, *Herbert Hoover's Latin American Policy* (1951); L. Ethan Ellis, *Frank B. Kellogg and American Foreign Relations, 1925–1929* (1961) and *Republican Foreign Policy, 1921–1933* (1968); Herbert Feis, *The Diplomacy of the Dollar, First Era, 1919–1932* (1950); Robert H. Ferrell, *American Diplomacy in the Great Depression: Hoover-Stimson Foreign Policy, 1929–1933* (1957), *Frank B. Kellogg—Henry L. Stimson* (1963), and *Peace in Their Time: The Origins of the Kellogg-Briand Pact* (1952); Peter G. Filene, *Americans and the Soviet Experiment, 1917–1933* (1967); Betty Glad, *Charles Evans Hughes and the Illusions of Innocence: A Study in American Diplomacy* (1966); Akira Iriye, *After Imperialism: The Search for a New Order in the Far East, 1921–1931* (1965); Robert Langer, *Seizure of Territory: The Stimson Doctrine* (1947); Elting E. Morison, *Turmoil and Tradition: A Study of the Life and Times of Henry L. Stimson* (1960); Dexter Perkins, *Charles Evans Hughes and American Democratic Statesmanship* (1956); Harold and Margaret Sprout, *Toward a New Order of Sea Power* (1940); Merze Tate, *The United States and Armaments* (1948); Joan H. Wilson, *American Business and Foreign Policy* (1971).

**FDR and Foreign Affairs**

Charles A. Beard, *American Foreign Policy in the Making, 1932–1940* (1946) and *President Roosevelt and the Coming of the War, 1941* (1948); James M. Burns, *Roosevelt: Soldier of Freedom* (1970); Robert A. Divine, *The Reluctant Belligerent: American Entry into World War II* (1965) and *Second Chance, The Triumph of Internationalism in America during World War II* (1967); Jean-Baptiste Duroselle, *From Wilson to Roosevelt* (1968); T. R. Fehrenbach, *F.D.R.'s Undeclared War, 1939 to 1941* (1967); Herbert Feis, *The Changing Pattern of International Economic Affairs* (1940) and *1933: Characters in Crisis* (1966); Lloyd C. Gardner, *Economic Aspects of New Deal Diplomacy* (1964); Edward O. Guerrant, *Roosevelt's Good Neighbor Policy* (1950); Waldo H. Heinrichs, Jr., *American*

*Ambassador: Joseph C. Grew and the Development of the United States Diplomatic Tradition* (1966) ; Cordell Hull, *Memoirs* (2 vols., 1948) ; Walter Johnson, ed., *Turbulent Era: A Diplomatic Record of Forty Years* (2 vols., 1952) ; Warren F. Kimball, *The Most Unsordid Act: Lend-Lease, 1939–1941* (1969) ; William L. Langer and S. Everett Gleason, *The Challenge to Isolation: 1937–1940* (1952) and *The Undeclared War, 1940–1941* (1953) ; James J. Martin, *American Liberalism and World Politics, 1931–1941* (2 vols., 1964) ; Julius W. Pratt, *Cordell Hull, 1933–1944* (2 vols., 1964) ; Basil Rauch, *Roosevelt: From Munich to Pearl Harbor* (1950) ; Bruce M. Russett, *No Clear and Present Danger: A Skeptical View of the United States Entry into World War II* (1972) ; Charles C. Tansill, *Back Door to War: Roosevelt's Foreign Policy, 1933–1941* (1952) ; Sumner Welles, *The Time for Decision* (1944) ; John E. Wiltz, *From Isolation to War, 1931–1941* (1968) ; Bryce Wood, *The Making of the Good Neighbor Policy* (1961).

Leland V. Bell, *In Hitler's Shadow: The Anatomy of American Nazism* (1973) ; Edward Bennett, *Recognition of Russia: An American Foreign Policy Dilemma* (1970) ; James V. Compton, *The Swastika and the Eagle: Hitler, the United States and the Origins of World War II* (1967) ; Robert Dallek, *Democrat and Diplomat: The Life of William E. Dodd* (1968) ; Henry L. Feingold, *The Politics of Rescue: The Roosevelt Administration and the Holocaust, 1938–1945* (1970) ; Saul Friedlander, *Prelude to Downfall: Hitler and the United States, 1939–1941* (1967) ; Alton Frye, *Germany and the American Hemisphere, 1933–1941* (1970) ; Allen Guttmann, *The Wound in the Heart: America and the Spanish Civil War* (1962) ; Brice Harris, Jr., *The United States and the Italo-Ethiopian Crisis* (1964) ; Arthur D. Morse, *While Six Million Died* (1967) ; Arnold Offner, *American Appeasement: United States Foreign Policy and Germany, 1933–1938* (1969) ; Richard P. Traina, *American Diplomacy and the Spanish Civil War* (1968) ; Hans L. Trefousse, *Germany and American Neutrality, 1939–1941* (1951) ; David S. Wyman, *Paper Walls: America and the Refugee Crisis, 1938–1941* (1968).

Reginald Bassett, *Democracy and Foreign Policy, the Sino-Japanese Dispute, 1931–1933* (1952) ; Dorothy Borg, *The United States and the Far Eastern Crisis of 1933–1938* (1964) ; Herbert Feis, *The Road to Pearl Harbor* (1950) ; A. Whitney Griswold, *The Far Eastern Policy of the United States* (1938) ; Walter Lord, *Day of Infamy* (1957) ; Armin Rappaport, *Henry L. Stimson and Japan, 1931–33* (1963) ; Sara P. Smith, *The Manchurian Crisis, 1931–1932* (1948) ; John Toland, *The Rising Sun: The Decline and Fall of the Japanese Empire, 1936–1945* (1970) ; Gerald E. Wheeler, *Prelude to Pearl Harbor, The United States Navy and the Far East, 1921–1931* (1963) ; Roberta Wohlstetter, *Pearl Harbor: Warning and Decision* (1962).

PART FOUR: A TIME OF WAR, AFFLUENCE, DISRUPTION, AND JUDGMENT

**World War II at Home**

Albert A. Blum, *Drafted or Deferred* (1967) ; Jacobus ten Broek, et al., *Prejudice, War and the Constitution: Japanese-American Evacuation and Resettlement* (1958) ; Lowell J. Carr and James E. Stermer, *Willow Run: A Study of Industrialization and Cultural Inadequacy* (1952) ; Bruce Catton, *The War Lords of Washington* (1951) ; Marshall B. Clinard, *The Black Market* (1952) ; Edward S. Corwin, *Total War and the Constitution* (1947) ; Roger Daniels, *Concentration Camps USA: Japanese Americans and World War II* (1971) ; John K. Galbraith, *Theory of Price Control* (1952) ; Jack Goodman, ed., *While You Were Gone: A Report on*

*Wartime Life in the United States* (1946); Robert J. Havighurst and H. Gerthon Morgan, *The Social History of a War-Boom Community* (1951); Reuben Hill, *Families under Stress* (1949); Eliot Janeway, *The Struggle for Survival* (1951); Gladys M. Kammerer, *Impact of War on Federal Personnel Administration, 1939–1945* (1951); Francis E. Merrill, *Social Problems on the Home Front* (1948); Donald M. Nelson, *Arsenal of Democracy: The Story of American War Production* (1946); Randolph E. Paul, *Taxation for Prosperity* (1947); Richard Polenberg, ed., *America at War: The Home Front, 1941–1945* (1968); Richard Polenberg, *War and Society: The United States, 1941–1945* (1972); Davis R. B. Ross, *Preparing for Ulysses: Politics and Veterans During World War II* (1969); Joel Seidman, *American Labor from Defense to Reconversion* (1953); Mulford Q. Sibley and Philip E. Jacob, *Conscription of Conscience: The American State and the Conscientious Objector* (1952); Herman Miles Somers, *Presidential Agency: The Office of War Mobilization and Reconversion* (1950); Walter W. Wilcox, *The Farmer in the Second World War* (1947); Lawrence Wittner, *Rebels Against War: The American Peace Movement, 1941–1960* (1969); Roland Young, Congressional Politics in the Second World War (1956).

**The Diplomacy and Military Action of World War II**

Gar Alperovitz, *Atomic Diplomacy: Hiroshima and Potsdam* (1965); Stephen E. Ambrose, *The Rise to Globalism: American Foreign Policy Since 1938* (1971); Robert Beitzell, *The Uneasy Alliance: America, Britain, and Russia, 1941–1943* (1972); William J. Bosch, *Judgment on Nuremberg: American Attitudes Toward the Major German War-Crime Trials* (1970); Russell D. Buhite, *Patrick J. Hurley and American Foreign Policy* (1973); James M. Burns, *Roosevelt: The Soldier of Freedom* (1970); Robert J. C. Butow, *Japan's Decision to Surrender* (1954); Diane Shaver Clemens, *Yalta* (1970); Robert A. Divine, *Roosevelt and World War II* (1969); Herbert Feis, *The Atomic Bomb and the End of World War II* (1966), *Between War and Peace: The Potsdam Conference* (1960), *Churchill, Roosevelt, Stalin* (1957), and *Japan Subdued* (1961); Lloyd C. Gardner, *Architects of Illusion, Men and Ideas in American Foreign Policy, 1941–1949* (1970); Gabriel Kolko, *The Politics of War: The World and United States Foreign Policy, 1943–1945* (1968); William L. Langer, *Our Vichy Gamble* (1957); William L. Neumann, *After Victory: Churchill, Roosevelt, Stalin and the Making of the Peace* (1969); Raymond G. O'Connor, *Diplomacy for Victory: FDR and Unconditional Surrender* (1971); Robert E. Sherwood, *Roosevelt and Hopkins* (1948); Gaddis Smith, *American Diplomacy during the Second World War* (1965); Henry Stimson and McGeorge Bundy, *On Active Service in Peace and War* (1948); Theodore H. White, ed., *The Stilwell Papers* (1948).

Stephen E. Ambrose, *Eisenhower and Berlin: The Decision to Halt at the Elbe* (1967) and *The Supreme Commander: The War Years of General Dwight D. Eisenhower* (1970); Omar N. Bradley, *A Soldier's Story* (1951); A. Russell Buchanan, *The United States in World War II* (2 vols., 1964); Dwight D. Eisenhower, *Crusade in Europe* (1948); Lenore Fine and Jesse A. Remington, *United States Army in World War II: The Technical Services—The Corps of Engineers: Construction in the United States* (1972); Kent Roberts Greenfield, *American Strategy in World War II* (1963); Kent Roberts Greenfield, ed., *Command Decisions* (1959); Haywood S. Hansell, Jr., *The Air Plan That Defeated Hitler* (1972); Basil H. Liddell Hart, *History of the Second World War* (1970); Hajo Holborn, *American Military Government* (1947); Martha Byrd Hoyle, *A World in Flames: The History of World War II* (1970); D. Clayton James, *The Years of MacArthur,*

Vol. I (1970); Gavin Long, *MacArthur as Military Commander* (1969); Jay Luvaas, ed., *DEAR MISS EM: General Eichelberger's War in the Pacific, 1942–1945* (1972); Walter Millis, *This Is Pearl!* (1947); Samuel Eliot Morison, *Strategy and Compromise* (1958) and *The Two-Ocean War* (1963); Forrest C. Pogue, *George C. Marshall* (3 vols., 1963–1973); Fletcher Pratt, *War for the World* (1950); Samuel A. Stouffer et al., *The American Soldier* (2 vols., 1949); Chester Wilmot, *The Struggle for Europe* (1952); Gordon Wright, *The Ordeal of Total War* (1968).

**Truman, Eisenhower, and the Cold War**

John Braeman et al., eds., *Twentieth Century American Foreign Policy* (1971); Seyom Brown, *The Faces of Power: Constancy and Change in United States Foreign Policy from Truman to Johnson* (1968); William G. Carleton, *The Revolution in American Foreign Policy* (1967); Council on Foreign Relations, *The United States in World Affairs*, 1945–1967, 1970 (24 vols., 1947–1972); Herbert Feis, *From Trust to Terror: The Onset of the Cold War, 1945–1950* (1971); Denna F. Fleming, *The Cold War and Its Origins, 1917–1960* (2 vols., 1961); John Lewis Gaddis, *The United States and the Origins of the Cold War, 1946–1947* (1972); Lloyd Gardner, Arthur Schlesinger, Jr., and Hans J. Morgenthau, *The Origins of the Cold War* (1970); Norman A. Graebner, *Cold War Diplomacy, 1945–1960* (1961) and *The New Isolationism* (1956); David Horowitz, *The Free World Colossus* (1965); Samuel P. Huntington, *The Common Defense: Strategic Programs in National Politics* (1961); Richard A. Johnson, *The Administration of United States Foreign Policy* (1971); George F. Kennan, *American Diplomacy, 1900–1950* (1951); Gabriel Kolko, *The Roots of American Foreign Policy: An Analysis of Power and Purpose* (1969); Joyce and Gabriel Kolko, *The Limits of Power: The World and United States Foreign Policy, 1945–1954* (1972); George Liska, *The New Statecraft: Foreign Aid in American Foreign Policy* (1960); William H. McNeill, *America, Britain, and Russia: Their Co-operation and Conflict, 1941–1946* (1953); Robert E. Osgood, *Limited War* (1957); Lisle A. Rose, *After Yalta: America and the Origins of the Cold War* (1973); John W. Spanier, *American Foreign Policy Since World War II* (1965); Edmund Stillman and William Pfaff, *Power and Impotence: The Failure of America's Foreign Policy* (1966); Adam B. Ulam, *Expansion and Coexistence: The History of Soviet Foreign Policy, 1917–1967* (1968); H. Bradford Westerfield, *Foreign Policy and Party Politics: Pearl Harbor to Korea* (1955); Arnold Wolfers, *Alliance Policy in the Cold War* (1959).

David P. Calleo, *The Atlantic Fantasy* (1970); W. Phillips Davison, *The Berlin Blockade* (1958); John K. Fairbank, *China: The People's Middle Kingdom and the U.S.A.* (1967); Herbert Feis, *The China Tangle* (1953); George C. Herring, Jr., *Aid to Russia, 1941–1946: Strategy, Diplomacy, the Origins of the Cold War* (1973); Robert Hunter, *Security in Europe* (1969); Henry A. Kissinger, *The Troubled Partnership: A Reappraisal of the Atlantic Alliance* (1965); Bruce Kublick, *American Policy and the Division of Germany: The Clash with Russia over Reparations* (1972); Walter La Feber, *America, Russia, and the Cold War, 1945–1966* (1967); Clarence G. Lasby, *Project Paperclip: German Scientists and the Cold War* (1971); Robert E. Osgood, *NATO: The Entangling Alliance* (1962); Glenn D. Paige, *The Korean Decision: June 24–30, 1950* (1968); W. H. Parker, *The Superpowers: The United States and the Soviet Union Compared* (1972); Robert Randle, *Geneva 1954* (1970); David Rees, *Korea: The Limited War* (1964); Dorothy Robins, *Experiment in Democracy: The Story of U.S. Citizen Organizations in Forging the Charter of the United Nations* (1971); John W. Spanier, *The Truman-MacArthur Controversy and the Korean War* (1965); Athan G. Theoharis, *The Yalta Myths:*

*An Issue in U.S. Politics, 1945–1955* (1970); Tang Tsou, *America's Failure in China, 1941–1950* (1963); Robert S. Walters, *American and Soviet Aid: A Comparative Analysis* (1970); Allen Whiting, *China Crosses the Yalu: The Decision to Enter the Korean War* (1960).

Dean Acheson, *Present at the Creation: My Years in the State Department* (1969); A. H. Berding, *Dulles on Diplomacy* (1965); James F. Byrnes, *Speaking Frankly* (1947); Herman Finer, *Dulles Over Suez: The Theory and Practice of His Diplomacy* (1964); Richard Goold-Adams, *The Time of Power* (1962); Charles E. Bohlen, *Witness to History, 1929–1969* (1973); Dwight D. Eisenhower, *The White House Years: Mandate for Change* (1963) and *The White House Years: Waging Peace, 1956–1961* (1965); Robert H. Ferrell, *George C. Marshall* (1966); Michael A. Guhin, *John Foster Dulles: A Statesman and His Times* (1972); George F. Kennan, *Memoirs* (2 vols., 1968–1972); Walter Millis, ed., *The Forrestal Diaries* (1951); Herbert S. Parmet, *Eisenhower and the American Crusades* (1972); Gaddis Smith, *Dean Acheson* (1972); Harry S Truman, *Memoirs* (2 vols., 1955–1956); Arthur H. Vandenberg, Jr., ed., *The Private Papers of Senator Vandenberg* (1952).

**The Affluent Society**

Jack Barbash, *The Practice of Unionism* (1956); Benjamin Haggott Beckhart, *Federal Reserve System* (1972); Lester V. Chandler, *Inflation in the United States, 1940–1948* (1950); R. E. Freeman, ed., *Postwar Economic Trends* (1960); Edward S. Flash, Jr., *Economic Advice and Presidential Leadership: The Council of Economic Advisers* (1965); John Kenneth Galbraith, *The Affluent Society* (2nd ed., revised, 1969), *American Capitalism* (1952), and *The New Industrial State* (1967); Alvin Hansen, *Economic Policy and Full Employment* (1947), *The American Economy* (1957), *Economic Issues of the 1960s* (1960), and *The Postwar American Economy* (1964); Jim F. Heath, *John F. Kennedy and the Business Community* (1969); Walter Heller, *New Dimensions of Political Economy* (1966); Edward Higbee, *Farms and Farmers in an Urban Age* (1963); Eliot Janeway, *The Economics of Crisis: War, Politics and the Dollar* (1968); Robert Lekachman, *Inflation: The Permanent Problem of Boom and Bust* (1973); David Lilienthal, *Big Business: A New Era* (1953); Herman P. Miller, *Rich Man, Poor Man* (1971); Mabel Newcomer, *The Big Business Executive* (1955); Ronald Radosh, *American Labor and United States Foreign Policy* (1969); Vernon W. Ruttan et al., *Agricultural Policy in an Affluent Society* (1969); Joel Seidman, *American Labor from Defense to Reconversion* (1953); George A. Steiner, *Government's Role in Economic Life* (1953); Robert L. Tyler, *Walter Reuther* (1973); Harold G. Vatter, *The U.S. Economy in the 1950s* (1963); Michael Wenk, S. M. Tomasi, and Geno Baroni, *Pieces of a Dream: The Ethnic Worker's Crisis with America* (1972).

Daniel J. Boorstin, *The Americans: The Democratic Experience* (1973) and *The Image: A Guide to Pseudo-Events in America* (1961); John Brooks, *The Great Leap* (1966); Commission on Population Growth and the American Future, *Population and the American Future* (1972); Lawrence A. Cremin, *The Transformation of the School: Progressivism in American Education, 1876–1957* (1961); Peter Drucker, *Age of Discontinuity* (1969) and *The New Society* (1950); Paul R. Ehrlich, *The Population Bomb* (1968); Philip M. Hauser, ed., *The Population Dilemma* (2nd ed., 1969); "Historical Population Studies," *Daedalus* (Spring 1968); Richard Hofstadter and Wilson Smith, *American Higher Education* (1961); David Lavender, *California: Land of New Beginnings* (1972); Max Lerner, *America as a Civilization: Life and Thought in the United States Today* (1957);

Marshall McLuhan, *Understanding Media* (1964); "Mass Culture and Mass Media," *Daedalus* (Spring 1960); C. Wright Mills, *The Power Elite* (1959) and *White Collar: The American Middle Classes* (1956); Larry K. Y. Ng, *The Population Crisis* (1965); William L. O'Neill, *Coming Apart: An Informal History of America in the 1960s* (1971); William Petersen, *The Politics of Population* (1964); David Riesman, Reuel Denney, and Nathan Glazer, *The Lonely Crowd* (1950); Bernard Rosenberg, *Mass Culture Revisited* (1971); Warren S. Thompson and David T. Lewis, *Population Problems* (5th ed., 1965); William H. Whyte, *The Organization Man* (1956).

Bennett M. Berger, *Working-Class Suburb* (1960); Hans Blumenfeld, *The Modern Metropolis* (1967); Donald J. Bogue, *Metropolitan Decentralization: A Study of Differential Growth* (1950); Benjamin Chinitz, ed., *City and Suburb: The Economics of Metropolitan Growth* (1964); Carl Condit, *American Building* (1968); William M. Dobriner, *Class in Suburbia* (1963); William M. Dobriner, ed., *The Suburban Community* (1958); Scott Donaldson, *The Suburban Myth* (1969); Herbert J. Gans, *The Levittowners* (1967) and *People and Plans: Essays on Urban Problems and Solutions* (1968); Mitchell Gordon, *Sick Cities* (1964); Jean Gottman, *Megalopolis: The Urbanized Northeastern Seaboard of the United States* (1961); Philip M. Hauser and Leo F. Schnore, eds., *The Study of Urbanization* (1965); Amos H. Hawley, *The Changing Shape of Metropolitan America: Deconcentration since 1920* (1956); Jane Jacobs, *The Death and Life of Great American Cities* (1961) and *The Economy of Cities* (1969); Robert C. Wood, *Suburbia: Its People and Their Politics* (1958).

## Postwar Politics

Barton J. Bernstein and Allen J. Matusow, eds., *The Truman Administration: A Documentary History* (1966); Jonathan Daniels, *The Man of Independence* (1950); Susan Hartmann, *Truman and the 80th Congress* (1971); J. Joseph Huthmacher, ed., *The Truman Years: The Reconstruction of Postwar America* (1972); Richard S. Kirkendall, ed., *The Truman Period as a Research Field* (1967); Allen J. Matusow, *Farm Policies and Politics in the Truman Years* (1967); Frank McNaughton and Walter Hehmeyer, *Harry Truman: President* (1958); Cabell Phillips, *The Truman Presidency: The History of a Triumphant Succession* (1966); Irwin Rose, *The Loneliest Campaign: The Truman Victory of 1948* (1968); Alfred Steinberg, *The Man from Missouri* (1962); Harry S. Truman, *Memoirs* (2 vols., 1955–1956); Margaret Truman, *Harry S. Truman* (1973).

Richard M. Freeland, *The Truman Doctrine and the Origins of McCarthyism: Foreign Policy, Domestic Politics, and Internal Security, 1946–1948* (1972); Robert Griffith, *The Politics of Fear: Joseph R. McCarthy and the Senate* (1970); Alan D. Harper, *The Politics of Loyalty: The White House and the Communist Issue, 1946–1952* (1969); Earl Latham, *The Communist Controversy in Washington: From New Deal to McCarthy* (1966); Seymour M. Lipset and Earl Raab, *The Politics of Unreason: Right-Wing Extremism in America, 1790–1970* (1970); Michael Paul Rogin, *The Intellectuals and McCarthy: The Radical Specter* (1967); Richard H. Rovere, *Senator Joe McCarthy* (1959); Athan Theoharis, *Seeds of Repression: Harry S. Truman and the Origins of McCarthyism* (1971).

Ronald J. Caridi, *The Korean War and American Politics: The Republican Party as a Case Study* (1968); Marquis Childs, *Eisenhower: Captive Hero* (1958); Robert J. Donovan, *Eisenhower: The Inside Story* (1956); Dwight D. Eisenhower, *The White House Years: Mandate for Change* (1963) and *The White House Years: Waging Peace, 1956–1961* (1965); Emmet John Hughes, *The Ordeal of Power:*

*A Political Memoir of the Eisenhower Years* (1963); Arthur Larson, *A Republican Looks at His Party* (1956); Herbert S. Parmet, *Eisenhower and the American Crusades* (1972); James T. Patterson, *Mr. Republican: A Biography of Robert A. Taft* (1972); Merlo J. Pusey, *Eisenhower the President* (1956).

David S. Broder, *The Party's Over: The Failure of Politics in America* (1971); Samuel Lubell, *The Future of American Politics* (3rd ed., 1965) and *The Revolt of the Moderates* (1956); Robert G. McCloskey, *The Modern Supreme Court* (1972); Arthur F. McClure, *The Truman Administration and the Problems of Post-war Labor, 1945–1948* (1969); Curtis MacDougall, *Gideon's Army* (1965); Norman D. Markowitz, *The Rise and Fall of the People's Century: Henry A. Wallace and American Liberalism, 1941–1948* (1973); Edward L. and Frederick H. Schapsmeier, *Prophet in Politics: Henry A. Wallace and the War Years, 1940–1965* (1970); Karl M. Schmidt, *Henry A. Wallace, Quixotic Crusader* (1960); David A. Shannon, *The Decline of American Communism* (1959); I. F. Stone, *The Haunted Fifties* (1960).

**Social Issues:
Civil Rights,
"the Movement,"
and Feminism**

James Baldwin, *Notes of a Native Son* (1957), *Nobody Knows My Name* (1961), and *The Fire Next Time* (1963); William C. Berman, *The Politics of Civil Rights in the Truman Administration* (1970); Archibald Cox, *The Warren Court: Constitutional Decision as an Instrument of Reform* (1968); Eldridge Cleaver, *Soul on Ice* (1968); Pete Daniel, *The Shadow of Slavery: Peonage in the South, 1901–1969* (1972); Richard M. Dalfiume, *Desegregation of the U.S. Armed Forces: Fighting on Two Fronts, 1939–1953* (1969); Foster R. Dulles, *The Civil Rights Commission, 1957–1965* (1968); Philip S. Foner, ed., *The Black Panthers Speak* (1970); Martin Luther King, Jr., *Stride Toward Freedom* (1958) and *Why We Can't Wait* (1964); C. Eric Lincoln, *The Black Muslims in America* (1973); Lionel Lokos, *House Divided: The Life and Legacy of Martin Luther King* (1968); Malcolm X, *Autobiography of Malcolm X* (1965); Neil R. McMillan, *The Citizens Council: Organized Resistance to the Second Reconstruction, 1954–1964* (1971); Carey McWilliams, *North from Mexico* (1948); August Meier and Elliott Rudwick, *CORE: A Study in the Civil Rights Movement, 1942–1968* (1973); Joan Moore, *The Mexican American* (1970); Benjamin Muse, *The American Negro Revolution: From Non-Violence to Black Power, 1963–1967* (1968); Wilson Record, *The Negro and the Communist Party* (1951); Charles E. Silberman, *Crisis in Black and White* (1964).

Philip G. Altbach, *Student Politics in America: A Historical Analysis* (1974); Jerry L. Avorn et al., eds., *Up Against the Ivy Wall: A History of the Columbia Crisis* (1968); Hal Draper, *Berkeley: The New Student Revolt* (1965); Roger Kahn, *The Battle of Morningside Heights: Why Students Rebel* (1970); Kenneth Kenniston, *Young Radicals: Notes on Committed Youth* (1968); Richard King, *The Party of Eros: Radical Social Thought and the Realm of Freedom* (1972); Christopher Lasch, *The Agony of the American Left* (1969); Laurence Leamer, *The Paper Revolutionaries: The Rise of the Underground Press* (1972); Seymour M. Lipset and Gerald M. Schaflander, *Passion and Politics: Student Activism in America* (1971); Robert James Maddox, *The New Left and the Origins of the Cold War* (1973); Norman Mailer, *The Armies of the Night* (1968); Gilbert Moore, *A Special Rage* (1972); William O'Neill, *Coming Apart: An Informal History of America in the 1960s* (1971); Ron E. Roberts, *The New Communes* (1971); Theodore Roszak, *The Making of a Counterculture: Reflections on the Technocratic Society and Its Youthful Opposition* (1969); Kirkpatrick Sale, *SDS*

(1973) ; Massimo Teodori, ed., *The New Left: A Documentary History* (1969) ; Irwin Unger, *The Movement: A History of the American Left, 1959–1972* (1974).

William Henry Chafe, *The American Woman: Her Changing Social, Economic, and Political Roles, 1920–1970* (1972) ; Nancy L. Cott, ed., *Root of Bitterness* (1972) ; Betty Friedan, *The Feminine Mystique* (1963) ; Charlotte Perkins Gilman (Carl Degler, ed.), *Women and Economics* (1966) ; Germaine Greer, *The Female Eunuch* (1971) ; Edward T. James, Janet Wilson James, and Paul S. Boyer, eds., *Notable American Women, 1607–1950: A Biographical Dictionary* (3 vols., 1971) ; Aileen Kraditor, ed., *Up from the Pedestal* (1968) ; Juanita Kreps, *Sex in the Marketplace* (1971) ; Gerda Lerner, ed., *Black Women in White America: A Documentary History* (1972) ; Gerda Lerner, *The Woman in American History* (1971) ; Kate Millett, *Sexual Politics* (1970) ; Mabel Newcomer, *A Century of Higher Education for American Women* (1959) ; Betty and Theodore Roszak, eds., *Masculine/Feminine* (1969) ; Anne Firor Scott, ed., *The American Woman: Who Was She?* (1971) ; Anne Firor Scott, *The Southern Lady: From Pedestal to Politics, 1830–1930* (1970) ; Patricia Cayo Sexton, *The Feminized Male* (1969) ; Andrew Sinclair, *The Better Half: The Emancipation of the American Woman* (1965).

**Science, Technology, and the Environment**

Sir Leon Bagrit, *The Age of Automation* (1965) ; Jeremy Bernstein, *The Analytical Engine: Computers, Past, Present, and Future* (1964) ; Eli Ginzberg, ed., *Technology and Social Change* (1964) ; Richard G. Hewlett and Oscar E. Anderson, Jr., *A History of the United States Atomic Energy Commission: The New World, 1939–1946* (1962) ; Richard G. Hewlett and Francis Duncan, *A History of the United States Atomic Energy Commission: Atomic Shield, 1947–1952* (1969) ; Robert Jungk (James Cleugh, trans.), *Brighter than a Thousand Suns: A Personal History of the Atomic Scientists* (1958) ; Norman Kaplan, ed., *Science and Society* (1965) ; Melvin Kranzberg and Carroll W. Pursell, *Technology in Western Civilization* (2 vols., 1967) ; David E. Lilienthal, *The Journals of David E. Lilienthal: The Atomic Energy Years, 1945–1950* (1965) ; John W. Logsdon, *The Decision to Go to the Moon* (1970) ; Emmanuel Mesthene, *Technological Change: Its Impact on Man and Society* (1970) ; William Rogers, *Think: A Biography of the Watsons and IBM* (1969) ; Michael Rose, *Computers, Managers, and Society* (1969) ; Walter Schoenberger, *Decision of Destiny* (1969) ; Carl F. Stover, ed., *The Technological Order* (1963) ; Aaron W. Warner, Dean Morse and Alfred S. Eichner, eds., *The Impact of Science and Technology* (1965) ; Norbert Wiener, *Cybernetics* (1948) and *The Human Use of Human Beings* (1954) ; Herbert F. York, *Race to Oblivion: A Participant's View of the Arms Race* (1970) ; Hugo Young, Bryan Silcock and Peter Dunn, *Journey to Tranquility* (1970).

Elizabeth Baker, *Technology and Women's Work* (1964) ; Jacques Ellul, *The Technological Society* (1964) ; Victor Ferkiss, *Technological Man: The Myth and the Reality* (1969) ; William Kuhns, *The Post-Industrial Prophets: Interpretations of Technology* (1971) ; Floyd W. Matson, *The Broken Image: Man, Science and Society* (1964) ; Herbert J. Muller, *The Children of Frankenstein: A Primer on Modern Technology and Human Values* (1970) ; James L. Penick, Jr., et al., eds., *The Politics of American Science, 1939 to the Present* (rev. ed., 1972) ; Don K. Price, *The Scientific Estate* (1965) ; Eugene B. Skolnikoff, *Science, Technology, and American Foreign Policy* (1967).

Lynton K. Caldwell, *Environment: A Challenge for Modern Society* (1970) ; Eugene N. Cameron, ed., *The Mineral Position of the United States, 1975–2000* (1973) ; Rachel Carson, *Silent Spring* (1962) ; Henry Clepper, *Professional For-*

*estry in the United States* (1971); Barry Commoner, *The Closing Circle* (1971) and *Science and Survival* (1968); David W. Ehrenfeld, *Biological Conservation* (1970); Paul R. and Anne H. Ehrlich, *Population, Resources, Environment: Issues in Human Ecology* (1970); Richard A. Falk, *This Endangered Planet* (1971); P. T. Flawn, *Mineral Resources* (1968); Frank Graham, Jr., *Since Silent Spring* (1970); John Hay, *In Defense of Nature* (1969); Seymour J. Mandelbaum, *Community and Communications* (1972); Eugene Odum, *Ecology* (1969); Paul Shepard and David McKinley, eds., *The Subversive Science: Essays toward an Ecology of Man* (1969); Sam H. Schurr, ed., *Energy, Economic Growth, and the Environment* (1972); Brian J. Skinner, *Earth Resources* (1969).

**Kennedy—Johnson—Nixon**

James M. Burns, *John Kennedy: A Political Profile* (1960); Aida DiPace Donald, ed., *John F. Kennedy and the New Frontier* (1967); Louise FitzSimons, *The Kennedy Doctrine* (1972); Robert F. Kennedy, *Thirteen Days: A Memoir of the Cuban Missile Crisis* (1971); Evelyn Lincoln, *Kennedy and Johnson* (1968); Kenneth O'Donnell, *Johnny, We Hardly Knew Ye* (1973); Pierre Salinger, *With Kennedy* (1965); Jack M. Schick, *The Berlin Crisis, 1958–1962* (1971); Arthur M. Schlesinger, Jr., *A Thousand Days: John F. Kennedy in the White House* (1965); Hugh Sidey, *John F. Kennedy: President* (1963); Theodore C. Sorenson, *Kennedy* (1965) and *The Kennedy Legacy* (1969); Richard J. Walton, *Cold War and Counter-Revolution: The Foreign Policy of John F. Kennedy* (1972); Tom Wicker, *JFK & LBJ: The Influence of Personality Upon Politics* (1969); William Appleman Williams, *The United States, Cuba, and Castro* (1962).

Leonard Baker, *The Johnson Eclipse* (1970); Rowland Evans, Jr., and Robert Novak, *Lyndon B. Johnson: The Exercise of Power* (1966); M. E. Gettleman and David Mermelstein, eds., *The Great Society Reader* (1967); Eric F. Goldman, *The Tragedy of Lyndon Johnson: A Historian's Personal Interpretation* (1969); Louis Heren, *No Hail, No Farewell* (1970); Lyndon B. Johnson, *The Vantage Point: Perspectives of the Presidency, 1963–1969* (1971); Hugh Sidey, *A Very Personal Presidency: Lyndon Johnson in the White House* (1968); Alfred Steinberg, *Sam Johnson's Boy: A Close-up of the President* (1968).

Louis M. Kohlmeier, Jr., *"God Save This Honorable Court!"* (1972); Leonard Lurie, *The Running of Richard Nixon* (1972); Bruce Mazlish, *In Search of Nixon* (1972); Earl Mayo and Stephen Hess, *Nixon: A Political Portrait* (1968); Reg Murphy and Hal Buliver, *The Southern Strategy* (1971); Richard M. Nixon, *Six Crises* (1962); Leonard Silk, *Nixonomics* (1972); H. D. Spalding, *The Nixon Nobody Knows* (1972); Richard Whalen, *Catch the Falling Flag* (1972); Garry Wills, *Nixon Agonistes: The Crisis of the Self-Made Man* (1971); Jules Witcover, *The Resurrection of Richard Nixon* (1970).

Richard J. Barnet, *Roots of War* (1972); Joseph Buttinger, *Vietnam: A Dragon Embattled* (2 vols., rev. ed., 1972); Bernard Fall, *Two Viet Nams: A Political and Military Analysis* (1967) and *Vietnam Witness, 1953–1966* (1968); Frances Fitzgerald, *Fire in the Lake: The Vietnamese and the Americans in Vietnam* (1972); J. William Fulbright, *The Arrogance of Power* (1967); Townsend Hoopes, *The Limits of Intervention: An Inside Account of How the Johnson Policy of Escalation in Vietnam Was Reversed* (1969); Irving L. Janis, *Victims of Groupthink: A Psychological Study of Foreign-Policy Decisions and Fiascoes* (1972); George M. Kahin and John W. Lewis, *The United States in Vietnam* (1967); David Landau, *Kissinger: The Uses of Power* (1972); John T. McAlister, Jr., *Viet Nam: The Origins of Revolution* (1969); John Norton Moore, *Law and the Indo-China War*

(1972) ; New York Times, *The Pentagon Papers* (1971) ; Ralph K. White, *Nobody Wanted War* (1968).

Chester Bowles, *Promises to Keep: My Years in Public Life, 1941–1969* (1971) ; John Kenneth Galbraith, *Ambassador's Journal: A Personal Account of the Kennedy Years* (1969) ; David Halberstam, *The Best and the Brightest* (1972) ; Roger Hilsman, *To Move a Nation* (1967) ; Jeremy Larner, *Nobody Knows: Reflections on the McCarthy Campaign of 1968* (1970) ; Jeb Stuart Magruder, *An American Life: One Man's Road to Watergate* (1974) ; Richard E. Neustadt, *Presidential Power: The Politics of Leadership* (1969) ; Chalmers M. Roberts, *The Nuclear Years: The Arms Race and Arms Control, 1945–1970* (1970) ; David Rodnick, *Essays on an America in Transition* (1972) ; James L. Sundquist, *Politics and Policy: The Eisenhower, Kennedy and Johnson Years* (1968) ; The Washington Post, *The Presidential Transcripts* (1974) ; Theodore H. White, *The Making of the President, 1960* (1961), *The Making of the President, 1964* (1965), *The Making of the President, 1968* (1969), and *The Making of the President, 1972* (1973).

# Index

1 2 3 4 5 6 7 8 9 10